AMERICAN SOVEREIGNS

American Sovereigns: The People and America's Constitutional Tradition Before the Civil War challenges traditional American constitutional history, theory, and jurisprudence that sees today's constitutionalism as linked by an unbroken chain to the 1787 federal constitutional convention. *American Sovereigns* examines the idea that after the American Revolution, a collectivity – the people – would rule as the sovereign. Heated political controversies within the states and at the national level over what it meant that the people were the sovereign and how that collective sovereign could express its will were not resolved in 1776, in 1787, or prior to the Civil War. The idea of the people as the sovereign both unified and divided Americans in thinking about government and the basis of the Union. Today's constitutionalism is not a natural inheritance, but the product of choices Americans made between shifting understandings about themselves as a collective sovereign.

Christian G. Fritz is a professor of law at the University of New Mexico School of Law, where he has held both the Dickason and Weihofen professorships. Fritz has a Ph.D. in history from the University of California, Berkeley, and a J.D. from the University of California, Hastings College of Law. He is the author of *Federal Justice in California: The Court of Ogden Hoffman, 1851–1891* (1991), a path-breaking work that analyzes the operation of the first federal district court in San Francisco. Fritz delivered the 2002 Justice William J. Brennan, Jr., lecture at the Oklahoma City University School of Law. Professor Fritz is a member of the American Society for Legal History and the American Historical Association, and he has served on the editorial boards of several law and history journals.

CAMBRIDGE STUDIES ON THE AMERICAN CONSTITUTION

SERIES EDITORS

Maeva Marcus, *George Washington University*
Melvin I. Urofsky, *Virginia Commonwealth University*
Mark Tushnet, *Georgetown University Law Center*
Keith Whittington, *Princeton University*

Cambridge Studies on the American Constitution publishes books that examine the American Constitution and offers a range of interpretations and approaches, from traditional topics of constitutional history and theory, case studies, and judicial biographies, to more modern and often controversial issues dealing with gender and race. While many estimable series have incorporated constitutional studies, none have done so exclusively. This series seeks to illuminate the implications – governmental, political, social, and economic – of the relationship between the American Constitution and the country it governs through a wide array of perspectives.

TITLES IN THE SERIES:

Mark A. Graber, *Dred Scott and the Problem of Constitutional Evil*

To Joe,
extraordinary friend and collaborator

American Sovereigns

THE PEOPLE AND AMERICA'S CONSTITUTIONAL
TRADITION BEFORE THE CIVIL WAR

CHRISTIAN G. FRITZ

University of New Mexico

CAMBRIDGE
UNIVERSITY PRESS

CAMBRIDGE UNIVERSITY PRESS
Cambridge, New York, Melbourne, Madrid, Cape Town, Singapore, São Paulo, Delhi

Cambridge University Press
32 Avenue of the Americas, New York, NY 10013-2473, USA

www.cambridge.org
Information on this title: www.cambridge.org/9780521125604

First published 2008
Reprinted 2009 (twice)
First paperback edition 2009

Printed in the United States of America

A catalog record for this publication is available from the British Library.

Library of Congress Cataloging in Publication Data
Fritz, Christian G., 1953–
American sovereigns : the people and America's constitutional tradition before the Civil War /
Christian G. Fritz.
  p. cm. (Cambridge studies on the American Constitution)
Includes bibliographical references and index.
ISBN 978-0-521-88188-3 (hardback)

  1. Constituent power – United States – History. 2. People (Constitutional law) – United States –
History. 3. State rights – United States – History. 4. Federal government – United States –
History. 5. Constitutional history – United States. I. Title. II. Series.
KF4881.F75 2008
342.7302' 9 – dc22   2007013827

ISBN 978-0-521-88188-3 hardback
ISBN 978-0-521-12560-4 paperback

Contents

Acknowledgments

All books have their own odyssey, frequently ending up far from where they began. This is particularly true of this work, which originated many years ago, in what was to have been a quick look at a neglected topic: American constitution-making in the nineteenth century. Research into that topic revealed ideas and arguments that made little sense in terms of the standard story of American constitutionalism. Curiosity about whether these apparently unorthodox views were unique prompted a wider study of all the convention debates of the latter half of the nineteenth century and eventually those before the Civil War as well. This reading only reinforced the puzzling existence of ideas and ways of thinking about written constitutions that were not idiosyncratic, but that continued to defy explanation in terms of the conventional account of American constitutionalism. The search to explain these ideas – their genesis and development – became this book.

The completion of this unintentionally long journey would not have been possible without the support and contributions of many people. Especially important has been help from the law school community at the University of New Mexico. A succession of deans – Ted Parnall, Leo Romero, Robert ("Desi") Desiderio, and Suellyn Scarnecchia – have generously offered both institutional and personal support that is gratefully acknowledged. The entire law library staff has been unfailingly helpful, and David Epstein and Eileen Cohen were particularly tenacious in acquiring materials through interlibrary loan – including items I was sure no one would lend us. Joseph Blecha and especially Torild Kristiansen deserve special mention for transcribing hundreds of tapes of notes dictated from convention debates and other sources, particularly in the early years of the research. Elodie Collins and Cindy Nee remained cheerful and helpful in providing never-ending copies of materials and fielding requests for assistance even as I made a pest of myself. Thanks are also due to Cyndi Dean and her staff for solving computer crises and saving more data than I had a right to expect.

Over the years, students in my American constitutional history seminar have proved a valuable sounding board, and feedback from them is much appreciated, particularly students in the seminars of spring 2006 and 2007. As the manuscript neared completion, several students offered excellent help in verifying citations and quotations under a tight deadline, for which I am most grateful. They included Barry Berenberg, Amber Chavez, Patrick Redmond, and especially Seth McMillan – whose compulsion to try to get things right rivaled my own pathology.

Among my law school colleagues who have invariably been supportive, three friends have offered extraordinary support. Em Hall not only read selected chapters and offered candid criticisms that helped clarify my thinking, but also provided much-appreciated empathy over the trials of a long-term project. Michael Browde and Jim Ellis read innumerable drafts of the entire manuscript over many years and were unstinting in their support of the project and the author. It is impossible to imagine completing this book without their help.

Many thanks to Barb Bergman, Joan and Fred Hart, April Land, Sally and Ted Occhialino, Scott Sandlin, and Ruth Singer. They saw little of the manuscript but much of the author during the research and writing of this book. Their friendship and encouragement contributed materially to its completion.

My debts extend far beyond the UNM law school community. I am extremely grateful to Tony Freyer and Reid Mitchell for critically reading earlier versions of Chapter 7. In addition, Deborah Celle, Dan Feller, Ron Formisano, John D. Gordan, Paul Kens, Maria McCulley, John Orth, Dave Reichard, John Phillip Reid, Bob Williams, and Mel Yazawa each read versions of the entire manuscript and provided a wealth of suggestions and comments. Their careful appraisals have helped make this a better book than it otherwise would have been, and I am profoundly grateful for their generosity and help. I thank David Szatmary for assistance in locating an elusive reference relating to events in Massachusetts in the 1780s.

Thanks are due to the sources listed in the Credits for permission to quote from materials in their collections. I also extend thanks for permission to use substantially revised versions of essays published elsewhere: "Recovering the Lost Worlds of America's Written Constitutions," 68 *Albany Law Review* (2005), 261–93; and "A Constitutional Middle-Ground Between Revision and Revolution: A Reevaluation of the Nullification Crisis and the Virginia and Kentucky Resolutions Through the Lens of Popular Sovereignty," in

Hendrik Hartog and William E. Nelson, eds., *Law as Culture and Culture as Law: Essays in Honor of John Phillip Reid* (Madison House, 2000).

At Cambridge University Press I have had the helpful guidance and encouragement of Lewis Bateman as my editor. He is directly responsible for facilitating a better book by giving me more time to develop the ideas in the manuscript. Thanks are also due to Shelby Peak, the production controller for the book, and to Janis Bolster, my production editor, who was both efficient and responsive during a tight production schedule. I am also appreciative of the contributions of Patterson Lamb at the copyediting stage.

A deep dept is owed to Maeva Marcus for her support and interest in the manuscript that became this book, as well as for being a model of how to combine scholarship and service to the wider academic community. Mark Tushnet also made helpful suggestions on an early draft for which I am most appreciative.

The book's production owes a debt of gratitude to Michiko Okaya, Director of the Williams Center Art Gallery at Lafayette College, for graciously facilitating the use of the Wolcutt painting for the cover artwork. In addition, thanks are due to Mark Franaszek for his expertise in producing the map for Chapter 3.

My deepest debt is to my wife, Marlene. This book could not have been written without her love and support. One measure of her commitment was continuous help with the book amidst the demands of a busy professional career of her own. Despite her many contributions, we both agree that someone else deserves the lion's share of credit for shaping *American Sovereigns*.

Eighteen years ago Joe Franaszek and the author were playing bocce ball in Albuquerque when the idea of a "short" study of state constitution-making surfaced in conversation. From that day until the writing of these words, Joe has been indefatigable in helping to develop the ideas, structure, and prose of what became the present book. Ever insistent that intellectual history should be explored in concrete terms of how people behaved, Joe has spent nearly as much time as the author in wrestling with the ideas explored in this book and making the prose as accessible as possible. His fingerprints can be found on virtually every page, and I can only partially express my gratitude for his remarkable collaboration and commitment to this book by offering him the dedication.

1 Prologue

This book is a history of an idea and of a people who tried to live by that idea. The idea is what we know today as American constitutionalism.[1] It defines "the people" as the sovereign whose written constitution grants and guides the legitimate exercise of government authority. The fact that the people, instead of a king, ruled in America justified the Revolution as well as the governments established in its wake. When New Yorkers pulled down the statue of George III in Battery Park shortly after Congress declared independence, they did more than reject British authority over America. Their action symbolized the replacement of the person of the king as the sovereign by the collective body of the people as America's new sovereign.

The Revolution stimulated the interest of Americans in their new governments and the people's relationship to them. Revolutionary leaders stressed the important role the people played in securing America's independence. In framing America's first constitutions, patriots celebrated the people's sovereignty. These ideals smoldered even after the Revolution ended and this heated revolutionary rhetoric soon permeated all regions and ranks of society. Government was no longer something that happened to people. In America it now became something that the people – by their consent and volition – brought into being. The people gave their consent through their conduct and their active participation reinforced the message that the people were America's new sovereign.[2]

Constitutional arguments about the people's sovereignty soon became familiar to ordinary Americans who knew these arguments because they participated in them zealously. Americans argued fiercely about the nature and the extent of their power as part of the collective sovereign, and seven decades later they were no closer to agreement over what the people's sovereignty meant than they were during the Revolution. Yet their disagreements produced a complex constitutional tradition that we have generally overlooked.

1

How the people could collectively act as the sovereign has remained a persistent puzzle. This elemental question shaped constitutional debates from the time of Independence. Yet, because the constitutional principle of the people's sovereignty has been largely overlooked, much of the reasoning driving these debates has been obscured.[3]

The emergence of a dominant understanding about American constitutionalism was not the result of a single defining event such as the federal constitutional convention. Rather, it developed incrementally through successive political controversies at the state and national levels that are the subject of this book. It is hoped that a rekindled interest in the significance of these past struggles may illuminate the continuing growth and development of American constitutionalism.

The constitutionalism of America during the decades following Independence differed from today's constitutionalism. The crux of this difference lies in the novel question that American constitutionalism faced in the wake of independence: how could a collectivity – a people rather than a monarch – rule as the sovereign over a region larger and more diverse than Europe? Moreover, how could that sovereign speak clearly with one voice on matters of state as well as national concern?

After the Revolution, few disputed that the people would rule as the sovereign speaking through written constitutions. But in putting this idea into practice, Americans parted company with one another. Their division did not end with the drafting and ratification of the federal Constitution. How the people should govern through constitutions surfaced in many hard-fought political controversies thereafter. Yet the promise of constitutionalism remained bright even as the nation grew and drifted toward disunion and civil war.

Today it is difficult to imagine a time when it was not widely assumed that the constitutional vision of the federal Framers epitomized American thinking on government. Invariably, we trace the roots of our constitutionalism back to the unique federal convention that met in Philadelphia during the summer of 1787. This singular focus on the federal Constitution assumes that little of constitutional importance happened at the hundred other state constitutional proceedings in America before the Civil War. If scholars give them any historical treatment, these other proceedings appear as variations on the constitutional themes of the federal convention.[4]

Those state proceedings, like the political controversies described in this book, raised questions about implementing the sovereignty of the people. They reveal very different views about the people as the sovereign from those reflected in the federal Constitution and dispel the notion that our prevailing constitutional view is an unbroken chain stretching back to 1787.[5] Indeed, many of our contemporary constitutional perspectives that echo those of the federal Framers were not inevitable; they did not become America's constitutional norms in 1787, or in 1800, or in 1840. Those norms emerged only after a protracted struggle. The views of the federal Framers predominate today not as a natural inheritance but as the result of conscious choices made over the years among competing visions.

The sovereign people's ability to change constitutions was frequently discussed, often exercised, and invariably disputed after the creation of the federal Constitution. Contrary to much scholarship, Americans vigorously debated whether "the people" could express their sovereign will in changing constitutions only by using government-sanctioned procedures.[6] Whether Americans found it necessary to use such procedures reflected contrasting views of the relationship of the people to their government. One view saw the people dependent on government and procedure while another view did not. Both views shared the general consensus of American revolutionaries that a majority of the people were the sovereign. Disagreement arose over how much power remained with "the people" and how much power "the people" relinquished to their elected officials.

It seems puzzling today that Americans once considered their sovereign to be the people acting collectively. Modern scholars suggest that sovereignty of the people was a rhetorical flourish lacking practical application as a constitutional principle. As a crucial "fiction," the people's sovereignty had enormous political influence.[7] But modern accounts of America's constitutional history neglect the constitutional authority once imputed to such a collective sovereign and as such they fail to appreciate the earlier existence of a widely held belief in collective sovereignty that lost sway only after the Civil War.

The lost view of sovereignty assumed that a majority of the people created and therefore could revise constitutions at will, and that a given majority of one generation could not limit a later generation. America's first constitutions, being an expression of the people's sovereignty, could not be turned against the majority of the people. Indeed, those constitutions frequently contained express provisions recognizing the broad scope of the people's authority. Such statements encouraged an expansive view of constitutional revision. The essence of the rule of law – that binding law exists above both the governors and the governed alike – was challenged by the idea that a sovereign people could not be bound even by a fundamental law of their own making.[8]

Under that expansive view, adhering to procedures specifying constitutional change provided one means of determining the will of the sovereign.

Nonetheless, constitutional text requiring special majorities could not prevail over the clear will of a majority to dispense with such requirements if that majority so desired. The key to legitimacy was whether constitutional change expressed the will of the collective sovereign, not adherence to specific procedures. While Americans frequently followed such procedures, for many those steps were simply useful, not indispensable. They were not the only legitimate tools available for a sovereign to articulate its will.[9]

For other Americans, once the people created a government, it became the conduit and the enforcer of that sovereign's will. If the people placed procedures in their constitution, they effectively exercised their unlimited power to limit themselves by those procedures. The people could not ignore the procedures they imposed upon themselves. This view of constitutionalism asserted that the people's unbounded power included the ability to bind themselves by their constitution and to bind future generations.

This constrained view of constitutional change made procedure the test of legitimacy. It assigned the people a passive role in making and altering constitutions, one that emphasized deference to elected leaders. Even advocates of a constrained view, however, dispensed with restrictive formal requirements when it seemed necessary. Their adherence to procedure was not absolute. They believed that government could enforce constitutional requirements for changing the constitution, but conceded that a majority of the people might deviate from specified procedures with the sanction of the government. Only when the government insisted on the formalities for change were the people required to follow them. Under this view government could repudiate change that defied stated procedures, but it could also validate constitutional revision under the people's authority that bypassed procedures.

Despite their consensus about the existence of the collective sovereign, Americans vigorously disagreed and, as the Civil War approached, forcibly disputed whether constitutional change was possible only through a process guaranteed by government. Both the expansive and the constrained views acknowledged the sovereign authority of the people. Each side accused the other of betraying the Revolution. Thus, the development that gave Americans their greatest pride in their new, postrevolutionary governments – written constitutions authorized by the people – also represented the most contentious aspect of their experiment with republicanism. Many leaders of the revolutionary movement became increasingly sensitive to the latent potential of sweeping changes made in the name of the people. After observing the operation of the legislatures under the first state constitutions, they became alarmed at the increasing influence of those who traditionally did not exercise positions of political leadership.

While American revolutionaries spoke with one voice in affirming the people's sovereignty, they did not speak with one voice about who counted as "the people." Initially, "the people" excluded women, those lacking property, Native Americans, and African Americans – even as the Revolution stimulated challenges to such exclusion.[10] Only in the course of the nineteenth and twentieth centuries would the definition of "the people" expand and become increasingly inclusive. As Americans wrestled with defining "the people," their answers to the question of who composed the collective sovereign varied over time and by place. Broader or narrower definitions of "the people" reflected different attitudes toward political participation, who should vote, and the perceived dangers of legislative majorities.

Even if a majority of "the people" – however defined – and not simply a faction took a given position, the issue became how that collective sovereign could express its will simultaneously and definitively. In a variety of disputes after Independence, Americans struggled to answer that question. The issue of the people's sovereignty arose in disagreements over such matters as taxes, court procedures, government reform, decisions to wage war, and the scope of dissent. The way the collectivity of the people acted as the sovereign was answered piecemeal. In those debates Americans tended to talk past one another. Some focused on the need for constitutional procedures before a collective sovereign could change the constitution. They also expected the existing government to be involved in the revision process. Others rejected such restraints on the people's sovereign authority. They believed that procedural restraints would make the servants, the elected officials, more powerful than the master, the sovereign people. In this view, a majority of the people possessed the inherent right to make constitutional changes, even independent of government.

American thinking about written constitutions can be traced through a series of events between the revolutionary era and the Civil War, beginning with the ways Americans employed the authority of the collective sovereign first to abolish and then to create governments during the Revolution. Part One of this book – "The People's Sovereignty in the States," (Chapters 2–4) – describes the origins and early application of the idea that the people were the sovereigns who created constitutional government in the states and on the frontier. This part concludes with Shays's "rebellion," a postrevolutionary struggle in Massachusetts over implementing the people's sovereignty.

The federal Constitution incorporated a particular version of rule by a sovereign people. Even so, as illustrated in Part Two – "The Sovereign

Behind the Federal Constitution" (Chapters 5–7) – the adoption of the federal Constitution reflected no consensus on how the people could express their sovereignty. Establishing constitutional government at the national level illustrates this lack of consensus, as do the events of another "rebellion," the Whiskey Rebellion in Pennsylvania, as well as the Virginia and Kentucky Resolutions, the Hartford Convention, and the Nullification crisis.

The final section of the book, Part Three – "The Struggle over a Constitutional Middle Ground" (Chapter 8) – explores the American puzzle of a collective sovereign, a sovereign that simultaneously rules and is ruled. Chief Justice John Jay commented on that novelty in 1793 when he said the American people were "sovereigns without subjects" who "have none to govern but themselves."[11] A definitive answer to the riddle of a collective sovereign still eluded Americans seventy years after Independence in the so-called Dorr "rebellion" in Rhode Island. The Epilogue of this book (Chapter 9) is not a summary of the work but rather seeks to identify broader themes in American constitutionalism before the Civil War, drawing from a consideration of the preceding chapters as a whole. It also suggests other avenues for further inquiry based on the findings of this study.

The events discussed in this book entailed *constitutional questions* as well as *questions of constitutionalism*. The political controversy over the Virginia and Kentucky Resolutions, for example, protested the constitutionality of laws passed by the Federalist Party that were aimed at their Republican opponents. Likewise, disputes between the North and South during the Nullification crisis involved sectional efforts to adjust the distribution of state and national power under the federal Constitution. These political and constitutional controversies also posed questions of constitutionalism – how to identify the collective sovereign, what powers the sovereign possessed, and how one recognized when that sovereign acted. Unlike constitutional questions, questions of constitutionalism could not be answered by reference to given constitutional text or even judicial opinions. Rather, they were open-ended questions drawing upon competing views Americans developed after Independence about the sovereignty of the people and the ongoing role of the people to monitor the constitutional order that rested on their sovereign authority.

This book tells a complicated story. Not everything "the people" did was an expression of their sovereign authority. The revolutionary idea of a collective sovereign suggested that the people might act in at least three capacities under a written constitution. First, the people *could* act as the sovereign, when, for example, they breathed life into a constitution. This was the most basic understanding of the role of the people. It encompassed not only the creation of a constitution but also its amendment, or revision, or even its "abolition." In their capacity as the collective sovereign, the people were not limited in revising or abolishing their constitution through constitutional revision procedures. As the sovereign they were ultimately free to use and invoke their authority as they saw fit.

In creating the new American constitutions, the people built a structure for a republican form of government. Because government was subordinate to the people and representatives were the people's agents, the people might act in a second capacity as "the ruler" to monitor the constitutional order established under their authority as the collective sovereign. One way they did this – but not the only way – was through the voting process in which they elected legislative representatives and state executives. These elections were not acts by a "sovereign." They were simply choices by "the ruler" to designate agents to run the government, much the way a sovereign king might select ministers. As electors, if the people believed their agents or the government acted outside the constitutional framework or undermined the constitutional order, or simply took steps that were imprudent or unwise policy, they could refuse to continue those agents of government in office.

In contrast to the people's function as "the ruler," American constitutions also contemplated a role for the people as "the ruled." In this third capacity the people – as individuals or in groups – had rights granted by the constitution to express their views on the policy and conduct of the government or even on the constitutionality of government actions. In making these expressions, the people did not act with the authority of the collective sovereign. When the people petitioned government or assembled to express their views they were simply engaged in a political role anticipated for the people in governments framed by the constitutional authority of the collective sovereign. Indeed, the commitment to a collective sovereign as a central tenet of the Revolution stimulated ever-broader claims and more inclusive definitions of who "the people" were and what rights they had in political participation.

Differentiating among the people acting as the collective sovereign, as "the ruler" acting within the constitutional framework, or as "the ruled" engaged in political participation was not easy because the distinctions were subtle.[12] Thus, it should not be surprising that Americans before the Civil War struggled to come to terms with the constitutionalism launched by the Declaration of Independence. Ideas of a collective sovereign were expounded and acted upon in the course of winning the Revolution. However, once the Revolution and the new American governments were justified by the authority of the people as the collective sovereign, the idea of the people's authority was not abandoned, even though Americans continued to struggle with what that idea meant.

The different roles the people could play under the concept of a collective sovereign were not a figment of a revolutionary imagination. It was part of a riddle inherent in the idea that a people actually could be the sovereign. That riddle remained unanswered even as America drew closer to civil war. The different dimensions of the people's authority had a natural tendency to blend into one another. This tendency was exacerbated during the heat of many political controversies. At such times, the ambiguity of the idea of the collective sovereign served to unify as well as divide Americans not simply on the expediency of policy, but also on the very basis of their Union.

The diverse events considered in this work share a unified theme. As political disputes the events raise unrelated constitutional questions. Considered in light of their implications for American constitutionalism, however, the events illustrate the dynamic, ongoing enterprise of giving life to the idea of a collective sovereign. This idea presented an important question for Americans then, and it remains just as vitally important today: what does it mean that in America "the people" rule?

PART ONE

The People's Sovereignty in the States

Independence created the need to frame new governments that reflected the legitimizing authority of the people. Steeped in English legal traditions, Americans engaged in constitution-making without completely appreciating the implications of that task. Revolutionaries agreed that the people were the new sovereigns of America who displaced the king. What that implied for traditional models of government and the relationship of the people to their new governments, however, only became clear to Americans at different times and in different ways. All of America's first written constitutions embraced the people's sovereignty and many of them expressed the inherent right of the people to scrutinize their governors and to effect constitutional change. Those constitutions reflected how deeply and widely patriots celebrated "the people" as the new sovereigns of America.

To a remarkable extent, the principles identified by America's constitution-makers resonated with Americans at the grassroots level. Far from centers of government, ideas that led to Independence and fueled the Revolution took hold among ordinary people. Reacting to local concerns while embracing the revolutionary cause, Americans made arguments drawn from the authority of the people's sovereignty, much like their state and national leaders.

The prevalence of ideas about a collective sovereign that invited challenges to the decision making of the newly created American governments inevitably triggered a reaction. Political grievances raised questions of constitutionalism when those who expressed disagreement with policies of state governments were denied the right to do so. Matters escalated as frustrated opponents of those policies increasingly took matters in their own hands. They asserted the right of the body of "the people" to check acts of

9

government that were believed to undermine the public welfare. In the late 1780s, Massachusetts witnessed a clash between Americans that advanced distinct views of what governments founded on the sovereign people meant in practice.

2 Revolutionary Constitutionalism

In the pouring rain on the morning of May 20, 1776, some four to five thousand American patriots – nearly 15 percent of the city's population – gathered in the State House Yard in Philadelphia. For three hours the crowd became "well-drenched" while hearing speeches and passing a number of resolutions directed at the colonial legislature due to meet in the State House later that day. They sent a clear message to the legislature.

The legislature's opposition to Independence threatened Pennsylvania's "Happy union with the other Colonies." By pledging allegiance to America's "mortal Enemy, the King of Great-Britain," the colonial government no longer represented the people. The crowd protested that because the legislature's authority came from the Crown, it lacked a crucial ingredient for constituting a legitimate government: "the Authority of the People." Establishing "a new Constitution, originating and founded" on that authority required a body representing the people. This was not the colonial legislature.

Recent events prompted the crowd's challenge to Pennsylvania's government. When it met ten days earlier at the State House, the Continental Congress called for new governments to be established if current ones were not "sufficient to the exigencies of their affairs." Moreover, on May 15 Congress added a preamble to the resolution calling for suppression of "every kind of authority" under the British monarch. Governments in America would now exist "under the authority of the people."

Many congressional delegates considered that preamble "a declaration of Independ[e]nce." John Adams, drafter of the preamble, thought its passage "the most important" vote "ever . . . taken in America." Years later he regarded it "a decisive Event" in the revolutionary struggle.

Adams was present in the Yard watching the activities of the crowd. He was gratified when the gathering punctuated the reading of Congress's resolution with "three Cheers" and "Hatts flying." While critics of this public meeting called the people's behavior "tyrannical," Adams thought they acted with "great order, Decency and Propriety."

Framing a new government turned "Every thinge up side down." Those gathered at the State House seemed to give "the Coup de Grace to the King's authority" in Pennsylvania. "The people" wanted to destroy the existing colonial government and replace it with a new one in which the people were the sovereign. For many Americans like Adams, "revolution principles" were not theoretical abstractions, but the basis on which "the whole government . . . stands."

Those principles reflected the emerging constitutional understandings of American revolutionaries. The fiction that government rested on the authority of the crown had been exposed. "Who ought to form a new constitution of government?" the Pennsylvania Journal asked two days later. The answer was simple: "The people."

The thousands of Americans taking to the muddy Philadelphia streets that morning were participating in a constitutional revolution as important as the military struggle against Britain. America's ability to resist British forces depended on united, legitimate governments in each former colony supporting independence. As the colonial governments were linked to the authority of the British sovereign they could not reflect the views of the legitimate sovereign for America: the people.

Despite the revolutionary nature of the crowd's resolutions and protest, the gathering did not ignore the need for a peaceful transition to the new sovereign. While the current legislature could not create the needed government, it could exercise "powers it has hitherto been accustomed to use, for the safety and convenience of the province, until . . . a new constitution . . . founded on the authority of the people, shall be finally settled."

Unlike previous sovereigns, the American sovereign was not a discrete person or group of people. In America the new sovereign was a collectivity: it was all the people. As the Reverend Samuel Cooper put it, "I am part of the sovereignty of my country." While the people as the sovereign drew universal support among the revolutionaries in 1776, constitutions drafted during the Revolution articulated how governments founded not on one sovereign, but on many, would operate.

Those constitutions transformed the idea of the people as the sovereign into a practical reality. This transformation reflected an emerging understanding of government that drew upon an existing constitutional tradition but pioneered a distinctive constitutionalism for America.[1]

GENESIS OF AMERICA'S NEW CONSTITUTIONALISM

The traditional model of government that Americans inherited on the eve of Independence rested on a hypothetical bargain struck in the mists of antiquity between a king and a people. In this bargain, the people were protected by the monarch in exchange for the people giving the king allegiance. This was a contractual relationship. American revolutionaries accused George III of breaching his implied duty of protection under that contract, thereby releasing the people in the colonies from their allegiance. The sovereign's breach of the hypothetical contract gave rise to the subjects' right of revolution. This right reflected a well-known justification for revolution under both natural law and English constitutional doctrine.[2]

Natural law included a right of revolution, and it imposed significant preconditions on its exercise. As suggested by the philosopher John Locke, the right of revolution arose only under the most dire circumstances. Americans considered that their plight met this test. On the eve of the Revolution, Alexander Hamilton justified American resistance as an expression of "the law of nature" redressing violations of "the first principles of civil society" and invasions of "the rights of a whole people." As expressed in the Declaration of Independence, natural law taught that the people were "endowed by their Creator with certain unalienable Rights" and could alter or abolish government "destructive" of those rights. For Thomas Jefferson the Declaration was the last-ditch effort of an oppressed people – the position in which many Americans saw themselves in 1776. Jefferson's litany of colonial grievances demonstrated that Americans were justified in exercising the natural law right of revolution.[3]

Although the Declaration and revolutionary rhetoric invoked the natural law right of revolution, natural law was not the sole justification for independence. English constitutional doctrine also supported the colonists' actions. By the 1760s, English law recognized what William Blackstone's *Commentaries on the Laws of England* called "the *law* of redress against public oppression." Like the natural law's right of revolution, this constitutional law of redress justified the people's resisting the sovereign. This law of redress arose from a contract between the people and the king to preserve the public welfare. This original contract was "a central dogma in English and British constitutional law" since "time immemorial." The Declaration's long list of grievances demonstrated that this bargain had been breached.[4]

This well-accepted law of redress justified a people's resisting unconstitutional acts of government. Liberty depended upon the people's "ultimate" right to resist. Unconstitutional commands breaching the "voluntary compact between the rulers and the ruled" could be "ignored" and arbitrary commands opposed with force. This right implied a duty on the part of the people to resist unconstitutional acts.[5] As Alexander Hamilton noted in 1775, government exercised powers to protect "the *absolute rights*" of the people, and government forfeited those powers and the people could reclaim them if government breached this constitutional contract.[6]

The law of redress had limits, like the right of revolution under natural law. The law of redress, like the right of revolution, was not an individual right. It belonged to the community as a whole, as one of the parties to the original constitutional contract.[7] It was not a means of first resort, or a response to trivial or casual errors of government.[8] Blackstone's *Commentaries* suggested that using the law of redress would be *"extraordinary"* – warranted, for example, if the king broke the original contract, violated "the fundamental laws," or abandoned the kingdom. During the Stamp Act crisis of the 1760s the Massachusetts Provincial Congress considered resistance to the king justified if freedom came under attack from "the hand of oppression" and "the merciless feet of tyranny." A decade later the "indictment" of George III in the Declaration of Independence sought to end his sovereign reign over the colonies because he had violated the original constitutional contract.[9]

American Independence was justified by the period's conventional theories about the people's collective right to cast off an arbitrary king. Both natural law and English constitutional doctrine gave the colonists a right to revolt against the sovereign's oppression. But in rejecting George III, Americans had no ready replacement with a traditional claim on their loyalty. Few American revolutionaries worried about this. They assumed that the people themselves were the new and rightful sovereign, rather than a monarch. They would neither return to the colonial fold nor surrender their recently acquired sovereignty. In creating governments to replace those established under the authority of the king, Americans saw themselves as the sovereign. This perception supported a particular theory of legitimate government giving rise to a distinctive constitutionalism in America.

America's theory of government did not pioneer new intellectual ground. The idea of basing government on the people's authority and consent had clear seventeenth- and eighteenth-century roots. Even before the Revolution, some supporters of the American cause in Britain saw the colonists' struggle as vindicating "the rights of sovereignty...in the people themselves." American revolutionaries did not discover the people's sovereignty. They inherited that idea.[10]

While the theory of the people serving as sovereigns was not original to Americans, actually building governments on that foundation was a dramatic departure from prevailing practices. Most governments in the world at the time were monarchies or expressions of raw power. Few examples existed of a people deliberately creating their own government. Thus, Americans found themselves in a unique position. As a South Carolina pamphleteer observed, "Before us, no people were ever so intirely relieved from the control of hereditary rulers and arbitrary force," so that they could fashion their own governments.[11]

American constitution-making created governments resting on actions of the people instead of the hypothetical bargain underlying the British constitution. American constitutionalism's future orientation in contrast to English constitutionalism's tie to the past was momentous. It made America's revolution, John Adams noted, "the most compleat, unexpected, and remarkable of any in the History of Nations." The significance lay in what Americans did with the idea that the people were the sovereign – how they implemented it, struggled with its implications for the nature of their governments and society, and ultimately transformed the principle. Their chief innovation and enduring constitutional legacy came from actually involving the people in forming new governments.[12]

The Anglo-American world in the seventeenth and eighteenth centuries saw many constitutional texts drafted. However, a written constitution giving voice to a collective people speaking as the sovereign and directing government was different in theory and practice from previous constitutions. American constitutions were written enactments. The British constitution was a product of tradition and history; it was not enacted, but simply existed. The written American constitutions were the explicit and unilateral orders of the new American sovereign – the people. The textual basis – the necessarily written nature – of American constitutions was a crucial characteristic of the process of establishing governments. This written feature remained a hallmark of American constitutions.[13]

In America, written constitutions – and not custom and time-honored practice – generated constitutional principles. Chief Justice John Marshall's famous 1803 opinion articulating the power of judicial review in *Marbury v. Madison* featured the recurring theme of the written quality of the federal Constitution. Written constitutions expressed what the sovereign people wanted from their governments and governors. As William Patterson, a justice of the Supreme Court and strong Federalist, noted in 1795, American constitutions were "the form of government, delineated by the mighty hand of the people." The significance of a written constitution demonstrated that what Americans established were manifestations of rule by the people as the sovereign. If their wishes were not reduced to writing, how could one know that the sovereign people had spoken?[14]

The written constitutions adopted in the 1770s demonstrated – with a dramatic clarity rarely seen in the world before then – that Americans possessed a unique opportunity. Independence, as Thomas Paine explained in his enormously popular tract *Common Sense*, gave Americans the "power to begin the world over again." A congressional delegate from Connecticut, Oliver Wolcott, described America's constitution-making in 1776 as "Real" because it was not the theoretical expression of the people's will. The new American constitutions reflected principles made "by the People at large." "Few opportunities," observed *Salus Populi* in 1776, "have ever been offered to mankind of framing an entire Constitution of Government." In a Fourth of July oration in 1778, historian David Ramsay captured the novelty of America's constitutions: "We are the first people in the world who have had it in their power to choose their own form of government." Until the American Revolution, constitutions were "forced on all other nations" or "formed by accident, caprice," or "prevailing practices."[15]

What distinguished American constitutions from those of the Old World, according to James Madison, was their being based on "the legitimate authority of the people" rather than "the usurped power of kings." In Europe, constitutions reflected power granting limited liberty to the people. In America's former British colonies the reverse was true: constitutions were "charters of power" granted by a people enjoying the benefits of "liberty." Americans choosing government by writing constitutions demonstrated a new and unique understanding of constitution-making.[16]

REVOLUTIONARY CONSTITUTIONAL SETTLEMENT

From pulpits, in town resolves, in newspaper articles, as well as in their private correspondence, patriots before the Revolution presumed that the people made a government legitimate or illegitimate by giving or withdrawing their support.[17] In opposing the Stamp Act in 1765, the town of New London, Connecticut, explained that "every form of government rightly founded, originates from the consent of the people." A decade later, Virginian George Mason succinctly identified the "fundamental maxim" that all government power was "originally lodged in, and consequently is derived from, the people." This differed from the bargaining model of government reflected in natural law and English constitutional doctrine. Americans rejected the need to bargain with another sovereign or monarch. Rather, the people as the sovereign set the parameters of government in creating their constitutional order. When constitutional boundaries were exceeded, "the people have a right to reassume the exercise of that authority."[18]

America's sovereign, unlike other sovereigns, was a collective one. "Supreme, Sovereign, absolute, and uncontroulable Power . . . resides, always in the Body of the People," declared the Massachusetts legislature in 1776. It was this "collective body" that established the ultimate "authority of the state," observed the influential minister Samuel West in a sermon that same year.[19] By the time of Independence, American revolutionaries widely agreed that the collective people were the sovereign.[20]

Even reluctant patriots agreed that legitimate government rested on the people. Although South Carolinian John Rutledge still hoped for "an accommodation of the unhappy differences" with Britain, he recognized that "the consent of the people" was "the origin" of government. The people's "inherent rights" were central to the "merits of the dispute." Pennsylvania's congressional delegate John Dickinson, while opposing independence in June of 1776, agreed on the need for the "full & free Consent of the People" to "change a Government." A Declaration of Independence was unnecessary because the people were "establishing their Governments . . . as fast as they can."[21]

Finding that the people as the new sovereign could give life to new governments through written constitutions marked a shift in the nature of representation and the existence of inherent rights. The principle that the people were the sovereign changed the relationship of the governed to their governors. Because the people were the new sovereign, representatives and other governmental officers who served them were subordinate to the new masters, the people. As the sovereign, the collective people inherently could act independent of government and even alter or abolish it. Written constitutions expressed the will of the collective sovereign.

During the first decade of constitution-making, the foundations of a revolutionary constitutionalism were firmly laid. The new American sovereign was not another monarch, but the people operating under written constitutions they created. These ideas logically followed from the text of the first state constitutions and the sweeping statements of leaders of the Revolution. Eventually, some Americans questioned the application of these constitutional principles and the idea that sovereignty was located in the people, not government.

In America, legitimate government was not the bargain between the people and a sovereign because in the new nation the two were fused. Americans readily noted this. "[A]ll power is . . . in the people," so that they could neither "give [it] up" nor have it "taken out of their hands," declared inhabitants of Albemarle County, Virginia. The state's bill of rights described government officials as the people's "trustees and servants," not as their sovereign. Not only would these officials "at all times be agreeable to" the people's desires, but they could also be called to "account" for abusing this trust. As citizens from Mecklenburg County, North Carolina, noted, the "principal supreme power is possessed by the people at large." On the other hand, the power of government officials, as the people's "servants," was "derived [from] and inferior" to that held by the sovereign people.[22]

The will of the collective sovereign, as expressed in the first state constitutions, invariably identified promoting the common good as the principal aspiration of American republics. South Carolina's 1776 constitution explained that governments were created for "the good of the people," and Maryland's 1776 constitution considered governments instituted "solely for the good of the whole." Georgia's 1777 constitution explained that it was "the people" for "whose benefit all government is intended." General John Sullivan observed in 1775 that "the Good of the People" was the object of government. A North Carolina congressional delegate echoed this position as well. The "happiness of society" was "the end and aim of all Government."[23] To advance this general welfare, many constitutional provisions prohibited government from giving special advantages to individuals or select classes.[24]

American constitutions enhanced the role of the people in scrutinizing governments and altered the understanding of how they did so. The traditional devices for scrutiny were petition, remonstrance, and instruction. Petitions (requests for governmental action), remonstrance (protests of governmental policy), and instructions (directives by voters to their representatives) were forms of political participation employed by colonial Americans. After Independence, however, those familiar tools that had been used in a system of a hierarchical government and social deference began to take on different implications. Revolutionary-era constitutions placed petitioners on a level more equal (if not superior) to that of those being petitioned. Still, to the extent that the use of petitions and remonstrances were a means of political expression, they largely expressed the people in their capacity of the ruled, as political participants. Instructions, however, soon acquired a different connotation, since under the new scheme of constitutionalism they more easily came to be seen as a communication from the principal to an agent. Instructions were more readily seen as directives from the ruler to those who in theory remained subordinate to the people.[25]

Many state constitutions acknowledged the subordination of government to the people, much as Virginia's 1776 constitution did. That constitution described public officials as the people's "trustees and servants" who were "at all times amenable to them." The first constitutions for Pennsylvania, Maryland, and Delaware echoed this sentiment. Massachusetts and New Hampshire used similar wording, stating that government officials were the people's "substitutes and agents . . . at all times accountable" to the people. This was not a burst of revolutionary enthusiasm. Massachusetts's 1780 constitution both provided for "instruction" and spoke of the right of the people to make "requests" (rather than "prayers") of the legislature. Instructing representatives and making requests of the legislature through "addresses, petitions, or remonstrances" indicated that government was the agent of the people.[26]

The idea that the sovereign should scrutinize government was not simply an aspiration expressed in many constitutions. Constitution-makers included specific measures and structural features to promote scrutiny. Their drafts reflected contrasting methods to monitor the operation of government. For example, Pennsylvania's 1776 constitution admonished the people to "pay particular attention" when choosing representatives. Freedom of the press under that constitution would enable the people to examine "the proceedings of the legislature, or any part of government."[27] Pennsylvania's constitution also established a single legislative body. The constitution designed a system for a check and balance between the people and the government. Pennsylvania's 1776 constitution-makers believed the people were sufficiently virtuous and that their vigilance would check any undue legislative or executive intrusions. The people should remain on guard against "Men of some rank" who, thinking liberty their private property, sought to "continue themselves and *favorites* in power."[28]

Pennsylvania's constitutional drafters recognized the utility of divided powers among government branches. Yet they concluded that a structural balance of government branches would not necessarily protect the common people from the rich and powerful. Only a virtuous people actively scrutinizing their government and rulers could ensure that government promoted the public welfare.

In contrast to Pennsylvania's approach, other states, such as Massachusetts, designed constitutions featuring checks and balances between government branches, rather than between the people and government. Such constitutional systems could be more self-regulating. They did not necessarily depend upon the people to take the initiative in scrutinizing government's operation. By checking each other, the various branches better promoted the public welfare.

These different approaches had remarkably common foundations. The difference was often one of emphasis. For example, most constitutions recognized the importance of the people's participation at the polls. The Massachusetts constitution contained a provision similar to one found in Pennsylvania's that encouraged the regular return of elected officials to their "private station" to forestall potential "oppression" of the people. "The People ought to have frequently the opportunity . . . of considering the Conduct of their Leaders, and of approving or disapproving," claimed John Adams. The constitutions of both Massachusetts and New Hampshire stressed the people's "constant observance" of lawmakers.[29] Political conservatives, such as Samuel Johnston of North Carolina, considered the people's role at the polls vital to preventing their representatives from "assuming more power than would be consistent with the liberties of the people." Pennsylvania's 1776 constitution instructed the people to watch their officeholders since they – and not their governors – held "the sole, exclusive and inherent right of governing and regulating" the state. The 1776 constitutions of Maryland and North Carolina basically incorporated this same instruction. The people under all these constitutions would play a role. In some states it was ongoing and active, even to the point of dispensing with traditional checks and balances of government branches. In others it was more passive and tended to be self-regulating.[30]

However the new American constitutions were structured and whatever their features, under them the sovereign was ultimately responsible for the government it created. This responsibility entailed the people's power to scrutinize government's operation. This idea was not consistent with the traditional limits and restrictions on public criticism of government that existed in England and in the colonies. Under English law, writings and speech that cast the government in a bad or false light, producing public disaffection with government, could be punished. Such seditious libel laws were not discarded upon the creation of American governments after the Revolution. Both state governments and eventually the national government under the federal Constitution would prosecute seditious libels.

Such laws increasingly seemed anachronistic because they conflicted with the central teaching of American constitutions that the collective sovereign had the right and duty to scrutinize government. A broader scope for criticism of government policies and officials in America developed growing force as a result of the concept that the people were now the sovereign and entitled to scrutinize government. The tension between freedom of speech and press and the government's self-preservation became harder to sort out with the rise of a legitimate political opposition. The first state constitutions provided minimal support for the logic that a government created by the collective sovereign had a right to protect itself against its creator.[31]

Participation by the collectivity of the people also posed a puzzle: how could all the people act as one, like a traditional sovereign? U.S. Supreme Court Justice James Wilson touched on the problem in 1793, describing the people in America as "a collection of original sovereigns." From the time of the Revolution, this difficult question generated conflict and profoundly shaped the structure of American constitutional thought. One answer to how all the people governed as the sovereign was that the collective sovereign expressed its will only through the use of procedural mechanisms. After creating governments based on their authority as the sovereign, the people henceforth were bound by their constitutions. Under this view, the written constitution and the government it created were the only channels through which the sovereign's will could be recognized.[32]

Others considered this procedural view an overly narrow conception of the people as the sovereign. For them, collective sovereignty meant that the majority of "the people" could express their will directly – just as they did during the events leading up to the Revolution. A sovereign could – but did not need to – use a constitution's formal mechanisms to express its will. Government was subordinate to the people. Although normally quiet and acquiescent, the people could, when they desired, act directly and independently of the existing government, or of constitutional procedures, to manifest their will.

These competing views of how the people as the sovereign articulated their will appropriated the universal acknowledgment that Americans used to support their Revolution. The idea that the people collectively were the sovereign – not a monarch or people serving in government positions – gave life and authority to the governments Americans created after Independence. It also implied that the new American sovereign – the people – retained power over the governments it created, including the ability to destroy that creation. This underlying principle of American constitution-making gave Americans considerable pride. But the idea that the people were the sovereign in America also introduced a worrisome potential: how could such governments be stable if subject to the will of such a collective sovereign? Moreover, the concept of a sovereign people called into question the continuing relevance of the right of revolution.

SOVEREIGNS AND SUBJECTS

After declaring independence, Americans believed the people acted directly and unilaterally to create constitutions that established their new governments. These constitutions did not arise out of a hypothetical bargain for rights with an equal or superior. Americans departed from existing notions of government, noted North Carolina revolutionary and future U.S. Supreme Court Justice James Iredell. Europeans believed that government was the result of "a contract between the rulers and the people." In this Old World view, the compact creating government "cannot be annulled but by the consent of both parties; therefore, unless the rulers are guilty of oppression, the people...have no right" to remake their government. American governments after the Revolution were "founded on much nobler principles." Americans "are known with certainty to have originated" government "themselves." The people could revise their government "whenever they think proper" and not only when the power was "oppressively exercised" by the "servants and agents" of the people. The people could change the government for the simple reason that "they think another form will be more conducive to their welfare."[33]

This new understanding of how to create legitimate government did not quickly or completely displace some Americans' talk of an implicit contract between the ruled and the ruler as the foundation of government. However, use of contract theory's bargaining metaphor seemed out of place when Americans were making their own constitutions. James Wilson's *Lectures on Law* explained that from the people's "authority the constitution originates: for their safety and felicity it is established: in their hands it is as clay in the hands of the potter: they have the right to mould, to preserve, to improve, to refine, and to finish it as they please." The people created constitutions. They could also destroy them. Wilson's observations suggest his excitement about the constitutionalism Americans had developed. In light of his later assessments of American government, it is likely that he did not fully appreciate the concept that if the people were the sovereign in the terms he described, the people would be a continuous, direct force for change.[34]

Drafting constitutions during the Revolution introduced Americans to the process of making governments. It led many to expect that as the sovereign they would have an ongoing right and obligation to act. Creating written constitutions expressed but did not exhaust the people's role as the sovereign. To many Americans, the people's sovereignty, like life, liberty, and property, might go unstated, but it remained an inherent right. For them, it made no sense that a government established by a constitution created by the sovereign people would become the sovereign in the place of the people. This attitude and expectation of an active role as the sovereign logically supported a right of the people to be more active in day-to-day government as well. This seemed particularly true to those once excluded from the arena of political discourse.

This aspect of American constitutionalism made some of America's traditional leadership fearful of "democratic excess." They worried that the idea of the people as the sovereign authorizing government would be stretched to facilitating increasing involvement of the people in day-to-day government decisions. As Theophilus Parsons, a prominent lawyer and future chief justice of the Supreme Judicial Court of Massachusetts, explained in 1778, "The idea of liberty has been held up in so dazzling colours," that some Americans were not "willing to submit to that subordination necessary in the freest States." Some American leaders feared that the common people would lose their proper sense of place in the postrevolutionary years. They occasionally returned to the earlier contract analogy describing government as an independent sovereign who contracted with the people and had rights against them.[35]

Despite the growing doubts of some about the people asserting a role as part of the sovereign, rhetoric that the people were America's sovereign seemed the coin of the American constitutional realm. Even those least comfortable with political democratization used the idea. In *Federalist No. 78* Alexander Hamilton identified judicial review as emanating from the principle that all legislative acts contrary to the will "of the people as declared in the constitution" were invalid. "To deny this would be to affirm that the deputy is greater than his principal; that the servant is above his master; that the representatives of the people are superior to the people themselves." Support for the unfettered right of the people to alter their governments even appeared in statements by Federalist justices of the U.S. Supreme Court. Chief Justice John Jay admitted the people were "truly the sovereigns of the country." Under the federal Constitution, Justice James Wilson noted, the people as the sovereign "reserved the Supreme Power in their own hands."[36]

All of America's revolutionary-era constitutions assumed that because the people were the sovereign they also legitimated and controlled government. Continental army officer John Laurens reflected this understanding in writing to his father, the president of Congress, from Valley Forge in 1778. Laurens described the power to revise constitutions as "inherent only in the people." This observation was a truism for American revolutionaries but would come under considerable strain after the struggle for independence was won.[37]

Americans believed that the people were simultaneously the sovereign and the ruled during constitution-making of the revolutionary era. This raised the question of whether the people, as the newly recognized sovereign in America, could ever "oppress" itself, justifying the right of revolution that Americans exercised in 1776. Invoking the right of revolution in the wake of declaring independence implicitly assumed the existence of two parties to the contract, one of whose breach warranted independence. But as America's new constitutions merged the ruler and ruled into one, they created anomalies in how and whether the right of revolution might apply in postrevolutionary America.

The constitutional logic of recognizing the people, not a king, as the sovereign implied the irrelevance of a right of revolution in America. This did not develop instantly or uniformly after the establishment of American governments. Some of the first state constitutions included "alter or abolish" provisions that mirrored the traditional right of revolution. For example, Maryland's 1776 bill of rights acknowledged that "whenever the ends of government are perverted, and public liberty manifestly endangered, and all other means of redress are ineffectual," the people could "reform the old, or establish a new government." New Hampshire's bill of rights borrowed that same language in 1784.[38]

Other state constitutions adopted different versions of this right to "alter or abolish" government that did not sound like the traditional right of revolution. In these provisions, the ability of the people to revise constitutions existed regardless of the traditional preconditions for the right of revolution. For example, Virginia's 1776 constitution protected the people's right to change government "inadequate" or "contrary" to its rightful purposes. The people could "alter, or abolish" government in Pennsylvania's 1776 constitution in any manner "judged most conducive" to the public welfare. Some of these provisions justified the people's acting outside governmental institutions. The people could alter written constitutions whenever and however they wished, even without strict compliance with existing procedures for change in the constitution. The people as the collective sovereign would play a unique role in America.[39]

Only five of the eleven states that drafted initial constitutions contained bills of rights with alter or abolish provisions. As bills of rights became more common, alter or abolish provisions appeared more frequently. Even state constitutions with alter or abolish provisions harkening back to the natural law precondition of oppression were not necessarily interpreted after the Revolution as limiting their use. Those provisions were construed to offer one example of a situation when the people could supersede government. However, they did not foreclose the people's right to alter or abolish government on other grounds.[40]

For example, in 1787, Maryland's legislators debated about whether that state's 1776 alter or abolish provision – that on its face looked like a traditional right of revolution – could be used by the people only if they were oppressed. Some Maryland legislators agreed that the people could resist their governors if those officials subverted the purposes of government as declared in the constitution. Yet this extreme situation was not an indispensable precondition. The Revolution, noted one legislator, William Paca, established that government's "power is derived from the people … to be exercised for their welfare and happiness." As "the judges" of when they think "it is not so employed," the people could "announce it by memorials, remonstrances, or instructions." Government officials risked being voted out of office if they ignored such efforts, "or if the magnitude of the case requires it," the people could resume "the powers of government." Thus, in one breath, Paca canvassed the possibilities of the people acting as the ruled by exerting political pressure, the ruler by exercising their electoral power, and the collective sovereign if they reclaimed their ultimate sovereignty.[41]

Increasingly, as Americans included it in their constitutions, the right of revolution came to be seen as a constitutional principle permitting the people as the sovereign to control government and revise their constitutions without limit.[42] In this way, the right broke loose from its traditional moorings of resistance to oppression. The alter or abolish provisions could now be interpreted consistent with the constitutional principle that in America, the sovereign was the people.[43]

After the Revolutionary War, Americans developed an appetite for histories that explained their victory in establishing a nation in which the people ruled as the sovereign. South Carolina revolutionary David Ramsay offered a popular account of the revolution in his state. Others, including Dr. Benjamin Rush, a signer of the Declaration of Independence, frequent pamphleteer, and essayist, considered but never completed such a project even though friends urged him "to undertake the work" of a history of the revolution in Pennsylvania.

Had Rush written his account it would have reflected his experience as "one of the firebrands" of the Revolution, who, as early as the 1760s while studying medicine at the University of Edinburgh, denounced "the absurdity of hereditary power." "[N]o form of government can be rational," he concluded, unless it was "the people" who were the sovereign. After returning to America, Rush participated in transforming the theory of the people's sovereignty into a practical reality by helping to organize the mass meeting in the State House Yard that John Adams so admired on that rainy day in May 1776. That meeting triggered the circumvention of the colonial government. In its place came rule by a committee of citizens that would eventually frame a government and constitution based "on the authority of the people only."

Although Rush's work to establish a government in which the people were the sovereign raised him to prominence and gained him a seat in the Continental Congress, his later thoughts about how this sovereign would rule undercut his political influence. Unlike fellow revolutionaries who helped displace Pennsylvania's colonial rulers, Rush publicly questioned whether government authorized by the people was the same thing as government power actually exercised by the people. Rush thought that it was not, becoming an unwelcome critic of the structure of government established in the state's first constitution.

An inveterate reformer, Rush began to crusade against the one-house legislature and lack of an executive veto that was part of the new constitutional structure. These "innovations" and "newfangled experiments," designed to make government directly controlled by the people, only produced "mob government." Rush thought that with time "the people" might develop a capacity for greater practical involvement in the affairs of government. These opinions, which cost him his seat in Congress in 1777, invigorated his efforts for another constitutional convention to revise the 1776 constitution, a process that took another thirteen years to accomplish.

Part of the problem was that it was not entirely clear how to call a new convention. The 1776 constitution anticipated the need for change. It provided for a constitutional convention every seven years only if a "Council of Censors" agreed by a two-thirds vote. This vote proved impossible to muster given political support for the 1776 constitution. This situation raised the question of whether the constitution's provision of a particular amendment procedure precluded changing it by other means. The constitution's bill of rights affirmed the people's "right to reform, alter, or abolish government in such manner" as the people "judged most conducive to the public weal."

After the Council of Censors refused to consider constitutional revision in 1783, Rush asserted that the Council's role in calling a convention under the 1776 constitution was not the exclusive means of altering that constitution. He expected that the people, much as they had done in 1776, could "easily" assemble a constitutional convention under their authority as the sovereign. All that was needed to initiate such a constitutional convention was "an appeal" from the legislature to the people of the state.

It took six more years before the opponents of the 1776 constitution came to dominate the legislature, so that such an appeal could be made. By March 1789 Rush hosted a meeting of advocates for a new constitution at his home, where they discussed how to overcome the 1776 constitution's apparent requirement that a convention meet only after a call by the Council of Censors. This planning led to the legislature's call for a constitutional convention because "the people have at all times an inherent right to alter and amend the form of government." The people could change the constitution "in such manner as they shall think proper." Limiting the people to the "too dilatory" procedures of the 1776 constitution involving the Council of Censors no longer reflected the people's will and frustrated their right as the sovereign to "alter or abolish" government. After many petitions favoring a convention were received by the legislature, a statewide election for delegates for that convention was held.

Rush was pleased with the constitutional convention's results. The new constitution's "reformation" of Pennsylvania's government gratified his "last political wish." The 1790 constitution altered many provisions of the 1776 constitution that Rush had opposed. In abolishing the Council of Censors, the 1790 constitution lacked any provision to govern constitutional amendment, although it included an alter or abolish provision similar to the one in the 1776 constitution. The language of that provision served to justify the legislature's call for a convention under the authority of the people when Pennsylvanians later sought to revise their 1790 constitution.[44]

AN ENDURING CONSTITUTIONAL LEGACY
OF THE REVOLUTION

The alter or abolish provisions of the first state constitutions reflected an American understanding that the people in a republic, like a king in a monarchy, exercised plenary authority as the sovereign. This interpretation persisted from the revolutionary period up to the Civil War. Although initially believing that the people could act at one discrete moment if subject to a tyrant's oppression, American constitution-makers began thinking that the people had a collective, ongoing, and inherent authority to change constitutions. For instance, even "conservative" constitutions of the postrevolutionary period, such as Massachusetts's 1780 constitution, preserved the people's right "to reform, alter, or totally change" government not only for their "protection" and "safety," but also whenever their "prosperity, and happiness require[d] it." Pennsylvania's 1790 constitution secured the "inherent" right of the people "at all times" to "alter, reform, or abolish their government, in such manner as they may think proper." Similarly, the preamble to Delaware's 1792 bill of rights recognized the people's "inherent" right "as circumstances require, from time to time" to "alter their constitution of government." When Connecticut replaced its colonial charter with a constitution in 1818, it recognized the right of the people "at all times" to alter government "in such a manner as they may think expedient."[45]

In fact, the creation of the federal Constitution reflected the belief that as the sovereign, the people were entitled to alter their forms of government without demonstrating the traditional preconditions of the right of revolution. While many supporters of the federal Constitution believed America to be in dire straits in 1787, the federal Constitution, unlike the Declaration of Independence, contained no litany of the misdeeds of the existing government to justify the constitution. As one scholar has put it, Americans understood by the late 1780s that "The people could properly amend whenever they deemed the status quo outdated or imperfect."[46]

Long after 1787, the principle that justified the Revolution, that the people were the sovereign, played a dominant role in the drafting of American constitutions. The principle of a collective sovereign defined the relationship of the people to their governments. A widespread understanding persisted in America that the people controlled constitutions and not the other way around. Constitutions drafted by new states joining the Union included the people's inherent right to change or abolish their governments. Often such provisions were not limited by the traditional preconditions of dire oppression. For example, Kentucky's 1792 constitution provided that the people could "alter, reform, or abolish" in any "manner as they may think proper." Four years later, Tennessee's bill of rights reflected that same language. Ohio's 1802 constitution declared that the people "have at all times a complete power to alter, reform, or abolish their government, whenever they may deem it necessary."[47] Constitutions drafted through the 1830s similarly expressed the people's freedom to "alter or abolish" governments.[48] These provisions routinely formed part of state constitutions through the nineteenth century and even persisted into the twentieth century.[49]

Modern scholars often dismiss alter or abolish provisions as glittering generalities. However, for many Americans before the Civil War these words meant something they no longer mean today. In that earlier day, alter or abolish provisions defined the relationship between the people and their governments. They were part of the constitutional heritage of the American Revolution. Americans had a natural right of revolution, as did every other people, but as the collective sovereign, Americans also possessed the inherent right to revise their constitutions. Not only did the people have constitutional sovereignty in America, but after the Revolution they freely exercised that authority. As a constitutional principle this power did not require a last-ditch effort of a desperate people.

In constructing their constitutions after they claimed independence, Americans did not seem to share a notion that took hold generations later of an unchanging constitution. Rather, as an expression of the sovereign people's will, a constitution could and should change frequently as the sovereign changed – over generations and as they increasingly learned about the "science of government." Constitutional revision was an important part of constitutional government. James Madison seemed to recall this shortly before his death in 1836. In explaining the lack of constitutional foundation for the doctrine of nullification, he tried to place in perspective the report he drafted for the Virginia Legislature in 1800 challenging the constitutionality of the Alien and Sedition Acts, quoting the language of his report that constitutional change diminished the "danger of degeneracy, to which Republics are liable as well as other Governments." While republics were subject to this corrosion, they were so "in a less degree than" other forms of government. Constitutional government would have a better chance to endure if its constitution was examined in light of the "fundamental principles" that constitution embodied. These principles were important, noted the *Federal Farmer* during the ratification of the federal Constitution, because "if a nation means its [governmental] systems ... shall have duration, it ought to recognize the leading principles of them. ... What is the usefulness of a truth in theory, unless it exists constantly in the minds of the people, and has their assent?"[50]

The American Revolution promised to forestall the inevitable demise of government. After the Revolution, a "frequent recurrence" to fundamental principles increasingly became associated with constitutional improvements, implicitly giving the people responsibility for monitoring the political process.[51] The revolutionary-era constitutions of Virginia, North Carolina, Pennsylvania, Vermont, and Massachusetts, as well as New Hampshire's second constitution in 1784, emphasized timely reforms from such "recurrence."[52] The people's participation in ongoing revision and formal constitutional adjustment was important. As "Demophilus" from Philadelphia argued in 1776, periodic constitutional review kept the government in "the hands of THE PEOPLE."[53] Nonetheless, for some revolutionary leaders a frequency of constitutional revision seemed more likely to undermine governmental stability than to shore up the country's commitment to republican principles.

Ultimately, Americans developed competing views over the ease of amending constitutions, while agreeing that their constitutions would continue to improve.[54] However, it was unclear whether amendments could occur without specific revision procedures in the constitution to be changed. Many Americans considered a specific procedure unnecessary. "[A]ny set of men" or even "any individual" could legitimately initiate a call for a constitutional convention, explained South Carolina pamphleteer Thomas Tudor

Tucker in 1784.[55] Because the people were the sovereign, revolutionary leaders like James Wilson argued, they "may change the constitutions whenever
and however they please." Wilson noted that this was the implication of what
it meant that "the supreme, absolute, and uncontrollable power remains in
the people." This was an important truth "far from being merely speculative." A strong proponent of the federal Constitution in Virginia's ratifying
convention, George Nicholas, reminded fellow delegates that "every people
had a right to change their Government" when they deemed it "inadequate
to their happiness."[56] This was true for many others as well. Even if revision
provisions existed, a majority of the people could bypass procedures in the
constitution. Indeed, several constitutions stated that revision could occur
in any manner the people saw fit.[57]

The common understanding that specific revision provisions were not a
prerequisite for constitutional revision was also reflected in how Americans
went about revising their first constitutions.[58] Americans routinely revised
their constitutions by citing the people's inherent right as the sovereign to
change their minds.[59] For example, Delaware's 1776 constitution prohibited
constitutional change unless a supermajority of the legislature consented.
Although it was silent about future constitutional conventions, that did not
stop the legislature from calling a convention in 1791 to draft a new constitution. After noting that "all government originates from the people," the
Federalist-dominated legislature broadly interpreted "the power of altering
and amending the constitution." They found support for this from the state's
bill of rights, which described the people's right to "establish a new, or reform
the old Government" whenever its ends were "perverted, and public Liberty
manifestly endangered."[60]

Demonstrating such a perversion of liberty in Delaware in 1791 would
have been difficult. But "Curtius" explained in the *Delaware Gazette* that
a convention was part of the people's inherent "power . . . of altering their
form of government." This power existed if government became inconvenient or failed to answer its intended "good purposes." Another Delaware
writer explained that such a convention reflected the people's "uncontrollable authority." On July 4, 1791, "Phileleutheros" advised that if the legislature failed to call a convention "there can be no constitutional, nor
legal reason assign'd, why [the people] cannot" act "independently" to hold
one "provided a decided majority of the citizens at large concur in the
measure."[61]

When constitutions specified procedures for their change, many Americans did not consider those means the exclusive method for revision.
For example, legislatures called constitutional conventions even though

different revision procedures were provided in the constitution they sought to amend.[62]

Changing constitutions without regard to revision provisions did not violate constitutionalism. It was inconsistent with American constitutionalism at this early period to believe that a constitution took precedence over the will of its makers or otherwise bound the people to specified procedures. The framers of the federal Constitution acted upon this belief when they sought the people's approval of the 1787 draft constitution without seeking the unanimous consent of the state legislatures as called for in the Articles of Confederation.[63]

THE PROCESS OF REVOLUTIONARY CONSTITUTION-MAKING

Americans struggled a great deal over how to exercise their sovereign power. More than a month before drafting the Declaration of Independence, Thomas Jefferson hoped Congress might recess. This would allow delegates to return home and help each state establish its "form of government." This activity was "the whole object of the present controversy," he noted. When Massachusetts initiated its constitution-making, John Adams agonized over staying in Philadelphia. Congress would guide the movement for independence, but those drafting a constitution in Boston would affect "the Lives and Liberties of Millions, born and unborn." The revolutionaries were alive, Adams noted to another correspondent, "when the greatest Philosophers and Lawgivers of antiquity would have wished to have lived."[64]

The novelty and significance of the people creating governments sparked considerable interest. Draft constitutions were widely circulated and discussed by many leaders of the Revolution. John Adams, for example, wrote to a number of correspondents about constitution-making and then published his *Thoughts on Government* in April 1776. He believed constitution-making "the most difficult and dangerous Part of the Business" of the Revolution.

Thoughts on Government reflected a concern shared by other revolutionary leaders. On one hand, the tract fully endorsed the constitutional premise that the people were the sovereign. On the other hand, once the sovereign established the new government, Adams opposed democratic political participation such as that advocated by Thomas Paine in *Common Sense*. Adams insisted that American governments incorporate "popular Principles and Maxims" and secure the welfare of the people. Under a leadership of their betters, the people should have a limited political role to play in these governments. For Adams, American governments were endangered if they lacked structural balance to check the untrammeled political participation of the people. Paine's advocacy of single-bodied legislatures to ensure rule by the people invited imbalance in Adams's view. In the "best" governments, Adams noted, "a few of the most wise and good" were deputized to act for "the many." Institutional checks such as two-bodied legislatures, executive veto, and an independent judiciary helped avoid the confusion that could result from a democracy. Governments with structural devices to calm the people's natural exuberance would instill "knowledge," inspire them with "dignity," and produce "good humour, sociability, good manners, and good morals." Education, for this purpose, "especially of the lower class of people," justified any expense.[65]

Adams initially worried that southern colonies did not fully accept the popular basis of republics. As events unfolded, however, he found that the "Spirit and Zeal" of the revolutionary cause in the South displaced "the Place of Fortune, Family, and every other Consideration, which used to have Weight with Mankind." Ironically, southerners might not be giving enough deference to the gentry for political leadership rather than giving them too much. Early American constitution-making was a balance between retaining a commitment to the constitutional dimension of a people as the sovereign while not allowing popular will to go unchecked by the governing hand of the "wise and good." Implicitly such a "governing hand" would temper the tendency of the people to see themselves as the rulers.[66] All in all, Adams was amazed at the populist nature displayed as Americans proceeded to craft their constitutions.

The American process of creating America's first constitutions has been questioned by scholars. Some suggest that Americans made no real constitutions during this period. This analysis finds that virtually all of these constitutions lacked the process of special constitutional conventions followed by popular ratification that seems so crucial to constitution-making today. Most modern observers question the legitimacy of early American constitutions because they did not take those procedural steps.[67] They assume that it took Americans until the 1780s to develop a "correct" understanding of constitutionalism. Americans during the revolutionary period are described as experiencing a "confusion" and "unfamiliarity" in creating constitutions. Engaged in "a hasty experiment," early state constitution-makers had not yet "fully learned to regard a written constitution as supreme fundamental law."[68] Supposedly, the first state constitutions "were not truly constitutional at all" because "a true constitution required its formation by a body appointed for that purpose alone, and then ratified by the people."[69] Although some Americans at the time called for constitutional conventions and others for popular ratification, most of America's first constitutions were drafted under exigent circumstances by revolutionary conventions without ratification.[70]

These state conventions guided revolutionary movements locally. They generally promulgated the first state constitutions. These conventions were not the "legislatures" of the colonial government. Instead, they were ad hoc bodies directing the patriot resistance. The revolutionary conventions made executive, legislative, and even judicial decisions and drafted the constitution for the revolutionary government. The consent of the people supporting the revolutionary cause gave these conventions their authority, including that needed to promulgate constitutions. Only after these constitutions established governments for the new states would formal legislative branches emerge.[71]

Early American constitution-makers knew what made a constitution legitimate. Many traced their new constitutions' legitimacy to special elections that preceded the conventions. The people elected these conventions with knowledge that one thing the convention could do was write the constitution. A legitimate constitution depended on whether the sovereign people authorized it, not whether a particular procedure was used or whether revolutionary conventions were free of other responsibilities, such as passing ordinary legislation. It was the people as the sovereign who authorized drafting those first constitutions that gave them their legitimacy, not whether they used procedures that matched what was later understood to be necessary to create fundamental law.[72]

The first conventions called to draft constitutions identified – in preambles and addresses – the people's role in supplying needed constitutional authority. The preamble to South Carolina's constitution noted its source in the "common consent" of the people. The bill of rights of Virginia's 1776 constitution was premised on the "power . . . vested in, and consequently derived from, the People," wording borrowed by other subsequent constitutions. The preamble to New Jersey's constitution noted that the people were the source of all "constitutional authority." Many postrevolutionary constitutions were no different in explaining the source of their authority, containing language in which the sovereign people expressly legitimated the new governments.[73]

Pronouncing the source of the constitution's authority did not always eliminate confusion about its legitimacy. For instance, South Carolina Governor John Rutledge resigned in 1778 because the legislature revised the constitution without "lawful Power" to do so. Such power was found "only, in the People." The perspective of the legislature was captured by John Lewis Gervais, a former member of the South Carolina legislature and future delegate to the Continental Congress. He agreed with Rutledge that only the people had the authority to adopt or change the constitution. However, since "every body" knew that the people elected the 1776 legislature "for the very purpose of altering the Constitution," their revisions did not lack legitimacy.[74]

The revolutionaries focused on substance, not form, in drafting constitutions. All but two of the eleven first state constitutions emerged from revolutionary conventions after representatives to those bodies were specially elected for that purpose or elected with the common understanding that they would create a constitution for the state. For example, the North Carolina Council of Safety called for an election in October 1776. The convention call made it clear that those elected would create a constitution, "the Corner Stone of all Law" for the state. Special elections in Delaware, Pennsylvania, Maryland, Georgia, New York, and Massachusetts selected similar revolutionary bodies that would put into place a state constitution. New Hampshire's provincial congress promulgated the state's 1776 constitution itself because it received a special mandate in the previous election to draft and adopt a constitution. New Jersey voters in 1776 understood they were voting for representatives who would create a new government.[75]

The two states that did not hold elections before their legislatures promulgated their initial constitutions were South Carolina and Virginia. Even without such elections, people in those states assumed that by electing representatives in favor of independence they were also authorizing the creation of a constitution, albeit a temporary one.[76] Indeed, Americans widely accepted the people as the source of constitutions even if they disagreed about the process of constitution-making.[77] As John Adams recognized as early as 1775, the key to creating governments in America was to acknowledge that "the People were the Source of all Authority and . . . Power."[78]

Today's view that legitimate constitutions require constitutional conventions followed by popular ratification would have been news to American constitution-makers of the revolutionary period. Few state constitutions were popularly ratified before the federal Constitution. Many after 1787 were also promulgated without ratification. Only one of the seven constitutions establishing new states in the Northwest Territory between 1801 and 1830 were ratified by the people. Of the 119 constitutions adopted between 1776 and 1900, forty-five of them (roughly 38%) lacked popular ratification. More than half of the nonratified constitutions were promulgated after 1800.[79]

Constitution-making eventually did become associated with popular ratification after a specially called convention drafted a constitution. However, such single-purpose conventions followed by ratification were only one means by which the people could authorize government during the eighteenth century and later. For example, the people's consent could take the form of permitting representatives in revolutionary conventions to create constitutions. It could also take the form of allowing delegates in a special convention to create a constitution. Finally, such consent could take the form that eventually became commonplace, of having the people ratify a draft constitution. In the first wave of state constitution-making, constitutional drafts were occasionally circulated for public comment before their final promulgation. Whatever tool of drafting was used for constitution-making, all of them reflected the popular conviction that the people were the indispensable creators of these constitutions and the only source of legitimacy for governments.[80]

While some Americans objected to constitutions framed without popular ratification or a special convention, this was not a common concern during the initial period of constitution-making. Concern about the necessity of such devices often came as an afterthought. For example, Virginia's 1776 constitution was adopted without a special convention or popular ratification. At the time neither James Madison (a member of the legislative committee that drafted the 1776 constitution) nor Thomas Jefferson (who produced several draft constitutions for consideration) raised questions about the legitimacy of Virginia's first constitution. Soon after its creation, Jefferson focused on its substantive features such as legislative apportionment, voting rights, and property rights that he wished changed rather than any perceived procedural irregularities that undermined the constitution's legitimacy. Only a decade later would Madison and Jefferson publicly question whether the creation of the constitution without popular ratification undermined its authority.[81]

The New Jersey 1776 constitution was also a target of later attention. In a judicial decision of 1802, a New Jersey court described the constitution as "framed by a convention never delegated for that purpose, and therefore never vested with competent authority." In 1827, New Jersey's legislature was urged to hold a constitutional convention to revise the 1776 constitution, which "went into operation by the mere force of public opinion and by the silent acquiescence of the people." This made it "unsanctioned by the People." Those views did not go unchallenged. Others asserted that citizens in New Jersey in 1776 understood their state's first constitution to rest on the authority of the people. They noted that officeholders under that constitution took an oath of allegiance "to the Government established in this State under the Authority of the People."[82]

During the Revolution, America's leadership learned that the will of the people could be expressed as often through direct action reflecting dire necessity as through expressions of will by formal votes. This lesson was a painful one because the expression of will through action, while powerful, was unavoidably ambiguous. George Washington's command of the American troops demonstrated this. Early in the war, Washington's largely untrained, volunteer army drawn from civilian life was stymied by the hardened, professional troops occupying Boston. Dislodging the British from the town seemed hopeless, but by March 1776, American soldiers were poised to stun their military opponents by a daring plan to fortify Dorchester Heights, overlooking Boston.

American citizen-soldiers entrenched artillery on the Heights despite the obstacle of building fortifications on ground "froze upwards of two feet deep, & as impenetrable as a Rock." The Americans worked feverishly to transport lumber and other materials to the Heights after Washington ordered them to act "as becomes men, fighting for every thing that is dear, and valuable to Freemen." To conceal their movements, the Americans lined their route of approach with bales of hay as they worked through the night to construct two forts on the Heights. The sound of their movements was also masked by the bombardment from Washington's artillery, which included a 13-inch mortar dubbed "Congress."

The next morning, the American achievement astounded the British. After viewing the fortifications through his spyglass, the commander of British forces in Boston, General William Howe, reputedly remarked, "The rebels have done more in one night, than my whole army could do in months." The citizen-soldiers had rendered the town indefensible. With his ships in the harbor and troops in the town now vulnerable to American guns on the Heights, Howe decided to evacuate Boston. By March 17 some 10,000 British troops were on transport ships that eventually took them to Halifax.

The success in retaking Boston seemed to confirm American faith in what a collective people could achieve. Although earlier troubled by the uncertain, fluctuating number of men he commanded as they came and went in accordance with (or in violation of) their terms of enlistment, Washington now expressed optimism. Even though many of his "Countrymen" once possessed "steady Attachment . . . to Royalty," he presently detected "a powerful change" in "the Minds of many Men" regarding "the Idea of Independancy." Two weeks after the British sailed out of Boston harbor, Washington predicted that "frequent appeals to the People" produced "no bad" and possibly "very salutary effects."

In spring of 1776, Washington directed his army toward New York, "a Post of infinite importance" to both sides. By April 13 he arrived in Manhattan to take command. Clearly, the challenge of defending New York was more daunting than what Washington faced at Boston. With naval and military superiority, the British could attack the Americans from almost all sides of Manhattan and Long Island.

After British troops landed a massive army on Staten Island in July and August 1776, it was only a matter of time before the American forces positioned along the Brooklyn Heights at the west end of Long Island came under attack. During the three-day Battle of Long Island, American troops were flanked and routed, forced to retreat to Manhattan, and eventually retired to White Plains. Some American troops fought bravely, but many others broke and ran.

What gave Washington greatest "surprize and Mortification" was seeing his troops flee Manhattan once the British landed at Kips Bay. He offered a prosaic account to the president of the Continental Congress, "I used every means in my power to rally and get them into some order but my attempts were fruitless and ineffectual." Others, however, recalled Washington physically lashing out at soldiers and angrily throwing his hat to the ground because of the Army's "disgracefull and dastardly conduct."

Washington feared that human nature might spell defeat for American Independence. Before experiencing the hardships of war, people "fly hastily, and cheerfully to Arms," he explained to Congress. But faced with difficult challenges the influence of "Interest" took over. To expect otherwise looked "for what never did, & I fear never will happen." Yet Washington did not abandon the revolutionary cause and he came to realize that most American soldiers and civilians who favored Independence continued to persevere.

Still, many of the Revolution's leaders shared Washington's mixed feelings about the combination of power and unpredictability exhibited by the people. On one hand, leaders shared the conviction that the people were the sovereign. On the other hand, particularly in dark moments for the revolutionary cause, they could not help worrying about how the new sovereign threatened that cause.[83]

POLITICAL DIMENSIONS OF THE PEOPLE'S SOVEREIGNTY

Despite their commitment to the idea that the people were the sovereign in America, those who led the Revolution were practical politicians. The protests against the British monarch found the people acting collectively outside the agency of government. The people's action provided legitimacy to revolutionary resistance.[84] Politics "out-of-doors" demonstrated the desires of the people. It also involved many who in ordinary times were expected to defer to their "betters."[85] Watching the "mob" begin "to think and to reason" both excited and worried some elites.[86] Nonetheless, many revolutionary leaders initially welcomed such popular action when directed at the British government. After the Revolution toppled the king's authority in America, however, those same leaders were uncertain about what a sovereign people might mean in the new American governments.[87]

John Adams described the quandary in 1776. Few doubted that "in Theory" the "Consent of the People" was "the only moral Foundation of Government." Where Americans might "carry this Principle" formed the real question. William Hooper, a conservative congressional delegate from North Carolina, raised similar concerns. What principles should govern, now that "the people at large" were "the source from which all power is to be derived?" How would these principles be implemented in the new American governments? For some, the people as the sovereign was not just a theoretical principle. They insisted it have practical application. Even Hooper conceded that acknowledging a sovereign people suggested a new way of thinking about government in America. "Rulers must be conceived as the Creatures of the people." Rulers were "made" for the "use" of the people and "accountable" to them. As such, those who held office were "subject to removal as soon as they act inconsistent with the purposes for which they were formed."[88]

During the war for independence, revolutionary leaders embraced the idea of rule by a sovereign people without displaying unconditional faith in them. George Washington is illustrative. His commitment to the people remained unshaken even with reservations about the new sovereign. General Nathanael Greene shared Washington's concerns about the character of the people. In late 1775 Greene advised Congress to make "the poorer sort of people as easy and happy . . . as possible" because "they are creatures of a day." They appreciated a small "present gain and gratification" more than "greater advantages at a distance." Such people avoided causes not quickly or easily won. Alexander Hamilton believed the common "multitude" displayed "contempt and disregard" for authority because they lacked "reason and knowledge." The "unthinking populace" were apt to grow "giddy" and "run into anarchy" if they were not kept "within proper bounds." Even so, most leaders of the revolutionary movement did not insist on having complete faith in the rationality, virtue, and trustworthiness of the people in order to accept the people as the sovereign of the new governments. Indeed, the revolutionaries' steadfast commitment to the people as the collective sovereign was separate and apart from what faith they placed in the political capacity of the people.[89]

Other American leaders expressed greater optimism about the people than Washington and Greene, focusing on the capacity of the people collectively.[90] Massachusetts lawyer Josiah Quincy, Jr., in describing America's grievances

to Parliament in 1774 declared that "THE PEOPLE" were "the only competent judges of their own welfare." In 1776, Thomas Jefferson explained
that as a general matter "the decisions of the people, in a body, will be more
honest and more disinterested than those of wealthy men." His contemporary in Massachusetts, Dr. Thomas Young, thoroughly embraced the ability
of ordinary people to act as the sovereign. Jefferson's neighbors in Albemarle
County, Virginia, believed in 1776 that most people "always aim at the public good." The anonymous author of a New Hampshire pamphlet in 1776
thought the people knew their "wants and necessities" and therefore were
"best able to rule themselves."[91]

Winning independence demonstrated that a people could successfully
rule as a collective sovereign and act as capable governors.[92] To New England farmer William Manning at the end of the eighteenth century, the
previous decade proved that the common people could make wise political
decisions for America. The people only needed sufficient information, which
he called "The Key of Liberty." Manning, and others who shared his views,
expected that as the sovereign, the people would play a broader political
role. Government could now be engaged in by "the Many."[93] Increasingly in
the nineteenth century, many Americans believed that "when facts are fairly
laid before the people . . . their decision will be right."[94]

Most leaders of the revolutionary era did not share this favorable assessment of the governing abilities of the people. A congressional delegate from
Connecticut in 1776 captured the typical view of eighteenth-century leaders.
The "unhappy Truth that People in general do not know their own happiness"
made it necessary for their leaders to secure it for them. When "powers are
vested wholly or partly in the collective body of the people," warned Alexander Hamilton, all one could expect was "error, confusion and instability."
Washington questioned the workability of popular government when those
"who act upon Principles of disinterestedness" were "no more than a drop
in the Ocean."[95]

Skepticism about the abilities of the people to serve in government did not
shake revolutionary leaders' belief that a sovereign people authorized government. Perhaps governing was similar to the attorney-client relationship.
In choosing a trial lawyer, the client retained plenary authority. Yet no client
expected that this power to choose meant the client possessed the skills to
conduct court proceedings independent of the lawyer. Thus, American leaders, such as the wealthy Virginian Landon Carter, could describe the mass
of people, on one hand, as "Idiots" and "ignorant Creatures." On the other
hand, Carter accepted the "premise" that government should "originate from
among the people."[96]

For many American revolutionary leaders, human nature did not bode well for the success of popularly based governments before the Revolution and their view of self-government after Independence gave them additional cause for concern about involving the people in government. In 1775 South Carolinian merchant Henry Laurens described "Back Woods-Men" who took their seats as legislators believing that government required "no more words than are necessary in the bargain & Sale of a Cow." The common people lacked sophistication, skill, and temperament. John Adams grew incensed when a former client congratulated him for supposedly abolishing the courts. The attitude of this "Wretch" horrified Adams. He feared for America's cause if "the Power of the Country should get into such hands" as this "common Horse Jockey." If Americans did not "guard against this Spirit" they would "repent" the Revolution.[97]

Many leaders, like Adams, wondered whether the people, although making the proper choice to cast off the British sovereign, possessed the public and private virtue needed for republican government. Republics hinged on the willingness of people to subordinate individual interests to those of the common good. In governments resting on such voluntary behavior, the character of the people assumed enormous importance. Nearly three months before the Declaration of Independence, Adams explained the problem: "public virtue is the only Foundation of Republics," but "Public Virtue cannot exist in a Nation without private [virtue]." Two months later, he worried that unless the people displayed more "pure Virtue," the blessings of liberty would elude Americans. On the eve of Independence, Adams thought the newly created governments needed "a Purification" from "Vices."[98]

For many revolutionary leaders, the threat of political democracy posed real dangers after Independence. In 1776, Edward Rutledge, a congressional delegate from New York, wanted to suppress "Popular Spirit." That same year, the Maryland revolutionary leader Charles Carroll saw "selfish men . . . busy every where striving to throw all power into the hands of the very lowest of the People in order that they may be their masters." The Virginian Landon Carter asked George Washington in 1776 if the revolutionary cause entailed a leveling of society. He overheard people say that independence not only promised freedom from the British, but "a form of Government . . . independnt of the rich men" allowing "eve[r]y man" to "do as he pleasd." For Carroll, Carter, and many other revolutionary leaders, "levelling" schemes were bad enough, but in addition, ordinary people might be misled by those with "desperate & wicked designs." By January 1777, James Otis, Jr., a prominent Boston lawyer and early advocate for the patriot cause, offered his opinion of the state of "measures & leaders": "When the pot boils, the scum will arise."[99]

Leaders of the Revolution expected that political control and guidance would come into the hands of a natural aristocracy. This reflected their world-view that drew sharp distinctions between the common people and those with education and social standing. George Washington lamented the "stupidity in the lower class," calling ordinary farmers "the grazing multitude." James Madison saw a difference between the leadership and the "middling sort of folks" as well as "the Common people." John Adams distinguished "Gentle-men" from "the Common People" and "simplemen." There were distinctions "among all orders and Degrees of Men," noted Adams. The "common Herd of Mankind" tended to choose ignorant and self-interested leaders instead of those with "Merit, Virtue, and public Spirit." It remained important for the people to show "a Decency and Respect, and Veneration" for "Persons in Authority." Otherwise, governments in which the people were the sovereign would fail. The potential tyranny of the many over the few made political leadership critical.[100]

Attitudes of revolutionary leaders toward the people varied. Most eighteenth-century American leaders agreed that the political involvement of the people should be limited. John Adams and Thomas Jefferson illustrate how those who differed in their view of the people could agree on rule by a natural aristocracy. Adams's distrust of the mass of the people contrasted with Jefferson's belief that the people could act in their best interests. On the eve of Independence, Adams worried about the people having "unbounded Power" since they, like "the Great," were "addicted to Corruption and Venal-ity." Nonetheless, Adams took a leap of faith and embraced the sovereignty of the people.[101]

On the other hand, Jefferson believed the people were "the mainspring" of the American nation. Their "good sense" formed the "only safe deposito-ries" of government. Nonetheless, Jefferson did not widely trust the people during the revolutionary era. Unlike the egalitarianism of Democrats of the Jacksonian period, Jefferson sought a limited role for the people in political affairs. Less than two months after writing the Declaration of Independence, Jefferson supported the indirect election of Virginia's senate as the means of choosing "the wisest men." The "choice by the people themselves is not generally distinguished for it's wisdom," he noted. It was "usually crude." He envisioned a filtering process – members of the "lower" house of the legislature should elect the senate. This "second choice" would "generally" select "wise men." Jefferson anticipated a natural aristocracy emerging from what he called "the rubbish."[102]

Jefferson's expressions did not make his faith in the people insincere any more than Adams's views made his commitment to the people equivocal. Instead, both reflected the way the idea of the common people as the ruler challenged ingrained social assumptions of many eighteenth-century Americans. Even as all could agree that it must be the people who as the sovereign would establish and legitimate government, America's revolutionary leaders were uncertain about the level of the people's involvement and who qualified as "the people" in a political sense. With time and growing confidence in the political capacity of ordinary people, American politics experienced a broad democratization in the course of the nineteenth century.[103] In the eighteenth century, however, even those sharing more benign views of the people, such as Jefferson and Dr. Young, were not inclined to grant the people a role in making political decisions and policy.[104] Although Jefferson eventually symbolized American democracy, in the eighteenth century he expected the people to be led by an educated, virtuous elite.[105]

Even the most sweeping defenders of the people's constitutional sovereignty – for example, James Wilson – did not expect ordinary citizens to participate in day-to-day governance.[106] The democratically inclined Dr. Young assumed that postrevolutionary leadership would be limited to those of "capacity and integrity." Although the common people lacked the education and experience to run government, Dr. Young and other revolutionary leaders anticipated that the body of the people would elect responsible leaders. When the people acted collectively they possessed the capacity to identify integrity and merit. They made this selection by voting and this, too, proved a matter of some dispute.[107]

Revolutionary leaders differed over whether to expand the relatively broad voting population of eighteenth-century America. In 1776, James Sullivan, a Massachusetts lawyer, judge, and later governor of the state, favored limiting representation on economic issues in proportion to one's wealth. However, on matters involving personal freedom and criminal punishment where "the poor and rich are alike interested," Sullivan opposed any property qualifications. John Adams disagreed. He was convinced that "very few Men, who have no Property, have any Judgment of their own." Sullivan's ideas threatened to "destroy all Distinctions," bringing "all Ranks, to one common Levell." A climate "afloat" with the "Spirit of Levelling" and the "Rage for Innovation" could ruin society. Adams was not alone in fearing a potential "Fountain of Corruption" from expanding the number of voters even as he remained committed to the constitutional principle of a sovereign people. In fact, the fear of unbridled democracy emphasized the extent of the commitment to the people's sovereignty because those fears did not lead to a repudiation of the principle.[108]

Despite their doubts about the mass of humanity, American leaders accepted some degree of the people's practical involvement in political affairs. Structuring that involvement became crucial. Filtering the popular will became an objective of numerous constitutional arrangements. Jefferson's idea of a two-step process for selecting the Virginia senate explicitly tried to screen out unqualified leaders. The idea of refining political leadership emerged early in the Revolution. In 1776, Josiah Quincy, a wealthy trader in semiretirement in Braintree, Massachusetts, developed and shared with John Adams his idea for a complex series of voting stages. This system would separate the participation of the "ignorant Multitude" from the "wise." While Adams did not endorse that particular scheme, it responded to his abiding fear that republican governments might not advance "Men of Learning" to positions of leadership. America should be led by those with "a liberal education" or at least some degree of "erudition in liberal arts and sciences."[109]

American constitution-makers faced the challenge of designing stable governments while also providing for popular participation. As students of history, they knew that coercive power could maintain order; yet they rejected this option. At the same time, their commitment to republicanism forced them to try to avoid the historical dangers of democratic governments. They sought to achieve stability without resorting to practices and powers that undermined republican governments. Constitution-makers struck that balance in the way they structured government to facilitate rule by the people. They also expressed a sovereign people's authority in constitutions drafted after Independence.[110]

An even greater difficulty emerged because of the powerful ideas stimulated by the Revolution. During the struggle for independence, certain words and concepts became familiar to the common people that needed to be "Properly explained" and "Soberly Considered," suggested Landon Carter. He touched on one of the most troubling aspects of the patriot cause from the perspective of its leaders. The Revolution produced a potent vocabulary that justified the end of British colonial rule. At the same time, that vocabulary established the criteria for evaluating any government's legitimacy. By 1777, the Pennsylvania revolutionary Dr. Benjamin Rush lamented that some Americans misused the language of their own sovereignty. There was no disagreement among Americans "that 'all power is *derived* from the people.'" But this idea, insisted Rush, did not mean "that all power is *seated* in the people."[111]

Sometimes the revolutionary leadership itself got swept up in the heady implications of the people as the new sovereign. Dr. Rush's distinction between sovereignty exercised by the people and rule by the people was often overlooked by other leaders. For example, Colonel Benjamin Hichborn delivered an oration on "civil liberty" in Boston in 1777. Such liberty, he declared, was "a power existing in the people at large, at any time, for any cause, or for no cause, but their own sovereign pleasure, to alter or annihilate both the mode and essence of any former government, and adopt a new one in its stead."[112]

NEW STATE CONSTITUTION-MAKING BEFORE
THE FEDERAL CONSTITUTION

Americans justified the Revolution as a legitimate step to establish their own governments in the thirteen former colonies. They were not reticent in contrasting their new state governments with the British colonial ones they rejected. The constitutions they adopted articulated a central idea – that governments were built by a new sovereign in America. With Independence, however, the significance of the people as the sovereign did not die. This idea was applied by Americans for years thereafter outside of the revolutionary context of the thirteen original colonies. The idea of the sovereign people transcended its roots in the revolt against the British, and after the war's end, it persisted to confront and confound American's own political leadership.

Constitution-making on America's frontiers illustrates the way the idea that the people were the sovereign truly became continental. After New York replaced the British colonial regime with a government established by the people, inhabitants of its own northeastern frontier claimed they were a separate people, entitled as were all people, to be sovereign. Many in the region that eventually became the state of Vermont participated in the struggle for American Independence. In 1777 they asserted they were a people entitled to their own government.

In words that echoed New York's assertion of independence from Britain, Vermonters in 1777 adopted a constitution declaring their independence from New York. "[A]ll power," the Vermont constitution noted, was "inherent in, and consequently derived from, the people." The people had the "sole, exclusive and inherent right" to create and govern their own state and the right to "reform, alter, or abolish" government "in such manner" as they felt "most conducive" to the public welfare. The sovereign people of Vermont did not recognize New York's legislature and governor as their agents. In addition to separating from New York, Vermont's constitution explicitly set out the people's relationship to their new state government. Government officers were the people's "trustees and servants, and at all times accountable" to the people who were able to instruct and petition their legislators. Vermont's claim for independence and the new government it created demonstrates that the idea ushering in the Revolution – that the people could rule as the sovereign – did not fade away.[113]

Vermonters were not the only ones making use of the idea of the collective sovereign. For example, delegates representing settlers along the western frontier of North Carolina in 1785 concluded that they too were "a people" entitled to a government of their own choice. They took that step by declaring themselves independent of the state of North Carolina and drafting a constitution for their presumptive state of "Franklin."

In establishing their state, delegates at their constitutional convention considered a draft constitution containing wide-ranging statements of American constitutional principles. Delegates prepared the draft after consulting "the thirteen Constitutions" of the American states and "the instructions of the people" in the region. Some of these delegates brought pocket-sized compilations of the existing state constitutions to the convention so they could create the most "Republican" constitution to date. The product of their efforts stated "principles, provisions, and restrictions" to protect "the ruled from ... the rulers." That draft constitution expected the people as the sovereign to actively "look in" on governmental proceedings and "judge for themselves" whether their rights were "infringed."[114]

The proposed constitution promoted widespread representation and political participation, as well as accountable government under strict scrutiny by citizens. Like the Vermont constitution, "the doors" of the legislature were "open" except when "the good of the commonwealth" required closing them. Widespread political participation would result not only from a very broad franchise, but also from unique mechanisms directly involving "the people." Abolishing property qualifications, all "free" males over twenty-one years of age could vote if they were state residents for six months. The constitution divided each county into multiple "districts" of approximately 100 voters. Each district elected three "Registers" to preside over elections and monitor voters within their district. In addition, a district could assemble "to consult for the common good, give instructions to their Representatives, or to apply to the Legislature for redress of grievances by address, petition, or remonstrance." The constitution gave extensive immunity from prosecution to everyone who examined the proceedings of the legislature.[115]

The draft constitution focused not only on public involvement in government but also on encouraging public virtue and morality. The constitution required that each citizen would receive a copy of the constitution, which, rendered into a catechism, would be taught in all the schools. The legislature could compel voters "to attend upon elections." Detailed voting provisions were designed to ensure "free" elections and prevent corruption "as much as possible." Moreover, the constitution avoided a monopolization of political power by imposing term limits and forcing incumbents to rotate out of many elective offices.[116]

By the time Americans won independence, the language of American constitutions encouraged citizens to think about themselves in novel ways. They were now the collective sovereign, responsible for creating constitutions and the governments formed under them. Unlike other peoples, Americans could direct government and expect it to abide their will. Far from the passive, theoretical role the people once had under the unwritten British constitution, America's written constitutions encouraged active scrutiny of government. The idea that the people were responsible for creating government – rather than merely being subject to it – was also unsettling. If the collective people made government, they also could destroy it. From its beginnings, American constitutionalism contained within itself this potential instability. Despite this instability the idea of the people as the sovereign was also the foundation for all of America's new governments.

3 Grassroots Self-Government

America's Early Determinist Movements

As delegates to the Continental Congress met in Philadelphia in the fall of 1775 they coordinated America's resistance to the world's greatest military power. Delegates were exhausted by meetings that stretched from morning until night, six days a week. They tried to find funds and supplies for Washington's newly formed army. Vindicating "the just rights and liberties" of the "great Continent" of North America required more than ringing words of rhetoric.

John Adams, one of Massachusetts's delegates, worked as hard as anyone. He funneled his energies into assessing the damage inflicted by British troops and fretted over how to acquire saltpeter – used in the production of gunpowder. As "Mistress of the sea," Britain could get saltpeter from many different places, but Americans would need to develop a domestic supply. Victory or defeat hinged on adequate production and Adams vowed "never to have Salt Petre out of my Mind."

In overseeing the war effort, Congress tried to get the colonies to work together. Even as Connecticut's delegates conceded on October 17 that "united Efforts" were necessary to protect America's "common Rights and Liberties," they squabbled with Pennsylvania's delegates over who was entitled to settle the Wyoming valley near the Susquehanna River. The failure of those two colonies to resolve their differences brought Congress into the controversy and proved a distraction.

Congress also responded to practical questions of how a people in revolt against an established government should approach self-government. On October 18, New Hampshire asked Congress about "administering Justice" and regulating "civil police." Congress advised calling "a full and free representation of the people," to establish "a form of government" best able to "produce the happiness of the people."

One week later, John Adams and his cousin Samuel, another delegate from Massachusetts, were introduced to James Hogg, a representative of the Transylvania land company of North Carolina. The promoters of Transylvania sought to establish a new colony west of the Allegheny Mountains (now generally referred to as the Appalachian Mountains), deep in the western wilderness of Kentucky in a region over which Virginia as well as North Carolina asserted authority. Investors in the Transylvania Company wanted Congress to recognize them as America's fourteenth colony with settlers "engaged in the same great cause of liberty" as other Americans. Five months earlier, delegates representing Transylvania's settlers had held a three-day convention that framed a government for the region.

Hogg met with other congressional delegates as well: Silas Deane from Connecticut, and Thomas Jefferson, George Wythe, and Richard Henry Lee from Virginia. According to Hogg, the delegates doubted that Congress would acknowledge Transylvania without Virginia's consent. Although Jefferson, Wythe, and Lee "seriously examined our map," they "gently hinted" that Transylvania belonged to Virginia.

Hogg wrote his fellow investors that they "would be amazed to see how much in earnest all these speculative gentlemen are about the plan to be adopted by the Transylvanians." Congressional leaders urged "that we may make it a free Government" and "threaten us with their opposition, if we do not act upon liberal principles when we have it so much in our power to render ourselves immortal." Hogg enclosed "a copy of a sketch" by John Adams, probably an early version of his Thoughts on Government *that offered advice on American constitution-making.*

Despite misgivings about Transylvania, the delegates were intrigued by the constitution-making of the frontier settlement. In his diary, John Adams noted, "They are charged with republican notions – and utopian schemes." Silas Deane thought Connecticut's government provided the "leading principles" for "any new state." Hogg thanked Deane for promising to describe "what part of your laws we might immediately adopt, and what [to] reject."

Settlers in isolated Transylvania anticipated Congress's suggestion to New Hampshire's delegates about how to form a government. While Transylvania never received Congress's blessing, the idea of self-government based on the consent of "the people" quickly became common currency. Opinions varied over who was entitled to act, but America's political leaders soon agreed that the underlying legitimacy of government rested on the people as the collective sovereign.[1]

Throughout the revolutionary period, Americans developed forms of governance based on consent and the people's sovereignty. From the well-known statehood efforts of Vermont, Kentucky, and Maine to the less well-known movements for the would-be states of "Westsylvania," "Transylvania," and "Franklin" to the frequently overlooked efforts at self-government in the Wyoming Valley, the Cumberland, and Watauga, these episodes had a distinctive constitutional pattern. Although historians consider them "separatist" movements driven by land-hunger, their participants are more accurately described as "determinists." While some settlers occasionally flirted with independence from the American union, most hoped their settlements would be recognized as new states. What settlers in these movements shared was an insistence on governmental self-determination.[2]

The Revolutionary War sparked a contagion of state-making. By 1782 James Madison relayed the caution of General William Irvine, stationed in the West, about the "avidity" and "industry" promoters used "to persuade the people to form new States." General Irvine also warned George Washington of western determinist movements. From Fort Pitt, Irvine described advertisements posted on trees setting a meeting date "for all who wish to become members of a new state on the Muskingum." A North Carolina congressional delegate suggested that the "Spirit of making new States" was "epidemic." For every petition Congress received seeking recognition as a new state, as many similar plans for statehood were afoot. By the war's end, even Continental Army officers got involved. Timothy Pickering and Rufus Putnam drafted a petition seeking compensation for officers and soldiers by "forming a *new state* westward of the Ohio." Pickering's scheme, which Washington endorsed, anticipated the migration of soldiers to "form a distinct Government" eventually to become "*one* of the confederated States of America." With peace negotiations and the army's demobilization the proposal was temporarily derailed.[3]

Exemplifying frontier efforts at self-government were the crude settlements established even before the Revolution in the Watauga and Holston region in what became eastern Tennessee. In the spring of 1770 James Robertson left his home in central North Carolina to explore that area and he soon brought his wife and newborn son to join the handful of settlers near the Watauga River. At the time, the North Carolina Regulator movement, a popular uprising aimed at colonial authorities, was about to face military suppression by the colonial governor William Tyron. Whether Robertson directly participated in the movement is unclear, but he certainly sympathized with the Regulators. He recalled that Tyron's "Tyranny" drove the people "into the woods," making them "mad enough to be ready to fight for their rights; set them to thinking, talking, consulting, acting." A dissenting religious tradition within the southern backcountry importantly influenced the organization of the Regulators' protest. The radical idea of focusing on

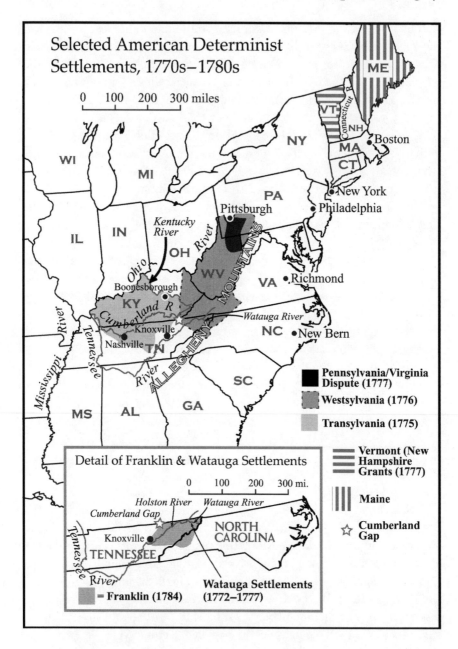

Selected American Determinist Settlements, 1770s–1780s

0   100   200   300 miles

Detail of Franklin & Watauga Settlements

0   100   200   300 mi.

Legend:
- Pennsylvania/Virginia Dispute (1777)
- Westsylvania (1776)
- Transylvania (1775)
- Vermont (New Hampshire Grants (1777)
- Maine
- ☆ Cumberland Gap
- = Franklin (1784)
- Watauga Settlements (1772–1777)

"the spirit within" encouraged independence and individual self-confidence, and it undercut customary deference to both religious and political authority. Many Regulators fled westward and some followed Robertson to Watauga in 1771.[4]

Robertson and the other settlers declined to leave their settlements even after British officials ordered them out. Rather, in May 1772, the settlers "unanimously" formed a committee "by consent of the people." Robertson and a dozen other delegates of the committee composed "Articles of Association." It established a five-person body to govern the settlement and resolve disputes because of the "want of a proper legislature." The settlers acted because they had no government and wished to "be considered as we deserve," not "as a lawless mob." They traced their legitimacy to the majority will of "the people." Two years after the formation of the Watauga Association, the royal governor of Virginia, the Earl of Dunmore, complained about "a set of people in the back of this colony" appointing magistrates and framing laws and "to all intents and purposes" erecting themselves into "a separate State." According to Dunmore, the Wataugans set "a dangerous example to the people of America" by establishing governments "Independent of His Majesty's authority."[5]

Uncertain about whether Virginia or North Carolina would claim jurisdiction over them, the Watauga settlers decided to follow the laws of Virginia to the extent "affairs would admit." A Virginia treaty with the Cherokees included the Wataugan settlements. After surveys placed them within North Carolina, Wataugans bought land from the Cherokees in 1775. They relied on the "precedent" established by "gentlemen of the law" who surely were "better judges" of legal requirements. This included Judge Richard Henderson, a former associate justice of the superior court for Granville County, North Carolina. On behalf of his Transylvania Land Company, Henderson had recently "purchased" from the Cherokees most of future Kentucky and much of Tennessee.[6]

As disputes between Britain and the colonies escalated, settlers on the Watauga formed a Committee of Safety, raised a company of volunteers, and suppressed potential loyalists as their contribution to "the common cause on the sea shore." Hoping "to share in the glorious cause of Liberty" they proclaimed "in open committee" their willingness to vindicate American rights. In 1776 the committee petitioned the revolutionary successor to the colonial government, seeking annexation. The settlers called themselves "the inhabitants of the Washington District." Without government "on the Frontiers," Watauga sheltered those who "endeavoured to defraud their creditors." Becoming part of North Carolina would help punish crime and supply the power to "enforce our laws under authority." Moreover, annexation would allow them to participate in the Revolution more directly.[7]

On August 22, 1776, North Carolina's revolutionary government recommended that Wataugans hold "a free and impartial Election" to select

delegates to represent the district in the legislature. Those delegates participated in drafting North Carolina's 1776 constitution. When the state incorporated their settlements into Washington County in 1777, the Watauga
Association came to an end.[8]

The Watauga experience reflected several themes common to determinist movements. First, Watauga illustrated how deeply constitutional ideas
of the revolutionary movement penetrated the general populace. All along
the frontier, from the New Hampshire grants to western Pennsylvania to
the Kentucky Bluegrass, determinists shared a common constitutional language. That language justified their self-government. Separated by hundreds
of miles and spread over remote locations, determinists reflected the arguments made for American Independence. The similarities in conventions
and meetings held by settlers reveal how widely a culture of constitutionalism spread among Americans. Determinists believed in the right of self-
government as resting on the consent of the people. As colonial governments
gave way to new states created after Independence, the activities of the determinists continued. Leaders of those new state governments thought that
determinists misinterpreted and misapplied the lessons of the Revolution.[9]

Second, North Carolina Regulators who went to Watauga were influenced by an evangelical Christianity reflecting the egalitarian and democratic themes of a long tradition of radical and dissenting Protestantism. The
emphasis of looking inward rather than to a religious hierarchy and being
emboldened to pronounce on matters of spirituality by virtue of individual judgment encouraged challenges to traditional authorities. Indeed, the
democratization of American Christianity formed an important underpin-
ning of determinism and reinforced the constitutional ideas released by the
revolutionary movement. The fusion of liberating notions of religious belief
with the expansive political and constitutional possibilities of the people's
sovereignty influenced many of the determinist movements from Vermont
to Pennsylvania to North Carolina.[10]

Third, Watauga's isolation encouraged settlers in the region to take matters into their own hands. They created an "Association" to compensate for
conditions they shared with other determinist movements: physical isolation
and lack of government. This state of nature had practical constitutional consequences for determinists. When government failed to protect life, liberty,
and property, a majority of the people were entitled to supply those crucial
deficiencies. Rather than seeking freedom from government, determinists
wanted government and more of it.[11]

Determinist movements usually arose in areas expected to raise revenue
from the sale of land, often the site of fierce struggles over land speculation

and jurisdictional controversies. Well into the 1780s, Congress looked to the sale of western lands as a source for reducing the national debt. In seeking to establish themselves as "a people" entitled to government, determinists seemed to threaten state authority with rebellion if not treason. In viewing determinist movements as a matter of jurisdictional authority over territory, state leaders did not recognize that determinists invoked the same source of legitimate authority that state governments rested on.[12]

As a practical matter, even before the Revolution, the distance and isolation of frontier western settlements from established seats of government suggested their eventual autonomy. The Revolution added powerful constitutional arguments to geographic ones in favor of forming new states out of western land. A central grievance of American colonists was their lack of political representation. Yet state leaders often turned a blind eye to meaningful representation for settlers in the western regions.

The question of America's western land could be approached from the perspective of what might benefit the existing thirteen states. On the other hand, some, like Thomas Jefferson, preferred to cast the question in what he called its "just form." "How may the territories of the Union," he asked, "be disposed of so as to produce the greatest degree of happiness to their inhabitants?" Others questioned the capacity of those on the frontier for republican government and suggested the need for a period of political "apprenticeship." That approach competed with recognition of the right of self-government celebrated by the Revolution. Ultimately, the Northwest Ordinance of 1787 adopted the principle of eventual equality for states formed out of territories, even if the process of statehood imposed a series of stages before full self-government was conferred.[13]

From an early period, ideas fostered by the Revolution challenged the notion of treating potential communities in the west as simply "territory" in the traditional sense of land under the dominion of existing states. Jefferson's draft constitution for Virginia in 1776 anticipated the creation of "new Colonies" out of the western regions of the state. He proposed that they be established "on the same fundamental laws" as those governing the state and made "free and independent" of Virginia and "all the world." Likewise, John Dickinson's initial draft of the Articles of Confederation in 1776 called for Congress to create "new colonies" out of western land "to be established on the Principles of Liberty." While Jefferson and Dickinson differed on whether Congress or individual states could create new western political subdivisions, they each reflected the ways in which the principles underlying the Revolution entered the debate over western lands.[14]

Determinists used these revolutionary principles to demand and justify their political independence and their right to equal treatment with established governments. Congress's approach to the issue of western lands illustrates that determinists were not unreasonable in expecting recognition. In 1780, Congress resolved that states eventually formed out of lands ceded to the United States would "have the same rights of sovereignty, freedom and independence" as existing states. Four years later, Congress stimulated determinist movements by passing an ordinance anticipating that new western states would be created on such "an equal footing" after "temporary governments" of a "republican" nature.[15]

Congress finally established a process for granting statehood to western territories under the Northwest Ordinance of 1787. Territories on the road to eventual statehood as units of government deserved equality with existing states. These territories would legitimate the constitutions and governments they formed to become a state through the same underlying source of sovereignty as each of the original thirteen states. The new states would emerge out of a "compact between the Original States and the people and States in the said territory." In ensuring the equality of new states to existing states, the ordinance reflected the central principle of the Revolution: that American governments rested on a sovereign people that created them. It was wrong as a matter of "justice or policy," declared James Madison, to deny new states equality with existing ones.[16]

Defining "a people" entitled to exercise sovereignty to form a state government defied easy answers. When eleven people gathered in 1785 at the remote town of Clarksville in the western Cumberland region as a convention composed of "a majority of the actual settlers of the town," it seemed a laughable attempt at self-government in the eyes of continental and state authorities. On the other hand, the thousands of inhabitants in the New Hampshire grants, who also claimed the right to form a state under their authority as a people were eventually vindicated in that position when Vermont was recognized as a state. Settlers in the New Hampshire grants thus succeeded in locating themselves along a continuum that justified their claim to the constitutional prerogatives of "the people" to form governments. Other determinist movements, however, found themselves at the opposite end of that continuum and accused of being a mere portion or faction of an existing people of the state. From the state's perspective, most groups of settlers lacked the authority possessed by a broader populace and society having existence since the colonial period.[17]

Despite the difference in numbers between the settlers in Clarksville and the inhabitants of the future state of Vermont, both movements justified their goals as an expression of the right of the majority of "the people" to create government. The argument by the settlers at Clarksville was the same as that of the determinists in the New Hampshire Grants, which in turn was the same as that made by American patriots during the Revolution. Determinists recalled the spontaneous and self-organizing origins of America's resistance to British authority that claimed to speak for "the people" and thereby acquired constitutional legitimacy. Determinists used the same constitutional principles employed by American revolutionary leaders. Those principles were shared by the common folk as well as their "betters" and they resonated with settlers on the most remote frontiers as much as they did with inhabitants in urban capitals.[18]

Despite their commitment to the establishment of new republican states in the west, many revolutionary leaders did not see determinist movements as involving the principles of the Revolution. When Vermont cited the Declaration of Independence in attempting to break away from New York, a congressional report in 1777 rejected this as an "unwarrantable" precedent. To recognize Vermont's claim would be "highly dangerous in its Consequences; since if it should prevail, and be carried into practice, it must inevitably destroy all Order, Stability and good Government."[19]

Americans could "alter or abolish" their governments but congressional leaders faced a quandary. The shoe was now on the other foot: for many revolutionary leaders, maintaining the status quo of newly established American governments was a more pressing concern than extending the logic of the Revolution's principles that might challenge those governments. Revolutionary leaders who defended the territorial integrity of existing states seemed to take positions similar to those held by the British during the Revolution– an irony not lost on some observers. London's *Gentlemen's Magazine* snidely remarked in 1785 that "the people of the western counties" in America "found themselves grievously taxed for the support of government without enjoying the blessings of it."[20]

TRANSYLVANIA

The writer for the *Gentlemen's Magazine* was unlikely to realize that some Americans in the West beyond the reach of taxation would have willingly paid taxes to get the "blessings" of government. Settlers pushing far into the western reaches of North Carolina and Virginia, in a wilderness area that formed part of the huge Transylvania land scheme, faced a precarious existence without governmental protection and security. Settlers in Transylvania – desperately isolated, ill-equipped, and constantly subject to

Indian attacks – displayed a remarkable instinct toward self-government that echoed the understandings of colonial American leaders in urban areas who were drifting toward a separation from Britain. The experience of settlers in Transylvania and the would-be "Proprietors" and promoters of the land scheme proved illustrative of how deeply the constitutional ideas that propelled the American Revolution penetrated remote regions and took hold among ordinary people.

Richard Henderson of North Carolina masterminded the Transylvania land scheme. He grew up in Granville County, where he practiced law while dreaming of a grand speculation in western lands. In 1768, the colony's governor, William Tyron, appointed Henderson associate justice of the Superior Court of North Carolina – a position he held until 1773. In 1770, Henderson and his court in Hillsborough became a prominent target of Regulators and paid the price for opposing "the people" by having his house, barn, and stables burned to the ground. He later organized a joint stock land company with eight other partners or "proprietors," some of whom also suffered at the hands of the Regulators.[21]

Operating in secrecy, Henderson sought territory for an ambitious scheme of colonization. In March 1775, Henderson arranged a sale of dubious validity for over 17 million acres in what is present-day Kentucky between the Ohio and Kentucky rivers and the Cumberland River from members of the Cherokee Nation. Colonial authorities regarded the land speculation as "Serious," demanding "the Attention of Government" before "valuable & extensive Territory will be forever lost to Virginia." The colonial governors of Virginia and North Carolina branded the "Transilvania" scheme a fraud by an "infamous Company of land Pyrates" and "freebooters."[22]

Future American revolutionaries responded in more mixed ways. Their reactions were colored by competing speculative claims. One Transylvania opponent in the fall of 1775 recalled that Virginians expressed "various oppinions" about Henderson's claim, including "Many" who "thought it go[o]d." One prominent speculator in western lands, George Washington, wrote of Henderson's scheme that "there is something in that Affair which I neither understand, nor like, and wish I may not have cause to dislike it worse as the Mistery unfolds." Washington seemed more awed by the scale of the plan than outraged at the illegality of Henderson's dealings with the Cherokees. Indeed, eight years earlier, Washington marveled about the "opening prospect in the back Country for Adventurers," predicting that those who neglected this "present oppertunity of hunting out good Lands" would "never regain it."[23]

It seemed like everyone wanted to get in on the expected riches from investments in western land. For instance, Patrick Henry and several other Virginians had also wanted to buy land from the Cherokees, and Henry in 1774 was sympathetic to Henderson's claim when the issue came before the Virginia convention. In April 1775, Henderson and other Transylvania proprietors wrote to Henry thanking him for his "exertions" to support their land claims. Henderson's group hinted at providing "more substantial evidence" of their gratitude, but nothing came of it. Henry's support turned to opposition after he became Virginia's governor. This opposition, as well as that from competing land schemes, contributed to the denial of the vast Transylvania claims by both Virginia and North Carolina. While the wheels of political influence turned slowly in Virginia's capital, settlers on the frontier took steps toward self-government.[24]

Henderson hired the frontier explorer Daniel Boone in 1774 to establish a fortified station at the site subsequently called Boonesborough deep in the Kentucky forest. Those going to such remote western regions were "fond of independency" and "democratical principles," remarked one observer. Even Henderson, in writing to a merchant in Scotland, admitted the particular "disposition that rules the people here." Americans "have ideas of liberty." They did not "stand in awe of rank and station" because they are "well informed, reasoning... perhaps the most of any on earth, because of the free intercourse between man and man that prevails in America." Then, with a touch of irony given his experiences in the late Regulation, the former judge assigned much of the independent-mindedness of the common people to "their free access to courts of law, as parties and jurors where they hear the rights of the subject nobly debated."[25]

Henderson decided to oversee his investment personally, anticipating what George Washington would learn "from long experience," namely, that "landed property at a distance from the Proprietor, is attended with more plague than profit." Settlers in the region claimed by the Transylvania Company, many of whom had migrated from western Virginia, vacillated between negotiating with the proprietors and challenging the company's claims. Henderson thought the proprietors would have their "rights acknowledged," making them "lords of the soil," even though he confessed being "much embarrassed" by the claims of settlers who were in "possession some time before we got here."[26]

When Henderson arrived at Boonesborough on April 20, 1775, after a treacherous trek through the wilderness, he was welcomed by "a voley of guns." At the time, the Boonesborough station consisted of fewer than

100 people. Several additional settlements completed the sparse concentration of white settlers in the area. They faced, by their own admission, dubious prospects of survival given Indian hostility and a lack of adequate shelter, supplies, and ammunition. A visiting Baptist preacher described one of their settlements a year later as "a row or two of smoky cabins."[27]

After Henderson arrived, he encouraged settlers to hold a constitutional convention and described that step as "exceedingly simple." "[T]he peoples" in the various settlements would send delegates "to act for them." On May 23, 1775, the convention met under the shade of a huge elm tree, which Henderson called "our Church, State-house, Council Chamber &c." In his opening address, Henderson told the delegates that "all power is originally in the people" and that their consent justified the convention. Eventually, nine bills were drafted during the three-day convention in addition to the compact organizing a frame of government.[28]

The Transylvania Compact was the "contract or agreement" between the proprietors and "the People" delineating "the powers" of each. This bargain between rulers and the ruled reflected a traditional understanding of government consistent with the proprietors' pretensions as "lords of the soil." Nonetheless, Henderson's acknowledgment of the underlying authority of the people's consent accorded with the concept that America's written constitutions represented the expression of the sovereignty of the people rather than a bargain with rulers. In any event, Henderson understood the need to respect consent if he wanted to attract settlers to the region and induce them to accept his company's land claims.[29]

The compact established annual election of delegates but allowed the proprietors to call special sessions in times of emergency. After Transylvania acquired "strength and maturity," legislative authority would be vested in three branches. First, the "Delegates, or Representatives, chosen by the people"; second, "a Council, not exceeding twelve men, possessed of landed estate, who reside in the Colony"; and finally, "the Proprietors," the nine members of the Transylvania Company. The plan for government also contemplated a supreme court and inferior courts. Although the proprietors appointed the judges of the supreme court, those judges were "supported by the People" and answerable to them for "malconduct." Inferior court judges, on the other hand, were to be "recommended by the people," but "approved" and "commissioned" by the proprietors.[30]

Although leaving much unclear, the compact granted "the People" considerable leeway and power. The government did not give proprietors veto authority. Writing to a distant outpost several months after the formation of the compact, Henderson assured its settlers that government rested on the people's approval. "We did not forget you at the time of making laws," he assured them. "[Y]our part of the Country is too remote from ours to attend our convention." The outpost "must have laws made by an Assembly of your own." Although he "prepared a plan," consent was both a practical necessity and the constitutional principle that conferred legitimacy on their government.[31]

A year after the Boonesborough convention, a newspaper reprinting the Declaration of Independence reached the settlement. When it was read to "the assembled garrison" they responded with "cheers and war-whoops" and "a big bonfire." John Adams wanted the Declaration to be properly "solemnized," including "Bonfires and Illuminations from one End of this Continent to the other." In the wake of the Fourth of July, city dwellers in Philadelphia, New York, and Boston did indeed celebrate with fiery tributes to independence. Thus, the response by settlers at Boonesborough might have been a month late, but was completely in step with their fellow revolutionaries back East.[32]

After concluding the Transylvania Compact, Henderson returned to North Carolina. He and the proprietors then petitioned Congress for Transylvania to become America's fourteenth colony and sent a proprietor of the company, James Hogg, to Congress.[33] Despite Hogg's efforts, Congress's was unwilling to act without the consent of both Virginia and North Carolina. Congressional delegates were intrigued by Hogg's stories and impressed by Transylvania's constitution-making. With time, accounts of resistance from local settlers to Henderson's land company foreshadowed the failure of the proprietors' scheme. By December 1775, the proprietors' Boonesborough agent struggled to gather a legislative quorum among the Transylvania delegates. "[D]isturbances and dissatisfactions" among "the people" produced the absences. On March 15, 1776, eighty-eight settlers in the Transylvania region petitioned Virginia for protection from the "insatiable avarice" of the proprietors who more than doubled the price of land from their initial asking price. "[A]nxious" to attain their "just rights and privileges" they dismissed the Transylvania Compact as the "oppressive designs" of "gentlemen stiling themselves proprietors." Henderson's prominent opposition to the North Carolina Regulators just a few years earlier also sparked resistance to the proprietors. Some settlers "revived the rallying cries of Regulators" in disputing the proprietors' claims based on title from the Cherokees. They insisted that the settlers' occupancy and settlement was the best evidence of ownership.[34]

By mid-June the proprietors dropped hopes of congressional action and approached the Virginia legislature as the "true friends of *America*" seeking

"the natural and inherent rights of mankind." They claimed it "absurd . . ."
to think of creating a separate Transylvania government within Virginia.
The Boonesborough convention merely created "temporary bye laws for
the good of their little community." Until Virginia could exert its authority, the
proprietors stood "ready to submit" to state government. In June 1776, the
Virginia legislature responded to the proprietors' claims by prohibiting them
from making financial demands on settlers in possession of disputed land
until a final determination was made of the company's claims. The legislature
eventually created a new county of Kentucky out of Transylvania and in
December 1778 declared the Transylvania claim void.[35]

VERMONT

Even under the rule of one sovereign – the British monarch – the American
colonies disputed their western frontiers. As Independence drew near, one
prominent conflict between New York and New Hampshire involved lands
that eventually became part of the state of Vermont. Prerevolutionary grants
of lands west of the Connecticut River by New Hampshire's governor met
with protests from New York authorities who insisted that the area granted
fell under New York's jurisdiction. That assertion did not deter settlement
of the disputed land.

In January 1775, Committees of Safety from some twenty-five towns in
the New Hampshire Grants region met in Manchester to solve the problem.
Their "Self-Preservation" required independence from New York. Under
"the strongest Necessity" they created "a civil and political Body" to regulate
their community. Invoking "the immutable law of self-preservation," another
convention at Westminster met in April 1775 and again renounced the
authority of New York's government.[36] News of the military clash between
British troops and American militia at Lexington and Concord interrupted
this convention at Westminster, but settlers reconvened at Dorset in 1776
and petitioned Congress. They asked to be recognized as the inhabitants
of the "New Hampshire Grants, and not as inhabitants of the province of
New York." They would do all in their "Power" for "the General Cause"
of American Independence. Another sixteen years elapsed before Congress
acted favorably on Vermont's petition. Unlike the smaller number of people frequently involved in other determinist movements, the Grants region
included nearly 20,000 settlers by the time of the Revolution.[37]

In 1775, Congress suggested "the respective assemblies and conventions
of the United Colonies" establish governments they deemed necessary. Ira
Allen, a leader of the Vermont determinists, described the people of the

Grants as having "governed themselves by Committees of Safety" eight years before the Revolution's start. On "revolutionary principles," the current 20,000 settlers of the Grants deserved the credit as "the *oldest*" self-governing community in America. In conformity with Congress's invitation, a convention in Westminster on January 15, 1777, declared the Grants "a separate, free and independent jurisdiction or state." The convention sent delegates to Philadelphia to represent the region in Congress. On March 17, 1777, a newspaper published a formal explanation of Vermont's status. America's Declaration of Independence "dissolved" the jurisdiction granted by the Crown to New York's government over the people of the Grants. Vermonters were in "a state of nature," lacking "law or government." Consequently, "a right remains to the people . . . to form a government best suited to secure their property, well being and happiness."[38]

Vermont determinists continued to invoke natural law even as they relied on legal and constitutional rights. For example, one key argument – the right, if not the duty, to resist tyranny and oppression – was rooted in English constitutionalism. Yet that right was also frequently expressed in terms of natural law. As the sermon before the convention that drafted Vermont's constitution expressed it, when the king broke his "compact" and "covenant" with the people and acted with tyranny, the people had a "divine warrant" to resist him under the "law of nature." By invoking natural law, Vermont determinists went further than most fellow Americans in embracing a theory critics called "the Vermont doctrine." Even before the Westminster convention met, Ira Allen described the consequence of rejecting British authority: "all power . . . naturally resolves back on the people." Allen saw "no reason why any county or counties, community or communities of people, may not assert their free and natural rights." Asserting that America's independence produced a state of nature troubled opponents of Vermont's determinist movement. Even more dangerous was suggesting that Congress invited "all such bodies of men" who considered "themselves returned to a state of nature" to create new governments.[39]

A public letter in April 1777 from Dr. Thomas Young, a Pennsylvania constitution-maker and an old friend of Ira Allen's brother Ethan, brought widespread notoriety to the Vermont doctrine. Although rebuffed by Congress, delegates returned from Philadelphia with a letter from Young addressed "To the Inhabitants of Vermont." Young urged them to establish a government after inviting all freeholders to select delegates to a constitutional convention. Having "taken the minds" of congressional leaders, the citizens of Vermont could not be refused by Congress, he promised. "You have as good a right to choose how you will be governed, and by whom, as they had." Young added that congressional acknowledgment of Vermont's legitimacy would come only after "you incorporate and actually announce . . . having become a body politic." Until then, Congress could not treat the region "as a free State."[40]

Congress denied having encouraged Vermont's determinists and accused Young of "gross misrepresentation." Still, one expression in his letter was uncontroversial. After recommending Pennsylvania's 1776 constitution as a model of constitution-making, Young described the collective sovereign. For Young, "the people at large" were "the true proprietors of governmental power." The people were "the supreme constituent power" and their representatives "the supreme Delegate power." While many revolutionary leaders did not share Young's enthusiasm for Pennsylvania's constitution, his identification of "the people" as the basis of American republics was widely accepted. Indeed, the people's sovereignty became the orthodox canon of American constitutionalism. John Adams and Benjamin Rush were only two revolutionary leaders who disliked the excessive democracy they associated with Pennsylvania's constitution. Yet they, with other leaders of the patriot cause, were committed to the sovereignty of the people. Though Young was branded "wicked" and "insolent," his description of the people as the "constituent power" ushered that term into American constitutional discourse.[41]

Vermont determinists defended their independence in the same terms that American revolutionary leaders explained the creation of new governments for the thirteen original colonies. When Congress ordered Vermont in 1779 to "abstain" from acting until jurisdictional claims over the region were settled, Vermont determinists accused Congress of missing a central constitutional point of the Revolution. Vermont's legitimacy, Ira Allen noted, did not rest on external authorization. Rather, the inhabitants of Vermont could therefore come "together and assume" the blessings of *"civil Government."* What gave authority to Vermont's government was the consent of the people of Vermont, not the actions of Congress or other states. Indeed, Vermont's governor sought to correct "mistaken Notions of Government," namely, that "a public Acknowledgement of the Powers of the Earth is essential to the Existence of a distinct, separate *State*." This view overlooked "that all Power originated from the People." If the image of unbridled people's sovereignty disturbed some American revolutionaries, they could not deny "the people" as the foundation of government any more than they could question the Revolution's validity.[42]

Vermont determinists described a self-conscious effort by "the people" of Vermont to establish a state by invoking the basis of republican governments.[43] They saw themselves as a distinct region outside the legitimate jurisdiction of New York. Possessing an identifiable population or "a people" entitled them to the same constitutional rights of self-government as other "peoples" in the American confederacy. Determinists were engaged in the legitimate creation of government. Opponents of Vermont determinists portrayed the issue as a matter of territorial rights of existing states.[44] Rather than seeing "the people" in action, they characterized the Vermont independence movement as the conduct of a faction of New Yorkers. They consistently described Vermonters as "Insurgents" and "Revolters" who wrongfully sought to "dismember" the state.[45] In 1777, New York's Committee of Safety claimed that "certain designing men" caused "a part" of the State to "revolt."[46]

In repudiating Vermont's independence movement, Congress said it represented the inhabitants of the thirteen "communities" of the former colonies as they "stood" at the formation of Congress. As declared by a congressional committee, "no number or body of people" were "Justified in Attempting to form and Establish any new Independant States within any part of these United States without the Consent of the State or States in which they are and were Included" when Congress was first established. Political reality dictated that Congress side with a key state during a war for independence. Nonetheless, the committee's support of New York nearly denied a basic premise of the Revolution: that "the people" constituted the sovereign foundation of government and thus always retained the authority to alter or abolish those governments.[47]

Different perceptions of the Vermont determinist movement stemmed less from disagreement over principle than whether shared principles were applicable. Samuel Adams illustrated how Americans could commit themselves to the principle of a collective sovereign and yet overlook its relevance in the context of Vermont. In 1780, Adams juxtaposed news that Massachusetts's draft constitution was ready "for the Inspection of the People" with efforts of the state to advance its "Right to the Land" in Vermont. Adams did not connect the authority of "the people" legitimizing Massachusetts's constitution and "the people" who framed a constitution and established a government in Vermont. Implicitly, Adams and other opponents of Vermont's determinist movement were not challenging the sovereign authority of the people as much as denying that Vermont determinists met the definition of "the people" who possessed constitutional authority to act. Determinists looked backward to why and how American revolutionaries justified independence, while their opponents looked forward in exercising the powers of states seeking their political independence as part of an American confederacy.[48]

WESTSYLVANIA

One revealing statehood movement involved determinists in settlements around what became Pittsburgh, an area claimed by both Pennsylvania and Virginia. The jurisdictional struggle began when Pennsylvania in 1773 made the region in dispute its Westmoreland County and Virginia responded by establishing the same area as its District of West Augusta. By December 1774 there were two parallel sets of magistrates, with subordinate officers, and two competing courts, "regularly or irregularly administering justice under the laws of two different governments." Despite concerns by Congress that the conflict undermined "the defence of the liberties of America," settlers in the region were zealous about the revolutionary cause – helping fuel their instincts toward self-government.[49]

Even before Congress declared independence, settlers organized Committees of Safety to resist British authority, reflecting steps taken by America's revolutionary leadership. On May 16, 1775, after news of the events at Lexington reached the Monongahela Valley, a public meeting in Westmoreland resolved that "there is no reason to doubt but the same system of tyranny and oppression will (should it meet with success in Massachusetts Bay) be extended to other parts of America." Therefore, it was every American's "indispensable duty" to "resist and oppose" the British, to which objective the settlers pledged their "lives and fortunes." By the end of May, one reluctant patriot complained of "nothing but musters and committees all over the country." In July 1775, an English traveler called the locals "Liberty mad." Inspired by the Boston Tea Party, settlers marched through Pittsburgh the following month, seized a quantity of tea being sold in "defiance of the Resolves of the Continental Congress," and burned it in front of a "Liberty pole."[50]

An independence movement for the area developed during the summer of 1776. A memorial from "the committee of West Augusta" to the Virginia House of Delegates explained that "the people" spontaneously selected delegates to "meet and consult" about whether the region should seek Congress's approval for a "new government" or whether settlers should organize by their "own authority, and send delegates to Congress to represent them as the fourteenth link in the American chain." Although both Virginia and Pennsylvania authorities repudiated determinist movements, the settlers invoking their right to organize government did not act without precedent. Only a few months earlier, revolutionary leaders in Philadelphia invoked the same principles of consent and authority of the sovereign people when they assembled in the State House Yard to bypass the colonial legislature and demand a constitutional convention.[51]

In the summer of 1776 settlers around Pittsburgh petitioned Congress to become "Westsylvania" and "the fourteenth Province of the American Confederacy." They felt, "as American Brethren and Associates," equally bound to the "arduous & glorious Cause of Liberty." Their present lack of "Regular Administration of Justice" and a "proper . . . system of Laws & regulations" entitled them to political independence. A "Mode of Polity & Government, adapted to their peculiar Necessities, local Circumstances and Situation" was impossible under the authority of Pennsylvania or Virginia some "five hundred miles distant and separated by a vast, extensive & almost impassable Tract of Mountains." Having "imbibed the highest and most extensive Ideas of Liberty," the inhabitants resisted "being partitioned or parceled out" between either state. Government existed only to preserve the welfare of the people, something neither state could guarantee.[52]

Shortly after the Declaration of Independence, Edmund Pendleton, leader of Virginia's revolutionary convention, responded to a petition by "some factious people on the Ohio" seeking "Separate Government." He thought Congress would not "dismember" any government without its consent. Nonetheless, forcing a union between the region and Virginia would be "exceedingly inconvenient." Because the region's independence was inevitable, Pendleton concluded that imposing Virginia's power over the area would not promote "the Good Purposes of Government." Opponents of the Westsylvania determinist movement thus conceded the grievances of isolation that underlay the statehood movement. In October 1776, the "committee of West Augusta" reiterated its concerns about a lack of "regular government" and "the administration of justice" to the Virginia House of Delegates.[53]

Even as Virginia and Pennsylvania disputed the location of their mutual boundary, each state claimed the region and resisted determinist challenges to their "ancient territory." This prompted Congress to request that both states refrain from disposing land until the boundary was settled. In November 1779, a Pennsylvanian urged fellow citizens "to stir, or Virginia will shortly sell" enough land for "three large Counties." Pennsylvania eventually created Washington County out of the disputed area.[54]

In 1780, a determinist movement led by local officials appointed by Virginia petitioned Congress to recognize "Inhabitants West of the Allegany Mountains" as a separate state. Petitioners wanted "that Freedom & Independence, due to all Freeborn Sons of Liberty, on which the present Contest

took it's rise." They only claimed "the Liberties & Blessings" that members
in Congress "wish to enjoy." Like earlier petitions, this one stressed the petitioners' distance from "Eastward" state governments. The petition alluded to
the congressional resolution of October 1780 declaring that "unappropriated
lands" of any state should "be settled and formed into distinct republican
states" having equality with preexisting states. Petitioners asserted that "the
people have a right" to "form new States" whenever "they can thereby promote their own Ease & Safty."[55]

The 1780 petition underscored for Virginia the seriousness of determinist
movements and the need to resolve the boundary issue with Pennsylvania. In
fact, in early 1782, Virginia's governor sought Madison's resignation as one of
the state's delegates in order to have him serve as a boundary commissioner.
Such work was "a matter of consiquence" even more important than congressional representation. Although Madison turned down the appointment,
pleading his weakness in "Mathematics," he, too, remained concerned about
the "scheme" of inhabitants in the region for "a separation of Govt."[56]

Determinist movements threatened Pennsylvania as well as Virginia. In
1781, settlers around Pittsburgh petitioned Pennsylvania's governor John
Dickinson and his executive council to intervene with Congress for relief.
The contest between Pennsylvania and Virginia should not render inhabitants "Subject to Military law." Although they would "lay down" their lives
"for the cause of America," they refused to have their liberty, property,
or their lives forfeited "on the will of a Commanding Officer and a Court
Martial." By November 1782, Dickinson and the executive council alerted
the Pennsylvania legislature about settlements on lands west of the Ohio
intended as "a fund" for "rendering justice to our deserving and suffering
officers and soldiers." The Pennsylvania legislature sent agents into the area
to remind "deluded" citizens of their "proper sense" of "Duty." Attempting to organize a new state within the boundaries of Pennsylvania was also
made high treason. Those convicted of the offense faced the death penalty
and confiscation of their estate. In addition, the Reverend James Finley,
a Scotch-Irish Presbyterian, was sent to western Pennsylvania on a secret
mission to stifle determinists.[57]

Despite Finley's efforts and the threat of treason, determinist sentiment
continued to percolate. Although Finley found some opposition to forming
a new state, "a considerable number" of inhabitants were "fond" of the idea,
including "some of ye clergy." In fact, Congress received a petition in late
January 1783 from settlers "on the west side of Laurel Hill and Western
Waters" seeking recognition as a "New State." They guarded the frontiers of
Pennsylvania, Maryland, and Virginia in the "common cause of liberty and

independence." Having earned the "Rights, Privileges, and Immunities of free Citizens of America" and living in an isolated region seemingly destined for separate government, they requested independence.[58]

Consistent with its position that determinist movements required the consent of existing states, Congress ignored the petition. James Madison, however, touched on a particularly sensitive point for determinists when he noted that the petitioners were upset that Pennsylvania prohibited "even consultations about a new State within its limits." Committed to viewing the matter as one of territorial jurisdiction, Pennsylvania and Virginia ultimately resolved their boundary dispute without reference to determinist arguments. At the end of the war, a joint survey placed much of the contested area within Pennsylvania.[59]

KENTUCKY, CUMBERLAND, AND FRANKLIN

The western regions of Virginia, North Carolina, and Pennsylvania featured some of the earliest determinist movements during the revolutionary period, among them Watauga, Transylvania, and Westsylvania. Those areas also saw renewed determinist activity in the 1780s, including efforts by the proposed state of Franklin and the Cumberland Association in western North Carolina as well as Kentucky's struggle to achieve independence from Virginia. Leading figures of the early determinist movements, including Richard Henderson and James Robertson, resurfaced in these new settings and were joined by other determinist leaders.

Even before Independence, settlers and explorers, in addition to those relying on Richard Henderson's Transylvania scheme, established a presence in the far reaches of western Virginia. One of the earliest determinist movements in that area – reflecting a dissatisfaction with the terms offered by the Transylvania proprietors – originated with settlers along the banks of the "Kentucke" River. Among them was George Rogers Clark, formerly of Albemarle County, Virginia. Clark initiated a call for a general meeting of settlers in early June 1776, at which time he anticipated that an assembly of "the people" would "Elect deputies" to negotiate with Virginia's Assembly. If "Valuable Conditions" were secured they would declare themselves "Citizens of the State otherways Establish an Independant Government." By the time Clark got to the meeting the gathered settlers had decided to petition Virginia's Assembly rather than follow Clark's preference of sending "Deputies under the authority of the people."[60] In their petition, the settlers around Harrodsburg repudiated "any power or prerogative" other than "the Convention of Virginia" to which they pledged allegiance. In seeking

Virginia's recognition as a separate district the petitioners supported the "laudable cause" of protecting "our common Liberty." Toward that end they elected a self-governing body, partly to serve as a committee of safety like those Americans were organizing elsewhere, but also to establish "good order" since without "Laws to Restrain or Power to Controul," vice could run rampant.[61]

Petitioners were determined to resist "a Detestible, Wicked and Corrupt Ministry." Two delegates to represent the expanse of Virginia's far western county of Fincastle was impracticable and insufficient. "[B]y the Free voice of the People" they sent George Rogers Clark and John Gabriel Jones to the Virginia convention to facilitate their representation. Clark presented petitions from Harrodsburg to the state's first legislature and sought his and Jones's recognition as representatives. The legislature did not seat them, but Clark and Jones succeeded in having the settlements west of the Alleghenies recognized as part of the new county of Kentucky.[62]

Neither the creation of Kentucky County nor the state's general policy of creating new western counties addressed the concerns of Virginia's far western settlers. Under Virginia's 1776 constitution, each new county was entitled to two delegates to the lower house of the legislature. The distance and extraordinary difficulty of getting to the state capital limited such representation as a practical matter in a legislature dominated by non-western delegates. Western grievances – including land distribution and absentee claimants, vulnerability to Indian attacks, and the lack of governmental services – seemed to be ignored by state authorities. That sense of neglect was compounded with the explosive influx of settlers to the Kentucky region. From a white population of only a few hundred in the spring of 1775, Kentucky's population grew to nearly 30,000 within a decade, a figure that doubled once more by 1788. The census of 1790 placed the region's population at 73,677. A Virginian captured the demographics by declaring in 1779, "People are Running Mad for Kentucky Hereabouts."[63]

Although some Kentuckians sought to retain the connection with Virginia, it became increasingly clear that their distance from the center of government required a self-sufficiency. By October 1779, "the Destressed Inhabitants of the county of Kentuckky" complained to the Virginia legislature about their sufferings "in settling and defending this extensive country" for "the benefit of the common charge." Their efforts left many of them without "so much as one cow" to support their families. They wanted "speedy redress" to avoid either "the disagreeable necessity of going Down the Mississippi" for "Spanish protection" or "becoming tennants to private gentlemen" who claimed large tracts of land in Kentucky.[64]

The threat of a Spanish connection reflected more than just frustration with policies deemed disadvantageous to the region. It also underscored the tenuous transportation links eastward to Virginia in comparison to the possibilities presented by the Mississippi River. Some revolutionary leaders, particularly George Washington, grasped this point as central to determinist movements that challenged Virginia. His advocacy of transportation schemes to link western and eastern sections of the state rested on the belief that its "consequences" for the Union were "immense – & more so in a political, than in a Commercial point." In 1785, Washington predicted that "unless we can connect the New States . . . with those on the Atlantic by interest," westerners would become "quite a distinct People." Effective east/west transportation was the key to "bind those people to us by a chain which never can be broken." The belated development of such transportation linkages and the continued vulnerability and isolation of Kentucky clearly fueled the determinist movements that eventually led to statehood.[65]

In 1780, settlers in Kentucky (or as they referred to themselves, "the people of that Part of Contry now Claim'd. by the State of Virginia"), petitioned Congress for statehood. Congress should either "form us into a Separate State" or provide adequate "Rules and regulations." Another petition sought recognition of the petitioners' political independence from Virginia and repeated the threat to move west of the Mississippi River under Spanish authority rather than remaining "slaves" to absentee land monopolists. Such petitions presented the challenge, as James Madison expressed it, of "extending the benefits of Government" and satisfying "the exigences of the people" in Kentucky while also preserving "the idea of Unity in the State."[66]

Even as Kentuckians sought relief, a determinist movement developed in western North Carolina. In May 1780, settlers along the Cumberland River, near what became Nashville, declared their inherent right to establish a government through a Compact and Articles of Agreement, echoing the Watauga Association. Although over 250 settlers signed the Cumberland Compact (including James Robertson), Richard Henderson played a major role. The compact coincided with the fading hopes for Henderson's Transylvania venture in Virginia, after which the company turned its attention to lands it claimed in North Carolina. Those proprietary interests were reflected in Henderson's opening of a land office when he reached the Cumberland. The instinct toward self-government, however, soon prompted the drafting of the Compact and Articles. The articles called for the election of a tribunal consisting of twelve "Judges, Triers, or General Arbitrators" to be replaced if "the people" were "dissatisfied." Their "remote situation" and lack of "proper offices for the administration of justice" deprived them of "regular proceedings at law." Their isolation justified a "temporary method of restraining the licentious" by the tribunal, but the legitimacy of their ad-hoc self-government rested on the "unanimous consent" of the settlers.[67]

The failure of Transylvania's claims in Virginia made Henderson cautious about challenging the political authority of North Carolina. According to the compact, settlers at Cumberland sought to become a county of the state. They predicated any future government in the region on "the people in general, or their representatives." Despite the politic phrasing, Henderson's claim to land in the Cumberland also met with failure. In May 1782, a committee of the North Carolina legislature denied Henderson's Cherokee purchase.[68]

Although failing to gain his speculative objectives through the compact, the government Henderson inspired in 1780 continued to guide the region. At one point, physical hardships drove so many people away that it seemed to one settler that "all administration of justice seemed to cease from amongst us." With settlers returning in early 1783 it seemed "highly necessary . . . to revive our former manner of proceedings, pursuant to the plan agreed upon at our first settling here." The Committee of Cumberland Association elected James Robertson chairman and announced they would operate until North Carolina granted them "the salutary benefit" of law "duly administered."[69]

If the Cumberland Association provided self-government without breaking away, North Carolina soon faced a movement seeking recognition as the separate state of Franklin. In 1784, the Watauga-Holston settlements, just west of what eighteenth-century Americans called the Allegheny Mountains declared their independence in the wake of the state's cession of its western lands to Congress. Determinism had surfaced in the region several years earlier. In the southwestern portion of Virginia, Arthur Campbell had led a determinist movement since 1780 seeking the independence of western portions of Virginia and North Carolina. Campbell, a former justice of the peace and county lieutenant, actively supported the Revolution and participated in the framing of Virginia's first constitution in 1776.[70]

In 1782, Campbell authored an *Address* to local settlers, rhetorically asking if they were "well served" by their representatives, if government was "wisely administered," and whether their "rights and Liberties" were secure. The *Address* grew out of perceived inequities in taxes enacted by a distant government. It described the people's relationship to their government in terms that reflected the common language of America's constitutions. According to the *Address*, "the power of Legislators is in [the] nature of [a] trust to form regulations for the Good of the whole" and is designed to "obtain the greatest Degree of happiness and safety, not for the few, but for the many." Occasionally, "rulers may exceed their Trust" and undermine "the majesty of the

People." As such, the people should examine if taxes went toward "the real Exigencies of the State" or merely fed the "Corruption" of self-interested rulers. The people should not remain "passive" under "Measures of Government." Campbell offered a reminder that "Your rulers . . . are only falable men. When they act well, honor and applaud; [w]hen wickedly, impeach and punish them."[71]

Beyond encouraging the people to scrutinize their leaders, Campbell raised the possibility that political independence might solve western grievances. Early in 1782, Campbell drafted a circular calling for a convention "to adopt such measures as may be adjudged proper by a majority" and advance their constituency "as members of the American Union." The call for a convention reinforced the source of its legitimacy. Campbell's plan called for the election of delegates at county courthouses, but another supporter, Colonel William Christian, suggested electing delegates at the muster of county militias, where more people would gather than those attending the courts. For Christian, it was important to have representatives deputized "by the People from whence all Power flows." Like Christian, Campbell stressed the importance of taking "the sense of the People" before acting.[72]

Although a convention did not immediately meet, the circular prompted much discussion. Campbell broached the idea of independence to John Sevier, a backcountry leader and one of the delegates from Watauga who helped draft North Carolina's first constitution. Sevier gave "this Important Subject" much thought. He welcomed a meeting of "the people at Large," since "all political Authority Originates with the Collective Body." In June 1782, Campbell wrote to Arthur Lee, one of Virginia's congressional delegates, explaining his support for the determinist cause. He guided his "political conduct" by two "principal landmarks: the Constitution and the voice of the people." Although Campbell received encouragement from westerners, the view from Virginia's eastern leadership was distinctly different. James Madison warned Thomas Jefferson about Campbell's "aggressions meditated on the territorial rights of Virginia." The convention Campbell called for eventually met in the summer of 1784, when settlers in the Watauga region of North Carolina declared their independence as the state of Franklin.[73]

Before that challenge to North Carolina's authority, Virginia faced another determinist movement in Kentucky during the spring and summer of 1782. Virginia's legislature received several petitions from that region renewing grievances over the lack of effective government. The petitioners based their claims on "the Rights of [the] Constitution." The petitions encountered a mixed reaction. Virginia's political leadership anticipated the eventual separation of Kentucky. While opposed to unilateral action by western settlers, many conceded the time had come to "plan for administering Justice" and extending "the other benefits of Government to that remote region." The attorney general of the state, Edmund Randolph, acknowledged legitimate grievances of Kentuckians. "It is enormous," he wrote to James Madison, "to bring criminals from the distance of 400 miles for trial, and to oblige the poor settlers to travel hither for the adjustment of their disputes, at the expence perhaps of . . . half . . . their little capital." Nonetheless, dividing the state without Virginia's consent was a different matter. Kentucky settlers broached such a severance in a petition sent to Congress in 1782.[74]

In their congressional petition, settlers emphasized that their remoteness both endangered "their rights" and made their incorporation as counties of Virginia impractical. They asserted that Virginia's colonial authority over the region "devolved on the United States" with the Revolution. As "subjects of the United States & not of Virginia," they asked to be admitted into "the federal Union" as a "separate and independent State." Arthur Lee called the petition an "insult" to Virginia. The theory of congressional control over western lands was "a groundless" and "idle supposition."[75]

Instead, the petition stimulated a debate, despite the suggestion of Lee and Madison that Congress lacked any basis to consider the petitioners' claims. According to them, Virginia's legislature and not Congress was the exclusive judge of Kentucky's potential separation. For Madison, the theory that the rights of the Crown devolved to the United States with independence was "so extravagant that it could not enter into the thots of any man." If Virginia's delegates summarily dismissed the Kentucky determinists' position, members of other delegations disagreed. John Witherspoon, a New Jersey delegate and Madison's "revered teacher" at Princeton, suggested that his former pupil must have been making a rhetorical point. Witherspoon accepted the devolution argument as did "many" other "sensible men." The American Revolution represented "the united and joint efforts of the thirteen States" and not "those of any one State." Indeed, a decade later Chief Justice John Jay noted that it was not an "uncommon opinion" during the revolutionary period that "unappropriated lands" did not pass – with the Revolution – "to the people of the Colony or States within whose limits they were situated, but to the whole people." Consequently, "the rights claimed and exercised by the crown devolved on all, and not any individual State." Witherspoon's New Jersey colleague, Abraham Clark, also suggested that Virginia's efforts to control western lands smacked of the colonialism underlying the Revolution. Virginia's attempts invited "another revolution" by settlers on the frontier. After inconclusive debate, Congress dropped the issue, but it resurfaced several months later in the context of Vermont's status.[76]

Sectional tensions and the politics between "large" and "small" states as well as land companies lobbying for perceived advantages in the disposition of western lands influenced the debate over Kentucky's congressional petition. Nonetheless, support from members of Congress, whatever its motivation, offered Kentucky determinists – as well as other determinist movements – additional legitimacy. The parallels between remote western settlements and the American colonies on the eve of the Revolution underscored the point that they were merely invoking rights validated with Independence. Kentucky determinists stressed their loyalty to the revolutionary cause and defended their competence to form their own governments. "Some of our fellow citizens may think we are not yet able to conduct our affairs, and consult our interest; but if our society is rude, much wisdom is not necessary to supply our wants, and a fool can sometimes put on his clothes better than a wise man can do it for him." Indeed, if "inexperience" disqualified them from their own "management," they worried there was no right under Virginia's 1776 constitution that "might be taken" away "upon the same principles." By allowing the settlers to form their own government, Virginia's legislature would "respect" its own constitution. Given the practical impossibility of Virginia authorities to make "wholesome laws" for Kentucky, determinists sought independence "to enjoy the freedom and blessings of our fellow-Citizens."[77]

In 1782, Hugh Williamson, a congressional delegate for North Carolina, compared his state's western land situation with Virginia's. He thought his state's "moderate" government over its western inhabitants meant they would be "among the last who will run riot." Williamson's prediction that North Carolina would avoid the contagion of new state-making was premature: even as he wrote, Arthur Campbell and others spearheaded an ambitious determinist movement. One supporter noted that movement stirred up "contentions" having "a powerful influence to set on foot free enquiry, and to bring about surprising advances in political knowledge." North Carolina's cession of its western lands to Congress in 1784 proved the catalyst for delegates to assemble from three western counties of the state in a convention that eventually led to the creation of the state of Franklin.[78]

The convention analogized its situation to that of the American colonies, justifying the independence of the western counties. For Arthur Campbell, "the events of 1776" and the constitutions written in their wake established "the *Basis*" for their actions. A committee of the convention recommended that the three counties create "an Association" consistent "with the modes and forms of laying out a new State." The report asserted Congress's authority "to countenance us in forming ourselves into a separate government" and reiterated the "right to keep and hold a convention from time to time."[79]

A subsequent convention met in December and adopted a temporary constitution for the state of Franklin, patterned on North Carolina's 1776 constitution. That convention believed North Carolina implicitly consented to Franklin's independence by ceding its western lands. Delegates thought Congress gave the Franklin movement "ample encouragement." They possessed an "inalienable right" to form themselves into "a new and independent State" and protect their "lives, liberties and property."[80]

Soon after Franklin's organization, a congressional petition initiated by Campbell and other determinists in Washington County, Virginia, sought recognition for "a free and Independent State" drawn from Virginia, North Carolina, and the future states of West Virginia, Georgia, Tennessee, Alabama, and Kentucky. They believed Congress was ready to extend "equal respect to the liberties" of inhabitants of western lands as to other Americans. As patriots, the petitioners claimed "the privileges of American citizens." In 1785, a determinist in Washington County considered developments in the State of Franklin "the fruits of the glorious American revolution!"[81]

Washington County determinists sent another petition seeking the creation of two separate states, one located in Kentucky and another near the upper waters of the Tennessee River. The petitioners expected annexation to Franklin, the "new Society forming itself back of North-Carolina," but sought "an orderly accession to Independence under the auspices of Congress." The petitioners were "Deputies" for the "People of this Country," who deeply appreciated "the advantages of local Constitutions." They acted under the principle "that any number of People under any government have an indefensible right to consult and provide for their proper interests," including making "such alteration in their present situation and government as they think will increase their happiness." They echoed early state constitutions in declaring that "individuals are not created for the pleasure of government, but [that] government is instituted for the happiness of individuals." Their petitions thus squarely rested on "the sovereignty of the People."[82]

Although Congress did not act on the petitions, both North Carolina and Virginia tried to suppress the determinist movements. In April 1785, North Carolina's governor, Alexander Martin, issued a "Manifesto" in response to the Franklin events, demanding that "all persons concerned in the said revolt . . . forbear paying any obedience to any self-created power" that was "not sanctified by the Legislature." Virginia's governor, Patrick Henry, denounced "the assumption of sovereign power" without "authority known in the American constitution." Henry worried that the Franklin example might become a "contagion" to Virginia's western counties. Arthur Campbell reported that efforts "against the friends for New States" produced a backlash "on account of the infringement of constitutional privileges."[83]

Franklin's governor, John Sevier, defended the determinists in letters written to each governor. Sevier wrote Martin that "necessity and self-preservation have compelled us to the measure we have taken." Sevier also assured Patrick Henry that "we are not a banditti, but a people who mean to do right, as far as our knowledge will lead us." If his advocacy of Franklin's independence was deemed "criminal," Campbell complained, then there was more than enough "guilt" to be shared with "many respectable characters in other Counties on the Western Waters." Campbell questioned how men bound "to support republican principles" could blame the determinists since they acted in a manner "strictly consistent with the Constitution." In addition, they acted in accord with "different Acts of Congress," those of "different Legislatures, [and] the opinions of the best statesmen in America." Franklin determinists also lobbied North Carolina's legislature, seeking "to participate in the fruits of the Revolution; and to enjoy the essential benefits of Civil Society under a form of Government" of their own making. They asked no "more than free people ought to claim, agreeable to Republican principles."[84]

Campbell claimed that Patrick Henry "first suggested" the "ideas" that encouraged Campbell's determinism – views that other leaders "fostered." In fact, in 1778, as Virginia's governor, Henry, reminded far western settlers that they were entitled to "free and equal representation" as well as "all the improvements in Jurisprudence and police which the other parts of the state enjoy." Campbell sensed that by the end of the war many American revolutionaries had "lost sight of the object they were contending for." It was essential to scrutinize government officials to make sure they were acting in conformity with "fundamental principles" as "expressed in the Constitutions."[85]

As a framer of Virginia's first constitution, Campbell believed his actions were constitutional and consistent with "republican principles." In 1785 Campbell wrote to a fellow Virginia constitution-maker, James Madison. In that letter, Campbell predicted the formation of many future American states and hoped the existing large states would be limited to "convenient" and "suitable bounds" with the remaining western lands divided "into proper divisions for free Communities." Crucial to maintaining the "bands of amity" among the growing number of states was revising state constitutions that might be "defective." When he and Madison helped create Virginia's 1776 constitution, Campbell considered it "a specimen of consummate wisdom." Ten years of operation revealed that constitution's "many defects," lessons that would allow Franklin's constitution-makers to "produce a Form . . . much superior" to Virginia's first effort.[86]

When Franklin held its second convention to adopt a permanent constitution in November 1785, Campbell helped draft a document, the so-called Frankland constitution, intended as an advance in American constitution-making. This constitution also underscored the continuing confluence of radical Christianity and the more direct participation of the people as "the ruler" under constitutions authorized by the collective sovereign. Prior to the convention, Campbell and the Reverend William Graham, the Presbyterian president of Liberty Hall Academy (the forerunner of Washington and Lee University), drafted a constitution providing for widespread political participation. Over spirited opposition, other delegates favored making the existing constitution based on the North Carolina constitution the permanent constitution for Franklin. The disagreement persisted in a vigorous debate that split Presbyterians in Virginia and North Carolina over the shape of constitutional government for Franklin.[87]

Eventually, the Washington County and Franklin determinist movements were suppressed. In June 1785, Virginia's governor, Patrick Henry, removed Campbell as county lieutenant and justice of the peace. He also signed an act making it "high treason" to establish "any government separate from or independent of the government of Virginia." Despite a few clashes, a threatened civil war between "New State" and "Old State" adherents never materialized in North Carolina. By 1789, John Sevier's Franklin government largely collapsed.[88]

Even as western determinist movements were contained, developments in New England not only threatened the governmental stability of that region, but illustrated the ongoing percolation of determinist movements – this time entailing the genesis of statehood for Maine. In October 1785, inhabitants of three northeastern counties of Massachusetts were invited to attend a "conference" to explore the possibility of creating from those counties "a separate government" and to test "the sentiments of the people on the subject." Three months later, a contributor to the *Massachusetts Centinel* identified the danger in such a "separate State" movement. The "evil" was not confined to Massachusetts since it might institute "a spirit of *novelty* and *revolution* in the interior part of several of our large states" potentially leading to "civil dudgeon."[89]

The failed determinist movements in North Carolina and Virginia subjected neither Sevier nor Campbell to political oblivion. Indeed, both were personally vindicated. After Edmund Randolph replaced Patrick Henry as Virginia's governor, the legislature concluded that Henry had exceeded his authority in depriving Campbell of his judicial office. Campbell was reinstated as justice of the peace for Washington County. John Sevier also experienced validation. After the state of Franklin collapsed, Sevier was elected to North Carolina's senate. And when western North Carolina achieved statehood as Tennessee, Sevier became its governor and most prominent political leader. [90]

Despite opposing Campbell's determinist objectives as Virginia's governor, Henry subsequently embraced Campbell's movement. By 1790 Henry reflected that "the people of Franklin" were entitled to gather in convention "to consult together for their own Good" and exercise "that Right to chuse a Form of Government." Being "cut off" from a government to which they could give consent, the people in Franklin possessed "all the Rights of Sovereignty over the District & Lands therein." Neither Congress nor "any other persons who understand the principles of the Revolution" could "controvert or deny" those rights. [91]

During the mid-1780s when Franklin determinists struggled with North Carolina, and Campbell led the independence movement in Virginia's Washington County, settlers in Kentucky sought to separate from Virginia. In May 1784, "an Inhabitant of the most remote part" of Virginia warned the state's governor about a growing movement to "revolt from Government." Kentucky's progress toward political independence – eventually successful while Franklin's bid was not – relied on many of the same arguments advanced by the Franklinites, Campbell, and other determinists. [92]

In December 1784, a convention of delegates meeting in Danville resolved that Kentucky's inhabitants had the same rights as "their Bretheren in the Eastern part of this State." Another Kentucky convention meeting in May 1785 drafted an address modeled on the Declaration of Independence, in which they identified their constitutional rights. One "self evident truth" was that government existed "for the ease and protection of the governed." As such, "whenever these ends are not attained, by one form of government" it is the "right" and "duty" of the people "to seek such other mode, as will be most likely" to ensure them government's "blessings." Isolation deprived them of "benefits of government" that every citizen "has a right to expect." Most people in the region, another Kentuckian assured Madison, thought they did not "at present enjoy a greater portion of Liberty than an American Colony" might have had "a few Years ago." [93]

In subsequent conventions Kentucky settlers continued to draw parallels to the Revolution. Their "sequestered situation," as a petition to the Virginia legislature in September 1785 put it, "precludes every Idea of a connexion, on Republican principles." Independence was necessary to enjoy "the inestimable blessings, which mankind may derive from the American Revolution." The settlers explained their tone: "it becomes Freemen when speaking to Freemen, to imploy the plain . . . unadorned Language of Independence."[94]

Using "plain" and "unadorned" words in their petition signified constitutional understandings of the people as the collective sovereign. As rulers as well as the ruled, the people were no longer supplicants to government officials and representatives, expected to "pray" deferentially for relief. Rather, as the new sovereigns of America, the people could petition government as equals if not as "masters" speaking to "servants." The tenor of such petitions reflected a different concept of the relationship between the people and their government since the Revolution.[95]

Indeed, to consider the "Language of Independence" as mere rhetoric misses important concepts of constitutionalism that many Americans acted on in framing constitutions and forming states during the revolutionary period. Determinist movements suggested one way in which the ferment of the constitutional ideas unleashed by the Revolution was manifested. The creation of "The Political Club" at Danville during the heyday of conventions seeking Kentucky's independence offered yet another example. Founded by political leaders of the region and constitutional convention delegates, members of the club regularly debated a wide range of political and constitutional issues.[96]

An even more energetic form of sharing constitutional understandings and a new way of thinking about government came from those willing to canvass remote settlements by horseback. It might entail wearing out "all the Stirrups at every Station" in order to dispel the "ignorance" and "blind obeyance which used to Characterize the Colonies." For one so motivated, it was "a pity" that some Americans had "lost sight of those principles" that "produced" the Revolution. Remembering those principles would "prompt" Americans to act "by every means within their reach."[97]

American revolutionaries agreed that the people as the sovereign justified their independence and the formation of new governments. As such, they did not agonize over defining "the people" during the initial transition from colonial to state governments. The revolutionary committees and conventions that oversaw the shift of political power from the British authorities in the thirteen colonies to the emergent American states were in a sense pouring new wine into old bottles. While the basis of revolutionary governments drew from the new experience of drafting written constitutions, each provisional and then state government simply displaced the political entity of its former colony and perpetuated the existing colonial boundaries. On the other hand, the claims of Vermont and other determinist movements seeking independence directly raised the question of creating state governments in addition to the original thirteen. Just how that creation should occur and who constituted "the people" forming the sovereign basis of such new governments confronted Americans at the same time they struggled for independence and as religious ferment in the backcountry shaped their views of self-governance.

Two of the most widely accepted premises of the American Revolution were that the people's consent legitimated government and that government retained its legitimacy by protecting and advancing the welfare of the people. As the sovereign source on which constitutions and governments rested, "the people" possessed enormous authority under the newly fashioned republics. The extent of that authority after the creation of government and how the people might act would soon be tested in dramatic events arising in western Massachusetts in the late 1780s. Even before the end of the Revolutionary War, however, Americans dealt with the threshold question of defining "the people" as the sovereign in a variety of frontier settings. Those early definitional struggles occurred far from the centers of government that received greatest attention. Americans wrestled over defining a sovereign people because determinist movements emerged contemporaneously with the revolutionary struggle and forced the issue. The terminology proved slippery but vital, and pitted the rights of "the people" against the jurisdictional authority of existing state governments. The struggle over the meaning of the constitutional vocabulary and principles employed by the people in the aftermath of the Revolution had only begun.

4 Revolutionary Tensions

"Friends of Government" Confront "The Regulators" in Massachusetts

Under arrest and awaiting trial, Dr. William Whiting pled his case to Massachusetts's Attorney General Robert Treat Paine in 1787. The two were hardly strangers. As a congressional delegate during the Revolutionary War, Paine had lobbied for the home manufacture of saltpeter – used in producing gunpowder and something that both Paine and John Adams considered of crucial military importance. Much of the success in stimulating domestic production of saltpeter they attributed to Whiting's efforts. At the time, Paine called him "my friend" and proclaimed that "the world knows your merit."

The doctor questioned the charges he faced. The Commonwealth accused him of encouraging the people's disaffection, hatred, and contempt of the government – the crime of sedition. Three weeks before his letter to Paine, the Massachusetts Senate recommended Whiting's removal from office for conduct "derogatory to Government."

As a prominent physician in revolutionary Massachusetts, Whiting had recently served as chief justice of the Berkshire County Court of Common Pleas. His judicial tenure came to an end in 1787 with his arrest after authoring two essays sympathetic to protesting farmers. Those farmers closed his court in Great Barrington until the state legislature considered their grievances. The closing came at "the point of Bayonets," Judge Whiting explained to the attorney general, and he yielded despite his great "aversion to mobs riots tumults & Insurrections."

He insisted that his essays defended the constitutional right of the majority of the people to correct government actions harmful to the public welfare. If lawful government action depended on the people's consent, argued Whiting, how could officials escape the scrutiny of the people? Consent and scrutiny were self-evident propositions of the Revolution and principles found in Massachusetts's 1780 constitution. Stripped of his judgeship, he pondered why it was now criminal "to avow such sentiments" when just ten years earlier no patriot would have "contradicted or denied them." His essays reflected basic themes central to the Revolution. Yet he stood accused as an enemy of the state for expressing those same ideas.

Whiting was no radical. A member of the Berkshire County elite since the Revolution, he served several years in the provisional legislature and then in 1775 as justice of the peace for Berkshire County. In the late 1770s, some revolutionaries challenged the legitimacy of his court's jurisdiction because it did not rest on a written constitution approved by the people. Whiting disagreed. He defended the authority of his court and presided as one of its judges. Now charged with aiding the forceful closing of his own court, he reminded the attorney general that during "that Dreary period" of the Revolution he preserved "the sacred fire of Lawful Government from being totally Extinguished in the County," despite "many threats and great hazard."

Writing to Paine was probably unwise. The doctor was part of Paine's busy schedule of "Trying & Convicting Traitors." And Whiting, as a member of the Massachusetts establishment, was especially dangerous for justifying the farmers' resistance on the basis of the state constitution.

A decade after Americans created their new governments, Whiting's fate was tied to two questions raised during the Revolution: what did it mean that the People were the sovereign in the new American nation and how did that sovereign make its will known? Answers to those questions that were unchallenged by many in 1776 were now to others the expression of sedition.[1]

Dramatic events unfolded in Massachusetts during the summer of 1786. Citizens petitioned for relief from state fiscal policies that placed farmers and small debtors under increasing economic pressure after the Revolution. When farmers' repeated appeals for relief went unanswered and the economic crisis deepened, countywide meetings were organized to present grievances. When those steps proved fruitless, protests focused on holding matters in abeyance until government responded to the farmers' plight and that of others in the state's rural communities.

This protest took the form of stopping county courts from meeting, effectively suspending debt collections that reflected trying economic times. Members of the state government and its defenders reacted to the meetings and court closings with a curious mixture of indifference and outrage. An *Address* of a Boston town meeting in November 1786 complained that many who disapproved of the actions of the farmers failed to provide "aid, in suppressing them." More militant observers urged an aggressive response to the farmers. After the state militia proved unreliable, Massachusetts's governor James Bowdoin sought to raise and fund a private army of over

4,000 soldiers. With this military force, the protests were effectively suppressed by February 1787. The aftermath of the conflict divided both the state and the nation. As a former governor of Massachusetts noted a few years after the event, "there was then ... a great diversity of sentiment respecting the measures ... to be pursued." Many observers of the controversy were troubled that citizens from the birthplace of American independence challenged their own government. Some saw in the protests the extent to which ideas unleashed by the Revolution might go if they were not constrained, while for others they demonstrated how far government strayed from the bright promise of a revolution in which the people played the role of the sovereign.[2]

While brandishing arms was not unusual during the Massachusetts controversy in 1786 and 1787, name-calling seemed the weapon of choice. The protesters thought they were exercising their rights as citizens to scrutinize, petition, and advise government. They called themselves "Regulators," harkening back to colonial protesters in the Carolinas who acted against the most tangible – and often the only – symbol of government at hand: local court proceedings. There were significant differences between Massachusetts "Regulators" and their earlier namesakes. However, this did not stop the Massachusetts protesters from describing themselves as Regulators.[3]

Regulators cast their opponents as government plunderers. Their opponents styled themselves the "Friends of Government." Friends derided the protesting farmers as "insurgents" engaging in a "rebellion" against the state.[4] Beneath this name-calling lay a deeper conflict. It formed part of a broader pattern of public unrest in America during the postrevolutionary period. The Massachusetts controversy reflected a continuing disagreement among Americans over what government – in which the people were the sovereign – meant in practice.[5]

The protests proved to Friends of Government the dangers of unchecked majorities – acting as a people and through a state legislature. Even if the "wise" were elected to govern, the actions of Regulators presumed that a majority of the people should exercise a continuous power in overseeing day-to-day operations. This role as the ruler could negate the virtuous guidance that Friends sought to provide government. Subordinating elected officials to popular oversight implied that the people could act whenever the need arose and not simply choose between candidates at election time. The suggestion that the people had constitutional authority for a direct regulation of their government profoundly disturbed Friends.

Events in Massachusetts illustrated the twin dangers that many Americans feared. Too much democracy might lead to anarchy. Yet excessive government force could stifle a democratic spirit and produce tyranny. Americans worried about both dangers. Friends of Government felt that events in Massachusetts provided evidence of anarchy. Regulators, on the other hand, saw the same events as evidence of oppression and tyranny. The plight of Dr. Whiting, for endorsing principles that Americans fought and died for only a decade earlier, reflected the gulf that separated such opposing perceptions.

Whiting's commitment to the promise of the Revolution was unshakable and he actively supported the patriot cause. He moved from Connecticut to Massachusetts before the Revolution and established his medical practice in Great Barrington. He soon became part of Berkshire County's political elite, led in part by lawyer Theodore Sedgwick, who served in the Continental Congress. Sedgwick later attained national prominence as a Federalist in Congress (rising to become Speaker of the House) and later served in the U.S. Senate. With Sedgwick's help, Whiting became a justice of the peace for the county in 1775, and later the presiding judge of the Court of Common Pleas.[6]

With the end of the Revolution, Whiting resumed his medical practice while still serving as a judge. In his medical rounds, he was exposed daily to "the Depressed State" of the people in western Massachusetts. The prosperity stimulated by the war was displaced by economic hardship. State policies creating a scarcity of hard currency made payment of debts burdensome and taxes heavier. Whiting assigned much of the blame for this shift in fortunes to unscrupulous men – some lawyers and "other Collecting officers" who avoided serving in the line of fire during the war, but who now advanced themselves in the race for wealth. By "constantly" harassing those of modest means by a "multiplicity of lawsuits" they added significantly to the "Distresses" of the time. Whiting did not retract these opinions, even when they put him at odds with his patron, Theodore Sedgwick.[7]

The two did not go their separate ways peacefully. Whiting accused Sedgwick of "Insidious" conduct. In return, Sedgwick accused Whiting of lying and betraying his old friends. After Whiting defended the Regulation, Sedgwick called his writing "a seditious libel" and urged Whiting's conviction for treason. Sedgwick thought that common people caught up in the Regulation were "to be pitied," but those "who drive them into excesses" – including Whiting, according to Sedgwick – were properly punished by "gibbets, & racks." Most of the Friends of Government, even those not intimately familiar with Whiting, also found the judge's writings highly objectionable.[8]

The economic hardship and political frustration experienced by farmers and others in rural communities of Massachusetts during the 1780s deeply affected Whiting. His assessment of the current state of affairs and sense of

who was harvesting the fruits of the Revolution differed dramatically from
that of Sedgwick.

UNDERLYING GRIEVANCES OF THE REGULATION

One postwar economic policy sought to resolve Massachusetts's revolutionary debt by increasing taxes. This approach might not have prompted the
controversy it did had it not also prohibited payment of debts by paper
money, reversing a policy dating back to the Revolution. The "hard money"
policy met with considerable favor within commercial and mercantile circles,
whose members also applauded the rejection of the practice of accepting
goods as legal tender and hence in satisfaction of debts. Those two measures
sent taxpayers scrambling to find sufficient coin currency to pay their debts.
In the tight credit market and economic depression that followed the war,
the absence of paper money and legal tender laws produced hardship and
resentment among debtors.[9]

The passage of these revolutionary-era fiscal measures encountered persistent, but ultimately futile, political resistance. Towns, particularly in rural
and western portions of the state, organized with the growing perception that
the Massachusetts constitution of 1780 marked a shift away from local control, largely centered in agrarian communities. Instead, Boston and eastern
commercial interests now seemed to exert undue influence on government.
In response, citizens in rural areas met and drafted instructions to legislators,
directed a stream of petitions to the legislature, and held meetings and conventions to articulate grievances and to request relief. Years of these appeals
were unavailing. By 1786, even the strongest supporters of the government's
policy, including Rufus King, then representing Massachusetts in Congress,
and John Adams, from his diplomatic posting in England, expressed views
in agreement with the judgment of the Salem lawyer William Pynchon that
the people were "labouring under grievous taxes and burdens." Alexander
Hamilton later observed that Massachusetts "threw her Citizens into Rebellion by heavier taxes than were paid in any other State."[10]

While the economic plight of farmers and small debtors produced support for the Regulation, it also attracted those who saw the state's fiscal
policies as illegitimately distributing wealth with punitive consequences for
the poorer segments of society. Many were struggling to pay off in hard currency debts that were created when paper payment was available, and they
felt victimized. They believed the state's policies were unjustly designed to
give a windfall to speculators. The manner chosen to retire the state debt
seemed to impose the heaviest tax burden on those with the least and did,

in fact, reward speculators in state securities. One farmer from Springfield predicted in 1786 that "the great men are going to get all we have." Even though the residents of Groton opposed "commotions," they asserted that the "greater part of the common people," while hanging onto their lands, "parted with their personal Estates, & are reduced to one & two Cows only." For Regulators and those sympathetic to their cause, the fact that a select few received special privileges and profits, while most of the community suffered, violated the purpose of government as stated in the state's constitution: to promote the general welfare rather than advance any one "class."[11]

Because organizing political meetings in large rural counties was more difficult than in closely populated urban settings, western representatives were hampered in coordinating their legislative goals. In addition, rural counties displayed an apparent political apathy that led to more frustration. Inland and western towns frequently failed to advance their legislative agenda by not sending representatives – prompted in part by the desire to avoid the cost of paying a legislator's salary. In 1786, for example, little more than 50 percent of western towns sent representatives to the legislature, while over 70 percent of eastern towns did so. Forgoing representation was not simply evidence of apathy; it also formed part of a wider New England pattern of protesting the failure of the legislature to provide economic relief. The decision of Regulators to boycott the legislature because they deemed it unresponsive to their complaints was a problematic strategy at best. Even those sympathetic to the grievances articulated by Regulators chastised western inhabitants for failing to exercise their electoral rights. The fact that westerners contributed to their plight, however, did not lessen their sense of frustration when the legislature failed to respond to their grievances.[12]

On the eve of the activities of the Regulators, what some people came to call the Regulation, the Massachusetts legislature rejected the implementation of paper money and any meaningful legal tender laws. Regulators saw this less as a rejection of their position than a result of the influence of wealth on the Senate. The constitution's property qualification for senatorial service – a freehold valued at £300 or a personal estate of £600 – ensured the exclusion of citizens of more modest means from that body. Moreover, unlike members of the House, who were elected by town meetings that could draft instructions for their representatives, senators were elected by counties. The perception that the size of senatorial districts undercut their accountability helped contribute to a movement seeking the abolition of the Senate.[13]

Regulators also focused on the prohibitive costs in the legal process of debt collection. Because court fees were fixed, smaller debtors often faced higher costs as a percentage of the underlying debt than did large debtors.

This made for "a most grievous oppression upon the people of the poor sort," noted Judge Whiting. In addition, the pay of court officials and lawyers was based on court fees. And like other costs under the state's fiscal policy, those fees were payable only in hard money. Use of a "loser-pays" fee system in which the prevailing creditor's costs were assumed by the losing debtor added insult to injury. For debtors, court costs could be "an amazing expence," even if the debt was undisputed. Even some lawyers acknowledged that fees in debt cases were exorbitant.[14]

To avoid such costs, farmers waged a long, but unsuccessful campaign for a debt confession act. Such an act allowed debtors simply to confess to indebtedness rather than go through a more elaborate judicial proceeding entailing costs and fees that were added to the amount they already owed creditors. A Confession Act of 1776 expired in 1778 and by the 1780s demand for a new confession act was "chronic." The legislature took its time in passing measures to reduce legal expenses. Whether or not litigation necessarily advanced the interests of creditors over debtors, the protesters resented paying avoidable costs in debt collection cases and blamed the judicial system (including lawyers) for this added expense.[15]

The criticism of government and the legal system united officeholders and lawyers in opposing Regulators. Abolishing the Senate would destroy needed legislative balance and stability, Friends argued. It also impugned the integrity and dignity of the senators. For their part, lawyers were sensitive to the heightened antilawyer rhetoric that accompanied complaints about the debt collection system.

The economic decisions of the Massachusetts legislature affected the state's citizens differently. The fiscal policies the state adopted were not neutral and were not perceived as such. For farmers burdened with paying off debt in hard currency during the postwar depression, it seemed as if the policies of flush economic times during the Revolution were unnecessarily and unfairly reversed. They wanted paper money and legal tender laws to ease payment for debt, much of it incurred when the use of paper currency was possible and formed an implicit part of the bargain in undertaking a debt. The scarcity of specie made payments in paper currency or equivalents in goods particularly necessary for those hit hard by the higher taxes. Without such alternatives or equivalents, debts increased as a practical matter because one had to pay more to purchase a lower face value of hard currency.

On the other side, politically powerful merchants successfully blocked efforts that would make their economic life more speculative by reintroducing paper currency. Those in business complained that if farmers prevailed on the form of payment for goods, a merchant "might be forced to take" paper currency or barter of goods that he "knows not what to do with." Ultimately, the merchant would need to convert such payments into hard currency himself, losing the difference between the face value of the debt actually paid and the real value of what such things would buy on the market.[16]

For Friends of Government, neither paper money nor the tender of goods to pay debts were acceptable solutions. Rather than having the merchant bear the risks of barter sales, they wanted the government to foreclose on the farmer and transform his assets into hard currency. They described paper money as "iniquitous in itself, pregnant of innumerable evils, both political and moral, contrary to the spirit of our constitution, and inconsistent with the rights of mankind." Regulators were guilty of seeking society's economic collapse by pressing for the return to paper money, a step Friends thought "would produce calamities without end."[17]

Friends were not simply making an economic argument. Rather, they attributed the discontent of the times to a decline in virtue. Even if the legislature reintroduced paper money, that would not solve the farmers' economic predicament because their laziness and addiction to "Luxury and extravagance" underlay their problems. Rather than paper money, what was needed, believed Friends, was a return to virtue by those clamoring against the postwar policies of hard currency.[18]

The way Friends of Government sought to cure the ills of the postwar American economy reflected social as well as economic theories. They hoped to preserve a familiar world in which they occupied political leadership within the state. With the war, new patterns of competition and creation of wealth emerged that were facilitated by paper currency. Those changes severely disrupted traditional forms of wealth and investment that Friends used as a measure of rank. Friends were heavily invested in the prewar market and fiscal system and thus sensitive to alterations in the structure of property rights accompanying the Revolution. The new economic landscape threatened both their wealth and accustomed place in society.[19]

Friends faced a problem of paying their own debts if Regulators were able to delay paying theirs. As such, Friends charged Regulators with repudiating their debts and seeking to redistribute wealth through a paper money economy. Friends refused to acknowledge that Regulators sought relief from economic distress by suspending rather than repudiating debts. The few members of the traditional establishment who publicly defended Regulators observed as much. As Judge Whiting explained at the time, most "poor Debtors" neither "denied nor refused" to pay their debts. Debts, he wrote, "ought to be paid when it is in the power of the Debtor to Do it." Postponing debts and temporarily suspending their collection were stopgap measures to prevent "the Lower orders of the people" from being "Reduced to absolute poverty and Slavery" in the postwar economic crisis.[20]

Regulators appreciated their economic interests as much as Friends did, and both sides considered their positions justified. For Regulators, the use of paper money during the Revolution not only responded to the exigencies of the times but was an essential key to a thriving economy in which all shared in the spread of prosperity and the promise of heightened commercial expectations. Facilitating trade and the exchange of goods required money, but the scarcity of hard currency naturally produced demands for printing paper money. Although paper money, if not properly managed, could cause inflation, Regulators felt such effects could be mitigated. Preventing the use of paper money was not the answer. Their belief that paper money encouraged participation in the growing American economy was not an isolated or unwarranted economic view at the time. Some prominent revolutionary leaders, such as Benjamin Franklin, considered paper money part of a viable fiscal policy. By 1786, a Friend of Government conceded that even individuals with "respectable Standings and Characters" supported paper money. The revolutionary economy demonstrated the success of paper money – it not only had helped attain Independence but also allowed many Americans who formerly found themselves on the economic margins to aspire now to greater financial advancement.[21]

Politically, economically, and constitutionally, the logic of favoring "hard money" and rejecting "paper money" was not self-evident after the Revolution. There was nothing inherently constitutional about hard money nor unconstitutional about paper money under the Massachusetts constitution. Rather, both forms of money represented competing examples of "class legislation." Both options represented choices that benefited some groups in society at the expense of others. In postrevolutionary Massachusetts, the protection of one group – the farmers – would come at a considerable cost to the other – the Friends of Government – and vice versa.[22]

If the desire of Friends to retain their social and economic standing deserved respect and government support, why shouldn't the same be true of the Regulators' wish to preserve their community standing by retaining their farms until they could pay their debts? For Regulators, changes made in the state's fiscal policy after the Revolutionary War, urged by some who became leading Friends, precipitated the economic hardships experienced by many Regulators. This shift in policy gave financial and social protection to some people during the postwar years. Yet the Regulators asked why the interests of other citizens, including the smaller debtors and farmers, should not be equally entitled to support in an independent America in which the people were now the new sovereign?

THE REVOLUTIONARY CONTEXT OF THE REGULATION

The controversy over economic policies in Massachusetts in the late 1780s had revolutionary roots. Over a decade earlier, on December 26, 1775, the town of Pittsfield in Berkshire County had petitioned the provisional state legislature to suspend Massachusetts's royal charter. The inhabitants of Pittsfield considered the charter an "abhorrence" to their concept of legitimate government. They wanted a "new Constitution" in which the people, not a monarch, were the sovereign.[23]

The provisional legislature disagreed. For one, the recent election of representatives to the legislature produced a government "more . . . under the influence and control of the people" than had ever existed in Massachusetts. Moreover, despite the perpetuation of the royal charter, judicial commissions would no longer be issued in the name of the king, but rather by "the Government and People" of Massachusetts. Pittsfield petitioners thought these responses missed the point. The people should construct their own constitution rather than support a government originating under the king's authority. Holding elections and altering the form of judicial commissions was not enough. Even if judicial commissions struck out "the King[']s Name," that was "Nothing whilst the foundation is unfixed" and the state lacked a new constitution, "the Corner stone of Government."[24]

The people of Pittsfield questioned the legitimacy of the provisional government until the state adopted a constitution. The necessity of interim governance, however, permitted the provisional legislature to "levy Taxes, raise an Army," and prepare for the "common defence." Nonetheless, with the rejection of the king's authority, any successor government lacked legitimacy until it received and reflected the consent of the people. The wartime need for a provisional legislature did not include the courts. Rather, the judicial system required a new foundation based on the people's adopting a constitution. Until then, judicial appointments lacked authority. Because the courts were the least crucial branch of government in resisting the British, stopping county courts from sitting became a recurring pattern to protest the unfinished work of constitution-making. Other counties also engaged in this activity, but Berkshire most consistently stopped courts between the Revolution and the formation of Massachusetts's constitution in 1780.[25]

The revolutionary-era court closings differed significantly from those of the postrevolutionary years. Court closings during the Revolution challenged the legitimacy of provisional government because it sought to determine judicial questions without a constitution under which the people authorized the courts. On the other hand, Massachusetts Regulators in 1786 stopped courts because they disagreed with policies they deemed illegitimate. They did not challenge the legitimacy of state government or the courts whose operations they suspended.

In 1778, as a justice of the peace for Berkshire County, Dr. Whiting defended his court's operation as part of the provisional revolutionary government. He acknowledged that the Declaration of Independence had ended colonial governments, including that from which his court drew its authority. He argued that Independence did not produce a state of nature, since there was still a *"union* or *compact* existing among the people" to regulate their affairs in an orderly way. The dissolution of the colonial government did not release members of society from their "allegiance" to the community's majority will. The agreement "to be governed" by the majority was "a sufficient and substantial foundation of government" and justified the continuation of the courts, despite their establishment under the British colonial regime. Whiting favored a new constitution for Massachusetts. However, until that new constitution was adopted, those who objected to the provisional government were bound to submit to the majority will that accepted the provisional government. Court closings by a minority were "unwarrantable and seditious," conflicting with the "ancient maxim, *vox populi* est vox Dei (the voice of the people is the voice of God)."[26]

One group of Americans who strongly supported Independence but rejected the Massachusetts provisional government's legitimacy included the Berkshire Constitutionalists. During the Revolution they disputed Whiting's argument that acquiescence by most Massachusetts inhabitants conferred legitimacy on the provisional government and its courts. As Thomas Allen, one of the Constitutionalists' leaders, put it, the Declaration of Independence placed Americans in a constitutional state of nature. This situation would end only after the people in Massachusetts created a new constitution. Consent to a government could not be implied or imputed through acquiescence, as it was under English constitutional theory. Creating governments in which the collective people, not a British monarch, were the sovereign created a new constitutional order for America – it was "a New thing under the sun."[27]

A constitution became effective only after receiving "the Approbation of the Majority of the people at Large," declared Allen. Such consent by the sovereign required positive action. The act of a sovereign creating government "is a Trust that Cannot be Deligated," warned Allen. After

establishing government, no "Rational Person" would blindly let it operate unchecked, the sovereign having renounced "a Right of Inspection
Approbation Rejection or Amendment." It was not possible for the people
as the sovereign to surrender their sovereign authority to others. Allowing
the provisional legislature to create a constitution by itself would be such a
surrender. It made that legislature "Greater than the people[,] their Master."
It contradicted the idea that after the American Revolution when it came
to government's actions, the people were encouraged to "see with your own
Eyes and Judge for your selves."[28]

The Constitutionalists' preoccupation with constitution-making by the
people was not an unusual concern in postrevolutionary America. Increasingly, it became clear to Americans that only the sovereign authority, the
people, could create constitutions that gave legitimacy to governments they
established. The Berkshire Constitutionalists were simply in step with, or
even ahead of, the times. Towns in Berkshire were among the first to call for
a new constitution. They insisted on more directly involving "the people."
Towns in eastern counties such as Suffolk, Middlesex, and Bristol, as well
as towns in Worcester County in the center of the state, came to lead the
demand for creating a constitution through a special convention.[29]

Calls for a special convention grew after the state's provisional government
proposed to create a constitution in September 1776. That proposal limited
the people's role to "Inspection and Perusal" of the final draft rather than
formally voting on ratification. If the people were to inspect the results of the
constitutional drafting process, the town of Norton in Bristol County insisted
that the drafters (who were also the legislators) be "Seperately Elected by
the people" for the "Special purpose" of drafting a constitution.[30]

Boston voters also rejected the proposal that the provisional legislature
draft the constitution without a special election. Wide input was needed
because a constitution affects "every Individual." The legislature should not
frame a constitution if it was not specially chosen for that purpose. Otherwise the people lost those opportunities of "consulting, aiding and assisting"
that went into producing a fundamental law that reflected their will as the
sovereign. Since the right to form a government "is essentially in the People,"
some towns demanded even greater popular participation, seeking county
conventions followed by a statewide convention at which "the wisdom of the
whole state may be collected" and "Extracted" into a constitution.[31]

Massachusetts resolved the dispute over constitution-making by holding
a special drafting convention with delegates selected by the people whose
product faced popular ratification. The convention called for ratification
by two-thirds of the people voting in the towns. The returns, however,

revealed considerable opposition to various parts of the constitution and even to the entire document. Nonetheless, a committee of the convention, by manipulating the vote count, declared that two-thirds of those voting approved of the constitution. In actuality, the vote in favor of ratification was probably closer to a simple majority – ultimately consistent with the traditional iteration of how to identify the voice of the sovereign people.[32]

Even if not ratified by two-thirds of the people, the 1780 constitution unequivocally established the majority of the people as the sovereign in Massachusetts. If the people directly created the state's constitution, the question now became the role of the people after the creation of government. As later events in Massachusetts and other states demonstrated, Americans disagreed about the role that the new sovereign might play as the ruler as well as the ruled under written constitutions expressing that sovereign's will.

In 1786, it would have been difficult to find an American supporter of Independence who did not believe that conventions or congresses acting during the Revolution reflected the "voice of the people." Now that the people were the acknowledged sovereign, would their voice be heard the same way? If the legislature gave voice to the people, would the addition of the people also speaking through a convention necessarily hinder the new American governments?

Many Massachusetts farmers in the 1780s blamed their distress on the hard currency requirements. They were upset that their voice was not being heard. With the legislature seemingly ignoring their plight, they turned to some of the mechanisms through which they, as the sovereign, had spoken in the past decade with great effect. In so doing, they ended up testing precisely how they, as part of the new sovereign, could communicate their will. The legislature was one means to express the will of the sovereign. They had used such a body during colonial times to send representatives to Boston to administer the colony. In addition, farmers and other citizens convened in additional venues to assert their will. While the colonial Massachusetts legislature might, as it did, condemn Parliament's passage of the Sugar Act (and the taxation it imposed) in 1764, this did not preclude the people of Boston from gathering in town meetings to express their views independent of legislative action.[33]

It was against this background that towns began holding their own meetings and conventions in 1786 when the Massachusetts legislature failed to respond to the hardships produced by its policies. The meetings and conventions focused on the farmers' economic woes. Meetings were held in "most of the towns" of the state for the purpose of "appointing members to meet in convention." County conventions could draw several members from each town, and at times over fifty towns were represented. Often conventions included "the most prominent" citizens of the region. Participating in the Hampshire County convention were current and former members of the legislature. The town of Springfield chose as a convention delegate a member of "one of the oldest and most respected families in the town." Not only did some county conventions attract prominent citizens, but most towns and counties in the state were represented in them. Many towns in the eastern counties of the state sent delegates, as did central and western counties. "[T]he General talk," noted one observer, "was County Conventions."[34]

CONTRASTING PERCEPTIONS OF CONVENTIONS

Friends of Government were outraged by this talk of conventions. They made two charges. First, that grievances against the government were exaggerated. Second, that even if reason for discontent existed, conventions initiated by the people were an impermissible means of expressing such grievances under Massachusetts's 1780 constitution. Their charges were closely related. Conventions were illegitimate attempts to displace the republican government the people established under their constitution. Convention participants were simply a minority of "Persons of small Abilities . . . and of no great Integrity" who were undermining public order by stirring up grievances against the state government. Merchant David Sewall explained this thinking in October 1786. The idea that conventions were legal was "a misapplication or misconstruction" of Massachusetts's 1780 bill of rights. Conventions should "always . . . be Opposed" as sowing "Seeds of Sedition."[35]

Bezaleel Howard, a minister in Springfield, observed that "many Gentlemen of the Law" considered conventions not only "Illegal," but tending "to Enflame the minds of the people." Indeed, the chief justice of the Supreme Judicial Court, Massachusetts's highest court, thought conventions served only to "counteract" the legislature and "excite treason and insurrection." A former justice of that court and future governor of the state, James Sullivan, belittled "the idea of a county convention being a legal body." He wanted such a misinterpretation of the law "exploded." John Adams tried to do so during his diplomatic posting to England. The resurgence of "County Conventions" in his home state, which had once admirably expressed the views of the people for Independence and liberty, now amounted to "seditious meetings" and prompted him to publish *A Defence of the Constitutions of Government of the United States of America*.[36]

The challenge by Friends to the conventions' legality reflected a particular belief about how the people were to rule as the new sovereign. With

Independence, Americans struggled to secure the fruits of the Revolution, which they did by creating republican governments. Resolutions passed in county conventions about policies adopted by the state government seemed out of step with the new political arrangements ushered in by the Revolution. Unlike 1776, Friends explained, no foreign sovereign held sway that would justify conventions involving themselves with government.

Conventions were appropriate in revolutionary times because they expressed the will of the people that could not otherwise be ascertained. During the war, conventions were needed to reach policy decisions and bypass a discredited governmental structure drawing authority from the British Crown. Then, as the former patriot leader Samuel Adams explained, "County Conventions" had "an excellent Purpose" and were "highly necessary." Since the Revolution, as some townspeople from Boston argued, "County Meetings" of "the People at Large" were no longer justified since the people's adoption of the 1780 constitution authorized a way to express their will through the legislature. For Samuel Adams, the establishment of "regular & constitutional Governments" made conventions "useless" and "dangerous." The people no longer needed conventions as a conduit to express their will. For Friends, county conventions were a questionable means of hearing that will. It seemed that duly enacted legislation, such as the hard money policies adopted by the state only a few years earlier, were a more certain expression of the people as the sovereign.[37]

The town of Cambridge reflected this attitude when it refused to send delegates to a Middlesex County convention to meet in August 1786. A convention was "justifiable," the town meeting resolved, only when the "powers of the State have been evidently and notoriously" used for "unconstitutional purposes." Conventions were inappropriate if the people possessed a "constitutional means of redress." The legislature established under the 1780 constitution provided the means for the people to rule as the sovereign and as far as Friends were concerned, it was the only way.[38]

Conventions or similar meetings unsanctioned by the legislature intruded into the business rightly entrusted to the legislature by the people's constitution. In that constitution, the legislature was the body selected by the people to represent their interests. Ratification of the state constitution vested that body with the authority to act in the name of the people. Allowing "self Created Conventions" to question the judgments of the legislature introduced a conundrum: who spoke for the people? Was it the legislature that the people established to speak day-to-day, or those who attended a convention at the people's behest? Such competing expressions of the people's will was not only confusing to the general administration of the state but also undermined the authority of those elected by the people to act on their behalf. For this reason, noted Governor Bowdoin of Massachusetts in September 1786, even "peaceable" conventions deliberating on state policy were a "very dangerous tendency."[39]

Few disputed that in America the people collectively were the sovereign. What divided Friends and Regulators was whether there could be multiple expressions of that sovereign will. The underlying question was whether the people retained the right to speak in the voice of the ruler even after they created government. On that issue the two sides divided.

Samuel Adams captured the sense of a collective sovereign – and that the collective sovereign should uniformly express its will – by noting that the people as the sovereign should "keep a watchful Eye over the Conduct of all" concerned with "Publick Affairs." Such "Attention is the People[']s great Security" against tyranny. A government established with "Constitutional Authority" gave the legislature "the Weight of Government lawfully exercised." Even the collective American sovereign owed "Respect" to "Constitutional Authority," Adams explained.[40]

For Adams, government's authority, or, as he put it, "Weight," came from the people sufficiently trusting it to act in their interest. That trust made it unnecessary to watch government's every move. County conventions needlessly encouraged a minute, critical examination of government. It seemed that such bodies would hobble America's unique system of representation in which each person who was ruled was also part of the sovereign who collectively authorized the government to rule. Encouraging faultfinding by the people of their government undercut that relationship.[41]

In 1788, George Minot, a lawyer who served as clerk of the Massachusetts House of Representatives during the Regulation, elaborated this idea in his *History of the Insurrections in Massachusetts*. Conventions tended to develop "lists of grievances," he complained. Those lists included judgments passed by conventions on officeholders. This "always weakened the government," he observed. Critique of actions taken by duly elected representatives of the people "wore a strong appearance of opposition to constitutional authority." Using a phrase popular among Friends, he thought county conventions undermined "the dignity of government."[42]

If Adams and Minot worried about the fragility of representative government, other Friends made a more technical argument. Some Friends concluded that because the 1780 Massachusetts constitution did not mention the people's ability to hold conventions, such meetings were "void of all authority." According to the chief justice of the Supreme Judicial Court, the constitution's silence on conventions demonstrated that such meetings

were "inconsistent with the nature of government, and substantially repugnant to our constitution." The 1780 constitution "parceled out . . . all power
that is to be exercised" in the government formed "under it." The failure of
the constitution to identify a role for conventions, observed "AN OTHER
CITIZEN," rendered "*all* conventions of the people . . . illegal" and "unconstitutional." Simply put, declared Governor Bowdoin, county conventions
were "anti-constitutional."[43]

The irony of the sudden obsolescence and illegality of conventions
was not lost on Regulators and critics of the government's fiscal policies.
Friends seemed to display self-serving inconsistency by calling conventions of the people, which facilitated their rise to power, unlawful assemblies engaged in acts "treasonable to the state." One Regulator responded
to this shift by reminding his readers that when the British were the
"*Rulers*, . . . Conventions of the people were lawful – they were then necessary." Indeed, those conventions were justified on constitutional grounds.
Now it seemed that Friends of Government were saying that "since I have
myself become a ruler," conventions "cease to be lawful" and "the people
have no right to examine into my conduct." Apparently, wrote one defender
of conventions, those who dared enquire into the "gross mismanagement"
of state government were "stigmatized as traitors, incendiaries" and "*vile
creatures*."[44]

From the perspective of Regulators, the conventions that preceded court
closings were entirely legitimate. Those who participated in conventions
renounced unlawful action even as they itemized their grievances. Conventions were a constitutional alternative to "mobs and unlawful assemblies,"
and those who used them were seeking relief in "a peaceable, orderly, and
constitutional way." The product of conventions – petitions – was a standard
means of the people as the ruled to express themselves politically. If denied
this means of expression, the people, as the ruler, had every right to hold
conventions under their authority to communicate with their agents in the
legislature. For Regulators, county conventions were a perfectly reasonable
means of allowing the people to speak to the legislature under the existing
structure of government.[45]

Although conventions organized resistance against the British authorities during the Revolution, delegates to conventions during the 1780s
saw nothing revolutionary in using them to formulate their grievances
to the state legislature. Rather, they believed they were acting in accord
with well-established American constitutional principles.[46] Article XIX of
Massachusetts's bill of rights enshrined these principles. It guaranteed the
people the right "in an orderly and peaceable manner, to assemble to consult

upon the common good; give instructions to their representatives," and petition the legislature for "redress of the wrongs done them, and of the grievances they suffer." Friends like George Minot argued that Article XIX did not mean what it said. It intended nothing more than town meetings, a common feature of Massachusetts's local government. Construing that provision to allow the people to examine the same policies deliberated on by the legislature made the legal authority of the state "uncertain."[47]

At least one Friend of Government, however, Noah Webster, conceded that "the town meetings and conventions" had "proceeded very constitutionally" given the existence of Article XIX. He blamed Article XIX for encouraging the Regulation by allowing conventions that deigned to "consult for the *common good* of the State, and arraign the conduct of the Legislature before their petty tribunals." The real problem lay with suggestive constitutional language. The "maxim" found in some state constitutions that representatives were the "servants" of the people was not only "a false opinion" and a "most dangerous" error, but also "repugnant to every idea of a free government."[48]

Confronted by such arguments, Regulators resisted this denial of rights guaranteed under the 1780 Massachusetts constitution. Convention delegates intended to "ensure redress" by vindicating constitutional "principles," including the constitution's guarantee that the common good of the people was the highest goal of the state. It seemed impossible that after framing governments citizens would be precluded from gathering to discuss issues of concern from which they sought relief (or even give direction to government), especially since Article IV of the bill of rights spoke of the "sole and exclusive" right of the people to govern themselves. That language could only mean that "every individual has a right to think and act for *himself*." For Regulators, the constitution articulated an active and ongoing role for the people that included overseeing elected officials. The bill of rights provided for the rotation of offices to prevent incumbents from becoming "oppressors" and it declared the people's right to a "constant observance" of the process of law-making.[49]

Indeed, a county convention in Worcester disputed the idea that conventions were "dangerous" and defended them on the grounds that all "orders of men" under republics had an inherent right to "assume the character of politicians." That characterization came close to making an explicit claim for the people to act as the ruler. The people had such a right in "a free government" notwithstanding how "ridiculous the proposition may appear to the conceit and arrogance of men, who think themselves born to domineer over their fellow creatures at pleasure." Even the "lowest orders of men" in America could "examine," "censure," and "condemn" the "conduct of their rulers."[50]

In addition, Article XIX specified the people's right to assemble and petition. In fact, given the long legal tradition of the right of petition before
the Revolution, American states incorporated it without question. That traditional right included a felt obligation of the government to respond to
petitions. Yet Friends suggested that county conventions were unconstitutional because the constitution did not authorize them by name, and were
not "orderly and peaceable" (as the constitution called for) because the legislature did not call them. To Regulators, such an interpretation seemed
strained given that a majority of the people formed the sovereign basis of
government. In defending their meetings, Regulators pondered additional
questions. Could the people air their grievances only with the government's
permission? Why should critiquing matters of governance slight the dignity of government? After all, were not the legislators the servants of the
people and not the other way around? Such inquiries underscored the gulf
separating the two camps. For each, the issue of conventions hinged on
the relationship of the people to their government and whether the people
played a more active or passive role in government.[51]

Those who gathered in conventions believed they acted with restraint and
authority. They also believed their actions were consistent with America's
commitment to the people's sovereignty. The same basis that justified the
Revolution – the sovereign people – legitimated American governments. The
formation of Massachusetts's constitution was not an irrevocable transfer
of the people's sovereignty to government or a delegation of constitutional
authority that deprived "the people" of their right to control that government.
Rather, in perhaps the most significant departure from Friends, Regulators
and their supporters thought "the people" – after ratifying the constitution –
retained inherent constitutional authority. Their ongoing authority as the
sovereign, made it impossible for the people's conventions to violate the
constitution.[52]

In asserting inherent, collective constitutional rights, Regulators assumed
that the people exercised direct and practical control over their government
and constitution. For them, voting during periodic elections expressed the
people's will in an initial way that did not foreclose other, more direct expressions of the people's sovereignty. This understanding underlay the reason that
Regulators claimed the authority to abolish the Senate despite the constitutional provision prohibiting revision until 1795. To Friends, such proposals
demonstrated the unconstitutional instincts of Regulators. For Regulators,
on the other hand, a constitution could not bind a sovereign people seeking to
change the fundamental law. Giving final control to constitutional text, as the

Friends proposed, would elevate process and procedure over the substantive authority of the people's role as the sovereign.

Friends and Regulators shared a crucial premise but reached different conclusions about the constitutional rights of the people and their appropriate relationship with government. While Friends denied the authority of the people to employ their sovereignty, they acknowledged that government rested on the people. For example, in 1787, Fisher Ames, a prominent Boston lawyer and later member of Congress, wrote a series of articles repudiating the notion that "all government is . . . actually held by the majority of individuals." Ames considered majority rule "incendiary" and "subversive of all government." Still, Ames conceded "that all lawful government is derived from the people" and that they constituted the "source and origin of power." Nonetheless, he denied any "residue of power" that "the majority of individuals" could exercise or "delegate to conventions" once governments were created.[53]

Contract law framed Ames's analysis. In creating government, the "whole people . . . expressly contracted with each individual, and each individual with the whole people." Consequently, "the servants of the public" were "constitutionally omnipotent" in exercising powers over "every subject" except those denied them in the bill of rights. Having accepted the contract, the people could not change their minds. "If consent once given, can be withdrawn at pleasure, then there is a lawful contract, without any lawful obligation: An absurdity which refutes itself. If the contract is binding upon the people, what right have the majority of individuals to annul or change it?" Government remained an irrevocable contract, "sanctified from violation." After Massachusetts's 1780 constitution, the relevant sovereignty rested with government. The "rulers," Ames argued, now "have all power; and there is no majority of individuals, or convention" that could "dispute their commands." Moreover, Regulators failed to recognize "that the right of self-defence belongs to rulers as plainly as to private men."[54]

By denying the people an inherent constitutional authority and asserting a right of self-defense for the state, Friends reversed the relationship between the people and government that Regulators identified in American republics. For Friends, the people existed subordinate to government. As such, representatives were the exclusive means of expressing the people's views. They rejected the suggestion that "the people" possessed a superseding authority. As "AN OTHER CITIZEN" said in September 1786, although "all power originates *from* the people, it does not remain *with* them" because the constitution "delegated" that power to the legislature.[55]

Regulators, however, could not fathom how their opponents attributed sovereignty to "The Government." Governmental sovereignty seemed untenable when the Massachusetts bill of rights "Solemnly Declared" that all power was "in the people" and that government officials were always accountable as "their Substitutes and agents." If delegates to conventions resented accusations of unconstitutional behavior, they were increasingly frustrated when their petitions were largely ignored. During October and November 1786, the legislature rejected most of the Regulator demands for paper money and legal tender laws, court reform, and potential constitutional revision. The legislature's unresponsiveness prompted Regulators to take more dramatic action.[56]

COURT CLOSINGS

When Regulators stopped courts – primarily the courts of Common Pleas – they expected that their sheer numbers would prompt the government to reconsider its policies. Massive crowds in and around courthouses made it impossible for proceedings to carry on normally. When courts opened despite "very large numbers of People" urging them not to, they frequently conducted no business and quickly adjourned. Regulators often conducted a military parade, apparently willing to risk battle. In fact, they counted on a sufficient turnout of citizens to claim they were the body of the people in action.[57]

The court-closing phase of the Regulation formally began on August 29, 1786, when some 1,500 farmers prevented the Court of Common Pleas at Northampton from opening without violence or loss of life. Although the huge crowd intimidated the court, the actions of Regulators belied their description, by the merchant Jonathan Judd, as a "mob." Instead, as became typical, Regulators at Northampton demanded a temporary suspension of the court until "the resolves of the convention of this county can have an opportunity of having their grievances redressed" by the legislature.[58]

Friends of Government uniformly reacted to court closings. After the Northampton event, Fisher Ames identified "the most radically wicked" rebellion "that ever disturbed the peace of mankind." The legislature's public address in November 1786 explained the stoppage of courts as the overthrow of "all order and government." The court closings were repeatedly equated with anarchy. To Friends and many later observers, the deliberate obstruction of the judicial process challenged the authority of the state. Despite the Regulators' frustration, surely they lacked legal – much less constitutional – justification for their actions.[59]

The traditional rationale for court closings as a remonstrance dating back to the colonial period underwent an important shift after the Revolution. Earlier court closings took place within the English constitutional tradition. Their justification rested on a sense of public morality and a breach of the implied contract between the people and their governors.[60] With the Revolution, however, written constitutions expressed the sovereignty of the people rather than the terms of government that supposedly bound them. Indeed, Massachusetts Regulators justified court closings by reference to Article VII of their state constitution. That provision proclaimed that "the people alone have an incontestable, unalienable, and indefeasible right to institute government; and to reform, alter, or totally change the same, when their protection, safety, prosperity and happiness require it."[61]

For Regulators, court closings did not overthrow the Massachusetts government but legitimately interposed the authority of the people – as the ruler – to temporarily suspend policies that were inherently wrong if not unconstitutional. They sought a moratorium during which the legislature could finally grant needed relief. Such dramatic intervention would alert the legislature – which was not the sovereign – to the discontents of the people that could be redressed before the people – as the sovereign – took matters into their own hands.

Friends of Government, on the other hand, disagreed that court closings were a constitutional effort to regain redress from the state government, a graduated response that culminated years of fruitless petitions to the legislature. Friends routinely described Regulators as irrational, supposedly intent on abolishing private property and redistributing wealth. To Fisher Ames they were a "mob" of "mad men and knaves," guilty of "a high degree of moral depravity" and full of "stupid fury." Abigail Adams considered the Regulation "popular tyranny," while for the merchant Stephen Higginson it was an "infection."[62] Such descriptions were repeated time and again because most newspapers supported the Friends. Disparaging remarks about Regulators were "freely handed about by the Government party." One contemporary observer thought that Regulators were deliberately misrepresented as "Profligate Licentious Banditi, Who wish to Destroy all Law and Government" in order "to Rouze" the "Powers of this State against them" and "Render them odious and Contemptible." Indeed, the campaign to discredit the character of Regulators was necessary because they were not, as depicted, "the Ragmuffins of the Earth."[63]

The highly charged atmosphere left little room to acknowledge shared ground. The lawyer and future governor of the state, James Sullivan, observed intense pressures for conformity in Boston due to the desire to punish the "Rebels." The "powers of Government" were "so united" that it was "dangerous even to be silent; a man is accused of rebellion if he does not loudly approve every measure as prudent, necessary, wise, and *Constitutional*. God knows where all will lead." John Quincy Adams reported to his mother, Abigail, from Harvard that "riots, insurrections, and anarchy" were the only topics of conversation in Cambridge. Ultimately, such attitudes encouraged the repression of Regulators and their allies.[64]

In closing courts instead of taking up arms against the state government, Regulators disproved the charge of rebellion. Their behavior frankly puzzled those sent to suppress them. General William Shepard, a leader of the government forces, was "surprised" on December 20, 1786, that Regulators failed to seize the well-stocked military arsenal at Springfield. Three months earlier, Regulators had closed the Springfield courts but did not attack the arsenal, even though Friends assumed they would. Another Friend with extensive military experience considered the arsenal "of infinite" importance and could not help wondering "in case the insurgents mean to make an experiment of their strength against government, will they hesitate to avail themselves of its contents?" On December 26, Regulators closed the county court at Springfield a second time, but left the arsenal untouched.[65]

The lack of interest in militarily engaging government forces was obvious from the decisions of some Regulators, including men like Daniel Shays and Luke Day who were officers during the Revolutionary War. Their more limited objectives of pressuring a shift in policy rather than overthrowing government was consistent with the many accounts of the orderly behavior of the Regulators. Indeed, after the first violent confrontation with government troops, many farmers defected from the Regulator movement because, according to one observer, "they had flatterd themselves it would never have come to Blood." Even Secretary at War Henry Knox conceded that "prudence" by Shays at the first Springfield closing "prevented an attack on the Government troops."[66]

The Regulators' nonmilitary objective sought relief from the government, composed of, after all, the servants of the people. From their perspective, they had patiently sent petitions for many years and most recently gathered in county conventions to discuss their situation and concerns. Apart from having their grievances ignored, their peaceful meetings in conventions were branded unconstitutional. Taking more direct action to prompt the government to respond to their problems seemed a reasonable next step. Indeed, believing the stoppages a temporary, limited action of defiance to alleviate hardships faced by a majority of the populace encouraged Regulators to believe they might not be prosecuted for closing courts. Even a Friend of Government conceded that Regulators regarded court closings "only as a mode of awakening the attention of the legislature" for "the redress of grievances."[67]

The limited objectives of the court stoppages were clear from the start. "The voice of the people of this County," announced Regulators in Middlesex, closed the court "until such time as the people shall have a redress of a number of grievances they labour under at present." The Regulators at _____ _____ _____ _____ forth these grievances in a "petition or remonstrance" to the next legislature. Likewise, the Springfield court closing on September 26, 1786, occurred under the direction of "the People collected now . . . for the purpose of moderating Government." Stopping the courts by a gathering of "the Body of People," Worcester Regulators noted, was for the "common good."[68]

The court closings did not constitute the long feared "western" uprising to overturn private rights and public order. In fact, all of the half dozen court closings in September 1786 – the busiest month for them – took place without physical violence. In reporting to Governor Bowdoin on the state of affairs in Berkshire County in early October, the lawyer Theodore Sedgwick noted that most people did not seem "disposed to Subvert the present government." A prominent Friend noted that after Regulators seized several houses in Worcester for temporary quarters, the homeowners retook possession and "gained their point" simply by insisting that Regulators leave. Even John Jay, then serving as secretary for foreign affairs for the Continental Congress, conceded that Regulators "abstained from Plunder" and apparently avoided "any outrages" except those "their Purpose made necessary."[69]

Although largely peaceful affairs, the court closings were an escalation. Regulators threatened more stoppages until the legislature responded to their demands. Adam Wheeler, in a public letter before the closing of Worcester County's Court of Common Pleas, captured the goal of many Regulators: "I had no intention to destroy the publick government, but to have those Courts suspended, to prevent such abuses as have of late taken place by the sitting of those Courts." The court closing provided more time to redress grievances "in a constitutional way."[70]

The court closing at Great Barrington, in Berkshire County, demonstrated a focus on regulation rather than overthrow of the legal system. On September 11, 1786, the day before the scheduled meeting of the Court of Common Pleas, Regulators physically occupied the courthouse. The following day, ostensibly to ensure the court's operation, a troop of militia entered the town, but "much the greatest part" joined the Regulators, reported the local Sheriff. Such sympathies placed the militia commander in an awkward position. A stalemate was averted by the court's decision to abide by the will of those present, a practice with precedent. All those favoring the closing of the court stepped to one side of the road while those opposed stepped to the other. Out of nearly 1,000 people present, roughly 800 opposed the court's sitting.[71]

Chief Justice William Whiting then perfunctorily opened and adjourned court. Regulators followed the judges to Whiting's home and demanded a signed agreement not to hold court "until the Constitution of Government shall be revised or a new one made." Although one judge refused, Whiting and two other judges signed. In addition, the Regulators released debtors in the Great Barrington jail. Henry Van Schaack, an eyewitness and prominent merchant, marveled that the "vast concourse of people" did not commit "one act of private outrage" despite being armed and on the move.[72]

The court's conciliation to the Regulators was not entirely unexpected. In fact, Whiting wrote a short tract signed "Gracchus" just before the Great Barrington court closing in which he acknowledged Regulator grievances. He hoped to avoid the court closing by making it "known to the people that those were the Sentiments of Some of the Court." Nonetheless, Whiting's views, as a later biographer understated, "brought upon him the dislike and displeasure of the friends of law and order." Indeed, after the court closing, Massachusetts congressional delegate Rufus King anticipated "the utmost indignation towards that unworthy magistrate the first Justice of Berkshire."[73]

Whiting began "Gracchus" by asserting that the purpose of government "is or ought to be the equal Protection, Prosperity, and Happiness of all its Subjects" – hardly unusual since every state constitution drafted after the Revolution contained such a statement. As a constitutional principle it could mean more to some than to others. For Whiting, the fundamental purpose of government was tied to the authority of the people. The people remained a living force in governments even after constitutions were established. If the people's welfare served as a paramount objective, then whenever some people could "enrich themselves by the same means that impoverishes and depresses" others, government "is either defective" or "the Laws are unjustly and unequally administered." According to a scholar of the revolutionary period, America needed a "rough equality of condition" since most Americans "took for granted" that republicanism was threatened if a "minority controlled most of the wealth and the bulk of the population remained dependent servants or landless laborers." At the time of the court closings, Whiting and many Regulators believed that "a set of overgrown Plunderers" were "tyrannizing over the rest of the people." If legislators could only see "with their own Eyes the Extreme poverty and Distress" of "Great numbers of the poorer Sort of people," they would immediately respond to Regulator complaints.[74]

For Friends, the farmers' options were limited to electing different representatives since even petitioning and formulating grievances in county conventions was unconstitutional. For Whiting and Regulators, however, not only were conventions legitimate, but other constitutionally justifiable alternatives existed that rested on the authority of the people in their capacity as the ruler. According to Whiting, if "baneful injustice and inequality" arose in a republican government, "it is the indispensable duty of the people to exert themselves, and persevere in their exertions until they get them effectually removed." Article V of Massachusetts's bill of rights "Expressly" made "Substitutes and Agents ... accountable" to the people, and "as no particular mode is pointed out for Calling them to an account," the majority had "a Right to adopt Such measures for that purpose" as they thought "best." Even a staunch Friend concluded that "the majority of the people" agreed with the Regulators "in principle."[75]

Unlike the Berkshire Constitutionalist minority, whose court closings Whiting opposed in 1778, Regulators were likely a majority of the eligible voters in 1786. If so, Regulators were entitled to invoke the sovereign authority of the people celebrated in America's constitutions, including Massachusetts's 1780 constitution. According to Whiting, the legislature should not "Reverse the opperation of this Right," expressed by temporarily suspending the courts, "by Endeavoring to Treat you as Rebbels and Traytors for attempting to Exercise it." Whiting spoke as one who had served as Great Barrington's delegate to the constitutional convention that produced the state's constitution.[76]

Friends described Whiting's position as reflecting grossly "mistaken" constitutional views about "favourite rights" associated with the Revolution. Even if parallels existed between the revolutionary struggle with Britain and the present dispute with the Massachusetts authorities, Friends accused the Regulators of failing to see the "difference in the circumstances of the people now and twelve years ago." The "maxim that all power is derived from the people" and that they influenced "all government" could be "perverted." Indeed, that principle presently produced "effects materially different" from those intended. Another Friend noted that "the people" had "far too much political knowledge."[77]

To the chagrin of Friends, part of the perversion of constitutional understandings could be traced to the state's 1780 constitution – largely drafted by John Adams. Adams served on the committee charged with drafting that

constitution, but he constituted a subcommittee of one and became the constitution's "principal Engineer." Regulators relied on many of the principles
Adams included in Massachusetts's bill of rights. Abigail Adams heard from
relatives complaining that the "excess of Liberty" that John's constitution
"gave the People has ruined them." Another Friend blamed the Regulation
on the state's excessively "liberal" constitution. The "revolution principles
and ill-judged declarations of right and power in the people with which the
constitution of this commonwealth abounds" inspired the people "with a
high sense of their importance as the source of all powers."[78]

A measure of the widespread acceptance of the expressions celebrating
the sovereignty of the people and their relationship to government can be
found in the sources that shaped the constitutional language Adams used
in Massachusetts's bill of rights in 1780. Adams's draft reveals considerable influence and borrowing from Virginia's and especially Pennsylvania's
1776 bills of rights. The contempt Adams had for the structure of government established by Pennsylvania's first constitution – which he considered hopelessly imbalanced – did not extend to its bill of rights. Indeed,
in drafting Massachusetts's "alter or abolish" provision, Adams closely followed Pennsylvania's language in emphasizing the purpose of government
as being for the common good "and not for the profit, honor, or private
interest of any one man, family, or class."[79] Moreover, while all three bills
of rights contained a provision articulating the need for "frequent recurrence" to fundamental principles, Massachusetts's constitution bore the
most resemblance to the model provided by Pennsylvania.[80] Finally, while
a provision asserting the people's right of assembly and instruction was not
found in Virginia's 1776 bill of rights, the language Adams incorporated bore
many similarities to the comparable provision in Pennsylvania's 1776 bill of
rights.[81]

Beyond expressing dismay at the invocation of such constitutional principles, Friends also denied that Regulators were a political majority. They
described them instead as a "faction" or "mob" or "rabble." For their part,
Regulators called themselves "the people" or "the body of the people." The
struggle over competing descriptions came from the shared acceptance that
a majority of the people formed the sovereign basis of constitutional governments. Even as he pursued Regulators, former Continental Army General
Benjamin Lincoln wondered how "upon republican principles" Friends
could "justly exclude them from the right of Governing" if they formed a
majority. Whiting was blunter. In America, government officials and representatives were the people's "Cretures and Servants" and obliged to respect
the will of the majority.[82]

When Whiting declared it a "Virtue" to "disturb the government" if the "liberties" of the people were endangered, Friends considered that expression an incitement to disorder rather than a statement of constitutional principle. For Whiting and Regulators, however, vigilance of government was what they had "always been taught" as orthodox "political Sentiments." Many American constitutions echoed that same idea. All "free Governments" entailed some "Degree" of "Disputes and Struggles." As the town of New Salem noted in a petition to Governor Bowdoin arguing for a resolution of the Regulation other than "with the point of the Bayonet," they worried as much about "Tyranny and oppression" as they did about "Anarchy and Confusion." Inevitably, a trade-off existed between greater governmental efficiency through the use of coercion and a republic governing with the people's consent. Before the Revolution, John Adams reminded fellow Americans of the maxim that "All Men would be Tyrants if they could" and urged a close scrutiny of government officials. Less than a decade after Independence, Whiting found himself in trouble for saying the same thing.[83]

GOVERNMENT RESPONSE AND REGULATOR REACTIONS

After the first court closing, Governor Bowdoin denounced the action as having "the most pernicious consequences" and tending "to subvert all law and government," "dissolve" the constitution, and "introduce universal riot, anarchy and confusion" inevitably leading to "absolute despotism." He called upon citizens of the state to "unite in preventing and suppressing all such treasonable proceedings." While some legislators shared his belief in the need for "vigorous measures," not everyone in government proved as eager to crush Regulators as some of Governor Bowdoin's more militant advisors. One group, later considered by George Minot, then the clerk of the House of the legislature, to be a "majority," initially resisted taking "coercive measures." According to Minot, they believed that "violent plans" would merely increase "uneasiness" and cause "the great body" of neutral citizens to be "disgusted with the government."[84]

Eventually, however, after some wavering, the legislature passed an act subjecting any militia officer or soldier with court-martial for joining a "mutiny or sedition," followed by a Riot Act that punished twelve or more armed men who gathered in public with property forfeiture, public whipping, and imprisonment. The legislature also suspended the writ of habeas corpus and gave the governor power to issue general search warrants. The suspension allowed the governor to hold anyone without bail when he deemed this necessary, notwithstanding "any law, usage, or custom to the contrary."

Moreover, the governor could arrest and imprison anyone suspected of being "unfriendly to government." This last measure, when coupled with another bill preventing "the making and spreading of false reports to the prejudice of government," effectively banned criticism of the state. Finally, the legislature offered pardons to Regulators who took an oath of allegiance to the state government.[85]

These legislative measures convinced Regulators that the people's basic liberties were under attack by their own government. They were reminded of the American Revolution. Regulators saw "an infringement" of rights "which many of us, in the late War with Britain, purchased at the Expense of Blood and Treasure." They expressed their "horror" at the suspension of habeas corpus, considering that step "dangerous if not absolutely destructive to a Republican Government." Another Regulator thought that suspension sought to punish "those persons who have stepped forth to assert and maintain the rights of the people." Heightened rhetoric by Regulators reflected their growing dismay at the government's actions, which seemed disproportionate to their own limited goals and moderation. The legislative response, however, was not the only reason Regulators were distraught.[86]

One event, taking place in late November 1786 after the suspension of habeas corpus, particularly angered Regulators and generated support for their movement. Under warrants issued by Governor Bowdoin, several hundred government troops took part in a raid under the command of Colonel Benjamin Hichborn, a Boston lawyer. Nine years earlier, Hichborn had celebrated the "power" of "the people at large, at any time, for any cause, or for no cause, but their own sovereign pleasure, to alter or annhilate both the mode and essence of any former government, and adopt a new one in its stead." Now in 1786 Hichborn's forces seized three Regulators from their homes in Groton, Middlesex County, slashing one across the knee with a sword and hauling them to jail forty miles away in Boston. The Groton arrests sowed the "seeds of war" and some Regulators were determined "to carry" their "point." Over thirty towns drafted petitions protesting the state's actions. Some petitions came from towns not particularly sympathetic to Regulators but whose residents objected to the raid. Even Friends acknowledged that Hichborn's action allowed Regulators to claim that "the liberties of the Commonwealth" were under attack. The raid helped convert Regulators into "sufferers seeking the redress of grievances, at the risque of every thing."[87]

The Groton raid marked the first forceful step taken against Regulators and was soon followed by a broader – and in their eyes, even more ominous – military campaign against them. The ineffectiveness of using militia troops to stop court closings – including their frequent defection to Regulator ranks – stymied Governor Bowdoin's attempt to use military force. Instead, Bowdoin formed a special army of some 4,400 troops under the command of General Benjamin Lincoln. Lacking legislative funding, Bowdoin and Lincoln turned to private sources. Boston merchants were asked to lend the government £6,000, the estimated cost of supplying the army for one month. A subscription list was circulated in early January 1787. Despite the governor's personal pledge of £250, contributions from the business community were initially sluggish. They picked up after General Lincoln went to "a club of the first characters in Boston" and appealed to their self-interest. Lincoln explained to George Washington that he "suggested" to the merchants "the importance of their becoming loaners of part of their property if they wished to secure the remainder." Within several days the full amount was collected.[88]

According to George Minot, the troops were formed because "a number of gentlemen, from a conviction of the necessity of maintaining good order, and from a consideration of the exigencies of government, voluntarily offered a loan to support the publick cause." Regulators saw the matter differently. From their perspective, they now faced a private army paid for by merchant and creditor Friends of Government created to crush debtors and farmers who had constitutionally expressed their legitimate grievances. They were rightly suspicious of the motives of Friends who financed the army: over half the contributors to Lincoln's private army were speculators in government securities who stood to gain if the policy of redemption was sustained. In addition, the mercenary aspect of the affair resurrected the revolutionary generation's fears of professional standing armies.[89]

Regulators sought to forestall the army by petitioning Governor Bowdoin. They promised not to disturb the December sitting of Worcester's county courts if the troops turned back and left "the people who have taken an active part in the late rising . . . unmolested in their persons and property." They fully expected to see the legislature "redress all" their "real grievances" at its next session. Bowdoin did not stop the army, much to the approval of more militant Friends. The militants hoped a forceful suppression of the uprising would further reduce political support for the legislative agenda

Once Lincoln advanced on Worcester, Regulators increasingly spoke of the conduct of "Public Affairs" having "a Direct tendency to involve the Common People in a State of Slavery and Poverty." They warned they would "defend themselves at the risk of their lives." One Regulator circular accused Lincoln of attempting "by the point of the sword" to "crush the power of the people." An assembly "in arms" was needed to defend "the rights" and "liberties of the people since our opponents by their hasty movements refuse to give us opportunity" to see the effects of petitions submitted. The crowning blow came on February 16, 1787, when the legislature passed a Disqualification Act. That measure prohibited Regulators from voting, serving on juries, holding political offices, teaching school, or keeping an inn for three years. Reverend Bezaleel Howard considered the act "severe and Tyranical."[91]

Even before the Disqualification Act, however, some Friends thought the state had gone too far. In early September 1786, the Salem lawyer William Pynchon questioned the policy "of cannons, arms, and apparatus of the kind" being deployed "in the country and among people" already suffering under heavy taxes and other burdens. From New York in October 1786, John Jay identified a "Spirit of Licentiousness" in Massachusetts, but worried that "the Charms of Liberty will daily fade" for those keenly intent on reestablishing order. By mid-December 1786, Henry Knox was troubled by the "unjust means" used to control Regulators. Knox did more than anyone to spread the alarm (and exaggerate the dangers) of the Regulation. Yet even he worried about Friends "who hold that if a measure be right in itself, one Should not be very delicate" about how "it is to be accomplished." Allowing the ends to justify the means was "infamous."[92]

The Disqualification Act particularly troubled some leading Friends. Rufus King pointed to "great & illustrious examples" against the "policy" of disfranchisement. James Warren, Massachusetts's Speaker of the House in 1787, thought government forces worried so much that Regulators would "destroy the Constitution" that Friends "violated it themselves." Withholding the franchise created a troubling inconsistency. General Lincoln, for one, predicted that a widespread voting disqualification encouraged further disorders and served to justify extralegal actions. Regulators were admonished to "seek redress in a Constitutional way, & wait the decision of the Legislature." Now, however, Regulators could accuse the government of having "cut them off from all hope of redress" and denied them "representation in that Legislative body, by whose Laws they must be governed."[93]

The measures used to suppress Regulators escalated the war of words and produced its own momentum. By the end of January 1787, the presence of an effective military force poised to punish the "rebels" set the stage for deadly confrontations avoided until then. On January 20, 1787, General Lincoln left Boston "in high spirits" and, as a Friend of Government put it, with "the whole of the monied men to support him." Even as Lincoln headed to Worcester to ensure the opening of that county's court session, over two thousand farmers began encircling General Shepard and his one thousand militia force guarding the military arsenal at Springfield. On the morning of

January 25, 1787, Daniel Shays led one of three different groups surrounding Shepard's position.[94]

Writing to General Lincoln, Shays offered to disband if Lincoln did the same. Standing down, according to the Regulators, would give the next legislature "a fair opportunity" to address the "Insupportable Burdens" from which "the people now in arms, in Defence of their Lives and Liberties" sought "Constitutional Relief." Lincoln replied that he had no authority "to make a Compromise with them & that if they really wished as they professed to prevent the shedding of Blood, the line of duty was clear before them – to lay down their arms & Submit to the Clemency of their Country." When Shays advanced his forces toward Shepard's troops and Regulators continued to approach despite warning shots, Shepard ordered cannon fire that killed four Regulators and wounded twenty more. The Regulators retreated with "precipitation & confusion" and without firing a shot.[95]

Lincoln's army arrived at Springfield two days later and spent the next week pursuing and essentially routing Regulator forces in bitterly cold weather. On January 30, Shays offered a written response to Lincoln's request that the Regulators lay down their arms. Shays conceded that "recourse to arms" by Regulators lacked the justification of the people's earlier acts of convening conventions and closing courts, but he noted "various circumstances" that prompted their actions. Potentially shooting at government forces – even if they constituted a private army – qualitatively differed from the earlier steps of asserting and underscoring grievances by an armed body of "the people." Even at this late date Shays urged a truce until the "united prayers" of Regulators were presented to the legislature "and we receive an answer," since someone had been sent "for that purpose."[96]

At the same time, Lincoln continued to receive petitions from towns sympathetic to Regulators seeking truces to allow the legislature to consider their grievances. By February 1787, Lincoln reported to Governor Bowdoin that Regulator opposition was "giving way" everywhere and they were "hourly surrendering themselves, giving up their arms & taking the Oaths." The widespread dispersal of Regulators ended whatever military threat they posed to the Massachusetts government. Although violent "mopping up" actions continued, most of the leaders of the Regulation fled the area and the state.[97]

After this daunting display of military force and lack of desire to fight on the part of Regulators, state officials initiated criminal prosecutions for sedition and treason. Mainly, however, the government used the occasion to publicly repudiate the Regulator position. Theodore Sedgwick thought the prosecutions had "a good effect" and he had no problem if those on trial faced capital punishment. Although more than a dozen Regulators were sentenced to death for treason and others received lesser punishments of fines and imprisonment, all of them were subsequently pardoned – except for two laborers who were executed. The perceived leaders of the Regulators, however, including Shays and others who fled the state, ultimately received pardons.[98]

Most attention (and deepest virulence) was reserved for leaders of the community, like Whiting, who sympathized with the Regulators. Dr. Whiting lost his judgeship, was fined £100, sentenced to seven months' imprisonment, and placed on bond for good behavior for five years. One of his judges described Whiting as "greatly overcome" by the sentence of the court and "confined to his Bed with Sickness" as a result. Within a week, over fifty Berkshire residents – including Friends of Government, but with Sedgwick conspicuously absent – petitioned the Governor to remit Whiting's prison sentence or a least allow him to serve it under house arrest. Whiting also requested a pardon, assuring the governor that his present "Troubles & Disgrace" were due to "Inveterate & Powerful Enemies" and that imprisonment in his present state of health would kill him. Although denied a general pardon, Whiting's prison sentence was remitted after less than two months' confinement.[99]

Sedgwick lectured Whiting on the depth of his transgression even before the doctor went to trial. After the Great Barrington court closing, Sedgwick accused Whiting of "urging a watchful attention" to government as well as encouraging the people "to pursue measures, which . . . will terminate in irretrievable ruin." Although "seditious libel," such opinions were "infinitely less reprehensible" than how and by whom they were communicated. The common people might not know better, but there was no excuse for Whiting to encourage incorrect constitutional ideas and views of government among those with "limited understandings." John Adams's cousin, Samuel Adams, shared Sedgwick's sentiments but opposed the widespread clemency ultimately granted Regulators and their supporters. According to Samuel, in monarchies "the crime of treason and rebellion" could be "pardoned or lightly punished; but the man who dares to rebel against the laws of a republic ought to suffer death."[100]

Despite Sedgwick's and Adams's views, many in Berkshire County continued to support Whiting. When the time came to elect delegates to consider the proposed federal Constitution, the townspeople of Great Barrington voted to send Whiting to the state's convention with instructions to oppose the constitution. At a town meeting, Whiting narrowly defeated Elijah Dwight, the candidate of those favoring ratification. Dwight was appointed to the

Court of Common Pleas for Berkshire County following Whiting's removal. After Whiting accepted his nomination as delegate and received the town's instructions, those in favor of the constitution maneuvered another town meeting – "a stormy one" – at which by a narrow vote the instructions were retracted and Dwight substituted in Whiting's place. For Theodore Sedgwick the change was a victory for "the side of truth and justice" while Whiting's supporters considered it the result of an illegal and "Pretended Election." Notwithstanding a half dozen remonstrances filed with the ratifying convention that met in Boston and signed by well over one hundred inhabitants of Great Barrington, Dwight was seated and proceeded to vote – as did Sedgwick, who represented Stockbridge – in favor of the constitution. Despite that setback, Whiting was elected the following year to represent Berkshire County in the state Senate.[101]

AFTERMATH OF THE REGULATION

The political aftermath of the Regulator movement did little to relieve those worried about the people playing a more active, direct, and widespread role in government. Increasingly, Friends realized the need to deal with "the constitutional importance of the people." The spring elections in 1787 saw Governor Bowdoin swept from office and replaced by the former governor and highly popular John Hancock, who won 75 percent of the votes cast. For many, the election tested opinions about the Regulation. Friends anticipated "probable evils" from "an alteration" of the gubernatorial "chair of office." Although the Senate remained a bastion of support for the position of the Friends, the composition of the House changed dramatically. Less than half of the House members retained their seats and numerous Regulators won elections at the town level despite the Disqualification Act, which the new legislature repealed in June. Theodore Sedgwick described that body in dichotomous terms: "On one side are men of talents & of integrity, firmly determined to support public justice and private faith, and on the other there exists as firm a determination to institute tender laws, paper money, to disband the troops and in short to establish inequity by law." In his view, it was too soon to tell which side would prevail.[102]

Friends also saw the elections as further evidence of the danger to good government posed by the release of popular tendencies by the Revolution. The dramatic shift in the legislature concerned them as much as if not more than the events of the Regulation. By May 1787, Henry Knox spoke of "mad democracy" banishing "reason Law, and patriotism" not only in Massachusetts but from "almost every Legislature." The election of former

Regulators and Hancock, with his "peculiar talent of pleasing the multitude," proved, according to the son of John Adams, the desperate state of affairs. John Quincy Adams accused Hancock of favoring "tender acts, paper currencies, and all those measures which would give the sanction of the law to private fraud and villany." After the election, Sedgwick offered a bleak assessment in a letter to Rufus King: "Every man of observation is convinced that the end of government security cannot be attained by the exercise of principles founded on democratic equality." He cautioned King not to be fooled by the "appearance of a temporary cessation of hostilities" since in fact, a "war is now actually levied on the virtue, property and distinctions in the community." It was a war, he added to another correspondent, waged "by the dregs and scum of mankind."[103]

The attack on Hancock and the dismay Friends felt about political affairs in Massachusetts stemmed from a distrust of the capacity of ordinary people. Sound political leadership required going beyond "the bulk of the people," according to Massachusetts lawyer Theophilus Parsons. As early as 1778, Parsons wanted to restrain the sometimes "dazzling" notion of the "idea of liberty." Parsons, later serving as chief justice of the state's Supreme Judicial Court, sought leadership qualities "most probably" found in "men of education and fortune." General Lincoln's son wrote a series of articles in 1784 identifying the key to republican governments as giving political authority to men of property and selecting leaders of "great wisdom and great virtue." For Massachusetts Friends after the Regulation, the state Senate continued to screen out many of the common and middling sort who lacked the higher property qualifications to serve in that body. As such, there were hopeful signs that the Senate could stave off tender laws and paper money. The House, however, proved another matter and the prospect of Regulators achieving through the political process what they failed to accomplish through court closings deeply dismayed Friends.[104]

For Regulators, and particularly the smaller farmers in their ranks, the postrevolutionary period seemed to suggest that they might play a greater role in political affairs than they experienced before the Revolution. If Lincoln's son wanted a government of "the Few" over "the Many," the unlettered farmer from Billerica, Massachusetts, William Manning, sought the opposite in his far more democratic vision elaborated in *The Key of Liberty*. Manning was incensed that workers remained intimidated by those "who could live without labor," namely, "the merchant, physician, lawyer, and divine, the philosopher and schoolmaster, the judicial and executive officers." A free government in America, according to Manning, required a reversal of the traditional deference to "a few leading men" and for common people not to "take for truth whatever they [the elites] say without examining or trying to see for themselves."[105]

In founding governments on the consent of the people and by herald-ing the principle that the people were the sovereign, Americans enunciated ideas that proved difficult to contain after Independence. Patterns of defer-ence were altered not only by the new ways of thinking about government unleashed with the Revolution, but by how those ideas were put into con-stitutional practice. Berkshire Constitutionalists, as well as Massachusetts townships generally, developed a commitment to widespread participation by the people in constitution-making. This experience produced a constitu-tion in 1780 that for Regulators and their supporters guaranteed the inherent rights of the people and their ongoing, active role in government. Indeed, even Friends recognized how text and principles found in the state's consti-tution could support positions they opposed.

Nonetheless, Friends expected a more limited role for "the people" in government, no matter how the people were defined for political purposes. They assumed that those given political and social deference in the past would continue to lead after the formation of governments based on the authority of the people. However, in the postwar American economy, members of the "natural aristocracy" found themselves competing with their "lessers" in new and strange ways. The emphasis on the role of "natural" leaders thus proved a hedge against the undesired competition for place that the Revolution introduced.[106]

The lessons of the Revolution supported the arguments of both Friends and Regulators. Thus, the conflict in Massachusetts underscored the confu-sion and difficulties that attended the constitutional debate over the basis of governmental legitimacy. Friends considered the objectives sought and the techniques employed by Regulators as beyond the pale of legitimate govern-ment, yet still thought hiring a private army an acceptable complement to the power of the state. For their part, Regulators refused to equate a govern-ment based on the people as the sovereign with one that completely subordi-nated them to their governmental agents in the manner asserted by Friends. Friends claimed that Regulators misunderstood the principles of American government and Regulators accused their opponents of betraying those same principles. Americans continued to struggle over the meaning of the peo-ple's sovereignty without acknowledging the possibility that each side could claim constitutional legitimacy. The events in Massachusetts were galvaniz-ing because of the arguments advanced by Regulators and their supporters. Regulators challenged the essence of what their opponents considered good government by invoking an inherent constitutional authority for the people to act and claiming a direct role for them in government. Friends depicted Regulators as the opposite of government – anarchy – and thus devoid of constitutional justification.

For Friends of Government across the country, and not just in Massachusetts, the Regulation showed how important it was to rein in misguided constitutional understandings and gain control of the meaning of American constitutionalism. Since the time of the Revolution, ideas drawing upon the authority of the people were used in increasingly dangerous ways. This authority could not be denied, but many American leaders believed the time had come to temper and constrain the more wide-ranging invocations of the people's sovereignty.

Such concerns significantly contributed to the movement culminating in the federal constitutional convention. Indeed, the combination of dissatisfaction with the Articles of Confederation and concern about the state of political affairs in America helped fuel the convention movement. Many proponents of a change in the national constitutional structure saw America on the brink of disaster by 1787. This perception largely drew from their dire view of events and measures since the Revolution that invoked the authority of the people. The Massachusetts Regulation dramatically illustrated the problem.

Ironically, in the course of attempting to constrain the ways the people might express their sovereignty, the federal Framers justified jettisoning the Articles of Confederation and bypassing its amendment provisions by invoking the people's authority. Relying on that authority, however, was not contradictory. Rather, it demonstrated how the people's sovereignty was open to many uses, allowing Americans with a wide range of political views to assert the constitutional authority of "the people."

PART TWO

The Sovereign Behind the Federal Constitution

After Independence, the authority of the people conferred legitimacy on the governments established by America's written constitutions, ensuring that the sovereign source of the federal Constitution became (and remained) an issue of prime importance. In fact, against the prevailing assumption that sovereignty was indivisible, the Federalist defense of the proposed constitutional structure rested on the authority of the collective sovereign.

As the sovereign, the people could divide and allocate powers as they wished between state and national governments while retaining their ultimate authority as the sovereign. Invoking the sovereignty of the people was crucial to the formation of a national government that replaced the Articles of Confederation. But unlike the state constitutions, it proved a more elusive task to identify the sovereign that authorized the federal Constitution.

Framers of the federal Constitution were more successful in harnessing the authority of the collective sovereign to establish a new national government than they were in restraining wide-ranging constitutional ideas about the role of the people after the formation of governments. A decade's experience with written constitutions produced different possibilities about the relationship between the people and their governments. Supporters of the federal Constitution hoped its formation would establish a constitutional order after which little would be heard of the sovereign people except in an attenuated, symbolic, and theoretical sense. Early experience with that constitution, however, proved otherwise. Just as the ideas, implications, and metaphors that surfaced with revolutionary-era constitution-making proved impossible to eject from questions of constitutionalism arising in the states, they proved equally persistent in controversies arising under the government established by the federal Constitution.

The broad arena within which the underlying sovereign of the federal Constitution might act introduced ambiguities and concerns that were not present in the state context. If Americans remained committed to the people's sovereignty, it was easier to see how the people might exercise that sovereignty at the local and state levels than in the national context. Moreover, the concept of the Union and its preservation introduced a constitutional value that increasingly placed it in tension if not in conflict with assertions based on the rights of the underlying sovereign of the federal Constitution. Despite such difficulties, Americans continued to wrestle with what it meant that their national as well as state governments rested on the sovereignty of the people.

5 The Federal Constitution and the Effort to Constrain the People

From London, John and Abigail Adams corresponded with Thomas Jefferson in Paris about events back home in Massachusetts in the summer of 1786. Inhabitants in the western part of the state were closing courts and protesting government policies they considered illegitimate. A letter from John Adams in late November assured Jefferson that the "Turbulence in New England" was no cause for worry. He predicted that it would give "additional Strength to Government" and that "all will be well." Jefferson replied that he doubted "things will go far wrong where common sense has fair play."

As the three received further reports from America, Jefferson remained complacent about the New England news, writing Abigail that he liked to see "the people awake and alert." Abigail, however, considered "the Tumults" serious and hoped Jefferson agreed that "most vigorus measures" were needed to "quell and suppress" them. Rather than "that laudible spirit which you approve," she wrote, "which makes a people watchfull over their Liberties and alert in the defence of them, these mobish insurgents are for sapping the foundation, and distroying the whole fabrick at once."

Jefferson focused on critical scrutiny by the people. "The spirit of resistance to government is so valuable on certain occasions, that I wish it to be always kept alive. It will often be exercised when wrong, but better so than not to be exercised at all. I like a little rebellion now and then. It is like a storm in the Atmosphere." By July 1787 Jefferson wrote his last letter to Abigail on the subject of the Regulation, hoping that "all the disturbances of your country are quieted" with "little bloodshed."

Several months later, Abigail replied that the state's "commotions" displaced Governor James Bowdoin – who presided over the suppression of the Regulators – with political "Rubbish." Still, the legislature demonstrated "a sense of justice" by defeating a paper money law.

John agreed with Abigail. In assessing the context of the Regulation he estimated that two-thirds of America's state constitutions would "produce Disorders and Confusion" if "not altered." Jefferson, however, quantified the operation of American governments as a success. By multiplying the length of time since Independence by the number of states, Jefferson described the Regulation as the only insurrection in nearly 150 years of experience with American republican government.

Thirty years later, John Adams claimed that Jefferson misunderstood America's history because his old friend and adversary did not feel "the Terrorism" of the Regulation. Adams conveniently forgot that his own European posting also made him a distant observer of events in Massachusetts. Their different views on the Regulation, however, were not a matter of direct experience. Rather, they reflected competing visions of the role and authority of the sovereign people on the eve of the federal constitutional convention.[1]

For those who saw America in 1787 in dire straits, the Massachusetts Regulation symbolized the depth of the problem. The events in Massachusetts were particularly troubling because they undermined an apparently stable state government. Unlike Rhode Island, *Pennsylvania*, or even Virginia, whose legislatures seemed infected by democracy, Massachusetts's government was firmly in the hands of a traditional leadership. That "rebellion" and "insurrection" broke out in a state with a balanced constitution underscored the dangers of America's general political instability. Moreover, Massachusetts's turmoil seemed symptomatic of conditions nationally. By September 1787, the *Pennsylvania Gazette* reported that "[e]very state . . . has its SHAYS, who either, with their pens – or tongues – or offices – are endeavouring to effect what *Shays* attempted in vain with his sword." A Bostonian Friend of Government warned that the "inflammable matter that lately made its appearance" in Massachusetts "is by no means confined to this part of the continent." In fact, the "most discerning" people in every state were "sensible that the same fuel is scattered throughout, and will easily catch."[2]

For those who blamed the Regulation on the misapplication of constitutional principles it was not farfetched to believe each state might face its own "SHAYS." Protesters in Massachusetts and in other states seemed to misunderstand the Revolution. Success in defeating the British called for a particular attitude on the part of the people toward states of their own making and officials of their own choosing. From the perspective of many American leaders, criticism of government, especially coordinated in conventions and protest in the form of court closings, seemed tantamount to anarchy.

On the other hand, a different understanding guided those who gathered in conventions. They not only sent petitions, remonstrances, and instructions but also took direct action to gain the attention of and give direction to their agents in government. They observed that state constitutions drafted after Independence broadly described the collective powers of "the people." Moreover, those constitutions identified a direct, ongoing relationship between the people and their government. Those documents encouraged a wide-ranging role for the people under American constitutionalism during and after the war. Americans who took such views to heart were out of step with others who thought about the people as the collective sovereign in more constrained terms.

Determinists and Regulators outraged many American leaders by claiming to be a majority of "the people" and challenging elected representatives and government policy. Determinist movements throughout the country identified inherent rights of "the people" when they created governments and demanded protection of the common welfare. In addition, relying on the people's right to scrutinize their governors encouraged Massachusetts Regulators to neutralize acts of government they considered illegitimate. For many, determinist movements and the Regulation were examples of misconstruing constitutional principles linked to the Revolution. For those troubled by that tendency, constitution-making at the national level provided an opportunity to correct misguided views.[3]

The traditional story of the formation of the federal Constitution emphasizes the weakness of the Articles of Confederation and imprudent state legislatures. Too many bad laws had been passed by unwise legislators possessing too little virtue. In addition, the federal Framers supposedly expressed a "matured" understanding of the constitutional implications of governments resting on the sovereign authority of the people. Both the process of creating the constitution and its contents are depicted as a natural evolution of thinking that culminated in a shared understanding of American constitutionalism.[4]

The creation and text of the federal Constitution displayed democratic instincts and squarely rested on the sovereignty of the people. Most scholars, however, have overlooked the different possibilities that existed at the time for expressing and implementing the concept of the collective sovereign in a written constitution. If the federal Constitution was extraordinarily "democratic" for the eighteenth century, it nonetheless reflected a more constrained version of the constitutional principle of the people's sovereignty emerging since Independence. The choices made by the federal Framers were shaped by their view of the state of America in 1787. Their perceptions led them to craft a constitution that deliberately muted a more expansive version of constitutional government based on the sovereignty of the people.[5]

Traditional accounts of the federal Constitution, therefore, overlook a crucial dimension of American constitutionalism: competing understandings of the meaning of governments resting on the people. The question became what a majority of the people (however "the people" was defined) could do and how they were authorized to act. Some Americans, including the federal Framers, sought constraints on wide-ranging invocations of the sovereignty of the people that seemed to threaten the republican experiment. Equally concerned, however, were other Americans who saw the expression of constitutional principles since Independence as validating and encouraging an active role for the people. From their perspective, it punished legitimate behavior sanctioned by the authority of the collective sovereign to stifle those who gathered to send petitions, remonstrances, and instructions to their legislators or to criticize government. In the end, the struggle over the federal Constitution and its initial amendments reflected an ongoing tension between different visions of constitutionalism for America.

SOURCES OF PESSIMISM BY THE 1780s

Americans planted the seeds for future political democracies by basing their first state constitutions on the sovereignty of the people. At the time, however, many revolutionary leaders, like the Virginian John Marshall and future chief justice of the U.S. Supreme Court, expected that their new republics would operate under the moral direction and traditional guidance of "a few of the wise & virtuous." They expected these elites to gravitate toward selfless and wise leadership – a quality they called disinterestedness. Because of their education and standing in society, this elite supposedly could overcome self-interest and parochialism to focus on the common good.[6]

The actual experience with governments based on the authority of the people in the decade since Independence, however, severely tested this vision of idealized leadership. By the 1780s, many revolutionaries feared that something was amiss. In 1784 the clergyman Jeremy Belknap worried that without the "grand prerequisite" of "public virtue" Americans were "not destined to be long governed in a democratic form." It was well enough to acknowledge the "good principle" that "there should be no power but what is derived from the people and exercised by their consent and for their benefit." Nonetheless, the people needed to "be taught . . . that they are not able to govern themselves." The republic's survival depended on government's being "kept up over" the people.[7]

Belknap's concerns were not uncommon at the time. In May 1786, Charles Pettit of Pennsylvania saw states succumbing to the "intoxicating Draughts of Liberty run mad." Americans were as "inattentive" to their "Dangerous Situation as a flock of Sheep" on their way to "a Slaughter Pen." One month later, according to John Jay, Americans were "going and doing wrong," a worrisome departure from their "fixed" determination to do good during the war. He anticipated a future of "evils and calamities." George Washington wrote James Madison in November 1786 that "No morn[ing] ever dawned more favourable than ours did – and no day was ever more clouded than the present!"[8]

Members of the traditional elite uneasily viewed the increasing involvement in government by those seemingly lacking the education and virtue necessary for impartial rule. The elite assumed that they had the necessary qualities entitling them to govern. After the Revolution, they found themselves challenged socially, economically, and politically in the new American states. Men of lesser status undermined their hold on the economy, if not the government. Politics now found a "former indentured servant" challenging a "college-educated attorney" for leadership. The elite feared these lesser men were using government to advance their particular interests. As one example, they pointed to the passage of debt relief laws by state legislatures that forced creditors – most of whom were members of the elite – to accept repayment in devalued paper currency. The elite viewed such laws as undercutting property rights and the obligation of contract. James Madison and other Federalists thought these policies demonstrated the unfortunate result of too much political participation by common folk as well as "middling sorts" since Independence. Madison was not alone in lamenting "democratic excesses" during the early period of American self-government.[9]

For many revolutionary leaders, the major problem of the 1780s was that formerly obscure men who assumed leadership roles during the Revolutionary War "found it very difficult to fall back in the ranks" thereafter. The problem was not just different leaders but that the common folk increasingly resisted deferring to their "betters." Of "all the evils which attend the republican form of government" in America, noted the *New York Daily Advertiser* in 1786, none had "more pernicious effects than the *insolence* which liberty implants into the lower orders of society." Particularly troubling was that ordinary people seemed to have adopted the illusion that they were as good as their "betters." The "Desire of Equality in all Things" was a dangerous symptom of the times, observed John Jay. This was not simply a lack of social deference. It had become incorporated in the constitutional structure of some states, such as Pennsylvania, where majority will seemed unchecked by deference to traditional leaders.[10]

The problem of deference to traditional leadership was long in coming. Early in the Revolution, New Yorker Gouverneur Morris warned that it was nearly "impossible to curb" the common folk. He derisively called them the "mobility." In organizing crucial resistance to British authority, ordinary people exercised significant power through committees and associations. After this experience, "[t]hese sheep, simple as they are, cannot be gulled as heretofore." The task for the traditional leaders would be "how to keep them down." The rising expectations of the common folk, which ideas of the Revolution and the constitution-making process encouraged, was now the greatest challenge to traditional elites. The foundation of the Revolution and the constitutions created in its wake – that the people, not a king was the sovereign – made "curbing" the people all the more difficult, particularly because the idea of the people as the collective sovereign penetrated the thinking of a wide cross section of Americans.[11]

Other members of the revolutionary generation – particularly those recently admitted into the councils of government or the new marketplace – took a more positive view of America's prospects. They did not think self-government since Independence necessarily placed America on the road to disorder and ruin. They sought to preserve the opportunities for a wider range of people to remain involved in government and the transformed economy. Those not drawn from the ranks of traditional leadership (based on wealth, education, or social standing) now found themselves part of the new legislatures and becoming players in the new economy. For them, America's situation hardly seemed dire. Policies like paper money laws helped create a currency essential to fuel the economic opportunities of an internal market developing after the Revolution. Providing debt and tax relief was government's job, and they thought state legislatures were not doing enough. The perceived inadequacy of state legislatures to address these concerns was as worrying to some as was the perception by others that those legislatures granted too much relief. That the federal Constitution – touted by supporters as an indispensable response to existing political and economic conditions – barely avoided defeat shows that many Americans did not share the Federalists' bleak vision of America in 1787.[12]

In early 1787, the Massachusetts lawyer Fisher Ames lamented, "The people have turned against their teachers the doctrines" invoked "to effect the late revolution." Like Ames, many who were alarmed about America's future worried about the troubling manner in which principles of the Revolution were being used. The Massachusetts Regulation buttressed the fear of a contagion of wrongheaded ideas reflected in a growing coordination among the determinist movements. John Adams thought "too ardent and inconsiderate pursuit of erroneous opinions of government" underlay the Regulation.[13]

An example of how traditional leaders felt challenged by misguided notions of constitutionalism surfaced early in 1787. The context was a debate in Maryland, a state with "the most conservative" constitution of the revolutionary era. Although ostensibly a controversy over paper money, the debate focused on whether the people could instruct their representatives. This issue, in turn, raised the question of the relationship of the people as the collective sovereign to their government. The fact that some legislators assigned a wide-ranging and active role for the people as the collective sovereign even under Maryland's "conservative" constitution underscored the state of affairs in thinking about American constitutionalism on the eve of the federal convention.[14]

The debate over instruction arose when the House of Delegates of Maryland's legislature proposed using paper money to cope with the state's public debt. After the state Senate rejected the proposed bill, the House published an *Appeal* to the public, asserting that both branches of the legislature were bound by the people's instructions. If the two branches disagreed, "you alone are to decide, and to you only can there be any appeal." The Senate denied that Maryland's 1776 constitution allowed "one branch" to appeal directly "to the people from the proceedings of the other." Instruction undermined the Senate's constitutional function to exercise its judgment free from the bias and passion of "large collected bodies of people."[15]

During the debate, Samuel Chase – a member of the House and later an ardent Federalist as well as justice of the U.S. Supreme Court – captured metaphorically the argument for instruction. Chase emphasized that both senators and members of the House were "*trustees* and *servants* of the people." Indeed, Maryland's "alter and abolish" provision in its 1776 bill of rights described all governmental officials as "the trustees of the public." The powers of both branches of the legislature were "*derivative* and *delegated*." "All *lawful* authority originates from the people, and their power is like the light of the sun, native, original, inherent and unlimited by human authority." On the other hand, the power of legislators and government officials "is like the reflected light of the moon" and "is only borrowed, delegated and limited by the grant of the people."[16]

How one viewed instruction reflected one's understanding of the relationship of the collective sovereign to their governors and ultimately to government itself. Chase's metaphor of the sun as the people and the moon as government embodied this idea. The collective people were the primary source of light and authority in America's constitutional order. It was necessary that they transmit their will, which they could do by instructing their legislators. That concept of the relationship between the sovereign and government had consequences for the sovereign's right to alter or abolish government, including a shift in thinking about the traditional right of revolution.

Chase's position on instruction illustrated this new understanding of the right of revolution. Maryland's constitutional provision declared it the right of the people "to reform" government "whenever the ends of government are perverted," liberty "manifestly endangered," and "all other" means of redress "ineffectual." It thus echoed a traditional formulation of the right of revolution based on extreme circumstances as a precondition for the right. As such, it contrasted with a right that might be exercised at the discretion of the collective sovereign as expressed in other American constitutions. Nonetheless, some Maryland legislators (including Chase) interpreted the 1776 provision to give a discretionary right to the people to alter or abolish government. Chase believed that as the sovereign the people were not barred from acting until liberty faced "*manifest* danger." The people need not wait until their action might prove "too late." Rather, "the right of the people to instruct the legislature is necessarily implied in the establishment, and is the very essence of our government." Another member of the House, William Paca, writing as *Publicola*, more fully elaborated and defended that position.[17]

According to Paca, the people as the "*supreme authority*" behind the constitution were the ultimate judge of the government they created. Their judgment was not limited to periodic elections. It certainly included such moments, but elective choices did not exhaust the people's authority. Paca used an analogy of agency to suggest that all representatives remained subject to the wishes of their principal, the people – the "creators" of government. Although Paca's analogies varied – sometimes representatives were called trustees and sometimes the "deputy" of a "principal" – he consistently suggested the subordination of the government and its officials to the people. In terms that rankled the traditional leadership, Paca asserted that the people exercised the same "command over their delegates and representatives, as they have over their *grooms* and *cooks*."[18]

For Paca, constitutional principles of the American Revolution established the right to instruct the Senate. The people were "the judges" of the appropriate exercise of governmental power "and when they think it is not so employed they may speak and announce it by memorials, remonstrances, or instructions." If ignored by the legislature, the people could vote out representatives "at a future election, or if the magnitude of the case requires it, by resuming the powers of government." There was no need for a specific right in the constitution. "[T]he very relationship between principal and delegate, implies and maintains" the people's right of instruction. This right was a fundamental "constitutional doctrine" of America's written constitutions.[19]

Judge Alexander Contee Hanson, writing as *Aristides*, rejected Paca's argument for the people instructing the legislature. "[N]o writer of established reputation," he asserted, ever construed the alter or abolish provision of Maryland's constitution as giving the people a constitutional right to instruct their representatives. Rather, the state's constitution was a "compact" that strictly bound the people to its terms unless they chose to invoke an ultimate right of revolution. The government's relationship to the people was not one of agency, much less the image of master to servant described by Paca. The idea of "the people being masters" Hanson dismissed as "one of the most incongruous, and absurd, that ever entered into a human brain." The more appropriate analogy was that of a partnership in which the people "place their affairs in the hands of agents ... who are in all cases to act according to their own judgment, so long as the partnership continues." "All power indeed flows from the people," he observed, but "the doctrine, that the power actually at all times resides in the people, is subversive of all government and law."[20]

Maryland's alter and abolish provision was "a striking lesson," claimed Hanson, that constitution-writers should never "use sentences or words without necessity or meaning." Maryland's constitution-makers never anticipated that a provision "asserting only a natural right" would "be construed into a positive institution." The "obvious meaning" of Maryland's "alter or abolish" provision was that "the interference of the people" by resuming their retained powers "dissolved" government. The Maryland debate over instruction ended inconclusively, but the issue would arise again, reflecting America's differences in understanding the role of the collective sovereign.[21]

SOLUTIONS TO AMERICA'S PERCEIVED DANGERS

Maryland's debate over "the rights of the people" to instruct their legislators signaled a shift in arguments by those concerned about what the Revolution had wrought. This shift appeared most dramatically among a growing number of American revolutionary leaders. They traced many of the problems of the postrevolutionary era to the failure of the new constitutions to attain an adequate balance between the need for leadership by a natural aristocracy (in which they included themselves) and the increased involvement of the people – particularly ordinary people. In addition, they stressed the need for the people to defer to those with education and accomplishment. At the very least the people should listen to their governors more and criticize them less. Leadership by this natural aristocracy could balance the two countervailing dangers of republicanism, either of which would be fatal. One side of this balance involved the tendency toward anarchy resulting from an excess of democracy. The other side of the balance was the danger of tyranny from too much government coercion applied to maintain order.[22]

The leadership problem was crucial because recent disturbances showed what would happen when the people were not properly led. If "the great Body of the people are, without Virtue, and not governed by any internal Restraints of Conscience," asserted Rufus King, "the Framers of our constitutions, & Laws" operated on unfounded assumptions. For Abigail Adams, the Massachusetts Regulation featured "[i]gnorant, wrestless desperadoes, without conscience or principals" leading "a deluded multitude" with imaginary grievances. Washington also feared that the "commotions & temper" of the Regulators were "melancholy proof" that "mankind left to themselves are unfit for their own government." Henry ("Light Horse Harry") Lee found that "the lower order" threatened "good government." Increasingly, revolutionary leaders called for guidance by a natural aristocracy.[23]

"[E]xtremely mistaken" notions about free governments were leading Americans astray, claimed John Adams in 1789. Like all American revolutionaries, he acknowledged that "the natural authority of the people alone" founded government. No "free government" could exist "without a democratical branch in the constitution." However, that branch needed to be balanced. Under constitutions where "there is no balance, there will be everlasting fluctuations, revolutions, and horrors, until a standing army, with a general at its head, commands the peace." The challenge was to create governments in which the people were the sovereign while avoiding the inevitable dangers from too much popular power, what he called "simple democracy."[24]

For Adams, a balance was impossible without properly using the "natural aristocracy" that came from differences in "property, family, and merit." This group could be "the most dangerous" threat to republics if given too much weight. But if "judiciously managed in the constitution," the natural aristocracy became "the greatest blessing of society" because it had "the greatest collection of virtues and abilities in a free government." Using the natural aristocracy appropriately meant putting "them all, or at least the most remarkable of them" into an upper branch of the legislature. This would effectively balance the three "orders" of government: "the powers of the one, the few, and the many." The talents and virtue of "the few" drawn from the natural aristocracy would check the more misguided and less thinking "many" of the general populace, while both the executive "one" and the lower legislative branch could restrain the upper branch's aristocratic tendency.[25]

After returning to Massachusetts from a European diplomatic post in 1788, Adams offered a bleak view of his state's politics. Elected leaders now were "much more selfish and much less skilful." Adams feared that virtuous leaders were being bypassed by lesser men. Although convinced the people were the source of government's legitimacy, their involvement should be less direct, freeing representation from popular pressure, and hopefully resulting in direction from a virtuous elite drawn from the natural aristocracy. Without such leadership, Henry Knox observed in 1787, state governments were "sources of pollution, which will contaminate the American name perhaps for ages." He felt "strong checks" were necessary to prevent capricious, "headlong conduct" resulting in "[a] mad democracy."[26]

All revolutionary leaders did not share Adams's diagnosis of America's political ills. Thomas Jefferson, for one, did not think the Regulation threatened "serious consequences." The events in Massachusetts simply reflected the criticisms and occasional upheavals that were a natural part of America's commitment to a collective sovereign. Even those who feared the Regulation, including John Adams, conceded the necessity of government's listening to "just complaints" as well as "imaginary grievances" of the people. Likewise, John Jay argued that in "free states, there must and ought to be a little ferment" to avoid the public mind from growing "languid" and the vigor of a republic from becoming "lost."[27]

According to Jefferson, the Regulation and other "late troubles in the Eastern states" highlighted the three choices all societies faced. First, to live without government; second, to live under governments where "the will of every one" exerted some degree of "just influence"; or third, to live under governments of force. Practicality ruled out the first possibility, except in small populations. The "curse" of coercion in the third choice, "a government of wolves over sheep," made that option unacceptable. This left establishing a government in which the people had "just influence." The American Revolution promised to show the world that governments based on the sovereignty of the people could exist without the threat of coercive power hanging over its citizens.[28]

Jefferson reflected a calm, reassuring attitude toward the Massachusetts disturbances. The Regulation did not call into question America's commitment to the people as the sovereign. Rather, he cast the disturbance as if it were a natural phenomenon, like a storm. "[A] little rebellion now and then is a good thing, and as necessary in the political world as storms in the physical." Hoping to avoid such disturbances was as futile as trying to stop the rain.[29]

Because American governments provided the people "a precious degree of liberty" they were susceptible to "turbulence." Government should not overreact. Turbulence reminded governors that they served the people and that government was encroaching "on the rights of the people." Disturbances were a symptom of a failure to listen to the people. Like nature's often-capricious destruction, the Regulation resulted in some "absolutely unjustifiable" acts. It was pointless, however, to take the matter personally – as had some Massachusetts officials. Complaining about the weather was understandable, but ultimately unavailing.[30]

Jefferson believed that governments should be "so mild in their punishment of rebellions, as not to discourage them too much." He did not consider the Massachusetts court closings evidence of an actual rebellion. Rebelliousness, in the sense Jefferson used it, did not imply overturning government, but grievances and opinions expressed clearly, possibly rudely, and even forcefully so that governors paid attention. Governments founded on "the people" inevitably entailed some amount of disorder and even occasional, sporadic violence. He remained confident that "the result of our experiment will be that men are capable of governing themselves without a master." Weighed against the prospect of living under "a government of force," Jefferson considered the Massachusetts "commotions" a minor inconvenience.[31]

Like Jefferson, James Madison believed the Massachusetts events were not to be taken lightly – they still destabilized government, but they did not rise to the level of a revolution. In Congress, Madison questioned the wisdom of sending troops to quell the Massachusetts disturbances because it was "rather difficult to reconcile" such action "with the principles of Republican Govts." From the start, Madison described Regulators as the "discontented," terminology he continued to use, along with the term "insurgents." He referred to the Regulation's "turbulent scenes," and the closest he came to calling it a rebellion was to refer to its "spirit." Like Jefferson, Madison analogized the Regulation to a natural phenomenon. In November 1787 Madison reported, "there remains a great deal of le[a]ven in the mass of the people." The analogy to yeast in bread implied that the people's restlessness rose and fell; it did not inevitably result in a fixed determination to overthrow government.[32]

Jefferson's acceptance of "tumultous meetings of the people" as legitimate and a small price to pay for a free society was distinctly a minority view. By the late 1780s, most revolutionary leaders were not willing to err on the side of disruption and "a little rebellion now and then." Rather, more force appeared a better choice since the balance already seemed to have tipped too far in the other direction. The danger now lay in government not exerting enough strength. In October 1786 Henry Knox wanted government "braced, changed, or altered" in order to wield more power. By December of that year Knox reported to Washington that the recent "commotions" brought "prodigious changes" in thinking. Washington agreed that the Regulation provided "evidence" of the lack of "energy" in American governments. The Massachusetts import merchant and banker Jonathan Jackson demanded a standing army to "cooperate with the well disposed, when things are taking a wrong, but violent turn." Others, like the Boston merchant, Stephen Higginson, felt the national government needed "more force" or "Insurgents will arise and eventually take the reins from us." The Regulation taught a clear lesson: the people must be "compelled by force to submit to their proper stations."[33]

MOVEMENT TOWARD THE FEDERAL
CONSTITUTIONAL CONVENTION

The movement to change the Articles of Confederation, which Madison, along with other Americans, clearly understood to be the first federal Constitution, raised doubts and uncertainties. The proposal for a Philadelphia constitutional convention was met with "great disagreement," noted Madison. Nonetheless, an advocate for a "more energetic" national government in November 1786 observed that "the idea of a special convention, appointed by the states . . . seems to gain ground." Henry Knox identified "different sentiments" on the issue. "[S]ome suppose" the Philadelphia convention would be "an irregular assembly, unauthorized by the Confederation." They thought it circumvented Article XIII of the Articles of Confederation, which "point[ed] out the mode by which any alterations shall be made." Madison noted that some in Congress believed that such a step would be "an extra-constitutional mode of proceeding" and an "interposition of Congs." In the end, George Washington expressed the view that carried the day and led to the convention. "[A]ll attempts to alter or amend" the Articles were misdirected. What was needed was replacement. To try to fix the Articles would "be like the propping of a house which is ready to fall." A convention might "not be legal," Washington admitted, but it was the quickest way to replace the Articles with a strong national government.[34]

General Washington's concern about the illegality of a constitutional convention was shared by lawyers as well. John Jay considered such a meeting "questionable." If the convention's authority came from the state legislatures, he concluded they probably were not "authorized either by themselves or others, to alter Constitutions." If the convention merely recommended a new draft constitution, this might "produce endless Discussions, and perhaps Jealousies and Party Heats." Jay recommended that the Articles be changed by employing the process of constitution-making used by numerous states: an express vote by the people authorizing delegates to establish a constitution. "[T]he People of the States" could hold state conventions that in turn would appoint delegates to a national convention authorized to create a new constitution without popular ratification. Such a convention would also violate Article XIII, but it would be legitimate. The change in the Articles would come "from the only Source of just authority – *the People*."[35]

In proposing a federal convention Hamilton anticipated the need for congressional approval and confirmation by the legislatures of "every State." Obtaining Congress's consent was proving difficult as Madison explained to Washington in late February 1787. Congress was "much divided and embarrassed" about the convention movement, he reported. Madison later wrote Edmund Pendleton that some objected to the congressional recommendation for a convention as "extraconstitutional" and considered it a step "without some regular sanction." Secretary at War Henry Knox also acknowledged that congressional concerns about "the legality of the proposed convention" persisted.[36]

While the federal convention was assembling in Philadelphia in the summer of 1787, Washington wrote Jefferson that "[m]uch is expected from it by some – but little by others – and nothing by a few." "That something is necessary, all will agree; for the situation of the General Governm[en]t (if it can be called a governm[en]t) is shaken to its foundation – and liable to be overset by every blast. In a word, it is at an end, and unless a remedy is soon applied, anarchy & confusion will inevitably ensue."[37]

WORK OF THE CONVENTION

Democracy and Filtration of Leadership

When delegates to the convention considered a structure for the new national government, they sought to avoid the imbalance they perceived in how democratic politics presently operated under state constitutions. In giving the people a role in a national democratic branch, they needed, as Edmund Randolph put it, to temper the "turbulence" and "fury of democracy." This required creating "sufficient checks against the democracy," noted James

McHenry. American governments were "too democratic," conceded George Mason. He observed that many in the convention were "soured & disgusted" by what they attributed to the unchecked democracy in the states. He feared that some delegates, rather than seeking to balance the exercise of democracy might be willing to undermine its operation by going to "the opposite Extreme." But as Mason noted early in the convention, "Notwithstanding the oppressions & injustice experienced among us from democracy; the genius of the people is in favor of it, and the genius of the people must be consulted."[38]

The frame of government that emerged from the convention established a national democratic branch in the House of Representatives. It balanced the power of this branch and built in mechanisms to promote deference to, and the influence of, traditional sources of leadership. Elbridge Gerry sought elections for the federal government that encouraged "men of honor & character" to participate. The federal Framers' final product echoed John Adams's earlier concern that a balanced constitution should preserve "Respect" and "Veneration" for "Persons in Authority." Ultimately, the structure the Founders proposed left the people arbiters of political legitimacy, but provided a means for the government to be led by an educated, virtuous elite.[39]

Within the convention, Madison expected that the House of Representatives would attract "the wisest & most worthy citizens." Nonetheless, because the House was so large, its members could be led astray by popular "fickleness and passion." The Senate would serve as a "fence" in restraining this democratic excess and the "transient impressions" of the House. Senate members respected for their "wisdom & virtue" and "firmness" could "seasonably interpose agst. impetuous counsels." Finding "the most distinguished characters, distinguished for their rank in life and their weight of property" to serve in the Senate, according to John Dickinson, was more likely to be achieved if state legislatures elected the Senate. John Rutledge agreed that a legislative election would be "more refined" and Oliver Ellsworth thought it would produce more "Wisdom" than an election "immediately by the people."[40]

Madison's model of leadership saw its development through a process of refinement. This view resonated with many other Americans at the time. Judge Alexander Hanson's argument against the people's instructing their state senate is a case in point. Those selected to rule because of their "superior talents" and who "devote their attention to the public affairs" could better judge matters than the people "in general." As another correspondent in the Maryland dispute noted, requirements for service in the state senate resulted in the selection of "the most *wise, sensible* and *discreet* men." Madison acknowledged the central role of the people in electing those having virtue and wisdom. It was possible "to refine and enlarge the public views, by passing them through the medium of a chosen body of citizens, whose wisdom may best discern the true interest of their country."[41]

The federal convention combined its hope for refined leadership with the expectation that structurally the national government would diminish the dangers of majority tyranny. It sought to do so by balancing authority and tempering the direct involvement by the people. The electoral college, the election of senators by state legislatures, and the control of factional politics through direct election of the House of Representatives from large districts – all reflected a government that muted the manifestation of the voice of the sovereign people in day-to-day political affairs. Many supporters of the constitution hoped that after ratification the collective sovereign would express itself only by electing representatives.[42]

Greater Governmental Power

Providing enough power to maintain what James Madison called "the internal tranquillity of the States" was another theme within the convention. Article IV of the federal Constitution guaranteed every state a "Republican Form of Government." It also offered protection against "domestic Violence," reassuring southerners fearful of slave uprisings and states elsewhere worried about disturbances like the Massachusetts Regulation. Giving the national government a "certain portion of military force is absolutely necessary," insisted Alexander Hamilton. The "guarantee clause" of a republican form of government, according to James Wilson, protected the states from "dangerous commotions, insurrections and rebellions."[43]

Domestic turbulence was utmost in many delegates' minds. Edmund Randolph considered their crucial "mission" as one of preventing "seditions," such as the Massachusetts "rebellion." According to Madison, New England "insurrections" represented a "danger" to which every state was "exposed." The constitution would provide a "real" military presence to save states from "anarchy," hoped Charles Pinckney. Mere "apprehension" of a "national force," John Langdon thought, would be "salutary" in "preventing insurrections."[44]

Still in Paris in November 1787, Thomas Jefferson detected that federal constitution-makers were overly "impressed" by the events in Massachusetts. In creating a new national government, delegates had the choice of either "light" or "heavy" government. "Heavy" governments overreacted with force when the legitimacy of their actions was challenged – as had Massachusetts officials during the Regulation. Jefferson favored a "light" government. For Jefferson, the Regulation produced "more alarm" than it "should have done." As Jefferson explained:

> God forbid we should ever be 20. years without such a rebellion. The people can not be all, and always, well informed. The part which is wrong will be discontented in proportion to the importance of the facts they misconceive. If they remain quiet under such misconceptions it is a lethargy, the fore-runner of death to the public liberty. . . . And what country can preserve it's liberties if their rulers are not warned from time to time that their people preserve the spirit of resistance? Let them take arms. The remedy is to set them right as to facts, pardon and pacify them. What signify a few lives lost in a century or two? The tree of liberty must be refreshed from time to time with the blood of patriots and tyrants.

By the time Jefferson made this observation, the federal Constitution – with a distinctive accent on government's coercive power – was under debate in America.[45]

Constitutional Revision

The clearest indication of how the federal Framers viewed the role and authority of the collective sovereign in a more limited fashion entailed their provision for constitutional change. Most significantly, the procedures in Article V were intended to be the exclusive means of changing the federal Constitution. Some state constitutions contained daunting revision provisions but often included statements of the people's right to alter or abolish their governments at will. Even without such text, many Americans, including some legislators in Maryland, thought that the people as the collective sovereign possessed that right. The federal Framers did not include alter or abolish language in the federal Constitution. Moreover, they rejected the assumption that the sovereign source creating that constitution retained an inherent right of revision. The Framers' position dramatically departed from an expansive view of the people's sovereignty.[46]

At the time the federal convention considered whether to draft amending provisions, only two states explicitly provided for the amendment of their constitutions. Some delegates thought an amending clause unnecessary. James Madison did not wish to trust to the "dangerous" practice of future amendments. Instead, he urged his fellow delegates to produce a carefully crafted constitution rather than leaving it to the future. Ultimately, the convention agreed with the arguments of Elbridge Gerry and George Mason. Gerry felt that the "novelty & difficulty" of their constitutional "experiment" required "periodical revision." Mason explained that if amendment could be made "in an easy, regular and Constitutional way" it avoided the need to change the constitution through "chance and violence."[47]

The convention's initial revision provision allowed amendment "whensoever it shall seem necessary" but gradually that language was replaced.[48] In its final version it specified exacting procedures for revision.[49] The constitution provided a two-step process for amendment. Amendments proposed by a two-thirds majority of both houses of Congress then required ratification by three-fourths of the state legislatures or special state conventions called for that purpose. Moreover, Article V also provided that two-thirds of the states could petition Congress to call a special convention for proposing amendments.

The high barriers to revision and absence of an alter or abolish provision provoked George Mason. No matter how "oppressive" the federal Constitution might become, complained Mason, the sovereign, "the whole people of America can't make, or even propose alterations to it." This was simply "a doctrine utterly subversive of the fundamental principles of the rights and liberties of the people." It violated a central tenet of American constitutionalism: that the collective sovereign could never surrender its power to alter or abolish constitutions and governments. Revising constitutions in a "regular and Constitutional way" included not only using procedures set forth in a constitution, but an inherent right of the collective sovereign to change it at will.[50]

Supporters of the constitution, such as Alexander Hamilton, did not deny "the right of the people to alter or abolish the established constitution whenever they find it inconsistent with their happiness." But having adopted a constitution, the sovereign pledged to adhere to its provisions, including those dealing with constitutional change. The collective sovereign could not act in a way "incompatible with the provisions in the existing constitution." "Until the people have by some solemn and authoritative act annulled or changed" the way it was to occur, "the established form" bound them "collectively, as well as individually."[51]

THE CONSTITUTIONAL PRODUCT
OF THE FEDERAL CONSTITUTION

In seeking to balance the promise of democracy with the wisdom of virtuous leadership, the Framers' constitution sought to control the people's use of power. The constitution guaranteed the people republican government, but minimized disturbances like the Massachusetts Regulation by enforcing domestic tranquility. Some Framers feared that if the people adopted the federal Constitution they would lose the right to alter or abolish governments at will. Several state constitutions explicitly protected this right in their bills of rights. Other state constitutions did so in practice without specific text. The federal convention's concern with controlling the people's use of power was reflected not only by what they placed in the constitution, but by what they omitted.

The federal convention showed little interest in a bill of rights. According to James Wilson, a bill of rights "never entered the mind" of most delegates. He did not remember hearing the subject "mentioned" until late in the convention. Even then, delegates considered it of "so little account" that the convention dismissed the idea "in a short conversation" without "a formal debate." The necessity of a bill of rights arose only a few days before adjournment when a motion to draft one was unanimously defeated.[52]

Whether or not a bill of rights in the federal Constitution would have simply duplicated "the natural rights of men not yet gathered into society," many state bills of rights did much more. They also addressed the constitutional relationship of the people to their government and specified the people's collective rights. James Madison admitted that a bill of rights could appropriately address "those rights which are exercised by the people in forming and establishing a plan of government" as well as rights the people "retained" in making a constitution. Nothing prevented the federal Framers from specifying the relationship of the collective sovereign that established the federal Constitution to the national government it was creating. State constitution-makers routinely did so in clarifying the relationship of the collective sovereign of the people of individual states to their state governments. In fact, when the first Congress drafted amendments as a federal bill of rights soon after ratification, it not only articulated individual rights comparable to those found in state constitutions but also included language addressing the relationship of the people to the national government in what became the Ninth and Tenth amendments.[53]

Among the principles that did not find expression in the federal Constitution at the time of its initial drafting were statements of the rights of the collective sovereign – their ascendancy over government, their right to scrutinize governors and their government, and their right to alter or abolish government at will. It was one thing to make a general concession that governors were the servants of the people and that the collective sovereign had the right to abolish government, but another to place words to that effect in the constitution. In the convention, Madison acknowledged that the collective sovereign could "alter constitutions as they pleased." It was, after all, "a principle in the Bills of rights," he noted. Still, the invocation of that right under state constitutions caused difficulties, as the Massachusetts Regulation demonstrated. Why tempt fate by including similar language in the federal Constitution?[54]

In fact, while "the people" appeared prominently in the Preamble to "ordain and establish" the federal Constitution, they soon left the stage after making an appearance – as "the People of the several States" – to elect members of the House of Representatives. Thereafter, "the people" disappeared from the text of the constitution. That absence formed a striking contrast to their presence in many state constitutions in which the people and their collective existence as the sovereign was repeatedly acknowledged – particularly, but not exclusively, in their bills of rights. Even when "the people" reappeared in the federal bill of rights drafted in the first Congress, the expression of the sovereignty of the people lacked the comparable wide-ranging expressions of the authority and rights of the collective sovereign that were found in state constitutions.[55]

In the end, the federal Constitution, and especially Article V, reflected an expectation that after the sovereign people ratified the new constitution, they would thereafter largely disappear.[56] Federalists invoked the power of the collective sovereign to establish the federal Constitution even as they worried about the implications of the people's authority.[57] Madison illustrated this tendency in *Federalist No. 49* when he extolled the people's sovereignty while cautioning that too active participation by the people in such constitutional adjustments could undermine the "veneration" needed for government's "stability."[58] In the end, all Federalists proclaimed the constitution could be adopted because the people were the sovereign.

CIRCUMVENTION IN THE CREATION OF THE FEDERAL CONSTITUTION

Federalists relied on the people as the collective sovereign to overcome the procedural obstacles in bringing the federal Constitution into being. One difficulty was the Articles of Confederation's requirement that any constitutional amendment be unanimously approved by all thirteen state legislatures. Rhode Island's refusal to attend the convention made fulfilling this requirement highly unlikely. No one denied that the Articles' specified process and procedures for constitutional revision stood in the way. But for Federalist Stephen Higginson, "expediency" overcame the fact that a convention did not seem "perfectly regular." Madison also justified the convention's *"unauthorized propositions."* "[I]n all great changes of established governments, forms ought to give way to substance." America's ability to secure republican governments required adopting the constitution. In achieving that goal, Madison and other Federalists insisted that it was unnecessary to use the Confederation's amendment procedure set out in Article XIII. Instead, ratification of the federal Constitution by the people was all that was needed for constitutional change under the authority of a collective sovereign.[59]

The federal Framers faced a larger challenge than just giving life to a new national constitution. They realized that action by the collective sovereign creating that national constitution would still leave conflicts with state constitutions. For instance, the federal Constitution's prohibition of state emission of coin and currency under Article I, Section 10, clashed with provisions of state constitutions that gave such power to their own legislatures. Simply adopting the federal Constitution would not suspend these state powers.

Maryland Anti-Federalist Luther Martin offered insight into this problem. In assessing the proposed ratification process, Martin noted that the federal Constitution would *"alter* the *constitution of this state."* Yet Maryland's constitution already provided the "mode by which . . . alterations were to be made" to that state's constitution. The collective sovereign creating the national constitution could not legitimately act for the collective sovereign of each individual state in changing their state constitution.[60]

Madison admitted during the federal convention that "powers given to the Genl. Govt." were "being taken from the State Govts." Shifting these powers required the people as the sovereign of the state to amend their state constitution at the same time they vested new powers in the national government by ratifying the federal Constitution. The proposal that the federal Constitution be ratified by each state through conventions of the people provided a means for the people to act simultaneously in changing state constitutions as the sovereign of their state and ratifying the federal Constitution as part of the collective sovereign of the national government.[61]

Ratification of the federal Constitution "by the supreme authority of the people themselves" was "indispensable," concluded Madison. In going back to the people, the ratification process would be playing out "revolution Principles," noted Alexander Hamilton. James Wilson echoed Madison's concern. The people in each state meeting in "a convention [were] the only power that can ratify the proposed system of the new government." Even opponents of the constitution did not dissent from this crucial role of the people. George Mason considered action by the people "one of the most important and essential" aspects of bringing life to the convention's work. The national "concurrence" of the state "conventions of the people," Elbridge Gerry noted, "armed" the constitution "with power, and invested it with dignity."[62]

The people as the sovereign could simultaneously authorize the wholesale replacement of the articles and alterations to the state constitutions. As Madison explained in *Federalist No. 40*, the right of the sovereign people to alter or abolish their governments supplied any lack or "defect of regular authority" of the federal constitutional convention. A "rigid adherence" to the "forms," such as those set forth in the Articles of Confederation, would undermine the "transcendent and precious right of the people" as the sovereign over government. Madison suggested that complying with the Articles' amendment procedures was almost impossible. Some state constitutions authorized their legislatures to approve changes to the articles; others did not. In this latter case "a ratification must of necessity be obtained from the people."[63]

A similar concern, but one that operated slightly differently from the question of the authority to circumvent the Articles and alter the state constitutions, was the issue of ensuring that the collective sovereign of each state ratify the federal Constitution. Madison acknowledged that "the highest source of authority, at least paramount to the powers of the respective constitutions of the states" had to ratify the constitution. Madison explained that the federal Constitution made "essential inroads on the State Constitutions." So the state legislatures were "incompetent" to approve those changes. "[I]t would be a novel & dangerous doctrine that a Legislature could change the constitution under which it held its existence." As "the mere creatures of the State Constitutions," legislatures lacked the power of ratification, noted George Mason. They "cannot be greater than their creators." When a state constitution lacked explicit provisions for its own revision, Madison feared it made little sense to seek approval from legislators sworn to uphold the existing constitution. On the other hand, whether or not a state constitution required particular revision procedures, going directly to the people for approval would surmount "all difficulties" because "[t]he people were in fact, the fountain of all power." "They could alter constitutions as they pleased."[64]

Madison concluded that the federal convention could bypass amendment procedures specified by the Articles. In addition, each state ratifying convention could also circumvent any procedures set forth by a state constitution for constitutional amendment based on the sovereignty of the people. The rationale of using state ratifying conventions, as Madison and other delegates explained, was not that adopting the federal document would automatically dissolve state powers over federal matters such as legal tender. Rather, the people in the states would effectively amend their state constitutions by ratifying the federal document. That could not happen if drafters in Philadelphia or legislators in the states alone adopted the constitution. Altering the constitutional structure of existing federal and state governments required the validation of the sovereign people in the states. In effect, the ratifying conventions accomplished a global change in the state constitutions. Not only did those conventions serve to approve the national constitutional structure, but each particular ratification action amended the state constitution so as to grant the national government authority exercised until then by the various state governments.[65]

CONSTITUTIONALISM IN THE FEDERAL BILL OF RIGHTS

After the federal convention reported the constitution to Congress in September 1787, Congress sent it to the people of the states for ratification. The next two years witnessed heated debates over the draft constitution. Despite narrow margins of approval in such key states as Massachusetts, Virginia, and New York, Congress eventually certified that the federal Constitution had been ratified.[66]

The constitution's ratification in most states did not signal a national agreement on American constitutionalism. When the first Congress assembled in New York under the new constitution Americans seemed as divided as before about government by a collective sovereign. Everyone agreed that the people were the sovereign and that they exercised this sovereignty to give life to the new constitution, even though they had circumvented procedures specified by the prior constitution for its amendment. For some Americans, if the people were the sovereign they were also entitled to play a more prominent role in ruling the nation. This was disputed by those who considered the constitution a structure for "filtration" that would develop a new set of rulers in America. How the people would rule meant different things to different people in 1787, and these divergent views shaped American thinking about the collective sovereign for the next half-century. American constitutionalism did not coalesce in the aftermath of the Philadelphia convention. It merely continued a long, incremental journey in which Americans repeatedly tested and sorted out its meaning.

Part of America's odyssey to define its constitutionalism was reflected in the debates of the first Congress when it considered whether the just adopted constitution should be amended. A recurring objection to the constitution during the ratification debates was its failure to specify some of the important rights of the people. As one critic of the constitution put it, such provisions would "enumerat[e] . . . our prerogatives, as a sovereign people." Amending the constitution to include these prerogatives would help define the role the sovereign people rightly claimed as a participant in ruling the nation, as well as what rights they would enjoy as subjects of the government they formed to rule over them. Explicitly setting out these matters would ensure the people's rights would not become "unknown, forgotten or contradicted by our representatives, our delegates, our servants in Congress." A bill of rights could sum up much of what it meant not only that the people were the sovereign in America, but as the sovereign what role they could play as the national ruler and as the ruled.[67]

While not challenging the power of the collective people as the sovereign, the first Congress divided over whether amending the new constitution invited unwanted interference by that sovereign in governing the nation. Recent "serious embarrassments," such as the Massachusetts Regulation, demonstrated to some the dangers of the people being too ready to exercise their powers either to rule or, in being ruled, to resist lawful authority. Some congressional representatives feared that the people were unduly influenced by "artful, unprincipled, & disaffected" demagogues. Just as they had done with the simple, powerful, and easily misunderstood ideas found in state bills of rights, such rabble-rousers might confuse or mislead the people with respect to text found in the federal Constitution. As a result, some representatives feared amending the constitution with a bill of rights would be "a very unpropitious affair." Rather than allowing the rhetoric surrounding the constitution's ratification to settle, developing a bill of rights amendment, they worried, might "unhinge . . . the public mind."[68]

The image of a public misled by a bill of rights was utmost in the mind of Massachusetts Federalist Theodore Sedgwick. He proposed deleting the right to assemble from what eventually became the First Amendment. The word "assemble" was unnecessary because the right of speech necessarily included assembly, argued Sedgwick. A right to assemble "is a self-evident unalienable right which the people possess." It was "certainly a thing that never would be called in[to] question." Sedgwick was not appeased by a fellow Federalist, New Yorker Egbert Benson's explanation that the amendment enumerated a right "inherent" in "the people" and simply protected the right of assembly from "being infringed by the government." If they were to list a right to assemble, Sedgwick retorted, they might as well declare that "a man should have a right to wear his hat if he pleased."[69]

Federalist John Page of Virginia replied that in the past the people had been forced to take off their hats when appearing "before the face of authority." The words in the amendment were not trivial. Listing the right of assembly in the bill of rights was important because on "lawful occasions" the people had "also been prevented from assembling together." "[I]t is well to guard against such stretches of authority" by inserting the right to assemble in the constitution, Page insisted. Sedgwick remained unconvinced even though two years earlier, he – along with other prominent lawyers and judges – insisted that citizens lacked a constitutional right to assemble in conventions to draft grievances against the Massachusetts government for relief. As such, the Massachusetts Regulation illustrated that constitutional text could be problematic in two opposing ways. Its absence might encourage some to assume that no such right existed, but its presence might encourage the exercise of rights not easily controlled.[70]

While fear persisted about what a bill of rights might bring, it succumbed to the insistence that the federal Constitution was incomplete if it lacked, in contrast to the state constitutions, a bill of rights. From his diplomatic post in Paris, Thomas Jefferson considered the absence of a federal bill of rights a "principal defect" of the constitution. He believed that a "bill of rights is what the people are entitled to" whether the government empowered be state or national. "[N]o just government," he noted, "should refuse or rest on inference" what the rights of the people were under a government in which they were the sovereign. Jefferson's belief was shared by many who opposed the constitution. Proponents of a bill of rights felt such an amendment to the constitution was an important priority to ensure that a national government would not fail to protect the collective rights of the people against potential misdeeds that might arise because of vagaries in the constitution's language. A bill of rights protected the people's collective rights by setting forth the principles of an active, vigilant citizenry, who would always be aware of their duty to hold their representatives and governors accountable. In this way, the people could resolve questions of how they would govern and be governed through the constitution, rather than having to go outside the constitution and employ their powers as the sovereign.[71]

As a delegate to the federal constitutional convention, James Madison opposed inclusion of a bill of rights in the constitution. Later, as a delegate in the Virginia ratifying convention, he found considerable opposition to ratification because of the absence of a bill of rights. Despite reluctance to ratify on that score, the convention ultimately approved the constitution as drafted on an 89 to 79 vote, but with an expectation that a bill of rights would later be added. This irked one of the convention's delegates, Patrick Henry, who considered it a mistake to "enter into a compact of Government first, and afterwards settle the terms of the Government." In a letter to Jefferson, Madison reported it "probable" that a bill of rights would be added when the first Congress under the new constitution convened. He asserted he had always been in favor of a bill of rights" as long as it did not "imply powers" inconsistent with the government established by the federal Constitution.

He now favored a bill of rights "because I supposed it might be of use, and . . . not be of disservice." As a practical matter, in seeking election to the House of Representatives under the new constitution, he had promised to consider appropriate constitutional amendments.[72]

Madison traced how his attitude toward the federal bill of rights – whose champion he soon became – differed from Jefferson's by virtue of their respective vantage points. Madison considered Jefferson's advocacy for a federal bill of rights while serving as a diplomat in Paris as influenced by witnessing "abuses of power" by self-serving monarchs. America had disposed of this problem with Independence. Madison saw "no tendency in our governments" for such "danger." He considered it unlikely that in America "a succession of artful and ambitious rulers" would be able to "erect an independent Government" which would result in the "subversion of liberty." The experience with government after Independence under the various state constitutions was not a people suffering from "usurped acts of the Government" that imposed tyranny. Rather, the problem was the role the people had assumed under their state constitutions.[73]

In these constitutions, the sovereign established a system of democratic rule in which majorities in the state legislatures passed legislation harming the minority. As Madison explained to Jefferson: "Wherever the real power in a Government lies, there is the danger of oppression. In our Governments the real power lies in the majority of the Community, and the invasion of private rights is *ch[ie]fly* to be apprehended, not from acts of Government contrary to the sense of its constituents, but from acts in which the Government is the mere instrument of the major number of the constituents." The "danger of oppression" in postrevolutionary America lay not in the possibility of government abusing the people. Rather, it "lies in the interested majorities of the people" subjugating the minority. If a federal bill of rights was needed, it was this danger of majority rule, not the danger of government tyranny over the people collectively, that should be addressed. In his initial arguments for a new federal Constitution, Madison spelled out examples of such oppression of the minority, including "vicious legislation" passed by the state legislatures.[74]

Acting on these impressions, Madison proposed a series of constitutional amendments in the first Congress on June 8, 1789. He distilled these amendments from the many suggestions made by the state ratifying conventions. In conformity with his view that a federal bill of rights should serve to protect a minority against the actions of a majority, he primarily focused the bill on personal rights exercised individually rather than collective rights of the people.[75]

Madison's proposed bill did articulate certain common understandings about the people collectively. He proposed to amend the constitution to include language suggesting the extent of the collective sovereign's power: "[A]ll power is originally vested in, and consequently derived from the people," it would declare. In addition, "the people have an indubitable, unalienable, and indefeasible right to reform or change their government, whenever it be found adverse or inadequate to the purposes" for which the government was established. This wording never made it into the bill of rights that was ultimately adopted and in any event was qualified by Madison in later debate. This contrasted with many state bills of rights that had fulsome provisions not only setting out the powers of the sovereign but also expressing how the people as the ruler of the state, or as citizens of the state, could exercise collective rights.[76]

Madison's proposal avoided explicit descriptions of the role of the people, except for a provision that noted the collective right of the people to assemble and petition government. However, that provision omitted any mention of a right of instruction. Madison's proposal contained a version of what ultimately became the Tenth Amendment, reserving to the "states" powers not delegated to the federal government, but notably omitting a reservation of those powers to "the people." Nor did Madison's version of what became the Ninth Amendment refer to rights "retained by the people" in ensuring that the enumeration of rights in the constitution not be construed to deny other rights. In short, Madison's amendments primarily protected the individual from the majority – including religious belief and its exercise; free expression; freedom from providing army quarters; security against unreasonable searches and seizures; and entitlement to a speedy and public trial. Yet nowhere did Madison specify or provide protection for the rights of the collective people of the United States.[77]

The Virginia convention, for instance, suggested that the federal Constitution include an explicit statement of the subordination of government and elected officials to the people. Virginia wanted language that representatives were the people's "trustees and agents and at all times amenable to them." The New York convention proposed that the bill of rights for the national government declare that "the Powers of Government" could be "reassumed by the People, whensoever it shall become necessary to their Happiness." The omission of such principles in the bill of rights proposed by Madison led Aedanus Burke to dismiss the House's amendments as "frothy and full of wind, formed only to please the palate." The Madison-inspired bill of rights lacked any "solid and substantial" amendments that "the people expect," like the right of instruction. In contemplating the constitutional amendments produced by the first Congress in response to Madison's proposal, Virginian Anti-Federalist Richard Henry Lee complained that it was "too much the fashion now to look at the rights of the People" with extreme suspicion. In Federalists' hands "[t]he [E]nglish language has been carefully culled to find words feeble in their Nature or doubtful in their meaning!" The final text failed to express how, under a constitution in which the people were the sovereign, they would also rule and be ruled.[78]

The collective rights of the people as the ruler in America were not matters of mystery. A year before the first Congress's debate on a federal bill of rights, Elbridge Gerry advocated some of the essentials. Rather than "vague" statements, what Americans needed, according to Gerry, was an explicit declaration of "political axioms" and "established truths." Those "truths" included the existence of government for the common benefit of "the people" rather than any "class of men"; that "the origin of all power is in the people, and that they have an incontestable right to check the creatures of their own creation"; and that if representatives acted "contrary to the wishes" of their constituents, "the people have an undoubted right to reject their decisions [and] to call for a revision of their conduct." Gerry's litany echoed many state bills of rights that described a more active, ongoing role of the people serving as the ruler as well as the ruled in governments they established as the sovereign. It was a role that most Federalists who dominated the first Congress were unwilling to promote or describe in a federal bill of rights.[79]

Although Madison's proposal avoided general principles of constitutionalism and focused on individual rights of a minority beset by majority rule, disagreements among Americans over their constitutionalism did not fail to arise. No one contested the basis of American constitutionalism: that in America the people were the sovereign. This idea, Madison noted, was a matter of agreement "on all hands," but this unanimity did not signal a consensus on other aspects of that constitutionalism. For example, like many Federalists, Madison argued that the sovereign under the federal Constitution would be recognized as speaking only when the sovereign spoke in accord with the procedures the constitution set out for such communication or involvement. Whether the sovereign people under the constitution was bound in procedural chains arose quickly in the debate over adoption of a federal bill of rights. It surfaced in the issue of whether the people could amend the federal Constitution the same way they put it into place, by circumventing established procedures for amendment. Federalists answered this in the negative, asserting that Article V now established the only way in which the sovereign people could be recognized as amending their fundamental law. Anti-Federalists thought this interpretation contradicted the idea of the people's sovereignty. Moreover, it seemed paradoxical in light of how readily the Federalists ignored the procedures for amendment set forth in the Articles of Confederation.[80]

When Congress began to consider amendments to the constitution, the Anti-Federalist Theodorick Bland of Virginia introduced his state's request for another convention to revise the constitution. Madison and other Federalists insisted that the amending procedures of the constitution in Article V did not give Congress "deliberative power" on the issue until two-thirds of the remaining state legislatures joined such a petition. Bland, however, thought discussing the merits of a convention was not an "unconstitutional step." The South Carolina Anti-Federalist Thomas Tudor Tucker agreed. He had a different "point of view" from that of Madison on Article V. For Tucker, Congress needed to act if two-thirds of the states applied for a convention. Nonetheless, "if this should not happen, they were at liberty to exercise their discretion."[81]

James Wilson's reaction illustrated that not all Federalists assumed that procedures constrained the people's inherent right to revise their constitutions. Like other Federalists, Wilson spoke in sweeping terms about the authority of the sovereign people. In Pennsylvania's ratifying convention, for example, Wilson argued that sovereignty "*resides* in the PEOPLE, as the fountain of government." He also argued that "the supreme, absolute, and uncontrollable power *remains* in the people" and that they "may change the constitutions whenever and however they please. This is a right, of which no positive institution can ever deprive them." He continued to endorse this position in a metaphor he invoked in his Law Lectures of 1790. In those Lectures Wilson compared constitutions to clay in the hands of a potter. Just as a potter could shape the clay, "[a] majority of the society" was sufficient to "mould" and "finish" constitutions as "they please."[82]

Federalists supported Madison's motion simply to acknowledge Virginia's request of another convention in the House's Journal. That decision vindicated the position that Article V exclusively controlled constitutional revision. Madison's advocacy of a bill of rights revealed his commitment to the right of the people as the collective sovereign to revise their governments, but subject to the procedures specified in the constitution. Thus, Madison's language in his proposed declaration prefaced to the constitution – that "the people have an indubitable, unalienable, and indefeasible right to reform or change their government, whenever it be found adverse or inadequate to the purposes of its institution" – came with a crucial, if implicit, limitation. At this point in time, Madison did not endorse the right of the people to alter (much less abolish) constitutions independent of the governments they created. As he explained: "My idea of the sovereignty of the people is, that the people can change the constitution if they please, but while the constitution exists, they must conform themselves to its dictates."[83] Its "dictates" included the requirements of Article V. At this stage Madison shared the views of other Federalists such as Alexander Hamilton and George Washington in identifying constraints on constitutional revision by the sovereign people.

The Anti-Federalist Elbridge Gerry offered a different constitutional understanding of the collective sovereign. He responded that if, "while the government exists," the people "have no right to control it, it appears they have divested themselves of the sovereignty over the constitution." Rather than cede sovereignty to government, it was far more consistent with constitution-making since the Revolution to conclude that the people retained an inherent authority to exercise their sovereignty. Ultimately, this was compatible with the Anti-Federalists' rejection of the "fashionable language" that the "COMMON PEOPLE HAVE NO BUSINESS TO TROUBLE THEMSELVES ABOUT GOVERNMENT."[84]

The Select Committee that considered Madison's proposed amendments reported back and deleted the language regarding the people's right to "reform or change their government." Such a principle need not be added to the federal Constitution, even if it was qualified, as Madison asserted, by the "dictates" of Article V. Like other language articulating the source of government as resting on the sovereign people for whose benefit government existed, the committee was unwilling to insert text amplifying the relationship between the sovereign and the national government that emphasized the subordination of government to the people and the active role of the people to scrutinize their governors.[85]

Explicit recognition of the power of constitutional language emerged when the House debated whether the First Amendment should identify the right of the people to "instruct representatives." Concern about that provision entailed the perception that using such words might give the people overly broad ideas about their rights. The debate also reinforced the determination of some representatives to identify a more constrained constitutional role for the people.

The effort by Anti-Federalist Thomas Tudor Tucker to include language of instruction directly addressed the issue of the role of the collective sovereign. Moreover, that effort raised the question of how explicitly the constitutional principle of the subordination of the government to the people should be stated. Five years earlier Tucker had published a pamphlet defending the "undoubted right" of instructing representatives as a right "inherent in the people" that ought to be constitutionally recognized. Tucker's position rested on his understanding that "the people at large" were "the true sovereign." It also reflected his faith in their capacity to act reasonably in identifying and protecting their rights.[86]

Those favoring instruction argued that the people were entitled to express their views to their representatives. The Federalist John Page considered the denial of a right of instruction a "dangerous" and "subversive" doctrine. As he put it, "Our government is derived from the people, of consequence the people have a right to consult for the common good; but to what end will this be done, if they have not the power of instructing their representatives?" Page acknowledged that American republics were representative governments, not pure democracies. Still, instruction was "strictly compatible" with "the spirit and the nature" of "a government of the people." Although the people gave "part of their authority" to their representatives, "to refuse them the power of instructing their agents" seemed "to deny them a right." The Anti-Federalist Elbridge Gerry thought rejecting instruction repudiated the sovereignty in the people. Congress might as well "say that the sovereignty existed in the people" but not after "the establishment of this government."[87]

Opponents of instruction worried that the proposed amendment would "mislead the people" by suggesting that they could control legislative debates. Thomas Hartley of Pennsylvania thought instruction was "attended with danger" and liable to "great abuses." Likewise, the Federalist Jeremiah Wadsworth of Connecticut saw "a mischievous tendency" in the proposed amendment. Opponents of instruction characterized the debate as whether the independent judgment of representatives would be swept aside in favor of binding instructions. George Clymer of Pennsylvania claimed that a "constitutional right" to instruction meant "we are bound by those instructions." Madison also suggested that the issue of instruction implied their binding nature.[88]

Elbridge Gerry denied that a right of instruction necessarily meant they would be binding. Rather, representatives retained a "liberty to act" subject to not being reelected if they ignored the wishes of their constituents. Instruction only provided the people a "convenient" means of expressing themselves "to their agents." Another Anti-Federalist, Thomas Sumter from Virginia, complained that opponents of instruction "do not treat it fairly." According to Sumter, the underlying issue was whether representatives should "notice" instructions and "obey them as far as is consistent and proper." Although the amendment did not make instructions binding, Gerry nonetheless thought the people had the right to make them binding. He pointed out that "the friends and patrons of this constitution have always declared that the sovereignty resides in the people, and that they do not part with it on any occasion." That principle "seemed inconsistent with what gentlemen now asserted." "[I]f the people were the sovereign he could not conceive why they had not the right to instruct and direct their agents at their pleasure." Gerry also responded to those who argued that the people already possessed the right of sharing their views with their representatives: "if so, why not declare it?" Gerry saw "much good" in the amendment. "[T]he people will be encouraged to come forward with their instructions, which will form a fund of useful information for the legislature."[89]

Opponents of instruction wanted the wise and virtuous to rule because they thought the common people undermined representative government. Encouraging ordinary people to express themselves and offer opinions to representatives was the last thing that opponents of instruction wanted. George Clymer considered instruction "a most dangerous principle, utterly destructive" of an "independent and deliberative body." It undercut the judgment of men of "abilities and experience." While Elbridge Gerry doubted if "all the wisdom of this country is concentrated within the walls of this house," that presumption underlay the refinement of government leadership. Opponents of instruction did not share Gerry's faith that "unheard of and unseen" citizens could benefit American government by "a watchful observance of public men and public measures." Gerry's vision of "the people" interacting with their elected officials on a regular basis contrasted with a more passive and quiescent role for the people advocated by Madison and many other Federalists. Gerry and others simply disagreed with Madison's assertion in *Federalist No. 63* that representation under American constitutions necessarily implied *"the total exclusion of the people in their collective capacity from any share"* in the administration of government.[90]

The House decisively rejected a right to instruct (and hence refused to identify the relationship between the collective sovereign and their representatives as that between a principal and its agent). Thereafter it sent the following language as the basis of what became the First Amendment to the Senate: "The Freedom of Speech, and of the Press, and the right of the People peaceably to assemble, and to consult for their common good, and to apply to the Government for a redress of grievances, shall not be infringed." The Senate also agreed with the House's rejection of the right to instruct, but in addition, deleted the phrase "consult for their common good" and substituted the word "petition" for "apply." Those changes further emphasized a subordination of the people.[91]

Federalists did not betray the Revolution. Rather they questioned the constitutional settlement expressed in America's first constitutions. They never denied the fundamental principle that a majority of the sovereign people formed the foundation of constitutions. Indeed, Federalists embraced the authority of the collective sovereign as the means of establishing the federal Constitution. Yet many were reluctant to acknowledge, much less encourage, the role of the people as the ruler. The Federalist position, however, simply underscored the tension inherent in the American commitment to the sovereignty of the people. From the time of the Revolution the principle of a collective sovereign united Americans at the basic level of their constitutionalism, while it yielded different possibilities of how that authority of the people might or might not play itself out. Differences in how one cast the role of the people in relation to government could support a wide range of political objectives. The indeterminate nature of the constitutional implications of the sovereignty of the people that so confused Dr. Whiting during the Massachusetts Regulation also befuddled Anti-Federalists in the aftermath of the federal convention. In 1789, Richard Henry Lee lamented to Samuel Adams about the reversal of ideas associated with the Revolution. "But so wonderfully are mens minds now changed upon the subject of liberty" that it seemed as if "the sentiments which universally prevailed in 1774" were ancient "visions, and not the solid reason of fifteen years ago!"[92]

Politics and personal views changed, but commitment to the sovereignty of the people remained a constant, if confusing, consensus because of the principle's ability to convey different meanings over time. Nine months before declaring the people "that pure original fountain of all legitimate authority," Alexander Hamilton described sovereignty in New York as located in that state's government, not in the people. In advancing a legislative solution to Vermont's independence, Hamilton located sovereignty in government. Later, however, in justifying the federal Constitution, Hamilton invoked the sovereignty of the people. Equally indicative of the supple utility of the authority of the sovereign people was how conservative opponents of Pennsylvania's "radical" 1776 constitution bypassed its procedures for constitutional revision. They argued that "the people" as the sovereign could replace the existing constitution. Ironically the people's sovereign authority justified a new constitution in 1790 limiting the political role of "the people."[93]

In a similarly counterintuitive fashion, the Maryland Anti-Federalist Luther Martin rejected the collective right of the people to alter constitutions when he opposed the use of state conventions to ratify the federal Constitution. If adopted, the federal Constitution would "*alter* the *constitution* of *this State*; and as our constitution had pointed out a mode by which, and by which *only*, alterations were to be made," use of a state convention to ratify the federal Constitution was "a *direct violation*" of Maryland's constitution. Martin's position identified a sovereign that was not free to ignore the "mode" by which the constitution mandated the course of revision. In addition, he embraced a Lockean, prerevolutionary version of the right to "alter or abolish" governments. According to Martin, "once the people have *exercised their power in establishing and forming* themselves into a *State government*, it never *devolves back* to them, nor have they a *right* to *resume* or *again to exercise that power*, until such events take place as will amount to a *dissolution* of their *State government*."[94]

Such diverse positions illustrated the attraction of appeals to the sovereignty of the people even as they suggested ambiguity about the constitutional authority of the collective sovereign. The conflicting uses to which the people's authority was applied foreshadowed the continuing struggle among Americans over how they viewed that sovereignty. From London in late 1787 John Adams wrote Thomas Jefferson in Paris anticipating that the federal Constitution would not only "preserve the Union" but "bring us all to the same mode of thinking." Ultimately, however, the formation and ratification of the constitution confirmed the persistence of competing constitutional visions. The federal Framers anticipated a more passive role for the people in the document they drafted and deliberately avoided suggesting the people's ability to assume the role of the ruler. They claimed that henceforth the collective sovereign would be guided by established procedures. Even so, a different view of the people's sovereignty – one that posited a direct, active role for the people and stressed their ability to rule as well as be ruled – did not die with the constitution's ratification. As Benjamin Rush observed in 1787, although military conflict with Britain had ended, in terms of the American "revolution . . . nothing but the first act of the great drama is closed."[95]

It soon became clear in a dramatic struggle over a federal excise tax on whiskey that the federal Constitution had not put to rest divergent constitutional views. Those who protested the tax invoked the constitutional right of the people to petition government and gather to formulate their objections and grievances. Alexander Hamilton, who so eloquently championed the sovereignty of the people during the ratification of the constitution, saw no relevance in the people's sovereignty when it came to excise tax protesters. Now, only a few years later, Hamilton urged the criminal prosecution of people attending conventions that criticized the national government in which he served. He asserted that such conventions were unconstitutional and illegitimate. Despite John Adams's hope, Americans failed to reach agreement about the sovereign people, notwithstanding the efforts of Federalists to claim a uniform, singular understanding of its constitutional implications.

6 Testing the Constitutionalism of 1787

The Whiskey "Rebellion" in Pennsylvania

The summer of 1794 found President George Washington mobilizing an army to subdue opposition in western Pennsylvania to a whiskey excise tax – part of a major initiative of his administration. A call for militia from New Jersey, Pennsylvania, Maryland, and Virginia eventually formed an army of nearly 13,000 men – more troops than the general commanded during most of the Revolution. The necessity for this "resort to military coercion," according to Washington, came from "misguided or designing men" who were attempting "to poison and discontent the minds of the people against the government; particularly by endeavouring to have it believed that their liberties were assailed." In late September, Washington led a military expedition toward "the Country of Whiskey," accompanied by Alexander Hamilton, his secretary of the treasury and the author of the excise.

By early October, Washington and Hamilton reached the town of Carlisle, on the eastern side of the Alleghenies, where the general inspected militia troops. From Carlisle, Washington continued westward to Fort Cumberland, making more inspections and evaluating whether to lead the troops personally over the mountains into western Pennsylvania. If the formation of the army sufficiently dissipated opposition to the excise he could return to Philadelphia, where Congress would meet in early November.

From information gathered at Cumberland, it was "evident" to Washington "that the people in the Western Counties of this State" were "very much alarmed at the approach of the Army." Although this suggested he could safely return to the capital, Washington remained convinced that "nothing but coercion, & example will reclaim & bring" opponents of the excise tax "to a due & unequivocal submission to the Laws." Before heading back, Washington proceeded still further west to Bedford, a final staging area for the army and where he said farewell to his troops. He told them they were engaged in "a service" designed "to consolidate and to preserve the blessings" of the American Revolution.

At Bedford, Washington learned of the capture of seventy-three-year-old Herman Husband on the evening of October 20, 1794. Unlike some protesters of the excise, Husband had not roughed up tax collectors nor called for violent resistance to the excise. In fact, he was a committed pacifist. Nonetheless, Washington considered Husband one of the "Insurgents – or abetters of the Insurrection" responsible for threatening his administration and the federal Constitution. Washington hoped that "by Hook, or by Crook," Hamilton would send Husband and several others also arrested to Philadelphia for their "winter Quarters," where their prosecution might set an example for what one supporter of Washington called "the opposers of Government."

The oddity that Husband, an elderly man who attended some of the meetings organized to protest the excise tax, but who consistently argued against violent opposition to the government, became a key military target of Washington's administration was explainable. The answer lay in the ideas Husband spread through numerous pamphlets, tracts, and speeches criticizing the federal Constitution and the administration's fiscal policies. For Washington, Husband precisely fit the bill of one of those "designing men" the president thought were misleading the people and generating opposition to his administration that would not otherwise exist.

Husband disagreed with Washington's assumption that "the people" would have supported his administration but for "designing men." While he criticized Washington's policies and urged the repeal of the excise tax, Husband did not believe that scrutiny of and involvement in government was limited to natural leaders or those with educational and economic advantages. As he put it, the "natural Capacities" of "a good Mechanick, or good Farmer" meant that they were "also capable" of making "a good Assembly-man to rule the State."

In fact, Husband advanced a vision of American constitutionalism that challenged Washington's understanding of the relationship between the people and their national government. The constitutional truth Husband embraced was that "Government is formed in all Things for the Good of the People governed, and that it is their Right to choose all their Officers, as their Servants and Stewards." Before reviewing the draft federal Constitution of 1787, Husband "read over" the "former constitutions and bills of rights of the several United States." He had high hopes for the proposed federal Constitution because of the involvement of Benjamin Franklin and George Washington. In reading and then re-reading the draft, however, Husband became convinced that "the alteration was unfavourable to liberty" and that the Framers "were introducing tyranny."

Husband objected to the constitution because it failed to specify the sovereign authority of the people – whose general welfare and not the interests of select individuals was the sole object of government – the subordinate role of all officers of the federal government (including the president) as "trustees and servants of the people" who were "at all times accountable to them," and the people's ongoing right to scrutinize government and those officials, including the right to remove them from office and alter or abolish that government at will. Because the "common happiness of every individual" and not the enrichment of a "set of speculators" was the only "aim" of government, Husband thought the fiscal policies of Washington's administration were sorely lacking.

Husband's constitutional views were linked to his religious faith and millennialism. As the son of a well-to-do tobacco farmer in the Chesapeake Bay, Husband – like many others – underwent a spiritual change after hearing the captivating English evangelical George Whitfield preach in 1739. That experience led him on a lifelong search to look within himself to find religious meaning and to reject the hierarchies of established churches. Eventually, he came to believe that the New Jerusalem prophesied in the Book of Ezekiel would be fulfilled in America, triggered by Independence. He realized that some viewed him as "fanatical," but Husband simply believed that God chose America to be the site of the fulfillment of "the free principles of government," which included "all the first constitutions" of America's new states.

His struggle to perfect American governments and preserve the blessings of the Revolution ended with his arrest. Washington and Hamilton succeeded in capturing Husband, but they failed to make an example of him. Although prosecuted for seditious speech, a jury drawn from residents around Philadelphia found him not guilty. After seven months in jail, Husband was released and headed home to Bedford on May 12, 1795. He never made it. On his way out of Philadelphia, he collapsed, developed pneumonia, and eventually died on June 19.[1]

The emphasis on the authority of the people since Independence reinforced a constitutionalism that developed from the logic of a collective sovereign. If the sovereign people created constitutions that established governments, then those governments were necessarily subordinate to their creator, the people. For those who accepted that relationship between the people and their government, the people naturally played a role as the ruler to monitor government. In watching over their agents, the people could always give those agents instructions and, if need be, turn them out of office. Even when not acting in such a capacity, the people were entitled – as individual citizens and groups of citizens – to scrutinize the conduct of government in their capacity as the ruled. Under such a view, the rights to petition, instruct, and assemble to criticize government officials as well as to establish societies that questioned government policies all seemed appropriate behavior under a constitutional system in which the people were the ruler and the sovereign, as well as the ruled.

These views of the relationship of the people to their government that emphasized the role of the people as the ruler and an active role for the ruled were supported by a constitutionalism expressed in state constitutions.[2] That constitutionalism prompted some Americans to scrutinize their governments and seek greater participation for the ruled in political affairs. Other Americans – including George Washington and many of his fellow delegates to the federal constitutional convention – were troubled by that vision of constitutionalism. Particularly after the creation of the federal Constitution, the emphasis on the people as rulers seemed misguided and misplaced. In response, they advanced a relationship between the people and the government that came close to turning the constitutionalism drawn from the state constitutions on its head.

Even so, Washington and like-minded Americans did not reject the central tenet of American constitutionalism: that in America the people were the sovereign. Instead, those agreeing with Washington accepted the idea of a collective sovereign while resisting the conclusion that the people should play a role as the ruler after the formation of government. The federal Constitution was expected to channel the people and temper some of the exuberance of their involvement that had surfaced under state governments since Independence. Even as Federalists used the unlimited authority of the people as the sovereign to justify the formation of the federal Constitution, they provided a distinct understanding of the relationship of the people to government.

Some Federalists expressed this constitutional understanding by favoring the refinement of "natural" leaders under the national government, emphasizing elections as the primary if not exclusive means of how the people were to scrutinize government, and by opposing instruction and other direct means to influence representatives. Moreover, the relationship they described between the people and the national government did not spell out the expectations and rights of the collective sovereign – including the right to alter or abolish government – as did many state constitutions. Importantly, the relationship those Federalists described failed to emphasize the role for the people as the ruler to monitor the constitutional order established by the federal Constitution.

This description of the relationship between the people and government and the more muted version of the collective sovereign advanced by framers of the federal Constitution was immediately challenged during the debates over its ratification as well as during Washington's presidency. Debates in the first Congress over instructing representatives underscored competing views of what role the people should play in monitoring the national government. Those differences reflected some of the opposition to the federal Constitution itself. James Madison identified the reason many opponents of the proposed national government considered the absence of a bill of rights an important defect of the constitution. Madison observed that since the Revolution, many Americans had become "accustomed" to having state bills of rights "interposed" between them and government officials. Much of the language and many of the principles in those state bills of rights were not found in the federal Constitution.[3]

If language emphasizing the subordination of government to the collective sovereign or to the people as the ruler was missing in the federal Constitution, it continued to surface in the ways Americans described their governments – and not simply by former opponents of the constitution. Indeed, the persistence, if not the contagiousness, of the vocabulary of constitutionalism spawned by the Revolution is reflected in the opinions of two prominent Federalists and justices of the U.S. Supreme Court shortly after the ratification of the constitution. In *Chisholm v. Georgia* (1793), Chief Justice John Jay noted that after the Revolution, "sovereignty devolved on the people," who "truly" became "the sovereigns of the country." Thereafter, American "Governors are the agents of the people, and at most stand in the same relation to their sovereign, in which regents in Europe stand to their sovereigns." Likewise, Justice James Wilson noted the "confusion" from forgetting that "the Supreme Power resides in the body of the people." As "subordinate to the People," government in America could not be the sovereign. Overlooking this truth produced the "perversion" of governors wishing "to be considered as the sovereigns of the State" and was a "supercilious" attempt to attain "preeminence above the people."[4]

Thus, some Federalists like Jay and Wilson used language that reinforced the idea of government officials as agents of the people and rejected the concept that government, rather than the people, was the sovereign. By 1793, however, other Federalists, including Washington and members of his administration, suggested quite the opposite. By then, objections to a federal excise tax were culminating in the so-called Whiskey Rebellion in Pennsylvania. Protests against that excise tax were an early test of whether the relationship of the people to the national government some saw reflected in the federal Constitution should carry the day against the constitutionalism of the revolutionary-era constitutions.[5]

BACKGROUND OF THE WHISKEY EXCISE TAX PROTESTS

The broader context of the so-called Whiskey Rebellion illustrates how the struggle over the excise tax involved competing visions of American constitutionalism. Those differences surfaced when many of Pennsylvania's rural inhabitants resisted their state's fiscal and tax policies during the 1780s. During the postrevolutionary period, Pennsylvanians – and in particular rural farmers – suffered massive property foreclosures. These foreclosures stemmed from a condition that other states also faced: a severe shortage of money and credit.

In Pennsylvania, the shortage of hard currency affected Philadelphia merchants as well as rural farmers and had a ripple effect. As merchants sued country storekeepers to recover unpaid debts, storekeepers in turn sued their customers, who might well call in their own debts, contributing to a collapse of the network of credit crucial to the rural economy. Between 1782 and 1792 in the eastern county of Berks, some 3,400 writs of foreclosure were issued. That number was enough to foreclose two-thirds of the taxable population of the county. Matters were even worse in the western counties. During that same decade in Westmoreland County, over 6,000 writs of foreclosure were issued against goods and land for a population of some 2,800 taxpayers. In the decade of the 1780s more than half the citizens of that county whose property was foreclosed evidently lost their farms. By the decade's end they disappeared from Pennsylvania census rolls for the state's western regions.[6]

The economic hardships faced by the displaced farmers in western Pennsylvania were not simply the result of general economic conditions. Rather, they arose from government policies to redeem the war debt that reduced the supply of money and credit. In the postwar decades, although Pennsylvania's two main political factions clearly had their differences, both supported efforts to reduce the supply of paper money and public credit (as well as the enforcement of taxes to pay off the war debt). Farmers and others adversely affected by the constriction of the money supply blamed those policies for the mass of property foreclosures in the state. Moreover, they also clearly perceived government's policies as benefiting a select class of the population at the expense of those who were losing their farms and property because they could not pay their taxes.

Investors in the promissory notes that the Continental Congress had issued to soldiers, farmers, and others to fund the war were especially identified as reaping disproportionate benefits at the expense of the bulk of the populace. As those notes depreciated in value they were often sold by their holders to speculators at a fraction of their face value. Eventually those notes became consolidated in the hands of relatively few individuals – by 1790 over 96 percent of Pennsylvania's nearly $5 million in war debt certificates were held by some 400 people. The question of redeeming that debt offered the possibility of great profit for the note holders who lobbied for yearly interest payments on the notes and their eventual redemption at face value rather than the discounted price at which they might have been bought. The Pennsylvania legislature's decision to raise taxes tied to payments of interest and principal to those who held war debt notes placed more pressure on the money supply. At the same time it gave economic benefits to a few. For example, after the state's legislature issued $400,000 in paper money in 1785, two-thirds of that sum went directly into the Philadelphia bank accounts of sixty-seven note holders as payment of the yearly interest on their notes.[7]

Farmers viewed the adoption and implementation of state tax policies as a betrayal of the constitutional principles established by the collective sovereign in Pennsylvania's 1776 constitution. Pennsylvania's constitution clearly explained that government was "instituted for the common benefit" of "the people" and not for the special "advantage of any single man, family, or sett of men." In the 1780s, farmers sent a stream of petitions to the legislature objecting to the granting of benefits to a few at the expense and sacrifice of many others. The "spirit and design" of Pennsylvania's constitution, according to Herman Husband, was to make sure that "individual families or parties" did not particularly profit from the operation of government. As such, Husband was disappointed that the draft federal Constitution did not endorse the distribution of western lands in "small portions" to avoid the monopolization of vast tracts in the hands of individuals. Likewise, he wanted to force present holders of "large quantities" of land "to divide them equally at their death among their children and near relations." Husband's plan did not confiscate land to redistribute it equally but rather sought to avoid disproportionate concentration of land ownership in individuals. That policy would eventually promote greater overall equality in land holding.[8]

Policies that provided grossly disproportionate benefits for the few undermined the public welfare and subverted "the dearest rights of the people." Pennsylvania's constitution asserted that the people, as the collective sovereign of the state, had "the right to reform, alter, or abolish government in such manner as shall be by that community judged most conducive to the public weal." Additionally, as the constitution's preamble noted, whenever government failed to protect the public welfare, "the people" have a right to "take such measures as to them may appear necessary to promote their safety and happiness."[9]

In responding to their economic plight, Pennsylvania farmers did not act as the sovereign – they did not claim they were the body of the people in action who were invoking their right to alter or abolish government. In the early stages of their protest of government policies, they positioned themselves as the ruled, in launching a series of petition campaigns. Subsequently, however, their actions took on the role of the ruler in defying government policies that their agents, their legislators, had promulgated, but which arguably exceeded the authority granted them by the sovereign. The sovereign, the people, had given instructions – enshrined in the state constitution – not to favor the few over the many. The legislative agents were now blatantly violating those instructions.

Since both political factions in the state appeared united in supporting policies the farmers thought violated the state's constitution, farmers took steps to check the actions of their agents. Their strategy involved acting directly or with the cooperation of local county officials to thwart the collection of taxes tied to the redemption of the war bonds. To prevent the loss of farmers' property for nonpayment of taxes, county revenue officials declined to collect taxes, locally elected county justices rejected requests to prosecute delinquent taxpayers, juries failed to convict local officials for not collecting state taxes, and local constables refused to deliver warrants or arrest delinquent taxpayers. Even when tax prosecutions ended in convictions, farmers employed a technique that stymied auctions of property foreclosure sales. As tax officials explained, when their neighbors' property became subject to foreclosure, locals attended the foreclosure sale in large numbers but did not "offer to purchase" or "give a single bid." By such means, the farmers as some of Pennsylvania's rulers sought to negate laws they thought violated the state's constitution.[10]

Another method to frustrate the collection of taxes in Pennsylvania, employed in the fall of 1787 and continuing into the 1790s, was the closing of roads. This practice was dramatic not only because of the extraordinary effort expended to render roads impassable but also because of the self-inflicted hardship it imposed on the road-closers and their neighbors. Nonetheless, by digging ditches or holes, or by otherwise barricading roads, farmers sought to stop sheriffs' auctions from being held or at the very least to prevent the buyers of goods at such foreclosure sales from leaving with auctioned property. These road closings sought to disrupt if not stop the county courts from operating. Even if the road closings did not completely isolate the court, the obstacles offered a convenient excuse for nonattendance by witnesses, jurors, local constables, or other officials sympathetic to the farmers. While largely a backcountry phenomenon, the road closings, like the court closings during the Massachusetts Regulation, were by no means an essentially "western" occurrence. Indeed, roads were closed a mere twenty-five miles outside of Philadelphia.[11]

The road closings and other strategies of tax protest by rural Pennsylvanians signaled the frustration of the ruler with the policies of its wayward legislative agent. The frequent collusion of local officials in evading taxation, while partly a function of intimidation, seemed mainly a result of shared sympathies. Living in the rural communities made it easier to share the perspective that the economic burdens placed on farmers benefited a small "sett of men." By coordinating with the rural populace, local officials sent the message that the rulers did not recognize the legitimacy of the actions of government. Pennsylvania's political leadership, however, saw the protests as growing anarchy. As the bond speculator and soon to be elected Federalist representative to the first Congress Thomas FitzSimons put it, the tax protest simply caused "alarm."[12]

Pennsylvania's political leaders responded to the tax protests by passing laws to penalize government officials who refused to perform their duties. In addition, a new state constitution cut the electoral tie between county officials and the protesters. Instead of locally electing justices of the peace as under the 1776 constitution, the 1790 constitution gave the governor the power to appoint the justices. The new constitution also expanded the jurisdiction of the county court of common pleas (whose judges were also to be appointed by the governor) and gave that court oversight of the justices of the peace. Those justices were now removable not only on conviction of crimes or "misbehavior," but also "on the address of both houses of the legislature."[13]

Even before revisions to the state's constitution, some Pennsylvanians concerned about the tax protest and the threat it posed to investments in the war bonds participated in creating a new federal constitution. The constitution drafted in Philadelphia in 1787 authorized federally appointed revenue agents, prosecutors, and judges to oversee the collection of future taxes imposed by the national government. Moreover, it granted formidable powers to the president, to call up state militias for suppressing resistance – including tax protests – in any state.

The subsequent protest of Pennsylvania farmers and rural inhabitants to the federal excise tax was not unique – the tax faced widespread resistance in many other states. In that respect, the so-called Whiskey Rebellion did not occur because of conditions or attitudes unique to western Pennsylvania.

However, the tax protests in Pennsylvania and the Washington administration's efforts to suppress tax protesters presented a contrast in visions. Those who objected to the excise tax and eventually resisted its enforcement in Pennsylvania believed in a revolutionary constitutionalism that posited a real and active role for the people as the ruler in its relationship with government conceived of as the people's agent. Those in the federal government, on the other hand, considered the people's role at an end when they elected their representatives. Washington and his supporters associated that view with the formation of the federal Constitution. Although the constitution raised the question of the relationship of "the people" to a national government and not to their state governments, the underlying issues of constitutionalism were the same: what did the acceptance of a collective sovereign mean in terms of how the people might act as the sovereign, the ruler, and the ruled?

THE WHISKEY EXCISE TAX OF 1791

Before enactment of the federal excise tax, western Pennsylvania farmers resisted a state-imposed tax on whiskey dating from 1783. The effectiveness of farmers' efforts against the despised state tax led to its repeal. Their success illustrated the power of collective action. A "general Patriotic Convention" was convened in January 1787 in Pennsylvania's Washington County. The convention wanted "an amendment of the excise laws" and "particularly instructed" state legislators on their responsibility to relieve economic distress. Organizational efforts continued to seek a repeal of the tax. For instance, in 1790, a petition circulated in Pennsylvania's Westmoreland County. It expressed frontier residents' "general disapprobation" and "universal abhorrence and detestation" of the state excise tax, a reaction they thought Pennsylvanians generally shared.[14]

As a practical matter, the organized protests of the state excise rendered that tax a dead letter in western Pennsylvania. Settlers felt vindicated when the legislature repealed the state whiskey tax. Their protest also highlighted a growing division between rural Pennsylvania and more urbanized areas of the state. For instance, from Philadelphia, Dr. Benjamin Rush felt farmers were misdirecting their time and effort in looking toward government to relieve their economic distresses. Farmers spent too much time "attending Constitutional meetings at taverns" and not enough "improving their farms," which was where they should be looking for economic prosperity. The farmers' involvement in government led them to seek changes that came at the expense of the state as a whole. In this light, some Federalists in Pennsylvania considered the farmers' petitions for repeal of the state whiskey excise tax "clearly extralegal." The resort to organized protest was "a seditious remnant" of the earlier days of the Revolution, when the people sought to exert control over government. Now that the people could vote and express themselves during elections, they need not give directives to the government between elections.[15]

Coincidentally, two months after the Pennsylvania legislature repealed the state whiskey excise tax, a federal whiskey excise tax went into effect. The reaction to the federal tax, however, was not a coincidence. The disdain for a whiskey tax was rooted in more than the fact that it was an excise. Excise taxes were long-hated forms of taxation in the Anglo-American world, in no small measure due to the intrusive way they were collected and the sweeping powers they gave collectors. However, the depth of the opposition to the federal excise tax, among farmer and other rural inhabitants in Pennsylvania and elsewhere, arose from a clear understanding of how the excise would discriminate against them as opposed to a small number of larger distillers.[16]

The tax on spirits was a key part of Alexander Hamilton's finance plan for the national government. That tax would fund interest payments on the national debt, which would grow when the federal government assumed the states' war debt. Hamilton portrayed whiskey as an extravagance. Its taxation as a "pernicious" luxury, he asserted, would not only raise needed revenue but would also promote public health by curbing the consumption of alcohol. Americans – including those at the highest levels of political leadership – consumed enormous quantities of spirits at the time, but whiskey also served as a crucial medium of exchange in the economy of cash-poor rural areas. Given the long distance to markets, reducing the bulky harvest of grains into a compact distillation of whiskey was the only cost-effective way to move the product to market. It enabled one to be more than a subsistence farmer. Trading whiskey was the only practical way to get credit or currency to stay afloat, to pay taxes and debts, and to obtain needed supplies – it played a vital role in the economy of the western counties of Pennsylvania.[17]

Because of the extensive use of whiskey as currency, small farmers and laborers in Pennsylvania experienced the excise as an income tax. The law required federal revenue officers to collect the tax at the point of production of the whiskey, with payment in hard currency. This created a particular hardship for the western farmers, as they distilled whiskey to acquire hard currency. Nonpayment of the tax subjected distillers to fines that when not paid led to confiscation of the whiskey still. A further burden small distillers faced was the requirement to register stills, failure of which subjected them to fines they likely could not pay and once again led to seizure of the still. In contrast to how the excise affected the many small and individual distillers scattered in the backcountry, its operation offered distinct advantages to the handful of large distillers in urban areas. In depicting the excise as a tax on consumption rather than production, Hamilton shifted attention away from the particular burdens the tax placed on small distillers.[18]

For critics, the whiskey excise seemed ill conceived not only on the front end – in how it was to be collected – but also at the back end – in terms of where the collected tax would go. The excise ensured interest payments to holders of bonds and notes representing the nation's war debt. Many of these payments went to speculators, who managed to buy a great part of that debt for pennies on the dollar. These speculators' windfall would come at the expense of the farmer's participation in the rural economy. Inhabitants along the frontier, such as those in the western counties of Pennsylvania, considered themselves targeted by a disproportionate burden of the war debt.[19]

Protests of the excise tax prompted debates on its merits and the appropriateness of instructions to members of Congress. Just as it did under state constitutions, the issue of instruction raised the question of the nature of representation under the federal Constitution. That question arose when some state legislatures – in responding to protests against the excise – instructed their congressional representatives to vote against the measure.

In December 1790, North Carolina's legislature instructed its U.S. senators to "oppose every excise and direct taxation law" and to do so "strenuously" because such measures violated principles of a "republican economy." Samuel Johnston and Benjamin Hawkins, selected by the legislature as the state's senators under the provisions of the new federal Constitution, declined to follow the instruction. Both voted for the excise tax. Although the legislative instruction expressed "the sense of our fellow citizens" about the excise, the two senators felt that as members of the national legislature they ought to have a different focus. They should use their own "best Judgment" in matters concerning the national interest. On issues "affecting the State individually," however, they promised to give state legislative instructions "all that influence" the legislature could rightfully "expect."[20]

James Iredell, Senator Johnston's brother-in-law and a Federalist justice on the U.S. Supreme Court, endorsed that balance of local and national responsibilities. The legislature could lobby its senators against an excise tax because of its impact on the state. However, the legislature could not send binding instructions to state representatives with respect to the shape of national policy. Although the burden of discharging the national debt was "disagreeable to a great body of the people," Iredell thought the appropriate influence the legislature exerted on the senators was in selecting them – which it would do every six years. Once selected, senators should consider the national rather than merely the local interest.[21]

When the excise issue surfaced in the House of Representatives, some of North Carolina's representatives acknowledged the influence of legislative instructions. John Steele, a Federalist congressman and normally strong supporter of Hamilton, voted against the excise tax. His vote came from his sense of duty "to the people" of North Carolina and "to the Constitution," informed by the "opinion expressed" by the state's legislature in their instructions.[22]

The issue of instructions to congressional delegates in the 1790s raised the question of whether those elected to national councils were agents of those who elected them. Republican Senator William Maclay of Pennsylvania considered instructions a "responsibility" of senators as "servants of the public" and integral to the American system of republican representation. Federalists like Fisher Ames of Massachusetts considered that idea heresy. Debating a national excise tax both in state legislatures and in Congress invited "anarchy." Representation under the federal Constitution did not require multiple levels of discussion. Ames ridiculed the idea as coming from a "silly reliance" on "coffee house & congress prattlers" who suggested that representatives owed a special responsibility "to the people." From Ames's perspective, the use of instructions "disgraced . . . the history of popular bodies." Ames was not alone in his opposition. Senator Maclay observed that most other Federalist senators dismissed the idea of instruction. Senator Ralph Izard of South Carolina, for one, denied that legislatures had "any right to instruct at all." His fellow senator from Pennsylvania, Robert Morris, "violently opposed" the notion that they were subject to instruction.[23]

Nonetheless, many Americans were familiar and comfortable with the idea that the people could choose not only who would represent them but also how they would be represented on any particular matter. This practice surfaced under many state constitutions. In their view, there was nothing silly about thinking that the sovereign who created the federal Constitution would also play a similar role with regard to its representatives at the national level.

After Congress passed the federal excise tax in 1791, opposition seemed to increase. It surfaced in every state south of New York, with widespread resistance in North Carolina and Kentucky. The Treasury Department was hard-pressed to find people willing to act as tax collectors, particularly on the frontier. The difficulty of enforcing the law spread through the government. One lawyer identified the challenge of recruiting a U.S. attorney for Kentucky. "[T]he Excise is so very odious . . . no lawyer who has a reputation . . . will accept that Office." In those regions where opposition to the excise was so deep-seated that the effort to collect the tax was largely abandoned, organized protest was unnecessary. Western Pennsylvania became a testing ground because it seemed possible to overcome protests and to force compliance with the excise tax in that state while at the same time driving home an important lesson about the authority of the national government.[24]

EARLY PENNSYLVANIA PROTESTS, 1791–1792

Particularly alarming to Washington and Hamilton was the spread of organized protest against the excise tax. In meetings and conventions, people gathered to seek the repeal of the tax and to express their dissatisfaction. In mid-July 1791, one participant identified a "number of respectable characters" from Pennsylvania's Washington County who proposed meeting with "such gentlemen as chuse to come forward" to discuss the repeal of the excise. The participants would "state to the people at large some general objections" to the excise tax, take "their sense on that subject," and transmit it "to the general government."[25]

A little more than a week later, a meeting convened at Brownsville in Fayette County. Both Republicans and Federalists attended and decided the excise tax was "unequal in its operation" and particularly "oppressive and injurious to the inhabitants of the western country." Since the meeting represented only one county, they called for a multicounty convention to meet in Pittsburgh two months later. It would bring forth "the sense of the people" on the excise that could be expressed "with decency and firmness" in a petition to Congress.[26]

Following the Brownsville meeting, inhabitants of Washington County selected delegates to the Pittsburgh convention. The meeting recommended shunning excise officers and withholding "all aid, support and comfort." Some opponents of the excise tax would act on this language when they denied excise collectors "comfort" by tarring and feathering them. During the Pittsburgh convention on September 7, 1791, eleven delegates representing the western counties passed resolutions criticizing the fiscal policies of Washington's administration. "[U]nconscionable" bargains were permitted "where men seem to make fortunes by the fortuitous concurrence of circumstances, rather than by economic, virtuous and useful employment." The whiskey excise tax was "deservedly obnoxious" for discriminating "in its operations" and because duties would especially "fall heavy" on western regions. Their resolutions went to Congress as a petition.[27]

The petition was certainly an appropriate first step. Hugh Henry Brackenridge, a Princeton graduate, lawyer, and literary figure, participated in the convention. He was a former member of the Pennsylvania legislature and supported the federal Constitution, but broke with the Federalists soon after ratification, disagreeing with the federal excise tax. Criticizing the policy behind a law "after it is enacted, in order to procure a repeal" was just as legitimate as opposing its initial passage. Both actions were "constitutional." Stigmatizing excise officials who enforced a law such as the excise was consistent with republican principles and "public virtue," Brackenridge contended.[28]

Secretary of the Treasury Alexander Hamilton considered the Pittsburgh convention an "inflammatory" provocation. He particularly faulted the delegates for going beyond the excise tax and discussing the details of the government's fiscal policies. The convention's criticism, according to Hamilton, displayed an "unfriendly temper" toward the federal government. He did not see the activities of convention delegates as a legitimate expression of the right of citizens to scrutinize the operation of government. He denied the convention a right to seek reversal of congressional legislation, even if those delegates (representing the local leadership) thought the excise tax rewarded a small segment of the population at the expense of the many.[29]

Hamilton was also offended when the Pittsburgh convention's petitions were forwarded to him by Congress. Local revenue officials shared Hamilton's annoyance and attitude. John Neville, the Federalist inspector of the excise in western Pennsylvania, found it ridiculous when opponents of the tax declared "we are the people" and that Congress was "only our servants." The national government, he facetiously suggested, could hardly go wrong with "such able advisors" or "directors" who had little or no education or experience with government.[30]

Washington was troubled by the news of the protest meetings and conventions seeking repeal of the excise. He confided to his Secretary of State Thomas Jefferson that protest against the excise tax promoted disunion and "anarchy." It was a prelude to "monarchical government," he suspected. "[S]ubversion of the republican system of the Country," Hamilton had written him, would be the result of the "confusion" and "civil commotion" coming from these protests. This would drive the people into "the arms of monarchy." Proof could be found in the efforts to "embarrass ... the General Government & bring it under suspicion." The administration's opponents took "every opportunity" to do this. It seemed clear to the administration that encouraging poor farmers to protest the excise tax opened a back door to regaining a British-style monarchy in America. That was "the ultimate object" of protest organizers.[31]

Concern with the protest meetings in 1791 escalated with the news of another Pittsburgh convention in August 1792. Washington issued his first presidential proclamation on the subject of resistance to the tax as a result. Those in western Pennsylvania realized that protest of the excise tax came from directions other than those usually associated with public unrest. According to Excise Inspector Neville, the convention's twenty-four delegates included "leading men" and not "the rabble" of the region. After two days of "freely" debating the federal tax, delegates adopted resolutions and drafted a petition seeking its repeal. The petition was to be "signed by the people." The delegates acknowledged their "duty to persist" in "remonstrances" against the excise tax. They would employ "every other legal measure that may obstruct the operation of the [excise] Law." The people should sever social ties with anyone collecting the tax, treating them with the "contempt they deserve."[32]

The convention's determined stance against the excise tax alarmed the government and their supporters. The *Philadelphia General Advertiser* pondered the meaning of the convention's resolutions. Apparently concerned with the protesters' call to use "every other legal measure" to "obstruct the operation of the Law," the newspaper rhetorically asked, "Is not every measure tending to obstruct the operation of a constitutional law passed by legal representatives . . . illegal?" Hamilton responded by ordering the supervisor of the revenue for Pennsylvania, George Clymer, to gather "evidence" on convention participants including "the particulars of their behaviour" in anticipation of government prosecution. Their "persevering and violent" opposition, Hamilton feared, gave "the business" a "serious aspect," calling for "vigorous & decisive measures on the part of the Government" to suppress it. He urged the president to bring "the full force of the Law" against members of the convention, whom he called "the Offenders."[33]

Still, what law had the convention participants broken? Hamilton sought Attorney General Edmund Randolph's opinion on whether the delegates had committed an "indictable" federal offence. Hamilton also wrote Chief Justice Jay suggesting that advocating the obstruction of the excise law by "every legal measure" was a "contradiction in terms" and "a high misdemeanour." He wondered if when the federal circuit court next met in Philadelphia it should take notice of "the state of things" and "particularly the Meeting at Pittsburgh and its proceedings." He asked Jay whether the president should go to "the scene of commotion" in western Pennsylvania to emphasize the "criminality of such proceedings."[34]

Jay replied that "neither a Proclamation nor a *particular* charge by the court to the G[rand] Jury, would be advisable at present." Instead he thought it "more prudent" for Washington just to raise the issue in his next congressional address – allowing each branch to express its "sense" of the state of affairs. Washington ignored this advice. On September 15, 1792, the president issued a proclamation noting "certain violent and unwarrantable proceedings" in Pennsylvania that tended to "obstruct" the excise law. The meetings were "subversive of good order, contrary to the duty that every citizen owes to his country, and to the laws." They were "dangerous to the very being of a government." Washington warned against any further "unlawful combinations and proceedings . . . tending to obstruct the operation" of the excise tax.[35]

The proclamation was the handiwork of Hamilton, which Washington toned down. In his draft for the president, Hamilton had condemned the Pittsburgh meeting as illegal and criminal. Washington omitted that characterization, largely because Attorney General Randolph advised against it. The events in Pittsburgh did not warrant prosecution, what the attorney general called "a judicial movement." Assembling "to remonstrate, and to invite others to assemble and remonstrate to the Legislature, are among the rights of Citizens," noted Randolph. Indeed, they were rights most recently enumerated in the amendments to the new federal Constitution. Although some resolutions from the Pittsburgh convention displayed "a hostile temper," that was not a crime. However eager Hamilton was to punish the protesters, Randolph resisted using "a doubtful power" to suppress the protest. Instead, he favored limiting prosecutions to acts "infringing the peace." Randolph's conclusion implicitly recognized the capacity of the people under the constitution to participate politically and scrutinize the operation of government.[36]

After Washington's 1792 Proclamation, other developments soon shaped the debate over the federal excise tax and Washington's reaction to political criticism. On April 14, 1793, the "German Republican Society" was organized in Philadelphia, the first of many political groups that proliferated under a variety of names. Collectively they were referred to as "Democratic" or "Democratic-Republican" societies. Those societies insisted that the relationship of the people to their government – their agents – fully justified the scrutiny of the operations and policy of the national government. They criticized numerous policies of Washington's administration, including the excise tax.[37]

This additional criticism of the administration's policies surfaced at the same time that resistance to the collection of the tax hardened in western Pennsylvania. In early August 1794, Hamilton lobbied Washington to prosecute "delinquents and Offenders" with "vigour." Although an option existed for prosecuting violations of the federal excise tax in the local state

courts, U.S. Attorney William Rawle brought suit against over sixty western Pennsylvanian distillers in federal court in Philadelphia. When the U.S.
marshal – accompanied by the hated Federal Excise Collector John Neville –
started serving process for those suits in July 1794, it triggered the most dramatic and violent resistance to the excise tax.[38]

Pennsylvania's governor thought the service of process for federal prosecutions was "peculiarly inauspicious" and a "principal source of discontent."
Selecting the federal venue forced farmers in the western counties to trek
some three hundred miles over the mountains at harvest time to defend
themselves. The rumor that "[t]he Federal Sheriff was taking away people to
Philadelphia" helped fuel a spontaneous march on Inspector Neville's man-
sion at Bower Hall, demanding his resignation. That confrontation between
tax protesters and troops defending Neville in mid-July 1794 ended in a
shootout that killed several excise protesters and left Neville's home in ruins.
After this violence, a series of open-air meetings by opponents of the excise
tax were held to discuss the state of affairs and future action. Many leaders
of earlier, peaceful meetings in 1791 and 1792 counseled submission to the
law, but tempers still ran high. Protest leaders continued to urge resistance,
but even they only sought action "guided by reason, prudence, fortitude and
spirited conduct." The aftermath of Bower Hall ended with a show of firm,
but moderate, opposition to the excise. Some six thousand tax protesters
assembled outside Pittsburgh at Braddock's Field. On August 1, 1794, in
a massive but peaceful demonstration, the protesters marched through the
town largely without incident.[39]

From the start of the federal excise tax, sporadic violence had been
directed at revenue collectors – including tarring and feathering a few
unlucky collectors and offering physical threats and intimidation to others. In
addition, protesters tampered with the mails and repeatedly erected "liberty
poles" as a symbol of defiance to the excise tax. An opponent of the excise tax
noted that protesters made an important distinction "between an officer of
[the] excise and the officer of a court of justice." In fact, a precipitating cause
of the violence that spilled over at Bower Hall was that Inspector Neville
accompanied the U.S. marshal in the course of serving judicial process.[40]

Government officials (as well as most leaders of the meetings and conventions protesting the excise) joined in condemning the violence. However, they differed over the issue of using military force. Moreover, they
disagreed over whether criticism of the national government's fiscal policies
prompted the physical attacks on federal officers. Finally, they differed over
the danger that resistance to the excise tax posed to government – both
state and national. The day after the march through Pittsburgh, a revealing

meeting took place in Philadelphia between the president and members of his administration and Pennsylvania state officials. According to notes taken by Alexander Hamilton, Washington opened the meeting by announcing that everyone "understood" that events in western Pennsylvania struck "at the root of all law & order." He asserted that "the most spirited & firm measures were necessary to rescue the State as well as the general government from the impending danger, for if such proceedings were tolerated there was an end to our Constitutions & laws." The president noted he would call out the militia using his federal authority, but wanted Pennsylvania's governor, Thomas Mifflin, to take "some preliminary measures under the State Laws" because of delays in forming the federal military force.[41]

After Mifflin and his state colleagues remained "silent for some time," Washington's attorney general reinforced the hint, pointedly asking Alexander Dallas, the state's secretary of the commonwealth, if the governor possessed the authority to call up Pennsylvania's militia in the interim. Dallas replied that such power existed if the civil authorities were unable to enforce the laws. Mifflin later explained why he had not immediately granted Washington's wish: "In a free country" before one used "coercive authority" of "military power" to enforce the laws it was necessary to show that "the judicial power has in vain attempted to punish" lawbreakers. After Dallas's reply, Chief Justice Thomas McKean of Pennsylvania spoke up, declaring "his positive opinion, that the judiciary power was equal to the task of quelling and punishing the riots, and that the employment of a military force, at this period, would be as bad as anything that the Rioters had done – equally unconstitutional and illegal." Washington's frustration, if not anger, must have been palpable; the document recording the event ended with the statement: "Here the minutes of the conference suddenly terminate."[42]

While state officials eventually capitulated (five weeks later Governor Mifflin agreed to use military force against the protesters), five days after the federal and state conference, Washington issued another proclamation. He intended to raise an army to "suppress" the "fatal" spirit of resistance to the excise. Washington identified "combinations" and "irregular meetings" that "have tended to encourage and uphold the spirit of opposition" and the commission of "treasonable acts."[43]

PERCEPTIONS UNDERLYING THE SUPPRESSION OF THE PROTEST

In reacting to protesters of the excise tax in 1794, Washington adopted a view of the people under the federal Constitution that conceded they were the sovereign but denied them a role to play as the ruler. That understanding of the relationship between the people and their national government lacked a role for the ruler in scrutinizing government officials as its agents, much less offering direction to them. The shift in constitutionalism was so pronounced that it even questioned whether the ruled had rights under the federal Constitution to criticize government officials and policies of the national government, or even to petition and assemble.

Washington's reaction to the resistance to the excise in Pennsylvania rested on his characterization of the protest meetings in 1791 and 1792. Hamilton played a crucial role in shaping the president's view of those events. From the start of the meetings in 1791 and 1792 Hamilton lobbied Washington to use force, even as Washington worried that doing so would confirm the suspicion of his political opponents that Federalists welcomed the militaristic potential of the national government. Washington expected former Anti-Federalists to "cry at once 'The cat is let out; We now see for what purpose an Army was raised.'" By the time of the 1794 proclamation, however, Washington fully endorsed Hamilton's position.[44]

Hamilton saw a crucial link between the peaceful meetings in 1791 and 1792 and the violence and dramatic protests in 1794 that he termed "Treason." A connection existed because "influential individuals" in those early "formal public meetings" incited "a general Spirit of Opposition" leading to armed resistance against the tax. Members of the early meetings at Brownsville, Washington County, and Pittsburgh acted "without moderation or prudence" and were "justly chargeable with the excesses" leading to the current threat to "the foundations of the Government & of the Union." Criticism of the administration and the government revealed improper and treasonous motives.[45]

Hamilton shared these views in a lengthy letter to Washington in early August 1794. That letter – made public with the president's approval – summarized the previous three years of protests in western Pennsylvania. Hamilton's account refused to distinguish between peaceful protests and expressions of opposition to the policy of the excise from violence and ill treatment inflicted on excise collectors. Four months later, Washington blamed "riot and violence" on the "prejudice" and "artifice of men" seeking "an ascendency over the will of others."[46]

Leading opponents of the excise tax defended themselves against the accusations of Washington and Hamilton. Albert Gallatin, a future secretary of the treasury for two different administrations, questioned how "a circulation of opinions" could be called "criminal." "This doctrine, once adopted, would destroy the privilege, the constitutional privilege, of the citizens to assemble peaceably, to remonstrate, to discuss the measures of government, and to publish their thoughts." Gallatin distinguished between publishing "sentiments" or "an opinion merely" and "acting" or prompting "others to act." As such, "Whether the opinion be right or wrong, as long as it is only an opinion, everybody has a right to express it." By this standard, participation in the early meetings was "perfectly justifiable" and "not illegal or criminal."[47]

Likewise, William Findley, a representative from western Pennsylvania who would serve more than twenty years in Congress, could not believe that "a meeting to petition government respectfully" could be considered criminal "in any country" with "the least pretensions to freedom." Findley claimed that he and other participants at the Brownsville meeting conceded the constitutionality of the federal excise tax even as they opposed its policy. The "unjust and oppressive" operation of the tax did not make it unconstitutional. Still, citizens were entitled "to lay their grievances before Congress by petition" and seek the law's repeal.[48]

Henry Hugh Brackenridge later recalled that fellow lawyers at the 1791 Pittsburgh convention concluded that their actions were not treasonous. Even though the meeting went "to the utmost boundary of right reserved by the people," Brackenridge's description of the meeting's constitutional basis – the inherent, reserved right of the people – distinguished that activity from violent opposition to government, even if it was "the last step short of using actual force." In October 1794, as Washington's army made its way westward, Brackenridge disclaimed any "criminal" activity. He was willing to submit to "the closest examination" of his "conduct through the whole of the unfortunate crisis."[49]

Findley offered the most detailed justification of the people's right to monitor their governments as integral to American constitutionalism. Such a right was clearly recognized under state constitutions. He saw no reason that the people should not have the same right under the federal Constitution. Although conceding the "intemperate and impolitic" nature of some of the petitions, he denied any "influence" or "connection" between the Pittsburgh conventions and actual violence, which he condemned. Even if "popular meetings" were conducted with "indiscretion" and might "promote licentiousness," it did not follow that such meetings should be "prohibited by law or denounced by government." That reaction reduced "the people to mere machines" and subverted "the very existence of liberty." Republics inevitably entailed a dynamic tension between government and the people they represented.[50]

Findley challenged the premise of prominent Federalists that under a popularly based government the people exhausted their right of political expression by voting at election time. A "representative legislature" could not claim "implicit obedience." It was "absurd" to hold that simply "because our laws are enacted by our own representatives" the people "ought to submit to them without remonstrance" until those representatives "think proper to repeal them." That position erroneously assumed "that a government of representatives can never mistake the true interests of their constituents, nor be corrupted or fall into partial combinations." Both "the nature of man" and actual experience refuted the premise that legislatures were infallible.[51]

Findley expected protesters of the excise tax to be judged according to the underlying principles of American republics. Government was "valuable" only if it promoted "mutual happiness and security." For that reason, many state constitutions "expressly declared" that "the power of altering or amending governments" resided "in the people, who are the judges of their own happiness." They retained that authority "whether expressed in a written instrument or not." The people had the right to alter or abolish their governments. Implicit in that right as the sovereign, the people as the ruler or even the ruled could question the policy of proposed or enacted laws. Thus, opponents of the federal excise tax were not rebels engaged in treason. "If the people have a right to petition for the repeal of a law, or remonstrate against its injustice or inexpediency, surely they have a right to meet, publish their sentiments, and correspond... without the imputation of combining against the government."[52]

Petitions and remonstrances were crucial in governments in which the people were the sovereign. Avoiding violent confrontations with those governments depended on public "confidence" and required free communication between representatives and the people. Indeed, government officials who denounced "the liberty of expressing opinions" only increased public unrest. Massachusetts experienced its Regulation because the state failed to respond to "a long course of complaints and evident discontents." That unresponsiveness was similar to the congressional inattention underlying the whiskey protests. Implicitly, Findley described the dangers that could arise when the agents of the people refused to listen to the rulers or denied that the people could act in such a capacity.[53]

Though suppressed, the federal excise tax protesters in Pennsylvania – like the Regulators in Massachusetts – were ultimately vindicated. In the aftermath of the "Rebellion," the national government remained unsuccessful in collecting the tax. Moreover, after Thomas Jefferson's election to the presidency in 1800, the whiskey excise and all other federal internal taxes were struck down. At least until the Civil War, Americans developed a broad understanding that national excise taxes were only justified under dire circumstances. Yet it remained unclear what steps the national government might take when faced with vigorous resistance to its policies.[54]

COMPETING VIEWS OF CONSTITUTIONALISM
AND THE DEMOCRATIC SOCIETIES

At one level the debate over the excise tax raised the constitutional question of the scope and meaning of the First Amendment. That issue involved the legitimacy of political opposition within the particularly bitter context of American politics in the 1790s. Before the rise of political parties – with organization, structure, and perceived legitimacy – partisan politics operated in an arena in which political positions competed for acknowledgment as the one, true republican understanding. Political opposition, whether from Republicans or Federalists, triggered deep suspicion if not hostility.[55]

At another level, however, the debate over the excise tax raised the question of constitutionalism implicit in the issue of whether the people had a right to scrutinize government. Perception of the criticism leveled at the excise tax and other policies of Washington's administration hinged on one's understanding of the relationship of the people to the national government. If the people, as the sovereign, played a role as the ruler, then surely their scrutiny and even criticism of their governmental agents was justified. Denying that role and confining political expression to electoral choice prompted a rather different reaction to criticism of the administration. Significantly shaping that reaction was that such criticism came from "self-created" societies.

For Hamilton, the merits of the federal excise policy were "immaterial." Each citizen owed a "sacred duty" of "inviolable respect" to "the Constitution and Laws." That obligation included forgoing criticizing government because such criticism undermined government by breeding disrespect and legal disobedience. Defenders of Washington's administration considered "every embarrassment" to government officials "an opposition to the peace, freedom, and happiness of the United States." In private correspondence, Washington wrote that "no one denies the right of the people to meet occasionally, to petition for, or to remonstrate against, any Act of the Legislature." Still, Washington's public characterization and response to the 1791 and 1792 meetings displayed little commitment to even occasional remonstrances. The Federalist position thus reflected a narrower view of freedom of speech and the legitimacy of political opposition than Americans eventually accepted. More important, it also suggested a different view of constitutionalism.[56]

The debate triggered by Washington's condemnation of the Democratic societies revealed different views not only about political speech but also about American constitutionalism. The defense of the societies by Madison, Jefferson, and other Republicans reflected one understanding of the constitutional settlement of America's first written constitutions. On the other hand, the case against the societies advanced by some Federalists reflected a view of the people as the sovereign who played a limited role as the ruled and who had no role as the ruler. The controversy over the "self-created" political societies formed part of the broader, ongoing debate over the meaning of the collective sovereign and the relationship of the people to government – now considered in the context of the federal Constitution.[57]

Attack on the Democratic Societies

After the march through Pittsburgh in early August 1794, Washington saw societies spreading "mischief far and wide" intending to bring his government "into discredit." He saw the excise tax protests as the "first *formidable* fruit of the Democratic Societies." Washington's belief that the societies intended to "sap the Constitution" became public in his *Address* to Congress on November 19, 1794. Certain "self-created societies" and not merely "designing individuals" were responsible.[58]

The Federalist-dominated Senate quickly echoed Washington's sentiments. The Senate's response, primarily drafted by Rufus King of Massachusetts, connected the protests with societies "founded in political error" that were "calculated, if not intended, to disorganize" government. The House of Representatives, however, refused to endorse Washington's condemnation of the societies. After four days of debate it only expressed concern that misrepresentations of government might have led "individuals or combinations of men" astray.[59]

Some Federalists in the House wanted to censure the societies, but others conceded they were, as Thomas FitzSimons of Pennsylvania put it, "not strictly unlawful." Such Federalists were unwilling to reproach all societies, but only those "generally imprudent," heedless of "the truth," and engaged in "outrages against the law." Edmund Randolph considered self-created societies for "praise-worthy" purposes legitimate, but those for "improper" purposes illegitimate. Fisher Ames thought societies were justified where "town meetings are little known, and not practicable in a thinly settled country." Still, other Federalists thought societies could be "fatal to good order and true liberty," "reprehensible," or "mischievous in their consequences." Warning Americans about the dangers of misguided ideas spread by the societies, or as the Federalist William Murray of Maryland put it, to "hold out a caution to the thoughtless," became the purpose of the House's action.[60]

Federalists objected to the attacks on Washington's administration, but many focused on the fact that the societies existed outside of government. Individuals spontaneously forming groups that weighed in on the country's political affairs posed an entirely different danger. Implicit in the rejection of "self-created" societies was the position that denied the people a role as the ruler. The people were limited in acting on matters of government through the mechanism of their representatives. Considered together, representatives and the government were now the ruler.

The illegitimacy attributed to societies came from a view of representation that repudiated the need or authority of the people to express political opinions through self-created societies or groups. Federalists considered societies "powerfully competent" in mobilizing "resistance, or a change of the government," but *"unnecessary*, except as instruments of a revolution." During the American Revolution, grassroots organization was appropriate and even indispensable, but with the formation of American governments, self-constituted political groups lacked justification. Now that the American people formed "one Republican society," all "associations for promoting political views" were "useless . . . if not dangerous."[61]

Indeed, such societies undermined the proper relationship of "the people" to their governments. According to "A Federal Republican," since the Revolution "the constitutions and the laws of the country have clearly designated the mode in which the people are to be governed." Nothing in those constitutions "directly or by implication authorizes such associations" or warrants "any number of persons to form private clubs." Instead, constitutions made representatives the appropriate conduit for expressing the political views of the people. After creating their own governments, the people had no "interest" or "right to interfere" in government affairs other than "the preservation of the government." In postrevolutionary America, representatives were the constituent's "centinel," responsible for monitoring the "dangers" facing "the affairs of the Union." The job of citizens was to support government and not scrutinize it. Representatives were now the guardians of the governmental process.[62]

From that perspective the societies criticizing Washington's administration were highly problematic. Fisher Ames thought the "clubs" undermined "the real Representatives." Washington denounced the "arrogant presumption" of societies in "forming themselves into *permanent* Censors" to judge laws framed after "the most deliberate, and solemn discussion by the Representatives of the people." American liberties rested on "the virtue and vigilance of the people in their elections – and in this way alone." All other "modes of seeking redress of public grievances" simply made matters worse. Once the people's representatives passed laws for the common benefit, the community owed them "a strict and punctual obedience." Federalists disputed the necessity and propriety of what they regarded as overly suspicious scrutiny of government.[63]

The societies also undermined the appropriately submissive relationship of the people to their elected representatives by encouraging "a general influence and control upon the measures of government." Rather, the people should leave representation to their betters and not second-guess them. As only "a few" members of the societies made politics "a regular study," it seemed "impossible they should know much" about political affairs. The societies were dangerous because they encouraged the common people to forget their proper place.[64]

Beyond lacking authority and undermining representation, societies undercut the sovereignty of the people by embracing what Fisher Ames called "club sovereignty." Opposing a duly enacted law like the excise tax disrespected the sovereign people. Such challenges, noted Washington, threatened republican government and invited "anarchy and confusion" since anyone "may dislike another Law and oppose it with equal propriety until all Laws" were overthrown. Similarly, Hamilton, writing anonymously as "Tully," accused tax opponents of attacking the people. Since "the government is YOUR OWN work," by giving it support the people validated their "OWN POWER."[65]

Federalists occasionally attempted to reconcile their denunciation of the societies with freedom of speech. Representative Samuel Dexter of Massachusetts distinguished "false apostles of liberty" disturbing "the public peace" from legitimate expressions of opinion. Free speech required "a decent respect for the will of the majority." One of the most insidious dangers of the "clubs," Fisher Ames suggested, came from their tendency to generate "more complaints" against laws than their members ever "dreamed of." For Ames, wrongful speech included statements causing controversy or discontent with existing authority, in effect, precluding criticism of government altogether. Indeed, for Federalists, much of what the societies said was illicit speech.[66]

Justice John Blair of the U.S. Supreme Court also endorsed that position. The "scene of convulsive disorder" in Pennsylvania led Blair to consider the people's right to respond to perceived grievances. In charging a grand jury of the federal circuit court of Georgia in 1795, Blair acknowledged the right to petition for grievances, but his overarching message stressed the importance of stifling disagreement with government. He conceded that after "external obedience to the laws," citizens "have a right to think of them as they please, and even to *express* their opinion decently, yet strongly, as a mean[s] of obtaining an alteration." The "useful lesson" taught by the excise tax protests, however, was appreciating "how dangerous it is to indulge too freely discontent with respect to the measures of government." It would be "happy for the public if by fear," Blair noted, people might "be restrained from annoying the general peace" and "disturbing the orderly course of things." He worried that "if a minority can persuade themselves that they have a right to oppose a law enacted by the majority, with equal reason might they deny the existence of the law" and champion "the will of the few."[67]

Invoking majoritarianism was consistent with a narrower role assigned to "the people." Making elective representatives the exclusive repository of the people's sovereignty left no room for a concept of inherent or reserved rights of the people. As Justice Blair announced in his grand jury charge, "in such representation alone is displayed the majesty of the people" and anything undermining that delegated authority, "whatever pretences it may make to popular dignity," constituted "a presumptuous invasion of the rights of the people" and usurped "their sovereignty." Pennsylvania's troubles came from "an overstrained conception of liberty" that prompted some to presume to speak and act for the people. Blair's views thus echoed Benjamin Rush's assertion in 1787 that the people possessed sovereignty "only on the days of their elections." Thereafter, that sovereignty "is the property of their rulers, nor can they exercise it or resume it, unless it is abused." During the debate over the societies, "A Friend to Representative Government" conceded that "the people" were the "sovereign, but this sovereignty is in the whole people" and "cannot be exercised, but by the Representatives of the whole nation."[68]

A recurring theme in the Federalists' response to opponents of the excise tax was the value of using force to establish the dignity and authority of the new national government. Support of "the Laws," Washington wrote in his diary during the time he led troops toward the Alleghenies, was "an object of the first magnitude." Although intrinsically important, "obedience to law" and returning protesters "to a Sense of their duty" served a larger purpose. Washington's supporters in western Pennsylvania also hoped "that Government" would not be "insulted with Impunity."[69]

Federalists saw positive benefits in forcefully responding to protesters of the excise tax. By early September 1794, Fisher Ames thought the Pittsburgh "rebellion" could not "end badly for government, unless government flinches from its duty." On the eve of the army's march into Pittsburgh, Hamilton predicted that "the insurrection will do us a great deal of good and add to the solidity of every thing in this country." Demonstrating the national government's power and vindicating its authority might be expensive, but, he asked, "what is that compared with the object?" Likewise, Washington considered it money well spent to send a clear message to discourage "future attempts" to "sow the seed of distrust and disturb the public tranquility." Additionally, a military response would show the world, and particularly Britain, how America's new national government could support its laws and avoid "anarchy and confusion."[70]

Opposition to the excise tax and the appearance of the Democratic societies gave Washington's administration an opportunity to vindicate with force both the authority of the national government and the Federalists' constitutional vision. Stifling the "rebellion" and driving the societies out of existence reinforced the Federalist assertion of the proper relationship of the citizen to government and advanced the position of governmental sovereignty. One year after the suppression of "open insurrection," Justice James Iredell thought military force produced "[s]uccess beyond the most sanguine expectations." The end result taught a valuable "lesson to Governments and People" – at least from the Federalist perspective.[71]

Crushing opponents of the excise tax also produced a desired chilling effect on the Federalists' political opponents. Even as they discredited societies as agents of insurrection, Federalists recognized in them a more prosaic political danger. Fisher Ames predicted that Massachusetts societies would be "as busy as Macbeth's witches" before elections in undermining the Federalist Party. Ames wanted to forge a connection in the public mind between societies and the congressional "faction" responsible for "the discontents." In short, as Edmund Randolph wrote the president in late 1794, events in Pennsylvania offered the chance to wipe out the societies, a "prospect" that "ought not to be lost."[72]

Defense of the Democratic Societies

In defending the societies, James Madison, among others, acknowledged their legitimacy and denied their danger. By asserting the constitutionality of the societies, Madison challenged the assumption that legislative majorities of elected representatives embodied the sovereignty of the people. "The people" retained the authority to control governments they created. To deny that denied that the people were the sovereign. American governments not only rested on the governed but also justified their existence by preserving and protecting the common welfare of the people. Electing representatives as agents of the people took an important step toward that objective but did not displace the sovereignty underlying that representation. Denying legitimacy to societies scrutinizing and petitioning their government undermined the people's inherent rights.

Opponents of the censure argued that the people not only had a right but a duty to scrutinize government. Societies were constitutionally legitimate since the people had an ongoing role even after government established electoral representation. That position presumed that the people retained inherent rights. The principle behind the censure was a "pernicious" one, according to Madison, because the people as the collective sovereign had "reserved rights." "When the people have formed a constitution, they retain those rights which they have not expressly delegated." For Madison the "nature of republican government" meant that "the censorial power is in the people over the government, and not in the government over the people." Because government served the people, the people were free to petition and state their grievances. As a result, Washington's censure attacked both "the most sacred principle of our Constitution and of Republicanism" as well as "the essential & constitutional right of the Citizen."[73]

Some saw the censure in simpler terms: "The people have a right to think and a right to speak." For John Nicholas, the societies possessed a legitimate role "to watch the errors of the Legislature and Executive" and bring attention to what they considered government's "mistakes." The former attorney general of Georgia, Thomas Carnes, believed the censure undermined freedom of speech and he hoped "the day will never come, when the people of America" were unable "to assemble, and speak their mind."[74]

In defending themselves, the societies justified their formation in terms that reflected the constitutional vision and understanding of the collective sovereign that was under attack from Washington's administration. Repeatedly, the societies expressed the idea that in America, the people were the collective sovereign. That principle was central to the constitutions that founded the societies. Moreover, "the people" were constantly invoked – in resolutions, proclamations, petitions, and toasts offered by societies and their defenders. The Democratic Society of New York questioned whether it overstepped legitimate bounds. "Is it for assembling, that we are accused; what law forbids it? for deliberating, for thinking, for exercising the faculties of the mind; what statute has deprived us of the right? for the publication of our sentiments? where is the constitution that is prohibitory?" If the activities of the societies were neither illegal nor unconstitutional, the society asked, "By whom, then, ought we to have been constituted?" Implicitly, the authority of the people as the ruler justified the establishment of societies. As a Vermont defender of societies put it: *"when the people have deputed they are not defunct*; the sovereignty is not annihilated."[75]

Defenders of the societies also observed that despite opposing "self-created" societies, Washington seemed untroubled when the Society of

Cincinnati, the aristocratically inclined organization of Continental Army officers, was created in 1783. As the Democratic Society of the City of New York pointedly asked, "Was it thought *necessary* to obtain a *special act* of legislative power for the *exclusive* creation of the SOCIETY of CINCIN-NATUS...or *is that society* 'SELF CREATED?'" Shortly after Washington denounced the societies, Thomas Jefferson identified the "ingenuity" of Federalists in distinguishing Democratic societies seeking to advance constitutional principles of republics from the society of Cincinnati, "a *self-created* one, carving out for itself hereditary distinctions." As a writer for the *Philadelphia Independent Gazetteer* put it, "Whatever the United States might have been" before the American Revolution, "it is pretty evident" that since then "they are a great self created society."[76]

For the societies' defenders, the authority of the sovereign people seemed clear. The Constitution of the Democratic Society of the City of New York proclaimed that the constitutional "maxim" of the people's "alter or abolish" authority "is now considered a TRUTH" so obvious that explaining it was "superfluous." Writing as "Helvidius" in 1793, James Madison described the ultimate right of the people to abolish their governments as a principle "not only recorded in every public archive, written in every American heart, and sealed with the blood of a host of American martyrs," but "the only lawful tenure by which the United States hold their existence as a nation." For another defender, "the security of the people against any unwarrantable stretch of power" rested on "a jealous examination of all the proceedings of administration" and on "open expression of their sentiments." The writer concluded that if individual citizens were entitled to express opinions about public affairs, "surely the same right cannot be denied to a peaceable assemblage of a number of them." Other Americans urged the people not to place "implicit confidence in the integrity and wisdom of any set of men living," but persistently question their governmental leaders. That role "naturally" arose because in America the people were "at the same time, both sovereign and subject."[77]

Societies considered scrutiny essential: it was "the duty incumbent on every citizen" to either take part in government's "immediate administration" or through "advice and watchfulness" maintain its principles "by constant action." In July 1794, the Republican Society in Portland, Maine, described the "peculiar privilege" of Americans to monitor their public officials. Questioning that right seemed "absurd," to a Vermont society, when it came "from the tongue or pen of an American." Inspecting government stemmed from the people's relationship with their governors. Having "set up a government" the people should not "resign it" to "the hands of agents." Rather, it remained the "duty" of every citizen "to watch with the vigilance of a faith-ful centinel the conduct of those to whom is intrusted the administration of Government." Indeed, the German Republican Society of Philadelphia explained the need for public scrutiny "in a government where the peo-ple are supreme" since "who but they ought to be satisfied, that their agents have done their duty?" Keeping government leaders accountable, as trustees of the people's sovereignty, followed from the fact that sovereign authority remained in the body of the people.[78]

Such an active role assumed the capacity of the people to "think for them-selves." A New Jersey society rejected the "slavish doctrine" that political affairs were too complicated for common people. Likewise, the president of Vermont's Rutland County Democratic Society asserted that after "deliber-ate, unbiased investigation" the people "will decide rightly." Implicitly, James Madison expressed similar faith – if not in the common people, then in the republican experiment – during the congressional debate over the societies. Ultimately in republics, Madison concluded, "light will prevail over darkness, truth over error." Such confidence largely rested on an educated citizenry. Indeed, education was crucial where citizens were "judging" the "conduct of the rulers, and the tendency of the laws." The promise of American gov-ernment lay in the possibility, as the writings of Hugh Henry Brackenridge implied, that "the cobbler may become more than a cobbler." Herman Hus-band reached for that promise when he asserted that "good" farmers and mechanics were capable of leading government.[79]

CONFLICTING ATTITUDES TOWARD POPULAR PROTESTS

Ultimately, those who not only conceded that the people were the sovereign but could also act as the ruler as well as the ruled assigned them an active role in monitoring government and defended the consequences of vigorous polit-ical criticism. Political disruption and even some disorder could be tolerated to ensure the active involvement of the people. Even Federalists sometimes acknowledged that a free country inevitably entailed some upheaval. For example, Justice Blair identified the "peculiar advantage and disadvantage" of America's political systems. As "the natural price of freedom," disturbances did not necessarily undermine society's "good order." American government had demonstrated sufficient "energy" to restrain both "[s]light irregularities" and the wider disruption of the whiskey excise protests without frustrating "the most valuable object of the social compact."[80]

American political leaders differed in the value they assigned to order and the danger they saw from aggressive attempts to maintain stability.

Local leaders in western Pennsylvania protesting the federal excise tax in the 1790s did not urge insurrection against the national government any more than community leaders in Massachusetts sympathizing with the Regulators encouraged armed conflict against the state government in the 1780s. Yet during each of those "rebellions" some members of the establishment defended the legitimacy of aggressive expressions of grievances short of resistance by arms. When it came to actual insurrection, Washington and Hamilton as well as Madison and Jefferson agreed. They parted company, however, over the significance of popular pressure, including physical intimidation and occasional violence, and how best to respond to it.

For Washington and Hamilton, protests against the federal excise policy seemed like forcible resistance, the disintegration of law and order, and the rejection of constitutional government. Casting those who resisted the excise tax as anarchists led Federalists to label excise protesters "Shaysites." Hamilton and Washington believed the protesters posed a dire threat. As such, Federalists eventually endorsed a coercive military response to preserve republican government. Hamilton wanted an "outlawry" bill and treason prosecutions even as other Federalists supported lesser charges. An "outlawry" bill was needed in the aftermath of the protests because without "vigour every where" America's tranquility would be "of very short duration & the next storm will be infinitely worse than the present one."[81]

Madison and Jefferson, however, approached confrontations with government in the 1780s and 1790s differently. To them, the protests, agitation, and episodic violence in Pennsylvania and Massachusetts were temporary but expected upheavals in republican governments. Obviously, the people might be led astray and occasionally go to extremes. Although Madison did not suggest, as Jefferson did, the positive benefits of such upheavals, both of them anticipated only sporadic popular outbursts of limited duration. Even Jefferson's endorsement of "a little rebellion now and then" did not envision a thoroughgoing revolution.[82]

Significantly, Madison and Jefferson differed from Washington and Hamilton in how to respond to a roused public movement. For Madison and Jefferson, granting some political concessions seemed reasonable, as did a judicious use of amnesty to bring would-be "rebels" back into the normal political fold. In expressing reservations about a bill to provide compensation to those who suffered at the hands of excise tax protesters, Madison revealed his thinking about popular political protests. "A great body of people were commonly engaged in such disturbances," he noted, "who were not worth hanging, and to whom an established government usually held out an amnesty. By this means, great multitudes came in, and received pardon before the operations of chastisement began." That description assumed that such disturbances normally fell short of treason against the state.[83]

The danger in dealing with such upheavals was in reacting too soon and with excessive force. Jefferson thought that Washington resorted to "an appeal to arms" before efforts by civil authorities were "tried & *proved* ineffectual." For Madison, the response to both Regulators and whiskey excise tax protesters demonstrated the inclination of government to aggrandize its power at the expense of the people in the course of restoring order. As much as he disapproved of the violence associated with the protests against the tax, Madison saw a dangerous trend in how Washington's administration responded to events in western Pennsylvania. In December 1794 Madison wrote James Monroe suggesting "the general tendency of insurrections to increase the momentum of power." He reminded Monroe of "the particular effect" of recent events in Massachusetts and worried that "the same calamity was to be dreaded on a larger scale" in Pennsylvania.[84] In fact, both Madison and Jefferson thought Federalists deliberately manipulated the protests to enhance the national government's military power. Madison believed that if Washington had not "crushed" the excise protesters he would have made "a formidable attempt" to demonstrate that "a standing army was necessary for *enforcing the laws.*" Madison did not want the cure in restoring balance in republican governments to be worse than the disease of temporary instability.[85]

For Washington and Hamilton, resistance to the excise tax directly challenged the national government and colored their perception of events. The tax protests provided an opportunity to increase the strength of the government and give it added prestige. Hamilton evidently thought that an established government required "some signal display" of "its power of military coercion." The suppression of the whiskey "rebels" would send a clear message about the new government's ability to defend itself.[86]

If this exhibition of governmental power worried Madison, he also objected to what he regarded as the Federalists' use of the excise protests as a means to silence political opposition. According to Madison, "[t]he game" underlying Washington's condemnation was to connect congressional Republicans with "the odium of the insurrection" and the democratic societies. Even as Washington worried about Madison's getting "entangled with them, or their politics," Madison criticized the Federalist attack on the societies. He called Washington's denunciation of them "perhaps the greatest error of his political life."[87]

By the 1790s, the ways Americans viewed the people as America's collective sovereign produced distinctly different understandings of the Revolution and the constitutionalism Independence had inaugurated. Those favoring a limited role for the people in government during the excise tax protests saw the federal Constitution as the natural endpoint of the Revolution. Whatever the liberating potential of independence, the federal Constitution of 1787 established the final expression of constitutionalism and the appropriate relationship of the people to their governments. Vindicating that particular vision underlay the response of many Federalists to the events in Pennsylvania.

Reference to revolutionary constitutional principles, particularly those found in state constitutions, was not only unnecessary but potentially dangerous. Celebrations heralding the Declaration of Independence made many Federalists nervous. One reason for the whiskey excise protests, explained an officer sent to suppress them, was that "Americans seem so fond of the idea of revolutions, and changing government." This unhealthy revolutionary appetite revealed itself in the way many Republicans and members of the societies sympathetically responded to the French Revolution. Misguided attraction to principles of the American Revolution produced, as Justice Blair had explained in 1795, "overstrained" notions of liberty. When Federalists called liberty poles "anarchy poles," they were not only ridiculing the activity of erecting them but also denying their relevance after 1787.[88]

Many Federalists considered the excise tax protests part of a continuing effort by opponents of the federal Constitution to destroy the Union. Washington saw unrepentant Anti-Federalists plotting "to subvert the Constitution." Protests against the excise tax meant resistance to the national government, and in turn, the constitution. From this perspective, Washington and Hamilton were disinclined to offer any quarter to the protesters.[89]

On the other hand, for many Republicans and other Americans, the Revolution produced a dynamic legacy. Rather than a static historical event, the Revolution established principles in America's first constitutions that retained ongoing relevance. Exuberance over the French Revolution – particularly before it turned bloody – was simply a celebration of America's achievement in 1776: the displacement of a tyrannical monarch by the people as the collective sovereign. The ratification of the federal Constitution, however one felt about its distribution of powers, reinforced the fact that the national government – as well as America's state governments – rested on "the people." The construction of the new Capitol building in Washington, D.C., produced, as Jefferson later observed, "the first temple dedicated to the sovereignty of the people." At the end of his presidency, John Adams considered "the great body of the people" the "source of all legitimate authority," while at the start of his presidency Thomas Jefferson heralded "the will of the majority." Americans continued to agree that the people were the sovereign even as they disagreed about what that meant.[90]

COMPETING CONSTITUTIONAL VISIONS

The federal Constitution did not unify American constitutionalism. The narrow margin of ratification and calls for another convention underscored persisting differences in how Americans viewed written constitutions. While some Federalists, like John Adams, thought they saw a consensus emerging with the constitution, events proved otherwise. Americans continued to disagree (including Federalists among themselves) over the meaning of the collective sovereign in America.

Despite such disagreements, Washington's administration insisted that one particular view of the people's sovereignty possessed constitutional legitimacy. The protests over the whiskey excise tax gave Washington an opportunity to promote governmental sovereignty. Indeed, in the course of advancing his view of American constitutionalism, he established a precedent for the national government to protect and defend itself against "the people."[91]

Washington offered the quintessential expression of a constrained view of constitutional revision in his 1796 speech when he left public office. In his *Farewell Address*, Washington acknowledged the people as the sovereign, but in terms that limited their ability to act as that sovereign. In the *Address*, he identified "the right of the people to make and to alter their Constitutions of Government" as the "basis of our political systems." Nonetheless, Washington insisted that every constitution was "sacredly obligatory" on the people until changed "by an explicit and authentic act of the whole People." That "explicit and authentic" act could occur only through established procedural channels since any other constitutional change was revolutionary. As he put it, "The very idea of the power and the right of the People to establish Government presupposes the duty of every Individual to obey the established Government." Washington's description of the sovereignty of the people became associated – as it would for many others over time – with a view that denied the people, as the sovereign, the right to alter or abolish government at will. Indeed, his version of the sovereignty of the people helped transform a traditional constitutional statement into an assertion that sovereignty resided in the existing government.[92]

Washington's description of the "alter or abolish" principle did not go unchallenged. In an open *Letter* to Washington, the Pennsylvania printer William Duane sternly rebuked the outgoing president and accused him of reversing two decades of constitutional understandings about the sovereignty of the people in America. Duane, an Irish-American "radical," scandalized Federalists by his obnoxious attack on the revered figure of Washington. Nonetheless, Duane offered a common interpretation of the language found in many American constitutions. Because Washington urged "dogmas repugnant to free government," Duane accused him of forgetting he was "but a responsible agent" of the people.[93]

Washington's most egregious error, according to Duane, lay in misstating the "important principle" and "general truth" of American governments: "the right of the people to make and alter their constitutions." To those "unassailable" words, Washington improperly imposed the requirement of adherence to existing constitutions until changed by an "explicit and authentic act" of the people. The implication of Washington's "loose doctrine" subordinated the people to the existing government and its procedures for constitutional change. Putting government over the people rather than under them, according to Duane, suggested that government possessed "the only wisdom of the nation [and] that the people are not fit to know their own affairs, or judge how they are administered, or that the nation is a dependent creature on the government."[94]

To his own rhetorical question – "Are men to remain silent until called upon by their governmental agents?" – Duane emphatically answered in the negative. That response rested on the significance Duane attributed (but Washington denied) to constitutional language found in many American constitutions other than the federal one. That language described the people acting independent of government, emphasized their right to scrutinize their governors, and explicitly recognized them as America's sovereign.

The response to the so-called Whiskey Rebellion rationalized efforts by the national government to protect itself against perceived threats to its authority in defending an excise tax that lacked the support of many if not a majority of the American people. The argument that government possessed the power to protect itself, however, implied more of a sovereignty in the government than in the people.[95] Thus, as the nation's first president, Washington advanced an idea that ultimately undercut the supremacy of the sovereign people. Henceforth a tension remained between those who continued to emphasize government as inevitably playing a subordinate role to "the people" and those who elevated government – and in particular the national government – to a predominant position in the American constitutional order.[96]

Yet in many different contexts before the Civil War, Americans routinely asserted the right of the collective sovereign to act independent of government even if they disagreed about who or what constituted that sovereign. Indeed, after the excise tax protests, Americans continued to resist the trend of governmental sovereignty, with respect to both the federal and state constitutions. That resistance drew strength from a revolutionary constitutional settlement that embraced the people's sovereignty as the legitimizing foundation of American governments. The Revolution, the creation of the first state constitutions, the successful independence movements for new states, and the creation of the federal Constitution – all invoked the sovereign people for their justification.

Beyond putting the constitutional theory of the people's sovereignty into practice, Americans repeatedly relied on its authority in political disputes before the Civil War. During their political differences Americans reached for constitutional language that justified a challenge to those in government by those out of power. In particular, Americans insisted that the collective sovereign of the federal Constitution possessed a role – independent of government – in monitoring the constitutional order and maintaining its balance. The idea that the people had a legitimate right to a form of "interposition" to maintain that constitutional balance enjoyed support from leaders across political parties when they challenged the governmental policies of their opponents.

While such invocation of the authority of "the people" was frequently politically expedient, the position nonetheless rested on a solid foundation of constitutional understandings and practices since the Revolution. Moreover, much authority existed for the proposition that the sovereign source of constitutions could act independent of government without invoking the raw power of revolution. Despite the efforts of Washington and others to subordinate the collective sovereign of the people to the government, too much had been written, said, and done in the course of American constitution-making for there to be unquestioning acceptance of Washington's assertion in his *Farewell Address* – that the federal Constitution could be changed only by the procedures it provided. Ultimately, even Washington's enormous personal reputation proved no match against the practical political appeal of invoking the people's constitutional authority as America's sovereign.

7 Federal Sovereignty

Competing Views of the Federal Constitution

Death came for James Madison in his eighty-fifth year, only six days before the anniversary of American Independence in 1836. The day before he died, Madison refused stimulants offered by his doctors, who thought they might allow him to live until the Fourth of July, the day that other former Presidents – Jefferson, Adams, and Monroe – had died. Soon after six in the morning, Madison characteristically slipped off "quietly," unceremoniously.

His life ended with a brief, ambiguous comment that exemplified the controversy surrounding his final years. As recounted by his slave Paul, the former president took breakfast as usual, in his room, but had difficulty swallowing. He was asked, "What is the matter?" Madison seemed to abandon the effort to start the meal and the day as well, explaining before losing consciousness and his life, that he was experiencing "[n]othing more than a change of mind."

Madison spent much of his last years asserting that he had not changed his mind about some things – such as the Union, the federal Constitution, and that in America the people were the sovereign. Retirement from the presidency nineteen years earlier started peacefully enough when he moved from the White House to Montpelier, his estate near the foothills of Virginia's Blue Ridge Mountains. It was a time, his neighbor Thomas Jefferson assured him, to finally be "release[d] from incessant labors, corroding anxieties, active enemies and interested friends." Retirement promised a "return to your books and farm, to tranquility and independence."

As the years passed, Madison saw the circle of his fellow Federal constitution-makers shrink and his retirement become more difficult. When he left the presidency in 1817, he was one of thirteen delegates of the federal constitutional convention still alive. In 1825, he was one of six. Beginning the decade of the 1830s, he was the sole survivor. The start of that decade also witnessed the decline of Madison's Montpelier estate. It had become, as one observer noted after a visit shortly before Madison's death, "decayed and in need of considerable repairs." Nonetheless, the plantation still reflected a "gentlemanlike style of rural prosperity."

The problem was that as the 1830s began, there was precious little rural prosperity to be had. Time now seemed to be catching up with James Madison. Years of poor harvests and depressed agricultural markets placed him in a scramble to avoid bankruptcy, which he did mainly through his savings and by selling off slaves and his lands in Kentucky. He now complained of being crippled by rheumatism, going deaf in one ear, and losing his sight. With what time remained, Madison hoped to complete a work of increasing importance to him.

The project had begun fifteen years earlier. In 1821, Madison had decided to publish posthumously his detailed notes on the federal constitutional convention, after the posthumous publication of notes on the convention taken by Robert Yates, who had served as a delegate from New York. Yates's notes depicted Madison as inconsistent on the issue of state sovereignty, and Madison considered them plagued by "misstatement" and "incorrectness." It was important to challenge such "errors" and set the record straight.

As he entered his closing years, however, Madison counted on his convention notes for more than simply a historical corrective. With a deteriorating financial position, he pinned his hopes on the money that might be made with their publication. Apart from financial woes, as the 1830s unfolded, Madison encountered renewed charges of his alleged inconsistency.

Those charges surfaced in 1828, when a federal tariff of that year prompted a protest by South Carolina challenging the tariff's constitutionality. A friend entreated Madison to allow publication of letters Madison had written defending the tariff as well within Congress's commerce powers. Publication of the letters triggered personal attacks that made the ones he suffered as president pale in comparison. One Virginia newspaper accused Madison of distorting the constitution by a "far-fetched, ambiguous, irrelevant, and unsatisfactory" course of reasoning. Moreover, the newspaper charged that Madison's explanation of the constitution could not be trusted because what he wrote was "in direct hostility" to "the whole course of" his "reasoning for 40 preceding years." The theme of having changed his mind – and that his views about the founding were not entitled to credence – became a recurring and growing critique in Madison's closing years.

These personal attacks cast a pall over Madison's hope that his convention notes might clarify the achievement that was the federal Constitution. In 1833, one U.S. senator for Virginia, John Tyler, cited Yates's Notes on the Federal Convention *on the floor of the Senate. He noted Yates's assertion that*

*Madison wanted "to render the States nothing more than the provinces" of
the federal government. Tyler questioned how anyone could look to Madison
as an authority on the meaning of the constitution. The Tyler attack on "the
Last of the Fathers" was widely broadcast, particularly in Virginia. Madison
was aghast. A year later he wrote a former aide noting the wide recognition of
his role in drafting the constitution and that "my opinions, with the grounds
of them, are well known, being in print with my name to them." Yet many
Americans did not seem to care about his intent in his handiwork – few had
any "respect for my opinion" on the constitution.*

*At the time of his death, Madison hoped his notes on the convention might
give Americans an appreciation of their heritage of constitutionalism. He did
not want the notes to be used in partisan battles of the day but to serve as
a helpful reference "for general and future use." The full realization of that
hope remains an open question today.*[1]

The right to monitor the constitutional operation of government was a central
issue of American constitutionalism after the adoption of the federal Constitution. America's first four presidents – Washington, Adams, Jefferson, and
Madison – each struggled to address the issue. That issue revealed the fundamental disagreement among Americans about their country's unique governments and the day-to-day relation of those governments to the sovereign,
the people.

Disagreements typically arose in attempts to strike the balance of power
involved in the tension between the national and state governments. The constitution deliberately did not resolve that balance, and the tension between
the Union and the individual states remained a dominant concern before
the Civil War. Controversies over conflicting national and state powers were
"perpetually arising," observed Chief Justice John Marshall in 1819. They
would recur as "long as our system shall exist," the justice acknowledged. The
dynamic nature of federalism was inherent in that constitutional system.[2]

The Supreme Court's first two decades confronted federalism, but an
equally important struggle occurred outside of the court. This struggle arose
as Americans wrestled with the puzzle at the heart of the new federal system:
what did rule by a collective sovereign mean under a national constitution
when the people who held this sovereignty were also the sovereign of their
individual state governments? Three incidents illustrate how this aspect
of American constitutionalism was played out before the Civil War. Each
controversy – the promulgation of the Virginia and Kentucky Resolutions,
the meeting of the Hartford Convention, and the Nullification crisis, saw
Americans struggle with key questions of constitutionalism: who were "the

people" that underlay the national constitution and how could that collective sovereign act and be recognized in action? Historians typically treat these three episodes as unrelated political and constitutional disputes involving federalism. In fact, they involved much more because each shaped the ways the American sovereign could – as the concept of the people's sovereignty called for – monitor the constitutional operation of the national government.[3]

These three controversies saw Americans invoking a tool used before the Civil War but little seen today: the right of "interposition." Interposition sought reversal of national laws that some people thought unconstitutional. It involved many potential instruments and actions to maintain the constitution's health. It could involve individual citizens or groups of citizens. It might also involve the state legislatures, not acting as the sovereign, but as an instrument of the people to communicate concerns about the national constitution. Alexander Hamilton identified that role in *Federalist No. 26*. He described the state legislatures as naturally "jealous guardians of the rights of the citizens" of the state. In the new federal system, the state legislatures, observed Hamilton, could "sound the alarm to the people" when the national government exceeded its rightful powers.[4]

Public opinion, petitions, and protests as well as instructions to political representatives were some of the ways interposition could facilitate faithful execution of the constitution. Interposition could also involve resolving a constitutional controversy by seeking the revision of the constitution itself. James Madison described each of these options as "the several constitutional modes of interposition by the States against abuses of powers." The term "interposition" did not seem to prompt greater elaboration by contemporaries than what Madison provided. The word "interposition" did not carry the implication attached to it today that interposition nullified a law, the understanding attributed to it during its use in the sectional debates preceding the Civil War.[5] Rather, what Madison and his contemporaries meant by "interposition" seemed to come from its classic sense. As used in astronomical and scientific texts of the period, it described the movement of something between two other things in a relationship, so as to interrupt and bring attention to the essence of that relationship. In this sense, the moon interposed when it came between the earth and sun, allowing those on earth to reaffirm how the sun provided light to the earth.[6]

In a constitutional mode, interposition usually involved action by a third party coming between the people as the sovereign and the sovereign's agent, the government. This interposition was not a sovereign act, since the people as the collective sovereign did not take that step. It did not break the ties between the people and their government, as for example by nullifying laws.

Rather, the interposer, through public opinion, protests, petitioners, or even the state legislatures as an instrument of the people, focused attention on whether the government was acting in conformity with the people's mandates expressed in their constitutions. A successful interposition occurred when either the government backtracked, conceding that it had overstepped its constitutional boundaries as asserted by the interposition, or when the people in light of the interposition chose to change the constitutional order.

Since the agent of interposition was not "the people" as the sovereign, the interposer's action served as an alarm to the people and did not affect the legitimacy of the challenged action of government. The people in considering the claims of the interposer were not limited to the forms of change provided in the constitution. Because the sovereign had "ultimate authority" outside the "purview and forms" of the constitution, they could act, as Madison put it, to "explain, amend, or remake" the constitution. As the constitution's sovereign creator, the people were not subordinate to their creation, the national government. The people had a final authority. The federal Constitution was merely "a discription of those powers which the people have delegated to their Magistrates, to be exercised for definite purposes." Interposition alerted the people to whether the government, their agent, was acting in conformity with constitutional dictates. It remained up to the people as the collective sovereign whether to resolve matters by exercising their final or, as Madison put it, "ultimate" authority, which could also be exercised outside the "purview and forms" of the federal Constitution.[7]

The constitution divided governmental power between the national and state governments, a division creating a puzzle in identifying the sovereign of the federal Constitution. That puzzle was not encountered under state constitutions, whose sovereign was logically composed of the people of a given state. The federal Constitution, however, initially invited two different views of the collective sovereign that underlay that constitution. First, the underlying sovereign of the federal Constitution could be considered the people of the discrete states acting collectively. Alternatively, the people could be seen as one undifferentiated national American people. Both positions were plausible, but mutually inconsistent.

During the federal convention Madison argued that the sovereign was the people in the discrete states acting collectively. The draft constitution, he noted, sprang "not immediately from the people, but from the States which they respectively composed." During the ratification debate he identified the sovereign behind the constitution as "the people of America" but "not as individuals composing one entire nation; but as composing the distinct and independent States to which they respectively belong." Similarly,

in 1798, fellow Virginian John Taylor considered the need for federal constitutional amendments and described "the people in state conventions" as
"incontrovertibly the contracting parties" behind the constitution capable
of effecting such changes. In 1800 Madison described "the people composing" the political societies of their respective states acting "in their highest
sovereign capacity" as creating the constitution. Likewise, the constitutional
commentator St. George Tucker in 1803 described the foundation of the
constitution as resting on the consent of "the people of the several states,
separately, and independently taken, and expressed."[8]

Other Americans described one undifferentiated national people as the
sovereign, not the people of the discrete states acting collectively. James
Wilson at the Pennsylvania ratifying convention described the sovereign as
the people acting for themselves as "one great community." In 1793, Chief
Justice John Jay also expressed that view from his position on the Supreme
Court. It was "the people, in their collective and national capacity" who
brought the constitution to life. Justice Joseph Story's treatise on constitutional law reflected the same theme in denying that the constitution was not
a compact of independent states. This could not be, asserted Story, because
it was "[t]he people of the *United States*, not the distinct people of a *particular state*," who acted to create the constitution. This idea of a national
people creating the constitution gained additional currency through the oratory of Senator Daniel Webster. Reportedly, Webster enthralled listeners by
describing the formation of the American nation not by the people in separate states but rather by "the People of the United States, in the aggregate"
rising together to create a government.[9]

The idea that American constitutions were instructions by "the people"
as the sovereign could logically support either view of the founding: that it
was a national people or the people identified with individual states acting
collectively. Arguably, the idea of the people collectively acting through the
agency of their particular states better reflected American constitutionalism
before 1787. The manner in which the federal Constitution was ratified
demonstrated the people within individual states acting collectively: through
conventions of the sovereign people from the state in which they lived. Even
those who interpreted the constitution as granting broad national powers to
the federal government, such as Chief Justice John Marshall, described the
Founding in a voice much closer in tone to Madison's than Webster's.[10]

Because "the people" who created the national government could act as
a practical matter only through the agency of their states, the term "the
states" introduced a complexity that confused Americans at the time and has
confounded later observers as well. Like many Americans of his day, Madison

could describe the sovereign who gave life to the national government as "the states." Along with those Americans, Madison could be referring to three different things. Madison acknowledged that "the term 'States'" was ambiguous. First, the states, Madison noted, could mean individual state governments. Second, it could mean the people within a state as the sovereign of that state. Third, it could mean the people of the nation who lived in the different geographic areas known as "states." Madison's definition of the national sovereign encompassed this third meaning of the people in "the 'States.'"[11]

These different meanings of the term "the states" dictated how one might understand the federal Constitution as a "compact" among "the states." Under the first meaning attributed to "the states," the constitution could mean a compact of individual state governments.[12] The second meaning of "the states" implied the sovereign people of an individual state compacting with the sovereign people of other states to adopt the constitution.[13] For Madison, in using the third meaning of the term "the states," the constitution was a "compact" reflecting an agreement by the people of the individual states acting not as the sovereign of their own states. Rather, by acting in concert with the people of other states, they formed the collective sovereign of the national government they were creating. The collective people of the nation – while still identified in terms of the individual states in which they acted – was a different sovereign collectively than when those people acted as the sovereign of their respective states. This collective sovereign was the sovereign that created the federal Constitution and only a majority of that collective sovereign could alter or abolish the constitution.[14]

Madison's terminology demonstrated that describing the constitution as a compact did not necessitate accepting individual state governments or the sovereign people of individual states as the parties who created the federal Constitution. Rather, Madison's description of "the states" as parties to the federal compact envisioned a collective sovereign that created the constitution as defined neither in solely individual state terms nor in purely national terms. In the political climate of the 1830s, Madison came to occupy a middle ground between a "states rights" understanding of the constitution as a compact and a nationalistic view of the constitution as the product of an undifferentiated American people.

Because a "states rights" position became associated with the claim that individual states could act unilaterally as parties to the federal compact, some Americans rejected the use of the word "compact" to describe the constitution. For example, in denying that the constitution was a compact, Daniel Webster insisted that a national people and not "the states" created the constitution. In taking that position, the subtlety of Madison's views was overlooked – not only by many of his contemporaries but by subsequent scholars as well.[15]

Differences in the relationship of the collective sovereign to the national government it created persisted in disputes arising after the formation of the federal Constitution. These divisions tend to be analyzed today as reflecting different views of federalism. As Madison's efforts after the adoption of the constitution illustrated, they also reflected a second national division. This second division did not involve the relationship of various governments within a federal system but rather the relationship of the people to their various governments. The people's relationship to government also involved the authority of the sovereign to oversee the operation of the government it created.[16]

VIRGINIA AND KENTUCKY RESOLUTIONS

Many federal Framers – including Washington – hoped the people would be more subordinate, deferential to their national governors, and conscious of their passive role as the sovereign after the adoption of the federal Constitution. These hopes were soon disappointed. Stiff resistance met the attempt to collect the national government's first tax on a domestic product: an excise on whiskey. Those tax protests stimulated a wider and persistent debate over the people's relationship to that government.

Washington ultimately "crushed" the so-called Whiskey Rebellion, but this did not quell growing concerns about the relation of the people to their government. Washington's successor, John Adams, faced his own crisis in 1798 when Federalists in Congress passed several laws during a climate of agitation for war against France because of its interference with American shipping. One law, the Alien Act, allowed the president to deport aliens he deemed "dangerous to the peace and safety" of the nation or suspected of "treasonable or secret machinations." Its companion, the Sedition Act, permitted punishment of "false, slanderous, and malicious writing" that brought the president or members of Congress into "contempt or disrepute."[17]

Many opponents of Federalist policy were likely targets of both acts, but particularly the Sedition Act. Consequently, Republicans considered these acts a political attack. The Federalist bias of the American press diminished in the 1790s with the appearance of more newspapers taking a Republican slant. The Sedition Act threatened the Republicans' use of newspapers to counter their Federalist opponents. Besides the acts' effect on practical politics, they appeared to subvert the federal constitutional order. Republicans asserted that the Alien Act exceeded Congress's constitutional powers while the Sedition Act violated the First Amendment. Jefferson complained to Madison that both acts showed "no respect" for the constitution. Madison called the Alien Act "a monster" that would "for ever disgrace its parents," the Federalists. The act denied the people the "right of freely examining public characters and measures." [18]

Both acts prompted Madison and Jefferson to orchestrate protests. Most dramatic was a set of resolutions they drafted to be adopted by the legislatures of Virginia and Kentucky. Madison authored Virginia's Resolutions, while Jefferson developed a version for Kentucky. In passing the resolutions both legislatures expressed the judgment that the two federal laws were unconstitutional. Kentucky's Resolutions instructed the state's congressional representatives to seek the acts' repeal. The governor was to transmit copies to other state legislatures in hopes those bodies would adopt similar measures. Likewise, Virginia's Resolutions were sent to the state's congressional representatives and other state governors.[19]

Some contemporaries assumed (as have some subsequent scholars) that the resolutions sought to nullify the operation of the two objectionable federal laws in Virginia and Kentucky. This assumption discounts the resolutions' express purpose – to stimulate a coordinated national effort to repeal the laws through congressional action. The resolutions distinguished between a legislature's opinion of the constitutionality of national laws and action by the sovereign people to render those laws unenforceable.[20]

The Virginia Resolutions called the acts "unconstitutional" while the Kentucky Resolutions described them as "not law but utterly void and of no force." Those words, Madison later explained, simply emphasized the legislature's opinion of the acts. They did not constitute a nullification of the acts. Neither legislature asserted that their resolutions made the acts a dead letter, nor did either state take any action to resist the enforcement of the acts. The resolutions, as Madison pointed out, did not "annul the acts" because they came "from the Legislature only, which was not even a party to the Constitution." Only collective action by the people as the sovereign source of the federal Constitution could nullify the acts.[21]

Madison's explanations of the resolutions was echoed by John Breckinridge, the sponsor of the resolutions in the Kentucky legislature. He explicitly distinguished actions of the legislature from those that might be taken by the sovereign underlying the constitution. Because the people in the "co-States" who met in their state conventions were the "parties" to the constitution they were "*solely* authorized to judge in the last resort of the power exercised under that compact." However, when Congress – "merely the

creature" of the constitution – enacted laws "beyond the limits of the Constitution," states "ought to make a legislative declaration" affirming their
belief that because such laws were "unconstitutional" they were also "void
and of no effect." A wise Congress would respond by canceling "obnoxious laws." When – despite "representations" by "a majority of the States" –
Congress persisted in enforcing such laws, it was "the right and duty of
the several States," Breckinridge noted, "to nullify those acts" in order *"to
protect their citizens."* Presently, Kentucky's legislators were simply "firmly
express[ing]" their "opinions" and asking other states to "examine" the laws.[22]

A Kentuckian wrote Jefferson hoping that state authorities would get the
nation's attention by giving "solemnity to the voice of the people." When
Kentucky's legislature convened in early November 1798, the state's governor, James Garrard, urged legislators to assess "the conduct of the national
government" and to offer it appropriate "applau[se]" or "censure." The legislature should declare the state's support for the constitution and "protest
against all unconstitutional laws and impolitic proceedings."[23]

Kentucky's 1798 Resolutions called on its "Co-states" to declare the acts
"void and of no force." Virginia's Resolutions identified "the states" as the
"parties" to the constitution who could "interpose" to stop unconstitutional
acts. The resolutions were an interposition of each state legislature offering
its constitutional opinion. They were obviously not an ultimate intervention
by the people of the states themselves.[24]

Upon receiving the Kentucky legislature's resolutions, Jefferson forwarded a copy to Madison. Opponents of the acts nationwide should "distinctly affirm" the Kentucky Resolutions' "important principles." Hopefully
this would obviate the need of taking matters "to extremities." As Jefferson
wrote Virginia legislator John Taylor before Virginia's Resolutions passed, it
was premature to contemplate the ultimate step by the people. "[F]or the
present," he told Taylor, "I should be for resolving the alien & sedition laws
to be against the constitution & merely void." Virginia should ask other states
to make "similar declarations."[25]

Taylor agreed with Jefferson's request, recognizing that if the state and
national governments came into conflict it might force "the people in convention" to settle the matter. This approach reflected Taylor's belief that
when the people met in "a general convention" they were "the only genuine
and legitimate fountain of power" and the ultimate "corrector of unconstitutional" acts of the government.[26]

Like Jefferson, Madison believed a state legislature did not have the constitutional authority to nullify a national law. Five days after Virginia's legislature acted, Madison wrote Jefferson, concerned that in their "zeal" some

legislators might overlook "the distinction between the power of the *State*, & that of *the Legislature*, on questions relating to the federal pact." While states were "clearly the ultimate Judge of infractions" of the constitution, it did "not follow" that legislatures were "the legitimate organ" for rendering that ultimate judgment. Unlike the Articles of Confederation, state governments did not form the federal Constitution. Meetings of state conventions, like those that ratified the federal Constitution, were the appropriate mechanisms to invoke the "ultimate" right of the people to correct "infractions" by the national government. This was "especially" true, noted Madison, since the people in "a Convention was the organ by which the Compact was made."[27]

Both states' resolutions acknowledged the ultimate authority of the people as the sovereign to assess the constitutionality of acts of the government. Interposition by state legislatures operated differently from such final action by the people as a matter of last resort. Legislative interposition sought the repeal of unconstitutional laws by focusing attention on them. As Madison pointed out in the Virginia Resolutions, legislators were doing their "duty" to "watch over and oppose every infraction" of constitutional principles. Virginia's and Kentucky's legislatures were acting as Alexander Hamilton predicted they would during the ratification debate. State legislatures, asserted Hamilton, functioned as "jealous guardians of the rights of the citizens" to "sound the alarm to the people" if the national government exceeded its rightful powers. Hamilton also noted that after identifying excesses of "national authority" those legislatures could "communicate with each other" and "at once adopt a regular plan of opposition." By 1794, the Virginian John Taylor asserted that state legislatures had "as good a right to judge of every infraction of the constitution, as Congress itself."[28]

Many Americans considered the guardianship of the federal constitutional order an obligation extending well beyond state legislators and legislative action. The "true lesson" of "the Representative principle," Madison observed, taught "that in no case ought the eyes of the people . . . be shut" to "the conduct of those entrusted with power; nor their tongues tied from a just wholesome censure" of public officials. Ensuring the constitutional operation of government was the responsibility of individual citizens in addition to their state legislators.[29]

Protests against the Alien and Sedition laws preceding the resolutions in Virginia and Kentucky emphasized the duty of citizens to identify overreaching acts of government. On July 24, 1798, Clarke County, Kentucky, inhabitants considered national government officials "the servant[s] of the people." The people should "watch over" the conduct of their agents "with vigilance." They passed resolutions calling the Alien Act "unconstitutional" and the Sedition Act "abominable." Like other meetings protesting the acts, Clarke County's resolutions were sent to Congress and President Adams. On August 2, 1798, inhabitants of Montgomery County, Kentucky adopted resolutions similar to those of Clarke County. Four days later Kentucky's Woodford County also adopted resolutions urging citizens "to guard" against violations of their "Constitutional rights." A key framer of Kentucky's first constitution, the lawyer George Nicholas, denounced the Sedition Act in the *Kentucky Gazette* as unconstitutional. Exercising his "invaluable privilege of speaking and publishing" on the "conduct" of government officials, Nicholas addressed some four thousand to five thousand people gathered at Lexington in mid-August 1798. He told them that Americans "always have a right" to scrutinize "the public conduct of their servants."[30]

Grassroots opposition to the acts was not limited to Virginia and Kentucky. Congress also received a stream of petitions from counties in New York, New Jersey, and Pennsylvania. By the end of January 1799, the House of Representatives referred those petitions to a committee for a report. Virginia's congressional representative John Dawson predicted that the House might repeal the acts, but there was "no chance" the Federalist-dominated Senate would do so.[31]

When the committee reported, it defended the constitutionality of the acts, rejecting their repeal as "inexpedient." Federalists were unwilling to debate the issue. Republicans Albert Gallatin from Pennsylvania and John Nicholas of Virginia tried to urge repeal of the acts. Their advocacy was soon interrupted when Federalists "began to enter into loud conversations, laugh, cough &c. so that for the last hour of these gentlemen's speaking" they needed "the lungs" of a public auctioneer to be heard. Edward Livingston of New York also tried to talk, but "after a few sentences" the Speaker cut him off. "It was impossible to proceed." The report that the acts remain in force passed by a slim margin of 52 to 48.[32]

Despite local efforts, the effect on the national government seemed minimal. By September 1798, the Virginia legislator Wilson Cary Nicholas thought that actions by "town or county meetings will never produce the effect" of gaining national attention to the need for repeal. Only a month before, a Kentuckian also wanted "united and official action" by the legislature to supplement the other "constitutional measures" of letters, petitions, and remonstrances against the acts. Keeping government "within the just Limits of the Constitution," observed Virginia's congressional delegates, required "*wise* and *firm* State Measures."[33]

Instead of rallying other legislatures to protest the Alien and Sedition Acts, the Virginia and Kentucky Resolutions stimulated Federalist attacks.

George Washington dismissed criticism of the acts as purely political. Republican leaders were deaf to any arguments justifying the laws because they "have points to carry, from which no reasoning, no inconsistency of conduct, no absurdity, can divert them." Virginia's Resolutions had the tendency to "dissolve the Union." Washington's fears were echoed by other Federalists. For example, Massachusetts Federalist Theodore Sedgwick believed the resolutions were "a declaration of war" while his colleague Timothy Pickering thought they implied "a right to disobey" national laws.[34]

No other state legislature formally joined the protest of Virginia and Kentucky. Three months after the two states issued their resolutions, American state legislators revealed no "unanimity" about them. The negative responses of state legislatures to the resolutions reflected Federalist legislative majorities but obscured a frequently sizable Republican dissent. After North Carolina's legislature received Kentucky's Resolutions in December 1798, its House overwhelmingly passed a resolution condemning the Alien and Sedition Acts as a "violation of the principles of the Constitution" and called for the state's congressional delegation to support the repeal of the acts. The state's Senate, dominated by Federalists, handily defeated that resolution. In some cases, outnumbered Republicans boycotted proceedings and their views were normally not memorialized. In this way, the formal replies of states to the Virginia and Kentucky legislatures leave an impression of broader opposition to the resolutions than in fact existed.[35]

Legislative responses reflected the view – by no means universally held – that constitutional interpretation was "exclusively vested" in the federal courts and especially the Supreme Court. Federalists thought the legislatures of Virginia and Kentucky had no business assessing the constitutionality of the acts. Their legislative opinions were "unwarranted" and threatened to destroy the Union, undermine the national government, and introduce "discord and anarchy."[36]

Republicans questioned whether the judiciary was the sole interpreter of the constitution. A New York state senator insisted that his colleagues both "individually, and in a legislative capacity" were entitled to express their views about how the national government was operating. The Senate should "proclaim" the existence of unconstitutional acts. Keeping the national government within constitutional bounds was the responsibility of the state legislature as well as private citizens. Indeed, Republican legislators in Vermont thought the resolutions exemplified "the most pressing" duties of citizens "to guard with a watchful scrupulosity" against breaches of the federal Constitution. Guarding that constitution, "the great and impregnable bulwark" of America's "political salvation," could not be safely left to the federal government or its judiciary. Indeed, just a few years earlier, the Virginia Republican John Taylor insisted that the people of "the nation itself must watch over the constitution" and "preserve it from violation." Republican legislators were now being denied a right "daily exercised by individual citizens."[37]

In the face of negative legislative reaction, Virginia's and Kentucky's legislatures drafted rejoinders, aided by Madison and Jefferson. Kentucky's rejoinder consisted of a resolution passed in November 1799 clarifying that its intent was not to secede or "disturb the harmony" of the Union. Kentucky's legislature suggested that "the several states" (and by implication the people of "the several states") had the "unquestionable right" to nullify unconstitutional acts of the national government. Such a step could be exercised by the people as the sovereign who created that constitution. Kentucky's legislative protest of the Alien and Sedition Acts was a "SOLEMN PROTEST" intended to attract attention and bring corrective action. The state recognized that those acts were "laws of the Union" and the state would "bow" to such laws despite the legislature's opposition to them in a "constitutional manner."[38]

Initially, Jefferson was less conciliatory about the reception of the Virginia and Kentucky Resolutions than was Madison. For one thing, Jefferson displayed greater willingness to contemplate secession than did Kentucky's legislature. In August 1799, Jefferson wrote Madison about the right to dissent from actions of the national government. He could even imagine disunion (what he called "scission") if the government persistently ignored "the true principles" of the constitution. Jefferson's frustration was soon calmed, perhaps by a reminder of what he had written a year earlier when he opposed the talk of Virginia's and North Carolina's separation from the Union. In "every free & deliberating" society, Jefferson had observed, political differences were inevitable. Yet if the temporary dominance of one side justified the other in seceding, "no federal government" could "ever exist." Better, he counseled, to "keep together," "have patience," and gain political ascendancy. Madison evidently persuaded Jefferson to heed his own advice since Jefferson's draft for Kentucky's rejoinder omitted any reference to secession.[39]

In his draft for Virginia's response, Madison wanted to correct the "misconception" in the formal replies of state legislatures that Virginia's Resolutions threatened the Union. He insisted that states had a "right to interpose a *legislative* declaration of opinion on a constitutional point." Published in 1800, Madison's *Report* justified the resolutions as appropriate interposition to monitor the constitution.[40]

In his *Report*, Madison pointed out that Virginia's Resolutions only "communicat[ed]" to the other states its view that the acts were "unconstitutional." This communication was not improper, unconstitutional, or hostile to the Union. The resolutions reflected the "intermediate existence" of state governments "between the people" and the national government. Virginia's legislators exercised a right defended by the constitution's supporters – the right of scrutiny. Madison recalled that in 1788 Federalists insisted that the "vigilance" of state governments "would sound the alarm" at the first signs of "usurpation" by the national government. Virginia's legislature did its "duty" by signaling the people about these "alarming infractions of the constitution" represented by the Alien and Sedition Acts.[41]

Madison's *Report* surveyed the American practice of interposition. This practice was not a "novelty" for either individuals or state legislatures. Protests and declarations – by citizens or legislatures – were merely "expressions of opinion" to prompt "reflection" on the government's actions. Virginia's Resolutions were only one form of interposition. All Americans shared a responsibility to maintain the constitutional limits on government and vigilantly defend constitutional principles. There were many other legitimate means of interposing to preserve the constitution. In addition to state legislatures, "private citizens" could interpose to object to acts of the government they believed were unwarranted by the constitution.[42]

Declaring the acts unconstitutional did not exhaust the legislature's powers of interposition. State legislatures could have made a "direct representation" to Congress, explained Madison, either seeking the repeal of the "two offensive acts" or a revision of the constitution by amendment or through a constitutional convention. Interposition included all of these approaches for influencing the operation of the national government. They were some of the "several means . . . constitutionally open for consideration" as a legislative protest. Still, "the first and most obvious" step for Virginia's legislature was issuing its resolutions.[43]

The interposition by Virginia's legislature did not preclude the sovereign – being the people of the states that included, but was not limited to, those in Virginia – from using other "farther measures that might become necessary and proper." Among the "farther measures" for responding to unconstitutional laws was the sovereign's right to dictate a final constitutional solution. As Madison observed, "The authority of constitutions over governments, and of the sovereignty of the people over constitutions" meant that a sovereign people held greater authority than the governments they established. In America, "The people, not the government, possess the absolute sovereignty." These were "fundamental principles" that Virginia's and other

state constitutions "solemnly enjoined" Americans to observe. Virginia's legislature did nothing revolutionary by noting this ultimate right of the people
in their protest.[44]

The sovereign for the purpose of the federal Constitution was the people
of "the states." As the "sovereign parties" to the constitution, they supplied
that constitution's "genuine source" of legitimacy. Madison conceded that
"the term 'States'" was confusing because it was "sometimes used in a vague
sense, and sometimes in different senses." Nonetheless, this did not render
the term meaningless. In debates over the constitution, the term "the states"
referred to "political societies." Within that context, states could mean the
geographical extent of such political societies, or the government that those
societies established, or perhaps even the political society that operated
within the government.[45]

For purposes of identifying who gave life to the constitution (what Madison referred to as its "legitimate and solid foundation,") the term "the
states" meant "the people composing those political societies, in their highest sovereign capacity." Such a meaning was clear because that was how
the constitution was "submitted to the 'States'" for adoption. The people
of each state formed the sovereign of their respective state constitutions
but could not constitute the sovereign underlying the federal Constitution.
The sovereign people of one ratifying state needed the co-ratification by the
people of other states for the federal constitutional compact to take effect.[46]

The occasional assertion that state legislatures were the parties to the federal compact demonstrated "inaccuracies" in understanding the basis of the
constitution, concluded Madison. Since the people of the states ratified the
constitution as a collective body, they and not the state legislatures were
the "parties to the compact" that granted the national government power.
Whether to exercise the ultimate right of constitutional judgment under the
constitution, therefore, rested with "the American public."[47]

When Virginia's legislature considered Madison's proposed *Report*, debate
revolved around "the right of the Legislature to protest" the acts. Some Federalists argued that since the people were the sovereign, only they and not
the state legislatures should correct "violations" by the national government.
Madison responded that the legislature's right to issue "declarations of opinion" was an appropriate interposition by state legislators. Such interposition
was not the people invoking their ultimate right to resolve the matter.[48]

Although some Federalists described the people who created the constitution in national terms, Madison disagreed. Madison consistently described
the people of the states as the sovereign who gave life to the federal Constitution. Madison – like many other Americans – viewed the people as a collective

sovereign – made up of the people of the several states. Madison believed Federalists and Republicans basically "concurred" in their understanding that the people were the sovereign of the national government. In agreeing that the collective people of all the states were the underlying sovereign of the constitution, Madison and critics of his resolutions and *Report* shared more common ground than contemporaries acknowledged.[49]

This common ground was reflected by the *Minority Report* Federalists filed in the Virginia legislature in response to the 1798 resolutions. The *Minority Report* thought the "will of the majority" of "the people of united America" was the foundation and "first principle" of the "federal pact." The sovereign was thus "[t]he people of the United States" and "the American people." The Virginia Federalist Henry ("Light Horse Harry") Lee, anonymously writing the pamphlet *Plain Truth*, echoed Madison's description of the federal Constitution's creation. The constitution, Lee asserted, was "entirely the act of the people" and not the state governments. "It was sanctioned by the people themselves" who "assembled in their different states in convention." A Pennsylvania Federalist, Judge Alexander Addison, objected to Madison's *Report* and the Virginia Resolutions. Nonetheless, he agreed with Madison that "the people of the several states are the parties to the compact in the constitution." Only the people – "the *parties* to a compact" – could make the ultimate determination that the constitution had been violated, noted Addison. As merely another instrumentality of government, legislatures lacked this authority.[50]

The constitutionalism reflected by the resolutions presumed that the sovereign who adopted a written constitution had the final word on the constitutionality of government's actions. For many Americans, as for Madison, this was "a plain principle, founded in common sense, illustrated by common practice, and essential to the nature of compacts." Because "resort can be had to no tribunal superior to the authority of the parties, the parties themselves must be the rightful judges in the last resort, whether the bargain made, has been . . . violated."[51]

According to Madison, an "interposition of the parties, in their sovereign capacity" was justified only when unconstitutional acts of government "deeply and essentially affect[ed] the vital principles of their political system." This final resolution of the constitution by the people should not occur "in a hasty manner, or on doubtful . . . occasions." The Virginia Resolutions referred to a right and duty of the people of the states "to interpose" collectively in cases of the national government's "deliberate, palpable and dangerous exercise" of powers not granted to it by the constitution. Madison's analysis of the acts provided a justification for such ultimate interposition.[52]

The people of the states "as co-parties to and creators of the constitution" could exercise their ultimate authority by amending the constitution or finding other ways to express their constitutional understanding. Madison later conceded that the resolutions and his *Report* lacked specifics about "what mode the States could interpose in their collective character as parties to the Constitution." However, given "the object and reasoning" of those documents, specifics were "not necessary." "It was sufficient to show that the authority to interpose existed, and was a resort beyond that of the Supreme Court of the United States." If the sovereign people invoked their ultimate right to intervene, how they did so was their "own choice."[53]

Madison's *Report* rejected the Supreme Court as the federal Constitution's "sole expositor." Madison articulated two concepts of how the constitution was to be applied. The first was a broad view of who could authoritatively construe the constitution. The second was that in certain areas the court was the ultimate authority, the expositor whose construction would prevail as the last word, "in the last resort."[54]

Clearly, for Madison, the court was not the only entity that could authoritatively shape the constitution. During the ratification debates and during his service in the first Congress, Madison considered each of the three branches of the national government equally entitled to construe the constitutional authority of their own branch. "[T]he people" through the constitution granted "great powers" and "mark[ed] out the departments" or branches to exercise the delegated powers. The judiciary could not "mark[] out the limits of the powers of the several departments" because that would give it "greater powers" than the co-equal branches.[55]

In *Federalist No. 49*, Madison explained that because no branch could "pretend to [have] an exclusive or superior right of settling the boundaries between their respective powers," the ultimate ability to rectify constitutional "encroachments" among the branches of government was to "appeal to the people themselves." The people as the sovereign "can alone declare" the constitution's "true meaning and enforce its observance." This view did not change once the constitution was adopted. For example, Madison reiterated in 1789 his explanation that "[I]f the constitutional boundary of either [branch] be brought into question, I do not see that any one of these independent departments has more right than another to declare their sentiments on that point."[56]

Madison's concept of "departmental review" of the constitution had wide and continuing support.[57] It was consistent with an American constitutionalism that did not cede to the courts a monopoly in constitutional interpretation.[58] Even the emerging acceptance of judicial review was not inconsistent with the insistence that many other Americans – be they citizens or legislators – retained the right and duty to express their views about the constitutionality of actions of the government and participate in the guardianship of the constitution.[59]

The growing acceptance of judicial review was consistent with interposition. For instance even Hamilton's advocacy in *Federalist No. 78* depicted judicial review as a process of interposition that kept the constitutional order in check. For Hamilton it seemed reasonable to consider the federal courts as "an intermediate body between the people and the legislature . . . to keep the latter within the limits assigned to their authority." Judicial review at the state level was often described as a process of interposition. As a delegate to the New York constitutional convention in 1820 suggested, by invalidating unconstitutional acts the state judiciary formed a "shield between the rights of citizens and the encroachments of legislative power."[60]

That the Supreme Court was not the sole expositor of the constitution was not inconsistent with Madison's view that under certain circumstances, the Court was the final expositor, the one of "last resort." However, the Court's power here was limited. It could exercise such authority only in the cases that properly came before it. In deciding those cases the Court indeed had the final word on the constitution. Madison, for example, thought it appropriate for the Supreme Court to interpret the constitution "in the ordinary course of Government." In his *Report of 1800*, Madison elaborated on the limits of judicial review and the necessity of review beyond the Supreme Court in certain "great and extraordinary" cases. One limitation of judicial review involved unconstitutional acts of another branch that did not arise in a case "within the controul of the judicial department." Another situation involved "the Judicial Department" itself – if ever the judiciary "exercise[d] or sanction[ed] dangerous powers beyond the grant of the constitution."[61]

In these cases only the sovereign could determine whether the national government went beyond the people's grant of authority in the constitution. The people of the states who formed "the parties to the constitution" and not the departmental agents to which they "delegated authority" retained "the ultimate right . . . to judge whether the compact has been dangerously violated." This action by the sovereign people served as a check beyond judicial review. Their agents – public officials, representatives, and judges – could not exercise such authority for the sovereign. No single branch, including the judiciary, could make a decision to supersede "the authority . . . the sovereign parties to the constitution" might exercise.[62]

Madison's view that the Supreme Court was not the exclusive interpreter of the constitution was well within the mainstream of American thought at the time. The "doctrine" that only the Court could exclusively consider the constitutionality of national laws, wrote one Republican contributor to a Boston newspaper, took "from the people the ultimate sovereignty" and conferred it on their "agents." Another Republican contributor to the same paper saw a paradox because the people were America's collective sovereign. Insisting on a judicial monopoly for constitutional interpretation undermined that truth. If the people were truly America's sovereign it was "difficult" or even contradictory to credit the Federalists' argument that the people "*have no right to decide on any invasion of [their] constitutional powers.*"[63]

Independent of the constitutional right of the people as the sovereign to shape the constitution, there also existed a "natural right" to act when government took arbitrary and tyrannical steps. This was the "natural" right alluded to by Jefferson in his initial draft of the Kentucky Resolutions of 1798. Madison identified the same power in what he called "the *natural* right to resist intolerable oppression." The natural right justified any state or even a county "in shaking off the yoke," unilaterally invoking the power of self-preservation. Such a power differed from the people's authority to check the national government as the sovereign.[64]

In his first draft of the Kentucky Resolutions, Jefferson distinguished government's "abuse" of "delegated powers" from its exercise of powers not granted by the constitution. When government misused delegated powers, the people's "constitutional remedy" was to turn offenders out of office. In contrast, when the government exceeded its delegated powers other options existed. If undelegated powers were used, the states collectively – referred to by Jefferson as the "co-states" – could act. As "parties to the compact" the "co-states" were "solely authorised to judge in the last resort" whether Congress exceeded its constitutional powers. The federal government must accede to such action because as "merely the creature" of the constitution, the national government lacked such authority.[65]

Kentucky's legislature deleted Jefferson's reference to nullification in its 1798 resolutions, but retained the term "natural right." Notwithstanding its "natural right" to act independently, Kentucky rejected that option and sought to act with its "co-states." The legislature's emphasis on the national government as the creature of the constitution meant that government could not serve as "the exclusive or final *judge* of the extent of the powers delegated to itself." Giving that ultimate authority to government made "its discretion, and not the constitution, the measure of its powers." When Kentucky's legislature reiterated its position in the state's 1799 resolutions, it included Jefferson's reference to "nullification" but made it clear that "the several states" were the sovereign source underlying the constitution. Nullification by "those sovereignties" acting with their ultimate right of interposition was a "rightful remedy."[66]

Historians often consider the Virginia and Kentucky Resolutions a failure because no other state issued similar resolutions. Yet the interposition by these two states in 1798 and 1799 focused attention on the Alien and Sedition Acts, as interposition was designed to do. Consistent with the theory of interposition, in 1800 American voters went to the polls and chose between candidates who took opposing positions on those acts. Jefferson made "violations of the true principles" of the constitution a central campaign issue for the Republican Party. His election to the presidency and that of his followers to Congress reflected public opinion about the constitutionality of the Acts. Madison later concluded that the resolutions achieved "a triumph over the obnoxious acts, and an apparent abandonment of them forever."[67]

Americans continued to employ interposition in responding to federal legislation they believed violated the constitution. Following the lead of the first generation of Americans who lived under the constitution, subsequent generations employed the same constitutional tradition of interposition. However, as the revolutionary generation began to die off, the next generation tried to change that tradition, with fateful consequences.

THE HARTFORD CONVENTION

After the Republican victory represented by Jefferson's election in 1800, Federalists continued to dominate in the northeastern tier of states. Now as the opposition, they quickly adopted the tools they had so vigorously opposed when they were the party in power, such as the right of interposition. New England Federalists considered policies of Jefferson's successor to the presidency – James Madison – as unfairly and unconstitutionally burdening their region. Their grievances included economic policies involving a series of embargos as well as a war against Britain in 1812. The constitution clearly granted Congress authority to regulate commerce – this was one of the major arguments the Federalists used to promote adoption of the constitution in 1787. Now, however, New England Federalists considered this authority abused when employed by Madison in a manner they felt was destroying the commerce of their region. They sought to reverse Madison's policies and interposition was one tool in their arsenal.[68]

As early as 1808, citizens from the town of Northampton, Massachusetts, petitioned Congress and President Jefferson to repeal an embargo imposed in 1807. Other local committees distributed printed blank petitions for repeal. Seventy additional towns joined the remonstrance. The town of

Newburyport also sought repeal of the "unconstitutional" embargo. After not hearing from Washington, Newburyport Federalists in January 1809 petitioned Massachusetts legislators "as the more immediate guardians" of their "rights" to "interpose" on their behalf. A month later delegates from fifty-one towns in Hampshire County met in convention to address the administration's "shameful violations" of the constitution. Because "sovereignty resides in the people," the delegates noted that citizens rightfully could oversee the "conduct and measures" of their "Rulers." Boston also petitioned the legislature seeking its "interposition" to gain relief from national laws.[69]

In its 1809 winter session, Massachusetts's legislature responded to the calls for interposition. An "immense majority of the people" suffered from the embargo, it concluded. This required the use of "interposition to obtain relief." Legislators felt it their particular duty to warn their constituents of "all unconstitutional acts and usurpations of the national government." The legislature interposed by adopting four resolutions. The first declared the embargo unconstitutional and therefore "not legally binding on the citizens of this state." The second authorized a remonstrance to Congress urging the act's repeal. The third called for constitutional amendments giving "the commercial states their fair and just consideration." The last invited other legislatures to join in measures "to preserve inviolate" the constitutional union.[70]

Other states also used legislative interposition. In February 1809, Governor Jonathan Trumbull addressed Connecticut's legislature and presented town petitions against the embargo. Trumbull urged the legislature "to cast a watchful eye" on the federal government. It was their "duty" when Congress exceeded its constitutional powers "to interpose their protecting shield between the right and liberty of the people, and the assumed power of the General Government." The legislature responded by declaring the embargo unconstitutional and resolving to cooperate "zealously" with other states for constitutional amendments to protect New England's commerce. Rhode Island's legislature also pledged "to interpose" and to remain "vigilant in guarding" against unconstitutional acts of the government.[71]

In part because of these interpositions, Congress repealed the 1807 embargo in March 1809 . This brought only temporary relief to the region. A seriously divided Congress declared war against Britain in 1812, placing New England on the front line of the conflict because of its proximity to British-occupied Canada. Indeed, many New England Federalists opposed what they called "Mr. Madison's War."[72]

Another issue New England Federalists cited as evidence of unconstitutional actions by Madison's administration was the effort to nationalize state militias in the region. The governors of Massachusetts, Connecticut, and Rhode Island refused a federal requisition for troops on grounds it endangered their states and violated the constitution. They asserted (and an advisory opinion of Massachusetts's highest court agreed) that while the constitution authorized national service, state governors decided whether that service was warranted. In late 1814, Daniel Webster, then a congressional representative for New Hampshire, argued against a military draft that compelled members of state militias into federal service. "The operation of measures thus unconstitutional and illegal," Webster asserted, "ought to be prevented by a resort to other measures which are both constitutional and legal." Webster urged "the State Governments to protect their own authority over their own militia, and to interpose between their citizens and arbitrary power." Interposition was necessary, Webster later wrote his brother, because "[t]the people must look for protection to the *State Govts*." since the national government "cannot aid them – or will not – or both."[73]

Opposition to the war helped fuel the call for a multistate convention. Federalists asserted that a "rising of the New England people" was not "illegal or unconstitutional." For example, Federalist banker Charles Willing Hare of Philadelphia noted that measures taken under Madison's administration were "so violently and palpably unconstitutional" that they justified the "general right of the State Legislature to decide upon the proceedings of the National Government." The failure of citizen petitions and remonstrances led to calls for a multistate convention, an even more dramatic form of interposition than individual state legislatures interposing on behalf of their citizens. A South Hadley, Massachusetts, town meeting in December 1813 sought such a convention. That sentiment was echoed in a circular letter sent from the county of Hampshire in January 1814 to New England towns. The circular urged them to seek "a convention of all the northern and commercial states" with delegates "to be appointed by their respective legislatures." The circular wanted that convention to focus on the government's unconstitutional measures and consider constitutional amendments to guarantee New England its "due weight and influence" in the federal government.[74]

The Speaker of the Massachusetts legislature, Timothy Bigelow, noted in April 1814 that citizen, town, and county petitions to Congress and the president had been "tried in vain." Likewise, the individual efforts of the state legislatures of Massachusetts, Rhode Island, and Connecticut to interpose with the national government proved futile. Sending additional petitions would simply "invite contempt." Interposing by a gathering of a convention representing New England states seemed a logical next step.[75]

In October 1814, the Massachusetts legislature proposed that the New England states meet to discuss the region's grievances in a convention to be held at Hartford, Connecticut. With its Republican members boycotting, the Massachusetts legislature elected twelve delegates to the convention. Rhode Island's legislature sent four delegates while Connecticut's legislature selected seven. In addition, three counties (two in New Hampshire and one in Vermont) each sent one delegate. Of these twenty-six delegates, five were merchants and the remainder lawyers (with nine judges among them). Two delegates, Massachusetts's Nathan Dane and Connecticut's Zephaniah Swift, were legal treatise writers. George Cabot – perhaps the most respected leader of New England Federalism – presided over the convention. This was no meeting of the fringe of Federalist politics.[76]

As they assembled in Hartford on December 15, 1814, the delegates met behind closed doors. Three weeks later the convention adjourned, issuing a *Report*. The *Report* recommended that state legislatures ask the national government to use the federal taxes raised in northeastern states to defray the cost of that region's state militias – the high costs of which fell on the state governments. The *Report* also recommended state legislation to improve the efficiency of militias. Finally, the convention proposed constitutional amendments to protect New England's political influence within the Union.[77]

Amid these unremarkable steps of interposition, the convention broke new constitutional ground. The convention departed from traditional American constitutionalism by also suggesting in its first resolution that the five legislatures represented in the convention "adopt all such measures as may be necessary" to protect their citizens "from the operation and effects" of military drafts, including the possibility of conscription into the regular army. These drafts were unauthorized by the constitution, the convention concluded. The convention's *Report* implied that a state legislature could frustrate the operation of a national law that was unconstitutional. The Hartford *Report* asserted that the five state legislatures could act as "their own judges" and make "their own decisions" in neutralizing the military draft.[78]

The *Report* alluded to the Virginia and Kentucky Resolutions as support for this position. The author of the Hartford *Report*, most likely Harrison Gray Otis of Boston, paraphrased the Virginia Resolutions as establishing the right of a single state legislature to nullify unconstitutional national laws. The Hartford *Report* paraphrased from Madison's Virginia Resolutions (but without attribution) that "in cases of deliberate, dangerous, and palpable infractions of the constitution, affecting the sovereignty of a state, and the liberties of the people; it is not only the right but the duty of such a state to interpose its authority for their protection, in the manner best calculated to secure that end."[79]

This paraphrase of Madison's resolutions miscast Madison's argument (his authorship of the Virginia Resolutions had been revealed as early as 1809) in several crucial respects. First, Madison did not refer to the sovereignty of a state, with the implication that independent sovereign states created the constitution. Rather, it was the people in the states who were the sovereign who created the federal Constitution. Second, the resolutions carefully distinguished between actions by the people as the sovereign and actions by the sovereign's agents. As agents of the people, the legislature could not exercise the sovereignty of the people. Legislatures might interpose by protesting apparently unconstitutional national laws, but this was not an act by the sovereign that could nullify the law. Finally, the people as the sovereign who created the federal Constitution did have the authority to respond to unconstitutional acts. This required action by the collective people of the states – not a single state. Madison's resolutions and his *Report of 1800* recognized the possibility of nullification of a national law under the theory of American constitutionalism but only if the people in "the States" or the "Co-States" acted in a collective fashion.[80]

Federalist newspapers also differed from Madison's assumptions about who was the sovereign of the federal Constitution. A writer to the *Connecticut Spectator* in August 1814 characterized the constitution as "nothing more than a treaty between independent sovereignties." An article in the *Boston Daily Advertiser* exploring "The Nature of our Government" concluded that the "contracting parties" of the constitution "were SOVEREIGN STATES." Another article in the same newspaper admitted that the constitution was "submitted to the people" but stressed it was "ratified" by the "*States*." These articles emphasized that each state, independent of the other states, was a sovereign who created the constitution, rather than "the people" or "the people of the states" collectively.[81]

Republican newspapers, on the other hand, echoed Madison's views. For "Epsilon" of the *Washington National Intelligencer*, the constitution was not "a grant from the *states*, as sovereignties, but a grant of power by the *people* of all the states." The state and the national governments both derived their authority "from the people." A writer in the *Richmond Enquirer* in November asserted that "no state or set of states *has a right* to withdraw itself from this Union, of its own accord." Individual state secession was "Treason" unless a "*majority of States* which form the Union" consented to the withdrawal of "*any one*" branch of it."[82]

Federalist newspapers also asserted that Madison had previously endorsed resistance by individual states. In a series of articles addressed to "The President of the United States" in the *Boston Daily Advertiser* in November 1814, a writer examined "axioms" and "principles" that Madison allegedly "respected" and that New Englanders "*still*" respect." Among those principles were inherent limits on the national government to implement "odious and unconstitutional" laws. In such circumstances, "the State authority may enact that such supposed laws shall not be carried into effect." In support of that proposition the writer referred to Madison's Virginia Resolutions and quoted his contributions to the *Federalist Papers*. "You have shewn that, in your opinion, a State Legislature has a right to interfere, and oppose the Government of the United States, whenever it is dissatisfied with the *policy* which that Government may pursue." Madison's past political positions demonstrated, according to the writer, that he "thought such interference on the part of the State Government right and fit."[83]

Madison's *Federalist No. 46*, concerning "the authority of the State governments" to resist "ambitious encroachments of the Federal Government," provided New England Federalists fodder for accusing Madison of repudiating earlier principles of his political life. His views "*then* and *now*," according to one critic, "are wonderfully different!" New England Federalists misunderstood Madison's earlier explanations of interposition. In 1788 Madison wrote that constitutional violations by the national government allowed state legislators to sound a "general alarm." That alarm would initiate a "correspondence" among states in which "[p]lans of resistance would be concerted." Raising the alarm, as Madison did in opposing the Alien and Sedition Acts in 1798, was a far cry from the suggestion in the Hartford *Report* of resistance by a single state legislature.[84]

The controversy over the Hartford Convention centered on the loyalty of the participants, not their justification for concluding that a state could oppose acts of the national government. Before the Hartford Convention met, critics challenged their right to meet. "[T]hose traitors in Massachusetts," declared one, were gathered "for the purpose of severing the Union." Hartford raised "the standard of insurrection" of Daniel Shays and the Massachusetts Regulation, said another. Three years later, General Andrew Jackson regarded leaders of the convention as "traitors to the constituted Government" who deserved death.[85]

President Madison took a prudent approach to the Hartford Convention and did not give it official recognition. As the author of the Virginia Resolutions he was silent about the use of the resolutions to justify the convention's conclusions. In retirement at Monticello, Jefferson, like Madison, dismissed the convention and its leaders. Jefferson considered its leaders "venal traitors" trying to "anarchize" the nation by raising "the standard of Separation." The Hartford Convention demonstrated Massachusetts's political "degradation," he observed. Madison also focused on the loyalty of the delegates to the convention and those they represented. New England was "the source of our greatest difficulties in carrying on the war," he mused. Their antiwar stance explained why Britain continued to fight. New England's leaders were simply after "power" and they invited "revolt & separation."[86]

In contrast to privately speculating about motivations, Madison approved the dispatch of Colonel Thomas Jesup to keep an eye on the convention. From Connecticut, Jesup reported to the secretary of war that the convention included "the most determined opposition" to the government from "all ranks and classes of the *majority* of Massachusetts." He was certain that "open acts of hostility" awaited a "signal" from the convention. Alarmed, Madison ordered New York and New England volunteers to be ready to "put rebellion down" if the convention posed a threat to the national government.[87]

This action by the federal government was unknown to the Hartford delegates as they began their deliberations. Also unknown was that the major cause of their discontent would soon be resolved. News of Andrew Jackson's victory over the British at the Battle of New Orleans reached Washington along with indications that a peace treaty was nearing completion at Ghent. Pursuing what soon become a futile mission, a three-person commission from Massachusetts, including Otis, carried the convention's resolves to the nation's capital. They hoped to present the convention's proposals to the president. They also brought the Massachusetts legislature's plan for federal reimbursement of that state's militia expenses. News of the New Orleans victory and imminent prospects for peace spoiled their reception. Spoofed as the three "Wise Men of the East" and "*grievance deputies*," they became "a fine subject of jest & merriment."[88]

The meeting of Hartford delegates in a convention was little different from many other such interpositions. While some Federalists hoped the convention would offer more decisive recommendations, most New England Federalists seemed satisfied with the *Report*. Daniel Webster's assessment that the convention was "moderate, temperate & judicious" met with little dissent within his party. Webster thought Federalists in other states were "highly gratified" by the results. Another Federalist concluded that the convention made a "declaration of *principles*" by which "Legislatures and the people may direct their course." Eventually, only the Massachusetts and Connecticut legislatures endorsed the convention's proposed constitutional amendments. Although submitted to the House of Representatives in early

March 1815, the amendments were tabled without debate. Nine other state legislatures passed resolutions of disapproval.[89]

Although Republicans called Hartford delegates disunionists, neither the convention nor most Federalists endorsed secession. Threats of secession did surround the call for the convention and the Hartford *Report* acknowledged the possibility of the Union's "dissolution" but rejected that step for the moment. However, when Harrison Gray Otis conceived of a multistate convention in 1808 he anticipated it would be a "mode of relief" that would not be *"inconsistent with the union of these States."*[90]

Nonetheless, Hartford's delegates acquired the enduring stigma of disloyalty and disunion. More than a quarter century later, Otis was still defending the convention as "constitutional & peaceable." However, his participation in the convention doomed his candidacy for the Massachusetts governorship just as it undermined the Federalist Party.[91] When Otis later reflected on his declining political fortunes in 1820 as threats of southern secession surfaced, he wondered, "Is it not a queer world? Just as I have demonstrated that Massachusetts did not mean to break up the Union . . . it is about to be shown by Virginia" that disunion "is no crime." The Hartford Convention addressed a "question of *constitutional law*" over the respective powers of "the General and State Governments." Otis described its *Report* as "a manual of elementary principles." Hartford reflected the "self evident proposition" that in America "the right of the people" to assemble peacefully when they wanted was "universally recognized." Citizens could meet in "Convention or Caucus . . . however *inexpedient* may be their plans or proceedings; availing themselves only of the liberty of opinion and speech." Otis wondered why Hartford delegates "should be dealt with as a den of bandits."[92]

Otis could refute charges of secession, but he was hard-pressed to demonstrate that the Hartford *Report* simply reflected a traditional form of interposition. In defending the convention in the 1820s, Otis glossed over the implications of some of the *Report*'s recommendations by suggesting that "in substance," only two measures were proposed: federal funding for state militias and constitutional amendments. He did not discuss the *Report*'s call for individual state legislatures to resist national policies.[93]

Otis later saw the Hartford Convention as "restraining the tendency to excess" found in some of the petitions sent to the legislature and he denied any belief in *"nullification."* Otis did not acknowledge that as a member of the convention he endorsed the right of an individual state to pass legislation to frustrate the operation of a national law it deemed unconstitutional. He seemed unaware that the Hartford Convention's *Report* could have been used to buttress the claims of southern nullifiers were it not for the discredited reputations of the convention's delegates as disloyal secessionists. The southern nullifiers of the 1830s instead reached further back in time for a far more problematic justification in the Virginia and Kentucky Resolutions.[94]

THE NULLIFICATION CRISIS

In James Madison's final decade, he worried about the durability of what he had built during his time on the national stage. As one of the last surviving founders he was pleased that his work was celebrated. For example, one correspondent wrote to him in 1827 about the Philadelphia dinner at which glasses were raised to toast *"[t]he health and happiness of James Madison –* The father and guardian of the Constitution." Yet, as this decade continued, Madison realized that his legacy was in jeopardy. His recollections about the founding and the meaning of the federal Constitution seemed to carry no particular weight within the increasingly sectional nature of American politics. As he wrote a former aide two years before his death, few Americans seemed to have any "respect for my opinion." Madison's last years found him embroiled in controversies over matters he once considered of no enduring importance. One such issue involved Congress's power to impose a tariff on imports. He initially thought it was not "very serious" because "it involve[d] no great constitutional question." Now that issue seemed to threaten the stability of the Union.[95]

The divisiveness of the controversy over the tariff surprised Madison – particularly when he learned how differently his neighbors in rural Orange County, Virginia, thought about the tariff's constitutionality. It seemed clear to Madison that even if the tariff was questionable as a matter of policy, it was well within the constitutional power of Congress. The people of Orange County had been his steadiest supporters over the years. They cast their votes to send him to the Virginia legislature in 1776 as their advocate for Independence. Although they declined to reelect him in the next election after he failed to provide the traditional "spirituous liquors, and other treats," they later returned him to office. They sent him to the House of Representatives under the 1787 federal Constitution and elected delegates pledged to his presidency in 1809. After Madison's retirement in 1828, they once again selected him to serve as a delegate to revise Virginia's constitution. In 1831, however, they assembled within five miles of Madison's Montpelier estate and passed resolutions proclaiming the federal tariff unconstitutional. He considered those resolutions "most extraordinary," illustrating "how little" after all these years the constitution was understood even by his closest neighbors.[96]

Madison might have thought the tariff dispute would have no lasting significance because Americans had long struggled with sectional disputes – west versus east; north versus south; frontier versus settled areas. Madison spent much of his public career dealing with such disputes and their challenge to the federal union. During his presidency, for example, a federal embargo triggered complaints from New England states (expressed in part through the Hartford Convention in 1814) that federal policy unconstitutionally burdened their region. New Englanders acted out of a sense that political and constitutional imbalance within the Union placed them at risk. Now, hurt by tariffs imposed in 1828, South Carolina raised a similar objection. Its complaint echoed claims made by other southern states, such as Georgia and Virginia, that the tariff was unconstitutional because it primarily aided northern manufacturers rather than advancing a proper constitutional purpose of raising revenue for the nation. The tariff's protectionist motive and its tendency to make imports more expensive reduced government revenue as people bought less of the goods subject to the tariff. For tariff opponents, this demonstrated that Congress lacked a proper purpose in imposing the tariff, exceeding its constitutional authority. For many southerners it represented a perversion of the Union – one section was using its influence to transfer the earnings of southern agriculture to northern manufacturers. As one critic put it, the tariff rendered the agricultural society of the south "serffs," exploited by the weight the north was able to exert.[97]

The protests against the tariffs initially followed the traditional patterns of interposition that sought the repeal of unconstitutional laws. The effort was not limited to South Carolina. Protests came from counties, such as from Madison's neighbors in Orange County as well as from state legislatures, such as Georgia's petition to Congress seeking relief. Eventually, tariff opponents organized a national convention, the so-called Free Trade Convention, held in Philadelphia in September and October 1831. South Carolina sent a large delegation reflecting the view adopted by its legislature in 1825 that the tariff was "unconstitutional." Many other states, north as well as south, attended the convention. To no avail the convention adopted a memorial asking Congress to adjust the tariff. From the perspective of many in South Carolina, the convention avoided the central issue – it failed to address the concern that the tariff was only an example of what southern states would face in the future if the constitutional balance of the federal system was not restored.[98]

Years of trying to repeal the tariff brought little relief. Many South Carolinians concluded that the traditional tools of protest through interposition were not working. Petitions, remonstrances, and even the multistate convention were well-known means of interposition employed to review and protest actions of government. Their ineffectiveness on this occasion generated increasing frustration. By late 1831, one South Carolinian observed that citizens of his state had "petitioned, remonstrated and resolved" for "years" against the tariff. South Carolina's legislature did its "duty" in bringing attention to the tariff's "unequal and unconstitutional burden." Meeting with "other States" at the Philadelphia Free Trade convention was South Carolina's "last effort at redress." For tariff opponents the convention's failure made other steps necessary.[99]

One new step involved an approach that promised not only to redress the constitutional imbalance represented by the tariff but later federal measures that might unconstitutionally disadvantage the South. This step found a solution in the way the federal Constitution provided "checks against the abuse of power on the part of the absolute majority." The current tariff crisis did not stem from a flaw in the constitution's design but rather from the neglect of southern states "to make application of the proper remedy." For advocates of the next step, what had always been available was the use of the individual state veto.[100]

The names proponents used to describe the state "veto" seemed rather innocuous at first – the veto was a state's "protest," its "interposition," or its exercise of "reserved rights." As the heat of the national debate intensified, other, more dire names came into use. Proponents of the state veto were described as embracing "nullification, secession, disunion, and revolution." What distinguished the state veto from earlier proposals to rebalance the federal constitutional order was its national effect. The state veto was unlike the recommendation in the Hartford Convention's *Report of 1815*. Hartford's *Report* sought to regain the nation's constitutional equilibrium by asserting an individual state's ability to take "measures" opposing the "operation" of unconstitutional laws within its own borders. In contrast, the state veto proposed in the 1820s and 1830s anticipated that any single state could invalidate a national law for the Union as a whole. What also distinguished the state veto was that it seemed to be a solution advanced by prominent figures on the national stage rather than simply by local or regional leaders.[101]

The theory justifying the single state veto came from the pen of South Carolina's John C. Calhoun, the vice president of the United States. Calhoun's leadership in arguing that individual states could nullify federal law belied his earlier nationalist credentials. Educated at Yale and Connecticut's Litchfield

Law School, Calhoun served in the U.S. House of Representatives (1810–1817); as secretary of war under President Monroe (1817–1825); and as vice-president under John Quincy Adams and then under Andrew Jackson (1825–1832). A "war hawk" during Madison's administration, Calhoun favored the 1812 war against Britain and initially supported reducing the national debt and protecting America's new industries with a tariff in 1816. Like other South Carolina nationalists, Calhoun considered the 1824 and 1828 tariffs to affect the South disproportionately, insufficiently promoting the general welfare and the national objective of raising revenue.[102]

Calhoun's prior nationalism complicated his discovery of the state veto. He cast about for a "remedy" for the southern states' lack of influence under the constitution. It took several months before he saw his way "clearly" to reading into the constitution "a negative" power that could be exercised by each state over the laws of the nation. In November 1828, at the request of his state's legislature, Calhoun anonymously drafted what became known as the *South Carolina Exposition*, which the legislature endorsed by ordering its publication. Like Madison's *Report of 1800* for Virginia's legislature, South Carolina's *Exposition* focused attention on the power of the national government. The *Exposition's* justification of a state veto became a matter of national debate over whether the constitution included such a check on the national government. That debate raised many of the same questions that had been at issue during the controversy over the Virginia and Kentucky Resolutions and the Hartford Convention. In addition, the veto debate raised other sensitive and unsettled issues in American constitutionalism.[103]

One key question went to the core of American constitutionalism: the extent to which Americans were united – and still divided since the Revolution – about the meaning of a government in which the people were the sovereign. The scope of the controversy is best illustrated by several participants in the debate over the state veto – John C. Calhoun, its chief theorist, and Robert Hayne, U.S. senator from South Carolina who defended Calhoun's theory and later served as governor of South Carolina when it attempted nullification. Opposing the state veto was Daniel Webster, U.S. senator from Massachusetts. A final, at times reluctant, participant was James Madison. Both sides of the debate claimed that Madison's writings justified their positions. Madison often felt unable to set the record straight. His efforts to clarify that he had not justified a state veto were undermined by the heated debate.

Calhoun's *Exposition* explained that the veto was a narrow remedy found in the federal Constitution. It could be exercised when the national government used a power the constitution granted to achieve "one object" but "to advance another" and in so doing sacrificed the proper object to which that power was to be directed. This was a "perver[s]ion" of the constitution that was "insidious, and difficult to resist." According to Calhoun, the 1828 tariff presented an example of such a perversion. Congress had used its authority to exact a tariff. However, that tariff was not for the legitimate purpose of raising government revenue. Instead it was designed to benefit manufacturing states by placing commensurate burdens on southern agricultural states.[104]

Calhoun reasoned that the constitution's adoption in 1789 took previously independent states and subjected them to a federal regime that could exercise certain specified powers. The specified powers were exercised within a system of checks and balances, thereby preventing their abuse. By joining this federal compact with its scheme of balanced government, no state lost the power to determine for itself whether that constitutional agreement was properly applied, especially when the check-and-balance mechanism was failing. If such a failure meant a disputed exertion of federal power could not be constrained, the state could exercise its veto. The state's action could be rescinded under Article V, contended Calhoun, if three-fourths of the other states gave effect to the power that the vetoing state had disputed and nullified.[105]

Calhoun reconciled the veto with his nationalism by describing his theory as an interposition, something both envisioned and exercised by the federal Constitution's founders. Proponents of the state veto justified their reading of the constitution by finding words and actions of the federal Framers that they felt demonstrated a recognition of such a veto. Like other political mechanisms operating within the constitutional framework of the national government, such as political parties or the presidential cabinet system, important devices for sustaining the constitution did not have to be specified in the text. They could be fairly implied from the actions of the founders in implementing the constitution. Calhoun found just such proof for his theory in the Virginia and Kentucky Resolutions and Madison's *Report of 1800*. Calhoun credited the resolutions and Madison's *Report* as "the basis" of his discovery of the state veto. He cast the state veto as an interposition as equally justified as the interposition taken by Virginia's and Kentucky's legislatures in 1798.[106]

Calhoun's concept of a single state veto provoked a storm of controversy in part because it invoked the authority of Madison and Jefferson. For example, on the floor of the Senate, Robert Hayne described nullification by a single state veto as settled "Republican doctrine." He claimed it was not synonymous with disunion and he traced its origins to Madison's "celebrated 'Virginia Resolutions.'" This heritage alone ensured that the doctrine, like Madison's *Report of 1800*, would "last as long as the Constitution itself."[107]

Learning of such arguments, Madison felt compelled to enter the fray. Madison disavowed that neither he nor Jefferson was responsible for nullification, a doctrine with a "fatal tendency." Rather than protecting the diverse interests of the Union, Madison believed nullification put "powder under the Constitution and Union, and a match in the hand" of any faction, leaving it to their whim whether "to blow them up." Secession was a "twin" to the "heresy" of nullification, warned Madison. Both doctrines sprang "from the same poisonous root." The growth from this root would bring "disastrous consequences." By 1832, he noted how inexpressibly "painful" it was that Calhoun's doctrine might cause the constitution to be "broken up and scattered to the winds."[108]

Even before Madison went public with his opposition, he carried on a wide correspondence disclaiming any connection to the veto and trying to set the record straight. As his views became known, they prompted unpleasant attacks by advocates of the veto. After South Carolina acted on the propositions described in the *Exposition*, Madison felt powerless and hoped others would take up "[t]he task of combating such unhappy aberrations." Besides, he mused that his efforts were unavailing in bringing serious attention to his ideas on constitutionalism. Instead, Madison's explanations were met with silence or with dismissive statements that he was "enfeebled by age" and that his memory was too deficient to be of much credence.[109]

What made the "poisonous root" of the state veto and nullification so toxic was that it drew on the same principle that underlay American constitutionalism: that in America the people were the sovereign. A half-century after Americans established their governments on this principle, the concept remained as elusive as it was when it first energized the Revolution. The problem was that Americans remained divided on precisely how that sovereign could give effect to an expression of its will.

For purposes of the national government all agreed that the people were the sovereign – but how could they exercise their sovereignty? Proponents of the state veto, such as Calhoun, argued that the sovereign for purposes of the federal Constitution was the people in each individual state. As he explained, the constitution "when formed, was submitted for ratification to the people of the several States; it was ratified by them as States, each State for itself; each by its ratification binding its own citizens." Although each state independently bound itself to the Union, that did not mean they lost their independence.[110]

For Calhoun, the people were unquestionably the sovereign, yet this sovereign expressed itself through their organization into independent states. The people were the sovereign who created the independent states but it was these independent states who were the sovereign of the national government. Calhoun thought it insignificant that the constitution's preamble declared it was "ordained by the people of *the United States.*" Those words did not make a national people rather than the individual states the sovereign. Irrespective of the preamble's language, Calhoun noted that the constitution's "article of ratification" provided that "when ratified, it is declared *'to be binding between the States so ratifying.'*" This made "the conclusion ... inevitable, that the Constitution is the work of the people of the States, considered, as separate and independent political communities – that they are its authors – their power created it – their voice clothed it with an authority – that the Government it formed is in reality their agent – and that the Union, of which it is the bond, is an Union of States, and not of individuals."[111]

Opponents of the state veto, including Senator Daniel Webster, dismissed such arguments. In refuting South Carolina's Senator Hayne who accepted Calhoun's concept of the sovereign, Webster described a different sovereign. This sovereign was also "the people." The constitution was not "the creature of the States," observed Webster. It was created by a much greater entity – "The people of the United States." The American people "in the aggregate" formed the federal Constitution.[112]

By their act as the national sovereign they henceforth bound themselves to the terms of that constitution. Thereafter, any effort to alter the constitutional order required "submission to the laws" by compliance with the revision provisions of Article V. The attempt to change the operation of the constitution through other means – as for example by the theory of the state veto – necessarily relied on the natural law right of resistance to tyranny. There was no "middle course," no alternative between either complying with the constitution's procedural requirements or the people exercising the natural law right of resistance. Nullification by allowing each state a veto, argued Webster, simply represented "revolution or rebellion"; it could never amount to "constitutional resistance."[113]

As Webster's position illustrated, one's understanding of the nature of the federal union was shaped by how one described the sovereign that created the federal Constitution. The sovereigns envisioned by Webster and Hayne were each different from the sovereign recognized by the constitution's founder, James Madison. Madison thought both their concepts of the sovereign shared a "not uncommon" mistake in understanding the "true character" of the federal Constitution. Both Calhoun and Webster thought that only one of two options was possible – America either had "a consolidated Government" or "a confederated Government."[114]

Madison explained that the constitution created neither. It was not formed "by the governments of the component States" like the Articles of Confederation, as Calhoun maintained. Individual states were not the sovereign of the national government. "[N]or was it formed by a majority of the people of the United States, as a single community, in the manner of a consolidated Government," as Webster maintained. Therefore, the people in the individual states retained constitutional significance. As Madison explained, the constitution was "a mixture of both" consolidated and confederated governments. Neither Webster's claim that the American people in "the aggregate" were the sovereign who formed the constitution nor Calhoun's position that individual sovereign states were the parties creating the constitution accurately described the federal founding. Rather, "the undisputed fact is, that the Constitution was made by the people ... as imbodied into the several States ... and, therefore, made by the States in their highest authoritative capacity."[115]

States acting in their highest sovereign capacity were not the sovereign people of each state acting individually. According to Madison, a state acted in its "highest sovereign capacity" only when the sovereign people of a state acted in combination with the sovereign people of other states. Even though nearly thirty years had elapsed since he authored the Virginia Resolutions, Madison remained unshaken in the belief that the people of the states in their collective capacity had created the federal Constitution and were the sovereign of the national government. Nonetheless, much to his frustration, Americans in the 1830s began (and would continue) to describe the federal Constitution in the binary terms of either a consolidated or confederated government. Doing this ignored Madison's subtle concept of the constitution's formation.[116]

For Madison, the American sovereign was the people of each state acting collectively to adopt the federal Constitution. This resembled how state constitutions were ratified – by the people acting collectively and yet casting their votes in units of counties or precincts or even towns. The people of any one county, precinct, or town could not veto a state action. Madison thought the same principle applied at the federal level, precluding any single state from vetoing national laws as Calhoun asserted. Madison always considered the people of the states to mean the collective sovereign people of the states. Unlike Webster's theory of a national people, the people of each individual state were a crucial part of the underlying sovereign of the federal Constitution. Madison never suggested that the underlying sovereign, the parties to the federal compact, were the sovereign people of any individual state. The people of each state manifested their sovereignty within their states and ratified the federal Constitution in state conventions. Nonetheless, their authority to breathe life into that constitution was conjoined with the sovereign power of the people of other states acting in the same manner.[117]

One justification of Calhoun's theory was that the founding generation had used the state veto. Calhoun and Hayne frequently spoke of "interposition" in describing the state veto. They traced the veto's roots to the Virginia and Kentucky Resolutions, which interposed against the Alien and Sedition Acts. Calhoun characterized this interposition as having vetoed the acts. Madison's denial that the resolutions had that effect hardly impacted the debate. Calhoun, Hayne, and Webster, along with many other Americans by the 1830s, seemed confused about the nature and role of interposition in American constitutionalism. During the controversy, Madison tried to explain how interposition worked in theory, had been applied in practice with the Virginia and Kentucky Resolutions, and was not a justification for nullification by an individual state.

Madison identified two different types of "interpositions." The first was an interposition "against unjustifiable acts" of the national government that took place "within the provisions and forms of the Constitution." In this interposition, exemplified by the Virginia and Kentucky Resolutions, citizens petitioned and legislatures lodged formal protests. Appeals were made to citizens of other states to coordinate efforts to reverse the Alien and Sedition Acts or revise the constitution. In the process "[t]he people as composing a State, and the States as composing the Union . . . in fact, interpose[d]." The people acted "as constituents of their respective governments, according to the forms of their respective constitutions." In using the "forms" of the constitution the people exercised the franchise and their right of speech and assembly.[118]

This differed from a second type of interposition which Madison described as "not within the purview of the Constitution." Unlike interposition in which the people acted as constituents of government, here they acted "as the creators of their constitutions, and as paramount" to their constitutions and governments. Acting as the constitution's creators, they were unrestrained by the forms of the constitution. The Virginia Resolutions described, but did not exercise, this second form of interposition. South Carolina's "nullifying process" fit neither type of interposition. A single state veto could not constitutionally reverse national laws. And since only one state was acting, it could not be interposition by the sovereign people underlying the constitution because it did not involve an act by the collective sovereign of the nation.[119]

In repudiating the state veto as interposition, Madison still maintained, contrary to Webster, that states could interpose. Madison also reaffirmed the right of the people of the several states to act "in their highest authoritative capacity," as the creators of the federal Constitution, to check actions by the national government in excess of its delegated powers. Madison never repudiated the sovereign people's right, despite his concern that his earlier statements were being used to fashion a doctrine that threatened the Union.[120]

Madison distinguished the Virginia and Kentucky Resolutions from South Carolina's "nullifying process." South Carolina, Madison noted, did not distinguish the constitutional "right of *the parties* to the Constitution" to nullify national laws from the ability of "a *single* party" to withdraw from the Union in the face of oppression as an act of revolution. "[T]he *plural* term *States*," Madison noted of his *Report of 1800*, "was invariably used in reference" to actions taken by states and not by a single state. This meant that the collective sovereign, acting through the people in the states, could cancel a national law regardless of Article V's requirements for amending the constitution. This constitutional authority of the collective sovereign that had created the federal Constitution was obviously not available to an individual state and hence could not justify an individual state's veto. Any state could, however, abdicate its constitutional obligations by withdrawing from the Union "in extreme cases of oppression." This drew on a right of resistance, or what Madison called a right to "cast off the yoke" of tyrannical government by exercising "original rights." That step was revolutionary and outside the bounds of American constitutionalism.[121]

Madison was appalled by how veto proponents used his *Report*. That *Report* explained and justified the interposition by the Virginia and Kentucky legislatures but did not suggest that the people of a single state could constitutionally veto a national law. Nonetheless, Calhoun inferred this from Madison's *Report*. Madison replied that he had consistently referred to "the 'States'" when describing "the people . . . in their highest sovereign capacity" who had ratified the constitution. Likewise, he made the same reference when identifying the people's constitutional right to intervene in extraordinary circumstances when actions of government had gone hopelessly amiss. Madison's use of the plural – that it was the people of the states who were a collective sovereign – crucially distinguished his views from Calhoun's concept of a confederation of states, with each individual state a sovereign party to the constitution.[122]

Calhoun assumed that when Madison's *Report* and the Virginia Resolutions referred to the powers of the sovereign who created the constitution,

Madison meant powers exercised by the people within a single state. Reading the *Report* in this way affirmed Calhoun's belief that "a sovereign State as a party to the Con[stitutiona]l comp[ac]t" could nullify an unconstitutional federal law. Calhoun's theory asserted that each state was a sovereign of the national government and thus could act authoritatively and independently of the others and veto unconstitutional laws. Calhoun's reasoning drew from Madison's description that the collective people of all the states were the sovereign. Calhoun used this description to justify a state's veto. That argument failed to distinguish the power the collective sovereign possessed when acting as the sovereign from acts of interposition by portions of the people that might ultimately encourage a response by the collective sovereign.[123]

Consistent with Madison's *Report*, Calhoun recognized the people of "the states" as the sovereign who created the federal Constitution. However, Calhoun misunderstood Madison's justification of the Virginia legislature's 1798 interposition resolution. Madison explained it as an effort by the state legislature to "sound the alarm" to the collective sovereign of the nation, so that the people could resolve the constitutional difficulty by such actions as petitioning or instructing federal representatives, using the ballot to replace federal officials, or as a final resort, by acting collectively to change the constitution. Madison described the actions by the legislature and the people as involving, according to Calhoun, "the rights of *the State* to interpret the Constitution for itself" (emphasis added). This, however, was the right to take a position on the constitutionality of a federal act and to encourage the collective sovereign to use the tools at its disposal to resolve the constitutional dispute.[124]

Calhoun confounded this assessment of the rights of a state with the rights of the states collectively. In drawing support for his views from Madison's writings, Calhoun lacked precision about Madison's use of the singular or plural in referring to an action by a state or actions by states. Calhoun's imprecision probably stemmed from his preoccupation with establishing the limits of federal authority. He did not seem particularly concerned about distinguishing whether it was "the people" of a single state, rather than the people collectively among all the states, that was the sovereign who created the federal Constitution. Calhoun seemed quite willing to accept whatever advantage his argument for a state veto could gain from ambiguity. Failing to distinguish the powers of a state from the powers of the states contributed to such ambiguity. Similarly, ambiguity arose from failing to distinguish the people of each state as the sovereign who authorized their state constitution from the people of the union, collectively, who as sovereign gave life to the federal Constitution. Calhoun envisioned dual sovereigns – the people as the sovereign of the state, and each state as the sovereign of the federal union. This turned on its head Madison's view that the people were simultaneously the sovereign of their particular state and collectively the sovereign of the federal union.

In contrast to the ambiguity of Calhoun's argument on sovereignty, Calhoun was explicit about how a state veto could resolve a failure of the checks and balances built into the federal Constitution, which the tariff exemplified. He rejected the suggestion that the federal judiciary was able to check and balance congressional action on the tariff. The Court could not be the final and sole arbiter of the constitution in this situation. He did not believe the Court, as a branch of the national government, could properly act as a check upon the federal powers over a state.

The problem, according to Calhoun, stemmed from the fact that while Congress clearly had power over foreign commerce and could raise revenue for the nation, the 1828 tariff went beyond these powers. Congress had used a proper tool to advance a goal not within the constitution's scope. The tariff allowed one section of the country to use a proper power (the tariff) to achieve a goal that perverted the purposes of the union (by transferring the wealth of the agricultural South to the northern states). It was clear to Calhoun that the traditional checks and balances within the federal government's branches were unavailing in correcting this abuse. Both the congressional and executive branches had failed to address the problem. Neither could the federal judiciary resolve the abuse. "The Courts can not look in[to] the motives of legislators," Calhoun's *Exposition* noted. Under the judicial branch's interpretive function, "[t]hey are obliged to take acts by their titles and professed objects, and if these be Constitutional, they cannot interpose their power, however grossly the [tariff] acts may, in reality, violate the Constitution." In short, the Court could not properly redress Congress's use of a proper power to achieve an improper goal.[125]

The inadequacy of the court to resolve the problem of the use of a federal power to achieve an improper purpose demonstrated to Calhoun that no single branch of the government could exclusively decide the scope of its own powers. The courts held no monopoly in interpreting the constitution. Nor was the Court the final arbiter of whether the national government, of which it was a part, was operating within constitutional limits. Like all branches of government, the judiciary was subject to the ultimate decision of the sovereign to weigh in at the end and resolve constitutional disputes that were beyond the ability of the courts to resolve. This precluded the Court from having the final word on the federal constitutional order. Such final power could be exercised only by the sovereign, who under the federal constitution, according to Calhoun, was each individual state independent of the other states. The state veto was the means by which such final power could be exercised.

Calhoun cited the Virginia and Kentucky Resolutions as examples of states independently vetoing federal legislation. For him, the resolutions demonstrated that the constitution provided a proper check upon the power of the national government when the federal courts could not act as the sole expositor of the federal Constitution, as seemed to be the case in the tariff controversy. Madison rejected that this was the effect or significance of the resolutions. According to Madison, his *Report of 1800* made it "sufficiently clear" that the U.S. Supreme Court had "jurisdiction" of issues "between the several States and the United States" and that it provided "the *ultimate* decision" for "cases within the judicial scope of the Government." During the controversy over nullification through a state veto, Madison emphasized the role of the Supreme Court in interpreting the constitution. In both private and public letters dismissing the idea of a state veto, Madison cited *Federalist No.* 39 in which he had described the Court as an "essential" tribunal in resolving disputes over authority between the national and state governments. Judicial supremacy was "a vital principle" of the constitution, Madison asserted, and any who "denied or doubted" this were surely mistaken.[126]

But what was the logic of the Virginia and Kentucky Resolutions if the constitutionality of a national law was a matter for the federal judiciary? Why could the legislatures of Virginia and Kentucky interpose to bring before the sovereign – the people of the nation – the issue of the constitutionality of the Alien and Sedition Acts if it was the federal judiciary that made "the *ultimate* decision"? For Madison this was not a matter that would confound anyone who fairly reflected on the nature of the federal Constitution. Madison considered the Supreme Court's role as deciding issues "within" the scope of the constitution itself fairly clear. The Court's determinations were the "last resort" when one used "the purview and forms of the Constitution."[127]

The federal Constitution's provision of a final means of resolution for constitutional questions, however, did not and could not preclude the people collectively as the sovereign from deciding the constitutional issue for themselves. Even after a decision by the judiciary or other branch of the federal government, that fact did not diminish the power of the sovereign – the people of the states – as "the parties to the Constitution" from exercising their "authority *above* that of the Constitution itself" (emphasis added). Their authority "to interpose" existed regardless of "the decisions of the judicial as well as other branches of the Government." This was simply a matter of the unlimited power of the sovereign. As "the last resort of all" for challenging the proper meaning of the constitution, explained Madison, there could be no "tribunal above" the people in the states when they acted as the sovereign. As the "parties to the constitutional compact" they collectively could "decide whether" the constitutional compact they made was "violated."[128]

Madison described both the Court and the sovereign people as having ultimate authority regarding the constitution's meaning in "the last resort." He did not find this to be contradictory. To Madison's mind, the constitution allowed the judicial branch, using the forms and procedures established by the constitution, to check and balance the federal government's exercise of authority. Even so, the sovereign who gave life to the federal Constitution did not limit its own powers as the sovereign in adopting the constitution. The sovereign could use the forms and procedures of the constitution to redress any challenged exercise of government power – as the Virginia and Kentucky Resolutions attempted in prompting the people to use the rights of petition, speech, and the franchise to reverse ill-conceived government action. In the exercise of these forms of the constitution, the judiciary properly and ultimately interpreted the scope of the constitution. However, if the people acted outside the constitution's forms and exercised their power as the collective sovereign, the judiciary's determinations could not prevail.[129]

As a practical matter, the Supreme Court was the "surest expositor" of the constitution. The judiciary could act relatively quickly to construe the constitution under the forms and procedures for the operation of that branch of government. In contrast, action by the ultimate authority over the meaning of the constitution, the people collectively, was much more gradual. For example, it had taken that sovereign nearly two years to put in place the federal Constitution in 1789. Simply because there were physical difficulties in manifesting an authentic action by that collective sovereign did not preclude the power of that sovereign to act on constitutional questions.[130]

The key, of course, was authenticating an act of the sovereign. In November 1832, delegates for the people of South Carolina gathered in a convention and purported to nullify the tariff as unconstitutional. They did not rely on "what are called our natural rights, or the right of revolution," but insisted they were acting under "a CONSTITUTIONAL right." Under Madison's view of constitutionalism, had the people of South Carolina acted with the people of the other states rather than as an individual state, their nullification would have been an act of the sovereign that created the national constitution. Although occurring outside the "forms" of the constitution, if joined by a majority of the people of other states, that nullification would have constitutional legitimacy.[131]

As unilateral defiance by one state, South Carolina's nullification presented the dire prospect of disunion. Linking nullification with disunion dealt a heavy blow to the concept of the people as a meaningful monitor of the federal constitutional order. President Andrew Jackson's swift response to South Carolina's declaration made this clear. He issued a nullification *Proclamation* acknowledging the people's "indefeasible right of resisting acts which are plainly unconstitutional and too oppressive to be endured." Nonetheless, South Carolina took "the strange position" that a single state could "declare an act of Congress void" and "prohibit its execution." This was *"incompatible with the existence of the Union"* and *"destructive"* of the federal Constitution because the Union was not a "compact between sovereign States." Jackson concluded, as did Webster, that a national, American people as the sovereign had formed the national government. Madison disagreed with both Jackson and Webster on that point. Nonetheless, Madison agreed with Jackson that nullification through a single state's veto, like secession, was a "revolutionary act," not a constitutional right.[132]

In January 1833 Jackson engineered a congressional resolution to the crisis by suggesting a lower tariff yet greater enforcement power. Congress passed a Force Bill (enhancing presidential authority to collect federal revenues) as well as a Compromise Tariff (reducing tariff rates). After Jackson signed both bills, South Carolina nullified the Force Bill, but accepted the Compromise Tariff. These joint maneuvers and symbolic gestures effectively ended the confrontation between South Carolina and the national government. Later that year, Calhoun judged nullification a "success" and "indeed a triumph" because a political majority responded to the grievances of a minority.[133]

The various challenges to the Alien and Sedition Acts, embargos, and tariffs questioned the legitimacy of acts of the national government rather than the legitimacy of government itself. For many Americans, monitoring the constitutional operation of that government was an active responsibility of all citizens and not just their elected officials. As the sovereign, the people who created the constitution also served as its final arbiter. Interposition was inherent in American constitutionalism because, as Madison put it, the sovereign could always act outside the "purview and forms" of the constitution.

Madison and other Americans considered interposition very much in the same vein as Hamilton's description in *Federalist No. 26* that state legislatures would serve as "jealous guardians of the rights of the citizens" who would "sound the alarm to the people" when the national government exceeded its rightful powers. Individual states – through their citizens or legislatures – could assess the constitutionality of actions of the national government. Madison carefully distinguished between interposition identifying unconstitutional laws from any effort by individual states to nullify such laws. A single state lacked constitutional authority to nullify national laws or secede from the Union, Madison maintained. He considered the people of the states the ultimate judge of the constitutionality of acts of the government. This involved the ultimate constitutional authority to render national laws void or give constitutional text final meaning. It required the participation of a majority of the collective sovereign.

Because American constitutions expressed the voice of the people as the sovereign, the people could also directly weigh in on whether government acted consistent with their directions. Some Americans asserted that the Supreme Court was the sole authority to determine questions of constitutionality, but nothing foreordained such a monopoly. Before the Civil War, many Americans believed that individual citizens, state legislatures, and ultimately the people themselves – and not just the federal judiciary – played a significant role in ensuring the constitution's proper functioning. Interposition was a tool for scrutinizing the national government to ensure that it acted as desired by the sovereign people.

Interposition supplemented other devices built into the constitution itself to ensure the responsiveness of the government to the sovereign – such as periodic elections. Like elections, interposition could reflect the will of the people. Unlike elections, interposition served to clarify issues that simply voting for one candidate or another could not do in the context of an election. Interposition could bring voters' attention to matters that might help focus the exercise of the suffrage. The constitutional guarantee of voting did not preclude the use of more informal means such as interposition.

While interposition could be used to express a view on the constitutionality of a law it did not preclude the role of the Court as interpreter of the constitution. The judicial branch continued to play an important role in monitoring the operation of the national government. As a supplement to more formal and informal institutions of government, interposition was a sporadic tool available to the people when circumstances warranted the exercise of that authority. This informality gave it no lesser role than other informal devices such as political parties in a conception of constitutionalism shared by Madison and many other Americans before the Civil War.

Eventually, the concept of the Union of American states significantly shaped debates over constitutionalism. As preserving the Union became increasingly important to Americans, pressure mounted to restrict the role the people played as guardians of their sovereignty – at least in the context of the federal Constitution. Equating criticism of the national government with the threat of disunion initially surfaced during Washington's administration. Thereafter, both Federalist and Republican administrations leveled similar charges about their detractors. Branding as secessionists those who questioned the constitutionality of national laws effectively discredited political adversaries. It also served to narrow both who could actively engage in overseeing the constitutional operation of government and what processes could be employed in that undertaking.

The power of the idea that brought life to the American Revolution, that in America the people were the sovereign, thus became linked with the emerging power of the idea of the American Union. The idea of the American Union affected both sides of the debate over the Virginia and Kentucky Resolutions, demonstrating a growing attachment to the Union as a political concept. The increasing focus on the Union's preservation diverted attention from the notion that the national government owed its continued existence to the consent of the sovereign people who created it. Likewise, New England Federalists at the Hartford Convention were sensitive to accusations of disunion. By the time of the Nullification crisis, the grip that preserving the Union held on the American mind crossed party lines. Its importance rendered unfashionable earlier ruminations about the underlying sovereign basis of the constitution.

Andrew Jackson's determined opposition to nullification stemmed from his devotion to the Union. Nonetheless, he strongly adhered to majoritarianism, believed in the capacity of the people to govern themselves, and thoroughly embraced the people's sovereignty. Despite Jackson's commitment to the sovereignty of the people, however, he refused to recognize that principle when it placed the Union at risk. Madison's strenuous efforts during the 1830s to distance himself from the uses being made of his earlier defense of the Virginia and Kentucky Resolutions revealed a similar motivation. Jackson's and Madison's reactions illustrate how ideas that implicitly questioned the perpetuity of the Union were increasingly regarded as heresy.[134]

A perpetual union, however, contradicted the idea that government was a creation of the people. If created by the sovereign people, government could not be beyond the control of the people. Yet the idea of an irrevocable union repudiated this underlying authority of the people. The strength of the notion of a permanent union grew as the revolutionary generation passed away. Increasingly, Americans knew of only one America and many became committed to its preservation at all costs. The concept of an unchallengeable union restricted the people from invoking their authority as the sovereign to correct actions by their agents in the government.[135]

The Struggle over a Constitutional Middle Ground

By the 1840s, Americans had devoted more than sixty years to thinking about the authority of the sovereign to revise constitutions. The documents they drafted, the way they described the nature of their governments and political institutions – as well as debates over constitutional revision – all reflected their constitutional understandings. The decades following the Revolution witnessed Americans continuing to draw directly upon their authority as the sovereign to create and revise their constitutions. In effect, Americans practiced what their constitutions preached about the authority of the collective people to "alter or abolish" their governments at will.

This authority of the people's sovereignty was frequently expressed in terms of alter or abolish provisions in some of America's first written constitutions and in succeeding ones as well. Some of those provisions in state constitutions echoed the traditional requirements of dire political circumstances before invoking the right of revolution. But even such wording, as the experience with Maryland's 1776 constitution demonstrated, could be interpreted to allow the people to exercise their sovereignty without preconditions. This tendency epitomized how Americans supplanted the last-ditch right of revolution with an ongoing, inherent right of the people to revise their constitutions after Independence. This right rested on the sovereignty of the people under American constitutionalism rather than either natural law or the view of government as a bargain between the governed and governors. The understanding that the people could change their governments at any time and for any reason developed from the explicit recognition that republican governments in America were rooted in the people's sovereignty.[1] In 1793, when Virginia's highest court declared the state's 1776 constitution fundamental law legitimately created, one judge asserted that "the people have a right by a convention, or otherwise, to change the existing government." The "example of all America in the adoption of the federal government, and that of the several states in changing their state constitutions" provided clear evidence of that proposition.[2]

The inherent authority of the people to effect constitutional revision emerged even in the absence of alter or abolish provisions. In 1801, under New York's 1777 constitution (that lacked specific provisions for constitutional change), the state's legislature called a convention without first putting the question before the voters. Twenty years later, New York's Governor DeWitt Clinton criticized the failure to take that initial step when the state considered holding another constitutional convention. In November 1820, Clinton recommended a "double check" to "carry into effect the sovereign authority of the people" – namely, submitting the issue of a convention to popular vote and its draft constitution to ratification.[3]

The New York bill calling for a convention in 1821 did not submit the question to the people, prompting a veto by the state's Council of Revision. In his opinion for the council, Chancellor James Kent stated that there could be "no doubt of the great and fundamental truth, that all free governments are founded on the authority of the people, and that they have at all times an indefeasible right to alter and reform the same" as "their wisdom" might direct. Indeed, just two years earlier, Chief Justice John Marshall considered it "settled" that in America the people "may resume and modify the powers granted to government."[4]

In drafting and revising nineteenth-century constitutions, American constitution-makers repeatedly acknowledged that alter or abolish provisions were *"practical"* principles that gave American republics their *"distinctive* character."[5] In Virginia's 1829 convention, James Monroe observed, "Ours is a Government of the people: it may properly be called self-government. I wish it may be preserved forever in the hands of the people. Our revolution was prosecuted on those principles, and all the Constitutions which have been adopted in this country are founded on the same basis." In Pennsylvania's 1837 constitutional convention, one delegate described the alter or abolish provision as "a living and governing principle" and asserted that the people "have never parted with their inalienable right to alter, reform, or abolish their government." Even delegates who refused "to join in the wild shout – *Vox Populi, Vox Dei* – the voice of the people is the voice of God!" believed, along with "every true republican" that "the people are the only true source, from which power can emanate."[6]

Debate over a proposal for a ten-year moratorium on constitutional amendments in Pennsylvania's 1837 convention reflected the consensus about the sovereign authority in America. Such a moratorium, asserted one delegate, conflicted with the people's inherent "right to alter, reform or abolish their government, in such manner as they may think proper." Accordingly, "When the people feel the need of a change, and see in your constitution the assertion of their right to make such change, whenever they may deem fit, they will not always wait five or nine years, for the opportunity of doing it in a particular mode." Preserving "peace, order, and republican government" meant giving "the people the sovereignty" and "its exercise at all times." Although frequently disagreeing with the first speaker, another delegate joined in opposing the moratorium. Equally "averse to tying up the hands of the people," he thought "they ought not to be debarred from having their wishes carried into effect" whenever they wanted to change the constitution. By a substantial majority the convention rejected the ten-year time limit.[7]

With the inherent authority of the people to change constitutions well established by the late eighteenth century, later movements for constitutional revision turned to the same source. For example, after North Carolina's legislature repeatedly refused to call a convention, a contributor to the *Western Carolinian* in 1821 suggested that the people "should assemble in convention without the legislative sanction, and adopt such measures as the present and future welfare of the state . . . requires." Constitutional revision by "a majority" of the people bypassing the existing government, noted another writer, was "obligatory on the whole state" as a "legal act." Ever since the Revolution, James Madison and other leaders repeatedly underscored that the majority of "the people" formed the ultimate sovereign in America.[8]

Indeed, American constitution-makers continued to recognize the authority of the people to legitimize constitutional revision. Although he later denied the inherent right of the people to change their constitutions, during Massachusetts's 1821 constitutional convention Daniel Webster said that he "knew no principle that could prevent a majority, even a bare majority of the people, from altering the constitution." A delegate in Virginia's constitutional convention of 1829 explained that the lack of revision provisions in Virginia's 1776 constitution meant that it could not, "strictly speaking, be changed *according to law*." Rather, subsequent constitutional revision was "justified by that supreme and paramount law, the *salus populi*." Ultimately, the sovereign people "supplied the only mode, by which the original right of the people to meet in full and free Convention to reform, alter, or abolish their form of government, could be exercised." The delegate emphasized that the practical authority of the people to change their government outweighed the subordinate role the legislature played in the process of constitutional change. "If the substance of the thing, to wit: the ascertainment of the public will, is accomplished, it is needless to stickle about forms." James

Madison had made the same point forty years earlier in justifying the federal constitutional convention.[9]

Numerous prominent constitutional commentators writing before the 1840s endorsed the inherent authority of the people to revise constitutions outside of existing procedures or without the consent of the government. In 1803, St. George Tucker's edition of Blackstone's *Commentaries* described alter or abolish provisions as expressing "a fundamental principle in all the American States, which cannot be impugned, or shaken." The people could never be deprived of "the right of resuming the sovereign power into their own hands, whenever they think fit." A constitution "may indeed provide a mode within itself for its amendment; but this very provision is founded in the previous consent of the people," and if government undermined the public welfare, "the people will probably find the necessity" of resuming their "sovereignty" in order to correct such abuses. Another constitutional commentator, William Rawle, the former U.S. attorney for Pennsylvania who vigorously prosecuted whiskey excise tax protesters in the 1790s, likewise noted in 1825 that the people could "at any time alter or abolish the constitution they have formed." While it might be "most convenient to adhere" to existing revision provisions, they were "not exclusively binding."[10]

In 1833, Nathaniel Chipman, in his treatise on *Principles of Government*, explained that since both state and national governments derived their powers from "the people," the people still retained their "sovereign capacity" and "right to alter, to enlarge, or limit the powers of both, or either, as they shall think will best promote the public good." Even Justice Joseph Story in his constitutional *Commentaries* in 1833 identified the "general, if not universal" understanding that "the majority of the people" could change their state constitutions "in the manner prescribed by the constitution, or otherwise provided for by the majority." According to Story, the Declaration of Independence was "an act of original, inherent sovereignty by the people themselves, resulting from their right to change the form of government, and to institute a new government, whenever necessary for their safety and happiness." And when William Sullivan published an instruction manual in 1836 on "political power" he made a point of noting that in America "the people are the sovereign." He introduced his work by noting that the ultimate authority "resided in those who instituted" governments. They retained "the exclusive right to judge whether power, established for its benefit, is constitutionally exercised" and "the absolute right to amend, and even to abolish, an existing system, and substitute any other."[11]

Constitutional conventions in the 1820s and 1830s also recognized the supremacy of the people's authority in constitutional revision. A delegate to Delaware's 1831 convention acknowledged that while the legislature called the present convention, the authority underlying their convening came "directly" from "the power of the people, without any aid from the legislature." Moreover, delegates to Pennsylvania's 1837 convention suggested that constitutional amendments became "a part of the fundamental law of the land" when accepted by the people.[12] Another Pennsylvania delegate echoed the long articulated idea that "the people had at all times the right to alter, abolish, or reform their government, and to do that by means of a majority; because it was a right inherent in the people." Unlike "the old world" where "you cannot take up at pleasure the foundations of your Government, and improve its form," noted a Virginia delegate in 1829, Americans possessed that constitutional authority.[13]

In fact, delegates in Pennsylvania's 1837 convention acknowledged the right of the people to alter their governments independent of any revision provision the convention drafted. As one delegate put it, "The majority of the people, we all know, have the right at any time, to revise the constitution under which they live; and they could do so, as they have done in the present instance, without any provision being inserted in the constitution." It seemed obvious to another delegate that "any rules" for future constitutional revision "will be disregarded by the people" whenever "a change shall appear to them to be desirable." If "a majority of the people" ratified a constitution while circumventing constitutional procedures, "who will say that it is not law – law as valid and as binding as any that you have power to incorporate into the constitution now?" When "the people rise in their might to prescribe new rules for their own government" those rules became the law of the land.[14]

The prospect of conventions unauthorized by the existing government was particularly unsettling to some. Critics of "conventionizing schemes" described delegates to one such convention in Virginia in 1825 as "inciters to anarchy and disunion."[15] It was one thing for government to bypass provisions by invoking the inherent rights of the people but quite another for conventions independent of government to claim that authority. Scholars have considered self-created conventions "illegal" or "extra-legal."[16] Moreover, they have questioned the legitimacy of such conventions, describing "alter or abolish" provisions as "theoretical fluff" reflecting the rhetoric of the American Revolution and a natural law tradition.[17] Their characterization, however, overlooks the constitutional dimensions of the people's sovereignty. Even when conventions were unauthorized by the legislature, they relied on the same principled basis as did the existing government when it justified circumvention.[18]

The legitimacy of revising constitutions that lacked provisions for constitutional change, of revising constitutions in contravention of existing procedures for constitutional change, and, ultimately, of revising constitutions without the permission of the existing government, all came from the same source: the authority of the sovereign people. The people's sovereignty justified constitutional change when constitutions (state or federal) were silent about the means for revision or when it seemed appropriate to bypass existing procedures. More controversial was the notion that such change could occur independent of the existing government, in particular without the permission of the legislature. However, the insistence by some Americans that legitimate revision required the consent of the existing government raised, for other Americans, the troubling implication of governmental sovereignty. Insisting that the will of the legislature prevailed over that of "the people" undermined the people's inherent authority. It also struck many Americans as inverting the acknowledged constitutional principle since Independence: that only the people – not government – possessed inherent sovereignty and that governors remained the people's servants.

From the start, constitutional conventions meeting without the authorization of legislatures routinely sought legitimacy from the inherent rights of the people. In Staunton, Virginia, in 1816, convention organizers acted on the alter or abolish language of Virginia's 1776 bill of rights. When nearly fifty delegates from most of the counties of North Carolina met at Raleigh on November 10, 1823, many of those who gathered without the consent of the state government thought that a "majority of the people" possessed "an inalienable right to revise and alter their constitution whenever they please." Prior to Virginia's 1829 convention, legislators representing the western portion of the state asserted "an indubitable right" of a majority of the people to gather "in a body & organize a convention" if the legislature failed to act. Georgia's 1833 convention, which met to revise the state's 1798 constitution, was preceded by a series of conventions unauthorized by the legislature. A supporter of that reform movement wrote in 1832 that "the people have an undoubted right, in their sovereign capacity, to alter or change the form of their government, whenever in their opinion it becomes too obnoxious or oppressive to be borne." In 1833, a "Reform State Convention" meeting in Harrisburg, Pennsylvania, cited the 1790 state constitution's alter or abolish provision as permitting the people to "rise in the majesty of their power" if the legislature failed to call a convention. They were justified in initiating a convention effecting a "peaceful, tranquil revolution" by "public opinion." In 1834 that convention reconvened and urged the legislature to hold another convention.[19]

In 1836, a convention in Maryland claimed that the people could change their government "at any time" and "in any manner" even though Maryland's "alter or abolish" provision spoke of constitutional alterations only when the ends of government were "perverted" or liberty "manifestly endangered." Delegates argued that such preconditions put the people of Maryland in an "extraordinary position" different from all other Americans, "who have control over their constitutions." In agreement, "the largest meeting of the mechanics and workingmen ever convened in the city of Baltimore" resolved that "The power to amend, change or abolish the constitution is inherent in the people, and any vested delegation of authority to a legislature is no relinquishment of the sovereignty of the people so to alter, amend or abolish the constitution in *any* manner and at *any* time, as may to them seem most fitting." Maryland's constitution was an *"act of limitation of the people upon their agents"* under which the people never relinquished "the inalienable right to annul or abolish" that act. The sovereignty of the people justified recalling that authority and convening a convention.[20]

In 1837, a select committee of the Maryland legislature declined to respond to the convention movement by recommending a bill to make it "a high crime and misdemeanor for citizens to conspire against the constitution of the state." The chairman of the committee, Charles Ridgely, made it clear that the committee did not approve of revising the state's constitution "in a mode unknown to the constitution" and, in fact, regarded such action as "an unlawful act." While wishing to "fortify the state against such assaults, there is very great danger of running into the other extreme, and consolidating, in the hands of the executive, powers dangerous to civil liberty." Of the two dangers, Ridgely saw "more to fear from the latter than the former." The committee report concluded that Maryland's "institutions emanate immediately from the people" and that "whenever the majority of the people require a change, to promote the common good, it ought to and will be made." In the meantime, existing law ensured that revision within the state would occur in "a peaceful and constitutional mode." The report thus reflected the appeal of the majority principle of American constitutionalism even among those who sought to limit constitutional change to existing procedures.[21]

In August 1842, delegates, "appointed by the citizens" of twenty western counties in Virginia, met in convention to protest the political representation granted their region under the state's 1829 constitution. Frustrated by the legislature's unwillingness to hold another constitutional convention, the so-called Lewisburg Convention, which met for three days, appointed a committee to consider "suitable subjects for its action." Although the committee reported that they hoped their grievances would be remedied "under the

forms of the present constitution," they concluded that "the existing inequality is alone to be remedied by a recurrence to those fundamental principles
which declare that a majority of the community" had a "right to alter or
abolish in such manner as shall be judged conducive to the public weal."
The committee proposed resolutions, approved by the circumvention convention, urging constitutional revision. If the legislature did not call a convention, a member of Virginia's upper house warned in early 1844, "it will
then be the duty of the people to . . . do for themselves what their servants
or agents refused to do."[22]

Conventions unsanctioned by the present government generated an
alarm. They mainly served to pressure legislatures into calling constitutional
conventions and displayed a recurring pattern: a series of mass meetings
and conventions urging constitutional change under the veiled threat that
if the existing government did not act, the people would take matters into
their own hands. Except for events in Rhode Island in the 1840s, that threat
rarely offered serious challenge to existing governments. Nonetheless, even
the suggestion that conventions might act independently by invoking the
people's inherent sovereignty prompted government officials to deny the
legitimacy of any gatherings of "the people" unsanctioned by the existing
government.[23]

By the 1820s, the principle that the people retained the inherent right
to revise their governments seemed to encourage comprehensive constitutional change and the expression of majority will. Debates over constitutional
revision in constitutional conventions before the Civil War reflected both
issues and divided delegates who favored making the revision process more
accessible to the people from those who feared its destabilizing potential.
Ultimately, delegates agreed that "the people" should retain a realistic degree
of control over the means of modifying their governments and constitutions,
even if constitutional change should not occur for light or trivial reasons.
In that important sense, all constitution-makers remained committed to the
people's sovereignty.[24]

From the 1820s to the 1840s constitutional revision shifted away from
a predominant reliance on conventions. With one exception, every state
between 1820 and 1842 holding a constitutional convention inserted a provision for amendment if one did not already exist in its constitution.[25] In
addition, all the constitutional conventions leading to statehood between
1820 and 1842 included an amendment procedure in their constitutions.[26]
A delegate to New York's 1821 convention touted the benefits of making
amendments "without resorting to the difficult and dangerous experiment of
a formal Convention." In Massachusetts's convention that same year, Daniel

Webster explained that "the permanency of the constitution" was promoted by the absence of a provision for future conventions. Future conventions were unnecessary since "the great outlines" of the existing 1780 constitution were so well "established," but "plain sensible and useful" amendments could still occur. Other delegates shared Webster's desire for "sufficient security" against changes prompted by "temporary excitement" of the populace.[27]

Virginia's 1829 convention was the lone exception to the trend of adding amendment provisions. Some delegates to that convention opposed what they described as America's "mania" and "fever for Constitution-making." They considered constitutional revision inherently dangerous and subversive of order. As such, it should be generally discouraged. One Virginia delegate lamented a shift since the eighteenth century, when America's first written constitutions were "regarded by the rest of the world as little less than a miracle." Now, however, the people, "with no practical oppressions, but as if hunting for theoretical grievances, have become unsettled and dissatisfied with the old Government." The urge for constitutional innovation reached the point, the delegate complained, that "every pettifogger in the State, who cannot write a declaration in debt, without the aid of a form, will consider himself qualified, at a moment's warning, to draft you out a new Constitution . . . according to the latest fashion." Edmund Randolph compared adding an amendment procedure to "introducing into a marriage contract a provision for divorce." It prompted the people "to be dissatisfied with their Government." Even so, Randolph conceded the people's inherent power of constitutional revision. He questioned the "necessity" of an amendment provision because whenever the people wanted constitutional change nothing would prevent them from "doing as they please." After his speech, the convention rejected an amendment provision.[28]

Delegates concerned about unnecessary constitutional changes frequently alluded to the dangers of the popular will. Occasionally, even the principle of the sovereignty of the majority of the people came under attack, as, for example, when senate electors in Maryland denounced "this heresy of the absolute and controlling power of a numerical majority" to effect constitutional change. At other times, delegates in constitutional conventions articulated the necessary preconditions to the people's inherent right of revision that were reminiscent of the traditional right of revolution. Daniel Webster insisted that no constitutional changes should occur unless "a real evil existed." A delegate in North Carolina's 1835 convention echoed Webster by asserting that constitutions should "never be altered" unless "absolutely necessary" or "the emergency is great." And earlier, in Virginia's 1829 convention, Edmund Randolph identified several preconditions before legitimate

constitutional change could occur: "the grievance must first be clearly specified, and fully proved; it must be vital, or rather, deadly in its effect; its
magnitude must be such as will justify prudent and reasonable men in taking
the always delicate, often dangerous step, of making innovations in their fundamental law; and the remedy proposed must be reasonable and adequate
to the end in view." Such prerequisites for constitutional revision ultimately
ran counter to the trend since the Revolution of acknowledging the people's
unqualified right of constitutional change.[29]

Indeed, Virginia's position in questioning the people's inherent right of
revision departed from America's constitutional tradition. Cautioning against
perceived dangers of amendment was different from formally denying the
means of adjusting fundamental law. By and large, America's constitution-
makers – including Daniel Webster – conceded the principle that the people's
sovereignty – expressed by a majority – remained the ultimate constitutional authority. Delegates worried about the political implications of majority will, however, were somewhat mollified that most amendment provisions
required more than majority votes and even successive votes of the legislature. Moreover, amendment provisions provided an alternative to potentially
more sweeping revision through constitutional conventions. A delegate to
North Carolina's 1835 convention captured the widespread, if at times grudg-
ing, acceptance of the people's inherent authority: "That the deliberate will
of the people ought ultimately to prevail, no one will deny; but that the
temporary will of a majority, which may be produced by the effervescence
of the moment, ought to do *whatever it pleases* – set up and put down the
constitutions from day to day – no man can be so extravagant as to desire."[30]

By the late 1830s, Americans had considerable experience drawing upon
the people's inherent authority to justify constitutional revision in the absence
of provisions for change or revisions that did not follow constitutional procedures. In 1837, James Buchanan – a lawyer, senator from Pennsylvania, and
future Democratic president – justified constitutional conventions meeting
under the direct authority of the people's sovereignty. The issue of the constitutional authority of the sovereign people had surfaced repeatedly since
the 1770s when western territories sought statehood and determinist settlements advanced their claims. Tensions were long-standing between the
rights of the people in territorial regions to act on their own initiative and
the authority of Congress to control the process under the Northwest Ordinance. Thus, when congressional debate turned to the issue of Michigan's
admission as a state in 1837, claims for the right of "the people" to sanction
self-government were hardly new. Without waiting for Congress to pass an
enabling act inviting the Michigan territory to organize itself for statehood,

the territory drafted a constitution in a constitutional convention held in 1835. The constitution proclaimed all political power "inherent in the people" and asserted their right to "alter" or "abolish" government "whenever the public good requires it."[31]

Speaking on the floor of Congress, Buchanan described the situation of a people confronted by a legislature that persistently refused to reform voting rights and political representation. Under those circumstances, Buchanan would seek "to persuade the people to hold a convention of their own" and "call upon them peaceably and quietly to exert their own sovereign authority in effecting a change in their form of government." Such a step was not "rebellion or revolution." What Buchanan imagined soon became a political reality in Rhode Island when reformers became convinced that constitutional change had to "[e]manate from the People by their meeting in Primary Assemblies to choose delegates to meet in Convention to form a Written Constitution for the State."[32]

Although the threat of direct constitutional revision by "the people" in the face of legislative inaction was hardly unknown, the unique circumstances in Rhode Island prompted the most dramatic occasion since the Revolution for what one contemporary called the "practical application" of the people's sovereignty. By 1841, the recalcitrance of entrenched political power disenfranchised more white males in Rhode Island than in any other state. This long-standing political grievance became especially disturbing to Rhode Islanders when so many other Americans widely participated in the presidential election of 1840.[33]

The Rhode Island debate crystallized America's competing perceptions of the implications of written constitutions. That struggle pitted those who acknowledged the practical manifestation of the people's sovereignty against those who increasingly located sovereignty in government itself. Proponents of government sovereignty insisted that the people needed to act with the consent of the existing government and according to constitutional provisions for change. Otherwise, their actions could be justified only by a successful revolution based on raw power. Their opponents, on the other hand, insisted that the people's sovereignty gave constitutional legitimacy to revisions that bypassed existing provisions for constitutional revision and that occurred without the government's consent. The struggle between these competing constitutional views of the sovereign authority of the people squarely raised the question of the existence of a constitutional middle ground between strict subordination to government and natural law–based revolutionary action.

8 The Collective Sovereign Persists

The People's Constitution in Rhode Island

During the morning of May 3, 1842, an "immense influx" of out-of-town visitors mingled with local townspeople to witness a special event in Providence, Rhode Island. The occasion was the inauguration of a new governor and legislature for the state. A procession of sixteen hundred people (some estimates put the number at three thousand) gathered in High Street, in front of Hoyle's Tavern. The gathering included recently elected officials and was led by a series of militia companies and "Volunteer corps" from around the state. The Providence Brass Band provided music. Bringing up the rear on horseback "two abreast" were members of different trades, such as the butchers, who in "white frocks" made "a very imposing appearance."

Spectators and celebrants "thronged the sides of all the avenues" staring at "the novel sight." They strained to catch a glimpse of the "immense assemblage" as it moved toward the State House, where the inauguration was supposed to take place. Even the most conservative estimates placed the number of those present at more than 20 percent of the city's population; others thought it exceeded 40 percent.

The inauguration prompted special attention because the state already had a governor and legislature. The existing government traced its authority to Rhode Island's colonial charter, which had served as the state's constitution since the Revolution. The 1663 charter permanently fixed the number of representatives each town could send to the legislature, despite significant shifts in later patterns of population growth in the towns. In addition, legislatures under the charter government imposed a property requirement for voting that eventually excluded many potential voters. The state's entrenched political forces spurned constitutional revision for nearly fifty years.

In 1841, a "Suffrage" party convened a constitutional convention. They justified that step because the people had the right to alter or abolish

246

*governments – a principle enunciated since the Revolution and incorpo-
rated in many of America's written constitutions. That convention drafted a
constitution and set it before the public. This "People's Constitution" (which
extended the vote to all white adult male citizens with one year's residence)
was subsequently ratified by a majority not only of those who met that qualification but apparently also by a majority of those entitled to vote under
the colonial charter. When it was clear that the constitution had passed, the
Suffrage Party proceeded to elect a governor and other officials.*

*On this early May morning the officials under the new constitution would
commence their duty of ruling the state as agents of the people. When the
procession arrived at its destination, which underwent a last minute change
from the State House, the military units publicly declared what most of the
celebrants already believed, namely, "the People are sovereign, and ... when
acting in their sovereign capacity [have] full power and lawful authority to
alter and change the form of government." In doing so, the people elected
Thomas Wilson Dorr as their new governor. He was their "commander-in-
chief" and they felt bound to defend the People's Constitution.*

*Three days after Dorr's inauguration, the charter governor, Samuel King,
arrived in Providence by steamboat from Newport. A much smaller military and civilian escort than Governor Dorr had received greeted him. He
also considered himself a commander-in-chief and his supporters, who styled
themselves members of a "Law and Order" party, were committed to defending the colonial charter. The emergence of two governments for Rhode Island
initiated a contest over what it meant in America in the 1840s to say that
governments ultimately rested on the sovereignty of the people.[1]*

In the aftermath of the People's Constitution, the Suffrage Party's struggles
in Rhode Island became a cause within the national Democratic Party, while
many Whigs took the Law and Order position. Congressional debate over
"the Rhode Island Affair" reflected the efforts of national parties to make
political capital out of the dispute. Democrats invoked Dorr's position in
their campaign against the Whig Party during the presidential election of
1844, calling for the support of "Polk, Dallas, and Dorr." But reactions to
the People's Constitution did not break down along strict party lines, either
nationally or within Rhode Island. While New York's Democratic leadership
strongly supported Dorr, southern Democrats, including most prominently
John C. Calhoun, objected to Dorr's position that a majority of the people could change their constitutions at will. In Rhode Island, Whigs and
Democrats, one observer noted, were "arrayed indifferently on either side
of the contest."[2]

Although enmeshed in politics, the struggle over the People's Constitution raised a crucial question of constitutionalism. Those debating "the Rhode Island question" acknowledged that it bore "little" on "the present strife of parties" in America. The question, noted a prominent Law and Order leader, did not involve "a controversy between adverse political parties, for political power." Rather, its "real merits" lay elsewhere. As the federal district court judge for Rhode Island put it, the issue involved a "great question of Constitutional law." What escalated the struggle for Law and Order supporters was that so many prominent lawyers and political leaders embraced "the grossest misconceptions" about "their constitutional rights." Indeed Dorr's position, worried one Law and Order advocate, was advanced "in sober earnest, by men in high places as well as by men in low places" and received "quite too much sympathy." Women also actively supported Dorr. When someone "educated" like Marcus Morton, a former justice of the Massachusetts Supreme Judicial Court and recently a two-term governor of that state, endorsed Dorr, matters were clearly at a dangerous pass. The "practical application" of Dorr's doctrine was "fatal to popular liberty." Americans courted "the vortex of *revolution*" by abandoning "true" principles of constitutional reform.[3]

Likewise for Dorr's supporters, the debate over the Rhode Island question involved the "fundamental principles of our entire system of American institutions." The question was "not one of mere local interest, but one of free government." Whether the power to revise governments "resides in the governing or the governed" could not be "too often presented to the American people, as long as it remains a disputed point by any considerable portion of American citizens." If Dorr's opponents saw revolution in his position, Dorr's supporters considered denying his views a repudiation of the "living principle" that in America the people, not government, were the sovereign. Relegating the sovereignty of the people to "a theory" stripped the principle of its constitutional authority. For both sides the matter raised a central issue of American constitutionalism: could the people as the sovereign act without the consent of their government?[4]

When the controversy reached the U.S. Supreme Court in *Luther v. Borden* (1849), both sides agreed that "the true principles" of American government were at stake. Law and Order lawyers sought to "purify the political atmosphere" and "clear men's minds from unfounded notions and delusions" by repudiating the claim that the people had an inherent right to change their governments. Lawyers for Dorr, on the other hand, sought to vindicate the position that the people's sovereignty existed not "in mere form and theory" but also "practically, effectually and actively." Neither side got exactly what they wanted and the court's decision did not end the struggle over America's "true principles." The Rhode Island question illustrated how Americans in the 1840s continued to differ in how they understood the constitutional legacy bequeathed by the Revolution.[5]

EARLY EFFORTS AT CONSTITUTIONAL REVISION
IN RHODE ISLAND

Rhode Island's 1663 colonial charter dictated political representation based on townships that over time produced disproportionate representation. Moreover, the state's legislature tied the franchise to land, eventually requiring ownership of real property valued at $134 before one could vote or hold office. In the agrarian setting of the colonial period, over 75 percent of white adult males were eligible to vote before the Revolution. The trend toward industrialization and urbanization after the Revolution, however, increased the number of non-landowners and intensified interest in removing the $134 requirement and adjusting political reapportionment. By 1841, only 40 percent of the white adult males in Rhode Island could vote and a small number of towns, consisting of less than half of the state's citizens, elected more than two-thirds of its representatives. After 1830, when Virginia repealed its freehold requirement, Rhode Island was the only state with a general landowning requirement for voting. By the 1840s, the charter represented a hidebound approach to voting and political representation dramatically out of step with the rest of Jacksonian America.[6]

Because the charter provided no means for its alteration, reformers regularly asked the legislature to initiate constitutional revision. Between the 1790s and 1820s, efforts to reapportion the legislature proved unavailing, with rural legislators preserving their political power by refusing to amend or replace the charter. A legislative report in 1829 rejecting the expansion of the vote typified the concerns of defenders of the state's charter. The report's author, Benjamin Hazard, asserted that the state's stability rested on property requirements and that Rhode Islanders were not "infected with the rage of the times for constitution-making." Eligible voters respected "the wise institutions of their ancestors" too much to change them "lightly" for "new models of constitutions, which have nothing peculiar to recommend them, except the unsubstantial allurement of being framed after the revolution." The charter enshrined the principal insight of "the whole science of legislation and jurisprudence," namely, the importance of protecting the rights of property. Property requirements were an essential barricade against the landless as well as "the common mass of emigrants" from foreign lands. Most of those without the requisite property "reduced themselves to that condition by their own improvidence, extravagance, or vices" and hence were "unfit" to control "the property or rights of others."[7]

Pressure for constitutional change mounted given such attitudes, especially during the 1830s. One suffrage reformer, the carpenter Seth Luther,
wondered if Rhode Islanders who paid taxes, but who were denied the vote,
"gained by the revolution" anything more than "a change of masters in that
respect?" Renewed reform efforts led to the creation of the Constitutional
Party in 1834, seeking a constitutional convention. Although the legislature
held a convention that year, it avoided fundamental revision; in fact, it could
not even agree on a draft constitution.[8]

Despite its failure, the latest reform movement saw Thomas Wilson Dorr
emerge as a leading figure in the state's constitutional revision struggle. Dorr
wrote an *Address to the People of Rhode Island* that challenged the legitimacy of the charter government and questioned why Rhode Island was the
only state without a written constitution coming "directly from the *free* and
sovereign People." The "inherent right" of the people to establish a constitution "in their original, sovereign capacity" seemed a proposition beyond
doubt and judicially validated for half a century.[9]

Even Dorr's critics conceded his "intellectual ability" and his leadership
brought the movement enhanced respectability. Dorr came from a well-
connected Rhode Island family and received a privileged education. His
father, Sullivan Dorr, was a wealthy merchant, a trustee of Brown University,
and a leader of the state's Whig Party. Dorr's mother, Lydia Allen, ensured
the family's social standing through her ancestry back to William Harris,
who accompanied Roger Williams to Providence in 1636. Dorr's education
included study at the Providence Free School, the Latin Grammar School,
Phillips Exeter Academy, and Harvard College. After graduating at the top
of his class, Dorr left Cambridge for New York, where he studied law under
the renowned Chancellor Kent. In addition, Dorr later clerked in the office
of one of Rhode Island's leading lawyers, John Whipple. Following admission to the bar in 1827, Dorr practiced in Providence and then briefly in
New York City, specializing in commercial and maritime matters. In New
York, Dorr met future supporters of his cause, including John L. O'Sullivan,
later editor of the *Democratic Review*, and the legal reformer, David Dudley
Field. Dorr's professional reputation also aided his entrance into politics. In
1834, he was elected to Rhode Island's legislature as a Whig representing
Providence. However, disagreements with the "doctrines of Whigs and Federalists" on the regulation of banks led to a political "change of sentiment"
that cost him reelection in 1837.[10]

Even before his drift toward the Democratic Party, Dorr expressed his
understanding of the people's inherent right to make constitutional changes.
In 1831, he wrote to a correspondent, "Mankind are disposed to wait and

to suffer long before they attempt political revolutions; but their delay and acquiescence sanctify no abuses, confirm no tyrannies; and a recurrence to the popular sovereignty is always a right and true remedy, tho not usually resorted to till others have failed." Ultimately, "the actual, living majority of the day possess the true sovereignty of the country, & have a right to investigate, review & amend its political Constitution, & to accommodate it to the just demands & necessities of the people." Not only were such views part of American constitutional thought since the Revolution, but they were relied upon by others seeking revision of Rhode Island's charter long before Dorr entered the field.[11]

In 1797, the Federalist George R. Burrill justified revision through the inherent power of the people. No fringe thinker, Burrill was a prominent Providence lawyer and a well-connected member of the legislature. His brother served as state attorney general, chief justice, and United States senator. Burrill distinguished the government from a written constitution and both from what he called *"the constitution paramount."* Just as government existed subordinate to a written constitution (which only the people could authorize), so too a written constitution occupied a subordinate position to "the constitution paramount" – that is, *the immediate work of God, and a part of nature itself.*" Burrill expressly traced "the constitution paramount" to "the principles and immutable maxims of free government," foremost among them being the people's sovereignty.[12]

During the Rhode Island suffrage movement, reformers also asserted that legitimate constitutional revision did not require the consent of the legislature. George Burrill reaffirmed this point in 1807. In 1818, the Federalist journalist James Davis Knowles explained that the people in their "sovereign and corporate capacity" were entitled to hold a convention if the legislature failed to act. Other editorials reminded the legislature that "the people are competent to form a convention for themselves, without the authority of their *high mightinesses.*" In *An Address on the Right of Free Suffrage,* Seth Luther reiterated the right of "the whole people" to make a constitution by assembling in "primary meetings" to appoint delegates to a convention.[13]

THE SUFFRAGE MOVEMENT AND COMPETING CONSTITUTIONAL CONVENTIONS

After the setback of the 1834 convention, Rhode Island's constitutional reform movement stalled until its resurgence during the presidential campaign of 1840 between Whig William Henry Harrison and the incumbent

Democrat Martin Van Buren. Widespread political participation during that election – with an extraordinary 80 percent voter turnout – underscored the political powerlessness of many Rhode Islanders. The 1840 election precipitated the rise of the Rhode Island Suffrage Association, whose efforts again drew Thomas Dorr into a leadership role. The Association warned the charter government's legislature: "WE KNOW OUR RIGHTS, AND KNOWING, DARE MAINTAIN THEM." Although the Suffrage Party prompted a call for a constitutional convention, the legislature limited participation to those entitled to vote under the charter. Convinced that this Landholders' (or Freemen's) Convention slated to meet in November 1841 would, like those of 1824 and 1834, fail to embrace constitutional reform, the Suffrage Party decided to hold its own People's Convention. The party called upon all white adult males to vote in town elections on August 28 to select delegates to convene one month before the Landholders' Convention.[14]

The Suffrage Party invoked the right of the people "from time to time to assemble together, either by themselves or their representatives, for the establishment of a republican form of government." Withholding the vote from a "majority" of the people was "anti-republican" and justified Rhode Islanders to act "in their original, sovereign capacity" without the consent of the legislature. Ironically, the Suffrage Party invoked Washington's *Farewell Address* for the proposition that "the basis of our political institutions is the right of the people to make and to alter their constitutions." Suffrage proponents predicted, perhaps naively, that a constitution framed by the People's Convention, if accepted by a majority, "will be promptly acquiesced in by the minority; will be vigorously sustained; and will become, without delay, the undisputed, paramount law" of the state. A Massachusetts lawyer later suggested that the people of Rhode Island had "in their sovereign capacity, instituted for themselves a form of Constitution" in a "wise and prudent manner." As such, they "had every reason" to believe from "past history" and "the experience of sister republics" that their new government would be "universally respected."[15]

Delegates to the People's Convention gathering in the Masonic Hall at Providence on October 4, 1841, included many "respectable" persons eligible to vote under the charter government and "prominent" professionals.[16] Even a Law and Order advocate thought that most of the delegates "were undoubtedly well-meaning persons."[17] Their ranks included: Samuel Y. Atwell, an attorney and current member of the legislature who had most recently served as Speaker of the House of Representatives; Dutee J. Pearce, former attorney general of Rhode Island, federal district attorney, and six-term congressman; and Joseph Joslin, a Newport attorney who served as the convention's president.[18] Dorr took the principal role in drafting the People's Constitution, after which the convention adjourned to allow public comment on its draft.[19] Alexander Hill Everett of Massachusetts, a protégé of John Quincy Adams, thought the constitution "very judiciously drawn" and that the convention offered "pretty good proof that the Sovereignty of the People is not with us, as it has been in some other countries, a mere name, but a substantial, and practical reality." With more than half a century's "practice" with "American Principles of constitutional law" it seemed to Everett that "when the People are permitted to act for themselves, there is no great danger of their being led into any material error."[20]

In drafting the People's Constitution and during the Suffrage movement generally, considerable disagreement existed over how widely to extend the vote. If members of the Suffrage Party agreed that too many people were disenfranchised under the charter, they differed over whether race or any property requirements should limit the franchise. Eventually, the convention recommended that all white adult males with one year's residence were eligible to vote for political offices but retained the property qualification for voting on financial questions. Dorr opposed the racial exclusion, but many in the Suffrage movement believed that not doing so jeopardized ratification. Pragmatism ultimately prevailed over principle. Implicitly that dispute raised the question Dorr asked the convention: "Who are the people?"[21]

Although that question prompted different answers among Americans generally, the other question of constitutionalism identified by Dorr – What have the people "a right to do?" – found universal agreement among the delegates. The People's Convention articulated the principle of its legitimacy in the third section of the bill of rights:

> All political power and sovereignty are originally vested in, and of right belong to, the people. All free governments are founded in their authority, and are established for the greatest good of the whole number. The people have therefore an unalienable and indefeasible right, in their original, sovereign, and unlimited capacity, to ordain and institute government, and in the same capacity to alter, reform, or totally change the same, whenever their safety or happiness requires.

In virtually every particular, this statement of the people's sovereignty was unremarkable. Most American state constitutions contained similar statements and language. The provision in the People's Constitution served as a lightning rod only because Dorr's supporters invoked the alter or abolish principle to legitimate the new constitution and displace the charter government.[22]

Dorr insisted that nothing he and his supporters said or did was "inconsistent" with governmental order in Rhode Island. Dorr pointed out that Article XIV of the People's Constitution called for the continued operation of the charter government so as to facilitate "transition to the new order of things in legislative matters…without confusion or violence." For that reason the election of officials under the new government would take place only four months *after* the ratification of the People's Constitution. The decision to delay the election had unintended consequences, but it reflected Dorr's claim that his supporters appealed "not to the cartridge-box but to the *ballot box*." It also belied the charge by Law and Order advocates that Dorr and his followers planned to seize power by force.[23]

At the end of December 1841, nearly 14,000 people ratified the People's Constitution – well before the Landholders' Convention adjourned in February 1842. Only fifty-two votes were cast against the People's Constitution due to the boycott by supporters of the charter government. Two weeks before the referendum, Dorr speculated that "we ought to have more than 12,000 votes to place the result beyond all doubt or cavil. 13,000 will do this. 14,000 will make a triumphant majority." The Suffrage Party thus claimed that the People's Constitution received more than 2,400 votes over a simple majority of the state's estimated 23,142 white adult males, including a majority of those eligible to vote under the charter. Even with the possibility of fraudulent voting, from which elections under the charter government were hardly immune, Dorr's supporters identified a considerable mandate for the People's Constitution.[24]

Law and Order forces, however, dismissed the People's Convention as "illegal & revolutionary" and having no "pretense of authority." That convention had acted "in violation of the rights of the existing government," whose consent was necessary for the creation of a new constitution. However, Samuel Atwell, the Suffrage Party leader currently serving in the charter legislature, urged fellow legislators to determine whether in fact a majority of the people had adopted the People's Constitution. His position rested on the substantive authority of the people's sovereignty. "There is no fundamental law which prescribes the mode of alteration of our government, and when a majority of the people, the real sovereigns in this State, who have the power to alter that form of government desire to make an alteration, any one mode in which they choose to do it, would be as valid as another." Most of his fellow legislators disagreed and refused to entertain the possibility that a majority of "the people" – however defined – might have ratified the People's Constitution.[25]

After the People's Convention adjourned in October, to allow comment on a draft constitution, it reconvened in the State House in mid-November to finalize the constitution.[26] The Landholders' Convention, meeting in Providence on November 1, 1841, could have adopted constitutional reforms of the earlier convention. The possibility for constitutional reform prompted some delegates to the People's Convention (including Dorr) to serve as delegates in the Landholders' Convention as well. As a member of the Landholders' Convention, Dorr proposed to include in the bill of rights the principle of the people's sovereignty and the right of the people to revise their governments. Other delegates objected that such "abstractions" were "unnecessary and improper – and not strictly true." Dorr countered that America's founding "fathers" had "clung" to such "general principles." Dorr's efforts to enshrine those principles in the proposed constitution failed, as did his motion to adjourn the Landholders' Convention because the ratification of the People's Constitution "by the people in their original and sovereign capacity" made the People's Constitution "the paramount law" of the state.[27]

In offering some concessions to the constitutional reformers, the Landholders' Constitution did not redistribute as much political power as did the People's Constitution. Moreover, it retained the real property requirement for naturalized citizens. Like the People's Constitution, the Landholders' Constitution reflected prejudices of the day by excluding nonwhite voters and limiting the vote to native-born adult men. The legislature permitted all those to whom the franchise would be extended under the Landholders' Constitution to vote on its ratification scheduled for March 21–23, 1842.[28]

Law and Order supporters of the Landholders' Constitution touted its broad voting privilege while exploiting nativist and anti-Catholic feeling. The *Providence Journal* told Rhode Islanders that the Landholders' Constitution "extends suffrage for which you originally contended," whereas "foreign elements" in the People's Constitution "would neutralize your power and effectiveness." The newspaper's editor insisted that ratification of the Landholders' Constitution – in the wake of the People's Constitution – represented a crucial time "to choose" between "conservative checks, or foreigners responsible only to priests." A broadside urged "Friends of the Charter" to reject "the extension of suffrage, and secure the old Government!" Ironically, charter defenders and opponents of the Landholders' Constitution combined to defeat it by a narrow margin.[29]

After March 23, 1842, Rhode Islanders faced a choice of either implementing the People's Constitution or sustaining the charter government. After the rejection of the Landholders' Constitution, the "only question" between Dorr and his opponents, according to one Law and Order observer, was whether the People's Constitution "should or should not be recognized as the paramount law" in the state. Samuel Atwell made a final attempt on March 30 to avoid competing constitutions by urging the resubmission of the People's Constitution to those allowed to vote on the Landholders' Constitution one week before. After the legislature overwhelmingly rejected that motion, both Law and Order forces and Dorr's supporters anticipated a showdown with elections slated for both governments less than three weeks later.[30]

THE STRUGGLE FOR GOVERNMENTAL
LEGITIMACY IN RHODE ISLAND

In retrospect, the four-month hiatus between the ratification of the People's Constitution in December 1841 and subsequent elections under that constitution proved a crucial miscalculation that undercut the chances of Dorr's success. The provisions for political transition in the People's Constitution reflected Dorr's expectation of peaceful constitutional change. He simply assumed that a majority vote in favor of the People's Constitution would be recognized as a legitimate transfer of authority from one government to the next. He greatly underestimated the charter government's tenacity for retaining power. In early April 1842, Dorr still believed that confrontation between the two governments would produce nothing more than "a paper-war."[31]

Faced with the impending organization of a government under the People's Constitution, Law and Order forces aggressively acted on two fronts early in April. First, the charter legislature passed "An Act in relation to offences against the sovereign power of the State" that imposed severe penalties for supporting the People's Constitution. Dubbed the "Algerine Law" for its harshness reminiscent of the former potentate of Algiers, the act made it treason to hold office under the people's government, subjecting offenders to life imprisonment. Under the Algerine Law even voting for the People's Constitution, much less serving in its government, invited criminal prosecution. Members of Dorr's government who posted bail after being arrested under the Algerine Law forfeited that bail if they continued to act under the People's Constitution. "Let our men go to jail," Dorr advised, while asserting he would never post bail. This strategy made it increasingly hard to follow Dorr's leadership.[32]

In addition, the charter government's governor, Samuel King, sought federal intervention and "precautionary measures" from fellow Whig, President John Tyler. Tyler replied that under the federal Constitution he could not anticipate "insurrectionary movements," but would respond to a request for military assistance given "actual" insurrection. Although federal troops were not sent to Rhode Island, that possibility worked in favor of the Law and Order forces.[33]

Even as the charter government lobbied President Tyler, Dorr's supporters appealed to prominent Democratic senators and lawyers, including William Allen of Ohio, Thomas Hart Benton of Missouri, and Levi Woodbury of New Hampshire. Allen told the president that "the majority of the people in R[hode] I[sland] were in the right upon every known principle of public liberty." Benton "fully" admitted "the validity of the constitutional movement by the people in Rhode Island." Levi Woodbury, a former judge and governor of New Hampshire as well as future justice of the U.S. Supreme Court, thought it put "the whole fabric of our American liberties" on "sand" to deny the people's right, independent of the legislature, "to make a Constitution . . . when & how they please." Two years later, a congressional House report investigating presidential "interference . . . in the affairs of Rhode Island" endorsed the people's right to alter or abolish without the consent of their existing government.[34]

Dorr claimed the Algerine Law was "very generally condemned" even by his opponents as "impolitic, unnecessary & unjust" and considered "null and void" because it conflicted with the People's Constitution. Although Dorr dismissed the act as only intended *"to frighten the common sort of folks,"* prosecutions under the law undercut his support. Dorr's supporters were also subjected to other forms of pressure: butchers received "notice that they are to lose customers" and Law and Order forces sought "to induce landlords to turn their tenants out of their homes" and discharge "every man from employment" who supported the Suffrage Party. As one protégé of Dorr observed, "The screws are to be put on without mercy." Under those circumstances the turnout for the election under the People's Constitution on April 18, with Dorr running unopposed for governor, was lighter than the vote for the constitution's ratification. Two days later Samuel King won reelection as governor under the charter.[35]

The gubernatorial elections of Dorr and King placed the two governments in opposition. Soon after his election, King authorized armed "volunteer police companies" in Providence and began aggressively prosecuting Dorr's supporters under the Algerine Law. Dorr got off to a less propitious start. On May 3, 1842 – the day specified in the People's Constitution for the transfer of governmental authority – Dorr's supporters paraded to the State House in Providence. Locked out of the chamber in which they placed the final touches on the People's Constitution, they moved to an "unfinished" foundry building for their inauguration ceremony and held a two-day legislative session. The "Foundry Legislature" abrogated the Algerine Law and authorized a delegation to proceed to Washington. Delegates were to inform President Tyler that the people of Rhode Island had "formed a written constitution" and "peaceably organized a government." Urged by supporters to lobby Tyler personally, Dorr left for Washington after the legislature adjourned.[36]

Dorr's departure avoided his arrest by charter officials, but he did not convince President Tyler to recognize the legitimacy of the People's Constitution during a meeting on May 10. However, one day earlier, Tyler urged the charter government to offer amnesty for adherents to the People's Constitution, followed by a new convention organized on "somewhat liberal principles." A "resort to force" only promised years of animosity since "one-half of your people" were involved in the "recent proceedings." "A government," Tyler suggested, "never loses anything by mildness and forbearance to its own citizens" given the alternative of "the shedding of blood." Tyler's efforts to prevent a collision between the two governments failed when both sides refused to back down. Dorr grew increasingly convinced of the need to resist the charter government.[37]

After meeting with the president, Dorr went to New York City where Democrats warmly welcomed him and he received promises of troops to support his constitutional position. Emboldened by this reception, Dorr returned to Providence on May 16 by train and addressed a cheering crowd, numbering by one account three to four thousand people. During Dorr's speech he brandished a sword given to him in New York, declaring his willingness to die with it in his hand defending the People's Constitution.[38]

Over the next few days, Dorr's forces seized two cannons from the Providence armory – relics from the Revolutionary War – and several hundred of his supporters positioned themselves to capture the state arsenal, then defended by a comparable number of Law and Order forces. After the defenders refused to surrender, Dorr ordered the cannons discharged, but with powder dampened by age they misfired.[39] Thereafter, the would-be besiegers dispersed and retreated. Although the numbers arrayed on both sides were nearly equal at the arsenal, Law and Order supporters conceded that at any time since Dorr's return to Rhode Island from New York "his entire force" could have been militarily "routed and overwhelmed in twenty minutes" by available government forces. Indeed, Dorr's melodramatic sword-waving speech and the march on the "forewarned, reinforced, and impregnable" arsenal seemed more like a staged, ritualized effort to intimidate the charter government than a determination to make war on its defenders (who included members of Dorr's immediate family).[40]

Despite the bloodless confrontation at the arsenal, Dorr's apparent willingness to take "all such means as the occasion shall demand" against the charter government alienated his more moderate supporters, including several members of the people's government who promptly resigned. As they put it, "Our men will not kill their own citizens." Still, they assured Dorr that resignation did not mean a "surrender" of their belief in "the right of the people to form and establish a government" as had been accomplished by the People's Constitution. Indeed, three weeks before Dorr's sword-waving speech, his articulate defender from within the charter legislature, Samuel Atwell, declared that the alter or abolish principle was "at the foundation of all liberty, and he was ready to die for that principle with sword in hand." Still, Atwell would not "sacrifice the peace of the State to establish that principle."[41]

After the arsenal standoff, Dorr left the state, eventually returning to New York. One week later, a close associate reported from Providence how "completely have the minds of many been turned by recent misfortunes." He wrote Dorr, "Your idea of using force must be abandoned entirely – there is no hope in that remedy now." Despite the growing de facto control of the state by the charter government, that reality did not resolve the underlying question of the legitimacy of the People's Constitution. Indeed, after the arsenal confrontation, former president Andrew Jackson wrote a correspondent, "The people are the sovereign power and agreeable to our system they have the right to alter and amend their system of Government when a majority" so desires.[42]

In exile from Rhode Island, Dorr rallied his supporters despite "recent events." The People's Constitution did not lose its legitimacy "by a *failure* of arms, or the resignation of those elected to office under it." Dorr wanted to return to Rhode Island and reconvene his legislature on Independence Day at Chepachet, a northwestern village near the Connecticut border. As that date approached, Law and Order forces made preparations and on June 25 the charter legislature proclaimed martial law. Dorr called upon his supporters to sustain the People's Constitution "by all necessary means." As Dorr and those still willing to march with him approached Chepachet, charter forces vastly outnumbered them. After it appeared that "the people of Rhode Island" were unwilling "to assert their rights," Dorr dismissed his followers, believing that most of those who voted for the People's Constitution were now "opposed to its further support by military means." Dorr went into exile once more, this time in New Hampshire.[43]

The political aftermath of the averted military confrontation produced a major concession. In late June, the charter legislature called for a constitutional convention to meet at Newport in September 1842. The constitution that convention drafted (which those loyal to the People's Constitution dubbed the "Algerine Constitution") considerably expanded the suffrage beyond that permitted under the charter and more equitably redistributed political representation. Nonetheless, Dorr urged a boycott of the convention and its constitution since he regarded the People's Constitution as the state's legitimate fundamental law. Despite a low turnout, the new constitution was ratified overwhelmingly in November 1842.[44]

By the end of 1842, the political issues of suffrage and reapportionment were overshadowed by the struggle over issues of constitutionalism regarding the legitimacy of the People's Constitution. The Algerine Constitution responded to many demands for constitutional reform of the charter. But the means sought to attain that reform – the convening of the People's Convention and ratification of the People's Constitution – transformed events in Rhode Island and their significance for the rest of the country.

What now took center stage was whether, in America, a majority of the people as the sovereign was constitutionally entitled to alter their governments whenever and however they chose, even independent of the existing government. All sides identified this as "the Rhode Island Question."[45] The Algerine Constitution explicitly rejected the people's right to alter or abolish their governments and insisted on following established procedures for constitutional revision after prior consent from the legislature.[46]

Despite conceding military defeat, Dorr returned to Rhode Island determined to defend the People's Constitution after a new government was formed under the Algerine Constitution. When he reached Providence on October 31, 1843, charter officials arrested and eventually tried and convicted Dorr of treason. Sentenced to life imprisonment at hard labor, Dorr remained in jail until February 1845, when public pressure prompted his release. From the time of his arrest until the Supreme Court rendered its decision in *Luther v. Borden*, Dorr sought legal vindication of the People's Constitution.[47]

DEBATE OVER "THE RHODE ISLAND QUESTION"

The issues raised by the People's Constitution transcended the judicial arena. Many Americans considered the Rhode Island question a "most exciting" and "interesting" public issue. The debate over "the Rhode Island Question" pitted competing understandings of the constitutional significance of the Revolution for American government. The two sides of the debate clearly articulated contrasting views of the meaning of American constitutionalism by the 1840s.[48]

The Constitutional Argument of Dorr's Supporters

For Dorr, the "momentous event" of the American Revolution transferred sovereignty from the English monarch to the American people and profoundly altered the relationship of the people and their governors. Thereafter, the people of each state were invested with "the right of sovereignty" and "equally entitled to a voice" in framing their constitutions. Dorr echoed Chief Justice Jay's earlier description of the Revolution as having "devolved" sovereignty "on the people" and making Americans "equal as fellow citizens." A lawyer thought it "a great pity" that "the first great principles" of the American Revolution were "so easily forgotten by some." The Law and Order forces apparently believed the "only change our fathers accomplished by the Revolution, was a change of *masters*" and not "the establishment of a great principle."[49]

For Dorr's supporters, written constitutions altered "the nature" of government. Before the Revolution, government was often described as a contract or bargain between the people and their rulers, but that theory, according to Henry Williams – the lawyer and Democratic congressman from Massachusetts – was "not the doctrine of our revolution." Rather, the people's sovereignty formed the "solid foundation" underlying Independence and America's new governments. In America "the people are the authors of government" and their consent alone gave it rightful existence. American "governors and men in authority" were "but the mere agents and servants of the people."[50]

The people's sovereignty provided constitutional significance to the Declaration of Independence. The people's right to alter or abolish their governments was not a "rhetorical" flourish during a period of "great excitement," but according to Dorr, a statement of constitutional principle authorizing the people to resume government "whensoever it shall become necessary to their happiness."[51] The people had "the full right, at any time, and at all times, in their primary capacity, to 'alter, amend, or abolish' the forms of government under which they live." It was one of "the fundamental principles and time honored maxims of American Constitutional 'law and order.'"[52] Defenders of the People's Constitution saw the widespread incorporation of this right in American constitutions as "evidence of the highest degree" that it reflected "the public law of America."[53] The inherent right of a majority of the people to alter or abolish their governments was not "new or singular," but rather "sound doctrine" from the nation's best legal minds for over fifty years. Until the "recent troubles" in Rhode Island, Dorr's supporters observed, "no one" in America "denied the truth of these doctrines."[54]

Dorr's supporters distinguished "between a mere right of revolution resting on physical force, and a right of a majority to change government in the
exercise of that political sovereignty which the majority of [the] community
embodies." As a result, Americans, unlike other peoples of the world, were
"not bound to wait for usurpation and tyranny" in order to change governments and "perfect" constitutions.[55]

The American right to alter or abolish justified constitutional changes
made without the consent of the existing government or in compliance with
constitutional revision provisions. Indeed, nine prominent lawyers (including Dorr, John P. Knowles, who later became the U.S. District Court judge
for Rhode Island, Thomas F. Carpenter, a prominent leader of the Providence bar and former major-general of the state's militia, and Joseph K.
Angell, a well-known legal treatise writer) rejected the idea of "necessary
permission" from the legislature. Such permission was "an English doctrine" without application in America, "where the sovereignty resides in the
people."[56] The American people were "the judges" of both the "*time* of
exercising this sovereign power" and the "*mode* of proceeding." The lawyers
assured their readers that the People's Constitution was "rightful, and not
against law."[57] Likewise, former governor of Massachusetts Marcus Morton
questioned if any "friends of free government" would agree that "the people can *only* make or amend their Constitutions by the permission of their
rulers?" The lawyer Benjamin Hallett called the necessity of governmental
consent "anti-American." Although it might be "convenient" or "desirable"
to make constitutional changes with the blessing of the existing legislature
it was not indispensable. Another lawyer, Benjamin Cowell, after reviewing
the opinions of "the most able and distinguished expounders of Constitutional law," concluded that the people "can change the form of government
whenever and in *what manner soever* they please."[58]

Only the sovereign people could create constitutions and they retained
their sovereign authority even after constitutions and governments were
established. According to the *Nine Lawyers' Opinion*, that made legislators
the agents of the people. Even as an agent could act for his principal, "the
source of power remains" with the principal. "The greater power inherent
in the People, by virtue of their sovereignty, to form a Constitution, involves
the less power," namely "the *way* and *manner*" the people chose to direct
their agent.[59]

The authority that made legislative permission optional also implied that
the sovereign could not be strictly limited by existing constitutional revision
provisions. The people retained "absolute sovereignty over all Constitutions
and prescribed modes of amendment." Therefore, revision provisions could

not "impair" the "right of the People at large to make alterations in their organic laws in *any other* mode, which they may deem expedient." Where procedures for constitutional revision existed, the people "are *not* bound to proceed in the manner prescribed" for amendment, even though "this may be most *convenient* or expedient," but instead "they may rightfully proceed in the mode or manner which they deem most proper." Henry Williams reminded congressional colleagues that constitutional revision provisions "do not confer the right" but only provide the "means" of "exercising a prior right" based on the people's sovereignty. As such, the lawyer Benjamin Hallett noted, "The form prescribed is mere direction to the agents; not a bar to the people. If the necessity arises, the people may act." In the final analysis, American constitutions drew their "validity and binding force of law" neither from "the manner in which, nor the persons by whom" they were formed, but rather from the "assent" of "the people."[60]

The Constitutional Position of Law and Order Advocates

Law and Order advocates described the assertion of the people's inherent rights as "a string of absurdities" and "visionary theories" promoting constitutional misconceptions. Elisha Potter, a lawyer and Whig representative to Congress from Rhode Island, called peaceable revolution a "misnomer." He dismissed reliance on alter or abolish provisions because they were merely theoretical statements that "'sovereignty' resides in the people, the whole people, and that they have a right to resume the powers of government, and to alter or change the constitution." Virtually "no one denies" such assertions that were found "in almost all the State constitutions." Such "declarations of natural rights" reflected "the loose and unmeaning" tendency of state constitutional language. Potter noted that in the Algerine Convention, he opposed Dorr's proposal for an alter or abolish provision as "out of place in a constitution." According to other Law and Order delegates, such a provision put a powder "magazine beneath the fabric of civil society" which might "explode it without warning." Rhode Island's Whig senator and former yarn manufacturer, James Simmons, asserted that any right to alter or abolish government only arose "when that government becomes harsh, unjust, and oppressive, and there exists no remedy through the existing government."[61]

Such a view of the alter or abolish provisions assumed, as one Suffrage lawyer observed, that Americans "acquired no rights in regard to government, by the Revolution, that the people under old governments did not possess." Indeed, federal district judge John Pitman described American government in pre-Revolutionary terms when he declared, "The citizen owes allegiance to the government" and "the government owes protection to the citizen." For Pitman, this model of bargained for exchange between governors and the governed was a binding contract between the parties. Having given their consent to government, was it necessary to ask if the people were "at liberty to withdraw that consent, to violate the rights of the government, and the duty of allegiance?" Certainly not, unless, like King George, the government "forfeits our allegiance by refusing its protection," the only circumstance that might warrant invoking "the right of revolution."[62]

Other Law and Order supporters also downplayed the significance of the Revolution. Chief Justice Job Durfee of Rhode Island's Supreme Court, who presided over Dorr's treason trial, described the Revolution as "a conflict between corporate bodies" in which the American "corporate people" acted "in every legal form in which it could act." For Orestes Brownson, a Democrat who initially supported the People's Constitution, but later opposed it, the Revolution "in fact was no Revolution." He found a continuity, "[h]istorically and legally considered," between America's present governments and their colonial and English antecedents. Another Law and Order sympathizer claimed America's Revolution was "directed entirely by duly organized assemblies and associations, legally constituted." Indeed, American constitutional developments since 1776, according to Daniel Webster, reflected "a peculiar conservatism" leading to changes "with the utmost care and prudence."[63]

Such efforts to "de-revolutionize" the American Revolution were hardly new; they surfaced in the course of Fourth of July celebrations during the 1780s and remained an enduring theme in American politics and historiography. For Dorr's supporters in the 1840s, however, denying the right to alter or abolish governments denied the constitutional legacy of the Revolution and accepted "English," "old world," and "ultra-slavish" doctrines elevating government and subordinating the people. In rejecting the alter or abolish principle, Law and Order advocates endorsed "not the American, but the European, theory of government." To Dorr it seemed "strange, in a republican country, to hear it gravely advanced that the people cannot exercise the great act of sovereignty in forming and reforming their government, without the permission of their servants." Indeed, in 1844, while Dorr was in prison, David Dudley Field wrote to assure him that "the principles of your movement were the principles of our revolution." Likewise, the lawyer and congressman Henry Williams recalled that the "denial of the people's right to govern was toryism" during the Revolution and wondered if such denial constituted "anything better now?" The lawyer John Bolles accused the Law and Order minister and president of Brown University, Francis Wayland, of "adopting the *parlor* conviction, that the people were wrong and the government right" without first "sifting the facts or weighing the principles."[64]

In fact, Dorr's supporters reasonably worried about the commitment of their opponents to the constitutional axiom of the people's sovereignty. While many Law and Order supporters agreed that "under the American system all power is in the people" – thereby conceding the people as the sovereign – they inevitably emphasized "the rights of the government" and the people's submission to government's decisions.[65] Francis Wayland told Americans not to fear "oppression from Government," but warned that the country still faced "the dangers which arise from the sliding of liberty into licentiousness." When Judge Pitman repudiated the People's Constitution, he spoke of "the first duty" of government to defend itself and resist doctrines "which go to its own destruction." Government officials and the people were equal only in the sense that both were subject to law. For "the great purposes of society" Pitman thought "some must command and others must obey." For Orestes Brownson, "Government is not only that which governs, but that which has the *right* to govern. The governed, then, are not only *forced* to obey, but they are morally *bound* to obey. Obedience is a duty." When John Quincy Adams came to Providence in 1842 to lecture on "The Social Compact" he stressed that once government was established, "the action of the people" was largely "confined to the mere process of *election*." Such descriptions were a far cry from the language in many state constitutions that encouraged the people to place their governors, the people's "servants," under strict scrutiny and described the people in their capacity as the ruler.[66]

Other Law and Order advocates, including Daniel Webster and John Whipple, insisted that the sovereignty of the people could only be expressed through established procedures and with the consent of the existing government. How Law and Order supporters acknowledged that "all power is in the people" concerned advocates for the Suffrage position. Benjamin Hallett thought Webster's and Whipple's "limitations and constructions" made the people "very great sovereigns, with very great powers, but without any possible *right* to exercise that sovereign power short of *rebellion* against the governments of their own creation!" The current debate seemed to raise the central question about sovereignty in America: "To whom does it rightfully belong? To governors or to the governed?"[67]

In opposing Dorr's constitutionalism, Orestes Brownson offered one of the most sweeping assertions of governmental sovereignty. While nominally agreeing that in America the people "are sovereign," he claimed their constitutions "limit their sovereignty and prescribe the mode in which it shall be exercised." Brownson's position echoed other Law and Order advocates who insisted that one generation could bind a later one in terms of the sovereign authority of the people. For Brownson, "the *Constitution is itself ultimate*" and essentially "is the sovereign." Since sovereign authority was inextricably linked to governance, the actual "force" that governs "is the sovereign."[68]

Not without cause, Dorr and his supporters accused their opponents of locating the people's sovereignty "in the organization, and not in those who organize; in the system devised by the people, and not in the people themselves." John O'Sullivan, the reform-minded editor of the *Democratic Review*, saw the Law and Order Party transferring sovereignty from "the actual, real, living, flesh-and-blood People" to the "political organization" of government." Henry Williams thought the Law and Order position shared the same ground as the rejected governments of "Europe" by investing sovereign authority in "the State" and "the governing class." O'Sullivan suggested that if Dorr was wrong about the people's right to alter or abolish their governments, then most state constitutions needed to be "re-written," the Declaration of Independence "cancelled," and the Revolution itself "rolled back."[69]

Law and Order forces were aghast at the implications of Dorr's views. They were variously characterized as "revolutionary," "against law," "utterly subversive," and tending to "anarchy" and "tyranny."[70] William G. Goddard, a Democrat and professor of moral philosophy at Brown University, considered the alter or abolish principle "fatal to popular liberty." "Once abandon the forms of law in this grave matter of making and altering constitutions of government, and you abandon all the principles of true constitutional reform." Horace Greeley's *New York Tribune* asserted that if Dorr's views took hold, "all Courts, all laws, all Constitutions, become the merest frost-work, which the next breath may dissipate, or which a bushel of votes, collected by a peddler on his rounds, may utterly set aside." For Francis Wayland, Dorr's position made no constitution "worth the parchment on which it is written." John Whipple declared in 1843 that Dorr's principles "necessarily" tended "to annihilate all government, and to destroy the peace of all society."[71] Giving "the slightest countenance" to the People's Constitution subjected all American government "to the unbridled license of a mob." Daniel Webster also considered Dorr's views anarchical, generating "tumultuary, tempestuous, violent, stormy liberty" only "supported by arms to-day, crushed by arms to-morrow."[72]

The Law and Order perception of the Suffrage position produced heightened rhetoric, but also lapses of judicial propriety.[73] Several judges whose courts would hear disputes arising out of the controversy actively and publicly took the Law and Order side. In January 1842, federal judge Pitman published a pamphlet, *To the Members of the General Assembly of Rhode Island*, urging suppression of Dorr's "revolutionary movement." Pitman also responded to the former governor of Massachusetts for advocating Dorr's "dangerous principles" and supporting the People's Constitution, "the fruitful parent of so many abominations." A writer under the pen name "Justice" complained that Pitman's "declarations" made it clear that "any legal question" arising in his court "involving the validity of the People's constitution, would be determined against the party" relying on that constitution. In short, the judge, "in advance of any judicial inquiry," prejudged the case.[74]

Pitman sent copies of his pamphlet to Justice Joseph Story, to distribute to his Supreme Court colleagues. He also asked if his publication gave him the reputation "of having become a *'political* judge.'" Story found the pamphlet "perfectly sound and just" and assured Pitman that "[i]f ever there was a case that called upon a judge to write and speak openly and publicly," the present circumstances qualified. Pitman's efforts to save Rhode Island from being "shaken, if not destroyed" by the Suffrage Party could hardly be "censured." "What is a Republican government worth," asked Story, "if an unauthorized body may thus make, promulgate, and compel obedience to a Constitution at its own mere will and pleasure?" When Story later charged the federal circuit grand jury in Newport on the law of treason, he offered "some preliminary observations upon the late alarming crisis in the public affairs in Rhode-Island" that were supposedly "wholly extemporaneous."[75]

Pitman wanted Story to lobby Secretary of State Daniel Webster for "precautionary measures" by the federal government to "open the eyes of the deluded among us." Story thought the charter government should have criminalized "any self-created convention to frame a Constitution for the State; and thus to have stopped the affair in the bud." "I could say much more, but I do not know whether the questions may not yet come before us in some shape judicially, and therefore forbear." In fact, Story did say more. Three weeks later, Story wrote Webster that he had no "doubt" that Dorr's supporters acted "without law and against law" and that President Tyler could constitutionally intervene without actual insurrection. "Of course, I do not wish to be known in this matter," he said; "my sole object is peace."[76]

Rhode Island's Supreme Court also denounced the Suffrage position in an open letter published in a Law and Order broadside entitled *Citizens of Rhode Island! Read! Mark! Learn!* Chief Justice Job Durfee and two associate justices, William R. Staples and Levi Haile, said they were duty bound "not to intermeddle with party politics, nor to volunteer our opinion on questions of law" that might come to them "officially." Nonetheless, the legality of the People's Constitution did not seem "to be of such class," nor did they "feel at liberty" in withholding their opinion. The judges declared any attempt to implement the People's Constitution as "treason against this State, if not against the United States." Durfee repeated that message in political stump speeches as well as in a charge to a grand jury even though some might accuse him of "indulging in feelings not usual to the bench."[77] Durfee acknowledged his partisanship in a letter to Rhode Island's congressional representative.[78] Ultimately, Law and Order judges rationalized their behavior because of the danger they perceived. Judge Pitman saw "an end to all constitutional freedom" and revolutions becoming "our daily food." Justice Story anticipated "a civil war" that would destroy Rhode Island. And Judge Durfee described America poised on "the brink of an awful gulf" threatened with a "final plunge" into "anarchy."[79]

The Broader Implications of the Rhode Island Debate

While extra-judicial activities reflected reactions to Dorr's views, the Law and Order forces did not simply predict disaster from such constitutional understandings. They also asserted that those understandings lacked legitimacy. Law and Order forces consistently described Dorr's constitutional views as "wild," "new," "radical," and "heresies."[80] The Algerine Convention rejected what some delegates called the "unheard of doctrine" that "the people have the right to change their government whenever they please." At best, Dorr's supporters were resurrecting ideas from the revolutionary period long since discredited. [81]

In accepting that characterization, scholars overlook the legitimacy of Dorr's constitutionalism.[82] Dorr's views about the people's sovereignty could be traced back to the Revolution and they remained an integral part of American constitutional discourse and practice thereafter – even as those understandings increasingly competed with other constitutional views. The uniqueness of the debate over the "Rhode Island question" lay not in the expression of constitutional principles but rather the particular circumstances of their application. Rhode Island's state government displayed extraordinary resistance to constitutional reform that in turn provoked America's most dramatic revision movement bypassing an existing government.

In their zeal to deny the People's Constitution, some Law and Order advocates even rejected the right of revolution. John Whipple argued that the "old right of revolution" was no longer an option in America. That right rested on "oppression from the government, for which there was *no other remedy* but force." According to Whipple, the federal Constitution "annihilated the right of revolution" by doing away with "all the causes, or reasons for it." "No law which any State can enforce, no oppression which any State government can practice, can be imagined so severe as to justify revolution." During congressional debate over the Rhode Island controversy in 1845, Lucius Q. C. Elmer of New Jersey, a Democrat and former federal district attorney, also asserted that Americans "surrendered" the right of revolution after ratifying the federal Constitution. In joining the Union "the people of Rhode Island" accepted the national government's authority "to put down revolution; and thus they had restricted their natural right of revolution." Moreover, while Orestes Brownson conceded the right "to resist civil government" in order to preserve "human freedom," he believed that "violent resistance" was "rarely, if ever, necessary or expedient."[83]

Rather than reject the right of revolution, most Law and Order advocates insisted that if the people formed "new constitutions contrary to the will of the existing government" they were not invoking "a legal or a constitutional right."[84] If the people invoked their "natural right of self-preservation" to effect constitutional change, it was "revolution, and nothing but revolution" – it could not be "half revolution and half not."[85] They argued that governments could be changed in only two ways: either by the consent of the existing government and in conformity with constitutional procedures for revision or through the right of revolution based on dire circumstances threatening the people's liberty.[86] By definition those two choices in changing governments excluded a middle course between adherence to procedures with legislative consent and revolution – the very position Dorr and his supporters identified as the people's inherent and constitutional right to alter or abolish their governments.

That middle course had already surfaced in the congressional debate over Michigan's statehood in 1837. In an exchange between senators John C. Calhoun and James Buchanan, Buchanan disagreed with Calhoun's insistence that government "must first give its assent, before the people can hold a convention for the redress of grievances," citing the alter or abolish language of the Declaration of Independence. Calhoun said he was not denying "that a convention of the people had power to put up and to throw down any and every form of government," only that such action was "a revolution." Buchanan questioned the binary choice of constitutional revision either by "an act of the Legislature authorizing a convention" or "open rebellion" and asked, "Is there no middle course?"[87]

Buchanan answered his own question by asserting that "the whole history of our Government establishes the principle that the people are sovereign, and that a majority of them can alter or change their fundamental laws at pleasure." This was neither "rebellion" nor "revolution," but "an essential and a recognized principle in all our forms of government." Michigan's territorial legislature might take the initiative in constitution-making but ultimately the people had "the right . . . to proceed without any legislative interference or agency whatever."[88]

Law and Order advocates insisted that constitutional change required both permission from the existing government and strict adherence to forms or procedures.[89] Daniel Webster told the Supreme Court that it was self-evident that "no new form of government can be established in any State, without the authority of the existing government." The "whole system of American institutions" established this. Likewise, his co-counsel John Whipple asserted that despite the people's right to "make and unmake constitutions" it was "clear" that "by the universal voice of every American Constitution . . . there are certain modes of exercising this power, prescribed by the people themselves, from which they cannot depart without annihilating all governments of law."[90]

Law and Order supporters sought to correct the "erroneous notions of liberty" that produced the People's Constitution. The People's Constitution rested on "a wrong construction – a misunderstanding of the principles laid down in the declaration of independence." Dorr's supporters, according to Law and Order forces, failed to appreciate the Declaration as "a revolutionary document, intended to justify a revolution." The common people, complained Orestes Brownson, "take words in their most obvious and most literal sense" without making necessary "refinements." One pro-Suffrage work was "so erroneous in its premises, so false in its conclusions," and "so dangerous in its doctrines" that Brownson thought it would inevitably "mislead" and "undermine the foundations of all proper respect for authority." The danger became "incalculable," another Law and Order advocate noted, "when, by a plausible use of certain familiar and captivating general principles, the public vision is distorted from an accurate perception of the truth," prompting "an attack upon the foundations of constitutional liberty."[91]

Defenders of the charter government invoked George Washington's *Farewell Address* when they insisted on an "explicit and authentic" act of the people for legitimate constitutional change and elevated adherence to forms to "a cardinal principle." The Algerine Convention adopted language from Washington's *Address* by asserting that "the constitution which at any time exists, till changed by an explicit and authentic act of the whole people, is sacredly obligatory upon all." The idea that constitutional revision was constrained by procedures surfaced by the 1780s and challenged the constitutional views held by many Americans both before and after Washington's *Address*. Indeed, the Algerine Constitution so thoroughly denied an expansive view of constitutional revision that it prompted Dorr's return to Rhode Island.[92]

For Dorr, the Algerine Constitution "effectively nullified" the "fundamental principles of American political truth" and "just constitutional law." Law and Order proponents subordinated the people "to the forms by which they are surrounded" and "the creatures of the State." Such ideas underlay "the Rhode Island *Precedent of 1842*" that Dorr and his supporters insisted "must not become a law." The Law and Order position rejected "the hitherto undenied sovereignty of the People." From the time he returned to Rhode Island to face trial for treason, Dorr defended his position and denied that the Algerine Constitution expressed the final word on the right of the people to alter or abolish their governments.[93]

STRUGGLE OVER THE "PRECEDENT OF 1842"

Dorr was sorely disappointed in seeking to justify the People's Convention and Constitution during his treason trial. The Rhode Island Supreme Court, presided over by Chief Justice Durfee, disallowed that line of defense. When Dorr was unable to raise his constitutional arguments, few spectators were surprised that the jury, charged by Durfee, found Dorr guilty. The fact the verdict came after three hours did not signify doubt; the jury *"immediately"* agreed on conviction, one juror noted, but delayed only to let the crowd *"disperse."* Another juror explained, *"There was nothing for us to do – the* COURT *made everything plain for us."* Dorr addressed the judges before his sentencing and accused them of complicity in a political prosecution. Though following "the forms of law," the trial lacked "the reality of justice" and was only "a ceremony preceding conviction." The court rejected "the doctrines of ' 76" and reversed "the great principles" on which the country was founded. Ultimately, the American people would have to "decide between us." Immediately thereafter, Durfee sentenced Dorr to life imprisonment at hard labor.[94]

Federal litigation from the Rhode Island controversy also came before Law and Order judges. Justice Story and Judge Pitman formed the federal circuit court hearing two cases challenging the legitimacy of the charter government and its actions under martial law. Those cases involved Martin Luther, a shoemaker who served as a town election official counting ballots during the April 1842 ratification vote for the People's Constitution, and his mother, Rachel. Under martial law, charter government forces entered Luther's house to arrest him for violating the Algerine Act, but instead found Rachel. Both Luther and his mother brought trespass actions for the search of their home. Presiding over the circuit court during its November session in 1843, Story refused to give a jury instruction suggesting the possible legitimacy of the People's Constitution. Instead he charged both juries that the charter government's actions were justified. Although one jury could not agree on a verdict and the other found for the defendants, by prior arrangement both cases were consolidated and sent to the Supreme Court for review.[95]

Dorr eventually considered the *Luther* case a better opportunity to argue the constitutionality of his position than the appeal of his treason conviction and he took charge of the *Luther* case. He wanted *Luther* brought on "the high ground" of the people's sovereign authority to make constitutional changes and not the "minor point" that Rhode Island's lack of revision procedures justified the People's Convention. The lawyer Silas Wright, Jr., a Democratic senator and soon to be governor of New York, considered "the Rhode Island question" the "most important" issue that "has ever been submitted for decision, in a judicial form, under our institutions." Dorr actively coordinated the Supreme Court appeal from his jail cell and upon his release from prison after twenty months of confinement. One Dorr supporter questioned the chances of judicial validation since "Judges always stick by the Govt. right or wrong." Still, Dorr remained optimistic during the six years between the circuit court decision and the Supreme Court's opinion in 1849. His legal brain trust included Benjamin F. Hallett, a leading Massachusetts lawyer and newspaper editor, Robert J. Walker of Mississippi, then secretary of the Treasury, and Nathan Clifford of Maine, U.S. attorney general and a future justice of the U.S Supreme Court.[96]

When the Supreme Court finally considered *Luther* during its January term in 1848 (after a series of postponements), the case assumed the proportions of a major showdown between Dorr's position and the position of his opponents. Released from prison three years earlier after a "liberation" ticket won the Rhode Island governorship, Dorr now sought vindication. Opposing Dorr's position before the court was John Whipple, Dorr's former legal mentor, and Daniel Webster, both active supporters of the Law and Order position.[97]

While Hallett lacked Webster's oratory, he offered a more substantive argument than did his opposing counsel. Webster, and especially his co-counsel John Whipple, principally relied upon disparaging characterizations of Dorr, his followers, and his cause. In his oral argument, Whipple described his former student as "insane" and filled with "wild," "fanciful," and "revolutionary" ideas. Dorr's supporters were "office-hunters," "fifth rate politicians," "blustering demagogues," "visionary theorists," and "political fanatics" who acted in a "cowardly, base and treacherous manner." Webster directed a less personal attack on Dorr, but also cast Dorr's views as beyond the pale of American constitutionalism.[98]

Instead of addressing the argument, Whipple and Webster focused on the supposed parade of horribles Dorr's position would produce. If the people possessed the "legal and peaceable right" claimed by Dorr, according to Law and Order advocates, a majority could overturn "not merely the ordinary laws, but the government and [the] constitution itself" by *sending in* their vote to any self-constituted meeting." Nothing prevented "changes being attempted every day, and the community would, of course, be kept in constant agitation by a few heated partizans." On the other hand, if the right of revolution formed the only alternative to constitutional change by adhering to procedures and with the government's approval, everyone would be safer since the people "will never undertake a *revolution*" without "good cause." Whipple and Webster never addressed the illogic of their position that the people would necessarily run amok under Dorr's "peaceable right," but inevitably act prudently under the right of revolution.[99]

Dorr's supporters emphasized that popularly based governments ultimately required faith in the capacity of the people for self-government. Fearing the people, noted Henry Williams, was nothing new in "the history" of America. It always surfaced among those "who distrust the people." Some disruption was inevitable. The real "wonder," for Williams, was that "there has been so little" disruption and that "the people have borne so much, so long, and so patiently." Indeed, another Dorr supporter, the lawyer Benjamin Cowell, disagreed with the Law and Order claim that recognizing the people's right to alter or abolish governments implied their "overthrow." Since the Revolution, "almost every" state bill of rights "recognizes this same principle." Yet the people had not abolished their governments, demonstrating they "will do right when left to themselves." And since "sovereign power must rest *somewhere*, it is safest to let it rest in the whole people."[100]

In contrast to Whipple's and Webster's *ad hominem* and dismissive arguments, Hallett spent three days analyzing the constitutional significance of the American Revolution and the sovereignty of the people. While Hallett drew from seventy years of constitutional commentary, political debate, and judicial decisions describing the basis and understanding of American governments, Webster's and Whipple's responses were strangely bereft of citations. Dorr reported that Law and Order advocates were "surprised" that Hallett came into court "with such 'a load of books,' when there are 'but few points in the case and but few authorities on the subject.'" Dorr suggested that his opponents did not look "far enough" and took "too much for granted."[101] Whipple's few citations did not address the authority of the people to alter their government but rather whether the Court should defer recognition of the People's Constitution to Congress or the executive branch. Webster did not cite his declaration twenty-eight years earlier, that "no principle" existed "that could prevent a majority, even a bare majority of the people" from "altering" their constitution. Moreover, neither Webster nor Whipple referred to an advisory opinion of a New York court two years earlier that the people could legitimize bypassing procedures for revising the state's constitution through subsequent ratification.[102]

Dorr anticipated the Court's judgment when he asserted that Law and Order advocates "do not claim a decision against us on the merits" but rather hoped "that, somehow or other" the Court would "have nothing to do with the People's Constitution." Indeed, the Supreme Court's opinion did not directly address the questions of constitutionalism raised by the case. Chief Justice Roger B. Taney delivered the 5–1 opinion of the Court, with Justice Levi Woodbury the lone dissenter. Taney held that actions taken by individuals under the charter government's declaration of martial law were justified, but he did not examine whether the People's Constitution established a legitimate government. Taney wrote that Hallett's argument raised "political rights and political questions" that the court considered beyond its jurisdiction and declined to answer.[103]

Although Woodbury dissented on the issue of martial law, he agreed with Taney's characterization of the appeal. Although several "subordinate questions" dealing with the invocation of the people's sovereignty were "a shade less political," in the end they were "still political." Because "disputed points in making constitutions" depended on "policy, inclination, popular resolves, and popular will," their resolution, Woodbury reasoned, belonged "to politics, and they are settled by political tribunals" rather than the courts.[104]

In not examining the legitimacy of the People's Constitution, the Court upheld the state government under the Algerine Constitution. This was a practical result given the political realities by 1849. The majority decision also justified the actions of Rhode Island's officials under martial law. However, on the issue of the inherent right of the people to change their constitutions and government, both the majority and the dissent – at least in dicta – supported Dorr's position. Taney concluded that no one "has ever doubted the proposition, that, according to the institutions of this country, the sovereignty in every State resides in the people of the State, and that they may alter and change their form of government at their own pleasure."[105] Taney's statement implied the right of the people to make revisions without abiding by "forms" or seeking the government's permission. The *Luther* opinion thus endorsed the Suffrage rather than the Law and Order side on the Rhode Island question when it regarded the people's inherent sovereignty to "alter and change" governments as indisputable, even though the Court declined to so rule.

Indeed, after the opinion, some Law and Order supporters acknowledged that the central question of whether a majority of the people could change government outside of existing laws "has not been decided." Dorr recognized that the decision did not "warrant the exultation" of his opponents "upon the supposed judicial overthrow of the Rhode Island cause." Rather, in Dorr's view the Court withheld its opinion on "the R.I. Question" because it believed that "the act of sovereignty, which the People of this state claim to have performed is a political and not a legal subject." A correspondent agreed with Dorr that the Court avoided "the main question" and reported that "intelligent Algerines" considered *Luther* to rest "not on the old principles of Law & Order, but on your principles of 'popular Sovereignty.'"[106]

Justice Woodbury, who in 1842 had proclaimed the right of the people, independent of legislatures, to make constitutions "when & how they please," now, as a member of the Court, described the competing constitutional legacy of the Revolution. Woodbury observed that Americans "honestly divide on great political questions." Although agreeing that political questions should not be adjudicated by the Court, Woodbury acknowledged the existence of many "different tastes as well as opinions in politics, and especially in forming constitutions." Likewise, Taney's majority opinion, by not dismissing inherent rights of the people as a visionary theory – as Webster and Whipple had urged – also recognized the legitimacy of more than one understanding of the people's sovereignty.[107]

After the oral argument, but before the decision in *Luther*, Dorr identified the challenge of his constitutionalism. "[T]he People," he noted, "are apt to forget the true origin of political power" when they grew "accustomed to see no other than that exercised . . . under prescribed & definite rules." The "all-important" work was keeping "the true doctrine of original and imprescriptible Sovereignty . . . distinctly in the view of each generation" and to reject entirely "the anti-republican and detestable Sophism of Sovereignty in the government." In that same spirit Hallett dedicated the *Luther* brief's publication to future generations of Americans taking up the cause of "the practical sovereignty of the people."[108]

After appearing before the Supreme Court, Hallett wrote Dorr suggesting that a compilation of "all the arguments, notes & authorities" dealing with "Popular Sovereignty" would make "a great manual" for the public. Dorr replied that he thought the Rhode Island controversy had given "salutary"

attention to that "great and too long forgotten Principle lying at the foundation of all governments" in America – the sovereignty of the people. Dorr
never wrote the manual Hallett proposed and when he died in 1854 at the
age of forty-nine, his health broken from his stay in prison, he left the matter
of preserving his constitutional views to others. Shortly before Dorr's death,
Rhode Island's legislature passed an act annulling the judgment of the state
Supreme Court in his treason trial. The fate of "the true doctrine" of the people's sovereignty rested in the hands of later generations of Americans.[109]

9 Epilogue

This book presented the history of an idea and of a people who tried to live by that idea before the Civil War – the idea we know today as American constitutionalism, defining "the people" as a collective sovereign. With Independence, Americans confronted how that collective sovereign could, like a king, speak clearly in one voice on local as well as on national concerns in a large and diverse country. One solution was to hear the voice of this sovereign through written constitutions.

This did not mean that the collective sovereign could be heard speaking primarily through a written constitution, as is the accepted wisdom today. During their Revolution and for a half-century thereafter, Americans were more open to the idea than we are today that a collective sovereign could rule without insisting on institutions or procedures to verify and discern the sovereign's will. This understanding made sense under an American constitutionalism that considered the people both the ruler and the ruled. But as memories of the Revolution faded, applying the principle of the collective sovereign's ability to act became a growing source of dispute.

The problem of determining the people's will was evident from the start, as illustrated by reaction to the news of Independence. John Hancock, president of the Continental Congress, wrote General George Washington on July 6 enclosing a copy of the Declaration of Independence. Hancock wanted Washington, then headquartered in New York City, to share the news with the army in whatever way Washington thought "most proper." On July 9, 1776, Washington ordered the brigades under his command to assemble at six o'clock that evening "on their respective Parades" when "the declaration of Congress" would be read in "an audible voice." Long after the event, one veteran recalled that at his encampment "a hollow square" formed by soldiers enclosed Washington "on horseback." After hearing the Declaration "in a clear voice" by one of Washington's aides, "three hearty cheers were given." Washington reported to Hancock that "the measure" had the "assent" of "both Officers and men" giving it "their warmest approbation."[1]

This choreographed, disciplined military celebration contrasted with the exuberance that Independence produced in other New Yorkers. Inhabitants of New York were deeply divided about the Revolution. Independence energized the town's American patriots. During the evening of the same day that Washington's soldiers heard the Declaration, a crowd of patriots, described by one newspaper as "the Sons of Freedom," gathered at the commemorative statue of the now-repudiated sovereign, George III. The twenty-ton gilded lead form of the British monarch on horseback rested near the waterfront. Erected in 1770, it dominated a green for playing bowls, a popular English game similar to bocce. A tall iron fence, posts capped by metal crowns symbolizing the British monarchy, encircled the slightly larger than life-sized, gold-plated statue and separated it from the bowlers.[2]

In the twilight, "the Populace," as one American officer put it, tore down the fence and, joined by some soldiers, affixed ropes to His Majesty's form and began to pull. A participating soldier recalled the ropes breaking on the first try, but the second attempt succeeded in toppling the monarch on horseback from his pedestal. The crowd then cut off the king's head and chopped up the statue. The other symbol of the deposed sovereign – the decorative crowns mounted on the fence posts – were twisted off and added to the rubble.[3]

The "ominous fall of *leaden Majesty*," described by the *New York Journal*, marked a new constitutional order presided over by the people. That constitutional order was at once both powerful and ambiguous. Days after the new sovereign destroyed symbols of the old, a crowd in the "thousands" gathered at noon on Broad Street in front of City Hall. They assembled after New York's revolutionary convention requested the Declaration be read before the general public. The crowd approved of what they heard "by loud acclamations" and proceeded to tear down the king's wooden coat of arms hanging above the building's courtroom and burn it in the street. A portrait of the king from the city's council chamber met a similar fate. Repeated loud "huzzas" accompanied the destruction of both these symbols of monarchy.[4]

Loyalists considered these insults to royal authority a desecration by an unruly mob. For patriots, the same incident represented rule by the new collective sovereign. One revolutionary leader had reservations. In his General Orders the day after the toppling of the statue, Washington noted the crowd's activity. He believed that "the persons" who pulled down the statue "were actuated by Zeal in the public cause." However, because participants, including those in the Army, took part in "riot and want of order," the General "disapproves the manner, and directs that in [the] future these things shall be avoided by the Soldiery, and left to be executed by proper authority."[5]

That supporters and opponents of Independence reacted differently to the statue's destruction on the bowling green was predictable. Yet, supporters of Independence were equally divided. Whether the now-independent people were free to act directly on their judgment or whether they should act only after employing procedures that expressed their sovereign will was a question that resonated for the next half-century. At times, Americans hesitated about a collectivity such as the people being the sovereign. This probably reflected the realization that American constitutionalism logically allowed the sovereign to discard the government and institutions the people created. The lurking potential of the people's authority over government introduced an inherent tension into that constitutionalism.

The people's authority as the sovereign was central to American constitutionalism despite knowing that "government is always something other than the actual people who are governed by it, that governors and governed cannot be in fact identical."[6] Nonetheless, this recognition did not inhibit the belief that the people collectively ruled. The source of Americans' greatest pride in their Revolution – the creation of new governments resting on written constitutions authorized by "the people" – also was the most worrisome aspect of their experiment with republicanism.[7] The people's authority, simultaneously legitimate and subversive, quickly spread among Americans with the Revolution and penetrated even the most remote reaches of America.[8] America's constitution-making proved that government could be something people created rather than something that simply happened to them. The experience of creating government left a lasting impression on the revolutionary generation.

Constitution-making after Independence reflected this revolutionary constitutionalism. It was revolutionary because, unlike government before 1776, it encouraged supporters in the struggle for Independence to believe they were fighting for themselves. They struggled not only to be ruled by a government of their own choosing, but for a government in which they collectively and actively played the role of a ruler. This promise was not extinguished with the winning of Independence and certainly not by the meeting of the federal Framers in Philadelphia four years after the war ended. America's struggle with constitutionalism suggests that the belief that practical sovereignty remained in the hands of the people persisted in the thinking of many Americans throughout the period leading up to the Civil War. The essence of practical sovereignty – the principle of the power of the people to destroy the constitution they created – finds its roots in the American Revolution.

We associate such sovereignty with the Revolution. Yet we have lost that idea as a viable principle in the constitutionalism we know today.[9]

Contrasting eighteenth-century constitutionalism with today's understandings suggests our current theory of what makes government legitimate was not inevitable. It did not develop in a "straight-line" from the Revolution to today, as is often depicted in constitutional histories. Controversies over the people as the sovereign and how they would rule were not resolved in 1776, or in 1787, or for that matter on the verge of the Civil War in 1860. American constitutionalism – of both the federal Constitution and the states – did not emerge from one defining moment or event. Rather, it grew incrementally over the course of political controversies within the states and at the national level. The constitutionalism that holds sway today is not a natural inheritance but the product of choices Americans made between shifting understandings about a collective sovereign.

This book has examined America's early struggles to give life to the collective sovereign. It suggests that the traditional accounts of America's constitutional history, theory, and jurisprudence neglect how real the concept of the people ruling as the sovereign was for many Americans before the Civil War. Most explorations of America's constitutionalism acknowledge the idea that the people are the sovereign under America's constitutions. Yet, soon after identifying that idea, most studies find it of no particular utility. Mere acknowledgment is made and such studies quickly move on to analyze seemingly inevitable rules and structures that impose procedural constraints on America's sovereign. This shift is unfortunate. It assumes away the central tension within American constitutionalism before the Civil War.

This epilogue suggests some directions for future enquiry raised by the narrative of this book that might return the study of American constitutionalism to the central role played by a collective sovereign. The epilogue is intended to be thought provoking. The ideas that place the people at the center of American constitutionalism deserve more careful and exacting exploration. Identifying some of these ideas here may stimulate new directions for research. These new directions might reintegrate into American constitutional history, theory, and jurisprudence the significance of the once-held belief that in America, the people were the sovereign.

One recent treatment that does place the people at the center of American constitutionalism is Larry Kramer's *The People Themselves: Popular Constitutionalism and Judicial Review* (2004). That work challenges the role judicial review plays in American constitutionalism today. It finds an alternative to judicial review in a tradition of "popular constitutionalism," which vests in the people responsibility "for interpreting and enforcing their constitution."

That work joins other scholarship demonstrating that the judicial monopoly over constitutional interpretation reflected in the past half-century was not central to America's constitutional experience for a great part of its history. The author argues that other forms of constitutional review, such as a displaced tradition of popular constitutionalism, might better and more faithfully serve Americans and their government today.[10]

His notion of popular constitutionalism is not synonymous with the idea of a collective sovereign, as that concept has been explored in this book. Both concepts overlap, but popular constitutionalism emerges as a subset of the more fundamental idea of a collective sovereign. Popular constitutionalism involves actions to interpret and enforce the constitution. Like popular constitutionalism, the idea of the collective sovereign could be and was used to interpret and enforce the constitution. However, the idea of a collective sovereign is a broader foundational principle that justified the creation, revision, and even the destruction of constitutions.

That popular constitutionalism fits within the broader idea of a collective sovereign is consistent with the depiction of popular constitutionalism's negative role. It allowed the people to veto the actions of government by protesting with sufficient vigor, forcing government officials to change their minds. The negative force of popular constitutionalism comes into play only when a constitution already exists. Its effectiveness against official action stems from its exertion of political pressure rather than from a recognition that government is the agent of the people. Indeed, popular constitutionalism would operate whether or not the people were the sovereign.

In contrast, the idea of the collective sovereign justifies, as the Founders demonstrated, the creation of constitutions as well as their destruction. Besides giving life to a constitutional system, the concept that the people were the sovereign defined the relationship between that sovereign and the government. Before the Civil War this idea cast government as the agent that was charged with the faithful execution of the constitutional order.

The collective sovereign could change the constitutional scheme using its inherent authority or it could take the actions described as popular constitutionalism, effectively vetoing the collective sovereign's agent, the government. As exercised by Americans after the Revolution, the people as the collective sovereign could ultimately act independent of government and not merely through a mediation with government. They could exercise that sovereignty even without using procedures specified in their constitutions or by their government.

One example of popular constitutionalism – the Republican reaction to the Alien and Sedition Acts – illustrates how the concept of the interpretative function of "the people" comes within the ambit of the authority of the collective sovereign. The protests, petitions, and resolutions against the acts sought to preserve "the people's active control of their government and their Constitution." Popular constitutionalism occurred when the political protest was resolved by the two parties "squar[ing] off in the election of 1800." Federalists were "decisively . . . repudiated" after the voters were offered "sharply drawn, alternative visions of the Constitution." "The American public, or at least that portion of it permitted to vote, opted for . . . the Republican understanding of constitutionalism."[11]

In fact, the controversy involved much more than a "kind of politics" attributed to popular constitutionalism.[12] The Republicans' protest did not merely assert the unconstitutionality of the Alien and Sedition Acts. As Madison's *Report of 1800* on behalf of the Virginia legislature observed, what was at stake was "[t]he authority of constitutions over governments, and of the sovereignty of the people over constitutions."[13] The election of 1800 could have reached an ambiguous result, or even ended in Republican defeat. Had that occurred, the constitutional principle of the collective sovereign (and not simply a form of pressure politics) would have permitted that sovereign to seek the end of the Alien and Sedition laws even outside of what Madison called "the provisions and forms of the Constitution."[14] The people were not precluded from recognizing an authentic expression of the voice of the sovereign people apart from that provided by the ballot box.

A preoccupation with popular constitutionalism as an alternative to judicial review leads to overstating and understating the role of the sovereign people in America's past. Kramer assumes that popular constitutionalism was part of the Anglo-American constitutional tradition well before 1776. His story of the struggle over American judicial review takes for granted an accepted role for the people in interpreting and enforcing their constitutions. Such a role, according to him, existed long before Americans framed their first constitutions.

The constitutionalism born of the Revolution was not merely a continuation of earlier practices under the unwritten British constitution. Rather, the Revolution marked a significant departure in thinking about what rule by a collective sovereign meant. The shared commitment to the people as the collective sovereign in America did not mean there was agreement about the details. How to come to terms with a collective sovereign – to identify when it had spoken and how it might act – were matters of dispute from the start of American constitution-making. Americans did indeed have "profoundly different ideas" about what it meant to say the people provided the foundation for legitimate government, but those differences were not "suddenly" discovered in the 1790s.[15]

Moreover, the history of American constitutionalism before the Civil War suggests that the role of the people in a "departmental theory" for interpreting the federal Constitution was not as muted, limited, and constrained as *The People Themselves* depicts. The book describes popular constitutionalism – with its consequences for modern day judicial review – as the people giving their support to various mediating government branches and institutions that also apply the constitution. Constitutional interpretation and enforcement is the result of dynamic interactions between the branches operating in a constitutional balance. This view sees the collective sovereign as bound in a web of government and constitutional procedures. Kramer's belief that such a sovereign could not express its will without the mediation of government institutions and procedures is belied by historical attitudes about the collective sovereign.[16] The fact is that for many Americans before the Civil War the collective sovereign was not procedurally bound. The belief in a powerful and direct role for the people as the sovereign is part of America's historical experience with written constitutions and should not be ignored. Greater fidelity to America's historical experience has the potential to return to American constitutional history, theory, and jurisprudence the crucial role played by the belief that in America, the people were the sovereign.

AMERICAN CONSTITUTIONAL HISTORY

Many accounts of America's constitutional history assume that the federal Framers understood written constitutions in the same way we do today. Supposedly after a decade of wandering in the wilderness of constitutionalism, Americans found their way and a "matured" constitutionalism was discovered. Their failure to utilize special constitutional conventions, the lack of constitutional amending provisions, and the inclusion of rhetorical principles having no apparent judicial enforceability were all signs of their immature constitutionalism. The advent of a "matured" vision is linked to the convention that produced the federal Constitution. Like the product of that convention, a "real" constitution was one drafted by a special convention followed by popular ratification to ensure that the document reflected the consent of the people.[17] Moreover, a "real" constitution provided for its amendment or change and avoided – like the federal Constitution – "glittering generalities" about the role of the people as the sovereign. In time this mature constitutionalism would displace all the earlier practices of creating constitutions.

The different answers to the same question of constitutionalism – offered by the federal Framers as opposed to the first state constitution-makers – have perpetuated a binary explanation of the American constitutional tradition. One tradition is supposedly represented by the experience with the federal Constitution and another represented by the experience with state constitutions. Twentieth-century scholars show little interest in examining constitution-making before 1787 in depth and in taking that process seriously.[18] Equally neglected are attempts to probe the meaning of post-1787 constitutional disputes that addressed the ways the people, as the collective sovereign, could exercise their sovereignty. Invariably, the state constitutional tradition is deemed less authentic because of its departure from the federal model.[19] This has led to the assumption that one need only study the federal Constitution to discover what American constitutionalism was then and is today.

This book examines American constitutionalism from 1776 *forward*. It suggests that America's experience with written constitutions belies the thrust of two traditional historical narratives dealing with the federal Constitution. One narrative considers the federal convention a constitutional watershed. It presents the convention and its product as the natural culmination of tentative thinking and experience with written constitutions since Independence. Under this view, the federal Constitution is the product of a broad, nationwide consensus, articulating ideas and practices adopted and refined by the states in the wake of Independence. That narrative competes with another one that casts the federal convention as a counterrevolutionary event, turning its back on the Revolution's promise. In this narrative, a privileged class created a strong national government to shore up their slipping economic and political position challenged by postrevolutionary practices and events. The convention and the constitution it produced reflected a struggle between those more democratically minded and a privileged elite.[20]

The history of the idea of the people as America's collective sovereign suggests an interpretation that accommodates both these perspectives. As demonstrated by the consensus narrative, Americans did unite and remained united in their commitment that the people were the sovereign.[21] And as suggested by the counterrevolutionary narrative, this broad consensus about the people allowed one's view of the collective sovereign to vary with the eye of the beholder. It facilitated divisions among Americans about precisely what collective rule meant. Different answers to that question appear in the efforts to make and revise constitutions well into the 1840s. These competing views were reflected in the struggles over constitutional government in which the people who were the collective sovereign under the constitution were also subject to that constitution. How to accommodate the simultaneous role of the people as the ruler with their role as the ruled was a central focus of American constitutionalism before the Civil War.

The so-called rebellions named after Daniel Shays, the whiskey excise tax protesters, and Thomas Wilson Dorr, for example, illustrate the struggle for an accommodation. These events were not, as generally portrayed today, aberrations. In each incident, Americans justified their actions through their authority as the sovereign people. This type of call for action was familiar from the Revolution. Its repeated use after the Revolution was unexceptional. Even the federal Framers utilized this same revolutionary-era claim when they redirected a convention – that Congress had authorized for revising the Articles of Confederation – to submit a new federal Constitution for an up or down vote. As with the "rebels" who justified their acts as those of the people, so too did the federal Framers. They brought about a new federal Constitution in defiance of the procedures America's first federal Constitution set out for altering its structure. They did so using the familiar refrain that this step was legitimate because it could be done by the people acting as the sovereign.

Constitutional changes authorized by the supposed will of the new collective sovereign presented a difficulty that constitutional theory could not answer but that Americans let actual practice resolve. For example, how did one know that it was the people who supposedly had spoken? Oftentimes, the test was simple. Because the governments formed under American constitutions were agents of the sovereign people, in practice many were willing to look to that agent to see if it recognized its "master's voice." This is what happened in the case of the federal Framers. Their attempt to displace the Articles of Confederation by circumventing procedures in the Articles succeeded because the Framers secured the concurrence of established governments.

In contrast, the so-called rebels – acting under the same constitutional principle of the collective sovereign as did the federal Framers – encountered opposition from established governments. For some, the government's failure to recognize the voice of its "master" indicated that the so-called rebels did not speak for the people. Many others disagreed and believed that proof of the voice of the people might come by other, less-formal, but equally compelling means. For Dr. Whiting, the people could be heard when they lined up on the road and demanded that his court not open. For James Madison, echoes of the voice of the people lay behind the action and resistance of state legislatures to interpose with the federal government in an effort to repeal unconstitutional laws.

Although often depicted as "losers" in their confrontation with existing governments, these "rebels" were largely vindicated in the political aftermath of each "rebellion." For Regulators in Massachusetts the next state election after the suppression of the "rebellion" saw Friends of Government and officeholders who had supported forceful measures against the Regulators defeated at the polls. Friends of Government lost control of the governorship as well as the lower house of the legislature. For the whiskey excise tax protesters, the next election after the federal government's military march into western Pennsylvania also swept from local and state office supporters of the Federalist administration. Four years later that state helped Jefferson displace the Federalist John Adams from the presidency in 1800. For Dorr, the government that resisted a more equal apportionment of representation and broader franchise soon capitulated and accepted a new constitutional order that looked very much like the one embraced by the popular ratification of the People's Constitution. In these instances the so-called defeated rebels expressed views that more closely reflected the mood of the people as demonstrated by the elections soon after the "rebellions."

Understanding that many Americans, and not just the federal Framers, continued to grapple with the significance of the people as the sovereign offers a new perspective on constitutional events and episodes taking place before the 1850s. During that time constitutional questions intertwined with political disputes and controversies. Rather than focusing on the political aspects of these controversies, the events examined in this book are viewed in the light they shed on the key question of constitutionalism – how Americans thought about their authority as America's collective sovereign.

Conventional accounts of the history of American constitutionalism are not false. They are simply incomplete. This book challenges some existing interpretations in setting out a broader framework. Still, much existing scholarship dealing with the period from the Revolution to the Civil War can be integrated into this broader framework. The story of many events and constitutional practices now dismissed as unimportant assume a new significance when supplemented by the broader sweep of constitutional developments at both the state and national level before the Civil War. This broader framework makes sense of many things that existing studies cannot explain or dismiss as aberrational or illegitimate.[22]

The three so-called rebellions reflect how the idea of the people as the sovereign captured the American mind. In each "rebellion" both sides argued that they acted for the people. Their conflict arose when they could not agree on the answer to the ambiguity posed by American constitutionalism – how does one know when the people have expressed their will? Some Americans insisted that only formal mechanisms could convey the people's will. Many others were open to the lesson taught by the American Revolution: that in addition to formal mechanisms, other means could just as effectively give voice to the people's will.

When "rebellion" arose, all sides sought to find the expression of the sovereign. Those who subdued by force the Regulators, the whiskey excise tax protesters, and the advocates of the People's Constitution remained true to their insistence on a formal expression of the people's will. They recognized and obeyed the voice of the people when the polls removed them from power shortly after they defeated the "rebels." For Friends of Government, a formal step to recognize the voice of the people was necessary, and when the polls supplied this, they respected it. For the so-called rebels, state-sanctioned elections reflected the will of the people but were not the only means of detecting that expression. After suppression, the "rebels" used the formal mechanisms their suppressors insisted were necessary to prevail.

The political aftermath of the "rebellions" reveals the depth of the commitment to American constitutionalism. As much as the Friends of Government detested the policies favored by their opponents, they proved their fidelity to the authority of the collective sovereign by their deeds and not just words. Their willingness to accept their defeat at the polls and to step aside for Regulators and those who were sympathetic to the Regulation was somewhat extraordinary. They might have refused to give up their hold on government or at least challenged the legitimacy of their political displacement. Instead, their capitulation was not merely a function of recognizing compliance with the formal steps of an election. Rather, it rested on an acknowledgment that the people had spoken and as the ruler that will could not be dismissed as lacking controlling authority.

The so-called rebellions also reveal an important constitutional value largely lost to us today. When the Massachusetts Regulators, protesters of the federal excise tax, and Dorr's supporters argued that government undercut the public welfare, they were not simply making rhetorical arguments. Rather, they invoked a constitutional principle that tested the legitimacy of government actions.[23] Distribution of economic benefits and burdens so that a select group received windfalls and special privileges unavailable to the rest was not simply unfair. It was unconstitutional. The constitutional argument was not rooted in a principle of egalitarianism or an expectation of a "leveling" of wealth. Nor was it an unorthodox constitutional position.

Testing the legitimacy of government actions relied on the constitutional value of the public welfare. Government, as the servant, should protect and serve the welfare of its principal, the sovereign people. This idea was deeply enshrined in American constitutions since the Revolution. Government's mandate, as those constitutions made clear, was not to favor the few at the expense of the many. The public welfare was the only justification for government. Policies that directly undermined that objective were tell-tale signs of a malfunction in the constitutional order. When this happened, the collective people as the sovereign could take corrective action as the ruler. Such intervention was consistent with the view that the people actually fashioned government and were not simply passive objects of government's actions. With Independence, government in America depended on the collective sovereign, and if that government operated in constitutionally suspect ways the sovereign was entitled to restrain its wayward servant.

This constitutional belief was reinforced by memories of the resistance preceding the Revolution. Before the Revolution, Americans criticized what they saw as corrupt practices in England that undermined constitutional government. They identified corruption in measures burdening the colonists and benefiting a few favored interests in government. The tax on tea, for example, while primarily objectionable as a precedent for unconstitutional taxation, also gave a monopoly to the East India Company, which discriminated against the colonists.[24] Now in their own country and under constitutions of their own making, some Americans once again perceived government action that smacked of favoritism and violated constitutional principle. They saw their welfare sacrificed (and their farms sold off) for the benefit of a few favored speculators. That situation justified the people in taking steps to redress practices inconsistent with the constitution and to assert their sovereign power.

Government's natural tendency to advance the favorites of the rulers was supposed to have worked differently under American constitutionalism. Under George III, the monarch as sovereign and his servants, the ministers, predictably rewarded themselves and their friends. On the other hand, in the American constitutional system, the people as the collective sovereign and acting as the ruler should reward themselves only generally. Under American constitutionalism, the sovereign should have promoted the public welfare and not perpetuated patterns of governmental favoritism experienced under the king.

The enrichment of a select few became a litmus test signaling a malfunction of the constitutional order. The Revolution taught that the people were fully justified in taking matters into their own hands to resolve such misuse of power. This experience of direct action was a fundamental part of American constitutionalism as well. The people as the sovereign were expected to scrutinize government and could act if government subverted the constitutional order. Often this power was acknowledged in constitutional text, such as in the alter or abolish clauses so common after the Revolution. Even without such provisions the people retained the authority to act. Similarly, the existence of procedures for constitutional amendment did not prevent the sovereign from revising the constitution in other ways.

The logic of Americans being their own sovereign was not shared by everyone. All could agree on the sovereignty of the people, but just what that principle meant eluded a shared understanding. At times Americans emphasized an actual, active, and ongoing role for the people while at other times the collective sovereign was depicted in more theoretical, passive, and residual terms. Some Americans insisted that even after the creation of constitutions, the people had a role to play as the ruler, while others rejected that view and insisted that the status the people now enjoyed was largely limited to being the ruled.

The collective sovereign's role in overseeing and scrutinizing government's operation was not resolved with the adoption of American constitutions. Efforts by the sovereign to instruct government outside the frame of elections seemed perfectly consistent with the idea that the people were the sovereign. Still, some objected to constituent instruction because it interfered with representation conceived as the exercise of sovereignty through the people's representatives. They sometimes used language suggesting that the government itself was the sovereign. Likewise, the idea of interposition raised similar concerns about how to oversee and scrutinize government. As with instruction, the level at which interposition occurred – by individual citizens, groups of citizens, or the state legislature – was sometimes a point of dispute. However, the broader question of how one conceived of the people as the sovereign still remained. Did the collective people have an active, direct, and ongoing role in the affairs of government after they created those governments? Or did they instead play a more passive role, limited to elections, with their representatives exerting the people's sovereignty for all intents and purposes? Clearly, this latter supposition risked contradicting the principle undeniably established by the Revolution: that in America the people – however one understood them – were the sovereign.

Rule by the collective sovereign shaped other choices Americans made about their fundamental law. For example, the separation of church and state was a feature of most American constitutions. It embodied attitudes toward religious freedom, but it also reflected the reality that America's sovereign was no longer an individual monarch. Unlike a king, whose faith served as the state religion, the American sovereign embraced many different religions and this fact alone confounded the idea of establishing a state religion. As

James Madison noted, the "multiplicity of sects" in America helped avoid the imposition of a single religious faith in America. Thus, some early state constitutions, although requiring support for an established church, refrained – as did the federal Constitution – from identifying a state religion.[25]

AMERICAN CONSTITUTIONALISM
AND CONSTITUTIONAL THEORY

A central teaching of American constitutionalism is that in America the people are the sovereign who rule through the means of written constitutions. This precept also is the foundation for American constitutional theory. For example, in some of the earliest of its thousand-plus pages offering an analytical framework for American constitutional law, one frequently cited treatise notes that "the oldest and most central tenet of American constitutionalism" is that "all lawful power derives from the people."[26] Similarly, another lengthy exposition on American constitutional theory traces its growth and application through the doctrine of judicial review. It notes that judicial review in America is based on a constitution deemed "a superior form of law established by the direct will of society" with its legitimacy drawn from "the people of the nation" having "the right to establish binding, enforceable principles for the governing of society."[27]

Although each work begins its analysis with the central idea that the people are the sovereign, both treatises have little more to say about the concept. The focus immediately shifts to the way this idea intended "to preserve their [the people's] freedom" by the development and use of formal procedures.[28] One effect of these procedures was to establish an "essential role in government" for courts through a system of "judicial sovereignty."[29] The reader learns little more about the idea of a collective sovereign. In their perfunctory treatment of the people's sovereignty, the treatises leave the impression that the idea of a collective sovereign had become a dead letter by the time of the adoption of the federal Constitution in 1787.

This book suggests that the idea of the people as the sovereign did not fade so quickly. Rule by America's collective sovereign was questioned from the start of American constitution-making, but little justifies drawing a straight line between early doubters of the people as the sovereign to our modern doctrines of constitutionalism. The doubters ultimately prevailed in limiting the people as a source of constitutional authority, but that result was not inexorable. Restraining the collective sovereign was not accomplished in 1787 with the adoption of the federal Constitution. Nor was it accomplished in 1794 with the suppression of the whiskey excise tax protesters, nor in the

1830s with the Nullification crisis, nor even by the 1840s with the suppression of Thomas Dorr and his followers.

The idea that the people were an active sovereign, expressing their sovereign authority outside the formally written constitution, retained vitality even as the nation approached civil war in the 1850s. The life of this idea is difficult for contemporary readers to appreciate. Hindering that appreciation is the fact that the English language lacks a word conveying the idea of the inherent energy and vital force of the people as a whole. We are left with the term "sovereignty," which suggests institutional power rather than the vibrancy of something held collectively by the people.

That the people were the sovereign, and a real one at that, was part of a frame of mind quite different from modern America's. To understand that earlier constitutional view, the modern reader must suspend present-day assumptions, most prominently the rule of law. The essence of the rule of law is that binding law exists above both the governors and the governed alike. This idea is inconsistent with the notion that a sovereign people could not be bound even by a fundamental law of their own making. Under the rule of law, the people are only theoretically the sovereign because they are bound by mandatory constitutional procedures. Today's assumption is that those procedures – such as elections or ratification votes – are the only way of identifying when that sovereign speaks.[30]

Those procedures were relatively new tools of democracy before the 1840s. Before then Americans oftentimes did not count heads to discern the voice of the people. During their struggle for Independence, American revolutionaries did not worry about numbers in a governmental setting to establish the legitimacy of their conduct. When patriots acted and came together in common cause they were "the people." No votes or polls were necessary to establish that fact – merely sustaining that belief was enough. In a similar manner, believing that the body of "the people" was "in motion" legitimized the first state constitutions even without a formal ratification vote. What validated rule by the people as the sovereign was that ultimately it worked as an expression of the people's will.

Scholars today often assume that proceduralism quickly became the touchstone of constitutional legitimacy in America.[31] This book questions the conventional understanding that proceduralism carried the day before the Civil War. How that constitutionalism came to embody principles that minimized the role of the people in monitoring the constitutional order was a far more complex process than most commentators suggest.

Attitudes toward the idea that the people were the sovereign shifted with the end of the Revolution. Once relieved of the dire wartime circumstances that helped maintain confidence that "the people" were in action, some Americans came to view the concept of a collective sovereign differently. For most, America's victory confirmed that the people could be the sovereign in more normal times. Their confidence came from their use of the people's sovereignty in defeating one of the most formidable empires in the world. They considered the Revolution an unquestioned success.

After the war, other committed revolutionaries, many drawn from the ranks of the colonial elite, reacted differently. They were disappointed at receiving even less economic, social, and political deference than they experienced before the Revolution. With peace, elites reflected on the unintended consequences of a collective sovereign altering their prerevolutionary standing. They developed an increasingly pessimistic view of the state of affairs in America.[32] Such musing increased the difficulty of sustaining the illusion of a united people. The rise of factions and incipient parties presented new challenges to identifying, recognizing, and giving effect to sovereign rule by "the people."

Yet Americans adjusted. They explored the use of institutional mechanisms to channel the sovereignty of the people. The legislature was one means of discerning the people's will. Conventions were another device. In addition, simply a gathering of the people expressing their will had also been recognized. The experience of the Revolution taught that procedures were useful, but not mandatory. Unlike today, many did not think the sovereign was limited in how it could express its will. Procedures designed for such expression – for instance, through election of representatives and legislative action or proceedings of a convention – were all tools the sovereign could use.

Such methods were not exclusive of other ways to govern, even if the procedures in constitutional provisions suggested otherwise. The sovereign could not renounce its powers by tying them up in a web of procedure. Before the Civil War, Americans could find the voice of the sovereign in multiple, often overlapping ways. People exercised their sovereignty in self-created county or state conventions as well through the ballot box. In dire circumstances they simply gathered of their own accord, as they did before and during the Revolution.

When Massachusetts farmers gathered at Springfield to close Dr. Whiting's court in 1786, they faced a militia also drawn from the people. Resolving whether the court would meet by having the people who desired the closing to step to one side of the road and those who opposed the closing to step to the other side literally made it clear where the people stood. The mechanism was not simply a means of discerning majority will, even though modern eyes tend to see counting as the objective. To participants, the display sustained the conviction that those assembled were the body of the people. That was how the Massachusetts Regulators consistently referred to themselves and why they considered themselves entitled to exercise the sovereignty of the people. They followed the well-known and widely accepted practice employed during the Revolution when committees of correspondence, public crowds, gatherings, and mobs that protested British actions expressed the will of the people. It was something you knew, recognized, and accorded legitimacy when you saw it.

All Americans agreed that the people created government. They differed over when that collective sovereign might be recognized as having exercised its authority. Some recognized a multitude of ways, none of them exclusive, in which the people could express their will. In their expansive view, the people could use the formal procedures articulated in a constitution to amend or dissolve that document. Such procedures were not indispensable and the people's will could be recognized in other ways. On the other hand, some took a more constrained view. For them the sovereign spoke only in conformity with procedures it set forth in advance. That was the exclusive way in which the sovereign's voice would be recognized and heard.

The implications of this divide about when the sovereign had spoken were significant. For instance, one implication was whether the people of a past generation could bind a future one. If the people were, in fact, sovereign, their hands could not be tied and their sovereignty limited by an earlier generation. During this period, many Americans believed that a constitution's expression of fundamental rights and requirements for revisions could not dictate those terms to future generations. The unborn sovereign people of a later period were at liberty – just as the revolutionary generation had been – to express their sovereign will. Thus, each generation of American sovereigns would govern in its own way.[33]

The idea that the voice of the collective sovereign could be heard only through use of specified procedures was also a matter of dispute. However, the dispute was situational rather than a matter of ideology. The idea was not the exclusive property of any one political party or faction. For example, Federalists argued at one time that a measure could be adopted by the sovereign in defiance of formal constitutional procedures. In pressing for the adoption of the new federal Constitution in 1787 they did defy such procedures. Similarly, during their resistance to the War of 1812, they felt perfectly justified in organizing a convention to change the constitution in a manner not provided by Article V of that constitution. Yet Federalists also pressed the idea of strict adherence to established procedures in other instances. They regularly invoked the violation of procedures by Republicans who sought to organize politically through the Democratic-Republican societies and resist the Alien and Sedition Acts. In return, Republicans could be found insisting on strict adherence to established procedures during Madison's presidency. A decade earlier, when their party did not hold the presidency, they were quite willing to dispense with strict procedures to resist the Alien and Sedition Acts.

The need for the collective sovereign to act exclusively through established procedures could serve many different ends. It divided Americans in no consistent way. Attitudes did not simply follow political divisions, as the debates over a bill of rights in the First Congress illustrated. This is also clear from the numerous instances of Americans condemning the sovereign acting outside of established procedures and later arguing that the sovereign could depart from such procedures when it chose. Foreshadowing the Civil War, disputes over when the sovereign had spoken split families and pitted brother against brother and fathers against sons. Such divisions occurred during the struggle over the right of the people to act on their sovereignty at the time of the Massachusetts Regulation in the 1780s. And these divisions persisted during the conflict over the People's Constitution in Rhode Island in the 1840s when Thomas Dorr confronted members of his own family who were defending the state arsenal.[34]

The need to bring together a diverse people over a broad geographic expanse helps explain why the idea that the people were the sovereign played such an important role in American constitutional discourse before the Civil War. It was a doctrine that united Americans of many different situations, interests, and views. All Americans could support the role of the people as the sovereign, not the least because in doing so, they were empowering themselves. However, once talk turned to specifics, that agreement risked breaking down. Americans adjusted to this accommodating aspect of their constitutionalism. They took advantage of that quality when it advanced their goals and ignored it if it got in their way. Americans struggled to chan-nel their inherent authority – at times to release it and at other times to constrain it.

During his presidency, James Madison dismissed the resolutions of the Hartford Convention that challenged the constitutionality of policies of his administration. He considered them adopted by unpatriotic critics of the national government. He did not consider the convention entitled to chal-lenge supposedly unconstitutional policies of his administration. This posi-tion effectively constrained the broader role of the collective sovereign to scrutinize actions of its agent, the national government. Yet two decades later he defended his drafting of the Virginia Resolutions, which had also protested national laws. His resolutions, he said, simply raised the issue for the collective sovereign of whether the acts of the national government were unconstitutional. It was an appropriate release of the authority of the people to scrutinize their government. In neither case did he offer specific details or explanation of the lurking constitutional authority of the collective sovereign.[35]

This vagueness is problematic for those hoping to find with precision the specific "intent" of a Framer. The Framer left little to grasp. For Madison, it "was sufficient" to recognize the central truth that under American constitutionalism the people were to rule as the sovereign. He left the details to take care of themselves. Americans took this approach during the fight for Independence. This strategy was vindicated with their military victory. The key in the fight for Independence was whether the constitutional axiom of a collective sovereign worked in practice, not whether it was theoretically consistent or logical.[36]

Proceduralism as a constitutional value competed with the idea that the people were America's sovereign. Soon after the formation of the federal Constitution, some Federalists suggested that ratification transferred sovereignty from the people to the government. Having ratified the constitution, the people would fade away for any practical purpose. In responding to the whiskey excise tax protesters in the 1790s, George Washington's administration argued that its actions were proper because the federal government had a right of self-defense against the protesters. That argument implied that government was now the substitute for the people. This view was not widely held until long after the revolutionary generation passed. For the federal Constitution to displace the people with the government would truly have been a counterrevolution. Such a version of the concept of the people as the sovereign anticipated Britain's constitutional monarchy of today. The collective sovereign, much like the constitutional monarch, would be called upon for symbolic actions but would have a restricted role in the day-to-day operation of government.

Ultimately, America's revolutionary generation – including such leaders as James Madison – rejected government sovereignty well into the 1830s. Even as Madison defended the federal union against the threats of nullifiers, the last of the Founding Fathers never renounced his commitment to the bedrock principle that American governments – state and federal – were subject to rule by the people as their sovereign. To give government the status of a sovereign itself would repudiate the constitutional revolution that accompanied Independence.[37]

Madison's stance was not unique in the 1830s, as the struggle of Thomas Dorr and the People's Constitution demonstrated. Similarly, the constitutional melt-down of the Civil War, while significantly altering the terms of constitutional debate, did not banish the idea that the people were the sovereign. After the war just as before it, the argument that the national government now exercised the sovereignty the people once held was challenged as inconsistent with the constitutional legacy of the Revolution. Today, we may well have lost a sense of how a collective sovereign could rule. For many Americans before the Civil War, however, it seemed a very real possibility.

JURISPRUDENTIAL IMPLICATIONS

No Founding Father is cited in the Supreme Court's interpretation of the constitution more often than James Madison, the "Father of the Constitution." Yet, for all the importance the Court places on Madison's writings, the Court's jurisprudence reflects a curious anomaly. In many significant areas in which the meaning of the constitution is still at issue the Court seems to look to Madison with a blind eye. It screens from its consideration ideas articulated by Madison that do not comport with today's understanding of constitutionalism.

One of the areas in which the meaning of the constitution is still at issue involves the nature of the sovereignty underlying the federal Constitution. In dealing with that question the Court is divided. Some justices find a national American people in aggregate as the sovereign. This view reflects the understanding most forcefully advanced by Daniel Webster in the 1830s. Other justices consider the people of the states individually as the sovereign who formed the federal Constitution. This alternative view also reflects an understanding articulated in the 1830s in the course of the Nullification crisis. The Court's division became apparent in the 1995 case of *U.S Term Limits v. Thornton*, which considered whether a state could impose term limits upon its congressional representatives.[38] Seeking to find a single, unambiguous answer to who the federal sovereign was results in the Court's making a binary choice. The Court's division assumes that either a single national people or the people of the individual states reflects the "correct" view of the history of the constitution's founding.

Entirely missing in the Supreme Court's jurisprudence is James Madison's understanding of the founding. For Madison, it was the people in the states in their collective capacity who exercised sovereignty in ratifying the constitution. He specifically rejected the idea that the sovereign was an aggregated national people and that the sovereign was the people of individual states. Madison occupied a middle ground between these two alternate descriptions. Arguably, he best exemplified how most Americans understood the federal founding before sectional tensions in the 1830s produced a bifurcated constitutionalism pitting a national against a states' rights orientation. By defining the American sovereign as either of two extreme positions that brought the nation to civil war, the Court overlooks how most Americans understood the federal founding before they became locked into positions that led to the Civil War. An appreciation of Madison's understanding in the context of the *Thornton* case would suggest the invalidity of term limits to the extent it represented the action of a single state rather than a majority of the people of the states, who as the federal sovereign were free to impose whatever constitutional limitation they wished.

Another example of the anomaly in the Supreme Court's jurisprudence is its treatment of the constitutional system of checks and balances – the interplay between the three branches of government as well as striking a balance of power between the state and national governments. While the Court acknowledges Madison's contribution to that constitutional system, it ignores the intricacy of how the system operated in Madison's understanding. As this book has shown, Madison envisioned that under the constitution the people as the sovereign would have a real and direct role in maintaining the balance of the constitutional order. The three branches of government – as agents of the sovereign – were not self-regulating and not the sole players in the constitutional order. Rather, the people as the sovereign who gave life to the federal Constitution retained a role in maintaining constitutional balance. As Madison put it, such a retained role might well be expressed "within the forms" of the constitution through such traditional means as elections, petitions, conventions, and the like. The collective sovereign could also directly intervene and assert its authority as the sovereign without the need for its will to be mediated by government institutions or channeled by the existing branches of government. The consent of those branches or elected governors was not necessary for the sovereign to speak – if the sovereign chose to speak in the "ultimate" resort it was free to do so.

Another anomaly is the Supreme Court's assumption that the only means of restoring the constitutional balance rests with the judicial branch. The concept of interposition in the context of the federal Constitution before the Civil War saw a wide range of activities taken by nonjudicial actors to keep the national government within constitutional bounds. Moreover, Madison's assertion that the sovereign people could act in the last resort rested on the belief that the people's authority as the sovereign was – as an ultimate constitutional matter – not constrained or confined within the "forms of the constitution" or the judicial branch. Unlike today, Americans before the Civil

War did not assume that the only mechanism for restoring constitutional balance and monitoring the constitutionality of the national government rested with the judicial branch.[39]

The Supreme Court's treatment of Madison's writings overlooks the middle position he took in identifying the sovereign that created the federal Constitution. From this, the Court seems to ignore Madison's description of that sovereign's direct role in monitoring the constitutional order. These are more than simply blind spots in the Court's jurisprudence. Rather, the Court fails to acknowledge crucial features in the history of American constitutionalism. This reflects a central point: Americans have little faith in the idea of a collective sovereign. Our attenuated notion of the people as the sovereign is now a pale imitation of the place "the people" occupied when the constitution was formed and as it was elaborated and understood by many Americans before the Civil War.

The collective sovereign today has no practical role to play in the operation of government. This should not obscure the fact that earlier generations of Americans, including the federal Framers, would not recognize our sovereign. They might agree that the role they expected for the sovereign seems impractical in today's world, but this does not alter the fact that eighteenth-century constitution-makers believed a collectivity could be a sovereign. That we choose not to follow the directions of their thought is our choice. However, remaining ignorant of the meaning they attributed to a constitutionalism in which the people were the sovereign is quite another choice – particularly if we think we are relying upon their "intent" in construing the constitution they launched. Even if it seems inadvisable to reclaim their understanding of the role of the people in the constitutional order, recognizing the origins of the current system could expand the currently truncated framework of constitutional analysis so characteristic of the Court today. Indeed, acknowledging the significant role that a collective sovereign actually played in American history could help reshape our understanding of American constitutionalism. Moreover, returning to American constitutionalism its central idea of a collective sovereign provides a cogent reminder of the constitutional legacy the revolutionary generation bequeathed to later Americans.[40]

CONSTITUTIONAL LEGACY OF THE REVOLUTION

A deep-seated commitment to the principle of the collective sovereign underlay the constitutional experiment of American governments after Independence. That experiment involved balancing the interests of a sovereign with the needs of the government the sovereign created and to whom that sovereign was also subject. Members of the revolutionary generation such as James Madison and many other Americans were committed to that balance. This balance created an inherent tension in American constitutionalism that is arguably the most important constitutional legacy of the Revolution.

In replacing the king with "the people," leaders of American Independence understood the risk they took. As students of history, they appreciated the vulnerability of democracies and most of them placed little faith in the capacity of ordinary people to wield political power wisely. Nonetheless, leaders of the revolutionary cause believed the only legitimate foundation for their new governments was the people. The risk they took was creating republican governments with a popular basis, designing them to avoid degenerating into anarchy.

Although elite patriot leaders worried about the possibility of anarchy, they were also profoundly aware of the dangers of government tyranny that sparked their Revolution. The memory of abuses by British authorities made it important that a newly independent American people not trade one form of tyranny for another. If the possibility of an ungovernable "people" spelled trouble, so too did the prospect of government becoming a power unto itself. If so empowered, government might run roughshod over the collective sovereign, undermining the welfare of the people.

Remarkably, leaders of America's Revolution remained committed to the people's sovereignty even when it became increasingly clear how dangerous that idea could be when harnessed to advance policies they opposed. As they struggled to channel and curb the use of the argument that the people were the sovereign, they did not repudiate the authority of America's collective sovereign. Most revolutionary leaders sought to navigate between the specter of anarchy and the danger of tyranny. Maintaining this middle course was difficult in the face of temptations to use government's power to suppress criticism and unruly behavior of the people.

The Massachusetts Regulation, the whiskey excise tax protests in Pennsylvania, and the constitutional controversy in Rhode Island each involved American governments – state as well as federal – facing protests from organized groups of their citizens. In each instance the claim that the protest reflected the body of the people in action was met with contempt. In each instance protests against government policies were suppressed, with the expectation that such response would discourage comparable movements in the future.

Yet these suppressions were not simply about restoring stability and "law and order." Even the strongest supporters of the governments beleaguered by these three disturbances questioned government reaction as potentially dangerous. Hiring a private army to pursue Regulators in Massachusetts or marching a large army into western Pennsylvania appeared draconian and boded ill for the American experiment of governments resting on the people. Crushing citizen protest of government policies with military force raised the possibility of government tyranny that was just as dangerous as the threat of anarchy.

To the modern observer, the actions by the protesters in closing courts, punishing tax collectors, or celebrating a new government not created under the old constitution were all illegitimate acts. For Americans living before the Civil War this was not so clear. A gathering of the body of the people might be a crude way to express popular views. Often such a gathering formed only because of frustration that other steps had gone nowhere. Some degree of commotion, intimidation, and even sporadic violence was not unexpected. Americans before the Civil War accepted that public behavior tainted by some amount of physical intimidation and violence could be justified and might be entitled to a degree of toleration and cautious restraint from government. Americans believed there was a significant difference between determined rebellion that warranted decisive action and clumsy protest with unruly behavior that deserved a more tempered response from government. Preserving law and order need not come at the cost of a free society, and agents of government ought to exercise restraint in using coercive power.

All free nations contained, as Madison put it, an essential natural leaven. Unilaterally stamping out every instance of the people in action simply reflected the tyrannical ways of the Old World. Americans turned their backs on such tyranny with their Revolution. They instead embraced the challenge of maintaining a constitutional order requiring a continuous tension between generations of American sovereigns and their governments. If agents took protest personally and exaggerated the threat such protests posed to the need for order, that agency might well come to an end in a country in which the people were the sovereign.

Occasionally the sovereign did not express its will in ways government officials found congenial. An excited populace protesting real or perceived grievances was an expected part of free government. Sporadic popular "risings" and effervescent activity of the people required governments as agents of the sovereign to act with wisdom as well as force. A combination of firmness and conciliation, along with a judicious use of amnesty, could best calm such protests. Overreaction risked tyranny and might ultimately provoke the people's right to alter or abolish government.

Many prominent American leaders supported the government during the Massachusetts, Pennsylvania, and Rhode Island protests, but were troubled by the government's lack of proportionate response. All too often it seemed those governments were unduly coercive. Maintaining "law and order" at all costs and fiercely defending the "dignity" of government posed a significant danger to America's constitutional order. Leaders like James Madison identified a heavy responsibility that those in government owed to their sovereign to pilot a course between the twin dangers of anarchy and tyranny. Anything less would have abdicated the constitutional promise of the Revolution and repudiated the fact that in America the people ruled.

Key to Abbreviations

AA	Peter Force, ed., *American Archives: Consisting of a collection of authentick records, state papers, debates, and letters and other notices of publick affairs*... (9 vols., Washington, 1837–1853).
AAS	American Antiquarian Society, Worcester, MA
ADA	L. H. Butterfield, ed., *Diary and Autobiography of John Adams* (4 vols., 1961).
AFC	L. H. Butterfield et al., eds., *Adams Family Correspondence* (8 vols., 1963–).
AHR	*American Historical Review*
AJLH	*American Journal of Legal History*
AP	Robert J. Taylor et al., eds., *Papers of John Adams* (13 vols., 1977).
AW	Charles Francis Adams, ed., *The Works of John Adams* (10 vols., Boston, 1850–1856).
BA	Berkshire Athenaeum, Pittsfield, MA
BR	Helen E. Veit et al., eds., *Creating the Bill of Rights: The Documentary Record from the First Federal Congress* (1991).
BU	Brown University, Providence, RI
CA	Herbert J. Storing, ed., *The Complete Anti-Federalist* (7 vols., 1981).
CHS	Connecticut Historical Society, Hartford, CT
CRNC	William L. Saunders, ed., *The Colonial Records of North Carolina* (10 vols., Raleigh, NC, 1886–1890).
CVSP	W. P. Palmet et al., eds., *Calendar of Virginia State Papers* (11 vols., Richmond, 1875–1893).
DHRC	Merrill Jensen, ed., *Documentary History of the Ratification of the Constitution* (21 vols., 1976–).
DHSC	Maeva Marcus and James R. Perry, eds., *The Documentary History of the Supreme Court of the United States, 1789–1800* (8 vols., 1985–2007).

DU	Duke University, Durham, NC
FAW	W. B. Allen, ed., *Works of Fisher Ames* (2 vols., 1983, orig. published New York, 1854).
GMP	Robert A. Rutland, ed., *The Papers of George Mason, 1725–1792* (3 vols., 1970).
GWW	John C. Fitzpatrick, ed., *The Writings of George Washington from the Original Manuscript Sources, 1745–1799* (39 vols., 1931–1944).
HKC	Francis S. Drake, ed., *Life and Correspondence of Henry Knox* (Boston, 1873).
HL	American Historical Association, *Letters of Stephen Higginson, 1783–1804* (Washington, DC, 1897).
HP	Harold C. Syrett, ed., *The Papers of Alexander Hamilton* (27 vols., 1961–1987).
HU	Harvard University, Cambridge, MA
IC	Griffith John McRee, *Life and Correspondence of James Iredell* (2 vols., New York, 1857–1873).
JAH	*Journal of American History*
JCC	Worthington Chauncey Ford, ed., *Journals of the Continental Congress, 1774–1789* (34 vols., 1904–1937).
JCP	Robert L. Meriwether et al., eds., *The Papers of John C. Calhoun* (27 vols., 1959–2003).
JER	*Journal of the Early Republic*
JMP	Herbert A. Johnson et al., eds., *The Papers of John Marshall* (12 vols., 1974–2006).
JP	Julian P. Boyd et al., eds., *The Papers of Thomas Jefferson* (33 vols., 1950–).
JQAW	Worthington Chauncey Ford, ed., *Writings of John Quincy Adams* (7 vols., 1913–1917).
JW(F)	Paul Leicester Ford, ed., *Writings of Thomas Jefferson* (10 vols., New York, 1892–1899).
JW(L)	Andrew A. Lipscomb, ed., *Writings of Thomas Jefferson* (20 vols., 1903–1904).
LC	Library of Congress, Washington, DC
LDC	Paul H. Smith, ed., *Letters of Delegates to Congress, 1774–1789* (26 vols., 1976–2000).
LMC	Edmund C. Burnett, ed., *Letters of Members of the Continental Congress* (8 vols., 1921–1936).
LP	Philip M. Hamer, ed., *The Papers of Henry Laurens* (16 vols., 1968–2003).
LV	Library of Virginia, Richmond, VA
MdHS	Maryland Historical Society, Baltimore, MD
MHS	Massachusetts Historical Society, Boston, MA

ML	[William C. Rives and Philip R. Fendall, eds.], *Letters and Other Writings of James Madison* (4 vols., Philadelphia, 1865).
MP	William T. Hutchinson et al., eds., *The Papers of James Madison* (17 vols., 1962–1991).
MPP	James D. Richardson, ed., *A Compilation of the Messages and Papers of the Presidents* (10 vols., Washington, DC, 1896–1899).
MSA	Massachusetts State Archives, Boston, MA
MW	Gaillard Hunt, ed., *The Writings of James Madison* (9 vols., 1900–1910).
NA	National Archives, Washington, DC
NCDHR	North Carolina Division of Historical Resources, Raleigh, NC
NHS	Newport Historical Society, Newport, RI
NYPL	New York Public Library, New York, NY
NYU	New York University, New York, NY
PMHB	*Pennsylvania Magazine of History and Biography*
RFC	Max Farrand, ed., *The Records of the Federal Convention of 1787* (revised ed. in 4 vols., 1937, repr. 1966).
RIHS	Rhode Island Historical Society, Providence, RI
RKC	Charles R. King, ed., *The Life and Correspondence of Rufus King* (6 vols., New York, 1894–1900).
RSUS	*Records of the States of the United States, Constitutional Series*, (Microfilm), Library of Congress.
RSV	E. P. Walton, ed., *Records of the Council of Safety and Governor and Council of the State of Vermont* (8 vols., Montpelier, VT, 1873–1880).
SAW	Harry Alonzo Cushing, ed., *The Writings of Samuel Adams* (4 vols., 1904–1908).
SD	William F. Swindler, ed., *Sources and Documents of United States Constitutions* (11 vols., 1973–1979).
TC	Francis Newton Thorpe, ed., *The Federal and State Constitutions Colonial Charters, and Other Organic Laws of the States, Territories, and Colonies Now or Heretofore Forming the United States of America* (7 vols., 1909).
UM	University of Michigan, Ann Arbor, MI
VHS	Virginia Historical Society, Richmond, VA
VSM	Henry Cruger Van Schaack, ed., *The Life of Peter Van Schaack, LL.D., Embracing Selections from his Correspondence and other Writing During the American Revolution and his Exile in England* (New York, 1842).
WAL	*Warren-Adams Letters, Being Chiefly a Correspondence among John Adams, Samuel Adams, and James Warren* (2 vols., 1917–1925).

WebP(C)	Charles M. Wiltse, ed., *The Papers of Daniel Webster, Correspondence* (7 vols., 1974–1986).
Web(SFW)	Charles M. Wiltse, ed., *The Papers of Daniel Webster, Speeches and Formal Writings* (2 vols., 1986–1988).
WHS	Wisconsin Historical Society, Madison, WI
WMQ	*William and Mary Quarterly*
WP(CS)	W. W. Abbot and Dorothy Twohig, eds., *The Papers of George Washington, Confederation Series* (6 vols., 1992–1997).
WP(RWS)	Philander D. Chase et al., eds., *The Papers of George Washington, Revolutionary War Series* (16 vols., 1985–).
WW	Robert Green McCloskey, ed., *The Works of James Wilson* (2 vols., 1967).

Notes

CHAPTER 1. PROLOGUE

1. One definition of constitutionalism is "a complex of ideas, attitudes, and patterns of behavior elaborating the principle that the authority of government derives from and is limited by a body of fundamental law." See Don E. Fehrenbacher, *Constitutions and Constitutionalism in the Slaveholding South* (1989), 1.
2. The people's sovereignty is the theory and practice of associating the legitimacy of written constitutions and the governments they create with "the people." Although a term not commonly used by contemporaries, the "people's sovereignty" is preferable to "popular sovereignty." "Popular sovereignty" is a pejorative term associated with justifying the perpetuation of slavery. It also suggests transient popular whims. The alternative use of the "people's sovereignty" avoids both those negative connotations. It captures the serious thought that Americans before the Civil War gave to how a collective entity, the people, could act as the sovereign.

   Apart from the challenges of interpreting eighteenth-century constitutional text from the distance of the twenty-first century, much constitutional language and many political "keywords" of the revolutionary era experienced shifting and competing understandings within their own day. See, for example, Rodgers, *Contested Truths*; Ferguson, *Reading*, 6 (asserting that no language was "fraught with more contestation than that used in the early republic"). On the difficulties of assigning singular meaning in the interpretation of written text, see H. Aram Veeser, ed., *The Stanley Fish Reader* (1999). For the transformative power of the idea of volition that accompanied the American Revolution, see James H. Kettner, *The Development of American Citizenship, 1608–1870* (1978).
3. Larry Kramer asserts that the federal Framers believed that the people played a central role in shaping their constitutional tradition and that this view was a "background norm" supposedly "widely shared and deeply engrained" among eighteenth-century Americans. See Kramer, *People*, 53. This argument overlooks a central tension in American views on constitutional government since Independence. Americans did not "suddenly" discover in the 1790s that they entertained "profoundly different" ideas about constitutionalism. Rather, their ideas about the appropriate role of the people competed from the very beginning even as they agreed that the people were the ultimate source of sovereignty in America. See Kramer, *People*, 94.

   Akhil Reed Amar also emphasizes the importance of the authority of the people to the federal Constitution and depicts a constitutional founding relatively free from contentious disputes over the practical meaning of a sovereign people both before and after 1787. See Amar, *America's Constitution*. The failure to recognize these early disagreements on constitutionalism has led some scholars to consider them a subsequent development. See, for example, James A. Henretta, "Foreword: Rethinking the State Constitutional Tradition," 22 *Rutgers L. J.* (1991), 827 (identifying a novel "doctrine of activist popular sovereignty" in the 1820s).

4. For several recent exceptions to this focus on the federal Constitution, see Tarr, *State Constitutions* and Dinan, *Constitutional Tradition*.

5. The assumption of such a linkage largely rests on extending the findings of Gordon S. Wood's enormously influential *The Creation of the American Republic, 1776–1787* (1969) beyond the focus of its study on the period from Independence to the formation of the federal Constitution. For an elaboration of pervasive assumptions in the scholarship of historians, political scientists, and lawyers contributing to such a view, see Fritz, "Fallacies." See also Tarr, *State Constitutions*, 90 (noting that "a distinctive state constitutionalism continued even after 1787").

6. See, for example, Kyvig, *Explicit* (assuming the inevitability of formal mechanisms for constitutional change).

7. For the classic study of the sovereignty of the people as a "fiction," see Morgan, *Inventing*. See also Elkins and McKitrick, *Federalism*, 482 (describing the sovereignty of the people as "the most formidable abstraction of the Revolutionary era").

8. For the place of the rule of law in English thought of the seventeenth and eighteenth centuries, see Reid, *Rule of Law*.

9. On how America's first state constitutions encouraged constitutional practices at odds with our contemporary commitment to procedure and the rule of law, see Christian G. Fritz, "Recovering the Lost Worlds of America's Written Constitutions," 68 *Albany L. Rev.* (2005), 261–93. Alan Tarr has usefully reminded us that the modern assumption of "a fundamental incompatibility between majority rule and the protection of rights, as well as between individual rights and the common good," was not shared by those who framed the first state bills of rights. See Tarr, *State Constitutions*, 80.

10. For an account of how the revolutionary movement encouraged an expanding definition of "the people," see Nash, *Unknown*. That expansion was an inherently dynamic process and forms part of the broader and important story of how American political life became more democratic. But that story is *not* the subject of this work.

11. *Chisholm v. Georgia*, 2 U.S. 419 at 471–72 (1793) (John Jay).

12. Akhil Reed Amar has aptly noted that the idea of the sovereignty of the people raised "'mind-bending' questions." Amar, *America's Constitution*, 292.

CHAPTER 2. REVOLUTIONARY CONSTITUTIONALISM

1. The account of the State Yard Meeting draws on John Adams to James Warren, May 15, 1776, and May 20, 1776, *AP*, IV:186–87, 195–97; Autobiography of John Adams, *ADA*, III:383; John Adams, "Novanglus," 1774, *AW*, IV:14–15; Caesar Rodney to Thomas Rodney, May 17, 1776, *LMC*, I:455; May 10 and 15, 1776, *JCC*, IV:342, 357–58; Anonymous, *The Alarm: or, an Address to the People of Pennsylvania on the Late Resolve of Congress*, 1776, in Hyneman and Lutz, *Political Writing*, I:321–27; James E. Gibson, "The Pennsylvania Provincial Conference of 1776," 58 *PMHB* (1934), 312–41; J. Paul Selsam, *The Pennsylvania Constitution of 1776: A Study in Revolutionary Democracy* (1936), 112–23; David Hawke, *In the Midst of a Revolution* (1961), 129–38; Richard Alan Ryerson, *The Revolution Is Now Begun: The Radical Committees of Philadelphia, 1765–1776* (1978), 211–16; Steven Rosswurm, *Arms, Country, and Class: The Philadelphia Militia and "Lower Sort" During the American Revolution, 1775–1783* (1987), 93–96; "Introduction," Handlin, *Popular Sources*, 53.

2. See J. W. Gough, *Fundamental Law in English Constitutional History* (1955), 88–91, 162–64; Richard L. Bushman, *King and People in Provincial Massachusetts* (1985), 4, 51–53; Marston, *King and Congress*, 6, 17–20.

  For the legal and constitutional basis for the American revolutionary position, see Reid, *Constitutional History*; John Phillip Reid, "The Irrelevance of the Declaration," in Hendrik Hartog, ed., *Law in the American Revolution and the Revolution in the Law* (1981), 46–89 (finding appeals to natural law unnecessary and the Declaration of Independence "irrelevant" for justifying the Revolution). But Americans still invoked natural law when advancing the legal and constitutional basis of their Revolution. See, for example, New Hampshire 1776 Constitution,

Preamble, *TC*, IV:2451 (New Hampshire constitution-makers asserting their "natural and constitutional rights and privileges"); Larry R. Gerlach, "Power to the People: Popular Sovereignty, Republicanism, and the Legislature in Revolutionary New Jersey," in William C. Wright, ed., *The Development of the New Jersey Legislature from Colonial Times to the Present* (1976), 28 (New Jersey Grand Jury in 1776 finding liberty "defined and protected by Law" but nonetheless "Built on the Rights of human Nature"); Thomas C. Grey, "Origins of the Unwritten Constitution: Fundamental Law in American Revolutionary Thought," 30 *Stan. L. Rev.* (1978), 893 (identifying "the traditional idea of a legally binding and unwritten constitution" as central to the American revolutionary argument); Reid, *Constitutional History*, I:89 (acknowledging that "everyone agreed" that the right to self-defense was a natural right).

3. Alexander Hamilton, "The Farmer Refuted," [Feb. 23], 1775, *HP*, I:136; Declaration of Independence, *TC*, I: 3–4 ("endowed by their Creator"). For the constraints on the natural law right of revolution, see Julie Mostov, *Power, Process, and Popular Sovereignty* (1992), 59 (observing that natural law provided "a way of limiting the arbitrary power of the government" and "preventing popular consent from becoming too direct or overt"); Conkin, *Self-Evident*, 22 (suggesting that Locke "carefully restricted the practical import of popular sovereignty").

   For the way Americans perceived their plight in 1776, see Maier, *American Scripture*, 77–90.
4. William Blackstone, *Commentaries on the Laws of England* (4 vols., Oxford, 1765–1769, facsimile ed., repr., 1979), I:238; Reid, "Irrelevance," 72 ("central dogma"). For this contractual basis, including the Lockean "social contract" and the non-Lockean "original contract," see John Phillip Reid, "'In Our Contracted Sphere': The Constitutional Contract, the Stamp Act Crisis, and the Coming of the American Revolution," 76 *Colum. L. Rev.* (1976), 21–47; Reid, *Constitutional History*, I:132–58, II:53–64. See also Blackstone, *Commentaries*, I:47–48, 183, 238; New Jersey 1776 Constitution, Preamble, *TC*, V:2594 (identifying the king's breach of the contract).
5. Reid, *Constitutional History*, III:140. See also Maier, *Resistance*, 3–48; John Phillip Reid, "In a Defensive Rage: The Uses of the Mob, the Justification in Law, and the Coming of the American Revolution," 49 *N.Y.U. L. Rev.* (1974), 1066 (noting that John Adams, "one of the most law-minded" American revolutionaries, "accepted the necessity of crowd action when constitutional 'fundamentals are invaded'").
6. Alexander Hamilton, "The Farmer Refuted," [Feb. 23], 1775, *HP*, I:88. Seventeenth-century English thinkers differed on the necessity of a breach before invoking the right of revolution. See, for example, Conkin, *Self-Evident*, 21 (quoting Algernon Sidney that the people could always "meet when and where" they wished and "dispose of sovereignty as they will"); Stephen Holmes, "Precommitment and the Paradox of Democracy," in Jon Elster and Rune Slagstad, eds., *Constitutionalism and Democracy* (1988), 199 (quoting speech in British parliamentary debates (Oct. 28, 1647), asserting that "all the people, and all nations whatsoever, have a liberty and power to alter and change their constitutions if they find them to be weak and infirm"); Maier, *Resistance*, 35 (quoting John Milton that the people might keep or overthrow their king "as seems to them best," and even *"though no Tyrant"*). In the end, Americans justified independence on the classical precondition of dire necessity.
7. See Reid, *Constitutional History*, I:111 (identifying the collective right of the people "to preserve their rights by force and even rebellion against constituted authority"), III:427n31 (quoting Viscount Bolingbroke that the *"collective Body of the People"* had the right to "break the Bargain between the *King* and the *Nation*"); Maier, *Resistance*, 33–34 ("Private individuals were forbidden to take force against their rulers either for malice or because of private injuries, even if no redress for their grievances were afforded by the regularly constituted government").
8. Some commentators endorsed the right of resistance if Parliament "jeopardized the constitution," but most identified the need for oppression and tyranny before its exercise. See Reid, *Constitutional History*, III:121 ("jeapordized"), 427n31; Maier, *Resistance*, 33–35.
9. Blackstone, *Commentaries*, I:243 (*"extraordinary"*), 238 ("fundamental laws"); Reid, *Constitutional History*, I:112 ("the hand of oppression"), III:309; Reid, "Irrelevance," 84 ("indictment").
10. Jack P. Greene, *Peripheries and Center: Constitutional Development in the Extended Polities of the British Empire and the United States, 1607–1788* (1986), 203 ("the rights of sovereignty")

(quoting the English radical John Cartwright in 1774). See also R. R. Palmer, *The Age of the Democratic Revolution: A Political History of Europe and America, 1760–1800* (2 vols., 1959–1964), I:213–35; Thad W. Tate, "The Will of the People in Eighteenth-Century America," in George R. Johnson, Jr., ed., *The Will of the People: The Legacy of George Mason* (1991), 21–54; Morgan, *Inventing*, 78–93 (asserting American colonists did not know of seventeenth-century antecedents of the people's sovereignty). On the English origins of the sovereignty of the people and consent as the basis of government, see Reid, *Constitutional History*, III:97–101, 107–10.

11. Tucker, "Conciliatory," I:629 ("Before us"). See also Maier, *American Scripture*, 34–35 (observing that in 1776 no governments existed "in which all authority rested on popular choice"); Wood, *Radicalism*, 243 (noting that America "became the first society in the modern world to bring ordinary people into the affairs of government – not just as voters but as actual rulers"); Wayne Franklin, "The U.S. Constitution and the Textuality of American Culture," in Vivien Hart and Shannon C. Stimson, eds., *Writing a National Identity: Political, Economic, and Cultural Perspectives on the Written Constitution* (1993), 10 (asserting that Americans had "virtually no practical experience" in drafting written constitutions before 1776).

12. John Adams to William Cushing, June 9, 1776, *LDC*, IV:178. On the theoretical role of "the people" under English constitutionalism, see Reid, *Constitutional History*, III:109 (describing the people's sovereignty as "mere theory"). For the American constitutional contribution, see R. R. Palmer, "The People as Constituent Power," in John R. Howe, Jr., ed., *The Role of Ideology in the American Revolution* (1970), 73–82; Gerald Stourzh, "Constitution: Changing Meanings of the Term from the Early Seventeenth to the Late Eighteenth Century," in Ball and Pocock, *Change*, 35–54; Thad W. Tate, "The Social Contract in America, 1774–1787: Revolutionary Theory as a Conservative Instrument," 22 *WMQ* (1965), 375–91.

13. See Franklin, "Textuality," 11 (arguing that Americans were "acutely aware" of the power of language and "written texts"); Jefferson Powell, *Languages of Power: A Source Book of Early American Constitutional History* (1991), 4 (describing "the connection between the American constitutions' written nature, their supreme legal authority, and their capacity to render definite and fixed the forms and limits of governmental power"). For earlier experience with constitutional texts, see Donald S. Lutz, *The Origins of American Constitutionalism* (1988), 23–49.

14. *Vanhorne's Lessee v. Dorrance*, 28 F. Cas. 1012 at 1014 (C.C. Pa. 1795). See *Marbury v. Madison*, 5 U.S. 137 at 176–80 (1803). Marshall's statement in *McCulloch v. Maryland*, 17 U.S. 316 at 407 (1819) that "we must never forget, that it is *a constitution* we are expounding," referred to a written one, a feature he emphasized in the opinion. In focusing on the emerging idea that constitutions constituted fundamental law, scholars have overlooked the significance of the written character of American constitutions after the Revolution. See, for example, Bernard Bailyn, *The Ideological Origins of the American Revolution* (1967), 67–69, 175–84, 189–93; Wood, *Creation*, 259–60, 266–68, 273–82, 290–91.

15. Thomas Paine, *Common Sense* (1776) in Philip S. Foner, ed., *The Complete Writings of Thomas Paine* (2 vols., 1945), I:45; Oliver Wolcott to Samuel Lyman, May 16, 1776, *LMC*, I:449; *Salus Populi*, "To the People of North-America on the Different Kinds of Government," [Mar. 1776], *AA* (4th Ser.), V:182; David Ramsay, *An Oration on the Advantages of American Independence, Spoken Before a Public Assembly of the Inhabitants of Charleston, in South Carolina, on July 4th, 1778*, in Hezekiah Niles, ed., *Principles and Acts of the Revolution in America* (New York, Chicago, and New Orleans, 1822, repr., 1876), 379. See also Tucker, *Blackstone's Commentaries*, I: Appendix, Note A, p. 4 (asserting that the American Revolution introduced "a new epoch" by "reducing to practice" what seemed to exist "only in the visionary speculations of theoretical writers").

16. James Madison, article written for the *National Gazette* entitled, "Charters," Jan. 18, [1792], *MP*, XIV:191–92.

17. See "Boston Orations," Apr. 2, 1771–Apr. 8, 1776, in Niles, *Principles*, 17–42; "Pittsfield Memorial," Dec. 26, 1775, in Handlin, *Popular Sources*, 61–64; Hyneman and Lutz, *Political Writing*, I.

18. "New London, "Connecticut Resolutions on the Stamp Act," Dec. 10, 1765, Merrill Jensen, ed., *English Historical Documents, American Colonial Documents to 1776* (1955), 670; George

Mason, "Remarks on Annual Elections for the Fairfax Independent Company," [ca. Apr. 17–26, 1775], *GMP*, I:231. The New London Resolutions invoked both the authority of contract and the constitutional right of resistance. For an elaboration of these ideas, see Reid, *Constitutional History*, I:16–17, 111–13, 132–58, 188, 216.

19. "Proclamation of the General Court, Jan. 23, 1776," in Handlin, *Popular Sources*, 65; Samuel West, "On the Right to Rebel Against Governors," 1776, in Hyneman and Lutz, *Political Writing*, I:419.

20. See Conkin, *Self-Evident*, 52 (describing "the almost unanimous acceptance of popular sovereignty at the level of abstract principle"); Morgan, "Popular Sovereignty," 101 (concluding the American Revolution "confirmed and completed the subordination of government to the will of the people"); Adams, *Constitutions*, 137 (asserting that statements of the "principle" of the people's sovereignty "expressed the very heart of the consensus among the victors of 1776"); Onuf, *Origins*, 22 (seeing the people's sovereignty "institutionalized" in the state constitutions); Wood *Radicalism*, 187 (identifying popular consent after the Revolution as "the exclusive justification for the exercise of authority").

21. "John Rutledge to South Carolina General Assembly," Apr. 11, 1776, in Niles, *Principles*, 326–27; "John Dickinson's Notes for a Speech in Congress," [June 8–10, 1776], John Dickinson's Notes on Arguments Concerning Independence," [July 1?, 1776], *LDC*, IV:166, 357. See also Wood, *Creation*, 362 (observing that in 1776, "no one doubted, even most Tories, that all power ultimately resided in the people").

22. "Additional Instructions from the Inhabitants of Albemarle," [ca. Sept.–Oct., 1776], *JP*, VI:291–92; Virginia 1776 Constitution, Bill of Rights, Sec. 2, *TU*, VII:3813 (elected officials were the people's "trustees and servants, and at all times amenable to them"); "Albemarle County Instructions Concerning the Virginia Constitution," [ca. Sept.–Oct. 1776], *JP*, VI:286; "Instructions to the Delegates from Mecklenburg to the Provincial Congress at Halifax in November, 1776," *CRNC*, X:870b ("principal supreme power" and "servants"). See also "Instructions to the Delegates from Orange in the Halifax Congress, to be held in November, 1776," *CRNC*, X:870f (those "delegated chosen or employed or intrusted by the people are their servants and can possess only derived inferior power"). Although some state constitutions included "Declarations of Rights," for consistency's sake they are described as bills of rights.

23. South Carolina 1776 Constitution, Preamble, *TC*, VI:3243; Maryland 1776 Constitution, Bill of Rights, Sec. 1, Nov. 3, 1776, in Papenfuse and Stiverson, *Decisive*; Georgia 1777 Constitution, Preamble, *TC*, II:778; Letter from William Hooper, Delegate from North Carolina to the Continental Congress, to the Congress at Halifax, Oct. 26, 1776, *CRNC*, X:866; John Sullivan to Meshech Weare, Dec. 12, 1775, Otis G. Hammond, ed., *Letters and Papers of Major-General John Sullivan* (3 vols., 1930–1939), I:142.

24. See, for example, Massachusetts 1780 Constitution, Bill of Rights, Art. 7; North Carolina 1776 Constitution, Bill of Rights, Sec. 23; Pennsylvania 1776 Constitution, Bill of Rights, Sec. 5, *TC*, III:1890 (government was for "the common good . . . and not for the profit, honor, or private interest of any one man, family, or class of men"), V:2788 (perpetuities and monopolies were "contrary to the genius of a free State"), 3082–83 (government was for the "common benefit . . . of the people, nation or community; and not for the particular emolument or advantage of any single man, family, or sett of men"). For the theme of protecting the public welfare in American law, see William J. Novak, *The People's Welfare: Law and Regulation in Nineteenth-Century America* (1996).

25. On the right to petition, see Mark, "Vestigial Constitution," 2203 (identifying in the first state constitutions a shift from understanding the right of petition as based on "hierarchical bonds of political society" to "the capacity to deal with one's representative as an equal, or even to treat the representative as a servant"). See also Higginson, "Short History," 142–66; Amar, *Bill of Rights*, 30–32; Edward C. Papenfuse and Robert C. Murphy, "But for the Sake of a Comma: The Constitution, the Bill of Rights, and Changing Perceptions of Peaceable Assembly and Representative Government in Maryland, 1765–1802," Maryland State Archives Homepage (1999).

26. Virginia 1776 Constitution, Bill of Rights, Sec. 2, *TC*, VII:3813 ("That all power is vested in, and consequently derived from, the people; that magistrates are their trustees and servants, and at all times amenable to them."); Pennsylvania 1776 Constitution, Bill of Rights, Sec. 4, *TC*,V:3082; Maryland 1776 Constitution, Bill of Rights, Nov. 3, 1776, Sec. 4, in Papenfuse and Stiverson, *Decisive* (declaring "all persons" with legislative or executive powers "trustees of the public"); Delaware 1776 Constitution, Bill of Rights, Sec. 5, *SD*, II:198; Massachusetts 1780 Constitution, Bill of Rights, Art. 5, Art. 19; New Hampshire 1784 Constitution, Bill of Rights, Art. 8, *TC*, III:1890, 1892 (asserting the people's right to "give instructions to their representatives, and to request of the legislative body, by the way of addresses, petitions, or remonstrances"), IV: 2454.

    Peter Hoffer asserts that American constitutionalism after the Revolution was shaped by equity principles that provided the metaphor of a trust to describe the relationship between the people and their governors. See Peter Charles Hoffer, *The Law's Conscience: Equitable Constitutionalism in America* (1990), 47–79. Americans invoked the trusteeship metaphor, but they also used the principle of agency to express the accountability of governors to the people. For the interchangeability of the use of trustee and agency analogies, see Yazawa, *Representative*, 65, 112–13, 142, 144.

27. Pennsylvania 1776 Constitution, Bill of Rights, Art. 14 and Sec. 35, *TC*, V:3083–84, 3090. See Daniel N. Hoffman, *Government Secrecy and the Founding Fathers: A Study in Constitutional Controls* (1981), 13 (arguing that the Revolution helped "reverse the old presumption in favor of secrecy . . . with a presumption in favor of publicity, based on the doctrine of popular sovereignty"). Pennsylvania's provision for a right to petition and instruct representatives was incorporated in the constitutions for North Carolina, Massachusetts, and New Hampshire. See North Carolina 1776 Constitution, Bill of Rights, Art. 18; Massachusetts 1780 Constitution, Bill of Rights, Art. 19; New Hampshire 1784 Constitution, Bill of Rights, Sec. 32, *TC*, V:2788, III:1892, IV:2457. Maryland's 1776 Constitution included the right to petition but not the right of instruction. See Maryland 1776 Constitution, Bill of Rights, Sec. 11, Nov. 3, 1776, in Papenfuse and Stiverson, *Decisive*.

28. "An Elector" [Thomas Young], *Pennsylvania Gazette*, May 15, 1776, quoted in Pauline Maier, "Reason and Revolution: The Radicalism of Dr. Thomas Young," 28 *American Quarterly* (1976), 234 ("Men of some rank"). See also Ryerson, "Republican Theory," 114 (arguing that the framers of Pennsylvania's 1776 constitution believed everyone "would act as vigilant watchdogs over the performance of their government, which consequently would have no need for institutional checks upon its actions"); Kruman, *State Constitution Making*, 84 (noting that constitution-makers "expected voters to scrutinize their representatives' behavior through regular and frequent elections"); Tarr, *State Constitutions*, 79 (describing how scrutiny was "facilitated by constitutional requirements that the legislature regularly publish votes and proceedings").

29. Massachusetts 1780 Constitution, Bill of Rights, Art. 8; Pennsylvania 1776 Constitution, Bill of Rights, Sec. 6, *TC*, III:1890–91 (to prevent those "vested with authority from becoming oppressors, the people have a right" at intervals "to cause their public officers to return to private life"),V:3083 (to restrain those "employed" in the state's "legislative and executive business" from "oppression" the people have the right "to reduce their public officers to a private station"); John Adams to Hugh Hughes, June 4, 1776, *AP*, IV:238 ("The people ought"); Massachusetts 1780 Constitution, Bill of Rights, Art. 18; New Hampshire 1784 Constitution, Bill of Rights, Sec. 38, *TC*, III:1892, IV:2457. See also Thomas Young to Aaron Davis, Jr., [1772], quoted in Henry H. Edes, "Memoir of Dr. Thomas Young, 1731–1777," *Publications of the Colonial Society of Massachusetts* (1910), XI:24 (describing government officials as "public servants"); Williams, "State Constitutions," 556 (noting that Pennsylvania's 1776 constitution intended to make the legislature "an open deliberative body accountable to the voters").

30. Samuel Johnston to James Iredell, Apr. 20, 1776, *CRNC*, X:498; Pennsylvania 1776 Constitution, Bill of Rights, Sec. 3; North Carolina 1776 Constitution, Bill of Rights, Sec. 2, *TC*, V:3082 ("sole, exclusive and inherent"), 2787; Maryland 1776 Constitution, Nov. 3, 1776, Sec. 2, in Papenfuse and Stiverson, *Decisive*. On Johnston, see Robert L. Ganyard, *The Emergence of*

North Carolina's Revolutionary State Government (1978), 68–69. For the way Pennsylvania's bill of rights repeatedly described government and its officials as subordinate to the people and constantly subject to their scrutiny, see Pennsylvania 1776 Constitution, Bill of Rights, Secs. 3, 4, 5, 6, 14, and 16, *TC*, V:3082–84.

31. See Martin, *Press Liberty*, 122–23 (describing "transformations" during the revolutionary era prompting a rethinking of "the very nature of government and the implications they had for the role of the press" with some Americans concluding that "A sovereign people required a steady flow of political information, constructive as well as critical, in order to be competent masters of their public servants; they required not a free press but a 'press of sovereignty'"); Smith, *Freedom's Fetters*, 146 (asserting that controversy over freedom of speech and liberty of the press after the Revolution "pivoted on the concept of the relation of the people to the government"). On English legal doctrines dealing with criticism of government, see Philip Hamburger, "The Development of the Law of Seditious Libel and the Control of the Press," 37 *Stan. L. Rev.* (1985), 661–765, while for the American context see Levy, *Free Press*; Norman L. Rosenberg, *Protecting the Best Men: An Interpretative History of the Law of Libel* (1986). For the classic study of the rise of a party system, see Hofstadter, *Idea*.

32. *Chisholm v. Georgia*, 2 U.S. 419 at 456 (1793).

33. James Iredell, North Carolina Ratifying Convention, July 24, 1788, in Elliot, *Debates*, IV:9.

34. James Wilson, "Of Government," *Lectures on Law* [1790–1791], *WW*, I:304. See also Rodgers, *Contested Truths*, 112 (asserting it became increasingly clear that the people's sovereignty had a "radical edge" involving the people's implicit authority to "dissolve political society into its individual, constituent atoms . . . and make their governments anew").

35. Parsons, *Essex*, I:486. For descriptions that implied limits on the collective sovereign, see Benjamin Rush, "Address to the People of the United States," Feb. 1787 in *DHRC*, XIII:47 (conceding the people's sovereignty but asserting "[t]hey possess it only on the days of their elections. After this, it is the property of their rulers"); "The Sovereignty Is in the People," Pennsylvania, *Gazette of the United States*, May 29, 1793 (repr. from the *Boston Columbian Centinel*) (while the "*Sovereignty is in the People*" it existed in an "implied" and "abstract" manner and they "never shall exercise it but to appoint their representatives"); *Boston Columbian Centinel*, Sept. 3, 1794 (describing "the *majesty of the people*" as vested "in the constitution" they adopted, but which sovereignty was only "rightfully exercised" by those they elected until "the stated periods of election, when the sovereignty is again at the disposal of the *whole people*"); Fisher Ames, "Laocoon I," *Boston Gazette*, Apr. 1799, *FAW*, I:194 (describing elections as the place where "the sovereignty of the citizen is to be exercised"); "The Mirror," "The Government of the U. States not a Democracy," *Baltimore Republican, or Anti-Democrat*, July 15, 1803 (claiming that under the federal Constitution the people "*vested* in a few men, *all sovereign power*" and had "no right to assemble collectively"); Horst Dippel, "The Changing Idea of Popular Sovereignty in Early American Constitutionalism: Breaking Away from European Patterns," 16 *JER* (1996), 36–37 (identifying an emphasis on elections as the sole expression of the collective sovereign).

36. *Federalist No. 78*, pp. 524–25 (Hamilton); *Chisholm v. Georgia*, 2 U.S. 419 at 471 (Jay), at 457 (Wilson) (1793).

37. John Laurens to Henry Laurens, May 12, 1778, *LP*, XIII:296. Scholars frequently dismiss the "alter or abolish" provisions because they seem to preclude judicial enforceability. See, for example, Lutz, *Popular Consent*, 61 (describing bills of rights provisions as "general admonitions with no specific legal content" lacking "the positive, binding force" of language used "in the constitution proper"); A. E. Dick Howard, "From Mason to Modern Times: 200 Years of American Rights," in Josephine F. Pacheco, ed., *The Legacy of George Mason* (1983), 102 (first state bills of rights contain "hortatory language" frequently "not capable of judicial application"); Dinan, *People's Liberties*, 6 (asserting that "the principle utility" of bills of rights "did not lie in their ability to serve as judicially enforced limitations" but instead "to impress upon governing officials the importance of upholding certain standards and guarantees and thereby prevent them from being violated"); Jack N. Rakove, "Thinking Like a Constitution," 24 *JER* (2004), 16–17 (asserting the first bills of rights were "not constitutional documents in the strict sense of the

term" and that the use "of the monitory 'ought' rather than the mandatory 'shall' illustrates" their "moral and political – as opposed to legal – purpose").

 But see Robert C. Palmer, "Liberties as Constitutional Provisions, 1776–1791," in William E. Nelson and Robert C. Palmer, eds., *Constitution and Rights in the Early American Republic* (1987), 66 (arguing that the "alter or abolish" provisions were "not guarantees" but "serious principles of government by which government was expected to abide").

38. Maryland 1776 Constitution, Bill of Rights, Sec. 4, Nov. 3, 1776, in Papenfuse and Stiverson, *Decisive*; New Hampshire 1784 Constitution, Bill of Rights, Art. 10, *TC*, IV:2455.

39. Virginia 1776 Constitution, Bill of Rights, Sec. 3; Pennsylvania 1776 Constitution, Bill of Rights, Sec. 5, *TC*, VII:3813,V:3083–84.

40. Only Virginia, Pennsylvania, North Carolina, Maryland, Delaware, and Massachusetts had bills of rights in their first constitutions and all but North Carolina's contained "alter or abolish" provisions. The first constitutions of New York, New Jersey, South Carolina, Georgia, and New Hampshire lacked bills of rights and Rhode Island and Connecticut retained their colonial charters.

41. Yazawa, *Representative*, 117 (William Paca to Alexander Contee Hanson, May 10, 1787).

42. For assumptions that the "alter or abolish" provisions were simply part of the "natural law tradition" or merely philosophical or political statements, see Garry Wills, *Inventing America: Jefferson's Declaration of Independence* (1978), 238 (discussing Jefferson's "natural right of revolution"); Leslie Friedman Goldstein, "Popular Sovereignty, the Origins of Judicial Review, and the Revival of Unwritten Law," 48 *Journal of Politics* (1986), 57 (identifying the "alter or abolish" right as one of the "Lockean principles" in the Declaration of Independence); McInnis, "Natural Law," 370 (considering "alter or abolish" provisions "evidence" of a "commitment . . . to natural law"); Suber, *Paradox*, 230 (calling alter or abolish provisions "an appeal to higher law").

 But see Harry L. Witte, "Rights, Revolution, and the Paradox of Constitutionalism: The Processes of Constitutional Change in Pennsylvania," 3 *Widener J. Pub. L.* (1993), 390 (arguing that Pennsylvania's 1776 "alter or abolish" provision "was not simply a formal, theoretical basis for government in general, but a power to be claimed by the people in real time and in real places"); Matthew J. Herrington, "Popular Sovereignty in Pennsylvania 1776–1791," 67 *Temp. L. Rev.* (1994), 576–77 (finding the "conventional wisdom" of revolutionary-era constitutional understandings "the opposite of today's: the people . . . possessed an inalienable right to alter their government" and constitutional procedures for revision "supplemented rather than supplanted the potential for constitutional change through organic expressions of popular will"); Amar, "Consent," 458 (arguing that between 1776 and 1787 "popular sovereignty principles in America evolved beyond the Lockean core of the Declaration and established the legal right of the polity to alter or abolish their government at any time and for any reason, by a peaceful and simple majoritarian process"); David C. Williams, "The Constitutional Right to 'Conservative' Revolution," 32 *Harv. C.R.- C.L.L. Rev.* (1997), 413–47 (asserting a constitutional right of revolution in theory).

43. See Robin West, "Tom Paine's Constitution," 89 *Va. L. Rev.* (2003), 1413–61 (arguing that Paine, in his *Rights of Man* in 1791, posited that American constitutional law manifested the will of the people, who could change it whenever they liked).

44. The account of the creation and revision of Pennsylvania's 1776 constitution draws on Benjamin Rush to Anthony Wayne, May 19, 1777, Benjamin Rush to John Montgomery, Nov. 15, 1783, Benjamin Rush to Charles Nisbet, Aug. 27, 1784, Benjamin Rush to John Adams, Feb. 12, 1790, in L. H. Butterfield, ed., *Letters of Benjamin Rush* (2 vols., 1951), I:148, 314, 336, 531; George W. Corner, ed., *The Autobiography of Benjamin Rush* (1948), 46; *Pennsylvania Evening Post*, June 27, 1776; Jacob Cox Parsons, ed., *Extracts from the Diary of Jacob Hiltzheimer, of Philadelphia* (Philadelphia, 1893), 151; [Benjamin Rush], *Observations Upon the Present Government of Pennsylvania. In Four Letters to the People of Pennsylvania* (Philadelphia, 1777), 15; Pennsylvania 1776 Constitution, Bill of Rights, Sec. 5, *TC*, V:3083–84; David Freeman Hawke, *Benjamin Rush: Revolutionary Gadfly* (1971); 142–61, 183, 187, 195–202, 270–71, 278, 386–88; Selsam, *Pennsylvania Constitution*; Brunhouse, *Counter-Revolution*, 221–27; *The*

Proceedings Relative to Calling the Conventions of 1776 and 1790. The Minutes of the Convention that Formed the Present Constitution of Pennsylvania (Harrisburg, PA, 1825), 129, 133; Roy H. Akagi, "The Pennsylvania Constitution of 1838," 48 *PMHB* (1924), 303–304.

45. Massachusetts 1780 Constitution, Bill of Rights, Art. 7, *TC*, III:1890; Pennsylvania 1790 Constitution, Art. IX, Sec. 2 (language retained in Pennsylvania's 1838 constitution), *TC*, V:3100, 3113; Delaware 1792 Constitution, Preamble (language retained in Delaware's 1831 constitution), *TC*, I:568, 582; Connecticut 1818 Constitution, Bill of Rights, Sec. 2, *TC*, I:537. The first constitutions have been described as "radical" or "conservative" according to the political participation they permitted. See, for example, East, "Conservatives," 353 (calling Massachusetts's 1780 constitution "a conservative regime"); Wood, *Creation*, 438 (describing Pennsylvania's 1776 constitution as "the most radical" of the first state constitutions); Ryerson, "Republican Theory," 133 (considering Pennsylvania's 1790 constitution more "conservative" than the 1776 constitution it replaced). But see Yazawa, *Representative*, 4, 7–8, 27 (questioning these traditional characterizations).

46. Amar, *America's Constitution*, 12–13.

47. Kentucky 1792 Constitution, Art. XII, Sec. 2 (containing language largely retained in Kentucky's constitutions of 1799 and 1850), *TC*, III:1274, 1289, 1312; Tennessee 1796 Constitution, Bill of Rights, Sec. 1, *TC*, VI:3422; Ohio 1802 Constitution, Art. VIII, Sec. 1, *TC*, V:2909.

48. See Indiana 1816 Constitution, Art. I, Sec. 2 ("in such a manner as they may think proper"); Mississippi 1817 Constitution, Bill of Rights, Sec. 2 ("in such manner as they may think expedient"); Connecticut 1818 Constitution, Art. I, Sec. 2 ("in such manner as they may think expedient"); Maine 1819 Constitution, Bill of Rights, Sec. 2 ("when their safety and happiness require it"); Alabama 1819 Constitution, Bill of Rights, Sec. 2 ("as they may think expedient"); Missouri 1820 Constitution, Bill of Rights, Sec. 2 ("whenever it may be necessary to their safety and happiness"); Michigan 1835 Constitution, Art. I, Sec. 2 ("whenever the public good requires it"); Arkansas 1836 Constitution, Bill of Rights, Sec. 2 ("in such manner as they may think proper"); Texas (Republic of Texas) 1836 Constitution, Bill of Rights, Sec. 2 ("in such manner as they may think proper"); Florida 1838 Constitution, Bill of Rights, Sec. 2 ("in such manner as they may deem expedient"), *TC*, II:1058, IV:2033, I:537, III:1646, I:96, IV:2163, 1930, I:269, VI:3542, II:664.

49. See, for example, Kentucky 1890 Constitution, Bill of Rights, Sec. 4, *TC*, III:1316 ("the people" have "at all times" the right "to alter, reform, or abolish their government in such manner as they may deem proper"); Oklahoma 1912 Constitution, Sec. II-1 ("the people" have "the right to alter or reform the same whenever the public good may require it").

50. William Peden, ed., *Notes on the State of Virginia* (1955), 118 (Thomas Jefferson describing Virginia's 1776 constitution in 1785 as being formed "when we were new and unexperienced in the science of government"); James Madison, "On Nullification," 1835–1836, *ML*, IV:404 ("danger" to "fundamental principles"); *Federal Farmer, Letter No. 16*, Jan. 20, 1788, *DHRC*, XVII:343.

51. See John N. Shaeffer, "Public Consideration of the 1776 Pennsylvania Constitution," 98 *PMHB* (1974), 434–35 (describing calls for regular revision as allowing the people to preserve constitutional values); Adams, *Constitutions*, 142–43 ("The people had to insist on a permanent role and be ready to intervene in the political process before it came to a violent halt. This could be achieved by frequent elections and timely reforms of the constitutional system"); Tarr, *State Constitutions*, 73 (suggesting the first state constitutions "relied primarily on the state's citizenry for enforcement of constitutional limitations, with annual election of legislators the key element of this process").

On the concept of a "frequent recurrence to fundamental principles," see Gerald Stourzh, *Alexander Hamilton and the Idea of Republican Government* (1970), 9–37; J. G. A. Pocock, *The Machiavellian Moment: Florentine Political Thought and the Atlantic Republican Tradition* (1975), 462–552.

52. See Virginia 1776 Constitution, Bill of Rights, Sec. 15; North Carolina 1776 Constitution, Bill of Rights, Sec. 21; Pennsylvania 1776 Constitution, Bill of Rights, Sec. 14; Vermont 1777

Constitution, Bill of Rights, Sec. 16; Massachusetts 1780 Constitution, Bill of Rights, Art. 18; New Hampshire 1784 Constitution, Bill of Rights, Sec. 38, *TC*, VII:3814, V:2788, V:3083, VI:3741, III:1892, IV:2457.

53. "Demophilus" [George Bryan?], *The Genuine Principles of the Ancient Saxon, or English[,] Constitution*, 1776, in Hyneman and Lutz, *Political Writing*, I:363.

54. See, for example, Madison's emphasis on stability versus Jefferson's willingness to accept regular changes, in Adrienne Koch, *Jefferson and Madison: The Great Collaboration* (1950), 62–96; Merrill D. Peterson, *Jefferson and Madison and the Making of Constitutions* (1987), 11–12; Holmes, "Precommitment," 202–21; David A. J. Richards, *Foundations of American Constitutionalism* (1989), 131–37; John R. Vile, *The Constitutional Amending Process in American Political Thought* (1992), 59–78; Mayer, *Jefferson*, 295–319.

   On the idea of improvements in constitution-making, see, for example, John Marshall to Arthur Lee, Apr. 17, 1784, *JMP*, I:120 (expressing the view that new constitution-making might now proceed with "more experience & less prejudice" than that which marked America's first written constitutions); Peden, *Notes*, 118 (Thomas Jefferson describing Virginia's 1776 constitution in 1785 as being formed "when we were new and unexperienced in the science of government"); James Madison to Caleb Wallace, Aug. 23, 1785, *MP*, VIII:355 (advising Kentucky constitution-makers to insert revision provisions because they inevitably lacked "the same lights for framing a good establishment now" as they would "15 or 20 Years" later).

55. Tucker, "Conciliatory," I:624.

56. James Wilson, Nov. 24, 1787, Pennsylvania Convention, *DHRC*, II:361–62; George Nicholas, June 6, 1788, Virginia Convention, *DHRC*, IX:999.

57. Virginia's 1776 constitution declared that "a majority of the community" could alter the government "in such manner as shall be judged most conducive to the public weal" and Pennsylvania's 1790 constitution spoke of the people's right to alter their government "in such manner as they may think proper." Virginia 1776 Constitution, Bill of Rights, Sec. 3, Pennsylvania 1790 Constitution, Art. 9, Sec. 2, *TC*, VII:3813, V:3100. See also West, "Right to Rebel" I:418–19 (asserting that only "the major part" of a community could make or alter constitutions); James Wilson, "Of Government," *Lectures on Law* [1790–1791], *WW*, I:304 (identifying a "majority of the society" as entitled to exercise the "sovereign power" of the people); Ronald M. Peters, Jr., *The Massachusetts Constitution of 1780: A Social Compact* (1978), 189 (identifying "[m]ajority rule" in Massachusetts's 1780 constitution as "the most important procedural principle" before which "all other principles must give way"); Reid, "Governance," 437 (documenting acceptance on the Overland Trail "that majority vote could suspend constitutional provisions or even overturn the constitution"); Amar, *America's Constitution*, 12 (noting that supporters of the federal Constitution in Massachusetts clearly accepted the majority principle for constitutional change in the face of the state's 1780 constitution specifying a two-thirds vote for its alteration).

58. Of the eleven colonies that drafted their first constitutions after the Revolution, only Pennsylvania and Massachusetts explicitly provided for constitutional amendment. Pennsylvania's 1776 constitution had a mechanism for future conventions every seven years to consider amendments and Massachusetts's 1780 constitution called for a vote on holding another convention in 1795 as well as a process for constitutional amendments requiring approval by successive legislatures and the people. See Pennsylvania 1776 Constitution, Sec. 47; Massachusetts 1780 Constitution, Chap. 6, Art. X, Articles of Amendment, Art. IX, *TC*, V:3091–92, III:1911, 1913.

   Delaware simply provided that its constitution should not be changed without the consent of a supermajority of each branch of its legislature, Maryland provided that no constitutional changes could be made unless a bill to do so passed successive legislatures, and Georgia authorized the legislature to call a convention if a majority of the voters in most counties agreed. See Delaware 1776 Constitution, Art. 30; Maryland 1776 Constitution, Art. 59; Georgia 1777 Constitution, Art. 63, *TC*, I:568, III:1701, II:785; Dan Friedman, "Tracing the Lineage: Textual and Conceptual Similarities in the Revolutionary-Era State Declarations of Rights of Virginia, Maryland, and Delaware," 33 *Rutgers L. J.* (2002), 1011 (noting a "dichotomy" between Maryland's "alter or abolish" provision in its 1776 constitution and the procedural restrictions on constitutional change it sought to impose).

The remaining six state constitutions (Virginia, South Carolina, North Carolina, New Hampshire, New Jersey, and New York) lacked specific revision provisions.

59. See, for example, James Quayle Dealey, *Growth of American State Constitutions: From 1776 to the End of the Year 1914* (1915), 32–33 (noting that Americans assumed "the people had the inherent right to change their form of government," a right "apparently superior" to "methods of change contained in the constitution"); Walter F. Dodd, *The Revision and Amendment of State Constitutions* (1910), 42 (describing the invocation of the inherent authority of the people when Georgia ignored constitutionally specified procedures for revising its 1777 constitution in 1788); Richard Lynch Mumford, "Constitutional Development in the State of Delaware, 1776–1897," (Ph.D. diss., Univ. of Delaware, 1968), 111 (quoting reliance on "the uncontrollable authority of the people" to revise Delaware's 1776 constitution despite the absence of revision procedures); Amar, "Consent," 481 (suggesting constitutional revision provisions in the first state constitutions "simply added an additional mode of amendment without in any way limiting the people's pre-existing background right to alter or abolish"); Hulsebosch, *Empire*, 393n25 (observing that even without an amendment provision in New York's 1777 constitution, "everyone assumed it could be amended in another convention").

Constitutional conventions in New York (1801, 1821, 1845), Rhode Island (1824), Virginia (1829, 1850), South Carolina (1778, 1790), North Carolina (1835), New Hampshire (1784), and New Jersey (1844) were all held without a preexisting constitutional provision providing for their call by the legislature. See Dealey, *State Constitutions*, 41–49; Dodd, *Revision and Amendment*; Peter J. Galie, *The Constitutional History of New York: A Reference Guide* (1991), 6–13; Conley, *Democracy*, 202–13; A. E. Dick Howard, *Commentaries on the Constitution of Virginia* (2 vols., 1974), I:9–13. See also Wesley W. Horton, "Annotated Debates of the 1818 Constitutional Convention," 65 *Conn. Bar J.* (1991), SI-11–12 (noting that Connecticut's legislature, which retained its colonial charter after the Revolution, summoned a convention in 1818 during which delegates declared that "the people are the only true sovereigns" and have "a right to alter it").

60. Claudia L. Bushman, Harold B. Hancock, and Elizabeth Moyne Homsey, eds., *Proceedings of the House of Assembly of the Delaware State 1781–1792 and of the Constitutional Convention of 1792* (1988), 832–33 ("all government"); Friedman, "Tracing the Lineage," 953 ("establish a new").

61. "Curtius," "Alteration of the Constitution," and "Phileleutheros," "To the good people of the Delaware State," in *Delaware Gazette and General Advertiser*, Dec. 11, 1790 and July 30, 1791. See also Delaware 1776 Constitution, Bill of Rights, Sec. 5, *SD*, II:198, 204 (providing in Article 30 that "No part of this constitution shall be altered, changed, or diminished without the consent of five parts in seven of the assembly, and seven members of the legislative council"); Mumford, "Constitutional Development," 108 (arguing that the dual justifications for invoking Delaware's "alter or abolish" provision "would be difficult to document from the affairs of Delaware from 1776 to 1791").

62. See Dealey, *State Constitutions*, 33 (referring to revision of Delaware's and Pennsylvania's eighteenth-century constitutions), 49 (referring to revision of Georgia's constitution in the 1830s and Maryland's constitution in 1850); Parkinson, "Circumvention" (documenting efforts before the Civil War to circumvent state legislatures that resisted constitutional revision by means of holding "reform" or "circumvention" conventions); Friedman, "Tracing the Lineage," 1011 (noting that every constitutional convention held in Maryland "was plagued by assertions that it was called in contravention to the existing constitutional provisions").

63. James Wilson as well as other Federalist leaders recognized the implications of the people as America's sovereigns by describing them as having "reserved" a "Supreme Power." Wilson's "short definition" of a republic was a government in which "the Supreme Power resides in the body of the people." *Chisholm v. Georgia*, 2 U.S. 419 at 457 ("reserved" a "Supreme Power" and "short definition") (1793). See also *Vanhorne's Lessee v. Dorrance*, 28 F. Cas. 1012 at 1014 (C.C. Pa. 1795) (Justice William Patterson emphasizing that since American written constitutions

were "the work or will of the People themselves, in their original, sovereign, and unlimited capacity" only the people could revoke or alter them); Gordon S. Wood, "The Political Ideology of the Founders," in Neil L. York, ed., *Toward a More Perfect Union: Six Essays on the Constitution* (1988), 23 (asserting that Federalists considered sovereignty "literally remaining with the people").

64. Thomas Jefferson to Thomas Nelson, May 16, 1776, *JP*, I:292; John Adams to William Cushing, June 9, 1776; John Adams to John Penn, Mar. 27, 1776, *AP*, IV:245 ("the Lives"), 79 ("when the greatest"). See also George Washington to John Augustine Washington, May 31[–June 4], 1776, *WP(RWS)* IV:412 (asserting that constitution-making "requires infinite care, & unbounded attention; for if the foundation is badly laid the superstructure must be bad"); Francis Lightfoot Lee to Landon Carter, Nov. 9, 1776, *LDC*, V:463 (noting that *Constitutions* employ every pen"); "Letter from William Hooper, Delegate from North Carolina to the Continental Congress, to the Congress at Halifax," Oct. 26, 1776, *CRNC*, X:866 (suggesting that North Carolina's first constitution would determine whether "posterity are to be happy or miserable").

65. John Adams to Horatio Gates, Mar. 23, 1776, *AP*, IV:59; *Thoughts on Government*, *AP*, IV:87, 91, 92. Adams's call for "balance" in government – represented by dual-bodied legislatures – was not a natural or self-evident proposition in constitution-making. Just as "paper money" policies acquired an unnecessarily pejorative connotation at the hands of their opponents, uni-cameral legislatures received similar castigation from Adams, Benjamin Rush, and others. See, for example, Nash, *Unknown*, 277–80.

66. John Adams to Abigail Adams, July 10, 1776, *LDC*, IV:423. See also Samuel Adams to Benjamin Kent, July 27, 1776, *SAW*, III:305 (surprised at how fast "Democracy" was supplanting an "Aristocratick Spirit").

67. See, for example, Lutz, *Origins*, 99 (calling the first state constitution-making "legislative activities" because it failed to use special conventions followed by popular ratification); Eugene R. Sheridan and John M. Murrin, eds., *Congress at Princeton: Being the Letters of Charles Thomson to Hannah Thomson, June–October, 1783* (1985), xxxiv (asserting that Massachusetts's 1780 constitution demonstrated that "a proper constitution" required a constitutional convention followed by popular ratification); Rakove, *Meanings*, 129 (claiming that most state constitutions before 1780 "rested on no authority greater than ordinary acts of legislation").

68. Gordon S. Wood, "Foreword: State Constitution-Making in the American Revolution," 24 *Rutgers L. J.* (1993), 921 ("confusion"); John V. Orth, "'Fundamental Principles' in North Carolina Constitutional History," 69 *N.C. L. Rev.* (1991), 1358 ("unfamiliarity"); Jack N. Rakove, "The Super-Legality of the Constitution, or, a Federalist Critique of Bruce Ackerman's Neo-Federalism," 108 *Yale L. J.* (1999), 1940 ("hasty experiment" and "fully learned").

69. Rakove, "Super-Legality," 1944 (" were not truly"); Rakove, "Thinking" 13 ("true constitution"). See also Bruce Ackerman, *We the People: Transformations* (1998), 38 (identifying legislatures as "the source of the existing state constitutions" created without special conventions and ratification); Amar, *America's Constitution*, 287 (state constitutions established without "some dramatically special vote" by the people were arguably "little more than fancy statutes").

70. For calls to create a constitution with a constitutional convention, see Return of Concord, Oct. 22, 1776, Return of Acton, Nov. 4, 1776, "Resolution of Worcester County Towns," Nov. 26, 1776, in Handlin, *Popular Sources*, 152–53, 157–58, 164–66, and for requests for popular ratification, see "Instructions to the Delegates from Mecklenburg and Orange Counties to the Provincial Congress at Halifax in November, 1776," *CRNC*, X:870d; "The respectful Address of the Mechanicks in Union, for the City and County of New-York," [May, 1776], *AA* (4th Ser.), VI:895.

71. See Morgan, *Inventing*, 231 (describing the dissolution of colonial assemblies and their resurrection in America as "popular congresses or conventions" exercising the "'real majesty' of the people by creating fundamental constitutions for new governments").

72. See Kruman, *State Constitution Making*, 1–33; Christian G. Fritz, "Alternative Visions of American Constitutionalism: Popular Sovereignty and the Early American Constitutional Debate," 24 *Hastings Const. L. Q.* (1997), 322–29.

73. South Carolina 1776 Constitution, Preamble, *TC*, VI:3243; Final Draft of the Virginia Declaration of Rights, [June 12, 1776], *GMP*, I:287; The Constitution as Adopted by the Convention, June 29, 1776, *JP*, I:379; New Jersey 1776 Constitution, Preamble, *TC*, V:2594. See also New Hampshire 1776 Constitution, Preamble, *TC*, IV:2451; Francis Hopkinson to Samuel Tucker?, July 23, 1776, *LDC*, IV:524 (noting that New Jersey's first constitution affirmed that "the source of all Government originates with the People at large").

    An early draft of Maryland's Declaration of Rights described "all government" originating "from the people." See Maryland 1776 Constitution, Bill of Rights, Sec. 1, Oct. 31, 1776, Papenfuse and Stiverson, *Decisive*. In September, Delaware's bill of rights noted that "the People of this State have the sole exclusive and inherent Right of government." See Delaware 1776 Constitution, Bill of Rights, Secs. 1 and 4, *SD*, II:197.

    Pennsylvania's constitution-makers followed Virginia in describing themselves as "the representatives of the freemen of Pennsylvania, in general convention met, for the express purpose" of framing a government who were entitled to promulgate the constitution by virtue of the "authority vested" by their constituents. See Pennsylvania 1776 Constitution, Preamble, *TC*, V:3082. North Carolina's constitution-makers declared that "all political power is vested in and derived from the people only." See North Carolina 1776 Constitution, Bill of Rights, Art. I, *TC*, V:2787.

    Members of Georgia's convention, "the representatives of the people, from whom all power originates" promulgated a constitution by virtue of the power delegated by them by the people. See Georgia 1777 Constitution, Preamble, *TC*, II:778. New York's 1777 constitution-makers repeatedly asserted they were acting "in the name and by the authority of the good people of this State." See New York 1777 Constitution, *TC*, V:2628, 2631, 2632, 2633, 2635, 2636–37.

74. John Rutledge to Henry Laurens, Mar. 8, 1778, *LP*, XII:528; John Lewis Gervais to Henry Laurens, Mar. 16, 1778, *LP*, XIII:4.

75. "Journal of the Council of Safety," Aug. 9, 1776, *CRNC*, X:696. See generally Adams, *Constitutions*, 68–93; Kruman, *State Constitution Making*, 20 (observing the first state constitution-makers "assumed" their work required "special popular sanction" and hence "generally called for special elections" before drafting constitutions); Donald S. Lutz, "State Constitution-Making, Through 1781," in Jack P. Greene and J. R. Pole, eds., *A Companion to the American Revolution* (2000), 279 (asserting that virtually all state constitutions between 1775 and 1781 were formed "usually after an election where it was made clear that the new legislature would also write a new constitution").

    On Delaware, see Mumford, "Constitutional Development," 51; on Pennsylvania, see Selsam, *Pennsylvania Constitution*; Shaeffer, "Public Consideration," 415–37; on Maryland, see *Proceedings of the Convention of the Province of Maryland, Held at the City of Annapolis, in 1774, 1775, & 1776* (Baltimore & Annapolis, 1836), 184; on Georgia, see Albert Berry Saye, *A Constitutional History of Georgia, 1732–1945* (1948), 96–99; on New York, see "Report of the Committee on the Resolution of the Continental Congress of the 15th of May relating to a new form of Government," *AA* (4th Ser.), 1338 (suggesting "the right of framing, creating, or remodelling Civil Government is and ought to be in the People"), Lincoln, *Constitutional History*, I:481–83, 178–83, Galie, *Ordered Liberty*, 36–37, Hulsebosch, *Empire*, 171; on Massachusetts, see Handlin, *Popular Sources*, Morison, "Struggle," 353–61; on New Hampshire, see New Hampshire 1776 Constitution, Preamble, *TC*, IV:2451–53; Susan E. Marshall, *The New Hampshire State Constitution: A Reference Guide* (2004), 6 (even without ratification the state's first constitution was created "by the body they had elected to set up a government"); and on New Jersey, see Gerlach, "Power to the People," 29, 31; Erdman, *New Jersey*, 24.

76. On Virginia, see "Resolutions of the Virginia Convention Calling for Independence," *JP*, I:291. See also W. F. Dunaway, Jr., "The Virginia Conventions of the Revolution," 10 *Va. L .Reg.* (1904), 567–86; J. R. Pole, "Representation and Authority in Virginia from the Revolution to Reform," 24 *Journal of Southern History* (1958), 23–24; Editorial Note, Independence and Constitution of Virginia, *MP*, I:175–76.

    On South Carolina, George Edward Frakes, *Laboratory for Liberty: The South Carolina Legislative Committee System, 1719–1776* (1970), 127 (identifying the Second Provincial Congress, which adopted South Carolina's 1776 constitution, as the only "form of representative government" and "the ultimate authority in the province"); Jerome J. Nadelhaft, *The Disorders of War: The Revolution in South Carolina* (1981), 34 (quoting a member of the legislative committee drafting South Carolina's constitution urging fellow legislators to explain "the indispensable necessity" for the constitution).

If legislators were elected with the authority of the people to declare independence in the name of the people, it begged the question of why they would not also have the authority to promulgate constitutions in the name of the people.

77. For the recognition of the people's sovereignty in Connecticut and Rhode Island, the two states that retained their colonial charters, see Adams, *Constitutions*, 66–68; Lovejoy, *Rhode Island*, 191–94; Charles S. Grant, *Democracy in the Connecticut Frontier Town of Kent* (1961), 128–40; Richard J. Purcell, *Connecticut in Transition: 1775–1818* (1963), 113–45.

Moreover, the debates over constitution-making in Massachusetts clearly reveal agreement on the people's sovereignty. See Handlin, *Popular Sources*; Peters, *Massachusetts Constitution*, 189 (analyzing the state's 1780 constitution as resting on the "pre-eminence" of the people's sovereignty).

78. Autobiography of John Adams, *ADA*, III:352. See also Thomas Burke to Henry Laurens, Apr. 28, 1778, *LP*, XIII:214 (defining a constitution as "a fixed rule of Conduct for all the powers of the State, which cannot be dispensed with, or Deviated from, unless the Collective Body of the People give special authority for that purpose").

79. Of the states forming the American union before the federal Constitution, only Massachusetts (1780) and New Hampshire (1784) were drafted by a convention and submitted for ratification. See Lutz, *Origins*, 105.

On the belated pattern of using constitutional conventions followed by formal popular ratification, see Albert L. Sturm, "The Development of American State Constitutions," 12 *Publius* (1982), 57–98. See also Lutz, *Popular Consent*, 67–68 (constitution-making by conventions followed by ratification deemed "an isolated instance" well into the nineteenth century).

80. See Proceedings of the Maryland Constitutional Convention of 1776, in Papenfuse and Stiverson, *Decisive*, Sept. 17, 1776; Shaeffer, "Public Consideration," 415–37.

81. For Jefferson's and Madison's later objections, see Thomas Jefferson to James Madison, Dec. 8, 1784, in James Morton Smith, ed., *The Republic of Letters: The Correspondence between Thomas Jefferson and James Madison, 1776–1826* (3 vols., 1995), I:354 (describing 1776 constitution as "an *ordinance*"); Peden, *Notes*, 125 (Jefferson asserting in 1785 that to make a legitimate constitution "the people must delegate persons with special powers"); "Notes for a Speech Favoring Revision of the Virginia Constitution of 1776," [June 14 or 21, 1784], *MP*, VIII:77 (Madison suggesting convention of 1776 lacked "due power from [the] people").

For Jefferson's correspondence at the time of Virginia's first constitution-making, see Thomas Jefferson to Thomas Nelson, May 16, 1776, Jefferson to George Wythe, [June? 1776], Jefferson to Edmund Pendleton, Aug. 13 and 26, 1776, *JP*, I:292–93, 410, 491–94, 503–506. Although Edmund Randolph reported that Jefferson questioned the authority of Virginia's convention to form a permanent constitution at the time, it seems more likely that such misgivings stemmed from substantive objections to the constitution drafted. See [Edmund Randolph], "Edmund Randolph's Essay on the Revolutionary History of Virginia, 1774–1782," repr. in 44 *Virginia Magazine of History and Biography* (1936), 43; Brant, *Madison*, I:252–56.

82. The judicial decision of 1802 was only belatedly reported in 1827. See *State v. Parkhurst*, 9 N.J.L. 427, 443 (1827); *Memorial, of the Convention of Delegates Assembled at Trenton on the 22nd of August 1827, on the Subject of Revising and Amending the Constitution of New Jersey* (*RSUS*, New Jersey, Reel 1, Unit 4), 3–4; Maxine N. Lurie, "Envisioning a Republic: New Jersey's 1776 Constitution and Oath of Office," 119 *New Jersey History* (2001), 3.

83. The account of the events at Boston and New York draws on "General Orders," Mar. 3, 1776, George Washington to Jonathan Trumbull, Sr., Mar. 14, 1776, George Washington to John Augustine Washington, Mar. 31, 1776, *WP(RWS)*, III:401, 471, 567; George Washington to Joseph Reed, Apr. 1, 1776, *WP(RWS)*, IV:11; George Washington to John Hancock, Sept. 16 and

2[5], 1776, *WP(RWS)*, VI:313, 394; William Heath, *Memoirs of Major General Heath* (Boston, 1798, repr. 1908), 70; Christopher Ward, *The War of the Revolution*, (2 vols., 1952), I:125–34, 202–59; David Hackett Fischer, *Washington's Crossing*, (2004), 7–12, 81–114.

84. For the role of mobs and public participation in the American Revolution, see Wood, "Mobs," 635–42; Barbara Clark Smith, "Food Rioters and the American Revolution," 51 *WMQ* (1994), 3–38; Reid, "Defensive Rage," 1043–91.

85. See Jesse Lemisch, "Jack Tar in the Streets: Merchant Seamen in the Politics of Revolutionary America," 25 *WMQ* (1968), 371–407; Maier, "Popular Uprisings," 3–35; Merrill Jensen, "The American People and the American Revolution," 57 *JAH* (1970), 5–35; Nash, *Unknown*, 199 (asserting the Revolution "accustomed ordinary people to think about themselves as agents of history rather than the passive recipients of whatever history had in mind for them").

86. Gouverneur Morris to Mr. Penn, May 20, 1774, *AA* (4th Ser.), I:343 ("mob"). See also Elbridge Gerry to the Massachusetts Delegates in Congress, June 4, 1775, in James T. Austin, *The Life of Elbridge Gerry* (2 vols., Boston, 1828, repr. 1970), I:78 (describing the people as "fully possessed of their dignity" as the collective sovereign and wondering how a "necessary" subordination of the people might be achieved). For the dismay that colonial elites felt about sharing power with humbler sorts during and after the Revolution, see Merrill Jensen, *The Founding of a Nation: A History of the American Revolution, 1763–1776* (1968), 628–30, 697–704; Maier, *Resistance*, 3–26; Jerome J. Nadelhaft, "'The Snarls of Invidious Animals,' The Democratization of Revolutionary South Carolina," in Ronald Hoffman and Peter J. Albert, ed., *Sovereign States in an Age of Uncertainty* (1981), 62–94; Michael A. McDonnell, "A World Turned 'Topsy Turvy': Robert Munford, *The Patriots*, and the Crisis of the Revolution in Virginia," 61 *WMQ* (2004), 235–70.

87. See Jackson Turner Main, "Government by the People, the American Revolution and the Democratization of the Legislatures," 23 *WMQ* (1966), 391–407; Hoffman, *Spirit*, 138–51; Paul A. Gilje, *The Road to Mobocracy: Popular Disorder in New York City, 1763–1834* (1987), 39–68; Joyce Appleby, "The Radical Recreation of the American Republic," 51 *WMQ* (1994), 679–83; Brendan McConville, *These Daring Disturbers of the Public Peace: The Struggle for Property and Power in Early New Jersey* (1999), 137–201.

88. John Adams to James Sullivan, May 26, 1776, *AP*, IV:208; "Letter from William Hooper, Delegate from North Carolina to the Continental Congress, to the Congress at Halifax," Oct. 26, 1776, *CRNC*, X:867. See also Larry R. Gerlach, ed., *New Jersey in the American Revolution, 1763– 1783: A Documentary History* (1975), 431 (noting "An Elector" in 1778 describing both branches of New Jersey's legislature as "creatures of the people"). For Hooper, see Ganyard, *Emergence*, 64, 71, 74–77.

89. General Nathanael Greene to Samuel Ward, Dec. 31, 1775, *AA* (4th Ser.), IV:483; Alexander Hamilton to John Jay, Nov. 26, 1775, *HP*, I:176–77. But see Forrest McDonald, *E. Pluribus Unum: The Formation of the American Republic, 1776–1790* (1965), 1 (asserting that American revolutionaries had to answer: "is man rational and virtuous or is he evil, is he to be trusted or not?").

   Varying levels of faith in the capacity of the people did not cause Americans to question, much less repudiate, their commitment to the idea that in America the people were the collective sovereign. Just who made up "the people" was a changing and shifting understanding that evolved over time. That political question was different from the question of constitutionalism explored in this book: that however they came be defined, "the people" were America's sovereign with the authority to make, alter, or abolish their constitutions.

90. For the communal connotation of "the people" for eighteenth-century Americans, see Clinton Rossiter, *Seedtime of the Republic: The Origin of the American Tradition of Political Liberty* (1953); James Madison, "Speech in the House of Representatives," June 8, 1789, *MP*, XII:203– 204 (describing rights in state bill of rights "which are exercised by the people" either in "forming and establishing" government or "retained" by them after the creation of government).

91. Josiah Quincy, Jr., *Observations on the Act of Parliament Commonly Called the Boston-Port Bill; with Thoughts on Civil Society and Standing Armies* (Boston, 1774), 30; Thomas Jefferson to Edmund Pendleton, Aug. 26, 1776, "Additional Instructions from the Inhabitants of Albemarle,"

[ca. Sept.–Oct. 1776], *JP*, I:504, VI:292; Anonymous, "The People the Best Governors: Or a Plan of Government Founded on the Just Principles of Natural Freedom," 1776, in Hyneman and Lutz, *Political Writing*, I:391. See also John Sullivan to Meshech Weare, Dec. 12, 1775, Hammond, *Letters of John Sullivan*, I:145 (asserting that the people could not have "any Thing but the true End of Government (viz their own Good) in View, unless we suppose them Idiots, or self-Murderors").

On Young, see Edes, "Memoir," 2–54; David Freeman Hawke, "Dr. Thomas Young – 'Eternal Fisher in Troubled Waters,'" 54 *New York Historical Society Quarterly* (1970), 7–29; Maier, "Reason," 229–49.

92. Even before the Revolution, colonial Americans sought to discover, express, and render government responsive to the will of the people. See, for example, Jack P. Greene, *The Quest for Power: The Lower Houses of Assembly in the Southern Royal Colonies, 1689–1776* (1963); Michael Kammen, *Deputyes & Libertyes: The Origins of Representative Government in Colonial America* (1969); Gary B. Nash, *The Urban Crucible: Social Change, Political Consciousness, and the Origins of the American Revolution* (1979); *Boston Gazette and Country Journal*, July 25, 1768 (anonymous writer asserting that "[h]owever meanly" some thought about the people, "the power or Strength of every FREE Country depends entirely upon the Populace").

93. Merrill and Wilentz, *Key of Liberty*, 137. See also Thomas Paine, *Rights of Man* (1791), in Foner, *Writings of Thomas Paine*, I:375 ("Every man is a proprietor in government and considers it a necessary part of his business to understand"); Benjamin Austin, *Constitutional Republicanism, in Opposition to Fallacious Federalism* (Boston, 1803), 173 (identifying "a dignity attached to every man's station in society, which should render him competent to judge on the utility of public measures"); Ruth Bogin, *Abraham Clark and the Quest for Equality in the Revolutionary Era, 1774–1794* (1982); Sharp, *Politics*, 53–91.

94. Anonymous, *To the People of Maine: Is It for the Interest of the District of Maine to Become a Separate State?* (n.p., 1816), 3. See also Rakove, "Structure," 261–94 (suggesting that broader participation of the people accompanied an acknowledgment of the legitimacy of public opinion); Wood, *Radicalism*, 364 (noting that "newly enlarged and democratized public opinion" was central to American life by the early nineteenth century).

95. William Williams to Jabez Huntington, Sept. 30, 1776, *LDC*, V:268 ("unhappy Truth"); Alexander Hamilton to Gouverneur Morris, May 19, 1777, *HP*, I:255; George Washington to John Hancock, Sept. 2[5], 1776, *WP(RWS)*, VI:394. On the importance of disinterestedness to leaders of the Revolution, see Wood, "Interests," 69–109.

96. Landon Carter to George Washington, May 9, 1776, *WP(RWS)*, IV:237 ("ignorant Creatures"), 238 ("premises"); Jack P. Greene, ed., *The Diary of Colonel Landon Carter of Sabine Hall, 1752–1778* (2 vols., 1965), II:795 (entry for Feb. 12, 1774) ("Idiots").

97. Henry Laurens to John Laurens, Jan. 22, 1775, *LP*, X:39; John Adams, "Autobiography," *ADA*, III:326 ("Wretch" to "repent"). See also Henry Laurens to John Lewis Gervais, Jan. 30, 1778, *LP*, XII: 225 (complaining, as president of the Continental Congress, of "running whole days into weeds of unmatured conversations from a want of able Members"); George Mason, "Remarks on the Proposed Bill for Regulating the Elections of the Members of the General Assembly," [ca. June 1, 1780], *GMP*, II:630 (describing "ignorant or obscure" representatives filling the legislature instead of "Men of Modesty & Merit").

98. John Adams to Mercy Otis Warren, Apr. 16, 1776, *AP*, IV:124; John Adams to Zabdiel Adams, June 21, 1776; John Adams to Abigail Adams, July 3, 1776, *AFC*, II:21, 28.

99. Edward Rutledge to John Jay, Nov. 24, 1776, Morris, *Jay Papers*, I:322 ("Popular Spirit"); Charles Carroll of Carrollton to Charles Carroll of Annapolis, Aug. 20, 1776, Charles Carroll of Carrollton Papers, MdHS ("selfish men"); Landon Carter to George Washington, May 9, 1776, *WP(RWS)* IV:236 ("a form of"); Charles Carroll of Carrollton to Charles Carroll of Annapolis, Aug. 23, 1776, Charles Carroll of Carrollton Papers, MdHS ("levelling" and "desperate & wicked"); John Eliot to Jeremy Belknap, Jan. 12, 1777 in "The Belknap Papers," *Collections of the Massachusetts Historical Society* (6th Ser.) (Boston, 1891), IV:104 (quoting Otis's response when asked about "present measures & leaders").

100. George Washington to Richard Henry Lee, Aug. 29, 1775, *WP(RWS)*, I:372 ("stupidity"); Richard Bridgman, "Jefferson's Farmer Before Jefferson," 14 *American Quarterly* (1962), 576 ("grazing multitude"); James Madison to William Bradford, Jan. 20, 1775, *MP*, I:135; John Adams to Joseph Hawley, Nov. 25, 1775, *AP*, III:316 ("Gentlemen" and "the Common People"); John Adams, *Defense of the Constitutions*, *AW*, VI:185 ("simplemen"); John Adams to Mercy Otis Warren, Jan. 8, 1776, John Adams to Jonathan Sewall, Feb. 1760, John Adams to Joseph Hawley, Aug. 25, 1776, *AP*, III:398 ("among all orders"), I:41("common Herd"), IV:496 ("Merit, Virtue"); John Adams to James Warren, Apr. 22, 1776, *LDC*, III:570 ("a Decency"). See also Parsons, *Essex*, I:491 (claiming that most of those "possessed of wisdom, learning, and a firmness and consistency of character" would be found among "gentlemen of education, fortune and leisure").

101. John Adams to Abigail Adams, July 3, 1776, *AFC*, II:28.

102. Thomas Jefferson to Richard Price, Feb. 1, 1785, *JP*, VII:630 ("mainspring"); Thomas Jefferson to Diodati, Aug. 3, 1789, *JP*, XV:326 ("good sense"); Peden, *Notes*, 148 ("safe depositories"), 146 ("the rubbish"); Thomas Jefferson to Edmund Pendleton, Aug. 26, 1776, *JP*, I:503–504 ("wisest men" to "wise men"). In later life Jefferson continued to divide the people "into two classes – the laboring and the learned." Thomas Jefferson to Peter Carr, Sept. 7, 1814, *JW(L)*, XIX:213 ("into two classes").

103. See Remini, *Jackson*, 338–43; Appleby, *Inheriting*, 26–55; Wilentz, *Democracy*. See also Robert H. Wiebe, *Self-Rule: A Cultural History of American Democracy* (1995), 28 (describing the gradual emergence of a concept of "atomized sovereignty" that displaced a communal view of the people).

104. See, for example, Sharp, *Politics*, 136 (asserting that late eighteenth-century "Republican leaders still embraced a system of representation that emphasized deference rather than democracy"); Wood, *Radicalism*, 106 (observing that postrevolutionary politics "retained a traditional patrician bias in regard to officeholding"); Wiebe, *Self-Rule*, 36 ("Champions of the state governments did not ask how the people might exercise greater power but which officials would exercise it best in the name of the people").

105. See Gordon S. Wood, "The Trials and Tribulations of Thomas Jefferson," in Peter S. Onuf, ed., *Jeffersonian Legacies* (1993), 407 (identifying Jefferson's assumption that "a natural aristocracy would lead the country"); Richard D. Brown, *The Strength of a People: The Idea of an Informed Citizenry in America, 1650–1870* (1996), 77 (analyzing Jefferson's educational plan for Virginia as intended "to unite mass popular education with the perpetuation of elite, albeit enlightened, rule"); Thomas Jefferson to John Adams, Oct. 28, 1813, Cappon, *Adams-Jefferson Letters*, 388 (proclaiming "natural aristocracy" as "the most precious gift" for "the instruction . . . and government of society").

106. See Geoffrey Seed, *James Wilson* (1978), 73 (concluding that Wilson did not conceive of a political system "in which the people determined the policy of the state").

107. Thomas Young, "To the Inhabitants of Vermont, a Free and Independent State, bounding on the River Connecticut and Lake Champlain," Apr. 11, 1777, *RSV*, I:395.

108. James Sullivan to Elbridge Gerry, May 6, 1776, partially repr. in *AP*, IV:212–13n2; John Adams to James Sullivan, May 26, 1776; John Adams to John Lowell, June 12, 1776; John Adams to John Winthrop, June 23, 1776, *AP*, IV:210 ("very few men"), 212 ("destroy" to "common Levell"), 250 ("afloat" and "Spirit of Levelling"), 332 ("Rage for Innovation"); John Adams to James Warren, July 7, 1777, *LDC*, VII:308 ("Fountain of Corruption").

109. Josiah Quincy to John Adams, June 13, 1776, *AP*, IV:305; John Adams to Joseph Hawley, Aug. 25, 1776, *AP*, IV:495 ("Men of Learning"); John Adams, *Defense of the Constitutions of America* (3 vols., 1787–88), *AW*, VI:185 ("liberal education" and "erudition"). See also John Adams to Mercy Otis Warren, Jan. 8, 1776, *AP*, III:398 (asserting that the people's virtue was shaped by the structure of government).

110. While American revolutionaries favored republics, they were wary of democracies. See Wiecek, *Guarantee Clause*, 65 (suggesting that republicanism "did not imply 'democracy' in the eighteenth-century sense to Madison"); Wood, *Creation*, 222 (asserting that for "most

constitution-makers in 1776, republicanism was not equated with democracy"); Wiebe, *Self-Rule*, 34 ("Except in the first flush of revolution, when enthusiasm for legislative power ran at its highest, to call the entire government a democracy condemned it").

111. Landon Carter to George Washington, May 9, 1776, *WP(RWS)*, IV:237; [Rush], *Observations*, 15. See also Rodgers, *Contested Truths*, 109 (observing that interpreting the vocabulary of a sovereign people left Americans to "struggle with words" known "to be treacherously unstable and yet too vitally needed simply to abandon"); Powell, *Languages of Power*, 22 (describing "a central feature" of talk about sovereignty during 1791 and 1818 as involving concepts "as contested and confusing as they were common in American political debate"); Ferguson, *Reading*, 179 (concluding that the "new language of the people heightened the dilemma as well as the stakes in how the people themselves might be seen").

112. Benjamin Hichborn, *Oration Delivered at Boston, March 5th, 1777*, in Niles, *Principles*, 47.

113. Vermont 1777 Constitution, Bill of Rights, Arts. 4, 5, and 6, *TC*, IV:3740. On constitution-making in Vermont, see Jones, *Vermont*; Williamson, *Vermont*; Hendricks, "New Look," 136–40; Onuf, "State-Making," 797–815; Aichele, "Vermont Constitution," 166–90; William C. Hill, *The Vermont State Constitution: A Reference Guide* (1992), 1–11.

114. "The Provisional Constitution of Frankland," 1 *American Historical Magazine* (1896), 51 ("thirteen Constitutions" and "the instructions"), 52 ("Republican" to "the rulers"); "Frankland Constitution," 53 ("look in"). Electors of delegates to Frankland's constitutional convention were urged "to consider maturely the nature of free and republican governments, and the constitutions of the thirteen original states." See "Resolutions of August Session, General Assembly, State of Frankland," 1785 repr. in *Massachusetts Centinel*, Jan. 21, 1786. See also Williams, *Lost State*, 30 (noting the presence of constitutional compilations).

For the text of the initial provisional Franklin constitution, closely modeled on North Carolina's 1776 constitution, see Williams, *Lost State*, 339–47.

115. Compare Sec. 5, "Frankland Constitution," 55–56 with Vermont 1777 Constitution, Sec. 12, *TC*, IV:3744; Sec. 38, "Frankland Constitution," 62. See also Secs. 4, 20–21, 22, 42, "Frankland Constitution," 55, 58–59, 62.

116. Preface, Secs. 11, 22, 28, 45, "Frankland Constitution," 51–53, 57, 59, 60, 62–63. See also Amar, *Bill of Rights*, 131 (identifying an eighteenth-century belief that bills of rights could "crystallize" constitutional principles "so that they could be memorized and internalized – much like Scripture – by ordinary citizens").

CHAPTER 3. GRASSROOTS SELF-GOVERNMENT

1. The account of Congress's activities during the fall of 1775 draws on Richard Henry Lee to Catherine Macaulay, Nov. 29, 1775, James Curtis Ballagh, ed., *The Letters of Richard Henry Lee* (1911), I:160; John Adams to James Warren, Oct. 21, 1775, *LDC*, II:226; Connecticut Delegates' Proposed Resolution, [Oct. 17, 1775], *LDC*, II:196; Oct. 17, 1775, *JCC*, III:297; Oct. 18, 1775, *JCC*, III:298; Nov. 3, 1775, *JCC*, III:319; "Memorial of Proprietors of Transylvania to Congress," Sept. 25, 1775, *AA* (4th Ser.), V:554; James Hogg to Richard Henderson, [Dec.] 1775, *AA* (4th Ser.), IV:544–45; John Adams, diary entry, Oct 18, 1775, *ADA*, II:218; Silas Deane to James Hogg, Nov. 2, 1775, *AA*(4th Ser.), IV:556–58; Silas Deane to James Hogg, Nov. 2, 1775, *LDC*, II:288; James Hogg to Silas Deane, Nov. 16, 1775, in Correspondence of Silas Deane, in *Collections of the Connecticut Historical Society* (Hartford, CT, 1870), II:319.

   Adams's *Thoughts on Government* was published in the spring of 1776, but earlier versions were circulating in private letters before then, including a "Sketch" that Adams sent to Richard Henry Lee on Nov. 15, 1775. See *AP*, III:307, IV:65.

   On the Wyoming controversy, see Louise Welles Murray, *A History of Old Tioga Point and Early Athens Pennsylvania* (1908), 221–99; Julian P. Boyd, "Attempts to Form New States in New York and Pennsylvania, 1786–1796," 12 *Quarterly Journal of the New York State Historical Association* (1931), 257–70; Robert J. Taylor, "Trial at Trenton," 26 *WMQ* (1969), 521–47.

2. Competitors for land – whether large speculators or modest settlers – routinely accused one another of illegitimacy. See, for example, George Washington to James Duane, Sept. 7, 1783,

GWW, XXVII:133 (lamenting the prospect of "a wide extended Country" being "over run with Land Jobbers, Speculators, and Monopolisers"); Virginia Delegates to Benjamin Harrison, Nov. 1, 1783, *LMC*, VII:365 (complaining of settlements by "lawless banditii and adventurers"); Petition of Zebulon Butler and Others to the Continental Congress, May 1, 1784, Robert J. Taylor, ed., *The Susquehannah Company Papers* (11 vols., 1930–1971), VII:402–403 (complaining of "a Banditti of men . . . who have no right or Claim to any Lands here"); Andrew R. L. Cayton, *The Frontier Republic: Ideology and Politics in the Ohio Country, 1780–1825* (1986), 7 (noting the perception that settlers and determinists resisted governance and "constituted a dangerous challenge to the social order of the young republic").

Some scholars dismiss the arguments of the postrevolutionary determinist movements as the "pretensions of unruly citizens" and "frontier separatists and other malcontents" threatening America's "common cause" by their "treasonable tendencies." See, for example, Onuf, *Origins*, xv ("pretensions"), xvi ("frontier separatists"), 3 ("common cause"), 37 ("treasonable tendencies"). Focusing on the jurisdictional disputes over territory that hampered the establishment of a union of sovereign states makes the territorial claims of determinists seem questionable if not baseless. See Peter S. Onuf, *Statehood and Union: A History of the Northwest Ordinance* (1987), 28–29 (asserting that determinist movements simply "represented efforts to wrest control of public lands from particular states"); Onuf, *Origins*, 38 (dismissing the invocation of the people's sovereignty as "conventional rhetorical flourishes"), 42 (describing the focus on constitutionalism in the debate over creating new western states as "fundamentally misleading").

3. James Madison to Benjamin Harrison, Nov. 15, 1782, *MP*, V:276; William Irvine to George Washington, Apr. 20, 1782, C. W. Butterfield, ed., *Washington-Irvine Correspondence* (Madison, WI, 1882), 109; Hugh Williamson to Alexander Martin, Nov. 18, 1782, *LMC*, VI:545 ("Spirit"); William Parker Cutler and Julia Perkins Cutler, eds., *Life, Journals, and Correspondence of Rev. Manasseh Cutler, LL.D.* (2 vols., Cincinnati, OH, 1888, repr. 1987), I:149 ("forming a *new* state"), 159 ("form a distinct" to "of America"). For Washington's endorsement, see George Washington to the President of Congress, June 17, 1783, *GWW*, XXVII: 17 (offering his views of "the general benefits of the location and Settlement now proposed"). On the Ohio Company, see Cayton, *Frontier Republic*, 12–32.

For other statehood efforts, see "The Memorial of the Inhabitants of the Country West of the Allegheny Mountains," repr. in Boyd Crumrine, ed., *History of Washington County, Pennsylvania, With Biographical Sketches of Many of its Pioneers and Prominent Men* (Philadelphia, 1882), 187–88; John Dodge to the Continental Congress, June 22, 1784, in Clarence Walworth Alvord, ed., *Kaskaskia Records, 1778–1790* (Collections of the Illinois State Historical Library, 1909), V:365 (asking to be placed "in the same condition as that of our fellow-citizens so that we may form a new state" and receive "the same right of power, liberty, and independence" of "other states").

4. Quoted in A. W. Putnam, *History of Middle Tennessee; Or, Life and Times of Gen. James Robertson* (Nashville, TN, 1859, repr. 1971), 25. On the Regulator movement, see Powell, *Regulators*, xxi-xxvi; Lee, *Crowds*, 13–96; Kars, *Breaking*, see especially 77–129 for the religious context of the Regulation. See also Rhys Isaac, *The Transformation of Virginia, 1740–1790* (1982), 260–69. On the Watauga Association and settlement, see J. G. M. Ramsey, *The Annals of Tennessee to the End of the Eighteenth Century; Comprising its Settlement, as the Watauga Association, From 1769 to 1777* (Charleston, NC, 1853, repr. 1999), 133–40; Albert V. Goodpasture, "The Watauga Association," 3 *American Historical Magazine* (1898), 103–20; John Preston Arthur, *A History of Watauga County, North Carolina* (1915, repr. 1992), 15–52; Mariella Davidson Waite, "Political Institutions in the Trans-Appalachian West, 1770–1800," (Ph.D. diss., Univ. of Florida, 1961), 12–51; Max Dixon, *The Wataugans* (1976).

5. "The humble petition of the inhabitants of Washington District, including the River Wataugah, Nonachuckie," [endorsed, Aug. 22, 1776], repr. in Ramsey, *Annals*, 135–36; Earl of Dunmore to Earl of Dartmouth, May 10, 1774, quoted in Dixon, *Wataugans*, 20.

6. "Petition of the inhabitants of Washington District," repr. in Ramsey, *Annals*, 135–36.

7. "Petition of the inhabitants of Washington District," repr. in Ramsey, *Annals*, 136–37.

8. "Journal of the Proceedings of the Provincial Convention and Congresses of North Carolina," Aug. 22, 1776, repr. in *CRNC*, X:702.

9. For how the Revolution changed the terms of debate see Humphrey, *Land and Liberty*, 136 (noting how tenants and landlords in the Hudson River Valley interpreted "Revolutionary language in their own way and used it to espouse far different goals"). For the spread of constitutional ideas among the German-speaking "Kirchenleute" (Church People) in Pennsylvania after the War that emphasized the scrutiny of government and participation by the common people, see Newman, *Fries's Rebellion*, 202 (observing how America's "governing elite" in the 1790s reacted with "surprise and chagrin" at how well the "Kirchenleute" "learned these lessons" and "how well they had taught their pupils"). See also Ferguson, *Reading*, 287 (noting that after Independence "the people imbibed" a "language of protest" and "were quick to use it in extending their democratic prerogatives").

10. See Nathan O. Hatch, *The Democratization of American Christianity* (1989), 31–32 (calling "the wave of charismatic religious innovators who served as heralds and prophets" of agrarian movements "one of the untold stories of American religious history"); Williamson, *Vermont*, 21 (identifying contemporaries who "saw clearly how religious and political agitations were coalescing" to support the Vermont movement toward independence); Alan Taylor, "Agrarian Independence: Northern Land Rioters After the Revolution," in Young, *Beyond*, 233 (observing that the Revolution's "dramatic unpredictability encouraged millennial anticipation" and stimulated "new possibilities" in the thinking of "common folks").

11. For the right to government and right to security under the English constitutional tradition, see Reid, *Constitutional History*, I:34–46.

   The county lieutenant for Virginia's Illinois County told local inhabitants not to bother exercising their right of representation since "[t]he great distance at which you find yourselves from the capital . . . does not permit you . . . to be present in the assembly which governs the state." "Speech of John Todd to inhabitants of Kaskaskia," May 12, 1779, *Kaskaskia Records*,V:84.

12. Struggles over land in the determinist movements did not pit lawless "squatters" against rightful title holders but against contesting land claimants making competing arguments. Settlers often justified their land claims on the grounds of possession, settlement, and improvement while facing opposition from frequently absentee claimants relying on title based on purchase. See, for example, "The Memorial of the Inhabitants of the Country West of the Allegheny Mountains," repr. in Crumrine, *History*, 187 (asserting that "by the Laws of Nature" settlers were entitled to land "as first Occupants"); Thomas Jefferson to Samuel Huntington, Feb. 9, 1780, *JP*, III:288–89 (identifying fears by settlers that "actual possessions may be made to give way to mere paper titles"); Fisher Ames to George Richards Minot, July 23, 1789, *FAW*, I:694 (conceding the difficulty of resolving land claims where settlers had "actually bought" land "and by labor [it] has become their own"); Taylor, "Agrarian Independence," in Young, *Beyond*, 224 (arguing that Americans' "devout commitment to private property" entailed disagreement over whether its legitimacy rested on title or labor).

   Ultimately, frontier acquisitiveness confirmed the Americanism of determinists because of the depth of that trait among the urban and eastern leaders of the revolutionary generation. See Charles Royster, *The Fabulous History of the Dismal Swamp Company: A Story of George Washington's Times* (1999). See also Philyaw, *Western Visions*, 99–100 ("Western lands appeared as a painless panacea that would cure congressional financial ills, and most members of Congress favored land sales as the most expedient means of reducing the debt").

13. Thomas Jefferson to James Monroe, July 9, 1786, *JP*, X:112; Chad J. Wozniak, "The New Western Colony Schemes: A Preview of the United States Territorial System," 68 *Indiana Magazine of History* (1972), 304 (referring to "the 'apprenticeship government' feature" of the Ordinance of 1787). On the territorial system, see Jack Ericson Eblen, *The First and Second United States Empires: Governors and Territorial Government, 1784–1912* (1968); Robert F. Berkhofer, Jr., "Jefferson, the Ordinance of 1784, and the Origins of the American Territorial System," 29 *WMQ* (1972), 231–62; Arthur Bestor, "Constitutionalism and the Settlement of the West: The Attainment of Consensus, 1754–1784," Robert F. Berkhofer, Jr., "The Northwest Ordinance

and the Principle of Territorial Evolution," both in John Porter Bloom, ed., *The American Territorial System* (1973) 13–44, 45–55; Robert S. Hill, "Federalism, Republicanism, and the Northwest Ordinance," 18 *Publius* (1988), 41–52; Jack N. Rakove, "Ambiguous Achievement: The Northwest Ordinance," in Frederick D. Williams, ed., *The Northwest Ordinance: Essays on Its Formulation, Provisions, and Legacy* (1989), 1–19; Philyaw, *Western Visions*, 95–119.

14. Third Draft Constitution, [before June 13, 1776], *JP*, I:363; Articles of Confederation, Draft, July 12, 1776, *JCC*, V:551. For the argument that public lands policy should protect legitimate settlers and constrain speculation, see Dorsey Pentecost to James Wilson, June 26, 1783, repr. in E. Douglas Branch, "Notes and Documents: Plan for the Western Lands, 1783," 60 *PMHB* (1936), 288–92.

15. Oct. 10, 1780, *JCC*, XVIII:915 ("have the same"); Ordinance of 1784, repr. in Onuf, *Statehood*, 47 ("an equal" to "republican"), 51 (noting that determinists considered the 1784 ordinance "an invitation to organize their own new states").

16. Ordinance of 1787, repr. in Onuf, *Statehood*, 62; July 11, 1787, *RFC*, I:584 ("justice or policy").

17. "Resolves of a Convention held at Clarksville, Jan. 27, 1785," William Clark Papers, 1 M 103 (microfilm ed., 1980, reel 39), WHS. Clarksville's gathering echoed Thomas Paine's image in *Common Sense* of a social contract emerging from "a small number of persons . . . dwelling in the midst of a wilderness." See Robert A. Ferguson, "The Commonalities of *Common Sense*," 57 *WMQ* (2000), 490.

18. On the organizational aspects of the Revolution, see Brown, *Revolutionary Politics*; Maier, *Resistance*.

Determinists buttressed their constitutional claims by recounting their sacrifices to the revolutionary cause, implicitly entitling them to the gratitude of other Americans. See Sarah J. Purcell, *Sealed with Blood: War, Sacrifice, and Memory in Revolutionary America* (2002), 78–83.

19. June 30, 1777, *JCC*, VIII:512.

20. *Gentlemen's Magazine*, Aug. 1785, quoted in Philyaw, *Western Visions*, 112.

21. On Henderson and his experiences during the Regulation, see William Stewart Lester, *The Transylvania Colony* (1935); Lee, *Crowds*, 66–68; Kars, *Breaking*, 158–60, 168–70, 182–86. On Henderson's partners in the Transylvania land scheme, see Archibald Henderson, "The Transylvania Company: A Study in Personnel," 21 *Filson Club History Quarterly* (1947), 3–21, 228–42, 327–49.

On the Transylvania determinist movement, see Lewis Collins, *History of Kentucky* (revised and enlarged, 2 vols., Covington, KY, 1874), II:498–520; George Henry Alden, *New Governments West of the Alleghenies Before 1780* (Madison, WI, 1897), 49–63; Archibald Henderson, "Richard Henderson and the Occupation of Kentucky, 1775," 1 *Mississippi Valley Historical Review* (1914), 341–63; Samuel C. Williams, "Henderson and Company's Purchase Within the Limits of Tennessee," 5 *Tennessee Historical Magazine* (1919), 5–27; Lester, *Transylvania*; Waite, "Political Institutions," 52–94.

22. William Preston to Lord Dunmore, Mar. 10, 1775, repr. in Reuben Gold Thwaites and Louise Phelps Kellogg, eds., *The Revolution on the Upper Ohio, 1775–1777* (1908), 3–4 ("Serious"); "A Proclamation by Governor Martin Against Richard Henderson and the Transylvania Purchase," Feb. 10, 1775; "Proclamation of Virginia Governor Dunmore," Mar. 21, 1775, *CRNC*, IX:1125 (Martin describing Henderson's dealings with the Indians as "illicit and fraudulent"), 1170 (Dunmore condemning Henderson's "unwarrantable and illegal designs"); Governor Martin to the Earl of Dartmouth, Oct. 16, 1775, Nov. 12, 1775, *CRNC*, X:274 ("freebooters"), 324 ("infamous Company").

For the background of the royal policy for distributing "vacant lands" within the colony and the Virginia convention's reaction, see "Petition of George Mason for Warrants for Lands in Fincastle County," "Resolution on Land Grants," [June 1774], [Mar. 27, 1775], *JP*, I:112–16, 162–63.

23. "Clark's Memoir," in James Alton James, ed., *George Rogers Clark Papers, 1771–1781* (Collections of the Illinois State Historical Library, 1912), VIII:209 ("various oppinions"); George

Washington to William Preston, Mar. 27, 1775, *GWW*, III:279 ("there is something"); George Washington to John Posey, June 24, 1767; George Washington to William Crawford, Sept. 21, 1767, *GWW*, II:458 ("opening prospect"), 469 ("present opportunity"). For Washington's western land speculations, see Slaughter, *Whiskey*, 75–89; Philander D. Chase, "A Stake in the West: George Washington as Backcountry Surveyor and Landholder," in Warren R. Hofstra, ed., *George Washington and the Virginia Backcountry* (1998), 175–81; Royster, *Dismal Swamp*, 69–72, 81–83, 130–31, 156–57, 192–93, 293–301, 311–13, 318–19.

24. Henderson and Company to Patrick Henry, Apr. 26, 1775, repr. in George W. Ranck, *Boonesborough: Its Founding, Pioneer Struggles, Indian Experiences, Transylvania Days, and Revolutionary Annals* (1901), 194–95. See also Thomas Perkins Abernethy, *Western Lands and the American Revolution* (1937), 131–32; Stephen Aron, *How the West Was Lost: The Transformation of Kentucky from Daniel Boone to Henry Clay* (1996), 59–68.

25. Sir William Johnson to the Earl of Dartmouth, Nov. 4, 1772, quoted in Richard White, *The Middle Ground: Indians, Empires, and Republics in the Great Lakes Region, 1650–1815* (1991), 315 ("fond of" and "democratical"); Richard Henderson to Cunningham Corbett, July 30, 1774, in *Letters to Col. Joshua Bell and Cunningham Corbett from Richard Henderson* (Annapolis, MD, 1775), 2–3.

26. George Washington to James Ross, June 16, 1794, George Washington Papers, NYPL; Richard Henderson to Transylvania Proprietors, June 12, 1775, repr. in Ranck, *Boonesborough*, 193 ("rights acknowledged" and "lords of the soil"); Henderson's *Journal*, May 8, 1775 ("much embarrassed"), Kentucky Papers, 1 CC 21 (microfilm ed., 1980, reel 74), WHS.

27. William Clark Diary, Apr. 20, 1775, entry, in Ellen Eslinger, ed., *Running Mad for Kentucky: Frontier Travel Accounts* (2004), 73 ("a voley"); quoted in Lester, *Transylvania*, 253 ("a row"). See also John Mack Faragher, *Daniel Boone: The Life and Legend of an American Pioneer* (1992), 120–23 (describing conditions at Boonesborough).

28. Henderson's *Journal*, May 4, 1775 ("exceedingly simple" to "act for them"), May 14, 1775 ("our Church"), Kentucky Papers, 1 CC 21 (microfilm ed., 1980, reel 74), WHS; Journal of the Boonesborough Convention, *CRNC*, IX:1269 ("all power").

29. Boonesborough Convention, *Journal*, *CRNC*, IX:1276 ("contract" and "the powers"); Richard Henderson to Transylvania Proprietors, June 12, 1775, repr. in Ranck, *Boonesborough*, 193 ("lords of the soil").

30. Boonesborough Convention, *Journal*, *CRNC*, IX:1277.

31. Richard Henderson to Joseph Martin, July 20, 1775, quoted in Lester, *Transylvania*, 96.

32. Ranck, *Boonesborough*, 53 ("the assembled" to "big bonfire"); John Adams to Abigail Adams, July 3, 1776, *AFC*, II:30. See also Faragher, *Daniel Boone*, 141 (describing the reaction to the news of American Independence at Boonesborough). For the celebratory bonfires in the East, see Desbler, "Declaration," 167 (Philadelphia), 172 (New York City), 175 (Boston).

33. Hogg emigrated from Scotland in 1774 and settled near Hillsborough, North Carolina, where his brother purchased a thousand acres on his behalf before his arrival. In addition to his activities for the Transylvania Company, Hogg played a leading role in founding the University of North Carolina in the late 1780s. On Hogg and the saga of his migration to America, see Henderson, "Transylvania Company," 3–21, and especially Bernard Bailyn, *Voyagers to the West: A Passage in the Peopling of America on the Eve of the Revolution* (1986), 499–544.

34. John Williams to Joseph Martin, Mar. 3, 1776, George Rogers Clark Papers, 16 J 54 (microfilm ed., 1980, reel 25), WHS "[D]isturbances"); "Petition of Transylvanians to the Virginia Convention," repr. in Ranck, *Boonesborough*, 241–43 ("insatiable avarice" to "stiling themselves proprietors"); Aron, *How the West Was Lost*, 64 ("revived").

35. "A Memorial of Richard Henderson and Others," *Journal of the Virginia Convention*, June 15, 1776, p. 126 ("true friends" to "rights of mankind"), 127 ("absurd[]" to "ready to submit"); *Journal of the Virginia Convention*, June 24, 1776, p. 154 (giving actual settlers on such land "to which there is no other just claim ... preemption, or preference, in the grants of such lands"). Due to the proprietors' "great expense" in buying the lands and settling them, the state awarded

the company 200,000 acres between the Ohio and Green rivers. This land was 200 miles from any current settlement and having no immediate value, brought no income to members of the company for more than twenty years. See Lester, *Transylvania*, 231 ("great expense").

For the creation of new counties out of Fincastle, see Hartwell L. Quinn, *Arthur Campbell: Pioneer and Patriot of the "Old Southwest"* (1990), 44–46; "Bills for Dividing Fincastle County," [Oct. 15 and 26, 1776], *JP*, I:569–76.

36. "The Proceedings of the Convention of the New Hampshire Settlers; Containing their Covenant, Compact, and Resolutions," 1775, *RSV*, II:493 ("Self-Preservation" to "political Body"); Convention at Westminster, Apr. 11, 1775, *RSV*, I:338.

37. "The Humble Address, Remonstrance and Petition of that part of America being situated south of Canada line, West of Connecticut River, North of the Massachusetts Bay, and East of a twenty mile line from Hudson's River, commonly called and known by the name of the N. Hampshire Grants," Jan. 17, 1776, *RSV*, I:19.

Responding to the Dorset Convention's petition, a congressional committee in June 1776 urged the petitioners to "submit" to New York without "prejudice" to their property rights and promised a "final determination" of their rights before "proper judges" after the Revolution. See William Slade, comp., *Vermont State Papers; Being a Collection of Records and Documents, Connected with the Assumption and Establishment of Government by the People of Vermont* (Middlebury, VT, 1823), 64.

On the determinist movement in Vermont, see Jones, *Vermont*, 345–93; Williamson, *Vermont*, 7–67; John A. Williams, ed., *The Public Papers of Governor Thomas Chittenden* (1969), 5–54; Onuf, "State-Making," 797–815; Onuf, *Origins*, 103–45; Marston, *King and Congress*, 243–49; Aichele, "Vermont Constitution," 166–90; Bellesiles, *Revolutionary*; Shalhope, *Bennington*. For Vermont's population see Williamson, *Vermont*, 14.

38. May 10, 1775, *JCC*, IV:342 ("the respective"); Ira Allen, *The Natural and Political History of the State of Vermont* (London, 1798), 76 ("governed themselves" to "the *oldest*"); "Adjourned Session at Westminster," Jan. 15, 1777, *RSV*, I:41 ("a separate"); "Vermont's Declaration of Independence," *Connecticut Courant*, Mar. 17, 1777, *RSV*, I:51 ("dissolved" to "happiness").

39. Aaron Hutchinson, *A well tempered Self-Love a Rule of Conduct towards others: A Sermon Preached at Windsor, July 2, 1777, Before the Representatives of the Towns in the Counties of Charlotte, Cumberland, and Gloucester* (Dresden, VT, [1779]), 19 ("compact" and "covenant"), 20 ("divine warrant" and "law of nature"); Ira Allen, *Some Miscellaneous Remarks . . .* (Hartford, CT, 1777), repr. in *RSV*, I:379 ("no reason why"), 380 ("all power"); Young, "To the Inhabitants of Vermont," Apr. 11, 1777, repr. in *RSV*, I:395 ("all such bodies").

40. Young, "To the Inhabitants of Vermont," repr. in *RSV*, I:395–96.

41. June 30, 1777, *JCC*, VIII:511 ("gross misrepresentation"); Young, "To the Inhabitants of Vermont," *RSV*, I:395 ("the people" to "Delegate power"); New York Delegates to Abraham Ten Broeck, Apr. 21, 1777, James Duane to Robert Livingston, June 28, 1777, *LMC*, II:336 ("insolent"), 390 ("wicked"). On Young's use of the term "constituent power," see Adams, *Constitutions*, 65. For departures by Vermont's constitution from Pennsylvania's 1776 constitution, see John N. Shaeffer, "A Comparison of the First Constitutions of Vermont and Pennsylvania," 43 *Vermont History* (1973), 33–43.

42. Sept. 24, 1779, *JCC*, XV:1098 ("abstain"); Ira Allen, "To the Inhabitants of the State of Vermont," July 13, 1779, *RSV*, I:439 ("together and assume"); Thomas Chittenden, "Proclamation," June 3, 1779, *RSV*, I:442 ("mistaken Notions" to "the People"). For evidence of popular ratification of Vermont's constitution, see Hendricks, "New Look," 136–40.

43. See, for example, Roger Sherman to Jonathan Trumbull, Apr. 9, 1777, *LMC*, II:321 (noting the petition for admittance as "an Independent State" by "The people on the New Hampshire Grants"); Young, "To the Inhabitants of Vermont," Apr. 11, 1777, *RSV*, I:394–96 (asserting the authority of "the people" to act).

44. New York, New Hampshire, and Massachusetts each claimed jurisdiction over areas Vermonters sought to make their own. See James Duane to Robert R. Livingston, June 26, 1777, William Whipple to Meshech Weare, Dec. 14, 1778, *LMC*, II:388 (noting arguments on the "merits" of

New York's "Title" to the area), III:534 (considering the outcome of the controversy as either placing the Grants under the "Jurisdiction" of New York or New Hampshire or being recognized as "a seperate State"); Samuel Adams to John Lowell, Sept. 15, 1780, SAW, IV:203–204 (noting that Vermont representatives claimed "the rights of sovereignty of an independent state" and urged Massachusetts to assert the state's "*title*" for "the lands in question").

    In 1774, Massachusetts's legislature appointed a special committee – its work falling mainly on John Adams – to marshal arguments for the state's territorial claims to the region. See ADA, III:303n3; AP, II:22–81; June 30, 1777, JCC, VIII:509 (Congress disclaimed authority to undercut "the rights and jurisdictions" of the states).

45. New York Delegates to Abraham Ten Broeck, Apr. 21, 1777, LMC, II:336 ("Insurgents" and "Revolters"); James Duane to John Jay, Aug. 22–24, 1778, Morris, *Jay Papers*, I:494 (worrying about "the Secret whisperings of the Advocates for our Revolters"); William Duer to Abraham Ten Broeck, Apr. 17, 1777, LMC, II:331(describing Vermonters as attempting "to dismember" New York).

46. "Committee of Safety of New York to Congress," Jan. 20, 1777, quoted in Allen, *History*, 87.

47. June 30, 1777, JCC, VIII:509 ("communities"); "Committee of Congress," Report, July 1778, LMC, III:345 ("no number").

48. Samuel Adams to James Lovell, Mar. 5, 1780, SAW, IV:180.

49. Boyd Crumrine, "The Boundary Controversy Between Pennsylvania and Virginia, 1748–1785," 1 *Annals of the Carnegie Museum* (1902), 518 ("regularly or irregularly"); "Virginia and Pennsylvania Delegates in Congress to the Inhabitants West of Laurel Hill," July 25, 1775, JP, I:234 ("the defence"). On the Westsylvania determinist movement, see Abernethy, *Western Lands*, 91–97, 136–48, 166–68, 173–79, 254, 268–73; Crumrine, *History*, 187–88; Crumrine, "Boundary Controversy," 505–24; Solon J. Buck and Elizabeth H. Buck, *The Planting of Civilization in Western Pennsylvania* (1939), 158–72; Alden, *Governments*, 64–68; John D. Barnhart, *Valley of Democracy: The Frontier Versus the Plantation in the Ohio Valley, 1775–1818* (1953), 48–51; Edgar W. Hassler, *Old Westmoreland: A History of Western Pennsylvania During the Revolution* (1900), 5–17; Mary Alice Ferry Diener, *The Honorable Dorsey Pentecost, Esquire* (1978); Brunhouse, *Counter-Revolution*, 113–15; Marston, *King and Congress*, 232–36.

50. "Westmoreland county meeting resolution," repr. in Crumrine, "Boundary Controversy," 519–20 ("there is no" to "lives and fortunes"); Arthur St. Clair to Governor John Penn, May 25, 1775, quoted in Hassler, *Westmoreland*, 15 ("musters"); entries of July 31, 1775, [Nicholas Cresswell], *The Journal of Nicholas Cresswell, 1774–1777* (1925), 99 ("Liberty mad"); quoted in Buck, *Pennsylvania*, 180 ("defiance").

51. Oct. 30, 1776, *Journal of the Senate of Virginia*, 18. For the Philadelphia meeting see Chapter 2.

52. "The Memorial of the Inhabitants of the Country West of the Allegheny Mountains," repr. in Crumrine, *History*, 187–88. For land distribution concerns, see Philyaw, *Western Visions*, 74–75.

53. Edmund Pendleton to the Virginia Delegates in Congress, July 15, 1776, JP, I:462 ("some factious" and "Separate Government"), 464 ("dismember" to "of Government"); *Journal of the Virginia House of Delegates of the Commonwealth of Virginia*, Oct. 24, 1776, p. 26 ("committee of West Augusta" to "justice").

54. *Journal of the Virginia House of Delegates of the Commonwealth of Virginia*, Oct. 28, 1776, p. 31 ("ancient territory"); Thomas Scott to Joseph Reed, Nov. 29, 1779, JP, III:208 ("to stir"). On Washington County, see Alfred Creigh, *History of Washington County From Its First Settlement to the Present Time* (Washington, PA, 1870).

55. Louise Phelps Kellogg, ed., "Petition for a Western State, 1780," 1 *Mississippi Valley Historical Review* (1913–14), 267 ("Inhabitants" and "that Freedom"), 268 ("Eastward"), 269 ("the Liberties" to "enjoy" and "the people" to "Ease & Safty"); Oct. 10, 1780, JCC, XVIII:915 ("unappropriated lands" to "republican states").

56. Benjamin Harrison to James Madison, Jan. 19, 1782, James Madison to Benjamin Harrison, Feb. 1, 1782, MP, IV:37 ("a matter"), 52 ("Mathematics"); James Madison to Benjamin Harrison, Nov. 15, 1782, MP, V:276–77 ("scheme" and "a separation").

57. "Memorial of the Inhabitants of the Town of Pittsburgh," [ca. Apr. 1781], repr. in Louise Phelps Kellogg, ed., *Frontier Retreat on the Upper Ohio, 1779–1781* (1917), 361 ("Subject to"), 362 ("lay down" to "Court Martial"); President John Dickinson and the Executive Council to Pennsylvania Legislature, Nov. 15, 1782, *Colonial Records of Pennsylvania*, XIII:426 ("a fund"); *MP*, V:277n9 ("deluded").

58. Quoted in Buck, *Pennsylvania*, 172 ("a considerable number"); Petition of Laurel Hill Inhabitants, Jan. 27, 1783, quoted in *MP*, VI:138n6 ("on the west" to "of America").

59. "Notes on Debates," Jan. 27, 1783, *MP*, VI:133–34. On the boundary resolution, see Crumrine, "Boundary Controversy."

60. "Clark's Memoir," in James, *Clark Papers*, VIII:209–10.

61. "Petition of the Inhabitants of Ketucke (or Louisa) River on the Western Parts of Fincastle County," June 7–15, 1776, in James Rood Robertson, *Petitions of the Early Inhabitants of Kentucky to the General Assembly of Virginia 1769 to 1792* (1914), 36–38.

62. "Petition of the Committee of West Fincastle of the Colony of Virginia, Being on the North and South sides of the River Ketucke (or Louisa)," June 20, 1776, in Robertson, *Petitions*, 39. The convention adjourned before Clark and Jones reached Virginia, but Clark still lobbied Governor Patrick Henry on behalf of the settlers. See "Bills for Dividing Fincastle County," Oct. 15 and 26, 1776, *JP*, I:566; Lester, *Transylvania*, 142–44; Abernethy, *Western Lands*, 165–66; Petition by John Gabriel Jones and George Rogers Clark, Oct. 1776, in James, *Clark Papers*, VIII:19 (urging the legislature send "Forces" to protect the settlements).

63. Quoted in Patricia Watlington, *The Partisan Spirit: Kentucky Politics, 1779–1792* (1972), 18 ("*People are Running*"). See also Lowell H. Harrison, *Kentucky's Road to Statehood* (1992), 1–18. During the first five years of the Revolutionary War, Virginia created thirteen new counties. See Philyaw, *Western Visions*, 73. For the westward migration out of Virginia, including Kentucky as a destination, see David Hackett Fischer and James C. Kelly, *Bound Away: Virginia and the Westward Movement* (2000), 135–201.

64. "Petition of the Destressed Inhabitants of the county of Kentuckky," [endorsed, Oct. 14, 1779], Robertson, *Petitions*, 45–46. See also Archer Butler Hulbert, ed., *Ohio in the Time of the Confederation* (1918), 138 (repr. "Petition of Kentuckians for Lands North of [the] Ohio River" to Congress in 1780 complaining that "almost the whole of the lands" in the region were held in "the hands of a few Interest[e]d men, the greater part of which live at ease in the internal parts of Virginia"); Philyaw, *Western Visions*, 93 (observing that "Virginia's westernmost settlers routinely peppered the legislature with grievances, and when their petitions were not satisfactorily answered, they advocated forming their own state on their terms").

65. George Washington to James Warren, Oct. 7, 1785, George Washington to Jacob Read, Nov. 3, 1784, *WP(CS)*, III:300 ("consequences" to "distinct People"), II:122 ("bind those people"). For a vivid sense of the difficulties and dangers of traveling to and from Kentucky, see Eslinger, *Kentucky*.

66. Kentucky Petition to Congress, May 15, 1780, repr. in Appendix D, Theodore Roosevelt, *The Winning of the West* (4 vols., New York, 1889–1896), II:398–99 ("the people of that Part" to "Rules and regulations"); Motion of Virginia Delegates on Kentucky, Aug. 24, 1780, *MP*, II:65n2 ("slaves"); James Madison to Edmund Pendleton, Oct. 2, 1781, *MP*, III:274 ("extending" to "the State").

      The passage of a Land Act in 1779 not only stimulated migration to Kentucky, but facilitated absentee land ownership and a growing concentration of land in fewer hands. See Abernethy, *Western Lands*, 224–25, 228, 249–51; Aron, *How the West Was Lost*, 71 (noting that within a year of the law's passage Virginia sold treasury warrants redeemable for nearly 2 million acres and in the next decade "millions of additional acres passed into the hands of nonresident purchasers").

67. "ARTICLES OF AGREEMENT, or Compact of Government, entered into by settlers on the Cumberland river, 1st May 1780," repr. in Putnam, *Tennessee*, 96–97. On the Cumberland determinist movement, see "Records of the Cumberland Association," 7 *American Historical Magazine and Tennessee Historical Society* (1902), 114–35; Henderson, "Richard Henderson," 155–72; Lester, *Transylvania*, 255–74; Stanley F. Horn, "The Cumberland Compact," 3

Tennessee Historical Quarterly (1944), 65–66; Barnhart, *Democracy*, 53–54; Waite, "Political Institutions," 95–135; Malcolm J. Rohrbough, *The Trans-Appalachian Frontier: People, Societies, and Institutions, 1775–1850* (1978), 24, 46–47.

68. "Cumberland Compact," repr. in Putnam, *Tennessee*, 98. On the eve of the North Carolina legislature's consideration of the Transylvania claims in the spring of 1782, Henderson still expected to make "a fortune Out of them." See Thomas Hart to Nathaniel Hart, Apr. 22, 1782, repr. in "Shane Collection of Documents: The Hart Papers," 14 *Journal of the Department of History of the Presbyterian Church in the U.S.A.* (1931), 353. Due to the money, expense, and risks taken by the proprietors, the legislative committee recommended that the company be compensated with other land, but like the compensation offered by Virginia, the lands granted by North Carolina provided little financial reward for the Transylvania Company. See Lester, *Transylvania*, 269–81.

69. Minutes of the Committee of the Cumberland Association, "Records of the Cumberland Association," 115–16.

70. On Campbell, see Quinn, *Campbell*; Peter J. Kastor, "'Equitable Rights and Privileges': The Divided Loyalties in Washington County, Virginia, during the Franklin Separatist Crisis," 105 *Virginia Magazine of History and Biography* (1997), 193–226. On the contemporary reference to the Allegheny, rather than the Appalachian Mountains, see Lester J. Cappon, ed., *Atlas of Early American History* (1976), 16–17.

71. *An Address to the Freemen of Washington County, Virginia*, [ca. 1782]" repr. in Quinn, *Campbell*, 129–31. James Montgomery, who subsequently brought Patrick Henry a copy of the address, asserted that Campbell "personally explained, enforced & inculcated its contents" to citizens of the county. See Patrick Henry Executive Papers, June 10, 1785, Box 1, Fldr. 18, LV.

72. Campbell's circular calling for the election of delegates from southwestern Virginia counties as well as northwestern counties of North Carolina is repr. in Williams, *Lost State*, 6 ("to adopt"); William Christian to Arthur Campbell, Feb. 19, 1782 ("by the People"), Draper Manuscripts, King's Mountain Papers, [Series DD, Vol. 9:32], WHS; "Deposition of Robert Preston, incorporating part of a letter from Arthur Campbell," Feb. 16, 1786 ("the sense"), *CVSP*, IV:93.

73. John Sevier to Arthur Campbell, Feb. 16, 1782, quoted in Quinn, *Campbell*, 75 ("this Important" to "Collective Body"); Arthur Campbell to Arthur Lee, June, 9, 1782, repr. in Williams, *Lost State*, 8; James Madison to Thomas Jefferson, Mar. 26, 1782, *JP*, VI:172–73. See also Edmund Randolph to James Madison, Dec. 27, 1782, *MP*, V:454 (reporting accusations that Campbell "fomented a separation of the back countr[y]").

74. "Petition from "Inhabitants of Kentuckey," [endorsed May 30, 1782], in Robertson, *Petitions*, 64 ("the Rights"); Edmund Pendleton to James Madison, May 27, 1782, *MP*, IV:277 ("plan for administering"); Edmund Randolph to James Madison, June 27, 1782, *MP*, IV:376.

75. Charles Thompson, "The Papers of Charles Thompson, Secretary of the Continental Congress," *Collections of the New-York Historical Society For the Year 1878* (New York, 1879), 145–46 (paraphrasing the petition), (Minutes for Aug. 27, 1782); Lee quoted in "Comments on Petition of Kentuckians," Aug. 27, 1782, *MP*, V:82–83 ("insult" to "supposition") .

76. "Comments on Petition of Kentuckians," Aug. 27, 1782, *MP*, V:83 ("so extravagant"), 84n6 ("revered teacher"); Charles Thompson, "Notes of Debates," Aug. 27, 28, 1782, *LMC*, VI:458–59 ("many" to "one State"); *Chisholm v. Georgia*, 2 U.S. 419 at 469 (1793) ("uncommon opinion" to "individual State") (John Jay); Charles Thompson, "Notes of Debates," Aug. 27, 28, 1782, *LMC*, VI:458 ("another revolution"). On the renewed debate over the issue of western land, see "Notes on Debates," Nov. 14, 1782, *MP*, V:273–74.

77. "Petition for a New State," *Maryland Journal*, Dec. 19, 1783, Draper Collection, Newspaper extracts, [Series JJ, Vol. 3:114–121], WHS ("Some of our" to "respect"); "Virginia Delegates in Congress to Benjamin Harrison, with Petition from Inhabitants of Kentucky," Feb. 20, 1784, *JP*, VI:554 ("wholesome laws" to "fellow-Citizens").

78. Hugh Williamson to Alexander Martin, Nov. 18, 1782, *LMC*, VI:545; quoted in George Henry Alden, "The State of Franklin," 8 *AHR* (1902–1903), 284 ("contentions" to "knowledge"). On the determinist movement in Franklin, see John Haywood, *The Civil and Political History of*

the State of Tennessee From its Earliest Settlement up to the Year 1796, Including the Boundaries of the State (1823, repr. Nashville, TN, 1891), 146–215; Alden, "Franklin," 271–89; Thomas Perkins Abernethy, *From Frontier to Plantation in Tennessee: A Study in Frontier Democracy* (1932, repr. 1967), 64–90; Williams, *Lost State*; Barnhart, *Democracy*, 61–65; Paul M. Fink, "Some Phases of the History of the State of Franklin," 16 *Tennessee Historical Quarterly* (1957), 195–213; Waite, "Political Institutions," 136–203; James W. Hagy and Stanley J. Folmsbee, "Arthur Campbell and the Separate State Movements in Virginia and North Carolina," 42 *East Tennessee Historical Society's Publications* (1970), 20–46; Rohrbough, *Frontier*, 25–26.

79. "Extracts from an Address to the Western Inhabitants," enclosed in Charles Cummings to the president of Congress, Apr. 7, 1785 ("the events" to "the *Basis*"), *Papers of the Continental Congress*, Microfilm Copy 247, Reel 62, NA; quoted in Williams, *Lost State*, 31 ("an Association" to "time to time").

80. Preamble, Constitution of the State of Franklin, repr. in Williams, *Lost State*, 339.

81. "The Memorial of the freemen inhabiting the county westward of the Alleghany or Appalachian mountain, and southward of the Ouasioto," Petition repr. in Williams, *Lost State*, 46 ("a free" to "the liberties"), 47 ("the privileges"); *Maryland Journal and Baltimore Advertiser*, Oct. 11, 1785 ("the fruits"). Campbell's movement to separate Washington County from Virginia dovetailed with the Franklin movement when he sought congressional recognition of statehood for a region that included Washington County. For the "murky and byzantine" connections between the two determinist movements, see Kastor, "Divided Loyalties," 193–226, 207 ("murky"). When Samuel Hardy transmitted a copy of the congressional petition to Patrick Henry, he identified Campbell as "the parent of the Scheme." See Samuel Hardy to Patrick Henry, Jan. 17, 1785, Patrick Henry Executive Papers, Box 1, Fldr. 5, LV. Scholars have coined the phrase "greater Franklin" to describe Campbell's plan. See, for example, Frederick Jackson Turner, "Western State Making in the Revolutionary Era," 1 *AHR* (1895–1896), 259.

82. "Petition to Congress from Washington County, Virginia, Apr. 7, 1785," repr. in Quinn, *Campbell*, 144 ("new Society"), 142 ("Deputies" to "local Constitutions"); "Citizens of Washington County, memorial to Congress," *Papers of the Continental Congress*, Microfilm Copy 247, Reel 62, NA ("that any number" to "the sovereignty of the People").

83. Governor Alexander Martin, "A Manifesto," Apr. 25, 1785, repr. in Williams, *Lost State*, 69–70; "Message of Governor Patrick Henry," repr. in Williams, *Lost State*, 52–53; Arthur Campbell to Patrick Henry, May 21, 1785, Patrick Henry Executive Papers, Box 1, Fldr. 17, LV. For Henry's efforts to suppress the determinist movement in Washington County, see Kastor, "Divided Loyalties," 214–22; "Abridgment of Politics in the Western Country," *Maryland Gazette*, Oct. 11, 1785, Draper Collection, Newspaper extracts, [Series JJ, Vol. 3:157–158], WHS.

84. John Sevier to Alexander Martin, Mar. 22, 1785, repr. in Cora Bales Sevier and Nancy S. Madden, *Sevier Family History, With the Collected Letters of Gen. John Sevier, First Governor of Tennessee* (1961), 60 ("necessity"); John Sevier to Patrick Henry, July 19, 1785, *CVSP*, IV:43 ("we are not a banditti"); Arthur Campbell to Patrick Henry, July 26, 1785, *CVSP*, IV:44 ("criminal" to "in America"); "Petition of the Inhabitants of the Western Country," Dec. 1787, repr. in Williams, *Lost State*, 349 ("to participate" and "more than").

   On John Sevier, see Katharine E. Wilkie, *John Sevier: Son of Tennessee* (1958); Sevier and Madden, *Sevier Family History*; Carl S. Driver, *John Sevier: Pioneer of the Old Southwest* (1932).

85. Arthur Campbell to Archibald Stuart, Feb. 27, 1786, Campbell Family Papers, DU ("first suggested"); Instructions from Governor Patrick Henry to John Todd, Dec. 12, 1778, in James, *Clark Papers*, VIII:85 ("free and equal"); Arthur Campbell to John Edmundson, Aug. 26, 1785, *CVSP*, IV:100 ("lost sight"), 101 ("fundamental principles" to "the Constitutions"). A call for a constitutional convention to meet west of the Ohio River in 1785 was similarly justified on the grounds that "agreeable to every constitution formed in America," Americans "have an undoubted right to pass into every vacant country, and there to form their constitution." See "Advertisement," Mar. 12, 1785, repr. in Hulbert, *Ohio*, 99.

86. Arthur Campbell to James Madison, Oct. 28, 1785, *MP*, VIII:383. Campbell was not alone in thinking that Americans would continually improve their constitutions. A Kentuckian anticipating a constitution for the region in 1785 solicited ideas from a Philadelphia correspondent for a "System of Government" that would prove "best adopted to the genius of our Country & the Times." Such rethinking of constitution-making was necessary because "Hurry & theoretical notions had too much influence" in the formation of America's initial constitutions. See James Wilkinson to James Hutchinson, June 20, 1785, "Letters of Gen. James Wilkinson Addressed to Dr. James Hutchinson, of Philadelphia," 12 *PMHB* (1888), 60.

87. On the features of the "Frankland" constitution, see Chapter 2. For the debate over the Frankland constitution and the Presbyterian influence on postrevolutionary constitution-making, see Quinn, *Campbell*, 82; Fink, "State of Franklin," 204–207; Alden, "Franklin," 274–75; Williams, *Lost State*, 94–98; Howard Miller, "The Grammar of Liberty: Presbyterians and the First American Constitutions," 54 *Journal of Presbyterian History* (1976), 142–64.

88. William Waller Hening, ed., *The Statutes at Large; Being a Collection of all the Laws of Virginia* ... (Richmond, 1823), XII:41 ("high treason"). See also Kastor, "Divided Loyalties," 215–19; Williams, *Lost State*, 269. For North Carolina Governor Richard Caswell's reference to potential civil war, see Williams, *Lost State*, 146–47. Campbell insisted he sought "separation" by "petition to the legislature," and not by force. Arthur Campbell to Archibald Stuart, Feb. 27, 1786, Campbell Family Papers, DU.

89. *Maryland Gazette*, Oct. 20, 1785 (reporting a call for a "conference" in the *Falmouth Gazette* to explore "separate government" and test "the sentiments of the people"); *Massachusetts Centinel*, Jan. 18, 1786. For the movement to separate Maine from Massachusetts, see *Collections of the Massachusetts Historical Society* (Boston, 1795), 25–40; P. Emory Aldrich, "Massachusetts and Maine, Their Union and Separation," 1 *Proceedings of the American Antiquarian Society* (1877), 43–64; "Brunswick Convention of 1816," *Collections and Proceedings of the Maine Historical Society* (Portland, 1891), 129–42; Edward Stanwood, *The Separation of Maine from Massachusetts* (1907); Ronald F. Banks, *Maine Becomes a State: The Movement to Separate Maine from Massachusetts, 1785–1820* (1970); Marshall J. Tinkle, *The Maine State Constitution: A Reference Guide* (1992).

90. See Kastor, "Divided Loyalties," 222–23 (noting that Campbell's "political exile was short" and that after his return to the legislature in 1786 to 1788 he developed "local preeminence in Washington County"). On Sevier, see Sevier and Madden, *Sevier Family History*; Driver, *Sevier*.

91. Patrick Henry to Joseph Martin, Mar. 10, 1790, Draper Collection, King's Mountain Papers, [Series DD, Vol. 11:87a], WHS.

92. James Speed to Governor Benjamin Harrison, May 22, 1784, *CVSP*, III:588–89.

93. Thomas P. Abernethy, ed., "Documents: Journal of the First Kentucky Convention, Dec. 27, 1784–Jan. 5, 1785," 1 *Journal of Southern History* (1935), 71 ("their Bretheren"); "To the inhabitants of the District of Kentucky," repr. in William Littell, *Political Transactions in and Concerning Kentucky, From the First Settlement Thereof, Until it Became an Independent State, in June, 1792* (Frankfort, KY, 1806, repr. 1926), 63–64 ("self evident truth" to "right to expect"); Caleb Wallace to James Madison, July 12, 1785, *MP*, VIII:322 ("at present").

94. Petition from "The Subscribers resident, in the Counties of Jefferson, Fayette, Lincoln, and Nelson, composing the district of Kentucky," Sept. 23, 1785, in Robertson, *Petitions*, 80–82. See also *Maryland Journal and Baltimore Advertiser*, Nov. 4, 1785. For the series of conventions leading to Kentucky's statehood, see Watlington, *Partisan Spirit*, 79–132; Harrison, *Road*, 19–47.

95. See Ruth Bogin, "Petitioning and the New Moral Economy of Post-Revolutionary America," 45 *WMQ* (1988), 391–425 (identifying an egalitarian expectation in petitions related to land distribution, debt, and taxes after the Revolution); Marco M. Sioli, "The Democratic Republican Societies at the End of the Eighteenth Century: The Western Pennsylvania Experience," 60 *Pennsylvania History* (1993), 290 (noting that postrevolutionary petitions "assumed the characteristics of political proposals put forth by citizens in whom power originates and is legitimated, citizens ready to rescind institutional bonds and propose an alternative form of government – no longer 'humble servants' but 'remonstrants'").

96. For the political club, see Thomas Speed, *The Political Club, Danville, Kentucky, 1786–1790* (Louisville, KY, 1894); Harrison, *Road*, 44 (noting the complaint of a lodger being kept awake by "a Political Club which met in the next room where we slept").

97. James Wilkinson to James Hutchinson, May 4, 1786, in "Letters of Wilkinson," 62.

CHAPTER 4. REVOLUTIONARY TENSIONS

1. The account of Whiting draws on William Whiting to Robert Treat Paine, Mar. 19, 1787, Robert Treat Paine Papers, MHS; Robert Treat Paine Diary, Apr. 20, 1787, MHS; Robert Treat Paine to William Whiting, Apr. 3, 1776, William Whiting Papers, MHS; "Address for the Removal of William Whiting & Others from Office," Feb. 28, 1787, Massachusetts Archives, Vol. 189:171–77, MSA; John Adams to James Warren, Oct. 21, 1775, *LDC*, II:225–26; John F. Schroeder, *Memoir of the Life and Character of Mrs. Mary Anna Boardman* (New Haven, 1849), 45–64; A. M. Smith, "Medicine in Berkshire," in *Papers of the Berkshire Historical and Scientific Society* (Pittsfield, MA, 1890), 116–17; *History of Berkshire County, Massachusetts, with Biographical Sketches of Its Prominent Men* (2 vols., New York, 1885), I:363; Robert J. Taylor, *Western Massachusetts in the Revolution* (1954), 82, 92, 95, 111, 144–45, 148, 170; Stephen T. Riley, "Dr. William Whiting and Shays' Rebellion," 66 *Proceedings of the American Antiquarian Society* (1957), 119–39; Richard D. Birdsall, *Berkshire County: A Cultural History* (1959), 214–58; Robert J. Taylor, ed., *Massachusetts, Colony to Commonwealth, Documents on the Formation of Its Constitution, 1775–1780* (1961), 101–105; Handlin, *Popular Sources*, 114, 203, 368; Van Beck Hall, *Politics Without Parties: Massachusetts, 1780–1791* (1972), 229, 310–16; Leonard L. Richards, *Shays's Rebellion: The American Revolution's Final Battle* (2002), 12, 14–15, 39–40.

2. Quoted in Isaac Backus, *An Address to the Inhabitants of New-England, Concerning the Present Bloody Controversy Therein* (Boston, 1787), 5 ("aid"); [James Sullivan], *Biographical Sketch of the Life and Character of His Late Excellency Governor Hancock* (Boston, [1793?]), 12 ("there was then"). See also Peter Thatcher to Thomas Cushing, Sept. 15, 1786, Cushing Family Papers, MHS (noting support in a town meeting that "favored the insurgents and was not disposed to do any thing to discourage or oppose them"). Many scholars assume the Regulators lacked a constitutional basis for their position. For the considerable literature, see Robert A. Gross, "White Hats and Hemlocks: Daniel Shays and the Legacy of the Revolution," in Ronald Hoffman and Peter J. Albert, eds., *The Transforming Hand of Revolution: Reconsidering the American Revolution as a Social Movement* (1996), 286–345.

   Scholars routinely consider the means employed by the Regulators to express their grievances – including conventions and court closings – as necessarily extraconstitutional. See, for example, J. R. Pole, *Political Representation in England and the Origins of the American Republic* (1966), 238–39; Wood, *Creation*, 319–28; Maier, "Popular Uprisings," 3–35; Onuf, *Origins*, 175 (asserting that the Regulation formed a "paradigmatic" example of the people using "extraconstitutional means to express their grievances").

3. See, for example, Sheriff W. Greenleaf to Governor James Bowdoin, [Sept. 1786] (describing how "the regulators (as they term themselves)" closed the Worcester courthouse); Sheriff L. Baldwin to Governor James Bowdoin, Sept. 12, 1786 (describing threats by a Concord protester to banish those "who did not follow his drum and join the Regulator[s] in two hours"), Massachusetts Archives, Vol. 190:235, 253–54, MSA.

   On the colonial "Regulators," see Richard Maxwell Brown, *The South Carolina Regulators* (1963); Powell, *Regulators*; James P. Whittenburg, "Planters, Merchants, and Lawyers: Social Change and the Origins of the North Carolina Regulation," 34 *WMQ* (1977), 215–38; Lee, *Crowds*, 13–96, court closings at 25, 53–54, 67; Kars, *Breaking*.

4. Friends also called Regulators "Shaysites" after their presumptive leader Daniel Shays. In fact, protest meetings, conventions to formulate grievances, and court closings were well under way before Shays made his first appearance. When actual confrontations with government forces did take place, eyewitnesses described Shays as only one of several Regulator leaders and one who seemed reluctantly caught up in events he would rather have avoided. See C. O. Parmenter,

History of Pelham, Mass.: From 1738 to 1898 (Amherst, 1898), 391–99; Taylor, *Massachusetts*, 157; Neville Meaney, "The Trial of Popular Sovereignty in Post-Revolutionary America: The Case of Shays' Rebellion," in Neville Meaney, ed., *Studies on the American Revolution* (1977), 213n45.

Still, the term "Shaysites" stuck at the time and has largely been embraced by historians ever since, with most scholars viewing the events in Massachusetts as a "rebellion" or "insurrection." Even the most recent study of the Regulation demonstrating the demonization of the Regulators by the Friends of Government describes them as "rebels." Richards, *Shays's Rebellion*.

A rare consideration of the Regulator movement that breaks free of the conventional historiography is Ronald P. Formisano, "Teaching Shays/ The Regulation," *Uncommon Sense* (Winter, 1998), 26 ("If Daniel Shays had not existed, elite Federalists would have invented him. In fact, they did create him, i.e., their interpretations in the newspapers and prints, which they largely controlled, made Shays into the leader of a movement and promulgator of doctrines, neither of which he was").

The term "Friends of Government" (interchangeably used with "Friends of Order") also stuck and continued in use after the Regulation and into the politics of the 1790s. See Stephen Higginson to John Adams, Aug. 10, 1789, *HL*, 768 (describing supporters of Federalist judges as "the good Citizens" and "the friends of government"); Sharp, *Politics*, 122 (noting George Washington's distinction between "friends, and foes of order, and good government").

5. For how the Massachusetts Regulation paralleled events in other states in the region, see David P. Szatmary, *Shays' Rebellion: A Making of an Agrarian Insurrection* (1980).

For revolutionary-era protests and court closings, see Freeman Hansford Hart, *The Valley of Virginia in the American Revolution, 1763–1789* (1942), 123–25; Crowl, *Maryland*, 92–110; Barbara Karsky, "Agrarian Radicalism in the Late Revolutionary Period (1780–1795)," in Erich Angermann, Marie-Luise Frings, Hermann Wellenreuther, eds., *New Wine in Old Skins: A Comparative View of Socio-Political Structures and Values Affecting the American Revolution* (1976), 87–114; Richard Maxwell Brown, "Back Country Rebellions and the Homestead Ethic in America, 1740–1799," in Richard Maxwell Brown and Don E. Fehrenbacher, eds., *Tradition, Conflict, and Modernization: Perspectives on the American Revolution* (1977), 73–99; John L. Brooke, "To the Quiet of the People: Revolutionary Settlements and Civil Unrest in Western Massachusetts, 1774–1789," 46 *WMQ* (1989), 425–62; Alan Taylor, *Liberty Men and Great Proprietors: The Revolutionary Settlement on the Maine Frontier, 1760–1820* (1990), 109–14; Bellesiles, *Revolutionary*, 245–57; Shalhope, *Bennington*, 188–91.

6. For Whiting's arrival in Massachusetts and participation in community affairs, see *History of Berkshire County, Massachusetts, with Biographical Sketches of Its Prominent Men* (2 vols., New York, 1885), I:363. On Sedgwick's career, see Richard E. Welch, Jr., *Theodore Sedgwick, Federalist: A Political Portrait* (1965).

7. William Whiting to [Robert Treat Paine], Feb. 1, 1787 (typescript copy), Robert Treat Paine Papers, MHS. Even a strong Friend of Government, the Salem lawyer William Pynchon, thought "Scarcity of cash" was "alarming." See diary entry, Mar. 3, 1786, in Fitch Edward Oliver, ed., *The Diary of William Pynchon of Salem* (Boston, 1890), 233.

8. William Whiting to Theodore Sedgwick, Sept. 10, 1785, Sedgwick Papers, MHS ("Insidious"); Theodore Sedgwick to William Whiting, Sept. 14, 1786, repr. in Riley, "Whiting," 136 (Sedgwick's accusations and "seditious libel"); Theodore Sedgwick to Pamela Sedgwick, June 24, 1786, Shays Rebellion Papers, MHS ("to be pited" to "gibbets, & racks"); Theodore Sedgwick to James Bowdoin, Oct. 5, 1786, Massachusetts Archives, Vol. 190:277–88, MSA (for Sedgwick's lobbying efforts).

Whiting advanced his constitutional views in "Gracchus" and "Some Remarks on the Conduct of the Inhabitants of the Commonwealth of Massachusetts in Interupting the Siting of the Judicial Courts in Several Counties in that State: To Which is Aded an Appendix Extracted From the Antient Romas History." See Riley, "Whiting," 140–59. After the Great Barrington court closing, Sedgwick sent his exchange of letters with Whiting and a copy of the "Gracchus" article to Governor James Bowdoin, and the state's attorney general had these documents during Whiting's trial. See Riley, "Whiting," 127.

9. On Massachusetts's fiscal policies, see Ferguson, *Power of the Purse*, 245–50; John J. McCusker and Russell R. Menard, *The Economy of British America, 1607–1789* (1985); Robert A. Feer, *Shays's Rebellion* (1988), 46–140; Richard Buel, Jr., "The Public Creditor Interest in Massachusetts Politics, 1780–86," Joseph A. Ernst, "Shays's Rebellion in Long Perspective: The Merchants and the 'Money Question,'" Jonathan M. Chu, "Debt Litigation and Shays's Rebellion," all in Gross, *Debt to Shays*, 47–99; Claire Priest, "Colonial Courts and Secured Credit: Early American Commercial Litigation and Shays' Rebellion," 108 *Yale L. J.*, (1999), 2440–42.

10. William Pynchon, diary entry for Sept. 9, 1786, in Oliver, *Diary*, 248–49; Alexander Hamilton, "Objections and Answers respecting the Administration of the Government," Aug. 18, 1792, *HP*, XII:238. See also Rufus King to John Adams, Oct. 3, 1786, *RKC*, I:190 (suggesting that Massachusetts had taxed "beyond what prudence would authorize"); John Adams to Thomas Jefferson, Nov. 30, 1786, *JP*, X:557 (describing the "Zeal" of the legislature in imposing taxes "rather heavier than the People could bear").

11. "The Spirit of the Times: Addressing the People of Massachusetts," *Massachusetts Centinal*, Oct. 25, 1786, repr. in George McKenna, ed., *American Populism* (1974), 69 ("the great men"); Petition of the Town of Groton to the General Court, [Sept. 1786], Worcester Collection, AAS ("commotions" to "two Cows only"); Massachusetts 1780 Constitution, Bill of Rights, Art. 7, *TC*, III:1890 (any one "class").

On the economic policies and their impact, see Priest, "Commercial Litigation;" Richards, *Shays's Rebellion*, 63–88, 75 (tracing £600,000 of Massachusetts's state debt, finding nearly 80 percent of it owned by speculators living in or near Boston, and nearly 40 percent of it in the hands of only thirty-five people); Sidney Kaplan, "Veteran Officers and Politics in Massachusetts, 1783–1787," 9 *WMQ* (1952), 50–51; Ferguson, *Power of the Purse*, 245 (describing the payment to creditors of the value of the bills they held at the time of their issuance rather than at the time of the debt a conferral of "unmerited gains upon individuals"); Woody Holton, "'From the Labours of Others': The War Bonds Controversy and the Origins of the Constitution in New England," 61 *WMQ* (2004), 297 (arguing that Massachusetts's legislature "attempted to transfer large sums from taxpayers to bond speculators and then refused to adopt tax and debt relief").

12. See J. R. Pole, "Shays's Rebellion: A Political Interpretation," in Jack Greene, ed., *The Reinterpretation of the American Revolution, 1763–1789* (1968), 419 (discussing the organizational advantages of seaboard representatives); Taylor, *Massachusetts*, 143 (noting the frustration of western inhabitants of Massachusetts that "their votes were not doing them any good"); Ronald P. Formisano, *The Transformation of Political Culture: Massachusetts Parties, 1790s–1840s* (1983), 30–31.

On the tendency to boycott and the pattern of sending representatives, see Szatmary, *Shays' Rebellion*, 48–49; Pole, "Shays' Rebellion," 423; Jackson Turner Main, *Political Parties Before the Constitution* (1973), 92–93; Holton, "Adversaries," 340–46.

Whiting lamented "that the People" had not awoken "Earlier from their political Slumbers," Whiting, "Some Remarks," repr. in Riley, "Whiting," 14. A county convention urged "every town" to "send Representatives" to the legislature and "every voter" to vote, "ADDRESS of the CONVENTION of the County of WORCESTER to the PEOPLE," *The Worcester Magazine* (4th of Nov. 1786), 405.

13. On the perception of the Senate, see Taylor, *Massachusetts*, 140 (describing senators as coming "from the well-to-do" who "were suspect from the start"); Karsky, "Agrarian Radicalism," 92 (noting that lack of "popular control" over the Senate contributed to calls for its abolition); Pole, *Political Representation*, 230 (describing the "mere existence" of the Senate as a "grievance"); Holton, *"Federalist 10*," 182 (asserting that "[m]any farmers believed the senate's immunity to accountability helped explain the harsh fiscal and monetary policies adopted in the mid-1780s"). For the Senate's unwillingness to provide the economic relief sought by the Regulators, see Jackson Turner Main, *The Upper House in Revolutionary America, 1763–1788* (1967), 170–73.

14. William Whiting, "Gracchus," repr. in Riley, "Whiting," 134 ("a most grievous"); "PETITION of the Worcester County CONVENTION to the GENERAL COURT," *The Worcester Magazine* (1st week of Oct. 1786), 334 ("an amazing expence" and asserting that "the exorbitancy of the fee table" was a universal complaint). On court costs, see Priest, "Commercial Litigation," 2418

(concluding that "the inefficiencies of the colonial courts suggest that the Shaysites' concerns with the court system were entirely legitimate"); Chu, "Debt Litigation," in Gross, *Debt to Shays*, 91 (noting that court records "understate the actual cost of litigation" borne by the loser).

15. Taylor, *Massachusetts*, 190n19 ("chronic"). See also Priest, "Commercial Litigation," 2447. Before the Confession Act, some suggested eliminating the Courts of Common Pleas and replacing them with other "courts of record" or with arbitration supervised by the justices of the peace. See, for example, Taylor, *Massachusetts*, 198n21; William Whiting, "Some Remarks," repr. in Riley, "Whiting," 155–56. Only after most of the court closings would the Senate pass a Confession Act. See Hall, *Politics*, 218.

16. Richard Cranch to John Adams, Oct. 3, 1786, quoted in David Szatmary, "Shays' Rebellion in Springfield," in Martin Kaufman, ed., *Shays' Rebellion: Selected Essays* (1987), 7 ("might be forced").

17. Szatmary, "Rebellion in Springfield," 12 ("iniquitous"); Backus, *Address*, 5 ("would produce"). See also Janet A. Riesman, "Money, Credit, and Federalist Political Economy," in Beeman, *Beyond Confederation*, 151 (observing that "demands for paper [money] seemed to possess sinister, leveling implications that frightened the genteel part of society"); William Pynchon, diary entry, Dec. 4, 1780, in Oliver, *Diary*, 80 (anticipating the repeal of "the iniquitous Tender Law").

18. Abigail Adams to Thomas Jefferson, Jan. 29, 1787, *JP*, XI:86 ("Luxury and extravagance"). See also James Sullivan, "Hints Addressed to the Serious Consideration of the People of the Counties of Bristol and Middlesex," in Thomas C. Amory, *Life of James Sullivan: With Selections from his Writings* (2 vols., Boston, 1859), I:193 (attributing fiscal burdens to "laziness and extravagence"); Benjamin Lincoln to George Washington, Dec. 4, 1786–[Mar. 4,] 1787, *WP(CS)*, IV:420 (tracing current economic troubles to a decline in "usual industry" and the rise of a "luxuriant mode of living").

19. See Wood, "Interests," 69–109; Banner, *Hartford*, 70–72, 81–83; Stephen Higginson to John Adams, Mar. 1, 1790, *HL*, 774 (describing financial reverses from current "vicissitudes"); Gordon S. Wood, "Launching the 'Extended Republic': The Federalist Era," in Hoffman and Albert, *Launching*, 16–20.

20. William Whiting, "Gracchus," 134 ("poor Debtors") and William Whiting, "Some Remarks," 145 ("ought" to "Slavery"), both repr. in Riley, "Whiting." See also Bruce H. Mann, *Republic of Debtors: Bankruptcy in the Age of American Independence* (2002), 182 (asserting that Regulators "petitioned not to be relieved of their debts but for reforms that would permit repayment on less destructive terms").

21. Charles Pettit to Benjamin Franklin, Oct. 18, 1786, *LMC*, VIII:487 ("respectable Standings"). See Bouton, "Road," 858–65 (describing how advocates of paper money believed it allowed them to participate in the postrevolutionary economy). On paper money during the colonial period, see E. James Ferguson, "Currency Finance: An Interpretation of Colonial Monetary Practices," 10 *WMQ* (1953), 153–80; Bernard Bailyn, *Faces of Revolution: Personalities and Themes in the Struggle for American Independence* (1990), 188 (concluding that paper money "was in most places a fiscally sound and successful means . . . not only of providing a medium of exchange but also of creating sources of credit necessary for the growth of an underdeveloped economy"); Clare Priest, "Currency Policies and Legal Development in Colonial New England," 110 *Yale L. J.* (2001), 1303–1405.

On positive views of paper money, see Leonard W. Labaree, ed., *The Papers of Benjamin Franklin* (37 vols., 1959–2003), I:139–57, XII:47–60, XXXIV:228–32; Bogin, "True Policy," 100–109.

On the Friends' concern about support for paper money, see Edward Carrington to Thomas Jefferson, June 9, 1787, *JP*, XI:408 (asserting that some who "owed not a shilling" supported paper money); Appendix B: Demands for Remedial Legislation, Feer, *Shays's Rebellion*, 540–46 (identifying calls for paper money in Massachusetts conventions of the 1780s).

22. Ferguson, *Power of the Purse*, 245 (suggesting that critics of the Regulation "failed to realize that it was touched off by financial policies which were as surely class legislation as any paper

money bill"); Richard L. Bushman, *From Puritan to Yankee: Character and the Social Order in Connecticut, 1690–1765* (1967), 117–21 (asserting that colonial Americans understood how paper money benefited some groups and not others).

23. "Pittsfield Memorial," Dec. 26, 1775; Handlin, *Popular Sources*, 61 ("abhorrence"), 64 ("new Constitution").

24. "Proclamation," General Court of Massachusetts, Jan. 19, 1776, *AA*, (4th Ser.), Vol. IV:834 ("more ... under"); *The Acts and Resolves, Public and Private, of the Province of the Massachusetts Bay; to which are Prefixed the Charters of the Province* (Boston, 1869–1922), V:484– 85 ("the Government"); "Pittsfield Petitions," May 29, 1776, Handlin, *Popular Sources*, 92 ("the King[']s" to "Government").

25. "Statement of Berkshire County Representatives," Nov. 17, 1778, Handlin, *Popular Sources*, 378 ("levy Taxes"). On the court stoppages, see Taylor, *Massachusetts*, 75–76; Birdsall, *Berkshire*, 221; Dirk Hoerder, *Crowd Action in Revolutionary Massachusetts, 1765–1780* (1977), 327; Brooke, "Revolutionary Settlements," 436–40; Brown, *Revolutionary Politics*, 215– 18.

26. William Whiting, "Address to the Inhabitants of Berkshire," 1778, in Taylor, *Documents*, 102 ("*union* or *compact*"), 103 ("allegiance" and "unwarrantable"), 104 ("to be governed"), 105 ("ancient maxim"). In describing the people joined in a fundamental compact, Whiting distinguished the civil or political society in which majority will ruled from any particular constitution or form of government. As the representative of Great Barrington, Whiting urged the provisional government to call a convention to draft a new constitution. See "Berkshire County Remonstrance," Aug. 26, 1778, in Handlin, *Popular Sources*, 366–68.

27. Thomas Allen, "A Vindication of the County of Birkshire in their Principles and Conduct, against the False and Malevolent Aspersions Cast on them by their Enemies, Respecting the present Mode of Government as it is Exercised in The State of Massachusetts Bay," in Theodore M. Hammett, "Revolutionary Ideology in Massachusetts: Thomas Allen's 'Vindication' of the Berkshire Constitutionalists, 1778," 33 *WMQ* (1976), 525 ("a New thing"). For Allen's leadership of the Berkshire Constitutionalists, see F. W. Grinnell, "Note on the Position and Influence of Thomas Allen and the 'Berkshire Constitutionalists' from 1774 to 1780 in Connection with the Massachusetts Constitution," 3 *Mass. L.Q.* (1918), 332–41; Richard D. Birdsall, "The Reverend Thomas Allen: Jeffersonian Calvinist," 30 *New England Quarterly* (1957), 147–65. On the vicarious consent under the British constitution, see Reid, *Constitutional History*, III:100 (describing consent "manifested by the acquiescence implied by an individual living in British society").

28. Allen, "A Vindication," 523 ("the Approbation" to "or Amendment"), 524–25 ("Greater than"), 527 ("see with").

29. See Taylor, *Massachusetts*, 77 (quoting a Pittsfield town meeting of Aug. 15, 1774); "Pittsfield Petitions," May 29, 1776, "Statement of Berkshire County Representatives," Nov. 17, 1778, Handlin, *Popular Sources*, 63, 90, 377–78.

30. Resolution of the House of Representatives, Sept. 17, 1776, Return of Norton, Handlin, *Popular Sources*, 99 ("Inspection"), 124 ("Seperately"). See also Return of Lexington, Return of Brookfield (consenting to the existing legislature drafting a constitution subject to ratification by a subsequently elected legislature), Handlin, *Popular Sources*, 150, 156–57.

31. Return of Boston (unanimously rejecting the proposal), Return of Stoughton, Handlin, *Popular Sources*, 136 ("every Individual" and "consulting"), 106 ("is essentially"), 107 ("the wisdom" and "Extracted"). For an elaborate plan for widespread popular participation at the local level, see Return of Bellingham, Handlin, *Popular Sources*, 161–62.

32. For the ratification count, see Morison, "Struggle," 353–411; Stephen E. Patterson, *Political Parties in Revolutionary Massachusetts* (1973), 233–47.

33. See Edmund S. Morgan and Helen M. Morgan, *The Stamp Act Crisis: Prologue to Revolution* (1953), 34–36.

34. *Massachusetts Gazette*, Aug. 14, 1786, quoted in Szatmary, *Shays' Rebellion*, 39 ("most of the towns" to "in convention"); Taylor, *Massachusetts*, 137 ("the most" to "the town"); "Reverend Howard's Narrative," 1787, repr. in Richard D. Brown, "Shays's Rebellion and Its Aftermath: A View from Springfield, Massachusetts, 1787," 40 *WMQ* (1983), 601 ("[T]he General"). See

also "Hampshire County Convention," *The Worcester Magazine* (3rd week of Sept. 1786), 294–95 (drawing delegates from fifty towns in the county for a four-day convention). Although opposing conventions, "An Inhabitant of Worcester County" put "the best construction upon their conduct" given "the character and reputation" of advocates for conventions). See *The Worcester Magazine* (2nd week of Sept. 1786), 283–84.

35. David Sewall to George Thatcher, Oct. 16, 1786, "The Thatcher Papers," 6 *The Historical Magazine* (2nd Ser., 1869), 257 ("Persons of" to "misconstruction" and "Seeds of Sedition"), 258 ("always . . . be Opposed"). See also Henry Van Schaack to Peter Van Schaack, Aug. 21, 1786, *VSM*, 126 ("supposed grievances" underlay a Berkshire convention).

36. "Reverend Howard's Narrative," 1787, repr. in Brown, "Shays's Rebellion," 601 ("many Gentlemen"); "CHARGE of the Chief Justice to the Middlesex Grand Jury," *The Worcester Magazine* (4th week of Nov. 1786), 406–407 ("counteract" to "insurrection"); Sullivan, "Hints," I:197 ("the idea" to "exploded"); John Adams to Richard Cranch, Jan. 15, 1787, *AW*, I:432 ("seditious meetings"); John Adams to James Warren, Jan. 9, 1787, *WAL*, II:281("County Conventions").

37. Samuel Adams to John Adams, Apr. 16, 1784, *SAW*, IV:296 ("County Conventions" to "highly necessary" and "regular" to "dangerous"); "Letter to the Committees of the Towns of Wrentham & Medway," March 1784, in *A Volume of Records Relating to the Early History of Boston Containing Boston Town Records, 1784 to 1796*, (1903), 12–14 ("County Meetings").

38. "County Convention! At a meeting of the freeholders and other inhabitants of the town of Cambridge, on Monday, July 24, 1786," *The Worcester Magazine* (1st week of Aug. 1786), 211 ("justifiable" to "redress").

39. Samuel Adams to Noah Webster, Apr. 30, 1784, *SAW*, IV:306 ("self Created Conventions"); "Message from Governor James Bowdoin to the General Court," Sept. 28, 1786, Massachusetts Archives, Vol. 190:270, MSA.

40. Samuel Adams to Noah Webster, Apr. 30, 1784, *SAW*, IV:305 ("Keep a watchful" to "Constitutional Authority").

41. See Pauline Maier, *The Old Revolutionaries: Political Lives in the Age of Samuel Adams* (1980), 41 (asserting that for Samuel Adams "once the people put men in office, their authority was to be honored without fail"). Adams conceded the people's "*whole* sovereignty" gave them an "uncontroulable essential right" to alter or abolish their constitution. Samuel Adams to John Adams, Nov. 25, 1790, *SAW*, IV:344. See also Feer, *Shays's Rebellion*, 91 (noting that Friends of Government recognized the right of individuals or groups to petition government directly, but thought the constitution did not justify any other representative body than the legislature).

42. George Richards Minot, *The History of the Insurrections in Massachusetts* (2nd ed., Boston, 1810), 26 ("lists" to "authority"), 175–76 ("the dignity"). Although Minot offered a temporizing account of the Regulation in his *History*, in his diary at the time he wanted Daniel Shays beheaded. See Richards, *Shays's Rebellion*, 159–62. On preserving government's "dignity," see George Washington to Henry Knox, Feb. 25, 1787, *WP(CS)*, V:52 (anxious about the military campaign against the Regulators and "the dignity of Government"); John Quincy Adams to John Adams, June 30, 1787, *JQAW*, I:31 (relieved that most legislators were "well-meaning men, who will support the dignity of the government").

43. "An OLD REPUBLICAN," *The Worcester Magazine* (3rd week of Sept. 1786), 295 ("void of all authority"); "CHARGE of the Chief Justice to the Middlesex Grand Jury," *The Worcester Magazine* (4th week of Nov. 1786), 406 ("inconsistent" to "under it"); "AN OTHER CITIZEN," *The Worcester Magazine* (1st week of Sept. 1786), 275 ("*all* conventions"); "Message from Governor James Bowdoin to the General Court," Sept. 28, 1786, Massachusetts Archives, Vol. 190:270, MSA. See also David Sewall to George Thatcher, Oct. 16, 1786, "The Thatcher Papers," 258 (a county convention was "a Body of Persons unknown in the Law or Constitution").

44. "A CITIZEN," "To the Citizens of Massachusetts. On CONVENTIONS," *The Worcester Magazine* (4th week of Aug. 1786), 262 ("treasonable"); "A FREEMAN," *The Worcester Magazine* (1st week of Oct. 1786), 337 ("*Rulers, . . .*" to "my conduct"); "Attleborough" [George

Brock], Letter to the *Independent Chronicle*, Aug. 31, 1786, quoted in Lienesch, "Reinterpreting Rebellion," 166–67 ("gross mismanagement"). For defending conventions, Brock was indicted for libel against the government but was subsequently pardoned. See Clyde Augustus Duniway, *The Development of Freedom of the Press in Massachusetts* (1906, repr., 1969), 142n1.

45. "Hampshire County Convention," *The Worcester Magazine* (3rd week of Sept. 1786), 295 ("mobs and unlawful"); "Middlesex County Convention," *The Worcester Magazine* (4th week of Oct. 1786), 357 ("a peaceable"). On renouncing unlawful action, see, for example, "Hampshire County Convention," *The Worcester Magazine* (3rd week of Sept. 1786), 294 (declaring their meeting "constitutional"); "The ADDRESS of WORCESTER CONVENTION to the PEO-PLE," *The Worcester Magazine* (1st week of Oct. 1786), 335 (urging the people to "remain orderly and peaceable").

   Although some county conventions continued to meet occasionally after the advent of the first court closings, *all* the closings in the five counties that stopped courts (Hampshire, Worcester, Middlesex, Bristol, and Berkshire) were preceded by county conventions that reiterated the grievances of earlier petitions.

46. On the use of public meetings to voice grievances, see Wood, *Creation*, 324–28; Brown, *Revolutionary Politics*, 210–17; Jensen, *New Nation*, 118–22, 141; Wood, "Mobs," 635–42. See also Jackson Turner Main, *The Antifederalists: Critics of the Constitution, 1781–1788* (1961), 59 (asserting that in Massachusetts by the mid-1780s, "the right to hold conventions was steadily affirmed"); East, "Conservatives," 359 (arguing that Massachusetts's 1780 constitution "recognized the legality of local gatherings to protest against undesirable legislation, and the right was promptly seized upon to the embarrassment of the new government itself"); Brooke, "Ancient Lodges," 293 (observing that "the conventions and the bodies of Regulators associated with them claimed popular sanction for their petitions and crowd actions, claims often rooted in votes taken in town meetings").

47. Massachusetts 1780 Constitution, Bill of Rights, Art. XIX, *TC*, III:1892 ("in an orderly"); Minot, *History*, 24 ("uncertain"). "An American" conceded the people could assemble under the constitution, but only "in their corporate capacities." See "CONVENTIONS! And PAPER MONEY!" *The Worcester Magazine* (4th week of Aug. 1786), 251.

48. [Noah Webster], review of [Jackson], *Political Situation*, *The American Magazine*, Sept. 1788, pp. 744–46 ("the town meetings" to "free government").

49. "The ADDRESS of WORCESTER CONVENTION to the PEOPLE," *The Worcester Magazine* (1st week of Oct. 1786), 335 ("ensure redress" and "principles"); Massachusetts 1780 Constitution, Bill of Rights, Arts. IV, VIII, and XVIII, *TC*, III:1890 ("sole and exclusive" and "oppressors"), 1892 ("constant observance"); "A CONVENTIONER," *The Worcester Magazine* (3rd week of Oct. 1786), 350 ("every individual"). Articles VIII and XVIII of the 1780 Massachusetts Constitution dealing with rotation and constant observance of governors prompted a Hatfield convention to assert, "We are a republick – government rests upon the shoulders of the people; therefore why should any be inactive in such a day as this, when perhaps their happiness and that of generations yet unborn, depend upon their exertions." "An ADDRESS from the CONVENTION, at HATFIELD," *The Worcester Magazine* (3rd week of Jan. 1787), 511.

50. "ADDRESS of the CONVENTION of the County of WORCESTER to the PEOPLE," *The Worcester Magazine* (4th week of Nov. 1786), 404–405 ("dangerous" to "their rulers").

51. Massachusetts 1780 Constitution, Bill of Rights, Art. XIX, *TC*, III:1892 ("orderly and peaceable"). On the right of petition, see Reid, *Constitutional History*, I:21–24, 99, 109, 190, 203, 319–20n7–18; John Phillip Reid, *The Concept of Representation in the Age of the American Revolution* (1989), 96–109; Higginson, "Short History," 142–66; Mark, "Vestigial Constitution," 2153–231. See also Feer, *Shays's Rebellion*, 90 (noting that some writers "insisted that conventions were essential" since under the constitution senators were elected only on a countywide basis); Brooke, "Ancient Lodges," 293 (asserting that Regulators "gathered under the protection of the state bill of rights to confer and to instruct and petition the legislature").

52. The inhabitants of the Town of Methuen, in the coastal county of Essex, asserted in October 1786, "we have a Constitutional Right to Assemble at all times in an Orderly & peaceable Manner" and cited Article XIX of the state's bill of rights. "Petition of the Inhabitants of the Town of Methuen," Oct. 2, 1786, quoted in Rock Brynner, "'Fire Beneath Our Feet': Shays' Rebellion and Its Constitutional Impact" (Ph.D. diss., Columbia Univ., 1993), 55. Indeed, "A MEMBER of CONVENTION" cited Article XIX of the state's bill of rights as establishing the principle "that the people may, in a decent manner, seek redress of grievances; or even alter, change, or destroy, when for the good of the people." Reverting "to the principles of the constitution, on certain occasions, is not only lawful, but a duty," *The Worcester Magazine* (1st week of Oct. 1786), 321.

53. "Camillus II," Feb. 22, 1787, *The Independent Chronicle, FAW,* I:63 ("all government is"), 64 ("subversive"), 65 ("incendiary" and "that all lawful" to "origin of power"), 66 ("residue" to "conventions"). Twenty years later, Ames considered it slanderous to deny that the Federalist Party did not embrace "the principle, that from the people is derived the sovereignty of the government," "The Republican IV," Aug. 6, 1804, *Boston Gazette, FAW,* I:301. On Ames, see Winfred E. A. Bernhard, *Fisher Ames: Federalist and Statesman, 1758–1808* (1965).

54. "Camillus II," Feb. 22, 1787, *The Independent Chronicle, FAW,* I:65–66 ("whole" to "whole people"), 66 ("the servants" to "every subject"), 67 ("If consent" to "violation"), 68 ("rulers" to "commands"); "Camillus IV," Mar. 8, 1787, *The Independent Chronicle, FAW,* I:85 ("that the right"). See also "Consideration," *Boston Gazette,* Feb. 17, 1783, quoted in Feer, *Shays's Rebellion,* 478 (in voting, voters were "delegating their sovereign power for the high purposes of government").

55. "AN OTHER CITIZEN," *The Worcester Magazine* (1st week of Sept. 1786), 275. See also Wood, *Creation,* 412 (noting the Friends of Government's argument that Regulators "must rely on their elected representatives for the redress of wrongs").

56. William Whiting, "Some Remarks," repr. in Riley, "Whiting," 146 (paraphrasing Massachusetts 1780 Constitution, Bill of Rights, Art. V, which provided: "All power residing originally in the people, and being derived from them, the several magistrates and officers of government, vested with authority, whether legislative, executive, or judicial, are their substitutes and agents, and are at all times accountable to them"). See *TC,* III:1890. On the legislative action, see Szatmary, *Shays' Rebellion,* 83–84; Minot, *History,* 67–68; Taylor, *Massachusetts,* 150–53; Feer, *Shays's Rebellion,* 249–65.

57. David Cobb to James Bowdoin, Sept. 13, 1786, Shays Rebellion Papers, MHS ("very large numbers" and reporting that after the Court of Common Pleas in Taunton opened but immediately adjourned, those who sought to prevent its sitting shouted, "a generous concession on the part of Authority"). See also "Bristol County Address," repr. in Grindall Reynolds, "Concord During the Shays Rebellion," in *A Collection of Historical and Other Papers by Rev. Grindall Reynolds, D.D. To which are added Seven of his Sermons* (Concord, MA, 1895), 203–204 (the "body of gentlemen" signing the "Address" threatened to close the Court of Common Pleas "until a redress of the present grievances shall be obtained").

    Although justices of the peace possessed limited jurisdiction over debts, the county Courts of Common Pleas were engaged in most debt collection. Meeting quarterly, those courts were composed of three associate judges and one chief judge, any three of whom formed a quorum. Appeals went to the highest court, the Supreme Judicial Court. Thus, Regulators focused their attention on the Courts of Common Pleas and occasionally the circuit sessions of the Supreme Judicial Court, which heard prosecutions for court closings. For the Massachusetts court structure and jurisdiction over debt matters, see L. Kinvin Wroth and Hiller B. Zobel, eds., *Legal Papers of John Adams* (1965), I:xxxviii–xliv; Taylor, *Massachusetts,* 27–33; Priest, "Commercial Litigation," 2442–48; William E. Nelson, *Americanization of the Common Law: The Impact of Legal Change on Massachusetts Society, 1760–1830* (1975), 15–16; William T. Davis, *History of the Judiciary of Massachusetts* (1900), 168–78.

58. Diary entry of Jonathan Judd, Jr., and Northampton Regulators quoted in Szatmary, *Shays' Rebellion,* 81 ("mob"), 68 ("the resolves"). See also Taylor, *Massachusetts,* 143–44 (quoting an

observer of the Northhampton court closing that it was conducted "with less insolence and violence, and with more sobriety and good order, than is commonly to be expected in such a large and promiscuous assembly").

59. "Lucius Junius Brutus II," Oct. 19, 1786, *The Independent Chronicle, FAW*, I:47 ("the most"); *An Address From the General Court, To the People of the Commonwealth of Massachusetts* (Boston, 1786), 38 ("all order"). For perceptions of court closings as a challenge to governmental order if not the introduction of anarchy, see John Quincy Adams to Abigail Adams, Dec. 30, 1786, *JQAW*, I:28 (asserting the Regulators sought to abolish the Court of Common Pleas); James Warren to John Adams, Oct. 22, 1786, *WAL*, II:278 (describing Massachusetts as being in "a State of Anarchy and Confusion bordering on Civil War").

60. See "The Remonstrance presented to the Common's House of Assembly by the Upper Inhabitants–1767," in Richard J. Hooker, ed., *The Carolina Backcountry on the Eve of the Revolution: The Journal and Other Writings of Charles Woodmason, Anglican Itinerant* (1953), 220 (South Carolina Regulators in 1767 claiming they only sought their "Birth-Right, as *Britons*"); "Regulators' Advertisement No. 4," Jan. 1768, in Powell, *Regulators*, 76 (North Carolina colonial Regulators declaring they associated "for regulating publick Grievances & abuses of Power" and "to inform one another & learn, know and enjoy all the Priviledges & Liberties that are allowed us" under "the present Constitution").

The North Carolina Regulation drew from British and colonial patterns of crowd behavior that showed a greater "tolerance" and legitimacy for a wide spectrum of violent dissent and behavior, including the concept of "careful riot" involving calibrated violence. Wayne Lee suggests the emergence of "norms of riot" in which "the rioters restrained violence, with respect to both its intensity and its target. "They preceded violence (or threats of violence) with petitions to authority, and during the riots they made pretensions to legality. As part of this latter element, the county courthouse had emerged as a focal point for colonial riot. In each riot there was significant participation, if not leadership, by individuals from the political elite," Lee, *Crowds*, xiii ("tolerance"), 3, 5 ("careful riot"), 18, 43 ("norms of riot" and "They preceded" to "political elite"), 49–50, 64, 93. Thus, although the underlying justification for their actions was different, the Massachusetts Regulation reflected many of the earlier strategies and techniques of colonial rioters.

Before Independence, even Alexander Hamilton expressed his support for the "regulation" of courts to protect the rights of debtors. See *A Full Vindication of the Measures of the Congress*, Dec. 15, 1774, *HP*, I:75.

61. Massachusetts 1780 Constitution, Bill of Rights, Art. VII, *TC*, III:1890. For citations to Article VII and other bill of rights provisions as justifying the actions of the Regulators, see "Answer of the TOWN of GREENWICH to the circular Letter from Boston," *The Worcester Magazine* (4th week of Nov. 1786), 422–23.

62. "Lucius Junius Brutus I," Oct. 12, 1786, "Lucius Junius Brutus II," Oct. 19, 1786, "Camillus IV," Mar. 8, 1787, *The Independent Chronicle, FAW*, I, 40 ("high degree of moral depravity"), 41("mob"), 50 ("mad men and knaves"), 83 ("stupid fury"); Abigail Adams to John Adams, Nov. 28, 1786, quoted in Szatmary, *Shays' Rebellion*, 73 (warning that history predicted that "popular tyranny" of the Regulators "never fails to be followed by the arbitrary government of a single person"); Stephen Higginson to Henry Knox, Nov. 25, 1786, *HL*, 743 ("infection"). See also Henry Knox to George Washington, Oct. 23, 1786, *WP(CS)*, IV:300 (describing Regulators as "desperate & unprincipled men"); Lienesch, "Reinterpreting Rebellion," 167 (noting that Friends "made a point of depicting the protests as hopelessly irrational," frequently describing Regulators as "mad-men and fanatics").

63. Reverend Howard's Narrative, 1787, repr. in Brown, "Shays's Rebellion," 602 ("the Ragamuffins"), 603 ("freely handed"); William Whiting, "Some Remarks," repr. in Riley, "Whiting," 142 ("Profligate" to "Contemptible"). A leading Friend of Government refused to call the Regulation "a rabble" since it drew from "the substantial yeomanry of the country." Noah Webster to James Bowdoin, Mar. 15, 1787, Bowdoin and Temple Papers, pt. 2, *Massachusetts Historical Society Collections* (1907) (7th Ser.), IV:181. An examination of the social composition of the

Regulators challenges the description of them as debt-ridden farmers, arguing that participation in the Regulation frequently did little to hurt one's social standing. See Richards, *Shays's Rebellion*, 44–55.

For newspaper bias against the Regulators, see, for example, Paul D. Marsella, "Propaganda Trends in the *Essex Journal and New Hampshire Packet*, 1787–1788," 114 *Essex Institute Historical Collection* (1978), 161–78.

64. James Sullivan to Rufus King, Feb. 25, 1787, *RKC*, I:214 ("Rebels" to "will lead"); John Quincy Adams to Abigail Adams, Dec. 30, 1786, *JQAW*, I:28. Sullivan served on the Superior Court of Judicature, Assize, and General Jail Delivery from 1776 to 1782 (renamed the Supreme Judicial Court in 1782). See Davis, *Judiciary*, 101–102, 174. See also Wehtje, "Boston's Response," 19 (describing the fear of Bostonians that the "anarchy" of the Regulation would lead to "tyranny").

65. Quoted in Szatmary, *Shays' Rebellion*, 99 ("surprised"); General John Brooks to James Bowdoin, Oct. 30, 1786, Shays Rebellion Papers, MHS ("of infinite" to "its contents"). See also David Humphreys to George Washington, Nov. 1, 1786, *WP(CS)*, IV:325 (expecting "leaders of the Mob" to "soon take possession" of the Springfield arsenal).

66. Ezra Stiles to George Washington, Feb. 7, 1787, *WP(CS)*, V:16 ("they had flatterd"); Henry Knox to President of Congress, Oct. 3, 1786, *JCC*, XXXI:752. For the title of Knox's office, see *JCC*, XXXI:895 ("Secretary at War"). An officer who helped suppress the Regulators but who had served with Shays during the Revolutionary War remembered Shays as "a brave and good soldier." See "Recollections of Park Holland and Family History," Typescript, 22–23 (1832), Holland Family Papers, MHS.

For Regulators' lack of interest in the arsenal, see Hall, *Politics*, 223 (noting that although the Regulators who closed the court at Springfield "had the run of the town for two days, they made no effort to seize the arsenal"); Szatmary, "Rebellion in Springfield," 13 (concluding that until very late in their conflict with state authorities, Regulators "had no intention of attacking" the arsenal).

67. Minot, *History*, 39 ("only as a mode").

68. Middlesex County Court Closing, Sept. 12, 1786, Springfield Court Closing, Sept. 26, 1786, Massachusetts Archives, Vol. 190:250 ("The voice of the people"), 255 ("set forth"), 290 ("the People collected"), MSA; Worcester Court Closing, Sept. 6, 1786, Massachusetts Archives, Vol. 190:236 ("the Body of People"), MSA.

69. Theodore Sedgwick to James Bowdoin, Oct. 5, 1786, Massachusetts Archives, Vol. 190:284, MSA ("disposed" and estimating that only 20 percent of the inhabitants of his county were truly "desperate and prepared for any evil purpose"); Artemas Ward to James Bowdoin, Dec. 7, 1786, Shays Rebellion Papers, MHS ("gained their point"); John Jay to Thomas Jefferson, Dec. 14, 1786, *JP*, X:597.

For the peaceful character of the court closings, see Szatmary, *Shays' Rebellion*, 58–59, 80; Feer, *Shays's Rebellion*, 185–235. While the largest and most dramatic court closings occurred in the far western counties of Hampshire and Berkshire, nearly half of all the stoppages took place in eastern counties, including Middlesex and Bristol, or in the middle of the state, in Worcester County. In addition, the coastal county of Plymouth preempted court closings by adjourning sessions during the height of court closings. For Plymouth, see Priest, "Commercial Litigation," 244n133.

70. Adam Wheeler, "To the PUBLICK," Nov. 7, 1786, *The Worcester Magazine* (4th week of Nov. 1786), 414.

71. Sheriff Caleb Hyde to Governor James Bowdoin, Sept. 13, 1786, Massachusetts Archives, Vol. 190:263 ("much the greatest part"), MSA. The method of identifying the will of the people had been used in a Berkshire County court closing in 1782. See Feer, *Shays's Rebellion*, 166 (describing how residents around Pittsfield in February 1782 assembled in two different groups to gather the sense in favor of closing the court). For the Great Barrington court closing, see Taylor, *Massachusetts*, 144–45; Riley, "Whiting," 125; Feer, *Shays's Rebellion*, 209–11; Charles J. Taylor, *History of Great Barrington, Massachusetts* (Great Barrington, MA, 1882), 305–306 (estimating the crowd at 2,000 persons, "four-fifths of whom were opposed to the sitting of the court").

72. Sheriff Caleb Hyde to Governor James Bowdoin, Sept. 13, 1786, Massachusetts Archives, Vol. 190:264 ("until the Constitution"), MSA; Henry Van Schaack to Peter Van Schaack, Sept. 18, 1786, *VSM*, 126 ("vast concourse"). Whiting's fellow judges were James Barker, Charles Goodrich, and Jahleel Woodbridge, the last being the judge who refused to sign.

73. William Whiting to Theodore Sedgwick, Sept. 13, 1786, in Riley, "Whiting," 135 ("known to"); Smith, "Medicine in Berkshire," 117 ("brought upon him"); Rufus King to Theodore Sedgwick, Oct. 22, 1786, Theodore Sedgwick Papers, MHS. Whiting's tract was entitled, "Some Brief Remarks On The Present State of Publick Affairs." Whiting said he wrote "Gracchus" and "Some Brief Remarks" toward the end of the week preceding the session of the Court of Common Pleas scheduled for Great Barrington on Tuesday, Sept. 12, 1786. See Riley, "Whiting," 123.

   Whiting's attitude toward Regulator grievances was not unique among the Massachusetts judiciary. At least two other justices of the peace in Berkshire County, one in Bristol County, and another in Worcester County were also sympathetic toward the Regulators and similarly faced removal from the bench. See Taylor, *Massachusetts*, 148, 201n62; "Address for the Removal of William Whiting & Others from Office," Feb. 28, 1787, Massachusetts Archives, Vol. 189:171–77, MSA.

74. William Whiting, "Gracchus," repr. in Riley, "Whiting," 131 ("is or ought to be" and "enrich themselves" to "unequally administered"), 132 ("a set of"); Wood, *Radicalism*, 234 ("rough equality" to "landless laborers"); Whiting, "Some Remarks," repr. in Riley, "Whiting," 142 ("with their own Eyes"). See also Richards, *Shays's Rebellion*, 164 (arguing that Regulators included "thousands of backcountry families" who responded to "a revolution that had failed them, one which in their judgment had merely shifted power from one set of 'plunderers' to another").

75. William Whiting, "Gracchus," repr. in Riley, "Whiting," 132 ("baneful injustice" to "removed"); Whiting, "Some Remarks," repr. in Riley, "Whiting," 153 ("Expressly" to "best"); Noah Webster to James Bowdoin, Mar. 15, 1787, Bowdoin and Temple Papers, pt. 2, *Massachusetts Historical Society Collections* (1907) (7th Ser.), VI:181 ("the majority").

76. Whiting, "Some Remarks," repr. in Riley, "Whiting," 153 ("Reverse"). See also Great Barrington Election Result, Aug. 27, 1779, Massachusetts Archives, Vol. 160:184, MSA.

77. Minot, *History*, 170 ("mistaken" and "favourite rights"); Henry Van Schaack, article critical of Regulators, Feb. 1787, repr. in Appendix D, *VSM*, 227 ("difference"); Henry Knox to Marquis de Lafayette, Feb. 13, 1787, quoted in Szatmary, *Shays' Rebellion*, 97–98 ("maxim" to "materially different"); Stephen Higginson to Nathan Dane, Mar. 3, 1787, *HL*, 754 ("far too much"). See also Wood, *Creation*, 374 (noting contemporary complaints that the "common distinction 'between power being *derived* from the people, and being *seated* in the people' was rapidly being dissolved in the years after Independence, as radical writers 'in the transition from monarchy to a republic' expanded and indeed 'bastardized' the principles of the Revolution").

78. John Adams to Edmund Jenings, June 7, 1780, *AP*, IX:388 ("principal Engineer"); Mary Cranch to Abigail Adams, Sept. 24, 1786, Adams Manuscript Trust, Microfilm, Reel 368, MHS ("excess of liberty" to "ruined them"); Henry Van Schaack, article critical of Regulators, Feb. 1787, repr. in Appendix D, *VSM*, 226–27 ("liberal" to "all powers"). See also "Camillus III," Mar. 1, 1787, *The Independent Chronicle*, *FAW*, I:72 (Fisher Ames lamenting, "The people have turned against their teachers the doctrines, which were inculcated in order to effect the late revolution"). For John Adams's contribution to the 1780 constitution, see Editorial Note, *AP*, VIII:228–36; Robert J. Taylor, "Construction of the Massachusetts Constitution," 90 *Proceedings of the American Antiquarian Society* (1980), 330–31; Robert J. Taylor, "Lawyer John Adams and the Massachusetts Constitution," 24 *Boston Bar Journal* (1980), 22 (speculating that no draft in Adams's hand of the constitution exists "because so inconsequential were the alterations made in it that it was sent right to the printer who discarded it after setting his type").

79. See Massachusetts 1780 Constitution, Bill of Rights, Art. 7, Pennsylvania 1776 Constitution, Bill of Rights, Sec. 5, Virginia 1776 Constitution, Bill of Rights, Sec. 3, *TC*, III:1890, V:3082–83, VII:3813. For Adams's contempt of the structure of government created by Pennsylvania's 1776 constitution, especially its single-bodied legislature, see Nash, *Unknown*, 277–80.

80. The version John Adams drafted drew from both Virginia's and Pennsylvania's bill of rights, but the emphasis on scrutinizing government mirrored the language in Pennsylvania's bill of rights. See Massachusetts 1780 Constitution, Bill of Rights, Pennsylvania 1776 Constitution, Bill of Rights, Virginia 1776 Constitution, Bill of Rights, *TU*, III:1892, V:3083–84, VII:3814.

81. See Massachusetts 1780 Constitution, Bill of Rights, Pennsylvania 1776 Constitution, Bill of Rights, *TU*, III:1892, V:3084.

82. For Friends' descriptions of Regulators, see, for example, Lienesch, "Reinterpreting Rebellion," 166 (observing the resentment of Regulators at being "stigmatized as traitors, incendiaries" and *"vile creatures"*). For Regulators' self-description, see, for example, "Bristol County Address," repr. in Reynolds, *Collection*, 203–204; Worcester Court Closing, Sept. 5, 1786, Springfield Court Closing, Sept. 26, 1786, Massachusetts Archives, Vol. 190:232 ("the Body"), 236 ("the Body of People"), 290 ("the People now at Arms"), MSA.

    Benjamin Lincoln to George Washington, Dec. 4, 1786[–4 Mar. 1787], *WP(CS)*, IV:433 ("upon republican principles"); William Whiting, "Some Remarks," repr. in Riley, "Whiting," 148 ("Cretures and Servants"). On respect for majority will, see also Wood, *Creation*, 412 (noting the announcement of the town of Boston that Regulators "must obey the majority"); Henry Knox to Theophilus Parsons, Mar. 29, 1785, in Main, *Antifederalists*, 104n6 (rejecting that "a very small minority" could "check the great Majority"); John McAuley Palmer, *General von Steuben* (1937), 340 (wondering if "the numerous militia" supported the Regulators "and a very small number of *respectable gentlemen* only" supported the government, "would Congress dare to support such an abominable oligarchy?"); Wiecek, *Guarantee Clause*, 23n19 (citing references to the majority principle in the idea of "republican popular sovereignty").

83. William Whiting, "Gracchus," repr. in Riley, "Whiting," 132 ("Virtue"); William Whiting to Robert Treat Paine, Mar. 19, 1787, Robert Treat Paine Papers, MHS ("always been taught"); William Whiting, "Some Remarks," repr. in Riley, "Whiting," 148 ("free Governments" to "Struggles); "Petition to the Governor of Massachusetts from the Town of New Salem," Jan. 18, 1787, repr. in Meaney, "Popular Sovereignty," 218 ("Tyranny" to "Confusion"), 219 ("with the point"); John Adams, "An Essay on Man's Lust for Power," [post Aug. 29, 1763], *AP*, I:81 ("All Men"), 83 ("Was there ever, in any Nation or Country, since the fall, a standing Army that was not carefully watched and contrould by the State so as to" prevent them from enslaving "the People").

84. "A Proclamation, By His Excellency James Bowdoin, Governour of the Commonwealth of Massachusetts," Sept. 6, 1786, *The Massachusetts Centinel* ("the most pernicious" to "treasonable proceedings"); Minot, *History*, 52 ("vigorous measures" to "the government"). In addition to being unsuccessful in having federal troops suppress the "rebellion," Governor Bowdoin encouraged legislative measures against the Regulators. For the failed congressional effort to militarily aid the Massachusetts government, see Joseph Parker Warren, "The Confederation and the Shays Rebellion," 11 *AHR* (1905), 42–67; Wiecek, *Guarantee Clause*, 33–45; Keith L. Dougherty, *Collective Action Under the Articles of Confederation* (2001), 103–28.

85. The Militia Act was passed on Oct. 24, 1786, the Riot Act on Oct. 28, 1786, the Habeas Corpus Suspension Act on Nov. 10, 1786, the False Reports Act on Nov. 16, 1786, and the Indemnity Act on Nov. 15, 1786. On the various acts, see Szatmary, *Shays' Rebellion*, 83–84; Feer, *Shays's Rebellion*, 253. For provisions on the suspension of habeas corpus, see Massachusetts 1780 Constitution, Chap. VI, Art. VII, *TC*, III:1910.

86. "Petition for a Pardon by Eli Parsons and William Smith," May 24, 1787, Massachusetts Archives, Vol. 189:425, MSA ("an infringement" to "Treasure"); "Norman Clark to James Bowdoin, Transmitting Petition to the General Court," Jan. 11, 1787, Massachusetts Archives, Vol. 190:301–303, MSA ("horror" to "Government"); Daniel Gray, "An Address to the People of the Several Towns in the County of Hampshire Now Under Arms," repr. in Ellery B. Crane, "Shays' Rebellion," 5 *Proceedings of the Worcester Society of Antiquity* (Worcester, MA, 1881), 88 ("those persons").

87. Benjamin Hichborn, *Oration Delivered at Boston, March 5th, 1777*, in Niles, *Principles*, 47 ("power" to "in its stead"); "Thomas Grover and Elisha Pondell to the People," Dec. 2, 1786, repr. in Crane, "Shays' Rebellion," 85 ("seeds of war" to "point"); Minot, *History*, 87 ("the liberties" to

"every thing"). On the Hichborn raid, see Richards, *Shays's Rebellion*, 19–21; Szatmary, *Shays' Rebellion*, 92–93; Feer, *Shays's Rebellion*, 320–21; Hall, *Politics*, 221. For Hichborn, sometimes spelled Hitchbourne, see *Sibley's Harvard Graduates*, XVII:36–44 (entry on Hichborn); John Adams, diary entry, Sept. 16, 1775, *ADA*, II:174n1. On the petitions of protest, see Richards, *Shays's Rebellion*, 21; Feer, *Shays's Rebellion*, 340–44.

88. Benjamin Lincoln to George Washington, Dec. 4, 1786–[Mar. 4, 1787], *WP(CS)*, IV:422 ("a club" to "remainder"). For militia defection to the Regulators, see Richards, *Shays's Rebellion*, 11. On the special army, see Feer, *Shays's Rebellion*, 345–60; Taylor, *Massachusetts*, 158–59; David B. Mattern, *Benjamin Lincoln and the American Revolution* (1995), 166–69.

89. Minot, *History*, 93 ("a number"). On support by speculators for Lincoln's army, see Richards, *Shays's Rebellion*, 78–79. Governor Bowdoin insisted that the funds raised were only for supplies and not the soldiers' wages. See Feer, *Shays's Rebellion*, 356n1.

90. "Copy of the PETITION which was sent to his Excellency the Governor, and the Hon. Council, on the 17th instant," *The Worcester Magazine* (4th week of Jan. 1787), 520 ("the people" to "real grievances"). See also Hall, *Politics*, 225 (noting the strategy of Friends in seeking a "smashing" military victory to undermine "the political power of the conventions and the Regulators").

91. "Petition of the Inhabitants of Amherst to the General Court," Jan. 12, 1787, repr. in Edward Wilton Carpenter, *The History of the Town of Amherst, Massachusetts* (2 parts, Amherst, MA, 1896), Part II:106 ("Public Affairs" to "Poverty"); "Petition of Town of Sutton to Governor Bowdoin," Jan. 17, 1787, Massachusetts Archives, Vol. 190:305 ("defend themselves"), MSA; Daniel Shays, Joel Billings, John Bardwell, John Powers, and Reuben Dickinson to Luke Day, [Jan.] 1787, Worcester Collection, AAS ("by the point" to "opportunity"); "Reverend Howard's Narrative," 1787, repr. in Brown, "Shays's Rebellion," 614 ("severe"). On the Disqualification Act, see Feer, *Shays's Rebellion*, 385–86; Szatmary, *Shays' Rebellion*, 106.

92. William Pynchon, diary entry for Sept. 9, 1786, in Oliver, *Diary*, 248 ("of cannons"); John Jay to Thomas Jefferson, Oct. 27, 1786, *JP*, X:488 ("Spirit"), 489 ("the Charms"); Henry Knox to George Washington, Dec. 17, 1786, *WP(CS)*, IV:400 ("unjust means" to "infamous"). On Knox's exaggeration see Forrest McDonald and Ellen Shapiro McDonald, *Requiem: Variations on Eighteenth-Century Themes* (1988), 72–73; Henry Knox to George Washington, Oct. 23, 1786, *WP(CS)*, IV:300–301 (claiming Regulators sought "to annihilate all debts public and private" and that the country faced "the horror of faction and civil war").

93. "Notes on [Congressional] Debates," Feb. 19, 1787, *MP*, IX:276 ("great & illustrious"); James Warren to John Adams, May 18, 1787, *WAL*, II:292 ("destroy"); Benjamin Lincoln to George Washington, Feb. 27, 1787, *WP(CS)*, IV:432 ("seek redress" to "governed"). See also Rufus King to Elbridge Gerry, Feb. 18, 1787, *RKC*, I:215 (expressing "some doubt" about the Disqualification Act); Hall, *Politics*, 232 ("The combination of repression, dissension, and rumors about the future led many persons who had opposed the Regulation to dislike as well the administration that had crushed it"). Even the staunch Friend of Government, the Boston merchant Stephen Higginson, thought the legislature might have "carried their resentment too far" in some aspects of its "energetic system of policy" against the Regulators. Stephen Higginson to Nathan Dane, Mar. 3, 1787, *HL*, 753.

94. Henry Jackson to Henry Knox, Jan. 21 and 28, 1787, quoted in Mattern, *Benjamin Lincoln*, 169 ("in high spirits"), 170 ("the whole").

95. Daniel Shays and Samuel Gray to Benjamin Lincoln, Jan. 25, 1787 ("a fair" to "Constitutional Relief"), Benjamin Lincoln to James Bowdoin, Jan. 26, 1787 ("to make"), Shays Rebellion Papers, MHS; Timothy Bigelow to Timothy Bigelow, Sr., Jan. 28, 1787, Houghton Library, HU ("precipitation & confusion"). For the Springfield arsenal confrontation, see Feer, *Shays's Rebellion*, 360–70; Szatmary, "Rebellion in Springfield," 13–17; Taylor, *Massachusetts*, 159–61.

96. Daniel Shays to Benjamin Lincoln, Jan. 30, 1787, repr. in Josiah Gilbert Holland, *History of Western Massachusetts. The Counties of Hampden, Hampshire, Franklin, and Berkshire* (2 vols., Springfield, MA, 1855), I:268 ("recourse" to "circumstances"), 269 ("united" to "purpose"). See also Rufus Putnam to James Bowdoin, Jan. 8, 1787, in Parmenter, *Pelham*, 396 (indicating that Shays did not regard stopping courts as an impediment to his potential pardon).

97. Benjamin Lincoln to James Bowdoin, Feb. 17, 1787, Shays Rebellion Papers, MHS. See also Rufus King to unknown correspondent, Feb. 10, 1787, Rufus King Papers, LC (describing the rout of Regulator forces at Petersham as "totally irregular and in all directions"). On the petitions and "mopping up" actions, see Feer, *Shays's Rebellion*, 382–407; Mattern, *Benjamin Lincoln*, 170–72; Welch, *Sedgwick*, 50–53.

98. Theodore Sedgwick to James Bowdoin, Apr. 8, 1787, Sedgwick/Bowdoin Letters [typescript copies], BA ("a good effect"). See also Theodore Sedgwick to Benjamin Lincoln, Apr. 30, 1787, Theodore Sedgwick Papers, MHS (having "no objection" to imposing the death penalty on Regulators). Sedgwick argued that a general pardon for Regulators would be an "abdication" of government encouraging "future insurrections." Theodore Sedgwick to James Bowdoin, Oct. 5, 1786, Massachusetts Archives, Vol. 190:287, MSA. For the prosecutions, see Feer, *Shays's Rebellion*, 409–47; Marion L. Starkey, *A Little Rebellion* (1955), 191–226; Edward W. Hanson, "Robert Treat Paine, Attorney General," 8 *Massachusetts Legal History* (2002), 95–123; Richards, *Shays's Rebellion*, 41. On the pardons, see John Dryden Kazar, Jr., "No Early Pardon for Traitors: Rebellion in Massachusetts in 1787," 33 *Historical Journal of Massachusetts* (2005), 109–38.

99. Increase Sumner to Elizabeth Sumner, Apr. 8, 1787, Increase Sumner Papers, MHS ("greatly overcome"); William Whiting to Governor Bowdoin and Council, May 7, 1787, Massachusetts Archives, Vol. 189:374, MSA ("Troubles & Disgrace" to "Enemies"). See also "Petition of Elijah Dwight and others to the Governor and Council," Apr. 9, 1787, Massachusetts Archives, Vol. 189:371–373B, MSA; "Remission of Doctor William Whiting's Sentence," May 12, 1787, Massachusetts Archives, Vol. 189:369–369A, MSA.

100. Theodore Sedgwick to William Whiting, Sept. 14, 1786, in Riley, "Whiting," 136 ("seditious libel" to "reprehensible"), 137 ("limited understandings"), 138 ("urging a watchful"), 139 ("to pursue"); William V. Wells, *The Life and Public Service of Samuel Adams, Being a Narrative of his Acts and Opinions, and of his Agency in Producing and Forwarding the American Revolution* (3 vols., Boston, 1865), III:246 ("the crime" to "suffer death"). See also Theodore Sedgwick to Governor Bowdoin, Apr. 8, 1787, Sedgwick/Bowdoin Letters [typescript copies], BA (seeking mercy for Regulators led astray by "the arts and seduction of others" rather than their own "depraved disposition").

101. Taylor, *Great Barrington*, 317–19 ("a stormy" and "Pretended" at 318); Theodore Sedgwick to Henry Van Schaack, Dec. 5, 1787, in *DHRC*, IV:384 ("the side of truth"), V:957–65.

102. William Williams to Henry Van Schaack, Apr. 25, 1787, *VSM*, 141 ("the constitutional importance"); Peter Van Schaack to Benjamin Lincoln, Apr. 8, 1787, quoted in Mattern, *Benjamin Lincoln*, 174 ("probable evils" to "chair of office"); Theodore Sedgwick to Nathan Dane, June 3, 1787, Shays Rebellion Papers, MHS ("On one side"). For the political fallout of the Spring election, see Feer, *Shays's Rebellion*, 455 (giving vote totals for Hancock); Hall, *Politics*, 227–55; Formisano, *Transformation*, 30 (describing the 1787 election as a "referendum of whether to be lenient or harsh" toward the Regulators).

103. Henry Knox to Mercy Warren, May 30, 1787, *WAL*, II:295 ("mad democracy" to "every Legislature"); John Quincy Adams to John Adams, June 30, 1787, *JQAW*, I:31 ("peculiar talent" to "villany"); Theodore Sedgwick to Rufus King, June 18, 1787, *RKC*, I:224 ("Everyman" to "the community"); Theodore Sedgwick to Nathan Dane, July 5, 1787, quoted in Main, *Political Parties*, 118 ("by the dregs").

104. Parsons, *Essex*, 1778, I:486 ("dazzling"), 490 ("the bulk of the people" and "most probably"); Benjamin Lincoln, Jr., quoted in Mattern, *Benjamin Lincoln*, 165 ("great wisdom"). For dismay at the legislative agenda, see Christopher Gore to Rufus King, June 28, 1787, *RKC*, I:227; James Madison to Edmund Randolph, Apr. 22, 1787; James Madison to Thomas Jefferson, Apr. 23, 1787, *MP*, IX, 395, 399; Stephen Higginson to Nathan Dane, June 3 and 16, 1787, *HL*, 756, 759. See also Richards, *Shays's Rebellion*, 119 (concluding that Regulators "emerged victorious" after the Regulation by bringing "speculators to heel" and stopping the shift of money "from the backcountry to Boston"); East, "Conservatives," 363n31 (noting that on Nov. 13, 1787, the House continued "an act suspending the laws for the collection of debts" by a vote of 116 to 74).

105. Merrill and Wilentz, *Key of Liberty*, 136 ("who could live" to "executive officers"), 139 ("a few leading men" to "themselves").
106. See, for example, Wood, "Interests;" Banner, *Hartford*, 70–72, 81–83; Stephen Higginson to John Adams, Mar. 1, 1790, *HL*, 776 (enclosing state Senate speeches giving an "Idea of the feelings and Views of those people who are opposed to Government").

CHAPTER 5. THE FEDERAL CONSTITUTION AND THE EFFORT TO CONSTRAIN THE PEOPLE

1. The account of the correspondence between Jefferson and John and Abigail Adams draws on John Adams to Thomas Jefferson, Nov. 30, 1786, Thomas Jefferson to John Adams, Dec. 20, 1786, Thomas Jefferson to Abigail Adams, Dec. 21, 1786, *JP*, X:557, 619, 621; Abigail Adams to Thomas Jefferson, Jan. 29, 1787, Thomas Jefferson to Abigail Adams, Feb. 22, 1787, Thomas Jefferson to Abigail Adams, July 1, 1787, Thomas Jefferson to David Hartley, July 2, 1787, *JP*, XI:86, 174, 515, 526; Abigail Adams to Thomas Jefferson, Sept. 10, 1787, John Adams to Thomas Jefferson, Oct. 28, 1787, *JP*, XII:112, 291–92; John Adams to Thomas Jefferson, June 30, 1813, Cappon, *Adams-Jefferson Letters*, II:346.
2. *Pennsylvania Gazette*, Sept. 5, 1787, *DHRC*, XIII:192 ("[e]very state"); [Jackson], *Political Situation*, 51 ("inflammable" to "easily catch"). See also Stephen Higginson to Henry Knox, Feb. 13, 1787, *HL*, 751. For concerns about America's political instability, see Wood, *Creation*, 465 (identifying impressions that state governments, "however well structured, no longer seemed capable of creating virtuous laws and citizens"); Rakove, *Meanings*, 34 (noting how the Regulation "signaled a deeper crisis" in political governance within the states). On how newspapers converted Shays and the Regulation into a symbol of disorder and anarchy, see Alexander, *News Coverage*, 99, 142–44, 169–70, 179–81, 187, 218; Peter S. Onuf, "Anarchy and the Crisis of the Union," in Herman Belz, Ronald Hoffman, and Peter J. Albert, eds., *To Form a More Perfect Union: The Critical Ideas of the Constitution* (1992), 274 (noting how the Regulation prompted anxiety over "the degeneration of democracy" and made Shays "an exemplar of 'tyranny' or 'despotism'").
3. For perceptions of determinist movements before the federal Constitution, see Humphrey, *Land and Liberty*, 128 ("Conspiracies of wide-spread frontier rebellion may have been a bit far-fetched, but they were not new in the 1790s, and they were not entirely unfounded").
4. See Fritz, "Fallacies," 1327–69. For a recent depiction of the federal Constitution as reacting to weaknesses in the Articles and the misdeeds of the states, see Calvin H. Johnson, *Righteous Anger at the Wicked States: The Meaning of the Founders' Constitution* (2005).
5. In emphasizing the democratic features of the federal Constitution Akhil Amar overlooks the fact that the draft of the federal Framers reflected a more constrained understanding of the people's sovereignty in comparison with more expansive possibilities for the role of the people and their relationship to government available at the time. See Amar, *America's Constitution*. A more expansive constitutional understanding had manifested itself in many American constitutions since the Revolution.
   For a critique of the federal Constitution as a democratic document, see Robert A. Dahl, *How Democratic Is the American Constitution?* (2001).
6. John Marshall to Arthur Lee, Apr. 17, 1784, *JMP*, I:120 ("a few"). On the concept of disinterestedness and expectations of deference, see Wood, "Interests," 69–109; Shalhope, *Bennington*, 179 (describing "an influx of gentlemen" to Vermont in the 1780s who "firmly believed in a traditional social and political order in which common people exhibited an unquestioning deference and respect toward their superiors").
7. Jeremy Belknap to Ebenezer Hazard, Mar. 3, 1784, in "The Belknap Papers," *Collections of the Massachusetts Historical Society* (5th Ser.) (Boston, 1877), 313 ("grand prerequisite" to "their benefit"), 314 ("kept up over"), 315 ("be taught" to "themselves").
8. Charles Pettit to Jeremiah Wadsworth, May 27, 1786, Jeremiah Wadsworth Papers, CHS ("intoxicating" to "Slaughter Pen"); John Jay to George Washington, June 27, 1786, in Jared

Sparks, ed., *Correspondence of the American Revolution; Being Letters of Eminent Men to George Washington* (4 vols., Boston, 1853), IV:135 ("going and doing" to "calamities"); George Washington to James Madison, Nov. 5, 1786, *MP*, IX:161 ("No morn[ing]"). See also John Marshall to James Wilkinson, Jan. 5, 1787, *JMP*, I:201 (considering the present political situation as casting "a deep shade over" the "bright prospect" of the Revolution); Robert A. Feer, "Shays's Rebellion and the Constitution: A Study in Causation," 42 *New England Quarterly* (1969), 388–410; Wehtje, "Boston's Response," 19–27.

9. Shalhope, *Bennington*, 185 ("former indentured servant" and "college-educated attorney"). On the social divide between traditional elites and those newly entering the political arena, see Labaree, *Patriots*, 94 (describing "a new group of merchants" drawn from the ranks of cord-wainers, chaisemakers, and leather-dressers who displaced an "older generation" of economic elites in Newburyport by the 1780s and 1790s); Wood, "Interests," 93–101; Appleby, *Inheriting*, 26–55; Humphrey, *Land and Liberty*, 111 ("Only after the Revolution could a former store clerk and farmhand replace two mighty landlords" in the Hudson Valley); Nash, *Unknown*, 178–89.

For Madison's and others concerns about democratic forces, see Wood, *Radicalism*; James Madison, "Vices of the Political System of the United States," Apr., 1787, *MPP*, IX:345–58; Charles F. Hobson, "The Negative on State Laws: James Madison, the Constitution, and the Crisis of Republican Government," 36 *WMQ* (1979), 215–35; Drew R. McCoy, *The Elusive Republic: Political Economy in Jeffersonian America* (1980); Rakove, *Meanings*, 345 (identifying "the great challenge," for Madison, "to curb the excesses of legislative misrule and the unruly surges of popular interest and opinion that made republican politics so tumultuous").

For the argument that a new consumer economy involving ordinary people helped politicize Americans and encourage the belief they were engaged in a common political cause, see T. H. Breen, *The Marketplace of Revolution: How Consumer Politics Shaped American Independence* (2004).

10. Edward Rutledge quoted in James Haw, *John and Edward Rutledge of South Carolina* (1997), 184 ("found it very"); *New York Daily Advertiser*, July 15, 1786 ("more pernicious"); John Jay to Thomas Jefferson, Oct. 27, 1786, *JP*, X:489 ("Desire of Equality"). See Nash, *Unknown*, 277 (describing how Pennsylvania's 1776 constitution "shocked and dismayed some patriot leaders").

11. Gouverneur Morris to John Penn, May 20, 1774, *AA* (4th Ser.), I:342 ("impossible" to "keep them down"). See also Woody Holton, *Forced Founders: Indians, Debtors, Slaves and the Making of the American Revolution in Virginia* (1999), 197 (observing that as "more and more smallholders and poor whites became convinced that they would soon be living in an 'Independent Republic,' some of them began to make specific demands about what that republic should look like"); Kars, *Breaking*, 209 (noting that "elite revolutionaries discovered that it was increasingly difficult to limit the aspirations of lower-class Americans, upon whom they relied for support in their struggle with Britain").

12. See Wood, "Interests," 70 (describing the 1780s as "a time of great release and expansion: the population grew as never before, or since, and more Americans than ever before were off in pursuit of prosperity and happiness"); Benjamin Franklin to Thomas Jefferson, Mar. 20, 1786, *JP*, IX:349 (asserting that during his "long Life" he could not remember ever seeing "more Signs of Public Felicity than appear at present throughout these States"); Bogin, "True Policy," 105 (describing New Jersey legislator Abraham Clark's plan for paper money in 1786 as "the mainspring for economic and social regeneration" and the "stimulation" for manufacturing in the state). See also Joyce Appleby, *Liberalism and Republicanism in the Historical Imagination* (1992), 210 (observing that "[t]he characterization of the 1780s as a period of crisis comes from the writers of the Constitution themselves, most particularly from the authors of the Federalist Papers").

13. Camillus III, *The Independent Chronicle*, Mar. 1, 1787, *FAW*, I:72 ("The people have"); John Adams to Richard Price, May 20, 1789, *AW*, IX:558 ("too ardent"). See also John Adams to Thomas Jefferson, Oct. 28, 1787, *JP*, XII:291–92 (asserting that two-thirds of the states "have

made Constitutions, in no respect better than those of the Italian Republicks, and as sure as there is an Heaven and an Earth, if they are not altered they will produce Disorders and Confusion").

14. For characterizations that Maryland's 1776 constitution was "the most conservative" of the first state constitutions, see Hoffman, *Spirit*, 269; Williams, "State Constitutions," 567; Nash, *Unknown*, 244.

15. "The Appeal of the House of Delegates," Jan. 16, 1787; "The Reply of the Senate," Jan. 20, 1787, in Yazawa, *Representative*, 35 ("you alone"), 48 ("one branch" to "the other"), 50 ("large collected"). See also Wood, *Creation*, 369 (calling the Maryland debate the "most important constitutional debate" before the federal Constitution). On the political history of Maryland, see Crowl, *Maryland*; Hoffman, *Spirit*.

    In 1784 a Maryland legislator announced to his constituents, "I shall consider it my duty to follow your instructions; and whenever I am timely apprized of any subject of importance, I shall endeavour to inform you of it, and take your direction thereon." Charles Ridgely, "To the Electors of Baltimore County," Nov. 5, 1784, in *Maryland Journal and Baltimore Advertiser*, Dec. 24, 1784.

16. Samuel Chase to his Constituents, Feb. 9, 1787, in Yazawa, *Representative*, 56 ("All *lawful*" to "of the people"), 57 (*"trustees* and *servants"*). Chase borrowed his figure of speech from James Burgh's *Political Disquisitions*. See Wood, *Creation*, 372n49. For Chase's political and jurisprudential shift, see Stephen B. Presser and Becky Blair Hurley, "Saving God's Republic: The Jurisprudence of Samuel Chase," 1984 *U. Ill. L. Rev.* (1984), 771–822.

17. Samuel Chase to his Constituents, Feb. 9, 1787, in Yazawa, *Representative*, 60 (*"manifest* danger" to "our government"). The full text of the Maryland 1776 Constitution, Bill of Rights, Sec. 4 provided: "That all persons invested with the legislative or executive powers of government, are the trustees of the public, and as such accountable for their conduct, wherefore, whenever the ends of government are perverted, and public liberty manifestly endangered, and all other means of redress are ineffectual, the people may, and of right ought, to reform the old, or establish a new government; the doctrine of nonresistance against arbitrary power and oppression, is absurd, slavish, and destructive of the good and happiness of mankind." See Nov. 3, 1776, Papenfuse and Stiverson, *Decisive*.

18. William Paca to the Citizens, Feb. 15, 1787, William Paca to Alexander Contee Hanson, May 10, 1787, in Yazawa, *Representative*, 63 (*"supreme authority"*), 65 ("deputy" and "principal"), 113 ("command over"). For an example of Paca's varying analogies, see William Paca to the Citizens, Feb. 15, 1787, in Yazawa, *Representative*, 62 (describing a representative as the people's *"trustee* or *deputy"*),.

19. William Paca to Alexander Contee Hanson, May 10, 1787, June 22, 1787, in Yazawa, *Representative*, 117 ("the judges" to "powers of government"), 137 ("[T]he very" to "maintains"), 135 ("constitutional doctrine").

20. Alexander Contee Hanson to the People, June 9, 1787, Alexander Contee Hanson to William Paca, July 12, 1787, in Yazawa, *Representative*, 125 ("[N]o writer"), 144 ("compact"), 141 ("the people being" to "human brain"), 144 ("place their" to "partnership continues"), 125 ("All power" to "government and law").

21. "Remarks on the Proposed Plan of an Emission of Paper, by Aristides," Feb. 26, 1787, in Yazawa, *Representative*, 175 ("a striking lesson" to "dissolved").

22. "Remarks on the Proposed Plan of an Emission of Paper, by Aristides," Feb. 26, 1787, in Yazawa, *Representative*, 176 ("the rights").

    On the call for a natural aristocracy, see, for example, John Adams, *A Defence of the Constitutions of Government of the United States of America*, AW, IV:289, 397–98; Henry Knox to George Washington, Oct. 23, 1786, *WP(CS)*, IV:301; Theodore Sedgwick to Rufus King, June 18, 1787, *RKC*, I:224; Alan Taylor, "Regulators and White Indians: The Agrarian Resistance in Post-Revolutionary New England," in Gross, *Debt to Shays*, 151 (quoting William Plumer to John Hale, Sept. 21, 1786, "The *few*, and not the many, are *wise*, and ought to bear rule"); Andrew Burstein, *Sentimental Democracy: The Evolution of America's Romantic Self-Image*

(1999), 140 (quoting sermon to Connecticut's legislature on the eve of its sending delegates to the federal convention urging the election of a "natural aristocracy").

23. Rufus King to Theodore Sedgwick, Oct. 22, 1786, *LDC*, XXIII:612 ("the great Body"); Abigail Adams to Thomas Jefferson, Jan. 29, 1786, *JP*, XI:86 ("[i]gnorant" to "deluded multitude"); Henry Lee to George Washington, Sept. 8, 1786, George Washington to Henry Lee, Oct. 31, 1786, *WP(CS)*, IV:240–41 ("the lower order" and "good government"), 318 ("commotions" to "own government").

24. John Adams to Richard Price, May 20, 1789, *AW*, IX:559 ("[E]xtremely"); John Adams, *Defence*, *AW*, IV:293 ("the natural"), 289 ("free government" to "the constitution"), 588 ("there is" to "the peace"), 289 ("simple democracy").

25. John Adams, *Defence*, *AW*, IV:287 ("orders"), 382 ("the powers of the one"), 397 ("natural aristocracy" and "the most dangerous" to "free government"), 398 ("property, family" and "them all, or at least").

26. John Adams to Thomas Brand-Hollis, Dec. 3, 1787, *AW*, IX:557 ("much more selfish"); Henry Knox to Rufus King, July 15, 1787, *HKC*, 96 ("sources of pollution"); Henry Knox to Mercy Warren, May 30, 1787, *WAL*, II:295 ("strong checks" to "mad democracy").

   On the desire to constrain the people, see Lutz, *Popular Consent*, 22 (asserting that Federalists, "while they placed sovereignty completely in the people, nevertheless would come to insist that institutions be so designed that consent was given much more indirectly"); Robert H. Wiebe, *The Opening of American Society: From the Adoption of the Constitution to the Eve of Disunion* (1984), 38 (noting that theoretically "the people were everything" but under actual operation of government "the sovereigns were asked to assume their proper place, and the more distant and esoteric the affairs of state, the more subdued their voice was expected to become"); Morgan, *Inventing*, 255 (asserting that revolutionary leaders sought to "subdue the unthinking many to the thoughtful few"); Michael G. Kammen, *Sovereignty and Liberty: Constitutional Discourse in American Culture* (1988), 24–25 (noting the emergence of "a more conservative perception" of the people's sovereignty in the 1780s, "namely, power may be derived from the people; but once they elect officials, the power is transmitted; and the people may not resume it unless magistrates abuse their authority"); Joyce Appleby, "Capitalism, Liberalism, and the United States Constitution," in A. E. Dick Howard, ed., *The United States Constitution: Roots, Rights, and Responsibilities* (1992), 65 (describing "the political problem" of the federal Framers as how "to bring the ignorant many under the guidance of the enlightened few" in a society that offered "repeated proof that ordinary white men in America were not humbled by their social deficiencies").

27. Thomas Jefferson to James Madison, Jan. 30, 1787, *JP*, XI:92 ("serious consequences"); John Adams to John Jay, Nov. 30, 1786, Letterbook, Adams Manuscript Trust, microfilm reel 112, MHS ("just complaints" and "imaginary grievances"); John Jay to Lord Lansdowne, Apr. 16, 1786, in Henry P. Johnston, ed., *The Correspondence and Public Papers of John Jay* (4 vols., New York, 1890–1893), III:190 ("free states" to "lost"),

28. Thomas Jefferson to James Madison, Jan. 30, 1787, *JP*, XI:92 ("the will of every one" and "just influence"), 93 ("curse" to "wolves over sheep").

29. Thomas Jefferson to James Madison, Jan. 30, 1787, *JP*, XI:93 ("[A] little rebellion").

30. Thomas Jefferson to James Madison, Jan. 30, 1787, *JP*, XI:92 ("absolutely unjustifiable"), 93 ("a precious degree" to "rights of the people"). In 1784, Dr. Thomas Tudor Tucker of South Carolina justified the greater rambunctiousness in a republic. "A despotic government is often both quiet and durable," wrote Tucker, because it deprived the people "of all opportunity of communicating their complaints, or deliberating on the means of relief." Under freer governments, the people "gain more strength of mind and independence of spirit" and "call louder" for a vindication of their rights. "This is called turbulence and caprice, but is in reality only a requisition of justice," the denial of which was the appropriate source "that the mischief is to be imputed." Tucker, "Conciliatory," I:616–17.

31. Thomas Jefferson to James Madison, Jan. 30, 1787, Thomas Jefferson to Thomas Brand Hollis, July 2, 1787, *JP*, XI:93 ("so mild"), 527 ("the result" to "commotions").

32. "Notes on Debates," Feb. 19, 1787, James Madison to James Madison, Sr., Nov. 1, 1786, James Madison to Thomas Jefferson, Apr. 23, 1787, James Madison to Edmund Pendleton, Feb. 24, 1787, Virginia Delegates to Edmund Randolph, Mar. 19, 1787, James Madison to James Madison, Sr., Feb. 25, 1787, *MP*, XI:277 ("rather difficult"), 154 ("discontented"), 398 ("insurgents"), 295 ("turbulent scenes"), 325 ("spirit"), 297 ("there remains"). Even Hamilton spoke of the benefits of executive pardons in "seasons" of insurrection or rebellion. *Federalist No. 74*, p. 502 (Hamilton). In 1800, however, Hamilton criticized John Adams for pardoning tax protesters in Pennsylvania in the 1790s as dangerous "tempori[z]ings" during "times of fermentation and commotion" rather than taking an "imposing attitude" in defending government. Alexander Hamilton, "Concerning the Public Conduct and Character of John Adams, Esq. President of the United States," Oct. 24, 1800, *HP*, XXV:228.

33. Thomas Jefferson to William Carmichael, Dec. 26, 1786, *JP*, X:633 ("tumultous meetings"); Thomas Jefferson to James Madison, Jan. 30, 1787, *JP*, XI:93 ("a little rebellion"); Henry Knox to George Washington, Oct. 23, 1786, and Dec. 21, 1786, *WP(CS)*, IV:301 ("braced"), 470 ("commotions" and "prodigious changes"); George Washington to James Madison, Nov. 5, 1786, *WP(CS)*, IV:332 ("evidence" and "energy"); [Jackson,] *Political Situation*, 161 ("cooperate"); Stephen Higginson to Nathan Dane, Mar. 3, 1787, *HL*, 753 ("more force" to "reins from us"), 754 ("compelled").

  For the perception of opportunities in the aftermath of the Regulation to strengthen government, see Stephen Higginson to Henry Knox, Jan. 20, 1787, *HL*, 744 (urging making "the most" of changes in public opinion "whilst the fire burns"); Ezra Stiles to George Washington, Nov. 9, 1786, *WP(CS)*, IV:353; Stephen E. Patterson, "The Federalist Reaction to Shays's Rebellion," in Gross, *Debt to Shays*, 117 (arguing that Federalists seeking a stronger central government "astutely saw the potential in exploiting" the Regulation). See also Brown, *Redeeming* (arguing that a primary catalyst for the federal convention was the weakness and inability of state governments to overcome resistance to tax collection).

34. James Madison to Edmund Randolph, Feb. 18, 1787, *MP*, IX:271 ("great disagreement); Samuel Osgood to John Adams, Nov. 14, 1786, *AW*, VIII:419 ("more energetic" to "gain ground"); Henry Knox to George Washington, Jan. 14, 1787, *WP(CS)*, IV:519 ("different sentiments" to "shall be made"); "Notes on [Congressional] Debates," Feb. 21, 1787, *MP*, IX:263 ("an extraconstitutional"); George Washington to John Jay, Mar. 10, 1787, *WP(CS)*, V:79 ("[A]ll attempts" to "ready to fall"), 80 ("not be legal").

  In the Preface to his notes on the federal convention, Madison clearly considered the Articles a constitution. Madison noted that New Jersey remained dissatisfied until "the new Constitution, superseded the old." James Madison, "Preface to Debates in the Convention," *Notes of Debates in the Federal Convention of 1787 Reported by James Madison* (Introduction by Adrienne Koch, 1966), 7. Madison also drafted the Virginia Legislature's resolution appointing delegates to the Philadelphia convention, authorizing them "to render the federal Constitution adequate to the exigenc[i]es of the Union." "Bill Providing for Delegates to the Convention of 1787," [Nov. 6, 1786], *MP*, IX:164.

  In Congress in 1783, Alexander Hamilton wanted a "general Convention . . . to strengthen the federal Constitution." "Remarks on the Calling of States Conventions," [Apr. 1, 1783], *HP*, III:314. Moreover, as reporter of the Annapolis Convention to Congress, Hamilton sought a Philadelphia convention "to render the constitution of the Federal Government adequate to the exigencies of the Union." "Address of the Annapolis Convention," [Sept. 14, 1786], *HP*, III:689. See also William Barton, *Observations on the Nature and Use of Paper-Credit* (Philadelphia, 1781), 37 (asking Congress to hold "a Continental Convention, for the express purpose of ascertaining, defining, enlarging and limiting, the duties and powers of their constitution").

35. John Jay to George Washington, Jan. 7, 1787, *WP(CS)*, IV:503 ("questionable" to "Party Heats"), 504 ("[T]he People of the States" to "*the People*"). Special state conventions were unnecessary for state constitution-making since a mechanism for electing delegates to the revolutionary conventions (with special authority to frame constitutions) was already in place. See Chapter 2.

36. "Address of the Annapolis Convention," Sept. 14, 1786, *HP*, III:689 ("every State"); James Madison to George Washington, Feb. 21, 1787, James Madison to Edmund Pendleton, Feb. 24,

1787, *MP*, IX:285 ("much divided"), 294 ("extraconstitutional" to "sanction"); Henry Knox to George Washington, Feb. 22, 1787, *WP(CS)*, V:47 ("the legality").

37. George Washington to Thomas Jefferson, May 30, 1787, *WP(CS)*, V:208 ("[m]uch is expected"). See also Henry Knox to George Washington, Mar. 19, 1787, *WP(CS)*, V:96 (favoring the creation of a new constitution rather than propping up "the present radically defective thing").

38. May 31, 1787, *RFC*, I:51 (Randolph) ("turbulence"), 58 (Randolph) ("fury"); May 29, 1787, *RFC*, I:27 (McHenry) ("sufficient checks"); May 31, 1787, *RFC*, I:49 (Mason) ("too democratic"); George Mason, Sr. to George Mason, Jr., June 1, 1787, *GMP*, III:892 ("soured & disgusted" to "opposite Extreme"); June 4, 1787, *RFC*, I:101(Mason) ("Notwithstanding").

39. May 31, 1787, *RFC*, I:50 (Gerry) ("men of honor"); John Adams to James Warren, Apr. 22, 1776, *LDC*, III:570 ("Respect" to "Authority"). See also Gary J. Kornblith and John M. Murrin, "The Making and Unmaking of an American Ruling Class," in Young, *Beyond*, 55 (suggesting convention delegates wanted a government whose "republican architecture would be supported by the pillars of deference, influence, and force"); Wood, *Creation*, 513 (calling the constitution "intrinsically an aristocratic document designed to check the democratic tendencies of the period"); Morgan, "Popular Sovereignty," 111 ("The founding fathers, uncertain about elections and instructions, placed their hopes for the country's future in giving government a structure that would filter the will of the people and extract a beneficent essence from the raw wishes of the majority").

40. June 23 and 26, 1787, *RFC*, I:388 (Madison) ("the wisest"), 421 ("transient impressions"), 422 ("fickleness" to "fence" and "firmness" to "impetuous counsels"), 423 ("wisdom & virtue"); June 7, 1787, *RFC*, I:150 (Dickinson) ("the most distinguished"); June 21, 1787, *RFC*, I:359 (Rutledge) ("more refined"); June 25, 1787, *RFC*, I:406 (Ellsworth) ("Wisdom" to "the people"). But see Rakove, "Structure," 265–66 (suggesting reconsideration of the idea that "the 'filtration of talent' would serve to recruit a new and more distinguished political elite and to insulate the national government from the populist excesses of the states").

41. Alexander Contee Hanson to the People, Apr. 1, 1787, "A Constituent" to the Printers, Mar. 8, 1787, in Yazawa, *Representative*, 96 ("superior talents" to "in general"), 78 ("the most *wise*"); James Madison, June 20, 1788, Virginia Convention, *DHRC*, X:1417 ("virtue" to "country"); *Federalist No. 10*, p. 62 ("to refine") (Madison). For Madison's system of refined leadership, see Garry Wills, *Explaining America: The Federalist* (1981), 223–47; Rosemarie Zagarri, *The Politics of Size: Representation in the United States, 1776–1850* (1987), 61–104. See also Colleen A. Sheehan, "Madison and the French Enlightenment: The Authority of Public Opinion," 59 *WMQ* (2002), 948 (arguing that Madison sought "the refinement and transformation of the views, sentiments, and interests of the citizens into a public mind guided by the precepts of reason" rather than ascertaining the "will of the majority"); Holton, "*Federalist 10*," 208 (arguing that Madison's theory of enlarging the political sphere helped dissipate "grassroots influence on government").

42. See Russell L. Hanson, "'Commons' and 'Commonwealth' at the American Founding: Democratic Republicanism as the New American Hybrid," in Ball and Pocock, *Change*, 166 (considering the constitution a shift from a concept "in which government was limited or held in check by the people, to one in which popular government itself was limited, if not altogether stymied, by its constitution"); Lutz, *Popular Consent*, 41 (suggesting "the word *sovereign* disappeared" from Federalist consent theory); Robert W. T. Martin, "Reforming Republicanism: Alexander Hamilton's Theory of Republican Citizenship and Press Liberty," 25 *JER* (2005), 29 (describing Hamilton's understanding of the people's sovereignty as "a limited conception" with the people exercising self-government "at a certain remove").

43. June 19, 1787, *RFC*, I:318 (Madison) ("the internal"); U.S. Constitution, Art. IV, sec. 4 ("Republican Form"); June 18, 1787, *RFC*, I:285 (Hamilton) ("certain portion"); July 18, 1787, *RFC*, II:47 (Wilson) ("dangerous commotions").

On how strong government appealed to Federalists, see Max M. Edling, *A Revolution in Favor of Government: Origins of the U.S. Constitution and the Making of the American State* (2003).

44. May 29, 1787, *RFC*, I:18 (Randolph) ("mission" to "rebellion"); June 19, 1787, *RFC*, I:318 (Madison) ("insurrections" to "exposed"); Aug. 18, 1787, *RFC*, II:332 (Pinckney) ("real" and "anarchy"); Aug. 17, 1787, *RFC*, II:317 (Langdon) ("apprehension" to "preventing insurrections").

45. Thomas Jefferson to William Stephens Smith, Nov. 13, 1787, *JP*, XII:357 ("impressed"); Thomas Jefferson to David Hartley, July 2, 1787, *JP*, XI:526 ("light" and "heavy"); Thomas Jefferson to James Madison, Dec. 20, 1787, *JP*, XII:442 ("more alarm" to "have done"); Thomas Jefferson to William Stephens Smith, Nov. 13, 1787, *JP*, XII:356 ("God forbid"). See also Lienesch, "Reinterpreting Rebellion," 180–81 (noting complaints by opponents of the constitution about a preoccupation with the Regulation during the ratification debate).

46. For debate over revision of the federal Constitution outside the terms of Article V and whether, in theory, it ought to be confined to those provisions, see, for example, David R. Dow, "When Words Mean What We Believe They Say: The Case of Article V," 76 *Iowa L. Rev.* (1990), 1–66; John R. Vile, *Contemporary Questions Surrounding the Constitutional Amending Process* (1993), 75–125; Amar, "Consent," 457–508; Monaghan, "Original Understanding," 121–77.

47. June 29, 1787, *RFC*, I:478 (Madison) ("dangerous"); June 5, 1787, *RFC*, I:122 (Gerry) ("novelty & difficulty" to "periodical revision"); June 11, 1787, *RFC*, I:203 (Mason) ("in an easy"). On the revision provisions of the first state constitutions, see Chapter 2. South Carolina's second constitution inserted a provision stating that no changes in the constitution were to occur without the consent of a majority of the legislature and New Hampshire's second constitution provided for a vote seven years after its creation on whether to hold a convention for constitutional revisions. South Carolina 1778 Constitution, Art. 44, New Hampshire 1784 Constitution, *TC*, VI:3257, IV:2470.

48. For initial inclusion of the language, see *RFC*, I:227, 231, 237, II:84, 133, and for how the language dropped out, see *RFC*, II:188, 555, 559, 578, 602, 662.

49. See Richard B. Bernstein with Jerome Agel, *Amending America: If We Love the Constitution So Much, Why Do We Keep Trying to Change It?* (1993), xii (observing that Article V has permitted formal ratification of the federal Constitution from 1791 to 1992 in approximately one-third of 1 percent of the more than 10,000 proposals for change). Given the obstacles Article V presents to formal change of the federal Constitution, it seems odd to describe the federal Framers as "leaving the door to future constitutional amendments wide-open." Amar, *America's Constitution*, 285.

    For the argument that formal revision of the constitution has been less important than other means by which the document has changed its meaning, see David A. Strauss, "The Irrelevance of Constitutional Amendments," 114 *Harv. L. Rev.* (2001), 1457–1505.

50. Sept. 15, 1787, *RFC*, II:629 (Mason) ("oppressive" to "liberties of the people"). See also Conkin, *Self-Evident*, 67 (arguing that Article V "violated popular sovereignty" by allowing amendments "solely by legislative action").

51. *Federalist No. 78*, pp. 527 ("the right" to "Until the people have"), 528 ("by some solemn" to "collectively") (Hamilton). Hamilton's position anticipated George Washington's *Farewell Address* nearly ten years later. See Spalding and Garrity, *Farewell Address*, 180 (Washington asserting that "the Constitution which at any time exists, 'till changed by an explicit and authentic act of the whole People, is sacredly obligatory upon all").

52. James Wilson, Nov. 28, 1787, Pennsylvania Convention, *DHRC*, II:387 ("never entered" and "mentioned"), 389 ("so little" to "formal debate").

53. "Draft Sketch of the Constitution," [Edmund Randolph and John Rutledge], July 26, 1787, *RFC* (Supplement):183 ("the natural rights"); James Madison, Speech in House of Representatives, June 8, 1789, *MP*, XII:203 ("those rights").

    Scholars have noted that state bills of rights contained a wide variety of provisions (a "potpourri of rights" according to Jack Rakove and "a jarring but exciting combination of ringing declarations of universal principles with a motley collection of common law procedures" according to Gordon Wood), but have not appreciated the constitutional significance of language that seemed merely rhetorical and judicially unenforceable. Rakove, *Meanings*, 306; Wood, *Creation*, 271. See also

Levy, *Free Press*, 184 (calling state bill of rights guarantees "namby-pamby" and "flabby" because they used the word "ought" instead of "shall"); James H. Hutson, "The Bill of Rights and the American Revolutionary Experience," in Michael J. Lacey and Knud Haakonssen, eds., *A Culture of Rights: The Bill of Rights in Philosophy, Politics, and Law, 1791 and 1991* (1991), 74–75 (describing the first state bills of rights as containing "all the contradictory and incoherent thinking about rights that existed before 1776").

54. Aug. 31, 1787, *RFC*, II:476 (Madison) ("alter constitutions" to "Bills of rights"). See also Wiecek, *Guarantee Clause*, 42 (describing the Guarantee Clause as part of "a contemporaneous process of delegitimizing the resort to violence by the people as an extralegal means of defending the community interest when government failed to do so"); Rodgers, *Contested Truths*, 65 (describing the federal bill of rights as "stripped methodically bare of every speculation about the origins of rights or the legitimacy of governments").

55. Preamble and Art. I, Sec. 2, Constitution of the United States, *TC*, I:19 ("ordain" and "the People of the several States"). See Hemberger, "Representations," 298 (suggesting that the federal Constitution's text "itself acts out the marginalization of ordinary citizens from politics"). The stage metaphor in the text owes a debt to Hemberger. See also Wood, *Creation*, 562 (asserting Federalists tried "to confront and retard the thrust of the Revolution with the rhetoric of the Revolution").

　　　Akhil Amar emphasizes the appearance of the words "the people" in the Preamble and the first ten amendments, but fails to appreciate how the people's sovereignty was far less expansively described in the federal Constitution and its bill of rights than in state constitutions. See Amar, *America's Constitution*, 5–53, 315, 321, 327, 420.

56. On the expectation that the people would fade away after constitution-making, see Joyce Appleby, "The American Heritage: The Heirs and the Disinherited," 74 *JAH* (1987), 804 (arguing that despite "the celebration" of the people's sovereignty in America, "the sovereign people were restrained once the Constitution was ratified"); Joshua Miller, "The Ghostly Body Politic: The *Federalist Papers* and Popular Sovereignty," 16 *Political Theory* (1988), 104 (arguing that Federalists "rendered the democratic vocabulary of popular sovereignty harmless" by ascribing "all power to a mythical entity that could never meet, never deliberate, never take action. The body politic became a ghost"); Donald J. Boudreaux and A. C. Pritchard, "Rewriting the Constitution: An Economic Analysis of the Constitutional Amendment Process," 62 *Fordham L. Rev.* (1993), 162 (describing the federal Framers as "depriving the majority of meaningful control over the content of the Constitution").

57. See Joshua Miller, *The Rise and Fall of Democracy in Early America, 1630–1789: The Legacy for Contemporary Politics* (1991), 113 (arguing that "[o]nce the Federalists had conjured an imaginary 'people' who could not challenge the power of the national government, they became bold in declaring that the people had the right to decide, to act, and even to overthrow the government whenever they chose to do so"); George Washington to Bushrod Washington, Nov. 10, 1787, *DHRC*, VIII:154 (describing representatives as the "Servants" if not "the creatures of the people").

58. *Federalist No. 49*, p. 340 ("veneration" and "stability") (Madison).

59. Stephen Higginson to Nathan Dane, Mar. 3, 1787, *HL*, 752 ("expediency"); *Federalist No. 40*, p. 265 (*"unauthorized propositions"* to "substance") (Madison). John Quincy Adams described ratification of the Constitution by only nine states "an open and bare-faced violation" of the Articles. John Quincy Adams to William Cranch, Oct. 14, 1787, *DHRC*, XIV:223.

　　　For subsequent characterizations of the constitution's framing by scholars, see, for example, Richard S. Kay "The Illegality of the Constitution," 4 *Const. Comment.* (1987), 57 (considering the constitution "the product of a blatant and conscious illegality"); Sanford Levinson, "'Veneration' and Constitutional Change: James Madison Confronts the Possibility of Constitutional Amendment," 21 *Tex. Tech L. Rev.* (1990), 2448 (asserting that Madison's argument justifying the constitution's ratification "made only the barest pretense" that it was "faithful to the requirements set out by the presumably binding Articles of Confederation"); Bruce Ackerman and Neal Katyal, "Our Unconventional Founding," 62 *U. Chi. L. Rev.* (1995), 476 (asserting the existence of "flagrant illegalities" in the formation of the constitution); Hemberger, "Representations," 297 (considering the framing of the constitution a "circumvention of existing rules and institutions"); Wills, *Evil*, 175 (denying that federal Framers circumvented the Articles of Confederation; rather, they "abolished that constitution"); McDonald, *States' Rights*, 20 (arguing that the Framers complied with the Articles "[i]n a manner of speaking"); Amar, *America's Constitution*, 506n5 (calling the federal convention "a lawful exercise of free expression, akin to a political pamphlet proposing future legislation or future withdrawal from a treaty").

60. Luther Martin, *The Genuine Information, Delivered to the Legislature of the State of Maryland, Relative to the Proceedings of the General Convention, Held at Philadelphia, in 1787* [Nov. 29, 1787], repr. in *RFC*, III:229 (*"alter* the *constitution"* to "be made").

61. Aug. 31, 1787, *RFC*, II:476 (Madison) ("powers given").

62. June 5, 1787, *RFC*, I:123 (Madison) ("by the supreme" to "indispensable"); June 18, 1787, *RFC*, I:301 (Hamilton) ("revolution Principles"); June 5, 1787, *RFC*, I:127 (Wilson) ("a convention"); July 23, 1787, *RFC*, II:88 (Mason) ("one of the"); Aug. 13, 1789, *BR*, 127 (Gerry) ("concurrence" to "dignity").

63. *Federalist No. 40*, pp. 263 ("defect"), 265 ("a rigid" to "right of the people") (Madison); July 23, 1787, *RFC*, II:93 (Madison) ("a ratification").

64. June 5, 1787, and July 23, 1787, *RFC*, I:126 (Madison) ("the highest"), II:92–93 (Madison) ("essential inroads" to "its existence"); July 23, 1787, *RFC*, II:88 (Mason) ("the mere creatures" to "creators"); Aug. 31, 1787, *RFC*, II:476 (Madison) ("all difficulties" to "as they pleased"). Nine years after the convention, Madison described the draft constitution as "nothing but a dead letter, until life and validity were breathed into it, by the voice of the people, speaking through the several state conventions." James Madison, "Debate in the House of Representatives," Apr. 6, 1796, *MP*, XVI:296.

65. A number of delegates expressed concerns about conventions of "the people." Oliver Ellsworth said he "did not like these conventions. They were better fitted to pull down than to build up Constitutions." They seemed part of "a new sett of ideas" having "crept in" since the Revolution. Charles Pinckney was also nervous about their use. Conventions were "serious things" that should not "be repeated." June 20 and July 23, 1787, *RFC*, I:335 (Ellsworth) ("did not like"), II:91 (Ellsworth) ("a new sett"); Sept. 15, 1787, *RFC*, II:632 (Pinckney).

66. The ratifying margins were Massachusetts (187–168), Virginia (89–79), and New York (30–27).

67. "A *True Friend*," Richmond, VA, Dec. 5, 1787, *DHRC*, XIV:376 ("enumerat[e]" to "servants in Congress").

68. June 8, 1789, *BR*, 89 (James Jackson) ("serious embarrassments"); John Fenno to Joseph Ward, July 5, 1789, *BR*, 258 ("a very unpropitious"), 259 ("artful" and "unhinge"). See also Noah Webster, *A Collection of Essays and Fugitiv[e] Writings* (Boston, 1790), 144 (expressing concern that bills of rights "give people an idea, that as individuals, or in town meetings, they have a power paramount to that of the Legislature. No wonder, that with such ideas, they attempt to resist law").

69. Aug. 15, 1789, *BR*, 159 (Sedgwick) ("is a self-evident" to "question" and "a man should"); *BR*, 159 (Benson) ("inherent" to "the government").

70. Aug. 15, 1789, *BR*, 160 (Page) ("before the face" to "stretches of authority"). See also Chapter 4.

71. Thomas Jefferson to James Madison, Feb. 6, 1788, *MP*, X:474 ("principal"); Thomas Jefferson to James Madison, Dec. 20, 1787, *MP*, X:337 ("bill of rights" to "inference"). See also Bogin, "True Policy," 109 (describing how Abraham Clark, a signer of the Declaration of Independence and New Jersey legislator in 1786, did not consider the people "subservient folk who mutely awaited legislation by their betters" but "a population of alert citizens who were aware of issues and ready to instruct their representatives").

72. Patrick Henry, June 24, 1788, Virginia Convention, *DHRC*, X:1477 ("enter into"); James Madison to Thomas Jefferson, Oct. 17, 1788, *MP*, XI:297 ("probable" to "disservice").

73. James Madison to Thomas Jefferson, Oct. 17, 1788, *MP*, XI:298 ("abuses of power"), 299 ("no tendency" to "the Government").

74. James Madison to Thomas Jefferson, Oct. 17, 1788, *MP*, XI:298 ("Wherever"), 299 ("danger" to "majorities of the people"); "Vices of the Political System of the United States," Apr. 1787, *MP*, IX:353 ("vicious legislation"). See also Rakove, *Meanings*, 313 (asserting that for Madison after 1785 "the problem of rights was no longer to protect the people as a collective whole *from* government but to defend minorities and individuals against popular majorities acting *through* government").

75. For the argument that the first ten amendments to the federal Constitution form an interconnected expression of the collective rights of the people, see Amar, *Bill of Rights*, 3–133.

76. Madison's Resolution, June 8, 1789, *BR*, 11–12 ("[A]ll power" to "the purposes").

77. See Madison's Resolution, June 8, 1789, *BR*, 11–14.

78. Amendments Proposed by the Virginia Convention, June 27, 1788, *BR*, 17 ("trustees and agents"); Amendments Proposed by the New York Convention, July 26, 1788, *BR*, 21 ("the Powers" to "Happiness"); Aug. 15, 1789, *BR*, 175 (Burke) ("frothy" to "people expect"); Richard Henry Lee to Francis Lightfoot Lee, Sept. 13, 1789, *BR*, 294; Richard Henry Lee to Patrick Henry, Sept. 27, 1789, *BR*, 299 ("[t]he [E]nglish language").

    The motion to include a right of instruction lost by a vote of 41 to 10 in the House. See *Gazette of the United States*, Aug. 19, 1789, *BR*, 177. In the Senate, it lost by a vote of 14 to 2, with the only two Anti-Federalists in that body voting in favor. See Bernard Schwartz, *The Bill of Rights: A Documentary History* (2 vols., 1971), II:1148.

79. Elbridge Gerry, "Observations on the New Constitution and the Federal and State Conventions," 1788, in Schwartz, *Bill of Rights*, I:484 ("vague" to "their conduct").

80. Aug. 14, 1789, *BR*, 129 (Madison) ("on all hands").

81. May 5, 1789, *BR*, 58 (Madison) ("deliberative power"), (Bland) ("no unconstitutional"), (Tucker) ("point of view" to "discretion").

82. James Wilson, Dec. 4, 1787, Nov. 24, 1787, Pennsylvania Convention, *DHRC*, II:472 ("*resides* in the PEOPLE"), 361 ("the supreme, absolute"), 362 ("may change"); "Of Government," *Lectures on Law* [1790–1791], *WW*, I:304 ("[a] majority").

83. James Madison, Aug. 15, 1789, *MP*, XII:341 ("My idea"). See also Maier, *American Scripture*, 195 (describing Madison's language as "a pared-down version" of Virginia's 1776 bill of rights because the people's "right to abolish government (as opposed to changing it) went unmentioned").

84. Aug. 15, 1789, *BR*, 170 (Gerry) ("while the government"); "An Old Whig," *CA*, III:20–21 ("fashionable language").

85. See Kenneth R. Bowling, "'A Tub to the Whale': The Founding Fathers and Adoption of the Federal Bill of Rights," 8 *JER* (1988), 240 (suggesting that the committee's report "reflected the Federalist viewpoint of 1789, that support of government stability rather than the right of revolution proved uppermost").

86. Tucker, "Conciliatory," I:620 ("undoubted right" and "inherent in"), 622 ("the people" and "the true sovereign").

87. Aug. 15, 1789, *BR*, 163 (Page) ("dangerous" to "their representatives"), 173 (Page) ("strictly compatible" to "deny them a right"); Aug. 15, 1789, *BR*, 170 (Gerry) ("say that the sovereignty").

88. Aug. 15, 1789, *BR*, 154 (Roger Sherman) ("mislead"); Aug. 15, 1789, *BR*, 151 (Hartley) ("attended" and "great abuses"); Aug. 15, 1789, *BR*, 156 (Wadsworth) ("a mischievous"); Aug. 15, 1789, *BR*, 164 (Clymer) ("constitutional right"). See also James Madison, Aug. 15, 1789, *MP*, XII:340 (denying that the people could give binding instructions to their representatives); Aug. 15, 1789, *BR*, 162 (Thomas Hartley) (asserting that instruction would undermine "the principle of representation" which he distinguished from a system of "agency").

89. Aug. 15, 1789, *BR*, 165 (Gerry) ("liberty to act" and "friends and patrons" to "any occasion"), 170 (Gerry) ("convenient" to "to their agents"), 152 (Gerry) ("seemed inconsistent" to "at their pleasure"), 166 (Gerry) ("if so" to "for the legislature"); Aug. 15, 1789, *BR*, 174 (Sumter) ("do not treat" to "consistent and proper").

90. Aug. 15, 1789, *BR*, 164 (Clymer) ("a most dangerous" to "and experience"), 166 (Gerry) ("all the wisdom" to "public measures"); *Federalist No. 63*, p. 428 ("*the total exclusion*") (Madison).

91. "House Resolution and Articles of Amendment," Aug. 24, 1789, and "Senate Amendments," Sept. 9, 1789, *BR*, 38, 46. For the significance of the debate over instruction, see Hemberger, "Representations," 307–15, especially 314–15 (arguing that after the changes, "[n]o longer were the people assured of their right to 'consult for the common good' – that was the government's job – and when citizens addressed the government, regardless of whether they did it as individuals or as a group, it would be as petitioners").

92. Richard Henry Lee to Samuel Adams, Aug. 8, 1789, *BR*, 272 ("But so wonderfully"). A correspondent of a Boston newspaper in 1790 offered a comparison of phrases once "fashionable" during the independence movement with those "of the present day." Among the competing phrases:

1775	*1790*
Vox populi, vox dei	Democracy is a Vulcano
The rights and privileges *of the People.*	"Checks and Balances."
The people competent to the mangement of their political concerens.	But few characters fit to govern.

Boston Independent Chronicle, Sept. 2, 1790, quoted in Merrill Jensen, *The American Revolution Within America* (1974), 171.

93. *Federalist No. 23*, p. 146 ("that pure") (Hamilton). See Alexander Hamilton, "Remarks on an Act Acknowledging the Independence of Vermont," Mar. 28, 1787, *HP*, IV:131 (asserting "that the sovereignty of the people by our constitution is vested in their representatives in senate and assembly"). On how conservatives in Pennsylvania invoked the authority of the collective sovereign, see Brunhouse, *Counter-Revolution*, 222; Ryerson, "Republican Theory," 130.

94. Martin, *Genuine Information*, repr. in *RFC*, III:229 (*"alter* the *constitution"* to *"direct violation"*), 230 ("once the people").

95. John Adams to Thomas Jefferson, Nov. 10, 1787, *JP*, XII:335 ("preserve the Union"); Benjamin Rush, "Address to the People of the United States," Feb., 1787, *DHRC*, XIII:46 ("revolution"). See also Hemberger, "Representations," 289 (describing Federalists as "claiming for their Constitution, and for the national government it created, a monopoly on the legitimate representation of the people"); Hulsebosch, *Empire*, 229 (describing Federalists as hoping that the people as "their sovereign could be educated, guided, and cajoled" and that Federalists' "interests could be linked to the sovereign's").

CHAPTER 6. TESTING THE CONSTITUTIONALISM OF 1787

1. The account of Washington's western expedition and the capture of Husband draws on Slaughter, *Whiskey*, 3, 190–221; George Washington, "Proclamation", Sept. 25, 1794, George Washington to Daniel Morgan, Oct. 8, 1794, Bartholomew Dandridge to Henry Knox, Oct. 9, 1794, *GWW*, XXXIII:509, 524, 525n31; Donald Jackson and Dorothy Twohig, eds., *The Diaries of George Washington* (6 vols., 1976–1979), diary entries, Oct. 17–18, 1794, Oct. 20, 1794, VI:193, 195; George Washington to Henry Lee, Oct. 20, 1794, *GWW*, XXXIV:6; George Washington to Alexander Hamilton, Oct. 26, 1794, *HP*, XVII:344; Robert Wellford, "A Diary Kept By Dr. Robert Wellford of Fredericksburg, Virginia, During The March of the Virginia Troops To Fort Pitt (Pittsburgh) To Suppress The Whiskey Insurrection in 1794," 11 *WMQ* (1902), 10; [Herman Husband], *Proposals to Amend and Perfect the Policy of the Government of the United States of America* (Philadelphia, 1782), 7, 10; [Herman Husband], *A Sermon to the Bucks and Hinds of America* (Philadelphia, 1788), ii, 9, 19–20, 28; [Herman Husband], *A Dialogue Between an Assembly-Man and a Convention-Man* (Philadelphia, 1790), 11–12; Mark H. Jones, "Herman Husband: Millenarian, Carolina Regulator and Whiskey Rebel" (Ph.D. diss., Northern Illinois Univ., 1982); Dorothy E. Fennell, "From Rebelliousness to Insurrection: A Social History of the Whiskey Rebellion, 1765–1802" (Ph.D. diss., Univ. of Pittsburgh, 1981), 192–226; William Hogeland, *The Whiskey Rebellion: George Washington, Alexander Hamilton, and the Frontier Rebels Who Challenged America's Newfound Sovereignty* (2006), 71–95, 207–36.

2. Many scholars overlook the emergence of an American constitutionalism by assuming America's first written constitutions simply reflected inherited political traditions. See, for example, Brooke, "Ancient Lodges," 296 (describing the "county convention movement" of the 1780s as the "purest form of the Commonwealth whig tradition"); Robert M. Chesney, "Democratic-Republican Societies, Subversion, and the Limits of Legitimate Political Dissent in the Early Republic," 82 *N.C.L. Rev* (2004), 1539 (describing the Democratic Societies of the 1790s as the "inheritors of the 'Radical Whig' tradition tracing back to the Leveller movement of Civil War-era England"); Robert W. T. Martin, "Reforming Republicanism: Alexander Hamilton's Theory of Republican Citizenship and Press Liberty," 25 *JER* (2005), 25 (attributing a "conventional Whig 'vigilance' (a suspicious jealousy of governmental power)" to the opponents of Federalists in the 1790s).

3. James Madison, Speech in Congress, June 8, 1789, *MP*, XII:200 ("accustomed" and "interposed").

4. *Chisholm v. Georgia*, 2 U.S. 419 (1793), 471 ("sovereignty devolved" to "of the country") (Jay), 472 ("Governors are") (Jay), 455 ("confusion") (Wilson), 457 ("the Supreme") (Wilson), 455 ("subordinate" to "sovereigns of the State") (Wilson), 461 ("supercilious") (Wilson).

5. Most studies of excise tax protests in Pennsylvania depict them as part of an eighteenth-century tradition of resistance linked to political principles invoked during America's struggle for Independence. See, for example, Alfred P. James, "A Political Interpretation of the Whiskey Insurrection," 33 *Western Pennsylvania Historical Magazine* (1950), 98 (describing meetings protesting the excise tax as employing "good American Revolution technique"); Jacob E. Cooke, "The Whiskey Insurrection: A Re-evaluation," 30 *Pennsylvania History* (1963), 345 (describing the excise protesters drawing on "an unfortunately literal reading of the Revolutionary creed"); Slaughter, *Whiskey*, 128 (identifying an "allegiance to Whig principles"); Steven R. Boyd, "The Whiskey Rebellion, Popular Rights, and the Meaning of the First Amendment," in *The Whiskey Rebellion and the Trans-Appalachian Frontier* (1994), 78 (asserting suppression of excise tax protests challenged a "long-standing tradition that citizens of a community had a right to resist the exercise of governmental power they deemed antithetical to their needs or desires through crowd action").

   Compare Cornell, *Other Founders*, 206 (identifying in the protest of the excise tax a "plebian populist constitutionalism, wherein the will of the people could be reconstituted spontaneously in local organizations such as the militia, the jury, or even the crowd"); Saul Cornell, "Mobs, Militias, and Magistrates: Popular Constitutionalism and the Whiskey Rebellion," 81 *Chi.-Kent L. Rev.* (2006), 900 (noting "the fluidity of American constitutional thought in the years immediately following ratification" during which "the limits of resistance within the new legal system created by the Constitution had not yet been worked out").

6. This paragraph and this remaining section is heavily based on Bouton, "Road," 855–87.

7. Bouton, "Road," 863.

8. Pennsylvania 1776 Constitution, Bill of Rights, Sec. 5, *TC*, V:3082–83 ("instituted" to "sett of men"); [Husband], *Bucks and Hinds*, 30 ("spirit and design" to "or parties"), 8 ("small portions" to "near relations").

9. Petition quoted in Bouton, "Road," 865 ("the dearest"); Pennsylvania 1776 Constitution, Bill of Rights, Sec. 5, Preamble, *TC*, V:3083 ("the right" to "public weal"), 3081 ("the people" to "happiness").

10. Quoted in Bouton, "Road," 874 ("offer to purchase" and "give a single bid"). Bouton describes the measures as a series of "concentric rings of protection" that farmers placed around their communities. Bouton, "Road," 867.

11. See Bouton, "Road," 855 (finding that some 62 road closings occurred in Pennsylvania between the fall of 1787 and the fall of 1795).

12. Pennsylvania 1776 Constitution, Bill of Rights, Sec. 5, *TC*, V:3083 ("sett of men"); quoted in Bouton, "Road," 876 ("alarm"). On FitzSimons's bond speculation, see Eugene Perry Link, *Democratic-Republican Societies, 1790–1800* (1942), 196–97.

13. Pennsylvania 1790 Constitution, Art. V, Sec. 10, *TC*, V:3098 ("misbehavior" to "of the legislature").

14. *Pittsburgh Gazette*, Feb. 17, 1787 ("general Patriotic" to "particularly instructed"); "Petition of Inhabitants of Westmoreland County – Excise on Liquors – 1790," quoted in Slaughter, *Whiskey*, 73 ("general disapprobation" and "universal abhorrence").

15. Benjamin Rush to William Linn, May 4, 1784, in L. H. Butterfield, ed., *Letters of Benjamin Rush* (2 vols., 1951), I:333 ("attending Constitutional"); Slaughter, *Whiskey*, 74 (noting Federalists described petitions as "clearly extralegal" and "seditious" because petitioners could vote and express themselves during elections).

    Governor Thomas Mifflin signed the repeal act on Sept. 21, 1791. See Fennell, "Whiskey," 57.

16. For the long-standing antipathy toward excise taxes, see Slaughter, *Whiskey*, 12–27.

17. Alexander Hamilton, "Report Relative to a Provision for the Support of Public Credit," [Jan. 9, 1790], *HP*, VI:99 ("pernicious"). On the consumption of alcohol see W. J. Rorabaugh, *The Alcoholic Republic: An American Tradition* (1979), 233 (estimating that by 1795, Americans above the age of fifteen consumed an average of nearly three gallons of distilled spirits per person per year). For the social and economic aspects of whiskey in western Pennsylvania, see Fennell, "Whiskey," 227–58.

    George Clinton, New York's governor, honored the French ambassador with a dinner "at which 120 guests downed 135 bottles of Madeira, 36 bottles of port, 60 bottles of English beer, and 30 large cups of rum punch." Rorabaugh, *Alcoholic Republic*, 48.

18. On the effects of the excise tax, see Hogeland, *Whiskey*, 64–70. The principal counties involved in the protests in Pennsylvania were Westmoreland, Washington, Fayette, and Allegheny.

19. For profits from speculation in the war bonds, see Ferguson, *Power of the Purse*, passim; Hogeland, *Whiskey*, 29–33.

20. Walter Clark, ed., *The State Records of North Carolina* (16 vols., numbered XI–XXVI, Raleigh, 1886–1907), XXI:962 ("oppose every" and "strenuously"); Samuel Johnston and Benjamin Hawkins to Alexander Martin, Feb. 22, 1791, Governors Letter Books, NCDHR ("the sense" to "expect").

21. "A Citizen of Pennsylvania," *Philadelphia Federal Gazette*, Feb. 1, 1791, repr. in *IC*, II:318 ("disagreeable").

22. John Steele, "Circular Letter," Jan. 27, 1791, Noble E. Cunningham, Jr., *Circular Letters of Congressmen to Their Constituents, 1789–1829* (3 vols., 1978), I:4 ("to the people" to "opinion expressed").

23. Kenneth R. Bowling and Helen E. Veit, eds., *The Diary of William Maclay and Other Notes on Senate Debates* (1988), Feb. 24, 1791, 389 ("responsibility" and "servants"); Fisher Ames to Thomas Dwight, Jan. 24, 1791, *FAW*, II:848 ("anarchy"); Fisher Ames to Alexander Hamilton, Jan. 26, 1797, *HP*, XX:487 ("silly" and "disgraced"); Maclay, *Diary*, diary entry, Feb. 24, 1791, 388 ("any right" and "violently").

24. "Extract of a letter from Kentucky Dated Lexington, Jan. 25, 1794," enclosed in Edmund Randolph to George Washington, Feb. 27, 1794, Misc. Letters, Dept. of State, M-179, reel 11, NA ("[T]he Excise"). On opposition to the excise tax, see Jeffrey J. Crow, "The Whiskey Rebellion in North Carolina," 66 *North Carolina Historical Review* (1989), 16; Mary K. Bonsteel Tachau, "The Whiskey Rebellion in Kentucky: A Forgotten Episode of Civil Disobedience," 2 *JER* (1982), 239–59; Linda G. De Pauw et al., eds., *Documentary History of the First Federal Congress of the United States of America* (1972–), I:656; Alan P. Litehizer, "The Whiskey Rebellion: Frontier Violence and Political Conflict in Revolutionary Pennsylvania (MA thesis, Univ. of North Carolina, 1994), 36; Philyaw, *Western Visions*, 130–36.

25. James Marshel to Albert Gallatin, July 16, 1791, Papers of Albert Gallatin, Roll 1, Frame No. 545, NYU ("number" to "government").

26. *American Daily Advertiser*, Aug. 17, 1791 ("unequal" to "western country"); Hugh Henry Brackenridge, *Incidents of the Insurrection in the Western Parts of Pennsylvania, in the Year 1794* (3 vols., Philadelphia, 1795), III:16 ("the sense" to "firmness"). On the participants, see William Findley, *History of the Insurrection in the Four Western Counties of Pennsylvania: In the Year 1794* (Philadelphia, 1796), 95–96, 293; Brackenridge, *Incidents*, in Steven R. Boyd, ed.,

The Whiskey Rebellion: Past and Present Perspectives (1985), 67; Slaughter, *Whiskey*, 111; R. Eugene Harper, *The Transformation of Western Pennsylvania, 1770–1800* (1991), 17–18, 77, 141; Russell J. Ferguson, *Early Western Pennsylvania Politics* (1938), 30, 115, 120, 133; James P. McClure, "'Let Us Be Independent': David Bradford and the Whiskey Insurrection," 74 *Pittsburgh History* (1991), 73.

27. Unidentified newspaper clipping, Aug. 23, 1791, repr. in *HP*, XVII:28–29n6 ("all aid"); "Minutes of the Meeting at Pittsburgh," Sept. 7, 1791, *Pennsylvania Archives*, 2nd Ser. (Harrisburg, 1876), Vol. IV:20 ("[U]nconscionable" to "employment"), 21 ("deservedly" to "fall heavy").

   For the Washington County meeting, see Fennell, "Whiskey," 46–48; R. Eugene Harper, "Rebellion Contained: A Socioeconomic Approach to the Whiskey Rebellion and the Role of the Local Elite," in *Trans-Appalachian Frontier*, 39–56.

28. Brackenridge, *Incidents*, III:15 ("after it" and "constitutional"), 21 ("public virtue"). On Brackenridge, see Claude Milton Newlin, *The Life and Writings of Hugh Henry Brackenridge* (1932, repr., 1971), 87–133; Daniel Marder, *Hugh Henry Brackenridge* (1967), 38–54. Although not formally a delegate to the 1791 convention, Brackenridge had "no objections to assist in drawing up the addresses proposed to the public, or to the representatives in Congress." Brackenridge, *Incidents*, III:17.

29. Alexander Hamilton to George Washington, Aug. 5, 1794, *HP*, XVII:31. For the composition of the delegates to the 1791 Pittsburgh convention, see Edwin G. Burrows, *Albert Gallatin and the Political Economy of Republicanism, 1760–1800* (1986), 341n53; Leland D. Baldwin, *Whiskey Rebels: The Story of a Frontier Uprising* (1939), 78–79; Fennell, "Whiskey," 48–49.

30. John Neville to George Clymer, Sept. 8, 1791, Oliver Wolcott, Jr. Papers, CHS ("we are" to "directors").

31. "Notes of a Conversation with George Washington," July 10, 1792, *JP*, XXIV:210 ("anarchy" and "monarchical"); Alexander Hamilton to George Washington, Aug. 18, 1792, *HP*, XII:252 ("[S]ubversion" to "opportunity"); George Washington to Alexander Hamilton, July 29, 1792, *HP*, XII:131 ("the ultimate").

32. John Neville to George Clymer, Sept. 8, 1791, Oliver Wolcott, Jr. Papers, CHS ("leading men" and "the rabble"); quoted in Raymond Walters, Jr., *Albert Gallatin: Jefferson Financier and Diplomat* (1957), 67 ("freely"); Findley, *History*, 44 ("signed"); "Broadside of Minutes of Aug. 21, 1791, Meeting" repr. in *HP*, XII:308n5 ("duty" to "Law"), 309n5 ("contempt").

   On the composition of the 1792 Pittsburgh convention see Slaughter, *Whiskey*, 115, 168–69; Ferguson, *Pennsylvania*, 27, 48; Burrows, *Gallatin*, 343; Baldwin, *Rebels*, 85–86; Findley, *History*, 44; *HP*, XII:308–309n5; Harper, *Transformation*, 78, 81–82, 85, 87–89, 99, 141, 147, 174. The petition to Congress is repr. in Henry Adams, ed., *The Writings of Albert Gallatin* (3 vols., Philadelphia, 1879), I:2–4.

33. *Philadelphia General Advertiser*, Sept. 1, 1792 ("Is not every"); Alexander Hamilton to Tench Coxe, Sept. 1, 1792, Alexander Hamilton to George Washington, Sept. 1, 1792, *HP*, XII:307 ("evidence" to "behaviour"), 311 ("persevering" to "the Government"), 312 ("the full").

34. Alexander Hamilton to George Washington, Sept. 1, 1792, Alexander Hamilton to John Jay, Sept 3, 1792, *HP*, XII:312 ("indictable"), 316 ("every legal" to "its proceedings"), 317 ("the scene" and "criminality").

35. John Jay to Alexander Hamilton, Sept. 8, 1792, *HP*, XII:334 ("neither" to "sense"); "Proclamation," Sept. 15, 1792, *GWW*, XXXII:150 ("certain violent" to "of a government"), 151 ("unlawful combinations"). For the final proclamation, see *HP*, XII:330–331n1. For Washington's willingness to accept Randolph's legal judgment, see George Washington to Alexander Hamilton, Sept. 7, 1792, *HP*, XII:332.

36. Edmund Randolph to Alexander Hamilton, Sept. 8, 1792, *HP*, XII:337 ("a judicial movement" to "the peace"). A federal grand jury failed to return true bills against any of the members of the Pittsburgh meeting. See Richard A. Ifft, "Treason in the Early Republic: The Federal Courts, Popular Protest, and Federalism During the Whiskey Insurrection," in Boyd, *Whiskey*, 168.

   Two years later, when Washington received a remonstrance from western Pennsylvania, Hamilton urged the attorney general, then William Bradford, to "examine carefully" if it did not "contain criminal matter" and if so to prosecute. Bradford doubted if the remonstrance was "a proper subject for a criminal prosecution, without some *extrinsic* proof of a seditious intention." Edmund Randolph to Alexander Hamilton, Henry Knox, and William Bradford, Apr. 14, 1794, *HP*, XVI:260n.2.

37. Eventually over forty-five Democratic societies were formed nationwide by 1800. See Link, *Societies*, 6, 13–15; Phillip S. Foner, *The Democratic-Republican Societies, 1790–1800: A Documentary Sourcebook of Constitutions, Declarations, Addresses, Resolutions, and Toasts* (1976), 7.

   For Washington and other Federalists, "the Seditious & desperate" who threatened America were aided by the Democratic societies, "odious associations" that were "despised ... by men of right heads." See Stephen Higginson to Alexander Hamilton, July 26, 1793, *HP*, XV:127 ("the Seditious"); Henry Van Schaack to Oliver Wendell, Dec. 14, 1794, *VSM*, 190 ("odious"); Fisher Ames to Thomas Dwight, Sept. 3, 1794, *FAW*, II:1047 ("despised").

38. Alexander Hamilton to George Washington, [Aug. 5], 1794, *HP*, XVII:52 ("delinquents").

39. "Governor Mifflin's Message to the Assembly," Sept. 2, 1794, *Penn. Archives*, IV:251 ("peculiarly inauspicious" to "discontent"); quoted in Ifft, "Treason," 170 ("[t]he Federal Sheriff"); "David Bradford To The Inhabitants of Monongahela, Virginia," Aug. 6, 1794, *Penn. Archives*, IV:112 ("guided"). For the attack on Bower Hall, see Slaughter, *Whiskey*, 176–83; Baldwin, *Rebels*, 110–28. William Hogeland argues that Hamilton, U.S. Attorney General William Bradford, and U.S. Attorney William Rawle conspired to develop a "plan" of federal prosecutions as the means to provoke "violence that would justify a federal military suppression." See Hogeland, *Whiskey*, 142. For the gathering at Braddock's Field and the march on Pittsburgh, see Slaughter, *Whiskey*, 185–88; Baldwin, *Rebels*, 141–71; Hemberger, "Representations," 321 (describing excise protesters as marching "peacefully" through Pittsburgh and making "no attempt to take the garrison"); Thomas P. Slaughter, "'The King of Crimes': Early American Treason Law, 1787–1860," in Hoffman and Albert, *Launching*, 94 (asserting that the "armed array" gathered at Braddock's Field "committed no act of violence toward the government").

40. Findley, *History*, 78 ("between"). See also Slaughter, *Whiskey*, 177–78.

41. "Conference Concerning the Insurrection in Western Pennsylvania," Aug. 2, 1794, *HP*, XVII:9 ("understood" to "& laws"), 10 ("some preliminary").

42. "Conference Concerning the Insurrection in Western Pennsylvania," Aug. 2, 1794, *HP*, XVII:11 ("silent"), 12 ("his positive"), 13n20 ("Here the minutes"); "Governor Mifflin's Message to the Assembly," Sept. 2, 1794, *Penn. Archives*, IV:254 ("In a free country").

43. George Washington, "Proclamation," Aug. 7, 1794, *GWW*, XXXIII:460 ("suppress" and "fatal"), 457 ("combinations" to "spirit of opposition"), 461 ("treasonable acts"). For Governor Mifflin's capitulation to the use of force, see "Address of Governor Mifflin to the Militia of Philadelphia," Sept. 10, 1794, *Penn. Archives*, IV:273–76.

44. George Washington to Alexander Hamilton, Sept. 17, 1792, *HP*, XII:390 ("cry"). For Hamilton's early desire to use military force to suppress excise tax protesters, see Richard H. Kohn, *Eagle and Sword: The Federalists and the Creation of the Military Establishment in America, 1783–1802* (1975), 158–61.

45. Alexander Hamilton to George Washington, Aug. 2 and 5, 1794, *HP*, XVII:16 ("Treason" to "Opposition"), 32 ("without moderation" to "the Union").

46. "Sixth Annual Address to Congress," Nov. 19, 1794, *GWW*, XXXIV:28 ("prejudice" and "artifice"), 29 ("riot" and "an ascendancy"). For Hamilton's letter, see Alexander Hamilton to George Washington, Aug. 5, 1794, *HP*, XVII:24–58.

47. Gallatin, *Writings*, III:5 ("a circulation" to "acting"), 6 ("others to act" to "perfectly justifiable"), 7 ("not illegal"). Gallatin, a Swiss-born immigrant, had served in the Pennsylvania legislature since 1790 and after the excise tax protests would be elected to both the U.S. Senate in 1793 (though not seated due to a challenge of his nativity) and the House of Representatives in 1795 as a Republican, where he served until 1801. He eventually became secretary of the treasury under both Thomas Jefferson and James Madison. On Gallatin see Walters, *Gallatin*, 59–63; Burrows, *Gallatin*. See Burrows, *Gallatin*, 346 (concluding that most organizers of meetings

and conventions protesting the excise did not engage in "illegal or violent measures"). See also Gallatin, *Writings*, III:8; Findley, *History*, 39–40, 104–105, and *passim*; Brackenridge, *Incidents*, III:25–27.

48. Findley, *History*, 42 ("a meeting" to "freedom"), 43 ("unjust"), 265 ("to lay"). On Findley see Robert M. Ewing, "Life and Times of William Findley," 2 *Western Pennsylvania Historical Magazine* (1919), 240–51; John Caldwell, *William Findley from West of the Mountains: A Politician in Pennsylvania, 1783–1791* (2000).

49. Brackenridge, *Incidents*, III:20 ("to the utmost" to "actual force"); Hugh Henry Brackenridge to the Army, Oct. 26, 1794, *Penn. Archives*, IV:427 ("criminal" to "crisis").

50. Findley, *History*, 47 ("intemperate" to "connection"), 48 ("popular" to "government"), 48–49 ("the people" to "liberty"). For Findley's opposition to violence toward government, see Findley, *History*, 59, 177, 285.

51. Findley, *History*, 50 ("representative" to "obedience"), 49 ("absurd" to "nature of man"). As evidence of the fallibility of representatives, Findley pointed to the Georgia legislature's recent involvement in fraudulent land speculation. Findley, *History*, 50–51. See also C. Peter Magrath, *Yazoo: Law and Politics in the New Republic, The Case of Fletcher v. Peck* (1966) (analyzing the Georgia land speculation precipitating the Supreme Court case).

52. Findley, *History*, 54 ("valuable" to "or not"), 50 ("If the people").

53. Findley, *History*, 49 ("confidence"), 55 ("the liberty"), 52 ("a long").

54. On the repeal of the excise and other taxes, see Slaughter *Whiskey*, 226.

55. See Marshall Smelser, "The Jacobin Phrenzy: Federalism and the Menace of Liberty, Equality, and Fraternity," 13 *Review of Politics* (1951), 457–82; Marshall Smelser, "The Jacobin Phrenzy: The Menace of Monarchy, Plutocracy, and Anglophobia, 1789–1798," 21 *Review of Politics* (1959), 239–58; John R. Howe, Jr., "Republican Thought and the Political Violence of the 1790s," 19 *American Quarterly* (1967), 147–65; Hofstadter, *Idea*; Donald H. Stewart, *The Opposition Press of the Federalist Period* (1969); Brooke, "Ancient Lodges," 275–76, 282–83; Cornell, *Other Founders*, 195–99; Albrecht Koschnik, "The Democratic Societies of Philadelphia and the Limits of the American Public Sphere, circa 1793–1795," 58 *WMQ* (2001), 615–36.

56. "Tully" No. IV [Sept 2, 1794]; "Tully" No. III [Aug. 28, 1794], *HP*, XVII:178 ("immaterial"),159 ("sacred duty"); "A Republican," *Gazette of the United States*, Aug. 5, 1794 (repr. from *Greenfield Gazette*) ("every embarrassment"); George Washington to Burges Ball, Sept. 25, 1794, *GWW*, XXXIII:506 ("no one denies").

   For understandings about the scope of freedom of speech in eighteenth-century America, see Smith, *Freedom's Fetters*; Levy, *Free Press*; Gregg Costa, "John Marshall, the Sedition Act, and Free Speech in the Early Republic," 77 *Tex. L. Rev.* (1999), 1011–47; Curtis, *Free Speech*; Martin, *Press Liberty*; Lendler, "Sedition Act."

57. See Stephen Higginson to Timothy Pickering, Aug. 13, 1795, *HL*, 789 (describing the representative's role as making judgments independent of "popular Opinion," which he called "interference"); Koschnik, "Societies," 625 (asserting that Federalists assumed that "the constitutional settlement" of the federal Constitution "successfully neutralized the popular impulses set free" by the American Revolution and both enshrined the people's sovereignty and deflected its more radical ramifications).

58. George Washington to Charles Mynn Thruston, Aug. 10, 1794, George Washington to Henry Lee, Aug. 26, 1794, George Washington to Burges Ball, Sept. 25, 1794, *GWW*, XXXIII:464 ("mischief"), 465 ("into discredit"), 475 ("first *formidable*"), 506 ("sap the Constitution"); "Sixth Annual Address to Congress," Nov. 19, 1794, *GWW*, XXXIV:29 ("self-created" and "designing").

   Despite the claims by Washington's supporters that political societies critiquing his administration were fomenting rebellion by resisting the excise tax, little evidence of such a connection existed. See, for example, Slaughter, *Whiskey*, 113, 164–65; Jeffrey A. Davis, "The Whiskey Rebellion and the Demise of the Democratic-Republic Societies of Pennsylvania," and Harper, "Rebellion," both in *Trans-Appalachian Frontier*, 22–38, 39–56; William Miller, "The Democratic Societies and the Whiskey Insurrection," 62 *PMHB* (1938), 324–49; Link, *Societies*, 148n108. Alexander Addison, a leading Federalist and state judge in western Pennsylvania,

questioned the conspiracy theory advanced by other Federalists. See Alexander Addison to
Henry Lee, Nov. 23, 1794, in Richard H. Kohn, "Judge Alexander Addison on the Origin and
History of the Whiskey Rebellion," in Boyd, *Whiskey*, 51–56.

59. "Address to President Washington," Nov. 20, 1794, *RKC*, I:579 ("founded"); Nov. 28, 1794,
Annals of Congress, 947 ("individuals"). On the Senate's reaction, see Joseph M. Lynch, *Negotiating the Constitution: The Earliest Debates over Original Intent* (1999), 138.

60. Nov. 24, 1794, *Annals*, 899 ("not strictly") (Thomas FitzSimons); Nov. 26, 1794, *Annals*, 931
("generally" to "the law") (Fisher Ames); [Edmund Randolph], *Germanicus* (Philadelphia,
1794?), Letter III:13 ("praise-worthy"); Nov. 26, 1794, *Annals*, 922 ("town meetings") (Fisher
Ames); Nov. 24, 1794, *Annals*, 899 ("fatal" and "reprehensible") (Thomas FitzSimons), 902
("mischievous") (William Loughton Smith); Nov. 25, 1794, *Annals*, 906 ("hold out") (William
Murray).

61. [Randolph], *Germanicus*, Letter VIII and XIII:28 ("powerfully" to "the government"), 67
("*unnecessary*"); *Baltimore Daily Advertiser*, Mar. 31, 1794, quoted in Link, *Societies*, 122 ("one
Republican").

62. Foner, *Sourcebook*, 159 ("the constitutions" to "private clubs"); [Randolph], *Germanicus*, Letter
IV:17 ("interest" to "of the government"), Letter XII:60 ("centinel" to "the Union").

63. Nov. 25, 1794, *Annals*, 923 ("clubs" and "real Representatives") (Fisher Ames); George Washington to Burges Ball, Sept. 25, 1794, *GWW*, XXXIII:506–507 ("arrogant" to "the people"); *Gazette
of the United States*, Feb. 1, 1792 ("the virtue"), July 13, 1793 ("modes" to "obedience").

64. Oliver Wolcott, Sr., to Oliver Wolcott, Jr., Mar. 26, 1795, in George Gibbs, ed., *Memoirs Of The
Administrations Of Washington And John Adams, Edited From The Papers Of Oliver Wolcott,
Secretary of the Treasury* (2 vols., New York, 1846), I:179 ("a general"); Alexander Balmain to
James Madison, Dec. 8, 1794, *MP*, XV:410 ("a few" to "know much").
    On the Federalist view of a narrower role for the people in the governing process, see
Slaughter, *Whiskey*, 133 ("The proper time and the *only* proper time for citizens to express
their political preferences was on election day"); James Roger Sharp, "The Whiskey Rebellion
and the Question of Representation," in Boyd, *Whiskey*, 127 (noting Federalist defense of "the
deferential system of representation with its notion that a selfless elite was best able to divine
the public good").

65. Nov. 25, 1794, *Annals*, 923 ("club sovereignty") (Fisher Ames); George Washington to Charles
Mynn Thruston, Aug. 10, 1794, *GWW*, XXXIII:465 ("anarchy" to "all Laws"); "Tully" No. I
[Aug 23, 1794], *HP*, XVII:135 ("the government"). Washington saw the loss of security for "life,
liberty" and "property" if groups challenged enacted legislation. George Washington to Daniel
Morgan, Oct. 8, 1794, *GWW*, XXXIII:523.

66. Nov. 27, 1794, *Annals*, 936 ("false apostles" to "the majority") (Samuel Dexter); Nov. 26, 1794,
Annals, 922–23 ("clubs" to "dreamed of") (Fisher Ames).

67. "John Blair's Charge to the Grand Jury of the Circuit Court for the District of Georgia," Apr. 27,
1795, *DHSC*, III:32 ("scene" and "useful lesson" to "course of things"), 36 ("external obedience"
to "alteration"), 33 ("if a minority" to "the few").

68. "John Blair's Charge to the Grand Jury of the Circuit Court for the District of Georgia," Apr.
27, 1795, *DHSC*, III:35 ("in such representation" to "liberty"); Benjamin Rush, "Defects of the
Confederation," in Dagobert D. Runes, ed., *The Selected Writings of Benjamin Rush* (1947),
28 ("only on" to "abused"); "A Friend to Representative Government," *Gazette of the United
States*, Apr. 4, 1794.

69. George Washington, diary entry, Oct. 9, 1794, *Diaries*, VI:185 ("an object"); George Washington
to Burges Ball, Aug. 10, 1794, *GWW*, XXXIII:463 ("obedience" to "their duty"); Jasper Ewing
to Charles Hall, Sept. 27, 1794, *Penn. Archives*, IV:380 ("that Government"). See also Charles
Royster, *Light-Horse Harry Lee and the Legacy of the American Revolution*, (1981), 117–68
(for Lee's commitment to the values of maintaining order and stability).

70. Fisher Ames to Thomas Dwight, Sept. 3, 1794, *FAW*, II:1047 ("rebellion"); Alexander Hamilton
to Angelica Church, Oct. 23, 1794, Alexander Hamilton to Rufus King, Sept. 22, 1794, *HP*,
XVII:340 ("the insurrection"), 259 ("what is that"); George Washington to Edmund Randolph,

Oct. 16, 1794, George Washington to Edmund Pendleton, Jan. 22, 1795, *GWW*, XXXIV:4 ("future attempts"), 99 ("anarchy").

71. James Iredell's Charge to the Grand Jury of the Circuit Court for the District of Virginia, Nov. 23, 1795, *DHSC*, III:77 ("open insurrection"), 78 ("[s]uccess" to "and People"). See also Hemberger, "Representations," 325 (arguing Washington and Hamilton understood the military expedition "was not to subdue an insurrection" but responded to the threat of "conflicting understandings of how the popular will would be expressed"); Brooke, "Ancient Lodges," 276 (describing a "competition for the public mind" in the 1790s "grounded in the terms of the constitutional settlement of the Revolution"); Chesney, "Treason," 1566 (arguing Federalists "made a point of explaining their position in terms of their understanding of representative government and popular sovereignty").

72. Fisher Ames to Thomas Dwight, Sept. 3, 1794, Nov. 29, 1794, *FAW*, II:1047 ("as busy"), 1082 ("faction" and "the discontents"); Edmund Randolph to George Washington, Oct. 11, 1794, Worthington Chauncey Ford, ed., *The Writings of George Washington* (14 vols., New York, 1889–1893), XII:474n1 ("prospect").

73. James Madison, Speech to Congress, [Nov. 27, 1794], James Madison to Thomas Jefferson, Nov. 30 and Dec. 21, 1794, *MP*, XV:391 ("pernicious" to "over the people"), 396 ("the most sacred"), 419 ("the essential").

74. Nov. 25, 1794, *Annals*, 910 ("The people have") (Abraham Venable), Nov. 25, 1794, *Annals*, 911 ("to watch" and "mistakes") (John Nicholas), Nov. 27, 1794, *Annals*, 941 ("the day") (Thomas Carnes).

75. Foner, *Sourcebook*, 34 ("Is it" to "constituted"); Link, *Societies*, 106n23 (*"when the"*). On invoking the people's sovereignty, see Foner, *Sourcebook*, 23, 64, 151, 237, 269, 275, 319; Cornell, *Other Founders*, 195–99.

76. "Address to 'Fellow Freemen,'" Jan. 26, 1795, Foner, *Sourcebook*, 194 ("Was it"); Thomas Jefferson to James Madison, Dec. 28, 1794, *MP*, XV:427 ("ingenuity" to "distinctions"); "Arbiter," *Philadelphia Independent Gazetteer*, Jan. 28, 1795.

77. Foner, *Sourcebook*, 151 ("maxim" to "superfluous"); "Helvidius" Number 3, Sept. 7, 1793, MP, XV:98 ("not only" to "a nation"); *Philadelphia General Advertiser*, May 16, 1794 ("the security"); William Littell to unknown correspondent, July 15, 1793, repr. in *Pittsburgh Gazette*, Aug. 10, 1793 ("implicit"), Aug. 3, 1793 ("naturally" to "subject").

78. Quoted in Link, *Societies*, 6 ("the duty" to "constant action"); Foner, *Sourcebook*, 267 ("peculiar"), 275 ("absurd" to "American"), 25, quoting *Boston Independent Chronicle*, Jan. 16, 1794 ("set up" to "of Government"), 57 ("in a government" to "their duty"). For the mandate for the people's scrutiny of government and government officials, see Foner, *Sourcebook*, 3, 238, 254, 256, 259, 335.

79. William Littell to unknown correspondent, July 15, 1793, repr. in *Pittsburgh Gazette*, Aug. 10, 1793 ("think"); Link, *Societies*, 163 ("slavish"); *Farmer's Library*, Aug. 8, 1796, quoted in Link, *Societies*, 161 ("deliberate" to "rightly"); James Madison, Speech to Congress, *MP*, XV:391 ("light will prevail"); Link, *Societies*, 7 ("judging" to "the laws"); quoted in Daniel Marder, "The Whiskey Rebels and the Elusive Dream," 14 *Southern Quarterly* (1976), 381 ("the cobbler"); [Husband], *Proposals*, 10 ("good").

80. "John Blair's Charge to the Grand Jury of the Circuit Court for the District of Georgia," Apr. 27, 1795, *DHSC*, III: 36 ("peculiar" to "social compact").

81. Alexander Hamilton to Rufus King, Oct. 30, 1794, *HP*, XVII:348–49 ("outlawry" to "present one"). See McDonald, *States' Rights*, 38 (describing the government's "display of will and strength" during which protesters "were arrested and treated badly enough so that they would remember to behave in the future").

For the way opponents of the excise tax were characterized, see Thomas P. Slaughter, "The Friends of Liberty, the Friends of Order, and the Whiskey Rebellion: A Historiographical Essay," in Boyd, *Whiskey*, 19 (called "'Shaysites'"); "George Washington to the Inhabitants of the Borough of Carlisle," Oct. 6, 1794, Washington, *GWW*, XXXIII:519 (hoping that "the delusion" would soon dissipate and that "reason will speedily regain her empire").

82. Thomas Jefferson to Abigail Adams, Feb. 22, 1787, *JP*, XI:174 ("a little rebellion").

83. James Madison, Speech in Congress, [Dec. 17, 1794], *MP*, XV:416 ("A great body"). In this respect Madison echoed the approach Herman Husband had suggested in granting the federal Constitution the "power to quell insurrections." Husband advised treating "the offenders" like "the law directs for stubborn children and servants, and on the people's submission, to treat them again with a fatherly tenderness, as penitent sinners, granting them general pardons and forgiveness, as far as the safety of the state will permit." [Husband], *Bucks and Hinds*, 25.

84. Thomas Jefferson to James Madison, Oct. 30, 1794, James Madison to James Monroe, Dec. 4, 1794, *MP*, XV:366 ("an appeal" to "ineffectual"), 406 ("the general" to "larger scale"). Albert Gallatin made a similar point during a speech at the Brownsville meeting on Aug. 28–29, 1794, suggesting that suppressing opponents of the government had "a tendency to make the people abject and the government tyrannic." See Brackenridge, *Incidents*, I:112 (recounting Gallatin's speech).

85. James Madison to James Monroe, Dec. 4, 1794, *MP*, XV:406 ("crushed" to *"enforcing the laws"*). See also Thomas Jefferson to James Madison, Nov. 16, 1794, Joseph Jones to James Madison, Nov. 19, 1794, *MP*, XV:379 (reporting that "conversation" in Philadelphia "ran high for a standing army"), 385 (hoping that the prompt muster of the militia would be "a stumbling block to advocates for a standing Army").

86. Edmund Randolph to George Washington, Aug. 5, 1794, quoted in Kohn, *Eagle and Sword*, 171, 366n133 (concluding that Randolph was quoting Hamilton). See also Alexander Hamilton to James McHenry, Mar. 18, 1799, *HP*, XXII:552–53 (insisting that government should look "like a *Hercules*, and inspire respect by the display of strength" whenever it "appears in arms"); July 10, 1798, *Annals*, 2146 (Harrison Gray Otis justifying the Sedition Act on grounds "every independent Government has a right to preserve and defend itself against" threats to "its existence").

87. James Madison to James Monroe, Dec. 4, 1794, *MP*, XV:406 ("[t]he game" to "the odium" and "perhaps") George Washington to Edmund Randolph, Oct. 16, 1794, *GWW*, XXXIV:3 ("entangled"). On the acclaim Madison received for defending the societies despite never apparently joining one, see "The Republican Society of South Carolina to James Madison," Mar. 12, 1794, *MP*, XV:279. Jefferson wondered how Washington "permitted himself to be the organ of such an attack on the freedom of discussion, the freedom of writing, printing, & publishing." Thomas Jefferson to James Madison, Dec. 28, 1794, *MP*, XV:427.

88. David Ford, Sept. 26, 1794, "Journal Of An Expedition Made In The Autumn Of 1794, With A Detachment Of New Jersey Troops, Into Western Pennsylvania, To Aid In Suppressing The 'Whiskey Rebellion,'" 8 *Proceedings of the New Jersey Historical Society* (1856–1859), 83 ("Americans seem"); "John Blair's Charge to the Grand Jury of the Circuit Court for the District of Georgia," Apr. 27, 1795, *DHSC*, III:35 ("overstrained"); Fennell, "Whiskey," 260 ("anarchy poles").

89. George Washington to Daniel Morgan, Oct. 8, 1794, Washington, *GWW*, XXXIII:523 ("to subvert").

90. Thomas Jefferson to Benjamin H. Latrobe, July 12, 1812, quoted in Talbot Hamlin, *Benjamin Henry Latrobe* (1955), 292 ("the first temple"); John Adams, "Reply of the President," Nov. 27, 1800; Thomas Jefferson, "First Inaugural Address," Mar. 4, 1801, *MPP*, I:312 ("the great body"), 322 ("the will").

91. See Randolph M. Bell, *Party and Faction in American Politics: The House of Representatives, 1789–1801* (1973), 59 (seeing an "ideological continuity" between Washington's response to opponents of the excise tax and John Adams's reaction to critics of his administration); Slaughter, *Whiskey*, 226 (considering Washington administration's response a precedent for "executive branch law enforcement"). See also Wills, *Evil*, 108 (noting that states or governments have "prerogatives" while people have "rights").

92. Spalding and Garrity, *Farewell Address*, 180 ("the right" to "established Government"). See also Kyvig, *Explicit*, 2 (asserting that by the time of the *Farewell Address* "American political

culture embraced George Washington's perspective on constitutionalism, including his view of constitutional reform").

93. [William Duane], *A Letter to George Washington* (Philadelphia, 1796), 16 ("dogmas"), 10 ("but a"). Some scholars have identified the vigorous defense of a free press and the Democratic clubs by "radicals" (including Irish-American editors) during the heated politics of the 1790s. See, for example, Margaret H. McAleer, "In Defense of Civil Society: Irish Radicals in Philadelphia During the 1790s," 1 *Early American Studies* (2003), 176–97. However, many of the so-called radicals merely presented a strident version of ideas found in many state constitutions, even those deemed by scholars as "conservative" documents.

94. [Duane], *Letter to Washington*, 16 ("important principle" and "the right of the people" to "unassailable"), 17 ("general truth" and "loose doctrine"), 22 ("the only wisdom").

95. See Lenner, *Federal*, 18–19, 22, 25, 28, 30, 32; Forest McDonald, *Novus Ordo Seclorum: The Intellectual Origins of the Constitution* (1985), 279–80.

96. Two years after Washington's *Farewell Address*, Pennsylvania witnessed yet another tax protest resulting in the so-called Fries's Rebellion, during which protesters justified their resistance on the right of the sovereign people to check their government. See Newman, *Fries's Rebellion*; Robert H. Churchill, "Popular Nullification, Fries' Rebellion, and the Waning of Radical Republicanism, 1798–1801," 67 *Pennsylvania History* (2005), 105–40. Although Newman describes the tax protesters as using "illegal methods and Revolutionary ideals" (ix) to create a "unique" form of "popular constitutionalism to demand the right of direct action" (41), their position drew from preexisting constitutional understandings that emerged with the creation of written constitutions in the 1770s and which many Americans routinely invoked well before Fries's Rebellion.

CHAPTER 7. FEDERAL SOVEREIGNTY

1. The account of Madison draws on Brant, *Madison*, VI:420n4, 520; Charles Jared Ingersoll, "Visit to Mr. Madison," *Washington Globe*, Aug. 12, 1836, repr. in *Richmond Enquirer*, Aug. 19, 1836; Yates Notes, June 29, 1787, *RFC*, I:471–72; James Madison to W. C. Rives, Oct. 21, 1833, *RFC*, III:521–24; James Madison to Joseph Gales, Aug. 26, 1821, *MW*, IX:68–70; Drew R. McCoy, *The Last of the Fathers: James Madison and the Republican Legacy* (1989), 122 (quoting *Richmond Inquirer* of Mar. 13, 1829), 156, 163–70.

2. *McCulloch v. Maryland*, 17 U.S. 316 at 405 (1819) ("perpetually arising" and "long as").

3. For the focus on federalism in the debates over the theory of the Union before the Civil War, see Wayne D. Moore, "Reconceiving Interpretive Autonomy: Insights from the Virginia and Kentucky Resolutions," 11 *Const. Comment.* (1994), 315–54; Kevin R. Gutzman, "A Troublesome Legacy: James Madison and 'The Principles of '98,'" 15 *JER* (1995), 571 (considering "the radical southern states' rights tradition" as "firmly based" on the writings of Jefferson and Madison and especially the resolutions of 1798); David F. Ericson, "The Nullification Crisis, American Republicanism, and the Force Bill Debate," 61 *Journal of Southern History* (1995), 255 (attributing to southern senators the perception that the resolutions were "glorious reassertions of states-rights principles"); Keith E. Whittington, *Constitutional Construction: Divided Powers and Constitutional Meaning* (1999), 72–112 (analyzing the Nullification crisis mainly as an issue of federalism); Lawrence M. Anderson, "The Institutional Basis of Secessionist Politics: Federalism and Secession in the United States," 34 *Publius* (2004), 1–18 (examining the influence of federalism on the secession movement leading to the Civil War); William J. Watkins, Jr., *Reclaiming the American Revolution: The Kentucky and Virginia Resolutions and Their Legacy* (2004), 55 (seeing in the resolutions "insights into the American experiment with self-government" that "remain instructive as we continue to debate the proper roles of the state and national governments").

Scholars who have examined how Americans disagreed over early understandings of the sovereign basis of the federal Constitution still consider the issue as a struggle over "creation myths" relevant only to the question of federalism. See, for example, Jack N. Rakove, "Making a

Hash of Sovereignty, Part I," 2 *Green Bag* (2nd ed., 1998), 35–44 (denying the utility of the word "sovereignty" for understanding American federalism); Rakove, "Making a Hash of Sovereignty, Part II" 3 *Green Bag* (2nd ed., 1999), 51 (asserting that while "[p]opular sovereignty may express a noble idea" as "an analytical principle" for understanding the American federal system, "it is vacuous"); Martin S. Flaherty, "John Marshall, *McCulloch v. Maryland,* and 'We the People': Revisions in Need of Revising," 43 *Wm & Mary L. Rev.* (2002), 1339–97, 1342 ("creation myth").

4. *Federalist No. 26,* p. 169 (Hamilton) ("jealous guardians" and "sound the alarm"). For the intervening and mediating sense of interposition in the eighteenth century, see Samuel Johnson, *A Dictionary of the English Language* (2 vols., London, printed by John Jarvis, 1786–1787). Interposition might embrace revision as well as reversal of laws deemed unconstitutional, but in the three incidents examined in this chapter, reversal of the laws in question was sought.

5. James Madison, "To 'A Friend of Union and State Rights,'" 1833, *ML,* IV:335 ("the several constitutional modes"). Analytically, nullification as the purported power of an individual state to veto a national law because of its unconstitutionality is distinguishable from interposition conceived as a broader range of actions taken to reverse such laws. See Diane Tipton, *Nullification and Interposition in American Political Thought* (1969), 7. Most of the scholarly literature, however, simply uses the term "nullification" and limits its use to imply the presumed right of an individual state to veto national laws or policies. See, for example, Richard E. Ellis, *The Union at Risk: Jacksonian Democracy, States' Rights and the Nullification Crisis* (1987), 4 (describing the Virginia and Kentucky Resolutions as asserting the right of states to "'interpose' or 'nullify' an act of Congress"); Wills, *Evil,* 148, 152 (calling Madison "an abettor" of nullification for using the "strong" and active word "interpose").

6. For the sense of "interpose" and "interposition" as something placed or put between two other things, see Johnson, *Dictionary; The Oxford English Dictionary* (2nd ed., 1989), VII:1130–31); Jedidiah Morse, *The American Universal Geography* (Boston, 1796), I:37 ("Only a small part of the convexity of the globe is interposed between us and the sun"); Noah Webster, *An American Dictionary of the English Language* (2 vols., New York, 1828) ("The interposition of the moon between the earth and the sun occasions a solar eclipse").

7. James Madison, "To 'A Friend of Union and State Rights,'" 1833, James Madison, "On Nullification," 1835/1836, *ML,* IV:335 ("ultimate authority" and "purview and forms"), 417 ("explain"); Cheshire, Massachusetts, Address upon presenting President Jefferson a gift on New Year's Day in 1802, repr. in L. H. Butterfield, "Elder John Leland, Jeffersonian Itinerant," 62 *Proceedings of the American Antiquarian Society* (1952), 224 ("a description").

8. *RFC,* I:314 (Madison) ("not immediately"); *Federalist No. 39,* p. 254 (Madison) ("the people of America"); John Taylor to Thomas Jefferson, June 25, 1798, *JP,* XXX:434 ("the people in state conventions"); "Report of 1800," *MP,* XVII:309 ("the people composing" to "sovereign capacity"); St. George Tucker, *View of the Constitution of the United States with Selected Writings* (Clyde N. Wilson, ed., 1999), 34 ("the people of the several states"). See also Rawle, *View,* 25 (opening his first chapter by identifying the "people of the states" as establishing the national government). Rawle had been appointed by George Washington to serve as the federal district attorney for Pennsylvania.

9. James Wilson, Dec. 4, 1787, Pennsylvania Convention, *DHRC,* II:472 ("one great community"); *Chisholm v. Georgia,* 2 U.S. 419 at 470 ("national capacity") (1793); Story, *Commentaries,* I:319 ("[t]he people of the *United States*); "Speech of Daniel Webster," Jan. 26–27, 1830, in Belz, *Webster-Hayne Debate,* 153 ("in the aggregate").

10. Most scholars suggest that Marshall viewed the federal Constitution's framing as resting on a national people, but a careful reading of his defense of *McCulloch v. Maryland* (1819) reveals his more consistent endorsement of the view that the people of the states framed the constitution. See Flaherty, "John Marshall," 1389 (observing that "as Marshall had been at pains to point out, 'the people of the United States' is properly understood to mean the peoples of the several states in their highest sovereign capacity"). For the scholarly tendency to attribute the federal Founding to a national people, see Rakove, *Meanings,* 163 (concluding that James Wilson, who

endorsed a view of a national people as the basis of the constitution, was a "better historian" than Luther Martin, who advanced the idea that sovereign states created the federal Union); Amar, *America's Constitution*, 33 (asserting that the federal Constitution "would shape a new continental nation whose sovereign would be a truly continental people").

11. For Madison's distinctions of the meaning attributable to "states," see "Report of 1800," *MP*, XVII:308–309 ("the term 'States,'"). See "Speech of John Rowan," Feb. 4, 1830, Belz, *Webster-Hayne Debate*, 269 (noting that "[m]uch confusion has arisen from the indiscriminate application of the word State to different and distinct subjects. Sometimes it is used to mean the government of the State, instead of the people in their political capacity").

12. For example, when Patrick Henry challenged Federalists during the Virginia ratifying convention to explain why the constitution's Preamble spoke of "*We, the People*, instead of *We, the States*," he suggested "the States" were "the agents of this compact," thus implying state governments as such "agents." Patrick Henry, June 4, 1788, Virginia Convention, *DHRC*, IX:930.

13. For example, when John C. Calhoun asserted that an individual state could unilaterally nullify a national law he described that action taking place through a convention that would represent the sovereign people of that state. See "Rough Draft of . . . the South Carolina Exposition," [completed ca. Nov. 25, 1828], *JCP*, X:510 (noting that while a state legislature – composed of governmental agents for the people – did not embody the sovereignty of the people of the state, it was clear "that a convention, fully represents" such sovereignty).

14. For overlooking the divergent meaning that "the states" possessed for contemporaries and that Americans at the time were often unclear about which possibility they were considering, see, for example, Lenner, *Federal*, 63 (asserting that "the extensive role of the states in the formation of the Constitution" proved to Jefferson and John Taylor that the states "remained sovereign"); Akhil Reed Amar, "Of Sovereignty and Federalism," 96 *Yale L.J.* (1987), 1452 (assuming that pre–Civil War descriptions of a "federal compact" necessarily entailed an understanding that "the People of each state were sovereign"). But see H. Jefferson Powell, "The Principles of '98: An Essay in Historical Retrieval," 80 *Va. L. Rev.* (1994), 738 (recognizing in "compact theory" both an inherent ambiguity and an intent to vindicate the people's sovereignty and to reject its reduction "to a theoretical premise of republican government of no pragmatic significance").

15. See, for example, Morgan, *Inventing*, 267 ("Madison was inventing a sovereign American people to overcome the sovereign states"); Cornell, *Other Founders*, 242 (assuming that Madison and Jefferson were talking about only "the rights of the state legislatures to judge constitutional matters"); McDonald, *States' Rights*, 82 (asserting that in the Virginia Resolutions Madison claimed that the federal Constitution "had been created by the states as states").

   In part, the difficulty of understanding Madison's constitutional thought stems from his often complex, if not convoluted, manner of expression (his contributions to the *Federalist Papers* being a notable exception). Only by carefully parsing his prose is it possible to piece together and offer a clear statement of his views on the nature of the sovereign underlying the federal Constitution and how the people as the sovereign could act as the ruler as well as the ruled. If this "de-construction" of Madison's prose offers a clarity lacking in his original iteration, it is submitted that the explanation of his thought offered in this work is consistent with and remains faithful to what he wrote.

16. For examples of scholarship exclusively equating "compact theory" to a states' rights justification for nullification and issues of federalism, see G. Edward White, with the aid of Gerald Gunther, *The Marshall Court and Cultural Change, 1815–1835* (abridged ed., 1991), 486–94; Elkins and McKitrick, *Federalism*, 719 (asserting that both the Virginia and Kentucky Resolutions embraced "a view of the Constitution as a compact among the several states"); Kurt T. Lash, "James Madison's Celebrated Report of 1800: The Transformation of the Tenth Amendment," 74 *Geo.Wash. L. Rev.* (2006), 185 (seeing a basic divide between "those who sought to construe the Constitution as a compact between the federal government and the *states* (and not the undifferentiated American people)"); *Web(SFW)*, I:571 (editors of the Webster Papers identifying the "dogma" of nullification as deriving "from an interpretation of the Constitution as a compact between sovereign states").

17. The four separate laws composing the so-called Alien and Sedition Acts are repr. in Smith, *Freedom's Fetters*, 438 ("dangerous" to "secret machinations"), 442 ("false" to "disrepute"). For additional background on the acts, see Curtis, *Free Speech*, 58–79; David Jenkins, "The Sedition Act of 1798 and the Incorporation of Seditious Libel into First Amendment Jurisprudence," 45 *AJLH* (2001), 154–213; Lendler, "Sedition Act," 419–44.

18. Thomas Jefferson to James Madison, June 7, 1798, *JW(L)*, VII:267 ("no respect"); James Madison to Thomas Jefferson, May 20, 1798, *JP*, XXX:359 ("a monster"); "Virginia Resolutions of 1798," *MP*, XVII:189–90 ("right of freely"). For newspaper coverage during the framing of the federal Constitution, see Alexander, *News Coverage*; Jeffrey L. Pasley, *"The Tyranny of Printers": Newspaper Politics in the Early American Republic* (2001).

19. Before the resolutions, Jefferson and Madison anonymously drafted several petitions protesting Federalist use of federal grand juries in Virginia that intimidated Republicans. They sought "redress" from the state's legislature, prompting a resolution in support by the legislature's lower house. For these parallel efforts of interposition and the genesis of the better known resolutions, see Adrienne Koch and Harry Ammon, "The Virginia and Kentucky Resolutions: An Episode in Jefferson's and Madison's Defense of Civil Liberties," 5 *WMQ* (1948), 145–76, especially 153 ("redress"); Mayer, *Jefferson*, 199–201. Jefferson and Madison kept their authorship of the resolutions secret, in part because "the very act of drafting these Resolutions was in violation of the Sedition Act." Mayer, *Jefferson*, 357n66.

20. For both contemporary and scholarly assumptions that the resolutions (and in particular that Jefferson and the Kentucky Resolutions) asserted a constitutional "remedy" of individual state nullification, see Frank Maloy Anderson, "Contemporary Opinion of the Virginia and Kentucky Resolutions," 5 *AHR* (1899–1900), 45–63, 225–52; Koch and Ammon, "Resolutions," 162 (arguing that Jefferson, but not Madison, embraced nullification by an individual state); Merrill D. Peterson, *The Jefferson Image in the American Mind* (1960), 63 (concluding that the resolutions "contained in embryo the idea of constitutional resistance by a single state to federal laws which in the view of that state transcended the compact of government"); Ellis, *Union*, 4 (asserting the resolutions formulated "a legal procedure or 'rightful remedy' by which the states could 'interpose' or 'nullify' an act of Congress"); Mayer, *Jefferson*, 201 (asserting that Jefferson's Kentucky Resolutions were "more radical" in "expressing the principle that the states might nullify – that is, treat as void – acts of Congress that they deemed unconstitutional"); Watkins, *Kentucky and Virginia Resolutions*, 75 (asserting that Jefferson "declared that a single state could nullify acts of Congress").

21. "Virginia Resolutions," Dec. 21, 1798, *MP*, XVII:190 ("unconstitutional"); "Kentucky Resolutions Adopted by the Kentucky General Assembly," Nov. 10, 1798, *JP*, XXX:552 ("not law"); James Madison to James Robertson, Mar. 27, 1831, *ML*, IV:166 ("annul the acts"). See also James Madison to Edward Livingston, May 8, 1830, *ML*, IV:80 (lamenting the "failure to distinguish between what is declaratory of opinion and what is *ipso facto* executory").

22. Breckinridge's legislative speech recorded in the *Frankfurt Palladium*, Nov. 13 and 20, 1798, repr. in Ethelbert Dudley Warfield, *The Kentucky Resolutions of 1798: An Historical Study* (New York, 1894), 93 ("co-States" to "the creature"), 94 ("beyond the limits" to *"protect their citizens"*), 95 ("firmly" to "examine").

23. Samuel Brown to Thomas Jefferson, Sept. 4, 1798, *JP*, XXX:510–11 ("solemnity); "Address of James Garrard," quoted from *Kentucky Gazette*, Nov. 14, 1798, in *JP*, XXX:534 ("the conduct" to "impolitic proceedings").

24. "Kentucky Resolutions Adopted by the Kentucky General Assembly," Nov. 10, 1798, *JP*, XXX:555 ("Co-states" and "void"); "Virginia Resolutions," Dec. 21, 1798, *MP*, XVII:189 ("the states" to "interpose").

25. Thomas Jefferson to James Madison, Nov. 17, [1798], Thomas Jefferson to John Taylor, Nov. 26, 1798, *JP*, XXX:580 ("distinctly affirmed" to "extremities"), 589 ("For the present" to "similar declarations").

26. John Taylor to Thomas Jefferson, [before Dec. 11, 1798], *JP*, XXX:601 ("the people in convention"); [John Taylor], *An Enquiry into the Principles and Tendency of Certain Public*

Measures (Philadelphia, 1794), 54 ("a general convention"), 49 ("the only genuine"), 53 ("corrector").

27. James Madison to Thomas Jefferson, Dec. 29, 1798, *JP*, XXX:606 ("zeal" to "Compact was made").

28. "Virginia Resolutions," Dec. 21, 1798, *MP*, XVII:189 ("duty" to "every infraction"); *Federalist No. 26*, p. 169 (Hamilton) ("jealous guardians" and "sound the alarm"); *Federalist No. 28*, p. 180 (Hamilton) ("national authority" to "opposition"); [Taylor], *An Enquiry*, 55 ("as good").

29. [James Madison], "Political Reflections," [Feb. 23, 1799], *MP*, XVII:239 ("true lesson" to "wholesome censure"). During the protests against the Alien and Sedition Acts, some argued that juries played a crucial role in determining the constitutionality of federal laws. See Kathryn Preyer, "*United States v. Callender*: Judge and Jury in a Republican Society," in Maeva Marcus, ed., *Origins of the Federal Judiciary: Essays on the Judiciary Act of 1789* (1992), 173–95.

30. "Clark[e] County Resolutions," July 24, 1798, repr. in Warfield, *Kentucky Resolutions*, 41 ("the servant[s]" to "vigilance"), 42 ("unconstitutional" and "abominable"); quoted in James Morton Smith, "The Grass Roots Origins of the Kentucky Resolutions," 27 *WMQ* (1970), 228 ("to guard" to "Constitutional rights"), 229 ("invaluable privilege"), 230 ("always have" to "servants"). On Nicholas, see Joan Wells Coward, *Kentucky in the New Republic: The Process of Constitution Making* (1979).

31. John Dawson to James Madison, Feb. 5, 1799, *MP*, XVII:225 ("no chance").

32. *Report of the Committee To whom were referred, on the 12th instant, Certain Memorials & Petitions Complaining of the Act, Intituled "An Act Concerning Aliens," and of Other Late Acts of the Congress of the United States* (Philadelphia, 1799), 15 ("inexpedient"); Thomas Jefferson to James Madison, Feb. 26, 1799, *MP*, XVII:244 ("began to enter" to "impossible to proceed"). For the geographical range of petitions sent to Congress, see Thomas Jefferson to James Madison, Jan. 30, 1799, *JP*, XXX:665–66; Elkins and McKitrick, *Federalism*, 615 (noting petitions "from everywhere" coming to Congress in early 1799 bearing "thousands of signatures").

33. Wilson Cary Nicholas to George Nicholas, Sept. 21, 1798, quoted in Dumas Malone, *Jefferson and His Time* (6 vols., 1948–1981), III:401 ("town or county"); "Philo-Agris," *Kentucky Gazette*, Aug. 22, 1798, quoted in Smith, "Grass Roots Origins," 236 ("united" to "constitutional measures"); Walter Jones and others to James Madison, Feb. 7, 1799, *MP*, XVII:228 ("within" to "Measures").

34. George Washington to Bushrod Washington, Dec. 31, 1798, George Washington to Patrick Henry, Jan. 15, 1799, *GWW*, XXXVII: 81 ("have points"), 89 ("dissolve"); Theodore Sedgwick to Rufus King, Mar. 20, 1799, Timothy Pickering to Rufus King, Dec. 14, 1798, *RKC*, II:581 ("a declaration"), 493 ("a right").

35. Theodore Sedgwick to Rufus King, Mar. 20, 1799, *RKC*, II:581 ("unanimity"). On North Carolina, see *JP*, XXX:557 ("violation") (Senate vote 31 to 9). For the split votes in repudiating the resolutions and the acts, see Anderson, "Contemporary Opinion," 46–47 (Maryland; House rejected Kentucky Resolutions 58 to 14, Virginia Resolutions 42 to 24), 53 (New Jersey; House perfunctorily dismissed the resolutions 20 to 15), 57 (New York; motion in House to declare sedition laws unconstitutional defeated 50 to 43, Senate rejected resolutions 31 to 7), 232 (Vermont; Legislature rejected Virginia Resolutions 104 to 52, Kentucky Resolutions 101 to 50). For the seven formal legislative responses of Delaware, Rhode Island, Massachusetts, New York, Connecticut, New Hampshire, and Vermont to the resolutions, see Elliot, *Debates*, IV:532–39. For legislative responses omitted in Elliot, *Debates* because they were not directed to be sent back to the Virginia and Kentucky legislatures (including those from Maryland, Pennsylvania, and New Jersey), see Anderson, "Contemporary Opinion," 52–54, 244–52.

36. See Anderson, "Contemporary Opinion," 46 (quoting Committee Report of Maryland House of Delegates describing the Kentucky Resolutions as containing "*sentiments and opinions unwarranted by the Constitution of the United States*"), 245 (resolutions of Pennsylvania House of Representatives declaring that "the people of the United States ... have committed to the supreme judiciary of the nation the high authority of ultimately and conclusively deciding upon

the constitutionality of all legislative acts"), 247 (resolutions of Connecticut General Assembly describing the Kentucky Resolutions as "calculated to subvert the Constitution and to introduce discord and anarchy"); Elliot, *Debates*, IV:533 (Rhode Island General Assembly) (describing "the very unwarrantable resolutions" of Virginia), 534 (Massachusetts Senate) ("exclusively vested"), 538 (New York Senate) (doctrines of the Virginia and Kentucky Resolutions were "destructive to the federal government"), 539 (New Hampshire House of Representatives) (constitutional interpretation "is properly and exclusively confided to the judicial department").

37. Quoted in Anderson, "Contemporary Opinion," 57 ("individually" to "proclaim"), 252 ("the most pressing" to "political salvation"); Taylor, *An Enquiry*, 54 ("the nation" to "violation"); quoted in Anderson, "Contemporary Opinion," 251 ("daily exercised").

38. "Kentucky Resolutions of 1799," Nov. 14, 1799, repr. in Warfield, *Kentucky Resolutions*, 125 ("disturb the harmony" to "unquestionable right"), 126 ("SOLEMN PROTEST" to "constitutional manner"). Madison, elected to the Virginia legislature in the spring of 1799, formulated Virginia's response, while Jefferson shared his views with Kentucky legislators. Madison and Jefferson collaborated by letter and in person about how to respond. See Koch and Ammon, "Resolutions," 155–60.

39. Thomas Jefferson to James Madison, Aug. 23, 1799, *MP*, XVII:258 ("scission" to "true principles"); Thomas Jefferson to John Taylor, June 4, 1798, *JP*, XXX:388 ("every free" to "ever exist"), 389 ("keep together" and "have patience"). For the argument that Madison exercised a moderating influence on Jefferson, see Koch and Ammon, "Resolutions," 165–69.

40. "Report of 1800," Jan. 7, 1800, *MP*, XVII:349 ("misconception"); James Madison, "To 'A Friend of Union and States Rights,'" 1833, *ML*, IV:335 ("right to interpose"). See also James Madison to Thomas Jefferson, Dec. 29, 1799, *MP*, XVII:297 (reporting on "the job of preparing a vindication of the Resolutions"). The seven formal replies are collected in Elliot, *Debates*, IV:532–39.

41. "Report of 1800," Jan. 7, 1800, *MP*, XVII:349 ("communicat[ed]" to "unconstitutional"), 350 ("intermediate" to "infractions of the constitution"). In a similar manner, ten years earlier Virginia's legislature protested that the national government lacked constitutional power to assume state debts. See "Virginia Resolutions on the Assumption of State Debts," Dec. 16, 1790, Henry Steele Commager, ed., *Documents of American History* (8th ed., 1968), 155.

42. "Report of 1800," *MP*, XVII:348 ("novelty" to "private citizens").

43. "Report of 1800," *MP*, XVII:349 ("direct representation" to "most obvious").

44. "Report of 1800," *MP*, XVII:349 ("farther measures"), 312 ("The authority of constitutions"), 336–37 ("The people, not the government"), 312 ("fundamental principles" and "solemnly enjoined"). See also Taylor, *An Enquiry*, 53 (asserting that since the "component parts of government" were "the creatures of the constitution," subjecting "the creator to the created" was "a reversal of the course of nature").

45. "Report of 1800," *MP*, XVII:310 ("sovereign parties"), 311 ("genuine source"), 308–309 ("the term 'States'" to "political societies"). It must be conceded that Madison's clarification of the term "the states" still left the "different senses" of the phrase somewhat vague.

46. "Report of 1800," *MP*, XVII:309 ("legitimate" to "submitted to the states").

47. Madison's marginal notes on Memorandum from an Unidentified Correspondent, [ca. Jan. 2, 1800], "Report of 1800," *MP*, XVII:302n4 ("inaccuracies"), 309 ("parties to the compact"), 312 ("American public").

48. James Madison to Thomas Jefferson, Jan. 9, 1800, "Memorandum from an Unidentified Correspondent," [ca. Jan. 2, 1800], James Madison to Thomas Jefferson, Jan. 4, 1800, *MP*, XVII:352 ("the right"), 301 ("violations"), 302 ("declarations").

49. James Madison to Thomas Jefferson, Jan. 4, 1800, *MP*, XVII:302 ("concurred").

50. *The Address of The Minority in the Virginia Legislature to the People of that State; containing a Vindication of the Constitutionality of the Alien and Sedition Laws.* (Richmond, 1799), 2 ("will of the majority" to "federal pact"), 12 ("[t]he people of the United States" and "the American people"); [Henry Lee], *Plain Truth: Addressed to the People of Virginia. Written in February 1799 – By a Citizen of Westmoreland County, (Virg.)* [Richmond, 1799], 20 ("entirely" to "in convention"); Alexander Addison, *Analysis of The Report of the Committee of the Virginia*

374 **Notes to Pages 206–207**

Assembly, on the Proceedings of sundry of the other States in Answer to their Resolutions (Raleigh, 1800), 6 ("the people" to "a compact"). Likewise, the Federalist William Murray, a member of Kentucky's legislature who opposed his state's passage of resolutions in 1798, explained that the federal Constitution "was not merely a covenant between integral States, but a compact between the several individuals composing those States." Murray's legislative speech in the *Frankfurt Palladium*, Nov. 13 and 20, 1798, repr. in Warfield, *Kentucky Resolutions*, 90.

For the likelihood that John Marshall was the primary author of the Virginia *Minority Report*, see Kurt Lash and Alicia Harrison, "Minority Report: John Marshall and the Defense of the Alien and Sedition Acts," 68 *Ohio St.L.J.* (2007), 435.

51. "Report of 1800," *MP*, XVII:309 ("a plain principle" to "violated").
52. "Report of 1800," *MP*, XVII:310 ("the interposition" to "occasions"); "Virginia Resolutions of 1798," *MP*, XVII:189 ("to interpose" and "deliberate").
53. James Madison, "On Nullification," 1835/1836, *ML*, IV:413 ("as co-parties" to "own choice").
54. "Report of 1800," *MP*, XVII:311 ("sole expositor" and "in the last resort").
55. *Annals of Congress*, House of Reps., 1st Cong., 1st Sess., p. 520 (June 17, 1789, James Madison) ("[T]he people" to "greater powers").
56. *Federalist No. 49*, p. 339 (Madison) ("pretend" to "observance"); *Annals of Congress*, House of Reps., 1st Cong., 1st Sess., p. 520 (June 17, 1789, James Madison) ("[I]f the constitutional boundary"). See also James Madison, "Helvidius" Number 2, [Aug. 31, 1793], *MP*, XV:83 (describing all three branches of the federal government as having "a *concurrent* right to expound the constitution").
57. On views of "departmental review," see Donald G. Morgan, *Congress and the Constitution: A Study of Responsibility* (1966); Kermit L. Hall, *The Supreme Court and Judicial Review in American History* (1985), 4 (describing a theory in which "the political branches had responsibility for political-constitutional controversies within their spheres, and the judicial branch assumed the role of settling legal-juridical questions, overseeing the rule of law"). Both Thomas Jefferson and Andrew Jackson embraced a departmental theory of judicial review. See Thomas Jefferson to Spencer Roane, Sept. 6, 1819, *JW(F)*, X:141 (describing his understanding that under the federal Constitution "each department is truly independent of the others, and has an equal right to decide for itself what is the meaning of the constitution in the cases submitted to its action"); Andrew Jackson, "Veto Message," July 10, 1832, *MPP*, II:582 ("It is as much the duty of the House of Representatives, of the Senate, and of the President to decide upon the constitutionality of any bill or resolution which may be presented to them for passage or approval as it is of the supreme judges when it may be brought before them for judicial decision"). For the argument that America's constitutional history supports a departmental theory of constitutional review featuring "the people themselves," see Kramer, *People*.
58. During the Nullification crisis, Martin Van Buren denied that the Supreme Court was "the exclusive expositor of the Constitution," especially in conflicts between the state and the federal government. In those instances, "it is the right of each party to judge for itself; not for the Federal Government exclusively." See "Resolves of the Legislature of New York," *State Papers on Nullification* (Boston, 1834), 140 ("the exclusive"), 147 ("it is the right"). Moreover, in his First Inaugural Address, Abraham Lincoln questioned the Supreme Court's interpretative finality because such power undermined the sovereignty of the people. See "First Inaugural Address," Mar. 4, 1864, Roy P. Basler, ed., *The Collected Works of Abraham Lincoln* (8 vols., 1953), IV:268 (observing that "if the policy of the government, upon vital questions, affecting the whole people, is to be irrevocably fixed by decisions of the Supreme Court . . . the people will have ceased, to be their own rulers, having, to that extent, practically resigned their government, into the hands of that eminent tribunal").

See also Pauline Maier, "The Road Not Taken: Nullification, John C. Calhoun, and the Revolutionary Tradition in South Carolina," 82 *South Carolina Historical Magazine* (1981), 10 (noting that some nineteenth-century Americans "yielded to the Supreme Court their role as guardian of the constitution," but others did not); Phillip Shaw Paludan, "Hercules Unbound: Lincoln, Slavery, and the Intentions of the Framers," in Donald G. Nieman, ed., *The Constitution, Law,*

and American Life: Critical Aspects of the Nineteenth-Century Experience (1992), 2 (reminding that "the practice of making the Court "the final arbiter in constitutional interpretation did not gather momentum until after the Civil War"); Dinan, *People's Liberties* (describing a wide-ranging conception of nonjudicial guardianship of constitutional rights in America before the twentieth century); McDonald, *States' Rights*, 224 (describing the notion of the Court as "the sole and final arbiter of constitutional controversies" the "truly revolutionary consequence" of the Civil War); Kramer, *People*, 8 (arguing that for most of American history "American constitutionalism assigned ordinary citizens a central and pivotal role in implementing their Constitution" and that "courts no less than elected representatives were subordinate to their judgments").

59. For the contingent and contested meaning of judicial review before the Civil War, see Tony A. Freyer, *Producers Versus Capitalists: Constitutional Conflict in Antebellum America* (1994); Powell, "Principles of '98," 740 (describing the "universe" of those deemed to hold constitutional interpretive authority as including "legislatures, juries, private citizens, and 'the people in their highest sovereign capacity'"). See also Gerald Gunther, "Judicial Hegemony and Legislative Autonomy: The *Nixon* Case and the Impeachment Process," 22 *U.C.L.A. L. Rev.* (1974), 34 (arguing that the decision in *Marbury v. Madison* (1803) "intended" not "to announce that every constitutional issue requires final adjudication on the merits by the judiciary," but that many constitutional issues are left to other branches); Engdahl, "Name," 457–510 (identifying eighteenth-century terminology and practice calling into question the modern assumption that a "supreme" court necessarily implied judicial finality).

60. *Federalist No. 78*, p. 525 (Hamilton) ("an intermediate"); Peter Livingston quoted in Dinan, *Constitutional Tradition*, 102 ("shield"). On early attitudes toward judicial review, see Maeva Marcus, "Judicial Review in the Early Republic," in Hoffman and Albert, *Launching*, 25–53; Gordon S. Wood, "The Origins of Judicial Review Revisited, or How the Marshall Court Made More out of Less," 56 *Wash. & Lee L. Rev.* (1999), 787–809, esp. 798–99 (suggesting that for many Americans in the 1790s, judicial review "remained an extraordinary and solemn political action, akin perhaps to the interposition of the states that Jefferson and Madison suggested in the Kentucky and Virginia Resolutions of 1798 – something to be invoked only on the rare occasions of flagrant and unequivocal violations of the Constitution"); William Michael Treanor, "Judicial Review Before *Marbury*," 58 *Stan. L. Rev.* (2005), 455–562.

61. "Report of 1800," *MP*, XVII:310 ("last resort"), 311 ("great and extraordinary" to "grant of the constitution"); *Annals of Congress*, House of Reps., 1st Cong., 1st Sess., p. 520 (June 17, 1789, James Madison) ("in the ordinary").

62. "Report of 1800," *MP*, XVII:311.

63. *Boston Chronicle*, Feb. 25, 1799, *Boston Chronicle*, Feb. 18, 1799, quoted in Anderson, "Contemporary Opinion," 58 ("doctrine" to "agents"), 62 ("difficult" to *"constitutional powers"*).

64. "Jefferson's Draft," Oct. 4, 1798, *JP*, XXX:539 ("natural right"). For Madison's description of what he called the "original" or "natural" right of resisting government, see James Madison to Joseph C. Cabell, Sept. 7, 1829; James Madison, "On Nullification," 1835/1836, *ML*, IV:46 (noting a possible recurrence to "original principles" in "shaking off the yoke"), 409 (alluding to "the *natural* right to resist intolerable oppression").

65. "Jefferson's Draft," Oct. 4, 1798, *JP*, XXX:539 ("abuse" to "the creature").

66. "Kentucky Resolutions Adopted by the Kentucky General Assembly," Nov. 10, 1798, *JP*, XXX: 555 ("natural right" and "co-states"), 550 ("the exclusive" to "measure of its powers"); "Kentucky Resolutions of 1799," Nov. 14, 1799, repr. in Warfield, *Kentucky Resolutions*, 125 ("nullification" and "the several states"), 126 ("those sovereignties" and "rightful remedy").

67. Thomas Jefferson to James Madison, Nov. 26, 1799, *MP*, XVII:280 ("violations"); James Madison, "On Nullification," 1835/1836, *ML*, IV:415 ("a triumph"). See also Amar, "Sovereignty," 1502 (arguing that public reaction to the acts "effectively transformed" the election of 1800 into "a popular referendum" on them).

68. On Federalist concerns over embargo policies and the war, see Herman V. Ames, ed., *State Documents on Federal Relations: The States and the United States* (1906, repr. 1970), 26–44;

J. C. A. Stagg, *Mr. Madison's War: Politics, Diplomacy, and Warfare in the Early American Republic, 1783–1830* (1983); Donald R. Hickey, *The War of 1812: A Forgotten Conflict* (1989).

69. *Newburyport Resolutions at a legal meeting of the inhabitants of Newburyport . . . holden at the Court-House on Thursday, the 12 of January 1809,* 13 ("unconstitutional" to "interpose"); *An Address to the People of the County of Hampshire, By a Committee Appointed for that Purpose* (Northampton, MA, 1809), 15 ("shameful violations"), 3 ("sovereignty resides" to "Rulers"); *Boston Town Records, 1796–1813* (1905), 240 (applying to the legislature, "as the immediate guardians of their rights & liberties" for "interposition"). See also Banner, *Hartford,* 298–99; Labaree, *Patriots,* 164–67.

70. [General Court], *An Address to the People of the Commonwealth of Massachusetts* (n.p., 1809), 6 ("immense majority" to "national government"), Houghton Library, HU; *The Patriotick Proceedings of the Legislature of Massachusetts, During their Session from Jan. 26 to March 4, 1809* (Boston, 1809), 52 ("not legally binding"), 53 ("the commercial" to "inviolate").

71. "Speech of Governor Jonathan Trumbull at the Opening of the Special Session of the [Connecticut] Legislature," Feb. 23, 1809, "Resolutions of the [Connecticut] General Assembly," Feb. 23, 1809, and "Report and Resolutions of Rhode Island on the Embargo," Mar. 4, 1809, in Ames, *State Documents,* 39 ("to cast"), 40 ("duty" to "General Government"), 42 ("zealously"), 44 ("to interpose" and "vigilant").

72. Thomas Dawes to Noah Webster, July 24, 1812, Noah Webster Papers, NYPL ("Mr. Madison's War"). See also Ames, *State Documents,* 27 (on the repeal of the 1807 embargo); Hickey, *War,* 46 (noting the passage of the declaration of war in the House by a vote of 79 to 49 and by 19 to 13 in the Senate).

73. "Speech of Daniel Webster on the Conscription Bill," Dec. 9, 1814, *Web(SFW),* I:30 ("The operation" to "arbitrary power"); Daniel Webster to Ezekiel Webster, Dec. 22, 1814, *WebP(C),* I:178 ("[t]he people must look"). On the resistance to a federal requisition for troops, see "Massachusetts, Connecticut, and Rhode Island and the Militia Question," in Ames, *State Documents,* 54–65; Donald R. Hickey, "New England's Defense Problem and the Genesis of the Hartford Convention," 50 *New England Quarterly* (1977), 587–604. The New England governors also argued that while President Madison could take personal command of the militias, if he did not, their officer appointees were entitled to lead the troops.

74. Thomas Dawes to Noah Webster, June 25, 1812, Noah Webster Papers, NYPL ("rising"); Charles Willing Hare to Harrison Gray Otis, Feb. 10, 1814, repr. in Samuel Eliot Morison, *The Life and Letters of Harrison Gray Otis, Federalist, 1765–1848* (2 vols., 1913), II:175 ("so violently"); "Circular letter," repr. in Noah Webster, *A Collection of Papers on Political, Literary and Moral Subjects* (New York, 1843, repr. 1968), 314 ("a convention" to "respective legislatures"), 313 ("due weight"). See also Banner, *Hartford,* 262–63, 314–18; "Resolution of Town of Amherst," Jan. 3, 1814, repr. in Edward Payson Powell, *Nullification and Secession in the United States: A History of the Six Attempts During the First Century of the Republic* (New York, 1897), 239 (asking the legislature "to take the most vigorous and decisive measures compatible with the Constitution to put an end to this hopeless war, and restore to us the blessings of peace"). In February 1814, the Massachusetts legislature received an additional thirty-five town memorials seeking the legislature's interposition. See "Report of Joint Committee to the Memorial of the town of Deerfield, and several other towns," Feb. 18, 1814 (Boston, 1814), 7–9.

75. Timothy Bigelow, *An Address, Delivered on the Third Anniversary of the Washington Benevolent Society* (Boston, 1814), 16 ("tried in vain" and "contempt").

76. See "Report of the Massachusetts Legislature," Oct. 15, 1814, and "Report and Resolutions of the Legislature of Rhode Island," Nov. 5, 1814, in Ames, *State Documents,* 78–79, 81. On the origins of the Hartford convention, see Banner, *Hartford.* For biographical data on the convention delegates, see Theodore Dwight, *History of the Hartford Convention: With a Review of the Policy of the United States Government, which led to the War of 1812* (New York and Boston, 1833), Appendix, 423–34; Samuel Eliot Morison, *Harrison Gray Otis, 1765–1848, The*

Urbane Federalist (1969), 358–62 (describing at 361, the convention as representing "the rul-
ing class" of New England). On Cabot, see David Hackett Fischer, *The Revolution of American
Conservatism: The Federalist Party in the Era of Jeffersonian Democracy* (1965), 2–6. Zephaniah
Swift published *A System of the Laws of the State of Connecticut* (Windham, CT, 1795) and
Nathan Dane later published *A General Abridgment and Digest of American Law, With Occa-
sional Notes and Comments* (8 vols., Boston, 1823).

77. The *Report* was repr. in Dwight, *Hartford*, 352–79. The proposed amendments included the
exclusion of slaves from the apportionment of representation and taxes, the necessity of a
two-thirds vote of Congress before new states were admitted, limits on imposing embargos or
passing measures affecting foreign commerce or declarations of war, precluding naturalized
citizens from federal office-holding, and preventing a two-term presidency or the election of
the president from the same state in succession.

78. Hartford Convention, *Report*, 376 ("adopt" to "effects"), 361 ("their own judges" to "their own
decisions").

79. Hartford Convention, *Report*, 361 ("in cases of deliberate"). See also "Virginia Resolutions of
1798," *MP*, XVII:189 (Madison's resolutions read "that in case of a deliberate, palpable and
dangerous exercise of other powers not granted by the said compact, the states who are parties
thereto have the right, and are in duty bound, to interpose for arresting the pro[gress] of
the evil, and for maintaining within their respective limits, the authorities, rights and liberties
appertaining to them"). For Otis as the principal drafter of the *Report*, see Morison, *Otis*, II:148;
Hickey, *War*, 277 (asserting the *Report* "was largely the work of Otis"). While the suggestion of
nullification broke new constitutional ground, the mere assembly of delegates at Hartford was
well within the conventional arena of recognized forms of interposition. Still, scholars overlook
the unorthodox recommendation of the Hartford *Report* while questioning the legitimacy of
the convention itself. See, for example, Wilentz, *Democracy*, 165 (describing the convention as
"extralegal").

80. Jefferson's draft of the Kentucky Resolutions, but not the resolutions as adopted by Kentucky's
legislature, expressed the hope that each state would "take measures of it's own for providing" that
the Alien and Sedition Acts would not "be exercised." "Jefferson's Draft [Kentucky Resolutions],"
[before Oct. 4, 1798], *JP*:XXX:541. For the revelation of Madison's authorship of the Virginia
Resolutions, see Koch and Ammon, "Resolutions," 148.

81. Quoted in Frank Maloy Anderson, "A Forgotten Phase of the New England Opposition to the
War of 1812," 6 *Mississippi Valley Historical Society Proceedings* (1912–1913), 180 ("nothing
more"), 184 ("The Nature" to "SOVEREIGN STATES"), 183 ("submitted" to "*States*").

82. *Washington National Intelligencer*, Dec. 7, 1814 ("a grant from"); *Richmond Enquirer*, Nov. 1,
1814 ("no state" to "branch of it").

83. *Boston Daily Advertiser*, "To the President of the United States on the subject of the New-
England Convention," No. II. "The Nature of Our Government," Nov. 15, 1814 ("axioms" to
"*still* respect"), No. III. "The Meaning of the Federal Compact," Nov. 16, 1814 ("odious" to
"carried into effect"), No. IV. "Mr. Madison's Opinion on State Sovereignty," Nov. 17, 1814
("You have shewn" to "right and fit").

84. *Federalist No. 46*, p. 320 (Madison) ("the authority" and "ambitious encroachment" and "general
alarm" to "would be concerted"); *Boston Daily Advertiser*, "To the President of the United
States on the subject of the New-England Convention," No. IV. "Mr. Madison's Opinion on
State Sovereignty," Nov. 17, 1814 ("*then* and *now*").

85. William Pope to James Monroe, Oct. 28, 1814, James Monroe Papers, NYPL ("[T]hose traitors");
Boston Independent Chronicle, Dec. 1814, quoted in Marshall Foletta, *Coming to Terms with
Democracy: Federalist Intellectuals and the Shaping of an American Culture* (2001), 34 ("the
standard of insurrection"); Andrew Jackson to James Monroe, Jan. 6, 1817, Harold D. Moser
ed., *The Papers of Andrew Jackson* (1994), IV:81. For the Republican press characterization
of the Hartford delegates as traitors, see Daniel R. Dzibinski, "The Politics of Power: The
Partisan Struggle Surrounding the War of 1812 and the Hartford Convention" (MA thesis,
Florida State Univ., 1999), 86–118. On New England secessionism, see David Hackett Fischer,

"The Myth of the Essex Junto," 21 *WMQ* (1964), 191–235; Banner, *Hartford*, 307; Gerard H. Clarfield, *Timothy Pickering and the American Republic* (1980); Kevin M. Gannon, "Escaping 'Mr. Jefferson's Plan of Destruction': New England Federalists and the Idea of a Northern Confederacy, 1803–1804," 21 *JER* (2001), 413–43.

86. Thomas Jefferson to Lafayette, Feb. 14, 1815, Thomas Jefferson to Henry Dearborn, Mar. 17, 1815, Thomas Jefferson Papers, LC; James Madison to Wilson Cary Nicholas, Nov. 25, 1814, James Madison Papers, LC.

87. Thomas S. Jesup to James Monroe, Dec. 31, 1814, repr. in Jack Alden Clarke, "Thomas Sydney Jesup: Military Observer at the Hartford Convention," 29 *New England Quarterly* (1956), 396 ("the most determined" to "signal"); quoted in Ralph Ketcham, *James Madison: A Biography* (1990), 595 ("to repel").

88. Winfield Scott to James Monroe, Feb. 15, 1815, James Monroe Papers, NYPL (*"grievance deputies"* and "a fine subject"); Hector Benevolus, *The Hartford Convention in an Uproar and the Wise Men of the East Confounded* (Windsor, VT, 1815). See also Morison, *Urbane Federalist*, 383–99 (describing the mission to Washington).

89. Daniel Webster to [William F. Rowland?], Jan. 11, 1815, *WebP(C)*, I:181 ("moderate" to "highly gratified"); Timothy Pickering to John Lowell, Jan. 23, 1815, repr. in Henry Cabot Lodge, *Life and Letters of George Cabot* (Boston, 1878), 562 ("made a declaration"). Fifteen years later, in the midst of rejecting the individual state veto during the Nullification crisis, Webster dismissed the Hartford Convention as only a series of "indiscreet sermons, frothy paragraphs, and fuming popular addresses" not entitled to further attention. "Speech of Daniel Webster," Jan. 26 and 27, 1830, Belz, *Webster-Hayne Debate*, 114.

   On other reactions to the Convention's *Report* at the time, see Banner, *Hartford*, 345–46; Hickey, *War*, 278–79. On the fate of the amendments, see Ames, *State Documents*, 86–88; *Annals of Congress*, House of Rep., 13th Cong., 3rd Sess., pp. 1269–70 (Mar. 3, 1815).

90. Hartford convention, *Report*, 355 (observing that "if the Union be destined to dissolution, by reason of the multiplied abuses of bad administrations, it should, if possible, be the work of peaceable times, and deliberate consent"); Harrison Gray Otis to Josiah Quincy, Dec. 15, 1808, repr. in Morison, *Otis*, II:5 ("some mode of relief").

   On the resistance to secession as a political option, see Banner, *Hartford*, 115–21, 304–305; Hickey, *War*, 269–70, 273–75; Morison, *Otis*, II:110–24; Fischer, *American Conservatism*, 175–77; Christopher Gore to Rufus King, Apr. 11, 1815, *RKC*, V:476.

91. Harrison Gray Otis to Noah Webster, May 6, 1840 ("constitutional & peaceable"), Noah Webster Papers, NYPL. On the stigma of participation in the convention and its effect on Otis's political career, see Morison, *Otis*, II:140, 163–64; Banner, *Hartford*, 348–49; Thomas Jackson Oakley to Daniel Webster, Apr. 12, 1823, *WebP(C)*, I:327.

92. Harrison Gray Otis to William Sullivan, Feb. 13, 1820, repr. in Morison, *Urbane Federalist*, 429 ("Is it not"); Otis' *Letters in Defence of the Hartford Convention, And the People of Massachusetts* (Boston, 1824), 66 ("question of constitutional law" to "Governments"), 52 ("a manual"), 37 ("self evident" to "universally recognized"), 57 ("Convention or Caucus" to "den of bandits").

93. Otis' *Letters in Defence*, 52 ("in substance").

94. Harrison Gray Otis to Noah Webster, May 6, 1840 ("restraining" and *"nullification"*), Noah Webster Papers, NYPL. Maryland's U.S. senator predicted that those declaring the tariff of 1828 unconstitutional and calling for state action to resist the law "will be looked at, as little less than a counterpart of the Hartford Convention" and "will sink in publick estimation." Samuel Smith to John C. Calhoun, July 5, 1828, *JCP*, X:393.

95. Newspaper clipping enclosed in letter from Charles J. Ingersoll to James Madison, Nov. 9, 1827 ("[t]he health"), James Madison Papers, LC; James Madison to Edward Coles, Oct. 15, 1834 ("respect for my opinion"), *ML*, IV:367; James Madison to Richard Rush, Dec. 4, 1820, *ML*, III:195 ("very serious" to "constitutional question").

96. James Madison, Autobiography, 4 ("spirituous liquors, and other treats"), James Madison Papers, *LC*; James Madison to Nicholas P. Trist, Sept. 23, 1831 ("most extraordinary" and "how little"), James Madison Papers, LC; McCoy, *Madison*, 152. For Madison's defense of the tariff's constitutionality, see James Madison to Joseph C. Cabell, Mar. 22, 1827, *ML*, III:571; Brant, *Madison*, VI:470–74.

97. "Rough Draft of . . . the South Carolina Exposition," [completed ca. Nov. 25, 1828], *JCP*, X:456 ("serffs"). See Willliam W. Freehling, *Prelude to Civil War: The Nullification Controversy in South Carolina, 1816–1836* (1966), 25–86, 138–40; Brant, *Madison*, VI:469.

98. "South Carolina on Internal Improvements and the Tariff," Dec. 16, 1825, Ames, *State Documents*, 140 ("unconstitutional"). For the campaign against the tariff, see Freehling, *Prelude*, 134–259; Chauncey Samuel Boucher, *The Nullification Controversy in South Carolina* (1916, repr. 1968), 1–45. On the "Free Trade" convention, see *Memorial of a Committee Appointed by the Free Trade Convention, Held in Philadelphia in September and October, 1831, upon the subject of the present tariff of duties*, Jan. 30, 1832, House Document No. 82, 22nd Cong., 1st Sess.; John C. Calhoun to Samuel D. Ingham, July 31, 1831, John C. Calhoun to Francis W. Pickens, Aug. 1, 1831, Albert Gallatin to John C. Calhoun, Jan. 23, 1832, John C. Calhoun to Francis W. Pickens, Mar. 2, 1832, *JCP*, XI:444, 446, 544–45, 558–59. A minority report of the convention sought the tariff's immediate repeal.

99. John C. Calhoun, "Draft Report on Federal Relations," [ca. Nov. 20, 1831], *JCP*, XI:508 ("petitioned" to "last effort at redress"). For the perceived failure of the Philadelphia convention, see John C. Calhoun to Francis W. Pickens, Mar. 2, 1832, *JCP*, XI:558–59.

100. "Rough Draft of . . . the South Carolina Exposition," [completed ca. Nov. 25, 1828], *JCP*, X:496 ("checks against the abuse" and "to make application").

101. "South Carolina Protest," Dec. 19, 1828, "Rough Draft of . . . the South Carolina Exposition," [completed ca. Nov. 25, 1828], *JCP*, X:535 ("protest"), 512 (asserting "the Constitutional right of the States to interpose in order to protect their powers"); John C. Calhoun to A. Griffin and Five Others, May 14, 1832, *JCP*, XI:585 ("reserved rights"); Daniel Webster, "The Constitution Not a Compact," Feb. 16, 1833, *Web (SFW)*, I:619 ("nullification"); Hartford Convention, *Report*, 376 ("measures" and "operation"). Unlike the proponents of the individual state veto in the 1830s, delegates to the Hartford Convention did not address the question of how their advocacy of resistance to a national law or policy would affect the operation of the Union.

102. On Calhoun, see Richard N. Current, *John C. Calhoun* (1963); John Niven, *John C. Calhoun and the Price of Union: A Biography* (1988); Charles M. Wiltse, *John C. Calhoun* (3 vols., 1944–1951). On the qualified nationalism in South Carolina in the aftermath of the War of 1812, see Freehling, *Prelude*, 89–133.

103. John C. Calhoun to Littleton Walter Tazewell, Aug. 25, 1827, Nov. 9, 1827, *JCP*, X:301 ("remedy" and "a negative"), 312 ("clearly"). See "Rough Draft of . . . the South Carolina Exposition," [completed ca. Nov. 25, 1828], *JCP*, X:444–534.

104. "Rough Draft of . . . the South Carolina Exposition," [completed ca. Nov. 25, 1828], *JCP*, X:446 ("one object" to "difficult to resist").

105. See "Rough Draft of . . . the South Carolina Exposition," [completed ca. Nov. 25, 1828], *JCP*, X:498, 522; John C. Calhoun to James Hamilton, Jr., Aug. 28, 1832, *JCP*, XI:634.

106. John C. Calhoun to William Campbell Preston, Nov. 6, 1828, *JCP*, X:431 ("the basis").

107. "Speech of Robert Y. Hayne," Jan. 25, 1830, Belz, *Webster-Hayne Debate*, 73 ("Republican doctrine" and "celebrated"), 74 ("last as long").

108. James Madison to Henry Clay, Oct. 9, 1830, James Madison to Edward Coles, Aug. 29, 1834, James Madison to Nicholas P. Trist, Jan. 18, 1833, James Madison to Joseph C. Cabell, Sept. 16, 1831, James Madison to Mathew Carey, July 27, 1831, James Madison to Nicholas P. Trist, May 1832, *ML*, IV:117 ("fatal tendency"), 357 ("powder" to "blow them up"), 268 ("twin" and "heresy"), 196 ("poisonous root"), 192 ("disastrous consequences"), 218 ("painful" and "broken up"). For Madison's illness and agonizing over nullification, see Brant, *Madison*, VI:489–90; McCoy, *Fathers*, 140, 151.

109. James Madison to Nicholas P. Trist, Feb. 15, 1830 ("the task of combating"); quoted in McCoy, *Fathers*, 154 ("enfeebled by age").
110. John C. Calhoun to James Hamilton, Jr., Aug. 28, 1832, *JCP*, XI:615 ("when formed").
111. John C. Calhoun to James Hamilton, Jr., Aug. 28, 1832, *JCP*, XI:616 ("ordained by the people" to "not of individuals").
112. "Second Reply to Hayne," Jan. 26–27, 1830, *Web(SFW)*, I:330 ("the people" to "people of the United States"); "Speech of Daniel Webster," Jan. 26–27, 1830 in Belz, *Webster-Hayne Debate*, 153 ("the aggregate").
113. "Second Reply to Hayne," Jan. 26–27, 1830, *Web(SFW)*, I:329 ("submission to the laws" to "constitutional resistance").
114. James Madison to Edward Everett, Aug. 1830, *ML*, IV:95 ("not uncommon" to "confederated Government").
115. James Madison to Edward Everett, Aug. 1830, *ML*, IV:95 ("by the governments" to "a mixture of both"); "Speech of Daniel Webster," Jan. 26–27, 1830, in Belz, *Webster-Hayne Debate*, 153 ("the aggregate"); James Madison to Daniel Webster, Mar. 15, 1833, *ML*, IV:293 ("the undisputed fact"). Like Webster, Calhoun characterized the dispute over the federal Constitution as a matter of "two opposite views," whether a "consolidated" as opposed to "federal" government was established. "Rough Draft of an Address to the People of South Carolina," [ca. Dec. 1, 1830], *JCP*, XI:266.
116. James Madison to Edward Everett, Aug. 1830, *ML*, IV:95 ("highest sovereign capacity").
    Scholars have cast the formation of the federal Constitution in binary terms of either a national people or the people of individual states. See, for example, Wood, *Creation*, 532–36 (describing the Federalists' identification of "the people" as the foundation of the federal Constitution, implicitly assuming such a reference meant a national people without considering an alternative basis for ratification other than individual states); Monaghan, "Original Understanding," 129 (asserting that the constitution as created rested on "'We the People' (nationally understood) *and* the several states (i.e., 'We the People' thereof) as independent political communities"). An example of this binary tendency among Supreme Court justices is *U.S. Term Limits v. Thornton*, 514 U.S. 779 at 846 (1995) ("The ultimate source of the Constitution's authority is the consent of the people of each individual State, not the consent of the undifferentiated people of the Nation as a whole") (Thomas, J., dissenting).
    For an appreciation of the existence of two competing views of "the people" as well as a states' rights view identifying individual states as the foundation of the federal Constitution among eighteenth- and nineteenth-century Americans, see Flaherty, "John Marshall."
117. See "Report of 1800," Jan. 7, 1800, *MP*, XVII:309 (explaining that "the people" who composed the political societies of their states acted "in their highest sovereign capacity" when they "ratified" the federal Constitution); James Madison to Edward Everett, Aug. 1830, "Of Nullification," 1835/1836, *ML*, IV:95 (describing the formation of the federal Constitution "by the States – that is, by the people in each of the States"), 409 (conceding that each state had a *natural* right to resist intolerable oppression" but that did not extend to "a *constitutional* right in a single State to nullify a law of the United States").
118. James Madison to C. E. Haynes, Aug. 27, 1832, [sketch enclosed in letter from] James Madison to W. C. Rives, Oct. 21, 1833, *ML*, IV:224 ("interpositions" and "within the provisions and forms"), 319 ("[t]he people as composing a State" and "as constituents").
119. James Madison to C. E. Haynes, Aug. 27, 1832, [sketch enclosed in letter from] James Madison to W. C. Rives, Oct. 21, 1833, *ML*, IV:224 ("not within the purview" and "nullifying process"), 319 ("as the creators").
120. James Madison to Daniel Webster, Mar. 15, 1833, *ML*, IV:293 ("in their highest"). Even very careful studies of Madison's thought have not appreciated the constitutional legitimacy Madison attributed to the exercise of interposition by the sovereign people in the last resort. See, for example, Brant, *Madison*, VI:477 (attributing a strict dichotomy of "two principles" governing Madison's thinking during the Nullification crisis: "the *natural* right of the people to throw off a tyrannical government, and their *constitutional* right to interpose through the collective

force of public opinion"); Ketcham, *Madison*, 397 (describing the Virginia Resolutions as "a moderate statement shunning the centrifugal tendencies of the more categorical resolves" of Jefferson); McCoy, *Fathers*, 136 (asserting that during the Nullification crisis Madison argued that the only remedy for the usurpation or abuse of power beyond the checks provided by the constitution "was extraconstitutional: a resort to the natural right of revolution"). The work that comes closest to appreciating Madison's endorsement of interposition is Lance Banning, *The Sacred Fire of Liberty: James Madison and the Founding of the Federal Republic* (1995), 386–91.

121. James Madison to C. E. Haynes, Aug. 27, 1832, James Madison to Edward Livingston, May 8, 1830, *ML*, IV:224 ("nullifying process"), 80 ("right of *the parties*" to "a *single* party"), 225 ("[T]he *plural* term" to "original rights"). For Madison's reminders of his plural use of "states," see James Madison to James Robertson, Mar. 27, 1831, James Madison to Nicholas P. Trist, Dec. 1831, Dec. 23, 1832, James Madison, "On Nullification," 1835/1836, *ML*, IV:166, 204, 228, 398.

122. "Report of 1800," Jan. 7, 1800, *MP*, XVII:309 ("the 'States'" and "the people . . . in their highest sovereign capacity"). After the *Exposition*, Madison reiterated that a determination of constitutionality beyond that of the U.S. Supreme Court would "necessarily derive its authority from the whole, not from the parts; from the States in some collective, not individual capacity." James Madison to Nicholas P. Trist, Feb. 15, 1830, *ML*, IV: 63.

123. "Rough Draft of . . . the South Carolina Exposition," [completed ca. Nov. 25, 1828], *JCP*, X:520 ("a sovereign State").

124. "Report of 1800," Jan. 7, 1800, *MP*, XVII:350 ("sound the alarm"); "Rough Draft of . . . the South Carolina Exposition," [completed ca. Nov. 25, 1828], *JCP*, X:502 ("the rights of the State").

125. "Rough Draft of . . . the South Carolina Exposition," [completed ca. Nov. 25, 1828], *JCP*, X:446 ("The Courts can not look" to "violate the Constitution").

126. [sketch enclosed in letter from] James Madison to W. C. Rives, Oct. 21, 1833, James Madison to Nicholas P. Trist, Dec. 1831, *ML*, IV:317 ("sufficiently clear"), 205 ("jurisdiction" and "between the several States"), 317–18 ("the *ultimate* decision" to "scope of the Government"); *Federalist No.* 39. p. 256 (Madison) ("essential"); James Madison to N. P. Trist, Dec. 1831, James Madison to Edward Everett, Aug. [28], 1830, *ML*, IV:211 ("vital principle"), 100 ("denied or doubted").

127. James Madison to Nicholas P. Trist, Dec. 1831, *ML*, IV:205 ("within" to "forms of the Constitution").

128. [sketch enclosed in letter from] James Madison to W. C. Rives, Oct. 21, 1833, "To 'A Friend of Union and State Rights,'" 1833, James Madison to Nicholas P. Trist, Dec. 1831, *ML*, IV:318 ("the parties" to "the Constitution itself"), 335 ("to interpose" to "branches of the Government"), 205 ("the last resort of all"); "Report of 1800," *MP*, XVII:310 ("tribunal above"), 309 ("parties to the constitutional compact"), 310 ("violated").

129. James Madison to Nicholas P. Trist, Dec. 1831, James Madison to unknown correspondent, 1834, *ML*, IV:205 ("the last resort").

130. James Madison to Nicholas P. Trist, Dec. 1831, James Madison to unknown correspondent, 1834, *ML*, IV:350 ("surest expositor"). In 1821 Madison endorsed the national judiciary as the appropriate interpreter of the federal Constitution, instead of "the States in their individual characters." James Madison to Spencer Roane, June 29, 1821, *ML*, III:223.

131. *Journal of the Convention of the People of South Carolina: Assembled at Columbia on the 19th November, 1832, and Again, on the 11th March, 1833* (Columbia, SC, 1833), 60 ("what are called" to "CONSTITUTIONAL right").

132. Andrew Jackson, [Nullification] *Proclamation*, Dec. 10, 1832, *MPP*, II:641 ("indefeasible right" to "execution"), 643 ("*incompatible*" to "*destructive*"), 648 ("compact"), 649 ("revolutionary act"). See also Ellis, *Union*, 48 (describing Jackson's view that secession was "a revolutionary right" that "could be suppressed" and his belief that "nullification and secession were virtually synonymous, for the one verged almost automatically into the other"). On equating nullification

to secession, see James Madison to Joseph C. Cabell, Sept. 16, 1831, James Madison to Edward Coles, Aug. 29, 1834, *ML*, IV:196 (rejecting the idea "that although a State could not nullify a law of the Union, it had a right to secede" and describing both doctrines as springing "from the same poisonous root").

133. John C. Calhoun to Maximilian LaBorde and others, Mar. 27, 1833, *JCP*, XII:150 ("success" to "triumph").

134. On Jackson, see Ellis, *Union*, 15–19; Remini, *Jackson*, xvii (asserting that "more than anything else" Jackson "believed in a virtuous people and was supremely optimistic about their capacity for self-government").

135. The quintessential expression of the perpetual nature of the Union was the Supreme Court's assertion that the United States was "an indestructible Union, composed of indestructible States." *Texas v. White*, 74 U.S. 700 at 725 (1868). On the idea of perpetual union, see Paul C. Nagel, *One Nation Indivisible: The Union in American Thought, 1776–1861* (1964, repr. 1980), 235–80.

PART THREE. THE STRUGGLE OVER A CONSTITUTIONAL MIDDLE GROUND

1. See Chapter 2. On debates in ten constitutional conventions before the Civil War over the role, especially the electoral role, of the people, see Scalia, *Jeffersonian Experiment*, 30 (identifying a division among delegates between those inclining "toward or away from a more democratic understanding" of the people's sovereignty).

2. *Kamper v. Hawkins*, 1793 WL 248 (Va. Gen. Ct.) 1 at 6 (Spencer Roane) ("the people" to "that proposition").

3. Lincoln, *Constitutional History*, I:623 ("double check"). See also Galie, *Ordered Liberty*, 66 (noting that in 1801 "[n]o attempt was made to present the question of whether or not to hold the convention; rather, the act called for the selection of delegates to such a convention").

4. Quoted in Lincoln, *Constitutional History*, I:624 ("no doubt"); *McCulloch v. Maryland*, 17 U.S. 316 at 404 (1819) ("settled").
   Kent thought it "may well be doubted" if the legislature could authorize a wholesale revision of the constitution without "a legitimate and full expression of the will of the people that such changes should be made." Quoted in Lincoln, *Constitutional History*, I:625. On Kent's opinion and the response of the legislature, see Galie, *Ordered Liberty*, 72–74. See also Erdman, *New Jersey*, 134–35 (identifying the early nineteenth-century "theory that only a convention elected by the people could presume to alter fundamental law").
   Eventually, the bill calling for a convention that produced New York's 1821 constitution included both of Clinton's checks. Clinton later described the people as "the source of all legitimate government" who acted in their "sovereign character" in approving the new constitution. Quoted in Lincoln, *Constitutional History*, I:753.

5. *Proceedings and Debates of the Virginia State Convention, of 1829–1830* (Richmond, 1830), 56 ("*practical*" and "*distinctive*"). See also *Debate on the Convention Question, in the House of Commons of the Legislature of North Carolina; December 18 and 19, 1821* (Raleigh, 1822), 56 (J. S. Smith insisting that the people's right "to alter their constitution at pleasure" must be accompanied with a "remedy" to "act upon it"); *Proceedings and Debates of the Convention of the Commonwealth of Pennsylvania, to Propose Amendments to the Constitution, Commenced and Held at Harrisburg, on the Second Day of May, 1837* (14 vols., Harrisburg, 1837–1839), I:117 (Earle asserting that "more order" and "stability of laws" existed under state constitutions in which "the people enjoyed practical sovereignty"), XII:92 (Brown taking it "for granted" that "any rules" the convention thought "proper to lay down in reference to future changes in the fundamental law, will be disregarded by the people . . . at any time when a change shall appear to them to be desirable").

6. Virginia, *Debates* (1829–1830), 429 (Monroe) ("Ours is a Government"); Pennsylvania, *Debates* (1837–1838), IV:328 (Woodward) ("a living"), I:343 (Woodward) ("have never parted"), VII:169 (Biddle) ("to join" to "can emanate").

7. Pennsylvania, *Debates* (1837–1838), XII:230 (Earle) ("right to alter" to "particular mode"), 231 (Earle) ("peace, order" to "at all times"), 232 (Porter) ("averse"). The vote was 78 against and 35 in favor. See also Scalia, *Jeffersonian Experiment*, 6 (identifying the "meaning of America's commitment" to the people's sovereignty as "frequently the primary" agenda issue of constitutional conventions meeting before the Civil War).

8. Quoted in Fletcher M. Green, *Constitutional Development in the South Atlantic States, 1776–1860* (1930), 207 ("should assemble" to "legal act").

9. *Journal of Debates and Proceedings in the Convention of Delegates, Chosen to Revise the Constitution of Massachusetts, Begun and Holden at Boston, November 15, 1820, and Continued by Adjournment to January 9, 1821* (Boston, 1821), 184 (Webster) ("knew no principle"); Virginia, *Debates* (1829–1830), 887 (Thompson) ("strictly speaking" to "stickle about forms"). Madison argued that "in all great changes of established governments, forms ought to give way to substance." *Federalist No. 40*, p. 265 (Madison).

10. Tucker, *Blackstone's Commentaries*, I:Appendix, Note B, 21("a fundamental principle"), 20 ("the right of resuming"), 18 ("may indeed" to "sovereignty"; Rawle, *View*, 12 ("at any time" to "binding").

11. Nathaniel Chipman, *Principles of Government; A Treatise on Free Institutions including the Constitution of the United States* (Burlington, VT, 1833), 285 ("the people"); Story, *Commentaries*, I:305 ("general, if not universal" to "by the majority"), 198 ("an act of original"); William Sullivan, *The Political Class Book; Intended to Instruct the Higher Classes in Schools in the Origin, Nature, and Use of Political Power* (Boston, 1836), 71 ("the people are the sovereign"), iii ("resided" to "any other").

12. *Debates of the Delaware Convention, for Revising the Constitution of the State, or Adopting New One; Held at Dover, November, 1831* (Wilmington, 1831), 228 (Hall) ("directly"); Pennsylvania, *Debates* (1837–1838), XII:69 (Brown) ("a part of"). See also XIV:95 (McDowell asserting that Pennsylvania's constitution "in the hands of the people, is as clay in the hands of the potter" and considering "the idea that they must not interfere with the fundamental law of the land" as a tyrannical constitutional notion).

13. Pennsylvania, *Debates* (1837–1838), II:189 (Agnew) ("the people had"); Virginia, *Debates* (1829–1830), 143 (Gordon) ("the old world").

14. Pennsylvania, *Debates* (1837–1838), XII:88 (Dickey) ("The majority"), 92–93 (Brown) ("any rules" to "own government"). The legitimacy of the majority of the "the people" to overcome constitutional provisions even surfaced on the Overland Trail. See Reid, "Governance," 437.

15. Quoted in Robert Paul Sutton, "The Virginia Constitutional Convention of 1829–30: A Profile Analysis of Late-Jeffersonian Virginia" (Ph.D. diss., Univ. of Virginia, 1967), 64 ("conventionizing" to "disunion").

16. See, for example, Green, *Constitutional Development*, 207 (describing such conventions as "Extra-legal or even illegal"); A. E. Dick Howard, "'For the Common Benefit,': Constitutional History in Virginia as a Casebook for the Modern Constitution-Maker," 54 *Va. L. Rev.* (1968), 846 (defeat of convention bills in the legislature led to "threats of resort to extra-legal remedies"); William M. Wiecek, "Popular Sovereignty in the Dorr War – Conservative Counterblast," 32 *Rhode Island History* (1973), 35 (describing the "extra-legal People's Convention" in Rhode Island); James A. Henretta, "The Rise and Decline of 'Democratic-Republicanism': Political Rights in New York and the Several States, 1800–1915," in Finkelman and Gottlieb, *Toward*, 62 (describing Thomas Dorr as leading "the most famous extralegal movement for a more equitable constitutional system").

Bypassing procedures with the concurrence of the existing government, however, escapes such a pejorative characterization. See James Willard Hurst, *The Growth of American Law: The Law Makers*, (1950), 207 (acknowledging that conventions in Pennsylvania in 1789, Delaware in 1792, and Maryland in 1850 were "called in disregard of unduly rigid procedures" of existing constitutions, but if an "irregularly initiated" procedure, "at least it was brought about through the legislature").

17. See, for example, Elisha P. Douglass, *Rebels and Democrats: The Struggle for Equal Political Rights and Majority Rule During the American Revolution* (1955), 69 (describing bills of rights

as setting "a standard of political liberty"); Parkinson, "Circumvention," 39 (recounting how opponents of circumvention conventions rejected the alter or abolish provisions as "theoretical fluff"), 42 (describing circumvention conventions as carrying "the sanctions of revolutionary tradition"); McInnis, "Natural Law," 367 (seeing in the bills of rights provisions "a belief in the natural right to alter or abolish the government"); Suber, *Paradox*, 230 (asserting that the alter or abolish provisions were intended as "an appeal to higher law").

18. Legislatures in the nineteenth century justified the circumvention of revision provisions by invoking the inherent sovereignty of the people. See, for example, *Journal of a General Convention of the State of Georgia, to Reduce the Members of the General Assembly* (Milledgeville, GA, 1833) (delegates disputing whether the legislature could "instruct or control the action of the people, through their delegates when in convention" since "the sovereign people" through their election of delegates had given the convention sanction to operate), 43 (Branham) ("instruct"), 8 (Crawford) ("the sovereign").

19. Parkinson, "Circumvention," 37 (describing the Staunton Convention); *Salisbury Western Carolinian*, Jan. 6, 1824 ("majority"); Robert D. Powell to Waller Halladay, Dec. 23, 1828 ("an indubitable" to "they please" and Powell noting that Virginia legislators also adopted "other expressions of the right of the majority to alter or abolish their form of government"), Halladay Family Papers, VHS; quoted in Fletcher M. Green, "Cycles of American Democracy," 48 *Mississippi Valley Historical Review* (1961), 11, citing *Milledgeville Southern Recorder*, May 31, 1832 ("the people have"); *Hazard's Register of Pennsylvania*, XII (Sept. 14, 1833), 169 ("rise in the majesty" to "public opinion"). After explicitly alluding to Justice William Patterson's definition of a constitution in *Vanhorne's Lessee v. Dorrance*, 28 F. Cas. 1012 at 1014 (C.C. Pa. 1795) as a product "delineated by the mighty hand of the people," the Harrisburg convention concluded that "the same hand that first delineated its features, may change them as the occasion of society require"). *Hazard's Register*, XII:168 ("the same hand"). See also *Hazard's Register of Pennsylvania*, XIII (Jan. 25, 1834), 56 (for the reconvened convention).

20. Quoted in Green, *Constitutional Development*, 241 ("at any time" and "in any manner"); Maryland 1776 Constitution, Bill of Rights, Art. IV, *TC*, III:1687 ("perverted"); quoted in Parkinson, "Circumvention," 111–12 ("extraordinary position"); "'Reform or Revolution' in Maryland," *Niles' Weekly Register*, Oct. 8, 1836, p. 95 ("The power" to "annul or abolish"). On Maryland's convention movement, see A. Clarke Hagensick, "Revolution or Reform in 1836: Maryland's Preface to the Dorr Rebellion," 57 *Maryland Historical Magazine* (1962), 346–66.

21. "Constitution of Maryland," *Niles' Weekly Register*, Apr. 1, 1837, p. 73–74 ("a high crime" to "constitutional mode").

22. "Proceedings of the Convention," Aug. 1–3, 1842, *Journal of the House of Delegates of Virginia, 1842–1843*, Doc. No. 29 (Richmond, 1842), 2 ("appointed by" and "suitable subjects"), 4 ("under the forms" to "the public weal"); *Journal of the Senate of the Commonwealth of Virginia*, Feb. 13, 1844 (Richmond, 1844), 136 ("it will then").

23. See, for example, Lincoln, *Constitutional History*, I:615 (convention in Canandaigua on March 1811 urging legislature to call a convention to amend property qualifications for suffrage under New York's 1777 constitution); Howard, "'For the Common Benefit,'" 846 (noting a resolution passed in Frederick County, Virginia, in 1827 demanding "the assembling of a full and free convention of the good people of this commonwealth" and a meeting in Hardy County warning the Virginia legislature of "the determination of the people of this county upon ulterior methods, should this, their last appeal, be disregarded").

24. Many new states drafting constitutions before 1820 omitted amendment provisions. See, for example, Ohio 1802 Constitution, Louisiana 1812 Constitution, Indiana 1816 Constitution, Illinois 1818 Constitution, *TC*, V:2901–13, III:1380–92, II:1057–73, II:972–1012. For the shared commitment to the people's sovereignty that produced different visions of the political role for "the people," see Scalia, *Jeffersonian Experiment*.

25. New York 1821 Constitution, Massachusetts 1821 Articles of Amendment, North Carolina 1835 Amendments, Pennsylvania 1838 Constitution, Rhode Island 1842 Constitution. See *TC*, V:2650, III:1913, V:2798, 3115, VI:3234.

26. Missouri 1820 Constitution, Mississippi 1832 Constitution, Tennessee 1834 Constitution, Michigan 1835 Constitution, Texas 1836 Constitution, Arkansas 1836 Constitution, Florida 1838 Constitution. See *TC*, IV:2162, 2062–63, VI:3439, IV:1940–41, VI:3541, I:277, II:679.

27. *Reports of the Proceedings and Debates of the Convention of 1821, Assembled for the Purpose of Amending the Constitution of the State of New York: Containing all the Official Documents, Relating to the Subject, and Other Valuable Matter* (Albany, 1821), 656 (Bacon) ("without resorting"); Massachusetts, *Debates* (1820–1821), 95 (Webster) ("the permanency" to "and useful"), 183 (Webster) ("sufficient security" and "temporary excitement").

28. Virginia, *Debates* (1829–1830), 773 (Brodnax) ("mania" to "latest fashion"), 789 (Randolph) ("introducing"), 790 (Randolph) ("to be dissatisfied" to "doing as they please"). The vote was 68 to 25.

29. Quoted in Parkinson, "Circumvention," 107 ("this heresy"); Massachusetts, *Debates* (1820–1821), 184 (Webster) ("a real evil"); *Proceedings and Debates of the Convention of North Carolina* (Raleigh, 1836), 349 (Gaston) ("never be altered" and "absolutely necessary"), 370 (Gaston) ("the emergency"); Virginia, *Debates* (1829–1830), 313 (Randolph) ("the grievance").

30. North Carolina, *Debates* (1835), 346 (Gaston) ("That the deliberate"). See Massachusetts, *Debates* (1820–1821), 184 (Webster asserting that he knew of "no principle that could prevent a majority, even a bare majority of the people, from altering the constitution").

31. Michigan 1835 Constitution, Art. I, Sec. 1 and 2, *TC*, IV:1930 ("inherent" to "requires it"). See also Harold M. Dorr, ed., "Introduction," in *The Michigan Constitutional Conventions of 1835–36: Debates and Proceedings* (1940), 3–52.

32. *Congressional Globe*, Senate, 24th Cong., 2d. Sess., "Appendix," p. 148 (Jan. 5, 1837) (Buchanan) ("to persuade" to "form of government"), 147 ("rebellion"); William Peckham to Thomas W. Dorr, Feb. 3, 1837 ("[e]manate from"), Dorr Correspondence, Rider Collection, Box 2, BU.

33. [John L. O'Sullivan], "Mr. Brownson's Recent Articles in the Democratic Review," 13 *The United States Magazine and Democratic Review* (Dec. 1843), 654 ("practical application").

CHAPTER 8. THE COLLECTIVE SOVEREIGN PERSISTS

1. The account of Dorr's inauguration procession and the state's two rival governments draws on *Providence New Age and Constitutional Advocate*, May 3 and 7, 1842; *Providence Daily Express*, May 2, 5, and 6, 1842; *Providence Daily Journal*, May 5, 6, and 7, 1842; *Providence Daily Evening Chronicle*, May 5, 1842; John Pitman to Joseph Story, May 4, 1842 (an observer hostile to Dorr estimating the procession at between 1,600 and 1,700 persons), Pitman-Story Correspondence, UM; *Compendium of the Enumeration of the Inhabitants and Statistics of the United States ... Sixth Census* [1840] (Washington, 1841); Arthur May Mowry, *The Dorr War: The Constitutional Struggle in Rhode Island* (1901, repr. 1970); Marvin E. Gettleman, *The Dorr Rebellion, A Study in American Radicalism: 1833–1849* (1973); George M. Dennison, *The Dorr War: Republicanism on Trial, 1831–1861* (1976); Conley, *Democracy*.

2. Francis Bowen, "The Recent Contest in Rhode Island," 58 *The North American Review* (Apr. 1844), 373 ("arrayed indifferently"). For the Rhode Island controversy's place in national politics, see Conley, *Democracy*, 357–60; Gettleman, *Rebellion*, 165–73; William Tyack to James K. Polk, Sept. 7, 1844, John O. Bradford to James K. Polk, Oct. 5, 1844, Samuel H. Laughlin to James K. Polk, Oct. 28, 1844, Herbert Weaver, ed., *Correspondence of James K. Polk* (10 vols., 1969–2004), VIII: 28 (reporting from New York that the Democrats were "all alive to Mass Meetings" and predicting that "Do[r]r will yet be the Govr. of Rhode Island"), 153–55, 237–40; Henry Clay, Speech in Lexington, June 9, 1842, Robert Seager, ed., *Papers of Henry Clay* (9 vols., and supp., 1959–1992), IX:708–16; Dexter Randall, *Democracy Vindicated and Dorrism Unveiled* (Providence, 1846).

On Calhoun's reaction, see John C. Calhoun to William Smith, July 3, 1843, *JCP*, XVII:284 (asserting "it would be the death-blow of constitutional democracy, to admit the right of the numerical majority, to alter or abolish constitutions at pleasure, regardless of the consent of the Government, or the forms prescribed for their amendment"). See also Thomas Wilson Dorr to Walter S. Burges, May 12, 1842 (observing that while some southern members of Congress were "with the People of *Rhode Island*" they were "not with *all* People in asserting a principle, which might be construed to take in the Southern blacks and to aid the abolitionists"), Dorr Correspondence, Rider Collection, Box 4, BU.

3. Bowen, "Contest," 373 ("little" and "the present strife"); William G. Goddard, *An Address to The People of Rhode-Island, Delivered in Newport, on Wednesday, May 3, 1843, in Presence of the General Assembly, on the Occasion of the Change in the Civil Government of Rhode-Island, by the Adoption of the Constitution, Which Superseded the Charter of 1663* (Providence, 1843), 39 ("a controversy" to "real merits"); John Pitman to Joseph Story, Jan. 26, 1842 ("great question"), Pitman-Story Correspondence, UM; Goddard, *Address*, 49 ("the grossest misconceptions"); [Orestes A. Brownson], "Democracy and Liberty," 12 *The United States Magazine and Democratic Review* (Apr. 1843), 385 ("in sober earnest"), 386 ("quite too much"); [John Pitman], *A Reply to the Letter of the Hon. Marcus Morton, Late Governor of Massachusetts, on the Rhode-Island Question. By One of the Rhode-Island People* (Providence, 1842), 3 ("educated"); Goddard, *Address*, 41–42 ("practical application" to "true"). See also John Pitman to Joseph Story, Apr. 7, 1842 (suggesting that perhaps it was just as well that the "disorganizing principles" had broken out first in Rhode Island, as opposed to larger states "where they might do more mischief"), Pitman-Story Correspondence, UM. On the support of women for the Suffrage movement, see Ronald P. Formisano, "The Role of Women in the Dorr Rebellion," 51 *Rhode Island History* (1993), 89–104, and for the denunciation of the historian George Bancroft for his support of Dorr, see [George Ticknor Curtis], *The Merits of T. W. Dorr and George Bancroft, As they are Politically Connected* (Boston, 1844).

   On Morton, see "Governor Marcus Morton: An Address Delivered January 13, 1905, by Hon. Nathan Whitman Littlefield," 7 *Collections of the Old Colony Historical Society* (1909), 75–92.

4. [John L. O'Sullivan], "The Rhode Island Affair," 10 *The United States Magazine and Democratic Review* (June 1842), 602 ("fundamental principles"); Henry Williams, *In Vindication of the right of the People of Rhode Island to amend their form of Government* [Providence, 1845], 14 ("not one"); *Letters of the Hon. C. F. Cleveland, and Hon. Henry Hubbard, Governors of Connecticut and New Hampshire, To Samuel Ward King, The Charter Governor of Rhode Island . . . Also, the Letters of the Hon. Marcus Morton . . .* (Fall River, MA, 1842), 2 ("resides in"); Benjamin F. Hallett, *The Right of the People to Establish Forms of Government. Mr. Hallett's Argument in the Rhode Island Causes, Before the Supreme Court of the United States, January, 1848* (Boston, 1848), 7 ("living principle" and "a theory"). See also [Orestes A. Brownson], "Origin and Ground of Government," 13 *The United States Magazine and Democratic Review* (Sept. 1843) (2nd article), 246 (considering the issue raised by the Rhode Island controversy "vital" and "fundamental" with the two sides "separated by an impassable gulf").

5. *The Rhode-Island Question. Arguments of Messrs. Whipple and Webster, in the Case of Martin Luther, Plaintiff in Error, versus Luther M. Borden and Others, in the Supreme Court of the United States, January Term, 1848* (Providence, 1848), 36 ("the true principles"), 55 ("purify" to "delusions"); *Hallett's Argument*, 62 ("in mere form" to "and actively").

6. Under the charter, each town received a fixed number of seats in the legislature. Newport sent six representatives; Providence, Warwick, and Portsmouth sent four. New towns were entitled to two representatives. See Rhode Island Charter, repr. in Mowry, *Dorr War*, 311; Chilton Williamson, *American Suffrage from Property to Democracy, 1760–1860* (1960), 25–26, 243; Lovejoy, *Rhode Island*, 16–17 (estimating that over 75 percent of Rhode Island's white adult males before the Revolution were eligible to vote).

   For the shift in demographics and its impact on voting and representation, see Gettleman, *Rebellion*, 6–7; Peter J. Coleman, *The Transformation of Rhode Island, 1790–1860* (1963, repr. 1985), 255–59; Williamson, *Suffrage*, passim, 242–45; Scalia, *Jeffersonian Experiment*, 6–8. For convention debates over the role of property in the exercise of the vote, see Scalia, *Jeffersonian Experiment*, 76–95.

7. "Report of Benjamin Hazard on the extension of suffrage, in 1829," in [Edmund Burke, comp.], *Interference of the Executive in the Affairs of Rhode Island* (June 7, 1844, *Congressional Globe*, House of Reps., 28th Congress, 1st Sess., Rep. No. 546), 379 ("infected" to "the revolution"),

384 ("the whole science"), 386 ("the common mass"), 385 ("reduced themselves" to "rights of others"). For the resistance to reapportionment, see Conley, *Democracy*, 184–213.

8. See Seth Luther, *An Address on the Right of Free Suffrage . . .* (Providence, 1833), 13 ("gained by the revolution"). For an account of the 1834 convention, see Conley, *Democracy*, 236–68.

9. [Thomas W. Dorr], *An Address to the People of Rhode-Island, From the Convention Assembled at Providence, on the 22d day of February, and Again on the 12th day of March, 1834, to Promote the Establishment of a State Constitution* (Providence, 1834), 11 ("directly from"), 12 ("inherent" to "capacity").

10. [Autobiographical Sketch] [Thomas W. Dorr], Aug. 1, 1845, Dorr Papers, BU. For details of Dorr's life and family, see Conley, *Democracy*, 249–50; Gettleman, *Rebellion*, 12–18; Dennison, *Dorr*, 14–24; Coleman, *Transformation*, 197–98.

On assessments of Dorr, see [Orestes A. Brownson], "Review of *Might and Right*," 1 *Brownson's Quarterly Review* (Oct. 1844), 532 (considering Dorr "a man of no mean intellectual ability, of firm principles, of ardent devotion to popular rights, a true-hearted patriot, and an honest man"); Jacob Frieze, *A Concise History of the Efforts to Obtain an Extension of Suffrage in Rhode Island; From the Year 1811 to 1842* (Providence, 1842; 3rd ed., 1912), 63 (describing Dorr's "good talents and acquirements").

11. Thomas W. Dorr to William B. Adams, May 30, 1831 ("Mankind") and Nov. 7, 1831 ("the actual"), Dorr Correspondence, Rider Collection, Box 1, BU.

12. "Extracts from the oration of George R. Burrill, delivered in Providence in 1797, in favor of a republican constitution," in *Burke's Report*, 273 ("the constitution paramount" to "free government"). On Burrill, see Conley, *Democracy*, 168–69.

13. Quoted in Conley, *Democracy*, 186 ("sovereign"); "Extracts from the *Manufacturers' and Freemen's Journal*, under dates of Nov. 27, Dec. 11 and 18, 1820, and Jan. 11, 1821," quoted in *Burke's Report*, 276 ("the people are"); Luther, *Address*, 24 ("the whole people" and "primary meetings").

14. *Preamble and Constitution of the Rhode-Island Suffrage Association, Adopted Friday Evening, March 27, 1840* (Providence, 1840), 9 ("WE KNOW"). On the 1840 presidential election, see Michael F. Holt, *The Rise and Fall of the American Whig Party: Jacksonian Politics and the Onset of the Civil War* (1999), 75. On Dorr's involvement with the People's Convention, see Conley, *Democracy*, 298–305; Joyce M. Botelho, *Right and Might: The Dorr Rebellion and the Struggle for Equal Rights* (1992), 29 (noting that Suffrage reformers referred to the 1824 and 1834 efforts as "do-nothing" conventions); Coleman, *Transformation*, 274; "A call to the people of Rhode Island to assemble in convention," in *Burke's Report*, 410–12; Mowry, *Dorr War*, 94–95.

The Suffrage Party advertised the impending elections through broadsides and hand-bills, and appointed their own town clerks and election officials to tabulate the results of the voting for delegates to the People's Convention, a process they repeated for the subsequent ratification of the People's Constitution.

15. "A declaration of principles of the Rhode Island Suffrage Association," in *Burke's Report*, 403 ("from time to time" to "anti-republican"); "A call to the people of Rhode Island to assemble in convention," in *Burke's Report*, 411 ("in their original"); "Resolutions adopted at a mass meeting of the friends of suffrage held at Providence, R.I., July 5, 1841," in *Burke's Report*, 408 ("the basis"); *Providence New Age Daily*, July 7, 1841, quoting from a resolution adopted by the Suffrage Association's convention of July 5, 1841) ("will be promptly"); [John A. Bolles], *"The Affairs of Rhode Island," Being A Review of President Wayland's "Discourse;" A Vindication of the Sovereignty of the People, and a Refutation of the Doctrines and Doctors of Despotism. By a Member of the Boston Bar* (Boston, 1842), 3–4 ("in their sovereign" to "universally respected").

16. Conley, *Democracy*, 309 ("respectable" and "prominent"). See also Richard M. Bayles, ed., *History of Providence County, Rhode Island* (2 vols., New York, 1891), I:83, 40, 57 (for Ariel Ballou, a prominent doctor and delegate from Cumberland who chaired the Bill of Rights Committee in the People's Convention and who served in the Rhode Island legislature for most of the decade after the controversy, for David Daniels, a lawyer and delegate from Smithfield who was later nominated for the position of attorney general under the People's Constitution, and for Aaron White, Jr., a prominent lawyer and delegate from Woonsocket); Abraham Payne,

Reminiscences of the Rhode Island Bar (Providence, 1885), 28 (for Walter S. Burges, a lawyer and delegate representing Little Compton, and Perez Simmons, a lawyer, delegate from Providence and future judge); *The Biographical Cyclopedia of Representative Men of Rhode Island* (Providence, 1881), 215–16 (for John R. Waterman, a long-time member of the legislature and delegate from Warwick).

17. [Curtis], *Merits*, 21 ("were undoubtedly").

18. For Atwell and Pearce, see *Biographical Cyclopedia*, 235, 258; Payne, *Reminiscences*, 97–102; Thomas Durfee, *Gleanings from the Judicial History of Rhode Island* (Providence, 1883), 115.

19. See *Providence New Age and Constitutional Advocate*, Oct. 8, 15, and 22, 1841, Nov. 19, 1841; *Providence Daily Journal*, Oct. 8, 11, 1841.

20. Alexander Everett Hill to editor of the *Providence New Age and Constitutional Advocate*, Nov. 8, 1841 ("very judiciously" to "material error"), Dorr Correspondence, Rider Collection, Box 3, BU.

21. "Speech of Thomas W. Dorr, on the right of the people of Rhode Island to form a constitution: delivered in the people's convention on the 18th day of November, 1841," in *Burke's Report*, 852 ("Who are"). On disagreements over extending the franchise, see Dennison, *Dorr*, 43–44; Petition to People's Convention, repr. in Botelho, *Right and Might*, 32 (seeking removal of the "white" qualification from the franchise); Paul M. Thompson, "Is There Anything 'Legal' About Extralegal Action? The Debate over Dorr's Rebellion," 36 *New Eng. L. Rev.* (2002), 401n97 (observing that while "all reformers agreed that the people were sovereign, and that a majority of the people could abolish their existing government and frame a new one at any time, and in any way, they were deeply divided over one significant issue: who were the people?").

22. "Speech of Thomas W. Dorr, on the right of the people of Rhode Island to form a constitution: delivered in the people's convention on the 18th day of November, 1841," in *Burke's Report*, 852 ("a right to do?"); People's Constitution, 1842, Article I of the Declaration of Principles, Rights and Duties, Sec. 3, repr. in Mowry, *Dorr War*, 323 ("All political power"). For an analysis of the People's Constitution, see Conley, *Democracy*, 309–14. The constitution is reprinted in Mowry, *Dorr War*, 322–46. See also Scalia, *Jeffersonian Experiment*, 25 (noting that by 1850, 80 percent of American constitutions included a statement of the people's sovereignty and over half of them contained an alter or abolish provision).

23. "Speech of Thomas W. Dorr, on the right of the people of Rhode Island to form a constitution: delivered in the people's convention on the 18th day of November, 1841," in *Burke's Report*, 860 ("inconsistent"), 860–61 ("transition"), 853 ("not to the cartridge-box"). The People's Constitution invested charter government officials with powers until the first Tuesday of May 1842, when their successors under the People's Constitution would be elected.

24. Thomas W. Dorr to Dutee J. Pearce, Dec. 13, 1841 ("we ought to have"), Dorr Correspondence, Rider Collection, Box 3, BU.

    For the election results, see Conley, *Democracy*, 315; Dennison, *Dorr*, 53; Gettleman, *Rebellion*, 54; *Providence New Age and Constitutional Advocate*, Jan. 7, 1842. The Suffrage Party calculated that 4,960 out of a total of 9,590 freemen voted for the People's Constitution, a calculation made possible because the ballots used asked voters to indicate if they were eligible under the existing laws of the state. See *Burke's Report*, 121, 204–205; copy of the ballots for the People's Constitution, repr. in Botelho, *Right and Might*, 4. Even Francis Wayland, the president of Brown University and strong critic of the People's Constitution, conceded that "a large portion of our citizens voted" for that constitution. Francis Wayland, *The Affairs of Rhode-Island. A Discourse Delivered in the Meeting-House of the First Baptist Church, Providence, May 22, 1842* (Providence, 1842), 15. As a supporter of the People's Constitution put it, that constitution had been "Framed by the People" and "adopted By the People." Silas R. Kenyon to Thomas Wilson Dorr, Mar. 1, 1842, Dorr Correspondence, Rider Collection, Box 4, BU.

25. Elisha R. Potter, Jr., to Dutee J. Pearce (copy), Dec. 20, 1841 ("illegal & revolutionary" and "pretence"), Potter Collection, RIHS; "Resolutions of the General Assembly relating to the people's constitution," in *Burke's Report*, 647 ("in violation"); *Providence New Age and Constitutional Advocate*, Jan. 28, 1842 (reporting on debates in the charter legislature) ("There is no"). Law and Order advocates took the position that the legislature could not examine votes in favor of the

People's Constitution "without yielding the question of right." Elisha R. Potter, *Considerations on the Questions of the Adoption of a Constitution, and Extension of Suffrage in Rhode Island* (Boston, 1842), 35 ("without yielding").

26. The People's Convention reconvened in Providence on Nov. 16, 1842, and for two days the proposed constitution was "carefully and deliberately read" with alterations suggested by delegates and "a number of improvements" made on the draft. See *Providence New Age and Constitutional Advocate*, Nov. 19, 1841.

27. *Providence New Age and Constitutional Advocate*, Nov. 12, 1841 (reporting on debates in the Landholders' Convention) ("abstractions" to "general principles"); *A Journal of the Proceedings of the Convention Called to Form a Constitution, for the State of Rhode Island. Providence, November, 1, 1841* (RSUS, Rhode Island, Reel 1, Unit 3) (Nov. 11, 1841), 28 (Dorr's amendments to the Landholder's bill of rights that were rejected), (Feb. 14, 1842), 40 ("by the people" to "the paramount law").

28. For the text of the Landholders' Constitution, see Mowry, *Dorr War*, 347–66. See also Conley, *Democracy*, 320–21; Mowry, *Dorr War*, 119–27.

29. *Providence Journal*, Mar. 7, 1842, quoted in Conley, *Democracy*, 321 ("extends suffrage" to "effectiveness"); editorial and broadside repr. in Botelho, *Right and Might*, 34 ("to choose" to "priests"), 35 ("Friends of the Charter" to "old Government"). See also Conley, *Democracy*, 323 (reporting Landholders' Constitution defeated by a vote of 8,689 to 8,013).

30. Frieze, *History*, 70 ("only question" to "paramount law"). The vote rejecting Atwell's motion was 59 to 3. Elections under the People's Constitution were scheduled for April 18, 1842, with charter government elections taking place two days later. See Conley, *Democracy*, 324–27.

31. Thomas W. Dorr to Aaron White, Apr. 4, 1842 ("a paper-war"), Dorr Correspondence, Rider Collection, Box 4, BU.

32. Thomas W. Dorr to Bradford Allen, May 1842 ("Let our men"), Dorr Papers, BU.
    On the activity of the charter government, see Conley, *Democracy*, 324; Gettleman, *Rebellion*, 90–92; Dennison, *Dorr*, 69–71. For the text of the statute, see *Burke's Report*, 133–35. Even Law and Order advocates thought the Algerine Law represented "fairly questionable" policy. Frieze, *History*, 56.
    For Dorr's waning support before the April elections, see Conley, *Democracy*, 337; Dennison, *Dorr*, 69–71.

33. "Two letters of Governor King to the President," in *Burke's Report*, 657 ("precautionary"); "Letter from the President, in reply to the foregoing letters of Gov. King," in *Burke's Report*, 659 ("insurrectionary" and "actual").

34. William Allen to Thomas Dorr, Apr. 15, 1842 ("the majority"), Thomas Hart Benton to Thomas W. Dorr, Apr. 16, 1842 ("fully" and "the validity"), Levi Woodbury to Thomas W. Dorr, Apr. 15, 1842 ("the whole fabric" to "how they please"), Dorr Correspondence, Rider Collection, Box 4, BU.
    The majority of a five-person committee chaired by Democrat Edmund Burke of New Hampshire produced *Burke's Report*, running nearly 1,000 pages in length. A minority report from the committee, the so-called Causin's Report, took the side of Whig President John Tyler and the Law and Order forces. According to the minority report, the people possessed no inherent rights to revise their constitutions "unsanctioned by law or the assent of the authorities of government." "Rhode Island Memorial," June 17, 1844, *Congressional Globe*, House of Reps., 28th Congress, 1st Sess., Rep. No. 581, p. 37.

35. Thomas W. Dorr to Levi Woodbury, Apr. 11, 1842 ("very generally" to "null and void"), Woodbury Papers, LC; Thomas W. Dorr to Aaron White, Apr. 4, 1842 (*"to frighten"*), William S. Burges to Thomas W. Dorr, May 9, 1842 ("notice that" and "The screws"), David Parmenter to Thomas W. Dorr, May 30, 1842 ("to induce landlords" to "employment"), Dorr Correspondence, Rider Collection, Box 4, BU.
    Even with a heavy rainstorm on the day of the election, Dorr received 6,359 votes for governor. See Conley, *Democracy*, 326–27. Dorr's slate consisted of several other lawyers, including William H. Smith for secretary of state, Joseph Joslin for state treasurer, and Jonah Titus for attorney general. See Gettleman, *Rebellion*, 84–85.

36. "An act to authorize the establishment of volunteer police companies in the city of Providence," repr. in *Burke's Report*, 819 ("volunteer police"); John Pitman to Joseph Story, May 4, 1842 ("unfinished"), Pitman-Story Correspondence, UM; *Burke's Report*, 469 ("formed" and "peaceably"). For the proceedings of the Foundry Legislature, see *Burke's Report*, 447–69; *Providence Daily Evening Chronicle*, May 5, 1842. For the mobilization of the charter government and utilization of the Algerine Law, see Conley, *Democracy*, 327–28, 334–37; *Providence New Age Weekly*, May 14, 1842 (reporting the arrests of Dorr supporters).

37. "Confidential letter of the President to Governor King," May 9, 1842, in *Burke's Report*, 676 ("somewhat liberal" to "shedding of blood"). See Conley, *Democracy*, 336–37 (arguing that "Dorr spoke of military action mainly in defensive terms," sought "outside aid only in response to outside intervention by federal troops," and used local militia sympathetic to his cause "primarily to protect himself and his associates from what he regarded as the unauthorized and invalid aggression of the defunct charter government operating under the Algerine Law that had been repealed by the Foundry Legislature").

38. See *Providence Daily Express*, May 17, 1842 (crowd estimate); Conley, *Democracy*, 335–37; Mowry, *Dorr War*, 166–74, 193–94; Gettleman, *Rebellion*, 113–15.

39. See Conley, *Democracy*, 340.

40. Frieze, *History*, 77 ("his entire" to "twenty minutes"); Dennison, *Dorr*, 86 ("forewarned"). The arsenal incident bore similarities to the court closings during the Massachusetts Regulation and the symbolic march through Pittsburgh by whiskey excise tax protesters. Apart from the use of the worthless, antique cannon, Dorr launched a flare to initiate the early morning march to the arsenal (which also alerted its defenders that he was on his way). In Jacob Frieze's pro–Law and Order version of the Rhode Island controversy published in 1842, he cited the use of the signal flare as evidence of Dorr's "utter ignorance of military affairs," but it was also consistent with the staged quality of the confrontation. Frieze, *History*, 79.

   One historian of the Rhode Island controversy concluded that Dorr "harbored a naive expectation that the armory's defenders" (who included his father, a younger brother, and two uncles) "would surrender without a fight," while another thought he "systematically" underestimated his opponents. Conley, *Democracy*, 339 ("harbored"); Gettleman, *Rebellion*, 120 ("systematically"). Other historians have also focused on the inept attempt on the arsenal. See, for example, C. Peter Magrath, "Optimistic Democrat: Thomas W. Dorr and the Case of Luther vs. Borden," 29 *Rhode Island History* (1970), 96 ("a comedy of errors,"); David Grimsted, *American Mobbing, 1828–1861: Toward Civil War* (1998), 216 (a "farce, which seemed more a test of will and public sentiment than a resort to force"); William M. Wiecek, "'A Peculiar Conservatism' and the Dorr Rebellion: Constitutional Clash in Jacksonian America," 22 *AJLH* (1978), 243 ("*opera bouffe* efforts").

41. *Providence New Age and Constitutional Advocate*, Apr. 2, 1842 ("all such means" as part of a resolution offered by Dorr at "one of the largest and most enthusiastic" meetings of supporters of the People's Constitution); Samuel Wales, Eli Brown, William Coleman, F. L. Beckford, John A. Howland to Thomas W. Dorr, May 18, 1842 ("Our men"), Dorr Correspondence, Rider Collection, Box 4, BU; Resignation Handbill, repr. in Botelho, *Right and Might*, 47 ("surrender" and "the right of the people"); *Providence New Age and Constitutional Advocate*, Apr. 30, 1842 ("at the foundation" and "sacrifice the peace").

42. Aaron White to Thomas W. Dorr, May 25, 1842 ("completely" and "Your idea"), Dorr Correspondence, Rider Collection, Box 4, BU; Andrew Jackson to Francis P. Blair, May 23, 1842, John Spencer Bassett, ed., *Correspondence of Andrew Jackson* (7 vols., 1926–35), VI:153 ("The people are"). Jackson also predicted that if President Tyler did send federal troops to Rhode Island "a hundred thousand of the sovereign people would fly to the rescue to sustain the peoples constitution." For the perception of the charter government's ascendancy, see Dennison, *Dorr*, 81–82; Conley, *Democracy*, 339; Gettleman, *Rebellion*, 125.

43. *Boston Daily Advertiser and Patriot*, May 31, 1842 (repr. Dorr's *Address* of May 21, 1842) ("recent events" and "by a *failure*"); June 25, 1842, "General Orders," repr. in [Francis Harriet McDougall], *Might and Right; By a Rhode Islander* (Providence, 1844), 265 ("by all necessary"

to "their rights"); dispersal order from Thomas W. Dorr, June 27, 1842, repr. in Frieze, *History*, 103 ("opposed").

The search of one home during that period of martial law precipitated the court case eventually heard by the U.S. Supreme Court as *Luther v. Borden* 48 U.S. (7 How.) 1 (1849). See Mahlon H. Hellerich, "The Luther Cases in the Lower Courts," 11 *Rhode Island History* (1952), 33–45. Anticipating numerous prosecutions for "insurrection and rebellion" the Rhode Island Supreme Court printed grand jury forms (prior to 1842 clerks wrote such indictments out by hand). See Grand Jury Indictment of Seth Luther, repr. in Botelho, *Right and Might*, 52.

44. See "Governor Dorr's address to the people of Rhode Island, August 10, 1843," in *Burke's Report*, 762–63. The Algerine Constitution extended the vote to most adult males (including blacks – a reward for their support of Law and Order forces), while retaining a real property requirement for naturalized citizens and in order to vote on matters of taxation or spending. See Mowry, *Dorr War*, 370–73; Conley, *Democracy*, 344–45, 351; Coleman, *Transformation*, 284–86. The vote for the Algerine Constitution was 7,024 to 51. See Conley, *Democracy*, 351.

45. See, for example, [John O'Sullivan], "The Rhode Island Question," 11 *The United States Magazine and Democratic Review* (July 1842), 70–83; [Pitman], *Reply to Morton*; Goddard, *Address*, 45; Potter, *Considerations*, 22 (stating the issue as "whether a majority of the whole people, without reference to any existing laws regulating the right of voting, have a right to change the government at any time and in any manner they choose").

46. Instead of an alter or abolish provision, Art. 1, Sec. 1 of the Algerine Constitution invoked Washington's *Farewell Address* in asserting "the right of the people to make and alter their constitutions of government; but that the constitution which at any time exists, till changed by an explicit and authentic act of the whole people, is sacredly obligatory upon all." Art. 13 of the Algerine Constitution provided for amendments only after two successive legislatures voted for changes, followed by popular ratification. See Mowry, *Dorr War*, 367–68, 384.

47. See "Governor Dorr's address to the people of Rhode Island, August 10, 1843," in *Burke's Report*, 762–63; Conley, *Democracy*, 351. Although arrested in Providence, Dorr was tried in Newport in late April 1844. See "Report of the Trial of Thomas W. Dorr," in *Burke's Report*, 865–1048.

After 1844, many Democrats throughout the country called for Dorr's release from prison and in 1845 Charles Jackson was elected governor of Rhode Island on a "Liberation" ticket, after which Dorr was released. See Conley, *Democracy*, 366–71. The Houghton Library, HU, holds a copy of "Dorr Liberation Stock" that was given to the library on April 4, 1845, by Judge Joseph Story.

48. John O. Bradford to James K. Polk, Oct. 5, 1844, Polk, *Correspondence*, VIII:154 ("most exciting"); [O'Sullivan], "Rhode Island Affair," 602 ("interesting"). See also Anonymous, *Facts Involved in the Rhode Island Controversy With Some Views Upon the Rights of Both Parties* (Boston, 1842), 3 (noting that the Rhode Island controversy "has drawn the attention and excited the interest of the great body of the American people").

49. "Speech of Thomas W. Dorr, on the right of the people of Rhode Island to form a constitution: delivered in the people's convention on the 18th day of November, 1841," in *Burke's Report*, 856 ("momentous event" to "a voice"); *Chisholm v. Georgia*, 2 Dall (2 U.S.) 419 at 471–72 (1793) ("devolved" to "fellow citizens"); Benjamin Cowell, *A Letter to the Hon. Samuel W. King, Late Governor of the State of Rhode-Island* (Providence, 1842), 5 ("great pity" to "a great principle"). See also Sidney S. Rider, ed., *The Right of the People of Rhode Island to Form a Constitution. The Nine Lawyers' Opinion* (Providence, Mar. 14, 1842), repr. in *Rhode Island Historical Tracts*, no. 11 (Providence, 1880), 69 (the Revolution passed "the sovereign power" from "the king and Parliament of England to the People of the State"); Williams, *Vindication*, 6 (asserting that with the Revolution "the right of governing passed to the people of Rhode Island in common with those of the rest of the country"); Mercy Otis Warren, *History of the Rise, Progress, and Termination of the American Revolution* (3 vols., Boston, 1805, repr. in 2 vols., 1988), II:629 (considering the Revolution to rest on "that sovereignty which cannot be ceded either to representatives or to kings").

50. *Debates and Proceedings in the State Convention Held at Newport, September 12, 1842, For the Adoption of a Constitution of the State of Rhode Island* (Providence, 1859) (*RSUS*, Rhode Island, Reel 1, Unit 4), 29 (Ennis) ("the nature"); Williams, *Vindication*, 7 ("not the doctrine" to "solid foundation"), 8 ("the people are" to "servants of the people"). The constitutional significance of the American Revolution formed a recurring theme in the three-day oral argument for the Suffrage position in the *Luther v. Borden* case. See *Hallett's Argument*.

51. "Speech of Thomas W. Dorr, on the right of the people of Rhode Island to form a constitution: delivered in the people's convention on the 18th day of November, 1841," in *Burke's Report*, 859 ("rhetorical" to "their happiness"). See also William Goodell, *The Rights and The Wrongs of Rhode Island: Comprising Views of Liberty and Law, Of Religion and Rights, As Exhibited in the Recent and Existing Difficulties in that State* (Whitesboro, NY, 1842), 7 (Dorr's position had "the sanction of American Constitutional law").

52. Anonymous, *Facts*, 34 ("the full right"); Goodell, *Views*, 39 ("the fundamental principles"). The right of revolution also had a basis in English constitutional theory of the eighteenth century. See Chapter 2.

53. [O'Sullivan], "Rhode Island Question," 77 ("evidence"). See also Williams, *Vindication*, 4 (noting that the alter or abolish "principle has been incorporated into the constitutions of most of the States"); *Hallett's Argument*, 37 (noting "the solemn incorporation of this fundamental principle in nearly every State constitution"); [Bolles], *Affairs*, 7 (concluding that existing state constitutions reveal the "doctrine" of the alter or abolish principle to be "universally adopted and promulgated"); Goodell, *Views*, 27 (considering the many alter or abolish provisions "not merely as expressions of correct principles, but as authentic quotations of CONSTITUTIONAL 'LAW AND ORDER' in America"); [McDougall], *Might*, 125 (describing the federal constitutional convention as "the first quiet, bloodless revolution" that "practically reaffirmed the truth, that 'it is the right of the people to alter, or abolish,' their constitutions of government").

54. Rhode Island, *Debates* (1842), 29 (Ennis) ("new or singular" and "recent troubles" to "these doctrines"); *Hallett's Argument*, 19 ("sound doctrine").

55. *Hallett's Argument*, 52 ("between a mere"); Williams, *Vindication*, 9 ("not bound" to "perfect").

56. *Nine Lawyers' Opinion*, 76 ("an English doctrine"). Besides Dorr, Knowles, Carpenter, and Angell, the other five lawyers who signed the *Opinion* were Samuel Y. Atwell, David Daniels, Levi C. Eaton, Dutee J. Pearce, and Aaron White, Jr. See *Biographical Cyclopedia*, 351, 265, 251–53, 235 (for Knowles, Carpenter, Angell, and Pearce); Payne, *Reminiscences*, 3–5, (for Carpenter); Bayles, *Providence County*, I:40, 57 (for Daniels and White); William Richard Cutter, ed., *New England Families: Genealogical and Memorial* (4 vols., 1915), IV:2096 (for Eaton).

    Walter S. Burges, who became the U.S. attorney for Rhode Island under the Polk administration (1845–49) and Rhode Island's attorney general (1851–54, 1860–63), was one of Dorr's lawyers at his treason trial and was entrusted with Dorr's private papers before he died. On Burges, see John H. Stiness, *Memorial Address: Walter Snow Burges* (Providence, 1892).

57. *Nine Lawyers' Opinion*, 73 ("the judges" to "*mode* of proceeding"), 76 ("rightful"). Law and Order supporters consistently charged the People's Convention and Constitution as being "without law." In rebutting that charge by the Rhode Island Supreme Court, one Dorr supporter asserted that the "main point" was whether the people had "done anything *against* law." "No one pretends that the People's Convention assembled by a law of the [legislature]. That body could pass no law *directing* the People, freeholders or non-freeholders, to make a Constitution. They could only *request* them to do so. What the Judges mean therefore is a repetition of the well known fact, that the People framed and adopted a Constitution, without any *request*, or, if it be preferred, without law." *Providence New Age and Constitutional Advocate*, Mar. 4, 1842.

58. *Letters of the Hon. Marcus Morton, and others . . .*, 14 ("friends" to "their rulers"); *Hallett's Argument*, 28 ("anti-American"), 51 ("convenient" and "desirable"); Cowell, *Letter*, 24 ("the most able" to "they please"). See also "Democratic State Convention, Dec. 20, 1842," in *Burke's Report*, 241–42 (resolving that "the original right of the people to make or alter their fundamental law at any time, without authority or a request of the existing government is an *American right*"); Anonymous, *Facts*, 33 (finding it "absurd" to argue "that no convention of the people can be valid, unless called by the existing authorities").

59. *Nine Lawyers' Opinion*, 72 ("the *source*"), 74 ("The greater power").
60. Thomas W. Dorr to Nathan Clifford, Jan. 24, 1848 ("absolute sovereignty" to "expedient"), Dorr Correspondence, Rider Collection, Box 12, BU; *Nine Lawyers' Opinion*, 78 ("are *not* bound" to "most proper"); Williams, *Vindication*, 8 ("do not confer" to "prior right"), 12 ("validity" to "the people"); *Hallett's Argument*, 51 ("The form prescribed").
61. Rhode Island, *Debates* (1842), 33 (Simmons) ("a string"); Goddard, *Address*, 49 ("visionary theories"); Elisha R. Potter, *Speech of Mr. Potter, of Rhode Island, on the Memorial of the Democratic Members of the Legislature of Rhode Island. Delivered in the House of Representatives, March 7, 9, and 12, 1844* (Washington, DC, 1844), 9 ("misnomer"); Potter, *Considerations*, 48–49 ("sovereignty resides" to "all the State constitutions"); Potter, *Speech*, 8 ("declarations" to "in a constitution"); Rhode Island, *Debates* (1842), 29 (Simmons) ("magazine" to "the existing government").
62. *Hallett's Argument*, 30 ("acquired no rights"); [John Pitman], *To the Members of the General Assembly of Rhode-Island* (Providence, 1842), 9 ("the citizen owes"), 14 ("at liberty" to "right of revolution").
63. "Charge of Chief Judge Durfee to the grand jury, at the March term of the supreme judicial court at Bristol, Rhode Island, 1842," in *Burke's Report*, 716 ("a conflict"), 709 ("corporate people" to "could act"); [Orestes Brownson], "Origin and Ground of Government," 13 *The United States Magazine and Democratic Review* (Aug. 1843) (1st article), 139 ("in fact was"), 138 ("[h]istorically"); Bowen, "Contest," 428 ("directed entirely"); *Arguments of Whipple and Webster*, 37 ("a peculiar conservatism"). Initially, Brownson regarded Dorr on "the *right side*" of the "great principle" involved in the controversy. Orestes A. Brownson to Thomas W. Dorr, May 14, 1842, Dorr Correspondence, Rider Collection, Box 4, BU.
64. *Nine Lawyers' Opinion*, 76 ("English"); "Governor Dorr's address to the people of Rhode Island, August, 1843," in *Burke's Report*, 743 ("old world"); Thomas W. Dorr to Dutee J. Pearce, Mar. 18, 1842 ("ultra-slavish"), Pearce Papers, NHS; Williams, *Vindication*, 5 ("not the American"); "Speech of Thomas W. Dorr, on the right of the people of Rhode Island to form a constitution: delivered in the people's convention on the 18th day of November, 1841," in *Burke's Report*, 861–62 ("strange"); David Dudley Field to Thomas W. Dorr, Mar. 16, 1844 ("the principles"), Dorr Correspondence, Rider Collection, Box 8, BU; Williams, *Vindication*, 12 ("denial" to "better now"); [Bolles], *Affairs*, 28 ("adopting the *parlor*").

    On efforts to "de-revolutionize" the Revolution, see David D. Van Tassel, *Recording America's Past: An Interpretation of the Development of Historical Studies in America, 1607–1884* (1960); Arthur H. Shaffer, *The Politics of History: Writing the History of the American Revolution, 1783–1815* (1975); Lester H. Cohen, *The Revolutionary Histories: Contemporary Narratives of the American Revolution* (1980); Len Travers, *Celebrating the Fourth: Independence Day and the Rites of Nationalism in the Early Republic* (1997).
65. *Arguments of Whipple and Webster*, 22 ("under the American"); [Pitman], *Reply to Morton*, 21 ("the rights"). See also Frieze, *History*, 9 (conceding "the republican maxim, that all the rightful powers of government are derived from the people"); [Pitman], *General Assembly*, 18 (asserting that the "great object of a written Constitution" was "to check the legislative power, and to give greater permanency to the fundamental law").
66. Francis Wayland, *A Discourse Delivered in the First Baptist Church, Providence, R.I., On the Day of Public Thanksgiving, July 21, 1842* (Providence, 1842), 15 ("oppression"); [Pitman], *General Assembly*, 9 ("the first duty" to "destruction"), 15 ("the great purposes"); [Brownson], "Origin and Ground, (1st article)," 135 ("Government is"); John Quincy Adams, *The Social Compact, Exemplified in the Constitution of the Commonwealth of Massachusetts* (Providence, 1842), 13–14 ("the action"). Brownson's lack of faith in the "virtue and intelligence of the people" proved to him that "they are *not* competent to govern themselves." [Brownson], "Democracy," 382.
67. *Arguments of Whipple and Webster*, 22 ("all power"); *Hallett's Argument*, 32 ("limitations" to "creation"); Williams, *Vindication*, 1 ("To whom").

    Dorr called Webster a Tory of "the rankest sort" for asserting that "the People of this country can make no changes of the government without the forms prescribed in the Constitution; and, where there is no written Constitution, without the permission of the Legislature!" Thomas W. Dorr to Aaron White, Jr., May 12, 1842, Dorr Correspondence, Rider Collection, Box 4, BU.

68. [Brownson], "Democracy," 382 ("are sovereign" to "shall be exercised"); [Orestes A. Brownson], "Popular Government," 12 *The United States Magazine and Democratic Review* (May 1843), 534 ("the *Constitution*" to "the sovereign"); [Brownson], "Origin and Ground, (1st article)," 133 ("force"). See also Potter, *Speech,* 11 (arguing that if "a bare majority have a right to alter the government in any manner they please . . . then, for the same reason, one generation could never bind another in any respect").

69. "Governor Dorr's Address to the People of Rhode Island, August, 1843," in *Burke's Report,* 741 ("in the organization"); [John L. O'Sullivan], "Note," 12 *The United States Magazine and Democratic Review* (May 1843), 540 ("the actual"); Williams, *Vindication,* 5 ("Europe" to "governing class"); [John L. O'Sullivan], "Political Portrait of Thomas W. Dorr," 11 *The United States Magazine and Democratic Review* (Aug. 1842), 203 ("re-written" to "rolled back"). See also Thomas W. Dorr to Benjamin Hallett and George Turner, Feb. 2, 1847 (asserting that the Law and Order cause rested "mainly on the principle, that in this country the sovereignty is vested in the government and not in the people"), Dorr Correspondence, Rider Collection, Box 11, BU; Cowell, *Letter,* 5 (accusing opponents of the People's Constitution of believing that sovereignty "rests in the Government of the State" and that "the Government is the *master* and not the *servant* of the People"). On O'Sullivan, see Edward L. Widmer, *Young America: The Flowering of Democracy in New York City* (1999).

70. See, for example, [Pitman], *General Assembly,* 4 (describing "the foundations of society" being uprooted); "Charge of Chief Judge Durfee to the grand jury, at the March term of the supreme judicial court at Bristol, Rhode Island, 1842," in *Burke's Report,* 716 ("anarchy"); *Arguments of Whipple and Webster,* 4 ("without law and against law"), 8 (claiming the "Dorr revolution established a new standard of rebellion"), 29 (describing Dorr and his supporters as "visionary and political fanatics"); Wayland, *Affairs,* 6 ("anarchy"), 7 ("utterly subversive"); Joseph Story to Daniel Webster, Apr. 26, 1842, *WebP(C),* V:202 ("against law"); Anonymous, *How the PEOPLE'S Constitution was made for Rhode-Island, without the aid of the Law or of the Legislature* (n.p., 1841) (describing the People's Constitution as a "gross attempt at revolution, and usurpation, conceived in folly, carried on by the alternate use of force, and fraud").

71. Goddard, *Address,* 41 ("fatal" to "constitutional reform"); *New York Tribune,* May 24, 1842, quoted in Dennison, *Dorr,* 115 ("all Courts"); Wayland, *Affairs,* 7 ("worth the parchment"); John Whipple, *Address of John Whipple, To the People of Rhode-Island, on the Approaching Election* (Providence, 1843), 4 ("necessarily").

72. *Arguments of Whipple and Webster,* 4 ("the slightest countenance"), 42 ("tumultuary"). See also Wayland, *Affairs,* 8 (worrying that "the flame which was almost kindled here, might have spread over all New-England"); Potter, *Speech,* 11 (conceding Dorr's position meant nothing could stop a majority of the American people from "making us one consolidated nation").

73. For the questionable behavior, see Hellerich, "Luther Cases," 42 (concluding that neither Story nor Pitman "heard the Luther Cases with open and unprejudiced minds"); John S. Schuchman, "The Political Background of the Political-Question Doctrine: The Judges and the Dorr War," 16 *AJLH* (1972), 125 (seeing "the collective activities of the local and federal bench" in Rhode Island "as a prime example of judicial interference in the politics of the people"); Wiecek, "Conservatism," 244 (asserting the judges "denounced the suffragist cause from their benches"); R. Kent Newmyer, *Supreme Court Justice Joseph Story: Statesman of the Old Republic* (1985), 365 (noting Story's determination to "defeat radical social change" and "strike a blow for social order, one that called into action all aspects of his authority as a circuit justice, political and educational as well as legal").

   For contemporary complaints of the Law and Order bias of the courts, see Anonymous, *Facts* (1842), 28 (describing Chief Justice Durfee's grand jury charge as "committing himself fully to the Charter party, although those arrested under that charge would be tried, and the constitutional question raised before him"); [McDougall], *Might,* 191 (asserting that "the direct and inevitable tendency" of the "course" of the Rhode Island judges was "to produce a pre-judgment against the people, and to obstruct fair trials, and unbiased verdicts, in cases likely to arise out of the contest").

74. [Pitman], *General Assembly*, 14 ("revolutionary movement"); [Pitman], *Reply to Morton*, 30–31 ("dangerous principles" and "the fruitful"); "Justice," *Providence New Age and Constitutional Advocate*, Feb. 11, 1842 ("declarations" to "judicial inquiry"). Although published anonymously, Pitman's authorship of the pamphlet quickly became known. See John Pitman to Joseph Story, Jan. 26, 1842, Pitman- Story Correspondence, UM.

75. John Pitman to Joseph Story, Jan. 26, 1842 ("of having become"), Pitman- Story Correspondence, UM; Joseph Story to John Pitman, Feb. 10, 1842, William W. Story, ed., *Life and Letters of Joseph Story* (2 vols., Boston, 1851), II:416 ("perfectly sound" to "will and pleasure"); *Charge of Mr. Justice Joseph Story, On the Law of Treason, Delivered to the Grand Jury of the Circuit Court of the United States, Holden at Newport, For the Rhode-Island District, June 15, 1842* (Providence, 1842), 5 ("some preliminary"), 3 ("wholly extemporaneous"). Story defined treason as including resistance to "the exercise of any legitimate authority of the Government in its sovereign capacity." *Charge*, 7.

76. John Pitman to Joseph Story, Mar. 30, 1842 ("precautionary" to "among us"), Pitman-Story Correspondence, UM; Joseph Story to John Pitman, Apr. 1, 1842, Story, *Letters*, II:418 ("any self-created"), 419 ("I could say"); Joseph Story to Daniel Webster, Apr. 26, 1842, *WebP(C)*, V:202 ("doubt" to "against law"), 203 ("Of course").

77. Job Durfee, Levi Haile, and William R. Staples, Mar. 2, 1842, "Opinion of the Judges of the Supreme Judicial Court, Upon the Legality of the so called 'People's Constitution'" in *Citizens of Rhode Island! Read! Mark! Learn!* (n.p. [Mar, 1842]) ("not to intermeddle" to "against the United States"), Broadside Collection, BU; "Charge of Chief Judge Durfee to the grand jury, at the March term of the supreme judicial court at Bristol, Rhode Island, 1842," in *Burke's Report*, 716 ("indulging"). See also Joshua B. Rathbun to Thomas W. Dorr, Mar. 4, 1842 (reporting on "a floundering speech from Judge Durfee at the Town House in this town against the people's Constitution"), Dorr Correspondence, Rider Collection, Box 4, BU.

78. Job Durfee to Elisha R. Potter, Jr., Mar. 14, 1842 (noting his determination that "the 'people's constitution' must go down" and to give the grand jury "our views of the illegality of the 'people's constitution'"), Potter Collection, RIHS. Durfee's son suggested that his father took the stand he did because the "friends of 'Law and Order' stood doubtful of the issue – wavering – anxiously asking the course to be pursued." Thomas Durfee, ed., *The Complete Works of the Hon. Job Durfee, LL. D., Late Chief Justice of Rhode-Island; With a Memoir of the Author* (Providence, 1849), xviii.

79. [Pitman], *Reply to Morton*, 19 ("an end to"); [Pitman], *General Assembly*, 4 ("our daily food"); Joseph Story to John Pitman, Jan. 14, 1845, Story, *Letters*, II:516 ("a civil war"); "Charge of Chief Judge Durfee to the grand jury, at the March term of the supreme judicial court at Bristol, Rhode Island, 1842," in *Burke's Report*, 715 ("the brink" and "final plunge"), 716 ("anarchy").

80. See, for example, *Arguments of Whipple and Webster*, 10 (describing Dorr's "new doctrine, emanating from a very novel source"), 14 (Dorr's arguments the product of "visionary theorists"); Potter, *Speech*, 9 ("new doctrine"), 13 ("radical opinions"); [Brownson], "Democracy," 386 (describing Dorr's views as "loose radicalism with regard to popular sovereignty"); John Pitman to Joseph Story, Jan. 26, 1842 (alluding to the "new views of the right of the people to make alterations in the fundamental law themselves"), Pitman-Story Correspondence, UM.

81. Rhode Island, *Debates* (1842), 29 (Simmons) ("unheard of doctrine").

82. For examples of the scholarly acceptance of the Law and Order perspective, see Mowry, *Dorr War*, 298 (considering Dorr's position "manifestly unjustifiable"); Robert L. Ciaburri, "The Dorr Rebellion in Rhode Island: The Moderate Phase," 26 *Rhode Island History* (1967), 87 (describing Dorr's means of revision "illegal and unconstitutional"); Wiecek, *Guarantee Clause*, 116 (describing Dorr's argument as "political theory"); Gettleman, *Rebellion*, 131 (claiming Dorr's views "had a large component of fantasy"); Dennison, *Dorr*, 139 (asserting that Dorr's views were an anachronistic attempt to recreate "the natural order"); Conley, *Democracy*, 317 (describing Dorr's position as a "radical doctrine of popular constituent sovereignty"), 375 (asserting Dorr's

view by 1842 was "an archaic and potentially dangerous relic" of the revolutionary era); Newmyer, *Story*, 359 (describing Dorr's position as a belief "that the American Revolution established a tradition of revolution"); Russell J. DeSimone and Daniel C. Schofield, comp., *The Broadsides of the Dorr Rebellion* (1992), 12 (asserting Dorr's position constituted "revolutionary doctrine" that was "a minority position held only by extreme democrats of the Revolutionary generation"); Kevin D. Leitao, "Rhode Island's Forgotten Bill of Rights," 1 *Roger Williams U. L .Rev.* (1996), 57n66 (asserting that Dorr "believed in an extreme version of popular sovereignty"); Grimsted, *Mobbing*, 209 (describing Dorr's ideas as "democratic rhetoric"), 217 (an example of "extraconstitutionalism"); Thompson, "Dorr's Rebellion," 413 (asserting that Dorr's supporters "updated and altered the eighteenth-century rights of resistance and revolution").

83. *Arguments of Whipple and Webster*, 30–31 ("old right of revolution" to "justify revolution"); *Congressional Globe*, House of Reps., 28th Cong., 2d Sess., p. 82 (Jan. 2, 1845) ("surrendered" to "right of revolution") (Elmer); [Orestes A. Brownson], "Origin and Ground (3rd article)," 13 *The United States Magazine and Democratic Review* (Oct. 1843), 374 ("to resist" to "expedient").

84. *Congressional Globe*, House of Reps., 28th Cong., 2d Sess., pp. 81–82 (Jan. 2, 1845) ("new constitutions" to "constitutional right") (Elmer). See also Frieze, *History*, 11 (conceding that the right of revolution was "theoretically recognized" in the federal Constitution, based on natural law, and available only as a matter of "absolute necessity"); Rhode Island, *Debates* (1842), 30–31 (Jackson) ("The right of revolution is a theoretical right, and one which the people will make practical whenever their grievances are sufficient").

85. "Charge of Chief Judge Durfee to the grand jury, at the March term of the supreme judicial court at Bristol, Rhode Island, 1842," in *Burke's Report*, 712 ("natural right" to "half not").

86. See, for example, Potter, *Speech*, 8, 11; Wayland, *Affairs*, 28; Pitman, *Reply to Morton*, 20–21; Potter, *Considerations*, 22–24.

87. *Congressional Globe*, Senate, 24th Cong., 2d Sess., "Appendix," p. 147 (Jan. 5, 1837) ("must first give" to "middle course") (Buchanan).

88. *Congressional Globe*, Senate, 24th Cong., 2d Sess., "Appendix," p. 147 (Jan. 5, 1837) ("the whole history" to "agency whatever") (Buchanan). See also Dorr, "Introduction," *Michigan Constitutional Conventions*, 48n1 (quoting Michigan's territorial governor, Stevens T. Mason, justifying the constitutional convention that acted without prior legislative authorization by noting it "emanated with and from the exclusive source of all political power; it had its origin in that declaration of your constitution which asserts, that government is instituted for the benefit, protection and security of the governed; its authority is the deliberate will of the people").

89. See, for example, Goddard, *Address*, 41 (asserting that where revision provisions exist changes must occur "according to the mode established" and where none exist revision could only occur "through the agency of the Legislature"); [Brownson], "Democracy," 383 ("The *people* in a legal or political sense . . . have no existence, no entity, therefore no rights, no sovereignty, save when organized into the body politic; and then their action is legitimate only when done through the forms which the body itself has prescribed"); Potter, *Considerations*, 34 (asserting that because Rhode Island's charter lacked a revision provision, legislative consent was necessary as "the only practicable way" to gain the consent of "the whole people").

90. *Arguments of Whipple and Webster*, 45 ("no new form"), 46 ("whole system"), 22 ("make and unmake" to "governments of law"). See also [Curtis], *Merits*, 10 (asserting that it was "absolutely indispensable that the existing government should superintend every amendment of the fundamental law"); Wayland, *Discourse*, 11 (insisting the people's sovereignty could only be expressed "according to the forms prescribed by the constitution").

91. Potter, *Speech*, 8 ("erroneous notions" to "justify a revolution"); [Brownson], "Origin and Ground, (1st article)," 134 ("take words"); [Brownson], "Review," 544 ("so erroneous" to "respect for authority"); [Curtis], *Merits*, 3 ("incalculable" to "constitutional liberty"), 36 (accusing the historian George Bancroft, by supporting Dorr, of deliberately using "the power of deception" on "the unreflecting").

92. Goddard, *Address*, 41 ("explicit and authentic"); Potter, *Speech*, 9 ("a cardinal principle"); Algerine Constitution, Art. I, Sec. 1, repr. in Mowry, *Dorr War*, 367–68 ("the constitution which"). See also [Pitman], *General Assembly*, 3 (invoking Washington's sentiments about constitutional change as America's "pure fountain of political wisdom and patriotism").

93. "Governor Dorr's Address to the People of Rhode Island, August, 1843," in *Burke's Report*, 743 ("effectively nullified"), 766 ("fundamental principles" to "constitutional law"), 743 ("to the forms" to "creatures of the State"); Aaron White, Jr., to Thomas W. Dorr, Sept. 1, 1842 ("the Rhode Island *Precedent*" to "sovereignty of the People"), Dorr Correspondence, Rider Collection, Box 5, BU.

94. "Report of the trial of Thomas W. Dorr," in *Burke's Report*, 999 ("*immediately*" to "*plain for us*"); "Dorr's Reply to the Court," in *Burke's Report*, 1044 ("the forms of law" to "conviction"), 1045 ("the doctrines" and "the great principles"), 1046 ("decide between us"). See also "Charge of Chief Justice Durfee," *Burke's Report*, 993 (declaring that the people of the United States were "sovereign only to the extent, and in the qualified sense" that the federal Constitution "expressly grants and defines"). On the trial and the hostility of the jury pool, see Dennison, *Dorr*, 104–107; *Burke's Report*, 865–1048; Conley, *Democracy*, 355; Gettleman, *Rebellion*, 161–62.

95. For the Luther litigation in the circuit court, see Hellerich, "Luther Cases;" "Bill of Exceptions," in *Burke's Report*, 357–76; Dennison, *Dorr*, 146–54.

96. Thomas W. Dorr to Nathan Clifford, Jan. 24, 1848 ("the high ground" and "minor point"), Dorr Correspondence, Rider Collection, Box 12, BU; Silas Wright, Jr., to Edmund Burke, Aug. 8, 1844 ("the Rhode Island" to "our institutions"), Manuscript Division, LC; Aaron White, Jr., to Thomas W. Dorr, Apr. 30, 1843 ("Judges always stick"), Dorr Correspondence, Rider Collection, Box 7, BU.

For Dorr's legal management, see George M. Dennison, "Thomas Wilson Dorr: Counsel of Record in Luther v. Borden," 15 *St. Louis U. L. J.* (1971), 398–428.

97. See Conley, *Democracy*, 366–68; Gettleman, *Rebellion*, 169–73. For the delays in hearing the case, see Dennison, "Counsel," 417–22. Whipple actively opposed the "liberation" ticket and any pardon for Dorr and his supporters. See Broadside, "Letter from Hon. Lemuel H. Arnold, in reply to the Letter of John Whipple, Esq." (May 1, 1845), HU.

98. *Arguments of Whipple and Webster*, 6 ("insane"), 14 ("office-hunters" to "visionary theorists" and "cowardly"), 29 ("fanciful" and "political fanatics"), 34 ("wild" and "revolutionary").

99. Potter, *Considerations*, 36 ("legal and peaceable" to "good cause").

100. Williams, *Vindication*, 13 ("the history" to "so patiently"); Cowell, *Letter*, 20–21 ("overthrow" to "whole people").

101. Thomas W. Dorr to Nathan Clifford, Jan. 24, 1848 ("surprised" to "for granted"), Dorr Correspondence, Rider Collection, Box 12, BU.

102. Massachusetts, *Debates* (1820–1821), 184 (Webster) ("no principle"). For the contrast in citations in the briefs, compare *Hallett's Argument*, 32–40, with *Arguments of Whipple and Webster*, 29.

The New York advisory opinion, which Hallett did cite, emphasized that the legislature was "not supreme," but "only one of the instruments of that absolute sovereignty which resides in the whole body of the people." "Report of the Justices of the Supreme Court, In answer to a resolution of the Assembly," *Documents of the Assembly of the State of New-York, Sixty-Ninth Session*, Vol. IV, No. 181 (Albany, 1846), 5; *Hallett's Argument*, 60–61. The opinion was reprinted in John Alexander Jameson, *A Treatise on Constitutional Conventions; Their History, Powers and Modes of Proceeding* (4th ed., Chicago, 1887), 663–66. Technically, the opinion took the form of a "communication" from the court to the legislature, which asked for an opinion even though New York's constitution did not provide for advisory judicial opinions.

103. Thomas W. Dorr to Nathan Clifford, Jan. 24, 1848 ("do not claim" to "the People's Constitution"), Dorr Correspondence, Rider Collection, Box 12, BU; *Luther* opinion, 46 ("political rights").

104. *Luther* opinion, 53 ("subordinate questions"), 54 ("a shade less" and "still political"), 52 ("disputed points to "political tribunals").

105. *Luther* opinion, 47 ("has ever doubted").
106. *Providence Daily Journal*, Jan. 12, 1849, quoted in Dennison, *Dorr*, 185 ("has not been"); Thomas W. Dorr to Benjamin Hallett, Jan. 15, 1849 ("warrant" to "legal subject"), Aaron White to Thomas W. Dorr, Feb. 17, 1849 ("the main question"), Dorr Correspondence, Rider Collection, Box 12, BU.
107. Levi Woodbury to Thomas W. Dorr, Apr. 15, 1842 ("when & how"), Dorr Correspondence, Rider Collection, Box 4, BU; *Luther* opinion, 50 ("honestly divide"), 51("different tastes").
108. Thomas W. Dorr to Estwick Evans, Apr. 12, 1848 ("[T]he People" to "in the government"), Dorr Papers, Manuscript Division, LC; *Hallett's Argument*, 71 ("the practical sovereignty").
109. Benjamin Hallett to Thomas W. Dorr, Feb. 11, 1848 ("all the arguments"), Thomas W. Dorr to Benjamin Hallett, May 11, 1848 ("salutary"), Dorr Correspondence, Rider Collection, Box 12, BU. On the legislature's annulment, see DeSimone and Schofield, *Broadsides*, 81 (repr. "An Act to reverse and annul the Judgment of the Supreme Court of Rhode Island for Treason, rendered against Thomas W. Dorr, June 25, 1844"); Conley, *Democracy*, 371. For a graphic account of Dorr's prison experiences, see [McDougall], *Might*, 283–87.

CHAPTER 9. EPILOGUE

1. John Hancock to George Washington, July 6, 1776, "General Orders," July 9, 1776, George Washington to John Hancock, *WP(RWS)*, V:219 ("most proper"), 246 ("on their respective" to "audible voice"), 258 ("the measure" to "approbation"); Alexander J. Wall, "New York and the Declaration of Independence," in *Narratives of the Revolution in New York* (1975), 29 (quoting the recollection of Zachariah Greene, "a hollow square" to "cheers were given").
2. *New York Journal*, July 11, 1776 ("the Sons of Freedom"). In 1774 John Adams described the statue as "very large, of solid Lead, gilded with Gold, standing on a Pedastal of Marble very high," Aug. 20, 1774, *ADA*, II:103.
3. Edward Bangs, ed., *Journal of Lieutenant Isaac Bangs, April 1 to July 29, 1776* (Cambridge, MA., 1890, repr. 1968), 57 ("the Populace"). Oliver Brown in a statement made in 1845 claimed to be in command of the soldiers who helped pull down the statue. See "Where is King George's Head?" *The Sons of the American Revolution Magazine* (Winter, 1998), 28. For the toppling of the statue see Desbler, "Declaration," 172; Arthur S. Marks, "The Statue of King George III in New York and the Iconology of Regicide," 13 *American Art Journal* (1981), 61–82; Barnet Schecter, *The Battle for New York: The City at the Heart of the American Revolution* (2002), 102–103. On the ritualistic "killing of the king," see Winthrop D. Jordan, "Familial Politics, Thomas Paine and the Killing of the King, 1776," 60 *JAH* (1973), 294–308; Peter Shaw, *American Patriots and the Rituals of Revolution* (1981), 14–25.
4. *New York Journal*, July 11, 1776 ("ominous fall"); *New York Constitutional Gazette*, July 20, 1776 ("thousands"); *New York Gazette*, July 22, 1776 ("by loud"); *New York Journal*, July 25, 1776 ("huzzas"). See also Desbler, "Declaration," 172–73.
5. George Washington, "General Orders," July 10, 1776, *WP(RWS)*, V:256–57 ("the persons" to "proper authority").
6. Morgan, *Inventing*, 282.
7. It is worth recalling Hannah Arendt's observation that "nothing threatens the very achievements of revolution more dangerously and more acutely than the spirit which has brought them about." Hannah Arendt, *On Revolution* (1963), 235.
8. See Chapter 3.
9. This book has argued that America's past reveals the existence of "constitutional dinosaurs" – ideas seriously discussed, considered, and acted upon, but which are foreign to our present constitutional understandings. If readers find the evidence for the existence of such "dinosaurs" compelling, the question naturally arises of how, when, and why such creatures went "extinct." An exploration of that question is the subject of a future book and beyond the scope of this present work.

    Preliminary research, however, suggests that while the Civil War crucially affected constitutional understandings pertaining to the authority of the collective sovereign to act independent of government, the war and its aftermath seems not to have rendered the "constitutional dinosaurs" extinct. Indeed, those ideas can be traced in debates over the meaning of American constitutionalism well into the late nineteenth century. Ironically, many of the constitutional understandings traced in this book appear to have been displaced and rendered beyond the constitutional pale only in the course of the Progressive movement of the early twentieth century.

10. Kramer, *People*, 53 ("popular constitutionalism"). Colonial historians and legal scholars will need to assess Kramer's claim that popular constitutionalism was a "background norm" that was "widely shared and deeply ingrained" before the American Revolution.

11. Kramer, *People*, 111 ("the people's active"), 137–38 ("squar[ing] off" to "understanding of constitutionalism").

12. Kramer, *People*, 83 ("kind of politics").

13. "Report of 1800," *MP*, XVII: 312 ("[t]he authority").

14. James Madison to C. E. Haynes, Aug. 27, 1832, *ML*, IV:224 ("the provisions").

15. Kramer, *People*, 94 ("profoundly" and "suddenly").

16. Kramer advances two assumptions that "must be taken as given" if Americans are to talk "sensibly" about popular constitutionalism today: first, "that 'the people' cannot act in an unmediated fashion on the national political stage" and second, "any mediation must ultimately be done through formal institutions of government." Larry Kramer, "Response," in "A Symposium on *The People Themselves: Popular Constitutionalism and Judicial Review*," 81 *Chicago-Kent L. Rev.* (2006), 1175.

17. Christian G. Fritz, "The American Constitutional Tradition Revisited: Preliminary Observations on State Constitution-Making in the Nineteenth-Century West," 25 *Rutgers L. J.* (1994), 952–60 (describing the assumptions underlying the federal constitutional focus by scholars).

18. There are, of course, exceptions, most notably Adams, *Constitutions*, Tarr, *State Constitutions*, and Kruman, *State Constitution Making*.

19. See Fritz, "Fallacies," 1327–69. For an examination of that state constitutional tradition and how and why state constitution-makers departed from the federal model, see Dinan, *Constitutional Tradition*.

20. See, for example, Larry E. Tise, *The American Counterrevolution: A Retreat from Liberty, 1783–1800* (1998), 419 (describing the federal Constitution as "a counterrevolutionary governing charter"); Calvin H. Johnson, *Righteous Anger at the Wicked States: The Meaning of the Founders' Constitution* (2005), 182 (concluding that the Federalists are appropriately considered "the true heirs of the Revolution").

21. Our more attenuated commitment to a collective sovereign – if not a more cynical view – says more about our loss of faith than the federal Framers' acceptance of the orthodox constitutionalism embraced today. See Chapter 5.

22. See, for example, Wills, *Evil* (depicting many of the controversies discussed in this book as discredited expressions of antigovernmentalism and anarchical instincts). This book has tried to examine old stories with new eyes. The effort was to "estrange the familiar" – because casting familiar historical events and episodes in terms that make them seem unfamiliar helps us see more in what we have taken for granted. See Anthony G. Amsterdam and Jerome Bruner, *Minding the Law: How Courts Rely on Storytelling, and How Their Stories Change the Way We Understand the Law – and Ourselves* (2000), 4.

23. For the recurring theme of protecting the public welfare, particularly in American common law, see William J. Novak, *The People's Welfare: Law and Regulation in Nineteenth-Century America* (1996).

24. On the resistance to the Tea Act, see Reid, *Constitutional History*, II:130–32, 229–31.

25. James Madison, "General Defense of the Constitution," June 12, 1788, *MP*, XI:130 ("multiplicity of sects"). See also Dinan's *People's Liberties*, 34 (distinguishing state constitutional support for an established church from establishing a state religion).

26. Laurence H. Tribe, *American Constitutional Law* (3rd ed., 2000), I:6–7 ("the oldest" and "all lawful").

27. John E. Nowak and Ronald D. Rotunda, *Constitutional Law* (7th ed., 2004), 8 ("a superior"), 4 ("the people" to "governing of society").

28. Tribe, *Constitutional Law*, 6 ("to preserve").
29. Nowak and Rotunda, *Constitutional Law*, 9 ("essential role"), quoting Robert McCloskey, *The American Supreme Court* (1960) ("judicial sovereignty").
30. It should be noted that John Reid's prodigious research and writing on the American Revolution interprets that event primarily through the lens of English law and constitutionalism rather than looking forward from the Revolution to trace the development of American constitutionalism. That perspective leads him to emphasize a smooth if not inevitable transition from arguments based on the rule of law advanced in the struggle against Britain to the postrevolutionary constitutional experience in America. See Reid, *Rule of Law*. This book suggests that matters were not so clear for many Americans, including lawyers, for a considerable time after the Revolution.
31. See, for example, Rodgers, *Contested Truths*, 66 (suggesting that the idea of "a reserve of *extralegal* rights" based on natural law "was already being abandoned" by the 1780s); Brooke, "Ancient Lodges," 296 (asserting that county conventions as "representations of the people" were "doomed to disappear" in the 1780s); John Phillip Reid, *Constitutional History of the American Revolution* (abridged ed., 1995), 104 (surmising that the rule of law was "the principle that led [Americans] to write constitutions" and which they "enshrined at the center of their state and federal constitutions").
32. See Wood, "Interests;" 77 (asserting that "for most of the founding fathers, popular political behavior in the states during the 1780s was very different from what they expected from their republican Revolution, and for them that difference was what made the 1780s a genuine critical period"); Nash, *Unknown*, 454–55 ("Having elbowed their way into the political system; having pried open legislative-assembly debates to public view; having institutionalized the rotation of offices, term limits, and annual elections; having elected their militia officers; and having known through intimate experience that they had been instrumental to the genesis and conduct of the Revolution, the common people did not easily give up what they had achieved").
33. See, for example, Randy E. Barnett, *Restoring the Lost Constitution: The Presumption of Liberty* (2004), 11–31 (arguing that the consent of the governed as the basis of the legitimacy of the constitution only binds those who themselves actually consent and not later, unborn generations).
34. See Chapter 8.
35. One possible insight is that the collective sovereign remains the underlying authority of government and central to the American constitutional tradition, but only surfaces in the course of concrete political struggles. To the extent we have become habituated to process and procedure we tend to forget how effectively and vibrantly the substantive value of the sovereignty of the people was invoked in the course of American history. For a twentieth-century vestige of the authority of the collective sovereign, see *Armstrong v. King*, 126A. 263 (Pa. 1924) (holding that popular ratification of proposals by the electorate can "cure" defects in constitutionally established procedures). Thanks to Bob Williams for bringing this case to my attention.
36. James Madison, "On Nullification," 1835/1836, *ML*, IV:413 ("was sufficient").
37. See Chapter 7.
38. 514 U.S. 779 (1995).
39. One difficulty in putting judicial review in historical context comes from the Court's tendency – shared equally by academics – of imputing the same meaning to words used both in the eighteenth century and in our own time. This tendency contributes to the assumption that judicial review and the monopoly over the interpretation of the constitution by the courts was inevitable. See, for example, Robert F. Nagel, *Constitutional Cultures: The Mentality and Consequences of Judicial Review* (1989), 2 (noting that "it is difficult for many, whether in or out of the academy, even to imagine any alternative" to judicial review). See also Engdahl, "Name," 457–510 (identifying eighteenth-century terminology and practice suggesting that a "supreme" court did not necessarily imply judicial finality).

When Daniel Webster ridiculed state interposition by stating how "preposterous" it was to leave constitutional interpretation "to four and twenty popular bodies," modern observers routinely concede Webster's point. Quoted in Belz, *Webster-Hayne Debate*, 138.

However, opponents of Webster's insistence on judicial monopoly were not advocating competing interpretations of the constitution as much as they were asserting the legitimacy of a constitutional understanding resting on the collective sovereign. If such an understanding could manifest itself and be recognized, American constitutionalism provided considerable support to give that understanding finality over the judiciary.

40. It seems likely that many Americans, particularly after the Civil War, rejected the high costs – incurred by the war – of invoking the underlying sovereign of the federal Constitution without the constraints of institutions and procedures. That shift may have altered perceptions of what henceforth would be considered constitutionally legitimate, but our current views of orthodox constitutionalism can not be inexorably linked to those of the founding generation of American constitution-makers.

It thus becomes more understandable that the doctrine of secession became vilified and stigmatized after the Civil War as the position of apologists for slavery. When Americans after the war stopped asking questions about the underlying sovereign basis of the federal Constitution in the manner they had before the war, it became increasingly commonplace to assume that postwar constitutional understandings had always been embraced by Americans – at least by right thinking Americans who properly understood America's constitutional tradition.

Selected Short Titles

The following short titles are used in the notes when a source has been cited in two or more chapters. Place of publication is provided for works published before 1900.

Adams, *Constitutions*
    Adams, Willi Paul, *The First American Constitutions: Republican Ideology and the Making of the State Constitutions in the Revolutionary Era* (1980).
Aichele, "Vermont Constitution"
    Aichele, Gary J., "Making the Vermont Constitution:1777–1824," 56 *Vermont History* (1988), 166–90.
Alexander, *News Coverage*
    Alexander, John K., *The Selling of the Constitutional Convention: A History of News Coverage* (1990).
Amar, "Consent"
    Amar, Akhil Reed, "The Consent of the Governed: Constitutional Amendment Outside Article V," 94 *Colum. L. Rev.* (1994), 457–508.
Amar, *Bill of Rights*
    Amar, Akhil Reed, *The Bill of Rights: Creation and Reconstruction* (1998).
Amar, *America's Constitution*
    Amar, Akhil Reed, *America's Constitution: A Biography* (2005).
Appleby, *Inheriting*
    Appleby, Joyce, *Inheriting the Revolution: The First Generation of Americans* (2000).
Ball and Pocock, *Change*
    Ball, Terence and J. G. A. Pocock, eds., *Conceptual Change and the Constitution* (1988).
Banner, *Hartford*
    Banner, Jr., James M., *To the Hartford Convention: The Federalists and the Origins of Party Politics in Massachusetts, 1789–1815* (1969).
Beeman, *Beyond Confederation*
    Beeman, Richard, Stephen Botein, and Edward C. Carter, II, eds., *Beyond Confederation: Origins of the Constitution and American National Identity* (1987).
Bellesiles, *Revolutionary*
    Bellesiles, Michael A., *Revolutionary Outlaws: Ethan Allen and the Struggle for Independence on the Early American Frontier* (1993).

Belz, *Webster-Hayne Debate*
  Belz, Herman, ed., *The Webster-Hayne Debate on the Nature of the Union: Selected Documents* (2000).
Bogin, "True Policy"
  Bogin, Ruth, "New Jersey's True Policy: The Radical Republican Vision of Abraham Clark," 35 *WMQ* (1978), 100–109.
Bouton, "Road"
  Bouton, Terry, "A Road Closed: Rural Insurgency in Post-Independence Pennsylvania," 87 *JAH* (2000), 855–87.
Brant, *Madison*
  Brant, Irving, *James Madison* (6 vols., 1941–1961).
Brooke, "Ancient Lodges"
  Brooke, John L., "Ancient Lodges and Self-Created Societies: Voluntary Association and the Public Sphere in the Early Republic," in Hoffman and Albert, *Launching*, 273–377.
Brown, *Revolutionary Politics*
  Brown, Richard D., *Revolutionary Politics in Massachusetts: The Boston Committee of Correspondence and the Towns, 1772–1774* (1970).
Brown, *Redeeming*
  Brown, Roger H., *Redeeming the Republic: Federalists, Taxation, and the Origins of the Constitution* (1993).
Brunhouse, *Counter-Revolution*
  Brunhouse, Robert L., *The Counter-Revolution in Pennsylvania, 1776–1790* (1942, repr. 1971).
Cappon, *Adams-Jefferson Letters*
  Cappon, Lester J., ed., *The Adams-Jefferson Letters: The Complete Correspondence Between Thomas Jefferson and Abigail and John Adams* (2 vols., 1959, repr. 1987).
Conkin, *Self-Evident*
  Conkin, Paul K., *Self-Evident Truths: Being a Discourse on the Origins & Development of the First Principles of American Government – Popular Sovereignty, Natural Rights, and Balance & Separation of Powers* (1974).
Conley, *Democracy*
  Conley, Patrick T., *Democracy in Decline: Rhode Island's Constitutional Development, 1776–1841* (1977).
Cornell, *Other Founders*
  Cornell, Saul, *The Other Founders: Anti-Federalism and the Dissenting Tradition in America, 1788–1828* (1999).
Crowl, *Maryland*
  Crowl, Philip A., *Maryland During and After the Revolution: A Political and Economic Study* (1943).
Curtis, *Free Speech*
  Curtis, Michael Kent, *Free Speech, 'The People's Darling Privilege': Struggles for Freedom of Expression in American History* (2000).
Desbler, "Declaration"
  Desbler, Charles D., "How the Declaration Was Received in the Old Thirteen," 85 *Harper's New Monthly Magazine* (1892), 165–87.
Dinan, *People's Liberties*
  Dinan, John J., *Keeping the People's Liberties: Legislators, Citizens, and Judges as Guardians of Rights* (1998).

Dinan, *Constitutional Tradition*
Dinan, John J., *The American State Constitutional Tradition* (2006).
East, "Conservatives"
East, Robert A., "The Massachusetts Conservatives in the Critical Period," in Richard B. Morris, ed., *The Era of the American Revolution* (1939), 349–91.
Elkins and McKitrick, *Federalism*
Elkins, Stanley and Eric McKitrick, *The Age of Federalism* (1993).
Elliot, *Debates*
Elliot, Jonathan, ed., *The Debates in the Several State Conventions, on the Adoption of the Federal Constitution* (5 vols., 2nd ed., Philadelphia, 1861).
Engdahl, "Name"
David E. Engdahl, "What's in a Name? The Constitutionality of Multiple 'Supreme' Courts," 66 *Ind. L. J.* (1991), 457–510.
Erdman, *New Jersey*
Erdman, Charles R., Jr., *The New Jersey Constitution of 1776* (1929).
Ferguson, *Power of the Purse*
Ferguson, E. James, *The Power of the Purse: A History of American Public Finance, 1776–1790* (1961).
Ferguson, *Reading*
Ferguson, Robert A., *Reading the Early Republic* (2004).
Fritz, "Fallacies"
Fritz, Christian G., "Fallacies of American Constitutionalism," 35 *Rutgers L. J.* (2004), 1327–69.
Galie, *Ordered Liberty*
Galie, Peter J., *Ordered Liberty: A Constitutional History of New York* (1996).
Gross, *Debt to Shays*
Gross, Robert A., ed., *In Debt to Shays: The Bicentennial of an Agrarian Rebellion* (1993).
Handlin, *Popular Sources*
Handlin, Oscar and Mary Handlin, eds., *The Popular Sources of Political Authority: Documents on the Massachusetts Constitution of 1780* (1966).
Hemberger, "Representations"
Hemberger, Suzette, "A Government Based on Representations," 40 *Studies in American Political Development* (1996), 289–332.
Hendricks, "New Look"
Hendricks, Nathaniel, "A New Look at the Ratification of the Vermont Constitution of 1777," 34 *Vermont History* (1966), 136–40.
Higginson, "Short History"
Higginson, Stephen A., "A Short History of the Right to Petition Government for the Redress of Grievances," 96 *Yale L. J.* (1986), 142–66.
Hoffman, *Spirit*
Hoffman, Ronald, *A Spirit of Dissension: Economics, Politics, and the Revolution in Maryland* (1973).
Hoffman and Albert, *Launching*
Hoffman, Ronald and Peter J. Albert, eds., *Launching the 'Extended Republic': The Federalist Era* (1996).
Hofstadter, *Idea*
Hofstadter, Richard, *The Idea of a Party System: The Rise of Legitimate Opposition in the United States, 1780–1840* (1969).

Holton, "Federalist 10"
  Holton, Woody, "'Divide et Impera': Federalist 10 in a Wider Sphere," 62 *WMQ* (2005), 171–211.
Holton, "Adversaries"
  Holton, Woody, "An 'Excess of Democracy' – Or a Shortage?: The Federalists' Earliest Adversaries," 25 *JER* (2005), 339–82.
Hulsebosch, *Empire*
  Hulsebosch, Daniel J., *Constituting Empire: New York and the Transformation of Constitutionalism in the Atlantic World, 1664–1830* (2005).
Humphrey, *Land and Liberty*
  Humphrey, Thomas J., *Land and Liberty: Hudson Valley Riots in the Age of Revolution* (2004).
Hyneman and Lutz, *Political Writing*
  Hyneman, Charles S. and Donald S. Lutz, eds., *American Political Writing During the Founding Era, 1760–1805* (2 vols., 1983).
Jackson, *Political Situation*
  [Jackson, Jonathan], *Thoughts Upon the Political Situation of the United States of America, In Which That Of Massachusetts is more particularly considered, With Some Observations on the Constitution For a Federal Government* (Worcester, MA, 1788).
Jensen, *New Nation*
  Jensen, Merrill, *The New Nation: A History of the United States During the Confederation, 1781–1789* (1950).
Jones, *Vermont*
  Jones, Matt Bushnell, *Vermont in the Making, 1750–1777* (1939).
Kars, *Breaking*
  Kars, Marjoleine, *Breaking Loose Together: The Regulator Rebellion in Pre-Revolutionary North Carolina* (2002).
Kramer, *People*
  Kramer, Larry D., *The People Themselves: Popular Constitutionalism and Judicial Review* (2004).
Kruman, *State Constitution Making*
  Kruman, Marc W., *Between Authority and Liberty: State Constitution Making in Revolutionary America* (1997).
Kyvig, *Explicit*
  Kyvig, David E., *Explicit and Authentic Acts: Amending the U.S. Constitution, 1776–1995* (1996).
Labaree, *Patriots*
  Labaree, Benjamin W., *Patriots and Partisans: The Merchants of Newburyport, 1764–1815* (1962).
Lee, *Crowds*
  Lee, Wayne E., *Crowds and Soldiers in Revolutionary North Carolina: The Culture of Violence in Riot and War* (2001).
Lendler, "Sedition Act"
  Lendler, Marc, "'Equally Proper at All Times and at All Times Necessary': Civility, Bad Tendency, and the Sedition Act," 24 *JER* (2004), 419–44.
Lenner, *Federal*
  Lenner, Andrew C., *The Federal Principle in American Politics, 1790–1833* (2001).
Levy, *Free Press*
  Levy, Leonard W., *Emergence of a Free Press* (1960, revised and enlarged ed., 1985).

Lienesch, "Reinterpreting Rebellion"
  Lienesch, Michael, "Reinterpreting Rebellion: The Influence of Shays's Rebellion on American Political Thought," in Gross, *Debt to Shays*, 161–82.
Lincoln, *Constitutional History*
  Lincoln, Charles Z., *The Constitutional History of New York* (5 vols., 1906).
Lovejoy, *Rhode Island*
  Lovejoy, David S., *Rhode Island Politics and the American Revolution, 1760–1776* (1958).
Lutz, *Popular Consent*
  Lutz, Donald S., *Popular Consent and Popular Control: Whig Political Theory in the Early State Constitutions* (1980).
Maier, "Popular Uprisings"
  Maier, Pauline, "Popular Uprisings and Civil Authority in Eighteenth-Century America," 27 *WMQ* (1970), 3–35.
Maier, *Resistance*
  Maier, Pauline, *From Resistance to Revolution: Colonial Radicals and the Development of American Opposition to Britain, 1765–1776* (1972).
Maier, *American Scripture*
  Maier, Pauline, *American Scripture: Making the Declaration of Independence* (1997).
Mark, "Vestigial Constitution"
  Mark, Gregory A., "The Vestigial Constitution: The History and Significance of the Right to Petition," 66 *Fordham L. Rev.* (1998), 2153–231.
Marston, *King and Congress*
  Marston, Jerrilyn Greene, *King and Congress: The Transfer of Political Legitimacy, 1774–1776* (1987).
Martin, *Press Liberty*
  Martin, Robert W. T., *The Free and Open Press: The Founding of American Democratic Press Liberty, 1640–1800* (2001).
Martin, "Reforming"
  Martin, Robert W. T., "Reforming Republicanism: Alexander Hamilton's Theory of Republican Citizenship and Press Liberty," 25 *JER* (2005), 21–46.
Mayer, *Jefferson*
  Mayer, David N., *The Constitutional Thought of Thomas Jefferson* (1994).
McDonald, *States' Rights*
  McDonald, Forrest, *States' Rights and the Union: Imperium in Imperio, 1776–1876* (2000).
McInnis, "Natural Law"
  McInnis, Tom N., "Natural Law and the Revolutionary State Constitutions," 14 *Legal Studies Forum* (1990), 351–72.
Merrill and Wilentz, *Key of Liberty*
  Merrill, Michael and Sean Wilentz, eds., *The Key of Liberty: The Life and Democratic Writings of William Manning, "A Laborer," 1747–1814* (1993).
Monaghan, "Original Understanding"
  Monaghan, Henry Paul, "We the People[s], Original Understanding, and Constitutional Amendment," 96 *Colum. L. Rev.* (1996), 121–77.
Morgan, "Popular Sovereignty"
  Morgan, Edmund S., "The Problem of Popular Sovereignty," in *Aspects of American Liberty: Philosophical, Historical and Political* (1977), 95–113.

Morgan, *Inventing*

Morgan, Edmund S., *Inventing the People: The Rise of Popular Sovereignty in England and America* (1988).

Morison, "Struggle"

Morison, Samuel Eliot, "The Struggle over the Adoption of the Constitution of Massachusetts, 1780," 50 *Proceedings of the Massachusetts Historical Society* (1917), 353–411.

Morris, *Jay Papers*

Morris, Richard B., ed., *John Jay, Unpublished Papers, 1745–1784* (2 vols., 1975–1980).

Nash, *Unknown*

Nash, Gary B., *The Unknown American Revolution: The Unruly Birth of Democracy and the Struggle to Create America* (2005).

Newman, *Fries's Rebellion*

Newman, Paul Douglas, *Fries's Rebellion: The Enduring Struggle for the American Revolution* (2004).

Onuf, "State-Making"

Onuf, Peter S., "State-Making in Revolutionary America: Independent Vermont as a Case Study," 67 *JAH* (1981), 797–815.

Onuf, *Origins*

Onuf, Peter S., *The Origins of the Federal Republic: Jurisdictional Controversies in the United States, 1775–1787* (1983).

Papenfuse and Stiverson, *Decisive*

Papenfuse, Edward C. and Gregory A. Stiverson, eds., *The Decisive Blow Is Struck: A Facsimile Edition of the Proceedings of the Constitutional Convention of 1776 and the First Maryland Constitution* (1977).

Parkinson, "Circumvention"

Parkinson, George Phillip, Jr., "Antebellum State Constitution-Making: Retention, Circumvention, Revision," (Ph.D. diss., Univ. of Wisconsin, 1972).

Parsons, *Essex*

[Parsons, Theophilus], *The Essex Result* (1778), in Hyneman and Lutz, *Political Writing*, I:480–522.

Philyaw, *Western Visions*

Philyaw, L. Scott, *Virginia's Western Visions: Political and Cultural Expansion on an Early American Frontier* (2004).

Powell, *Regulators*

Powell, William S., James K. Huhta, and Thomas J. Farnham, eds., *The Regulators in North Carolina: A Documentary History, 1759–1776* (1971).

Rakove, "Structure"

Rakove, Jack N., "The Structure of Politics at the Accession of George Washington," in Beeman, *Beyond Confederation*, 261–94.

Rakove, *Meanings*

Rakove, Jack N., *Original Meanings: Politics and Ideas in the Making of the Constitution* (1996).

Rawle, *View*

Rawle, William, *A View of the Constitution of the United States of America* (Philadelphia, 1825).

Reid, "Governance"

Reid, John Phillip, "Governance of the Elephant: Constitutional Theory on the Overland Trail," 5 *Hastings Const. L. Q.* (1978), 421–43.

Reid, *Constitutional History*
Reid, John Phillip, *Constitutional History of the American Revolution* (4 vols., 1986–1993).

Reid, *Rule of Law*
Reid, John Phillip, *Rule of Law: The Jurisprudence of Liberty in the Seventeenth and Eighteenth Centuries* (2004).

Remini, *Jackson*
Remini, Robert V., *Andrew Jackson and the Course of American Democracy, 1833–1845* (1984).

Rodgers, *Contested Truths*
Rodgers, Daniel T., *Contested Truths: Keywords in American Politics Since Independence* (1987).

Ryerson, "Republican Theory"
Ryerson, Richard Alan, "Republican Theory and Partisan Reality in Revolutionary Pennsylvania: Toward a New View of the Constitutionalist Party," in Ronald Hoffman and Peter J. Albert, eds., *Sovereign States in an Age of Uncertainty* (1981), 95–133.

Scalia, *Jeffersonian Experiment*
Scalia, Laura J., *America's Jeffersonian Experiment: Remaking State Constitutions, 1820–1850* (1999).

Shalhope, *Bennington*
Shalhope, Robert E., *Bennington and the Green Mountain Boys: The Emergence of Liberal Democracy in Vermont, 1760–1850* (1996).

Sharp, *Politics*
Sharp, James Roger, *American Politics in the Early Republic: The New Nation in Crisis* (1993).

Slaughter, *Whiskey*
Slaughter, Thomas P., *The Whiskey Rebellion: Frontier Epilogue to the American Revolution* (1986).

Smith, *Freedom's Fetters*
Smith, James Morton, *Freedom's Fetters: The Alien and Sedition Laws and American Civil Liberties* (1956).

Spalding and Garrity, *Farewell Address*
Spalding, Matthew and Patrick J. Garrity, *A Sacred Union of Citizens: George Washington's Farewell Address and the American Character* (1996).

Story, *Commentaries*
Story, Joseph, *Commentaries on the Constitution of the United States; With a Preliminary Review of the Constitutional History of the Colonies and States, Before the Adoption of the Constitution* (3 vols., Boston, 1833).

Suber, *Paradox*
Suber, Peter, *The Paradox of Self-Amendment: A Study of Logic, Law, Omnipotence, and Change* (1990).

Tarr, *State Constitutions*
Tarr, G. Alan, *Understanding State Constitutions* (1998).

Tucker, *Blackstone's Commentaries*
Tucker, St. George, *Blackstone's Commentaries: With Notes of Reference, to the Constitution and Laws, of the Federal Government of the United States; and of the Commonwealth of Virginia* (5 vols., Philadelphia, 1803).

Tucker, "Conciliatory"
  [Tucker, Thomas Tudor] "Philodemus," "Conciliatory Hints, Attempting, by a Fair
  State of Matters, to Remove Party Prejudice" (1784) in Hyneman and Lutz, *Political
  Writing*, I:606–30.
Wehtje, "Boston's Response"
  Wehtje, Myron F., "Boston's Response to Disorder in the Commonwealth, 1783–
  1787," 12 *Historical Journal of Massachusetts* (1984), 19–27.
Wiecek, *Guarantee Clause*
  Wiecek, William M., *The Guarantee Clause of the U.S. Constitution* (1972).
Wilentz, *Democracy*
  Wilentz, Sean, *The Rise of American Democracy: Jefferson to Lincoln* (2005).
Williams, "State Constitutions"
  Williams, Robert F., "The State Constitutions of the Founding Decade: Pennsylvania's
  Radical 1776 Constitution and Its Influences on American Constitutionalism," 62
  Temp. L. Rev. (1989), 541–85.
Williams, *Lost State*
  Williams, Samuel Cole, *History of the Lost State of Franklin* (1924, revised ed., 1933,
  repr., 1993).
Williamson, *Vermont*
  Williamson, Chilton, *Vermont in Quandary: 1763–1825* (1949).
Wills, *Evil*
  Wills, Garry, *A Necessary Evil: A History of American Distrust of Government* (1999).
Wood, "Mobs"
  Wood, Gordon S., "A Note on Mobs in the American Revolution," 23 *WMQ* (1966),
  635–42.
Wood, *Creation*
  Wood, Gordon S., *The Creation of the American Republic, 1776–1787* (1969).
Wood, "Interests"
  Wood, Gordon S., "Interests and Disinterestedness in the Making of the Constitution,"
  in Beeman, *Beyond Confederation*, 69–109.
Wood, *Radicalism*
  Wood, Gordon S., *The Radicalism of the American Revolution* (1991).
Yazawa, *Representative*
  Yazawa, Melvin, ed., *Representative Government and the Revolution: The Maryland
  Constitutional Crisis of 1787* (1975).
Young, *Beyond*
  Young, Alfred E., ed., *Beyond the American Revolution: Explorations in the History
  of American Radicalism* (1993).

Credits

American Antiquarian Society, Worcester, Massachusetts
Shays' Rebellion collection: Petition of the Town of Groton to the General Court ([Sept. 1786]), Daniel Shays et al. to Luke Day ([Jan.] 1787)

Berkshire Athenaeum, Pittsfield, Massachusetts
Sedgwick/Bowdoin Letters [typescript copies]: Theodore Sedgwick to James Bowdoin (Apr. 8, 1787), Theodore Sedgwick to Governor Bowdoin (Apr. 8 and 10 and May 10, 1787)

Brown University Library, Providence, Rhode Island
"Opinion of the Judges of the Supreme Judicial Court, Upon the Legality of the so called 'People's Constitution,'" in *Citizens of Rhode Island! Read! Mark! Learn!* (n.p. [Mar. 1842]), Broadside; Dorr Papers: Thomas Hart Benton to Thomas W. Dorr (Apr. 16, 1842), Orestes A. Brownson to Thomas W. Dorr (May 14, 1842), Walter S. Burges to Thomas W. Dorr (May 9, 1842), "Biographical Memoranda of Thomas W. Dorr" (Aug. 1, 1845), Thomas W. Dorr to William B. Adams (May 30 and Nov. 7, 1831), Thomas W. Dorr to Bradford Allen (May 1842), Thomas W. Dorr to Nathan Clifford (Jan. 24, 1848), Thomas W. Dorr to Benjamin Hallett (May 11, 1848, and Jan. 15, 1849), Thomas W. Dorr to Benjamin Hallett and George Turner (Feb. 2, 1847), Thomas W. Dorr to Dutee J. Pearce (Dec. 13, 1841), Thomas W. Dorr to Aaron White (Apr. 4, 1842), Thomas W. Dorr to Aaron White, Jr. (May 12, 1842), David Dudley Field to Thomas W. Dorr (Mar. 16, 1844), Benjamin Hallett to Thomas W. Dorr (Feb. 11, 1848), Alexander Everett Hill to Editor of the Providence *New Age and Constitutional Advocate* (Nov. 8, 1841), David Parmenter to Thomas W. Dorr (May 30, 1842), William Peckham to Thomas W. Dorr (Feb. 3, 1837), Joshua B. Rathbun to Thomas W. Dorr (Mar. 4, 1842), Samuel Wales, Eli Brown, William Coleman, F. L. Beckford, John A. Howland to Thomas W. Dorr (May 18, 1842), Aaron White to Thomas W. Dorr (May 25, 1842, and Feb. 17, 1849), Aaron White, Jr., to Thomas Dorr (Sept. 1, 1842, and Apr. 30, 1843), Levi Woodbury to Thomas W. Dorr (Apr. 15, 1842)

Commonwealth of Massachusetts, Archives Division
SC1/series 45X, Massachusetts Archives Collection, v. 160: p. 184; v. 186: p. 369; v. 189: pp. 171–77, 371–73B, 374–76, 425; v. 190: pp. 235, 236, 250, 253–54, 255, 263, 270, 277–88, 290, 301–3, 305

The Connecticut Historical Museum, Hartford, Connecticut
Jeremiah Wadsworth Papers: Charles Pettit to Jeremiah Wadsworth (May 27, 1786); Oliver Wolcott, Jr. Papers: John Neville to George Clymer (Sept. 8, 1791), Frederick Wolcott to Oliver Wolcott, Jr. (May 2, 1796)

Duke University, Durham, North Carolina
  Campbell Family Papers, Rare Book, Manuscript, and Special Collections Library: Arthur Campbell to Archibald Stuart (Feb. 27, 1786)

Houghton Library, Harvard University, Cambridge, Massachusetts
  Timothy Bigelow to Timothy Bigelow Sr., Springfield (Jan. 28, 1787); [General Court], *An Address to the People of the Commonwealth of Massachusetts* (n.p., 1809)

Library of Virginia, Richmond, Virginia
  State government records collection: Executive papers of Governor Patrick Henry, 1784–1786 (bulk 1785–1786), Record Group 3, Accession 39700

Maryland Historical Society, Baltimore, Maryland
  Charles Carroll Papers 1749–1832, MS 1932: Charles Carroll of Carrollton to Charles Carroll of Annapolis (Aug. 20 and 23, 1776)

Massachusetts Historical Society, Boston, Massachusetts
  Adams family papers: Mary Cranch to Abigail Adams (Sept. 24, 1786); Cushing family papers: Peter Thatcher to Thomas Cushing (Sept. 15, 1786); Robert Treat Paine papers: Robert Treat Paine diary (Apr. 20, 1787), William Whiting to Robert Treat Paine (Mar. 19, 1787); Sedgwick family papers: William Whiting to Theodore Sedgwick (Sept. 10, 1785); Shays' Rebellion papers: David Cobb to James Bowdoin (Sept. 13, 1786), Theodore Sedgwick to Pamela Sedgwick (June 24, 1786); Increase Sumner papers: Increase Sumner to Elizabeth Sumner (Apr. 8, 1787); William Whiting Papers: Robert Treat Paine to William Whiting (Apr. 3, 1776)

National Archives, Washington, DC
  Misc. Letters, Dept. of State: "Extract of a letter from Kentucky Dated Lexington, Jan. 25, 1794," enclosed in Edmund Randolph to George Washington (Feb. 27, 1794, Microfilm Copy 179, Reel 11); Papers of the Continental Congress: Charles Cummings to the President of Congress (Apr. 7, 1785, Microfilm Copy 247, Reel 62), "Citizens of Washington County, memorial to Congress" ([Nov. 18, 1784], Microfilm Copy 247, Reel 62)

Newport Historical Society, Newport, Rhode Island
  Pearce Papers: Thomas W. Dorr to Dutee J. Pearce (Mar. 18, 1842)

New York Public Library, New York, New York
  James Monroe Papers, Manuscripts and Archives Division, Astor, Lenox and Tilden Foundations: William Pope to James Monroe (Oct. 28, 1814), Winfield Scott to James Monroe (Feb. 15, 1815); George Washington Papers, Manuscripts and Archives Division, Astor, Lenox and Tilden Foundations: George Washington to James Ross (June 16, 1794); Noah Webster Papers, Manuscripts and Archives Division, Astor, Lenox and Tilden Foundations: Thomas Dawes to Noah Webster (June 25 and July 24, 1812), Harrison Gray Otis to Noah Webster (May 6, 1840)

New York University, New York, New York, and the National Historic Publications Commission
  Papers of Albert Gallatin, microfilm edition

North Carolina Office of Archives and History, Raleigh, North Carolina
  Governors' Letter Books, 10: Samuel Johnston and Benjamin Hawkins to Alexander Martin (Feb. 22, 1791)

Rhode Island Historical Society, Providence, Rhode Island
  Elisha R. Potter Jr. Papers, MSS 629 sg 3: Job Dufree to Elisha R. Potter Jr. (Mar. 14, 1842, Box 1, Folder 7); Elisha Potter Jr. to Dutee J. Pearce (copy, Dec. 20, 1841, Box 1, Folder 6)

Virginia Historical Society, Richmond, Virginia
  Holladay Family Papers: Robert D. Powell to Waller Holladay (Dec. 23, 1828)

William L. Clements Library, University of Michigan, Ann Arbor, Michigan
  John Pitman to Joseph Story (Jan. 26, Feb. 10, Mar. 30, and Apr. 7, 1842)

Wisconsin Historical Society, Madison, Wisconsin
  Draper Manuscripts

Index

Adams, Abigail, 101–102
  complaints about Massachusetts 1780
    constitution, 106
  correspondence with Jefferson, 119
  leadership problem with Regulation, 128
Adams, John, 43, 48, 190, 197, 201, 286
  on American Revolution, 15, 47, 59, 80
  and the common people, 40–42, 129
  concern re "unbounded Power," 41, 62
  consent of the people, 34, 38, 42, 186
  considering the conduct of leaders, 20
  on constitution-making, 11, 25, 31, 48, 152
  on high taxes, 84
  institutional checks and government balance,
    31–32, 133
  Massachusetts county conventions as
    seditious, 93
  on Massachusetts "Regulators," 120
  Massachusetts 1780 constitution drafting,
    105–106
  mistaken notions of government, 125, 128
  and public virtue, 40
  on scrutiny of government, 107
  selfishness of elected leaders, 129
  on Transylvania, 48
  use of natural aristocracy, 41, 128
Adams, John Quincy, 102, 221, 253
  Governor Hancock "pleasing the multitude,"
    114
  lectures on social compact, 265
Adams, Samuel, 48
  collective sovereign, 63, 95
  conventions, 94
  opposes clemency, 112
Addison, Alexander
  reply to Madison's *Minority Report*, 206
Alien and Sedition Acts, 29, 197–98, 204, 210,
  215, 226, 230, 232, 281–82, 294
  congressional committee report defends, 201

  petitions from counties to Congress, 201
  protests against, 200–201, 203
Allen, Ira, 60–62
Allen, Thomas, 90
Allen, William, 257
"Alter or abolish" provisions, 24–28, 30, 55,
  106, 127, 135–36, 155, 174, 182, 235,
  246–48, 253, 257, 259, 261–64, 266, 273,
  289, 300
  distinguished from right of revolution, 24,
    126, 269
  national debate over, 235
  omitted in federal Constitution, 137
Ames, Fisher, 179
  concern re the people, 124
  contract law analogy, 99
  on democratic societies, 177–78, 180
  on instructions, 165
  majority rule as "incendiary," 99
  on Massachusetts "Regulators," 100–101
Angell, Joseph K., 262
Anti-Federalists, 139, 146–51, 172
Articles of Confederation, 200
  Article XIII, 139
  federal convention could bypass amendment
    procedures, 140
  procedural difficulty with federal
    Consitution, 138
Atwell, Samuel Y., 252, 254, 256, 259

Belknap, Jeremy, 122–23
Benson, Egbert, 142
Benton, Thomas Hart, 257
Berkshire Constitutionalists
  among first to call for new constitution,
    91
  See also Massachusetts "Regulators";
    Whiting
Bigelow, Timothy, 212

Index